OSAMA BIN LADEN

AMERICA'S ENEMY IN HIS OWN WORDS

STATEMENTS BY OSAMA BIN LADEN

EDITED BY RANDALL B. HAMUD, J.D.

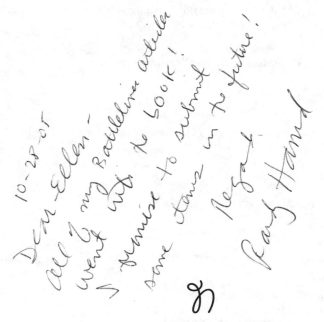

NADEEM PUBLISHING

SAN DIEGO, CALIFORNIA

Dedications

For: Mother, Ida, Tariq & Jimeel.
Thank you for your patience and support.

More information on Nadeem Publishing and the book—Osama Bin Laden: America's Enemy In His Own Words, can be found at the following websites:

http://www.nadeempublishing.com

http://www.osama-bin-laden-book.com

Published by Nadeem Publishing, 1200 3rd Avenue, Suite 1321, San Diego, California 92101. (800) 495-5589.
First edition.

Library of Congress Cataloging-in-Publication Data

2001012345

Hamud, Randall, B.

Osama Bin Laden: America's Enemy In His Own Words / Randall B. Hamud.— 1st ed.

p. cm.

Includes bibliographical references and index.

ISBN 0-9770935-0-6

1. Islam 2. Islam—Essence, genius, nature. Islam—History. I Title
297—dc22
Printed in the United States of America.
Edited by Randall B. Hamud, J.D.
Cover photo courtesy of AP/Wide World Photos.

Acknowledgements

Acknowledgements and
The Editor's Note
For The Reader

Ordinarily, the reader skims the Acknowledgements page because it usually thanks persons he or she has never heard of who assisted the editor or author in the preparation of the book. But there is nothing ordinary about either this book or its subject matter. Unfortunately, I am precluded from thanking by name those among the Muslim and Arab communities who assisted me in its preparation. They are all immigrants and naturalized citizens from the Middle East. They do not feel that they have the freedom to be identified by name as contributors to the publication of this book.

Since 9/11, the fear factor afflicting the Muslim community in the United States, and especially the Muslim Arabs, has been overwhelming. Random visits by F.B.I. agents, harassment by Immigration and Customs Enforcement agents, inclusion on no-fly lists, terrorist-threat warnings, and the unfortunate and unrelenting negative depiction of Muslims and Arabs in the media have taken a toll on their morale. Sadly, in today's America, Muslim immigrants do not enjoy the freedom of speech that those of us who are native-born enjoy in discussing subjects like Mr. Bin Laden, political Islam, and the subject of terrorism. Most of them wonder whether they will even be permitted to board commercial airliners the next time they fly. And they collectively hold their breath every time there is an elevated terrorist-threat level for fear of what might befall them if, God forbid, another 9/11 were to occur here in America.

They are intelligent and well educated, and they certainly would like to discuss these subjects in open forums without fear. Today, however, most of them find xenophobic America too reminiscent of the repressive regimes that drove them to this country in the first instance.

So, to those of them who assisted me in preparing this book, I say "*Shoukran*," (thank you). Without their skill, knowledge, and yes, personal courage, the book would not have seen the light of day. Their collective knowledge of Islam, Islamic history, Arabic history, and the Arabic and English languages have ensured that the reader will understand Mr. Bin Laden's words and the cultural and historical contexts in which they were uttered. Our hope is that after reading this book, the reader will know what we already know: that Islam is not the enemy.

Editor's Note

Though there is supposed to be a widely recognized system for the transliteration of Arabic to English, conventions vary from publication to publication. For example, compare different newsstand publications to see many variations in the names of individuals, locations and groups. In deference to clarity, I have elected to simplify the transliterated Arabic words as much as possible and to define them at every instance of their use for the convenience of the reader. For example, "*Kaba*" (destination of the *Haj* [not *Hajj*]) instead of "*Kaa'ba*," or "*Ka'aba*." Arabic is much too difficult a language to attempt to instruct the reader in its intricacies by crowding the text with pronunciation tools like hyphens, apostrophes, and reverse apostrophes. However, at the website located at *osama-bin-laden-book.com*, the verbal pronunciation of each of the transliterated words appearing in the Glossary may be heard.

Randall B. Hamud
San Diego, California
August 5, 2005

This Page Left Intentionally Blank For Notes

Table of Contents*

_____

*Although Mr. Bin Laden's statements in this book appear in chronological order from earliest to most recent, they may be read in any order.

In 1994, Sheikh Abdel Aziz ibn Baz was Saudi Arabia's most preeminent Islamic cleric. Unlike Shi'ite Islam, Sunni Islam lacks a hierarchy of Islamic clerics headed by a supreme cleric. However, in each Sunni venue, certain clerics garner respect because of their education and intellectual achievement. Sheikh Baz was such a man in Saudi Arabia. By issuing *Fatwas* (religious decrees), he informed his followers whether treated subjects were consistent with the teachings of the Holy Quran and the *Sunnah* (words and deeds of the Prophet Muhammud, peace be upon him, hereinafter "PBUH"). However, in Saudi Arabia, as in the other autocratic regimes of the Middle East, the clerics are on the government's payroll and are under government scrutiny. As civil servants, they are expected to support the government's policies, even in their *Fatwas*. If they fail to do so, then they are removed, or worse. Sheikh Baz is known for several *Fatwas* of political note. In 1979, he issued the *Fatwa* calling for *Jihad* (holy war) against the Soviet Union's invasion of Afghanistan. In 1990, he issued a *Fatwa* legitimizing the Saudi government's inviting of American military forces into Saudi Arabia for fear of imminent invasion by Iraq. In 1991 he and 400 other clerics and scholars issued an open letter to Saudi King Fahd seeking political reform, including the creation of a consultative assembly and the elimination of corruption. In 1993, he issued a *Fatwa* supporting peace with Israel and the transfer of some Muslim land to Israel in the name of peace.

In his 1994 letter, Osama bin Laden ("OBL") rails at Sheikh Baz for issuing false *Fatwas* and remaining silent instead of seeking reform in Saudi Arabia. Saudi corruption is rampant in the face of a silent Sheikh Baz. He has allowed the government to enact "man-made" laws, thereby making itself a "partner" of God. Crusader forces occupy the Arabian Peninsula, and instead of calling for *Jihad* (holy war), Sheikh Baz justified the occupation. He allows the persecution of non-governmental clerics and scholars who do not adhere to the government's policies. He has surrendered the *Al-Aqsa Mosque* in Jerusalem and the mosques at Mecca and Medina to the Judeo-Crusader armies. The Saudi regime is apostate and must be removed. It should not be able to rely on his *Fatwas* to resist true reform. OBL pleads with Sheikh Baz that the latter is old and should have piety at this stage of his life. He should look to Islamic history for the examples of early *Ulema* (Islamic scholars) who resisted previous autocrats. He should rely on the Quran rather than the corrupt, apostate Saudi rulers. If Sheikh Baz cannot find his conscience, then at the least he should remain silent.

CHAPTER 2 –

AN OPEN LETTER TO KING FAHD – 1995

PAGE 10

King Fahd of Saudi Arabia was debilitated by a stroke in late 1995, after which Crown Prince Abdullah acted as the defacto regent.

King Fahd died on August 1, 2005, and Abdullah succeded him. This letter was written to the King before his stroke. By 1995, OBL had become a vocal critic of the regime because of the introduction of American military forces into Saudi Arabia in August 1990, at the invitation of the Saudi government, which feared invasion by Iraq. In early 1991, already having been restricted to the city of Jeddah, OBL fled Saudi Arabia. He first traveled to Pakistan, then to Afghanistan, and finally later that same year, to Sudan, where he remained until 1996. In April, 1994, he organized and funded the Committee for Advice and Reform while in London, England, to continue the fight for the reform of the Saudi government. In 1994, the Saudi government responded by stripping OBL of his Saudi citizenship and freezing his substantial assets. The 1995 letter was signed by OBL but was directed to the King through the Committee.

OBL calls the letter a "frank manifesto," and it is very frank. He makes light of the government's "sedative" measures at reform and rails about its corruption and ineptitude. But the most serious criticism which OBL raises is his accusation that the government has violated the fundamental pillar of Islam: there is no god but God. By enacting "man-made" laws, it has made itself a partner of God much as Jews and Christians take others as lords. The regime is clearly apostate and must be removed. OBL cites as evidence a plethora of Saudi domestic laws to demonstrate his point, as well as Saudi Arabia's membership in the Gulf Council for Cooperation, which lists the *Sharia* (Islamic law) at the bottom of its list of controlling laws. The Saudi government has given billions of dollars to *Kufr* (non-believer) regimes like the Palestinian Liberation Organization, the Soviet Union and Syria. He claims these policies were driven by the Western powers. In Saudi Arabia itself, the King has created a failed economy. His family's corruption is unparalleled in the modern world. People in Saudi Arabia go without electricity while the royal palaces are aglow twenty-four hours a day. The government has failed to develop industries as alternatives to oil, thereby remaining under the dictates of the Western consuming nations. The Saudi government has purchased from these governments billions of dollars of unnecessary military equipment that it lacks the manpower to operate. In the 1991 Gulf War the performance of the Saudi military was dismal in spite of the billions the government had spent on weapons. OBL offers that American military forces remain in Saudi Arabia to protect the corrupt, apostate regime. The regime is not legitimate according to Islam. The King and his entire government must resign or else be removed.

CHAPTER 3 –

DECLARATION OF WAR AGAINST THE AMERICANS – 1996

PAGE 32

By 1996, OBL has migrated to Afghanistan, having been asked to leave Sudan, which had succumbed to United States, Saudi, and Egyptian pressure to remove him from that venue. American intelligence officials claim that while in Sudan in 1992, OBL and members of Al Qaeda agreed to attack U.S. forces in Saudi Arabia and the Gulf States. By 1996, OBL was on the United States government's radar screen. In December 1992, a bomb explosion in Aden, Yemen, had narrowly missed American soldiers en route to Somalia. This is alleged to have been OBL's first attack on U.S. personnel. Our government also suspected OBL of a role in the 1993 World Trade Center bombing and the 1993 killing of U.S. Rangers in Mogadishu, Somalia, during the famous "Black Hawk down" incident. In June 1996 a large truck bomb destroyed the U.S. military residence at the Khobar Towers in Dhahran, Saudi Arabia, killing nineteen U.S. service personnel. U.S. investigators are split on whether OBL's supporters were directly involved. But in August, 1996, OBL left no doubt that he was America's enemy because he declared war on us. Interestingly, he states that only U.S. military forces in the Middle East will be targeted.

OBL opens his declaration railing about the corrupt, apostate Islamic regimes of the Middle East. They have suspended the *Sharia* (Islamic law) and have invited the Crusader American military forces into the region, including Saudi Arabia. Oil is priced as the U.S. dictates. Unaffordable weapons systems are purchased from the American overseers. He notes prior attempts in 1991 and 1992 to notify the Saudi government of its transgressions, to no avail. The Saudi regime has enacted "man-made" laws and thrown its lot in with the infidel Crusaders. He calls for guerilla war against U.S. forces and for the boycott of American goods. To the Middle East's youth, he reminds them that they are the spear points of *Jihad* (holy war). They must become *Shaheed* (martyrs); death is but a pinch; 72 houris await them in Paradise. American misdeeds have nullified any treaty between the United States and Saudi

Arabia. Nor is the illegitimate regime authorized to sign a treaty with the United States. Reciprocity demands the blood of American soldiers. He also appeals to Islam's women to follow the example of the women of the Prophet Muhammad's (PBUH) early Companions.

CHAPTER 4 –

FATWA OF JIHAD (HOLY WAR) AGAINST AMERICANS – 1998

PAGE 60

This *Fatwa* (religious decree) was signed by OBL, Ayman al-Zawahiri (leader of the *Jihad* Group of Egypt), Abu-Yasir Rifa'I Ahmad Taha (Egyptian Group), Sheikh Mil-Harnzah (Jamiat-ul-*Ulema*-e-Pakistan), and Fazlur Rahman (Bangladesh *Jihad* Movement). It declares *Jihad* (holy war) against Jews and Crusading America. In 1996, OBL had declared war against the United States and limited the targets to U.S. military forces in Saudi Arabia and the Gulf States. Now, he and his cohorts extend the theater of operations to wherever Jews and Americans, military or civilian, are found.

The statement begins by noting that the Islamic see of Saudi Arabia is being assaulted by Crusader forces that are spreading like "locusts." The statement claims that nations attack Islam as people would fight over food. It itemizes three facts supporting "global *Jihad*:" 1) American occupation of Saudi Arabia and the Gulf States for the past seven years and the use of Saudi territory as a staging area for continuing aggression against Iraq; 2) continuing attacks on Iraq in spite of the sanctions that have cost the lives of over a million Iraqis; and 3) America's own economic and religious aims, an agenda to serve Israel by destroying Iraq and fragmenting Israel's neighbors. All of this manifests a declaration of war on Islam itself. Thus, it is obligatory on all Muslims to kill Americans and their allies, civilian or military, in any country in which they are found in order to liberate Islamic holy places in Jerusalem and Arabia from Jewish and Christian occupation.

CHAPTER 5 –

STATEMENT REGARDING AFGHANISTAN – OCT. 7, 2001

PAGE 64

The United States began its invasion of Afghanistan on October 7, 2001. It is unclear whether OBL issued this statement before, during, or after the initial stages of the invasion. Suffice it to say that the invasion was imminent at the time it was issued. OBL is in Afghanistan, which is about to bear the brunt of American military force. He does not seem to be worried about that prospect.

The statement is brief. He notes that on 9/11 the U.S. had been struck at its most vulnerable points. On that day, America tasted what Muslims have tasted for scores of years – humiliation and contempt. Millions of innocent children are dying in Iraq (from the effects of the United Nations imposed economic sanctions) even though the children have committed no sins. Israeli tanks invade Palestinian territories but the *Ulema* (Islamic scholars) of the corrupt Middle East regimes raise no criticisms. In the name of the war on terrorism, President Bush and his supporters fight Islam. America's use of nuclear weapons to kill hundreds of thousands of Japanese was justified, as are the deaths of millions of Iraqi children as a result of the Iraq sanctions. But when dozens are killed at the U.S. embassies in Africa, the hypocrites stand behind America. The world is now divided into two camps: the side of Faith (free of hypocrisy) and the side of the infidels (non-believers). America will never know security before Palestine is secure and the infidel armies leave Muslim lands.

CHAPTER 6 –

SECOND STATEMENT REGARDING AFGHANISTAN – NOV. 3, 2001

PAGE 68

The American invasion of Afghanistan is almost one month old. American forces and their Northern Alliance allies are easily defeating the ragtag Taliban forces. Air supremacy and guided bombs targeted by ground-based Navy S.E.A.L. and Army Special Forces teams assigned to Northern Alliance units are decimating Taliban resisters. Their frontlines of resistance around Kabul have been destroyed, and the Northern Alliance looks forward to seizing the Afghani capital in short order. On November 9, 2001, Alliance forces would seize Mazar-e-Sharif. Kabul would fall on November 12th. From a military standpoint, the Taliban's situation is desperate.

OBL begins by noting that since 9/11 the world has divided into two camps: those who support the attacks and those who denounce them. A similar split occurred after American's invasion of Afghanistan. Many Muslims opposed the invasion and most Christians did not. The war has a religious character. It is the opening round of the new Crusade. Muslims and Christians are hostile because of their creeds, and all Muslims now must ask themselves where they stand in this new order. Even President George W. Bush described the war as a Crusade(during a news conference in September of 2001). How can it be a war on terrorism when Muslims are slaughtered across the world in places like Palestine, Iraq, southern Sudan, Somalia, Kashmir, etc? In Chechnya, the Orthodox Russian "bear" feasts on Muslims. In Bosnia, even in the United Nations' safe havens, thousands of Muslims were murdered. Islam's enemies speak clearly, but the corrupt *Ulema* (Islamic scholars) and Islamic leaders are ashamed to support the *Mujahideen* (Islamic fighters). He implores his brothers in Afghanistan to continue the fight.

CHAPTER 7 –

THE "SMOKING GUN" VIDEOTAPE – DEC. 13, 2001

PAGE 74

Here, OBL is captured on videotape engaging several of his supporters in candid discussions about the war in Afghanistan, where the video was apparently made, and the planning for the 9/11 attacks. Up to this time, in several interviews with members of the press, OBL had been denying any involvement in 9/11. Present at the meeting are, among others, Al Qaeda spokesperson Suleiman Abu Ghaith and OBL's "number two," Dr. Ayman Al-Zawahiri. Dr. Al-Zawahiri is the ideological mentor of OBL, and after OBL, probably the second most wanted fugitive in the world. Mr. Abu Ghaith's claim to infamy is a message he posted on *Jihadi* websites in June of 2002. By adding up the long-term casualties among the Muslim masses in Palestine, Iraq, and Afghanistan, he concluded that Muslims have the right to slay 4,000,000 Americans, including 2,000,000 children, in order to inflict on the American enemy losses commensurate with those suffered by Muslims at the hands of America and her surrogates. He also stated that the Muslims had the right to use chemical and biological weapons in achieving that goal. He relied on religious law that provides for punishment of the infidel in the same way that the infidel treats the Muslim. Many people erroneously attribute Mr. Abu Ghaith's statement to OBL.

The transcript of the videotape is a "must read." In it, OBL admits advance calculations about the casualties that would be inflicted in the 9/11 attacks. He had only anticipated the collapse of the immediate areas where the plans struck. He claims he knew the date of the attacks as early as September 6, 2001. He claims that Muhammad Atta was the leader of the group. He states that except for Mr. Atta, none of the other hijackers knew about the mission until they boarded the planes.

CHAPTER 8 –

THIRD STATEMENT REGARDING AFGHANISTAN – DEC. 27, 2001

PAGE 84

By December 5, 2001, when the battle for Tora Bora began, the United States had toppled the Taliban government and taken Kabul, the Afghanistan capital. The remnants of the Taliban were fighting a delaying action in Kandahar, their last stronghold, as elements of their forces fled into neighboring Pakistan. The Tora Bora battle was over by December 20th. Osama bin Laden was suspected of having been in Tora Bora but was not killed or captured. His escape is attributed to the failure of General Tommy Franks to put American troops on the ground to seal the perimeter. In 2005, August Hanning, the head of German intelligence, said that OBL escaped from Tora Bora by bribing the local militias on whom the United States had relied to kill or capture him. By the time he issued his December 27th statement, OBL was far from Tora Bora, probably safely ensconced in the wild, untamed Waziristan province of northwestern Pakistan.

OBL chronicles the post 9/11 world as evincing the Crusaders' hatred for Muslims. He cites air attacks on innocent Afghanis and claims that *Mujahideen* (Islamic warriors) do not attack innocents. He claims 9/11 was a reaction to the plight of Muslims in Palestine, Iraq, Somalia, southern Sudan, Kashmir, and other venues. 9/11 was a blow to the U.S. economy, costing a trillion dollars. Democracy means freedom for whites and slavery for the Middle East. He relates tactical lessons learned in facing American forces and air power in Afghanistan. Because of the asymmetrical force levels between the warring parties, he advocates attacking the U.S.'s economic base. He notes a previous *ABC* interview in which he warned that the fight might be brought to the U.S. He mentions one of the 9/11 hijackers by name.

CHAPTER 9 –

STATEMENT TO AMERICA – OCT. 26, 2002

PAGE 94

By now, the United States has defeated the Taliban in Afghanistan and OBL and his Al Qaeda members are on the run, probably in western Pakistan. President Bush has begun to rattle his saber about Iraq and is preparing to lead America into war in that venue. Though a fugitive, OBL has been keeping his ear to the rail and takes this opportunity to address Americans directly. He does not realize that his complete statements are never broadcast to the American people because the Bush administration has convinced the media that he may be passing code words to his cohorts. Interestingly, the purpose of this statement is to inform Americans exactly why he is fighting them.

He begins by noting erroneous media reports about why he fights. He will tell Americans why he fights them and what he wants from them. He fights because we have attacked Islam. Israel's creation evoked a heavy price from the Palestinians. Muslim blood is spilled in Palestine, Somalia, Chechnya, and other venues and must be avenged. American military forces taint the holy places in Saudi Arabia, and oil is selling at paltry prices because of American pressure. U.S. citizens mourn the 3,000 lives lost on 9/11 but not the 1,500,000 Iraqi children who died because of the United Nations imposed economic sanctions. In Jerusalem, Israel plans to destroy the *Al-Aqsa mosque*, the third holiest site in Islam, the same site despoiled by Ariel Sharon's visit in 2000 while accompanied by a thousand bodyguards. Americans are not innocent. They elect their leaders, and therefore, support the anti-Islamic policies of their leaders. Americans can change the destructive policies if they desire, and their tax money pays for bombs that kill Muslims and helps Israel. God has given permission for Muslims to exact revenge; it is about reciprocity. The U.S. economy is a target. If Ariel Sharon can be a man of peace to President George W. Bush, then so can OBL. OBL also invites Americans to leave their debauchery and accept Islam, and also to distance themselves from the Jews who he claims control their economy. He reminds Americans that Ben Franklin warned against the influence of the Jews. The laws of the U.S. are "man-made" and are meant to protect only the wealthy. Accept God's Laws, and reject immorality and the exploitation of women. America's "friends" across the world are repressive regimes that suppress democratic aspirations. Israel possesses weapons of mass destruction but other countries who want them for their own protection are branded as criminals. Israel is the greatest violator of international law. You immunize your soldiers from the war crimes because of your crimes in Afghanistan, where 1,000 Afghanis and Arabs were deliberately suffocated in sealed cargo containers. After 9/11, you became just like the other repressive countries of the world, e.g., harsh new laws and Guantanamo Bay, Cuba. You are a nation of hypocrites. You are a nation without principles. Stop supporting the enemies of Islam across the world. Get out of our lands. Do not force us to send your soldiers back in coffins. You will lose Bush's Crusade. That is why we fight.

CHAPTER 10 –

CALL TO JIHAD – NOVEMBER 12, 2002

PAGE 104

This statement, though succinct, is bothersome because it documents the spread of terrorism across the world since 9/11. And in spite of reverses in Afghanistan, OBL has lost none of his bravado. He also acknowledges that supporters of the United States will be targeted and will pay a heavy price for their support.

OBL does not mention any military reverses. Rather, he recites follow-up attacks to 9/11: the terrorist attacks in Tunisia and Karachi aimed at German and French nationals, the attack on a French supertanker in the Arabian Gulf, the killing of U.S. Marines in Kuwait, the explosions aimed at the Australian patrons of a Bali nightclub, and the attack on the Moscow theater. OBL is proud that the zealous sons of Islam have committed these acts. Still, President Bush and Israel kill the innocent in Iraq and Palestine. He calls the White House occupants the greatest butchers of the age, citing two million deaths during the Vietnam War and several Bush administration members' roles in that War. Australia previously ignored warnings about what it had done in East Timor and the Bali bombings were a reminder. OBL promises to reciprocate for the killings of Muslims everywhere. *Jihad* (holy war) is upon you.

CHAPTER 11 –

STATEMENT TO IRAQIS – FEBRUARY 11, 2003

PAGE 108

This statement is meant to rally the Iraqis. OBL now finds the United States poised to invade Iraq in search of weapons of mass destruction that do not exist. He is in hiding, probably somewhere in western Pakistan. He prepares his followers for the imminent occupation of Baghdad, the old seat of the Islamic Caliphate, by the Crusader American forces, intent on looting Iraq and paving the way for Greater Israel. Muslims must fight for the sake of *Jihad* (holy war), seeking forgiveness and avoiding the "seven sins." He warns them to be wary of American air power and psychological warfare, but not to worry; American soldiers are cowards and lack morale. They fight for capitalists, usurers, the merchants of war, and President George W. Bush's personal grudges. He instructs future Jihadis in tactics to counter America's technological superiority. He specifically mentions his presence at Tora Bora and the counter-measures he and his men employed there. Close-order combat and martyrdom will be tactics of the first order in Iraq. In the coming fight, he authorizes Muslims to associate even with socialists to fight the Crusaders. He cautions future *Jihadis* not to decry the numbers; patience and heart will determine the outcome.

CHAPTER 12 –

SERMON FOR THE FEAST OF THE SACRIFICE – FEB. 16, 2003

PAGE 114

Here, OBL seeks to establish his credentials as an *Imam*, or Islamic cleric or scholar. Ironically, his seeking status as a cleric results from the corruption of the Middle East's *Ulema* (Islamic scholars) by the autocratic governments of the region. Throughout the region, they are civil servants employed by the governments. Thus, their *Fatwas* (religious decrees) hew closely to government policies. Though they are still highly educated in Islam and are graduates of respected Islamic teaching institutions, their objectivity is called into question. That allows lay persons like OBL, who are essentially self-trained in Islam, to fill the void of credibility by offering religious interpretations independent of the corrupted *Ulema*. Because Sunni Islam has no official hierarchy of clerics, as does Shi'ite Islam, any Muslim who appears to be educated in Islam can claim to be an Imam and seek to attract a flock. OBL is just such a phenomenon.

In this sermon in celebration of the Prophet Abraham's (PBUH) offering to sacrifice his own son if God demanded it, OBL credibly establishes his Islamic credentials. But he begins with the politics of the moment, reminding his flock of the creation of Israel and the Crusader wars of the last century. The war on terrorism is but an extension of the original Crusades of the 11th through 13th centuries which intended to destroy Islam. Iraq's invasion will be but the next step. American military forces are based in Saudi Arabia to divide and conquer it in order to establish a Jewish super-state. Palestine is an example of what awaits the region. Only *Jihad* (holy war) will save the *Ummah* (Islamic nation). Only the *Ummah*'s sins and retrenchment from Islam delays the *Holy Quran*'s promised victory over the infidels. He reminds his flock of the defeat of the Soviets in Afghanistan and localized victories in Afghanistan, Chechnya, Beirut in 1982, the bombings of the U.S. embassies in Africa, and other venues. He denies the White House rationale that he fights because he is jealous of America. He fights because of the evil that has befallen the *Ummah* at the hands of the infidels. He reminds them of 9/11, and that God guided the martyrs into the buildings, hitting the heart of the U.S. economy. 9/11 evoked the Crusaders' true hatred of Islam and awoke the *Ummah* to the need for unity and a new Caliph. 9/11 was a reaction to American policies. A small group of *Mujahideen* (Islamic warriors) brought America to its knees. The only restrictions on the youth's march to *Jihad* are corrupt *Ulema* (Islamic scholars) and rulers in the Middle East. The masses never pledged themselves to these rulers; rather, they are pledged to God. The rulers and their corrupt *Ulema* are allied with the infidels and rule by "man-made" laws. These rulers all were enthroned by the Crusaders. The *Holy Quran* teaches Muslims to free themselves from tyranny. He urges his flock to study the early Islamic scholars. Those scholars who refrain from *Jihad* are reacting to the pressures of the autocratic regimes, which have destroyed Islam and contemporary Muslim life. Now three factions characterize the Islamic world: the corrupt leaders and their supporters, those who compromised their values to protect themselves from these leaders, and those who remained steadfast but nonetheless remained unprepared for *Jihad* and *Hijra* (migration) to friendly Muslim venues. He notes that the "currency of God" is expensive, and regarding *Jihad*, a great divide exists between lectures and taking heads. Harkening back to the early experiences of the Prophet Muhammad (PBUH) and his Companions, he urges his followers to emulate them as his *Mujahideen* have emulated them. If anyone does not have what is required, then at least stand aside. *Jihad* is compulsory for the *Ummah*, even for the wealthy. He sees Afghanistan as a plus, a veritable swamp for America, the venue of a protracted guerilla war all which is very positive for the *Ummah*. The *Ummah* must unite.

CHAPTER 13 –

COMMENTS ON JIHAD – JULY 2003

PAGE 132

The Iraq War is now three months old. Although President Bush declared "mission accomplished" on May 1, 2003, he was wrong. At this writing, the Iraq theater of operations has deteriorated into a classic insurgency against the occupying American and Coalition forces and their Iraqi supporters. "IED" (improvised explosive device) has found its way into today's lexicon, and over 100,000 Iraqi civilians have paid the ultimate price for President Bush's invasion of their country. The bloodletting continues with no end in sight.

However, in July 2003, the immediate effects of the invasion were still rippling throughout Iraq and the insurgency was organizing. OBL needed to rally his followers to *Jihad* (holy war) in the face of reverses in Afghanistan and Iraq.

He recites that Islam has been in retreat since the fall of the Caliphate. He describes the five conditions necessary to restore the *Ummah* (Islamic nation) to a place of honor. The loss of Afghanistan is an especially damaging development because no Muslim country came to the defense of the Taliban, who, in OBL's view, had established a true Islamic state. Internecine warfare and international media slander brought down the Taliban rather than American guided bombs. The *Ummah* can reverse the course of events through *Jihad*, the individual obligation of every Muslim. Once sufficient numbers of *Mujahideen* (Islamic warriors) have taken to the field, then *Jihad* becomes a collective obligation of Muslims everywhere. Ignore the corrupt *Ulema* (Islamic scholars) who are civil servants to the Middle East's autocratic regimes and who stand in the way of *Jihad*. They are heretics. Because of the communications revolution, the *Ummah* today faces its greatest catastrophe because of the ability of the corrupt clerics to spread their corrupted messages. He calls on Muslims to boycott and banish them. There can be no Faith or Islamic rule if the ruler is a non-believer, as are the apostate leaders of Saudi Arabia and the Middle East generally. The survival of Islam depends on martyrdom. *Jihad* restores truth and abolishes falsehood. Even Prince Talal of the Saudi royal family admitted that the infidel American forces would not leave Saudi Arabia even if asked to do so by the Saudi government itself. Muslims have no choice but to fight the Crusaders.

CHAPTER 14 –

COMMENTARY ON THE 9/11 ATTACKS – SEP. 11, 2003

PAGE 138

Finally, two years to the day after 9/11, the world receives direct answers about OBL's involvement in those attacks from OBL himself. The world's most wanted fugitive taunts his hunters from his secret hideout, probably in western Pakistan, by calmly reiterating his own role in the planning of the attacks and the heroism of the hijackers themselves. The comments are intended as exhortations to the *Mujahideen* (Islamic warriors) everywhere that are facing American firepower. He reminds them and the world that a few committed *Mujahideen* hit American where it hurt the most, the economic super-structure.

He begins by commending the martyred youth who sacrificed themselves on 9/11. They inflicted heavy losses on the enemy and disrupted its plans for the conquest of Islam. He notes that plans existed for the Afghanistan and Iraq invasions six months before 9/11. 9/11 awoke Muslims to the need for *Jihad* (holy war). He personally knew the 9/11 hijackers, and he names each one of them. They were true believers, not corrupted by Western ways as are many youths. They learned their duty through the *Holy Quran* and the *Hadith* (words and deeds of the Prophet Muhammad [PBUH]). They held *Sharia* (Islamic law) preeminent over their own safety and over the corruptions surrounding them. They offered themselves to God and rejected Saudi Arabia's procrastinators, who were "too busy" for *Jihad*.

CHAPTER 15 –

SECOND STATEMENT TO IRAQIS – OCT. 12, 2003

PAGE 142

OBL now follows up his February 11, 2003, message to Iraqis, *infra*. Iraq is occupied, the insurgency is still embryonic, and weapons of mass destruction are nowhere to be seen. Casualties are enormous among the civilian population, but as a matter of official policy, the American military does not count civilian casualties. Thousands of Iraqis are headed to prison, including the notorious Abu Ghraib prison in Baghdad. The old seat of the Islamic Caliphate is occupied by the Crusader army. Matters could not appear to be worse, but in the eyes of OBL, Iraq presents an opportunity to focus *Jihad* (holy war) and attack the Crusaders. The time is opportune for attack.

He congratulates the Iraqis on their *Jihad*. America is now mired in the swamp of Iraq, just as it is mired in the swamp of Afghanistan. Because of his penchant for oil, President George W. Bush is easy prey. This is no time for peaceful, democratic solutions in dealing with the apostate governments of the Middle East, the Jews, and the Crusaders. *Jihad* is the rule, per God's Teachings. Those Iraqis who choose to participate in the municipal councils have gone astray, abiding by "man-made" laws rather than Islam. They have become polytheists obeying corrupt kings and *Ulema* (Islamic scholars) instead of God. Whoever assists the Crusaders is an infidel. The pending Iraqi government will be an American puppet, just like Hamad Karzai in Afghanistan. He takes a swipe at the "road map to peace" for Israel and Palestine as a ruse to stop the *Intifada*. He also urges Muslim women to play a role in *Jihad*. He exhorts the Iraqis not to fear the Americans, whose strength is weakening, militarily and economically. The 9/11 attacks cost the United States a trillion dollars, and its current budget deficit is 450 billion dollars. He reminds them of the sacrifices of the Muslims in Palestine, Chechnya, Kashmir, the Philippines, and Afghanistan.

CHAPTER 16 –

MESSAGE TO AMERICANS – OCT. 18, 2003

PAGE 146

Having recently issued a message to the Iraqis, OBL now turns his attention to his enemy, America. In exhorting *Jihad* (holy war) against America, he does not paint a nice picture of American society. In many respects, he is correct. Here in the United States, we seem to be adrift in a sea of immorality, exploitation of women, and xenophobia against not only Muslims but anything foreign. Minutemen vigilantes have been patrolling our southern borders looking for mostly Mexican undocumented immigrants traveling North to find jobs to support their families. The war on terrorism has become the weapon of choice by which America and Americans can attack people and cultures they do not like. OBL's depiction of our society reveals an intimate knowledge about our frailties.

He indicts the majority of Americans as vulgar and lacking good manners. They elect evil persons to office and find themselves enslaved to the rich and to the Jews, who use Israel's lie of democracy to promote American support for Israel. Israel's support is now paid for by Muslim blood and land and by America's economy and the blood of Americans. Iraq was no threat to America. President George W. Bush is an evil to all mankind; he stabs the truth with lies. He fooled Americans into invading Iraq and lied to the whole world in doing so. A nation consists of its ethics and morals. America is lost. President Bush has sent America's sons into the lion's den. He is out to steal Iraq's oil, just as early Americans killed the Native Americans and stole their wealth. But Iraq has turned President Bush's profits into losses, and he looks for a way out. He seeks mercenaries to do his bidding there, revealing America's own weakness. OBL resolves to retaliate against all parties who came to America's aid in Iraq, especially the United Kingdom, Spain, Australia, Poland, Japan, Italy, and the Gulf States that assisted in the invasion. American soldiers in Iraq are giving their lives for arms dealers and the White House's gang of corporations. OBL promises to continue martyrdom operations inside the United States until Americans abandon their folly. Baghdad will not fall; Americans will all die.

CHAPTER 17 –

STATEMENT TO THE ISLAMIC NATION – JAN. 4, 2004

PAGE 150

Broadening his focus, OBL now turns his attention to the entire *Ummah* (Islamic nation). His more recent messages had been directed to Iraqis and Americans. Of interest in this statement is that he has the currency and credentials to address the entire *Ummah*. He is supposed to be a terrorist who masterminded the deaths of 3,000 people on 9/11. However, most Muslims in the Middle East view him positively. He speaks more freely than they can in their repressive countries. He seems to be uncorrupted, as are his followers, none of whom has sought to collect the twenty-five million dollar reward placed on his head by the United States. He has focused the world on the grievances of the Islamic world, especially the plight of the Palestinians. He has sown the seeds of *Jihad* (holy war) in the minds of millions of Muslims, and now he seeks to cultivate what he has planted.

He notes that no weapons of mass destruction were found. The Crusaders occupy Baghdad, and now America wants to change the educational curricula in Muslim schools throughout the world. It wages a religio-economic war that will result in the occupation of the entire Gulf. He begs the *Ummah* to lend its ears to him so that he may save their lives. The West's struggle against Islam began centuries ago, and it is a matter of Faith versus falsehood. The only dialogue with occupiers is by war. In the past, only *Jihad* ended the Crusades. Today, Baghdad, tomorrow the Crusader forces will trample on the streets of Riyadh, and then the *Al-Haramain* (the holy mosques at Mecca and Medina). Do not defend your countries; defend Islam! The infidel rulers of the Gulf States brought the Crusaders into our lands. Having seen Saddam Hussein in jail, they now fear for their own safety at the hands of the Americans. Such leaders cannot defend Islam. Rulers are not qualified to rule if they do the bidding of the infidels and the *Ummah*'s enemies. Their historic corruption is of secondary importance to their loyalty to the new Crusaders. Islam must be injected into all walks of life, and leaders must hold Islam tightly and raise the banner of *Jihad*. He calls for an Islamic leadership council to fill the void of leadership. The first priority is to repel the new raid of the Romans that began in Iraq.

CHAPTER 18 –

OFFER OF PEACE TREATY WITH EUROPE – APRIL 15, 2004

PAGE 156

On March 11, 2004, bombs ripped through four crowed commuter trains in Madrid, Spain, killing 191 people and wounding 1,900. Islamic militant Moroccans who sympathized with OBL had bombed the trains in protest of Spanish Prime Minister Jose Maria

Anzar's support for the Iraq War and the stationing of Spanish troops in Iraq. A continuing investigation of the bombings by Spanish authorities has resulted in the trial of over a dozen Muslim militants in Spain, charged either with connections to the bombings or with connections to Al Qaeda. Mr. Anzar's actions in Iraq were extremely unpopular with the Spanish population. Two days after the bombings, they voted in the national elections and threw him and his government out of office. Control of the government passed to the new Prime Minister, Socialist Jose Luis Rodriguez Zapatero. He ordered the immediate withdrawal of Spanish forces from Iraq. OBL seeks to expand on the lessons taught by the Madrid bombings by offering all European countries a peace treaty. Spain accepted by its de facto withdrawal of its troops. The remainder of Europe rejected the offer. Whether the blanket rejection was a mistake remains to be seen.

OBL begins by noting that the western governments' definition of "terrorists" defines themselves. 9/11 and 3/11 were reactions. He asks why America's and Spain's dead innocents have value while dead Muslim innocents are worthless. Justice demands in-kind responses to violence, and those who begin the cycle are even more blameworthy. Your oppressive politicians are forcing your sons to be killed in Iraq. It is in the world's mutual interests to thwart the gang that occupies theWhite House. The Iraq War has generated billions of dollars for American corporations like Halliburton. Only the merchants of war are benefiting. Bloodsuckers like President George W. Bush and his ilk, the media giants, the United Nations and the corporations are the real dangers to the world. Responding to the recent positive events in Europe, he offers a peace treaty subject to renewal. He and his supporters will refrain from attacking those who refrain from interfering with Muslim affairs or attacking Muslims. The offer will be on the table for three months. Again, he notes that liars claim he hates freedom. Blood was spilled only after Russia invaded Afghanistan and later invaded Chechnya as well as America's invading of Afghanistan and Iraq. 9/11 occurred only after years of Palestinian suffering and America's occupation of Saudi Arabia.

CHAPTER 19 –

SECOND STATEMENT TO THE AMERICAN PEOPLE -OCT. 29, 2004

PAGE 160

This is OBL's second message to Americans. It was deliberately timed to affect the 2004 Presidential election, and it did. According to presidential candidate John Kerry, the broadcast of the videotape helped George W. Bush to be re-elected to the Presidency. Senator Kerry says that he was gaining in the polls until OBL's message was broadcast, then his gains flattened, and by Election Day on November 2nd, they had slipped. It was really quite amazing to see the world's most wanted fugitive take the time to choreograph a formal, videotaped presentation of his message while standing at a podium in front of colored cloth backdrop. He was calm, articulate, and menacing. He would tell Americans how he came to attack the World Trade Center. He would tell them how to prevent another 9/11. He would then offer his own view of the 2004 United States presidential election.

OBL begins by telling Americans how to prevent another 9/11. He facetiously comments that President Bush lies when he tells America that OBL and Al Qaeda hate freedom. If, in fact, they hated freedom, then they would have attacked Sweden. Free men do not forfeit their own security. Haters of freedom do not possess the defiant spirit of the youth who carried out the 9/11 attacks. He and his supporters fight because they are resisting oppression. As America kills their numbers, they will kill Americans in equal measure. He remains amazed that for three years after 9/11, Americans still allow President Bush to deceive them about the real causes of the attacks. OBL will now tell them the truth. He informs America that he first had the idea to hit the towers on seeing devastated high-rise buildings in Lebanon in 1982 after the American Sixth Fleet had just bombarded them. It was like seeing a crocodile eat a child. The crocodile only understands weapons. He then developed an intense desire to end tyranny and punish the oppressors. America's freedom and democracy meant the deaths of 1,000,000 Iraqi children during the sanctions period, and now bombs kill millions more. All this so that President Bush can remove Saddam Hussein, an old agent of America, and replace him with a new puppet in order to steal Iraq's oil. 9/11 was a reply to what had gone before it. Over the years, OBL had sought to enlighten Americans about the plight of the *Ummah*

(Islamic nation) and the grievances of the Muslims. He articulates specific interviews with identified, respected journalists as evidence of his earlier attempts at educating Americans. He dares today's media to broadcast some of those earlier interviews. He notes that thus far, he has achieved positive results. He and his *Mujahideen* (Islamic warriors) are well versed in dealing with the Bush administration because it is reminiscent of the repressive regimes of the Middle East with which they have had long experience. The Patriot Act and the fraud of the 2000 presidential election in America were imported from the examples of the autocratic Middle East regimes. He promises to bleed the United States to the point of bankruptcy. The White House's demands for new fronts in order to sate the appetites of America's corporations have helped Al Qaeda achieve results. We are on one team fulfilling America's economic goals. Al Qaeda's $500,000 expenditure for 9/11 cost the United States $500,000,000,000. The United States budget is in deficit, and the president asks for emergency funds for the Iraq and Afghanistan Wars. OBL and Muhammad Atta had agreed that twenty minutes would pass before the U.S. could respond to the 9/11 attacks. We did not think that President Bush would reward us with triple that time by reading a book about ramming to school children. "Black gold" — oil, has distorted President Bush's view of the world, and he sells out the national security to protect private interests. Welcome to the swamps of Iraq. President Bush is stained in blood for the sake of oil and private corporations. He cites a *Hadith* (words and deeds of the Prophet Muhammad [PBUH]) for the proposition that nations fail when they punish thieves but not kings. It will not matter whether President Bush or Senator Kerry is elected president. Your security is in your own hands. Any nation that does not menace us is secure.

CHAPTER 20 –

MESSAGE TO THE ISLAMIC WORLD – DECEMBER 16, 2004

PAGE 168

By now, the whole world is familiar with the abuse of Muslim detainees by the United States in Afghanistan, Iraq, and Guantanamo Bay, Cuba. Since 9/11, it has abandoned the moral high ground. Alleged terrorist suspects are seized in venues across the world and spirited away to brutal third-world countries for interrogation that certainly will include torture. The new word for such kidnappings is "rendition." Ironically, the destinations of many of these rendered suspects are Middle East countries like Egypt and Syria, whose interrogation methods are well-known throughout the Islamic world. It is a new world, a world of culture clash, of religious war between Christians and Muslims. OBL continues his effort to awaken the Muslims by offering them one of his most detailed messages. He seeks to galvanize them to action – *Jihad* (holy war).

There is much polarization in the Islamic world and much talk of bloodletting. But the fault is that of the corrupt rulers, not the *Mujahideen* (Islamic warriors). The rulers abdicated their responsibilities, disbelieve in God, and have committed major sins. For example, the Saudi rulers implement "man-made" laws and do not forbid the forbidden. The Middle East leaders have removed themselves from the fold of Islam. The Saudi people suffer while their leaders fatten their own pocketbooks. The regimes, and particularly Saudi Arabia, ally themselves with *Kufr* (non-believers) America and rule according to their whims rather than according to Islam. We who already possessed all of the material things that this life offers abandoned them in the cause of God. Muslims need only God. Steadfastness in Islam is the only happy ending. Follow the example of our glorious Prophet (PBUH) fourteen centuries ago. Deviation from Islam is apostasy. Obedience to rulers is not absolute; it is conditioned on adherence to Islam. Aspire to unity; for when Muslims abandon Islam, hatred ensues, which is the situation today. The Middle East countries play games in the name of free elections. Legislatures are forbidden because they make themselves partners with God and enact their own laws instead of His. It is the *Mujahideen* versus the *Kufr* Americans. Saudi Arabia's decision-makers reside in the White House, not Riyadh. The Middle East's corrupt rulers are succumbing to the demands of the Crusaders and changing the curricula at their Islamic schools. This is apostasy. The Saudi leadership is especially guilty, having thrown in with President George W. Bush's global Crusader alliance. In Iraq, America has removed Saddam Hussein, the local thief, and replaced him with George W. Bush, a global thief. The conflict is between the path of God and the apostate regimes of the Middle East and the Crusader alliance. Islam demands correction: the removal of the apostate rulers. There is no difference between the corrupt, apostate rulers of the Gulf States and Iraq's ruling stooges. The *Ummah* must rise up and make the necessary changes. Incredibly, we are accused of being

Zionist agents when, in fact, the corrupt, apostate rulers are the agents of Zionism. America does not deserve security because it continues to rain down on us death and destruction. Matters have gone beyond tolerance. Recall what happened to the Shah of Iran and the Romanian Ceausescu.

Preface

This book is about saving lives – yours, mine, and perhaps countless others. President Bush has recently acknowledged that Iraq has become the primary theater in the war on terrorism. He has told America that fighting terrorists in Iraq means that we will not have to fight them here.[1] However, recent events have proved him to be terribly wrong.

On July 7, 2005, three subway trains and a city bus were bombed in London, England, killing 56 people and wounding over 700. The bombings were carried out by four radical Muslim suicide bombers. Britain is our strongest ally in Iraq and has 8,500 troops on the ground fighting terrorists in that country's Southern provinces. Yet, that did not guarantee Britain's security. Quite to the contrary, a British think tank recently opined that Britain's alliance with the United States in the Iraq War increased Muslim hostility toward Britain and engendered an increased range of terrorist activity in Britain. Ironically, less than a month before the July 7th bombings, Britain's top intelligence officials had concluded that no group within Britain had the capability to mount a terrorist attack in the United Kingdom.[2]

I submit that the tragic events in London on July 7th bode ill for our own future here in the United States. Britain is an island nation of only sixty million people with a population of 1.8 million Muslims. It has stringent anti-terrorism laws. Its two security services, MI-5, the Domestic Security Service, and MI-6, the Special Intelligence Service, comparable to the United States' Central Intelligence Agency (C.I.A.), are models of cooperation in their counterterrorism intelligence-gathering efforts. They have been keeping a close eye on Britain's Muslim population since September 11, 2001. But even with these advantages, the British government was helpless to prevent the July 7, 2005 bombings.

Matters are even worse here in the United States. America has a population of approximately three hundred million people, thousands of miles of porous borders, and a Muslim population estimated to be between two and eight million people. Turf wars between the Federal Bureau of Investigation (F.B.I.), the C.I.A., and the Department of Homeland Security still plague our domestic counterterrorism efforts. America's security is nowhere near the level of security that the British enjoy, yet their gallant efforts fell far short on July 7th.

The lesson to be learned from this is that fighting terrorists in Iraq has actually *increased* not decreased the risk of future terrorist attacks here in the United States. The Bush administration has placed Americans into this mess because it failed to heed the advice of a Fourth Century B.C., Chinese military thinker. In the words of Sun Tzu: "Know the enemy and know yourself; in a hundred battles you will never be in peril."[3] Instead of venturing into Iraq, the administration should have been concentrating our efforts on the real enemy: Osama bin Laden.

The current war on terrorism officially began on September 11, 2001, when Osama bin Laden's Al Qaeda henchmen attacked the World Trade Center in New York City and the Pentagon in Washington, D.C. On that day, he became Public Enemy No. 1, and he still is to this day. He remains a free man who continues to release audio and videotapes thumbing his nose at America's military might and importuning the world's Muslims to rise up in *Jihad* (holy war) to combat the new Christian Crusader, America.

Unfortunately, America's invasion of Iraq has given Mr. Bin Laden's message deep traction in the Islamic world. Today, Muslim foreign fighters from all over the globe are flocking to Iraq to confront the new Crusader. Known in Arabic as *Mujahideen* (Islamic warriors), many of them will quite willingly die carrying out suicide bombing attacks against American and Iraqi forces. Islam teaches that Muslims who die in defense of the religion receive a one-way ticket to heaven after the "pinch" of death.[4] To die under such circumstances is to become a *Shaheed* (martyr).

Even more worrisome are the ones who do not die. Aside from the indigenous Sunni insurgency opposed to the American occupation, the *Mujahideen* from other countries do not necessarily remain in Iraq waiting to become casualties at the hands of American military forces. Many of them were sent to Iraq to be blooded and trained in the art of urban warfare, in the manufacturing of "improvised explosive devices," in exploiting the weaknesses of American military technologies and tactics, and in strategic and tactical countermeasures. Then they are sent back to their homes or to other venues throughout the world, including Europe and the United States, to ply their newly learned deadly skills wherever they might find Americans and America's supporters. Ironically, Iraq is proving to be a more efficient training ground for this generation of *Mujahideen* than was rural Afghanistan for Mr. Bin Laden and his generation of *Mujahideen*.[5]

As a Muslim and an Arab-American born in the United States, I am very pessimistic about the present prosecution of the war on terrorism. If anybody of importance in our government had paid any attention at all to Mr. Bin Laden's own statements for the past ten years, the current administration would not have taken such a drastically destructive detour into Iraq. I want to win the war on terrorism before it becomes a global holy war against Islam that America cannot possibly win, and I am not alone in that view.

I found an unlikely ally: the very man whose job it was to capture or kill Osama bin Laden. Michael Scheuer was a senior C.I.A. analyst who had been in charge of the search for Mr. Bin Laden from 1996 until his resignation from the C.I.A. in 2004. He resigned so that he could promote his new book about the war on terrorism: *Imperial Hubris: Why the West Is Losing the War on Terror*. In his book, Mr. Scheuer challenged the stereotypical negative depictions of Mr. Bin Laden as expressed by such Middle East experts as Don D. Chipman, Bernard Lewis, Victor David Hanson, Ralph Peters, Malise Ruthven, and Fareed Zakaria. They have collectively portrayed Mr. Bin Laden as a nihilist, a madman, a hater of freedom, and a product of a failed civilization, i.e., the Islamic world. To the contrary, Mr. Scheuer opined that Mr. Bin Laden exhibited patience; brilliance; managerial expertise; sound strategy; sound tactics; admirable character traits; eloquence; and the pursuit of focused, limited war strategies.[6]

I was more inclined to agree with Mr. Scheuer's view. After all, Mr. Bin Laden had perpetrated 9/11, no mean feat from somebody who was supposed to be hiding out in a cave somewhere in Afghanistan or Pakistan. And Mr. Scheuer apparently had gotten it right because he was concentrating on something that the other "experts" had missed – Mr. Bin Laden's own words, provided to him by the C.I.A.'s translation resources.

When I read Mr. Scheuer's important book, I found it repugnant that in our great democracy all of us Americans were not able to read Mr. Bin Laden's own words so that we could better understand this very dangerous man. Several factors led to this unacceptable situation. First, whenever he released a new audio or videotape, it was in the Arabic language. Ordinarily, the Arabic-language television network Al Jazeera would broadcast a portion (rarely all) of the statement on its network – in Arabic. Within a day or two, the Western media would offer crudely translated English-language snippets of what Al Jazeera had broadcast. However, Americans and other Western-world populations were never treated to his complete statements. The English-language snippets that found their way into our media were more soundbite than substance. Most of our media pundits ignored his words and expended their energies trying to figure out whether they and our Special Forces troops could locate Mr. Bin Laden by identifying rock formations in the background of the videotape.

The situation was made even worse by the United States government. It successfully discouraged the Western media, especially in the United States, from broadcasting Mr. Bin Laden's actual words, whether in Arabic or in English. The Bush administration's rationale was that his statements might contain "secret code words" issuing instructions to his terrorist minions across the world. The media succumbed to the pressure. After all, neither the media nor anyone else in the West wanted to be perceived as supporting Mr. Bin Laden or terrorism, either directly or indirectly.

The result was that until now most Americans remained totally ignorant about Mr. Bin Laden and his message. Thus, they believed

President Bush when he addressed a Joint Session of Congress on September 20, 2001, and told them that Mr. Bin Laden had attacked us because he hated our freedom.[7] That was untrue. Since 1994, Mr. Bin Laden has been telling us that he does not hate us because of our freedom. Rather, he claims to have righteous grievances that have resulted from certain foreign policies toward the Middle East and the Islamic world.

Since President Bush's speech, Americans have learned very little more about Mr. Bin Laden. We know that he is tall, perhaps 6'6"; he escaped from a place called Tora Bora, Afghanistan, in December 2001; and he may be hiding out in Afghanistan or Pakistan. I submit that if America really wants to win the war on terrorism, its citizens and goverment jointly need to follow Sun Tzu's advice and learn a lot more about him – other than just his mere physical description or his possible various previous locations – both of which might have changed radically in the past months.

Our need for more information about Mr. Bin Laden had reached critical mass on September 16, 2001, when President Bush used the word "crusade" to describe the war on terrorism at a news conference.[8] When he uttered that word, he played right into Mr. Bin Laden's hands. Since 1991, Mr. Bin Laden has been vociferously complaining that the United States has been engaged in a new Christian Crusade against Islam in the Middle East and in the Islamic world generally. Now a Christian, faith-based President had corroborated Mr. Bin Laden's message. Muslims have never forgotten the original Christian Crusades of the Eleventh through Thirteenth Centuries. If the Islamic world were to perceive the war on terrorism to be a new Crusade, then millions of Muslims worldwide would galvanize around Mr. Bin Laden and his message. The result would be an indefinite global holy war, not a focused war on terrorism with specific targets and specific goals.

That is why it is so important for Americans to read and understand Mr. Bin Laden's own words in their cultural and historical context. If they do so, they will see that his grievances actually arise from America's own foreign policies. Even more important, they will also find that those grievances are also harbored by the vast majority of Muslims, not only in the Arab Middle East but across the Islamic world. Perhaps if Americans had been privy to more information about Mr. Bin Laden before 9/11, we could have done more to prevent it. At the very least, we could have reviewed our foreign policies and corrected them so that Mr. Bin Laden's message would not have had so much resonance in the Islamic world.

Accordingly, I have compiled twenty of what I believe to be Mr. Bin Laden's most important statements over a ten-year period between 1994 and 2004. They have been translated into understandable English. For the first time, Americans will be able to study the real Osama bin Laden in his own words. They will clearly understand his thoughts, his grievances, and his goals, and therefore will clearly understand why 9/11 came as no surprise to either Mr. Scheuer or to anyone else in the government who was trying to stop Mr. Bin Laden. Perhaps that is the real reason why ex-White House counter-terrorism czar Richard Clarke apologized to the American people for failing to prevent 9/11 when he testified before the 9/11 Commission on March 24, 2004.[9]

In today's dangerous environment of color-coded threat levels, no-fly lists, and potential "dirty bombs" in our own backyard, the American people are entitled to all of the facts. In that way, they can take a proactive role in their own defense.

To know Mr. Bin Laden's words is also to know the true risks of the Bush administration's current approach to the war on terrorism. As aptly stated by Sun Tzu: "[T]here has never been a protracted war from which a country has benefited."[10] The longer the war on terrorism continues, the longer the world is at risk in this era of weapons of mass destruction. Unfortunately, President Bush has embarked on an indefinite and protracted war on terrorism. He himself has said that, "we may never sit down at a peace table to end this war."[11] He might have assured that result by his invasion of Iraq.

My thesis, then, is simple: the more everyone learns about Mr. Bin Laden the sooner we will defeat him and avoid a global holy war. By "defeat him," I do not mean to kill or capture him. As the reader will see *infra*, his words and his deeds will long outlive his natural life in an Islamic world which totally lacks modern heroes. In life or in death, Mr. Bin Laden's message and example will continue to motivate hundreds of thousands, if not millions, of the world's 1.2 billion Muslims – to engage in *Jihad* (holy war) against their perceived common enemy. What I mean by defeat is the complete discrediting of his message by changing the policies that created him in the first place. In that way, he will lose traction is the Islamic world and the *Mujahideen* [Islamic warriors] will go back home to their families.

And as you read the following pages, remember that neither Mr. Bin Laden nor his followers hate us because of our freedoms. They hate us because they believe that our government's foreign policies across the world have cost the lives of millions of Muslims. In their view, 9/11 was "blowback" for places like Palestine, Bosnia, Chechnya, Kashmir, the southern Philippines and many other venues in which Muslims are being persecuted and murdered.

Even the Mayor of London realizes the Western world's failed foreign policies have become the catalyst for terrorism. On July 19, 2005, barely after the dust of the July 7th bombings had settled, Mayor Ken Livingston commented about the then suspected link between the London bombers and Mr. Bin Laden's Al Qaeda network: "You've just had 80 years of Western intervention into predominantly Arab lands because of a Western need for oil. We've propped up unsavory governments; we've overthrown ones that we didn't consider sympathetic." Addressing the Palestinian situation, he continued: "If you have been under foreign occupation, and denied the right to vote, denied the right to run your own affairs, often denied the right to work, for three generations, I suspect if it had happened here in England, we would have produced a lot of suicide bombers ourselves."[12]

As a lawyer with a background in political science, as well as being an Arab-American and a Muslim, I hope to offer special insights into the policies that created Mr. Bin Laden, Islam, and the Arabic culture. And unlike many of the media's "ethnically correct terrorism experts," I have no private agenda that betrays my own ethnic and religious upbringing and subordinates me to today's faddish political ideologies. If you choose to turn this page, you will get the truth with no holds barred. Then you can make up your own mind about Mr. Bin Laden, about the conduct of the war on terrorism, and about what we need to do to win it today.

This Page Left Intentionally Blank For Notes

Introduction

Osama Bin Laden — The Man

Osama bin Laden's full name is Osama bin Muhammad bin Laden. He was born in the Malez neighborhood of Riyadh, Saudi Arabia, in 1957. Six months after his birth, his family moved to Medina. Mr. Bin Laden says that most of his life in Saudi Arabia was spent between Mecca, Jeddah, and Medina.[1]

His father, Sheikh Muhammad bin Awad bin Laden was born in Hadrmout, Yemen. As a young man, the senior Bin Laden came to Saudi Arabia in 1930 or 1931 to work as a laborer in the port of Jeddah. Ultimately, the senior Bin Laden built the largest construction company in Saudi Arabia. During the 1950's he was a favorite of the Saudi King Saud and actively encouraged close ties to the Sauds, the royal family of Saudi Arabia. He also enjoyed immensely good relations with King Faisal, King Saud's successor. Over the years, the senior Bin Laden's company was awarded gigantic construction contracts for royal palaces and the construction and refurbishing of the holiest sites in Islam, the *Masjid* (mosque) *Al-Haram* (site of the *Kaba*), located in Mecca; the *Masjid Al-Nabawi*, burial site of the Prophet Muhammad (peace be upon him, hereinafter "PBUH," words of grace that must attend any oral or written reference to any of the Prophets recognized by Islam), located in

Medina; and the *Masjid Al-Aqsa* on the *Al-Haram Ash-Sharif* (The Noble Sanctuary, also known as the "Temple Mount" in the Western world) in *Al-Quds* (Jerusalem). The elder Bin Laden liked to brag that during one day in his busy life he had been able to perform his obligatory Islamic prayers in each of the three mosques. Osama bin Laden himself proudly relates that his father rebuilt the *Al-Aqsa* mosque after a devastating fire in 1969.

Osama bin Laden's father had a total of ten wives, but no more than four at any one time, as is permitted by Islam. Osama apparently was either the seventeenth of fifty-five or fifty-seven children born to the elder Bin Laden and his many wives. Apparently there were twenty surviving sons and thirty half-sisters. Osama was the only child of the elder Bin Laden's tenth wife, a beautiful Syrian woman named Hamida al-Attas.

The senior Bin Laden insisted that all of his children live in one household. He was a strict disciplinarian, probably necessitated not only by cultural mores but also by the presence of so many children. As a devout Muslim, he maintained a strict religious and social code that applied to all of his children. He expected mature behavior from his sons even at an early age, hoping to encourage self-sufficiency and self-confidence.

The elder Bin Laden was killed in a helicopter crash in 1968 when Osama was eleven years old. By the time of his death, the elder Bin Laden was a multi-billionaire. Estimates of Osama bin Laden's inheritance have ranged between eighty and three hundred million dollars (U.S.).

Notwithstanding the loss of his father at such an early age, the younger Bin Laden happily passed his teenage years, even proudly having his own stable of horses by the time he was fifteen years old. He still brags of comfortably being able to ride a horse seventy kilometers (forty-two miles) nonstop. Such riding skills probably serve him well in his mountain hideouts in Afghanistan and Pakistan.

Osama bin Laden himself states that he studied economics at King Abdul Aziz University in Jeddah. Other sources state that he received a degree in civil engineering from the University in 1979. Another source says he received a degree in public administration in 1981.

The confusion about the nature of his degree is unimportant. What is important to the task of defining Bin Laden the man was the presence at the University of Professor Abdullah Yusuf Azzam, an Islamic scholar and early contributor to the development of political Islam.[2] Apparently, Osama bin Laden was introduced to the teachings of Professor Azzam while he matriculated at the University. Later, he and Professor Azzam would both find themselves in Pakistan and Afghanistan as *Mujahideen* (Islamic warriors) engaged in *Jihad* (holy war) against the occupying Soviet army. Professor Azzam was killed in Peshawar, Pakistan, in 1989 when the car in which he was riding exploded from a hidden bomb. Mr. Bin Laden's exposure to Professor Azzam at the University cannot be underestimated. It probably planted the seeds of political Islam that later grew into the Osama bin Laden of today.[3]

Of equal, if not more, importance to the presence of Professor Azzam at the University was the presence of Professor Muhammad Qutb, an eminent Islamic scholar and political philosopher. He was the brother of Sayyed Qutb, an Egyptian Islamic radical who had been executed in Egypt in 1966 for advocating the overthrow of President Nasser's secular government. As will be discussed below, Sayyed Qutb was probably the most influential, modern-day political-Islamist thinker. His writings continue to have a profound effect on reformist Islamic movements throughout the world. Because Professor Azzam and Professor Qutb both taught the University's required Islamic-studies courses, Mr. Bin Laden probably was familiar with the teachings of each of them.

Although contemporary sources disagree, apparently Osama bin Laden visited Lebanon in the early 1970s before graduation from university. Some sources describe him as a rich, Saudi playboy imbibing in his share of wine, women, and song in the very accommodating venue of Beirut. Whether the allegations about his lifestyle are true or not cannot be determined with any degree of certainty, as they are based mostly on uncorroborated gossip.

Of importance, however, is that in fact Mr. Bin Laden also visited Beirut sometime between 1975-1989 during the Lebanese Civil War. There, Mr. Bin Laden claims to have seen high-rise buildings that had been bombarded either by Israeli or United States military forces. In fact, Israel invaded Lebanon in 1982 and maintained a military presence there until 2000. And in 1983 the United States Navy bombarded Lebanese neighborhoods with shellfire from large-caliber naval guns. At any rate, Mr. Bin Laden admits in one of the statements reprinted *infra* that the stark images of devastated Lebanese high-rise buildings later gave him the idea for attacking the World Trade Center. Reciprocity is a common theme in Mr. Bin Laden's statements, and in his mind the collapsed Trade Towers were part payback not only for the destruction he had witnessed in Lebanon but also for other perceived transgressions against the Islamic world by Israel and the United States.

In 1974, at age eighteen, Mr. Bin Laden married his first wife, Najwah Ghanem. Reportedly, he married four other women, divorcing one of them. He has had perhaps twenty-four children. Najwah bore him eleven children, seven of them sons, including Abdallah, Omar, Saad, and Muhammad. All indications are that he led a devout life during this period in his life.

In addition to pursuing his education and starting his family life, after his father's death Mr. Bin Laden actively involved himself in the family's construction business. He became adept at administering construction projects. And like his father before him, he continued to maintain close relations with the Saudi royal family. It is noteworthy that after the senior Bin Laden died in the helicopter crash, King Faisal directly intervened in the Bin Laden family's personal affairs. The King placed the construction company in trust to ensure its continued operations and to guarantee financial stability to the Bin Laden children until the elder Bin Laden sons, led by Osama's half-brother, Salem, could manage the company themselves. Later, Prince Turki, the son of King Faisal, became the head of Saudi Arabia's General Intelligence Department, or G.I.D., comparable to the American Central Intelligence Agency, or C.I.A. He would work intimately with Osama bin Laden in assisting the *Mujahideen* (Islamic warriors) fighters in Afghanistan and Pakistan.[4]

Ironically, today's Osama bin Laden, the self-declared archenemy of the Saudi royal family, was one of their favorites during his early adult life. Like their father before them, the other Bin Ladens still reside in Saudi Arabia and continue to be counted among the royal family's inner circle of friends and business partners. In fact, immediately after 9/11 many Bin Ladens were on Saudi government-chartered aircraft that received special clearances from the United States government to transport them and many other Saudis out of the United States because of supposed concerns about their personal safety. The transport remains a matter of controversy, especially among law enforcement personnel whose questioning of the Bin Laden family members was short-circuited by their abrupt departure made possible by the Bush administration.[5]

Two watershed events in Islamic history marked the year 1979. First, in January the Shah of Iran was toppled by an Islamic reformist movement led by the Ayatollah Khomeini. Then in December the godless Soviet Union invaded Muslim Afghanistan. Both events profoundly affected Osama bin Laden.

In importance, the Afghanistan invasion occupies first position. In the crucible of the war against the Soviet invaders in Afghanistan, Osama bin Laden was forged into a steel-hardened Islamic warrior, or *Mujahid,* and a widely respected leader of men. Like it or not, Mr. Bin Laden performed superbly in Afghanistan. Like it or not, his efforts might even have been partly funded by the C.I.A., which through its surrogates, the Saudi and Pakistani intelligence agencies, funneled millions of dollars in aid and equipment to the *Mujahideen* (Islamic warriors) in a clandestine effort to counter the Soviets in Afghanistan.

Between 1979 and 1984, Mr. Bin Laden traveled widely between Afghanistan, Pakistan, Saudi Arabia, and the Gulf States, recruiting men as *Mujahideen* fighters to carry out *Jihad* (holy war) against the occupying Soviet army and raising millions of dollars for arms and equipment. He coordinated efforts by the Saudi G.I.D., and the Pakistani intelligence service, the Inter-Services Intelligence Agency, (I.S.I.), to funnel Saudi money and Arab *Mujahideen* fighters into the theater of operations. During this time, besides his close relationship with Prince Turki, Mr. Bin Laden also cultivated close relations with Prince Naif, Saudi Arabia's Minister of the Interior.

In 1980, C.I.A. chief William Casey and Prince Turki agreed that the United States would match dollar-for-dollar whatever aid Saudi Arabia contributed to the Afghani cause. By 1987, the United States had expended approximately 600 million dollars (U.S.) in support of the *Mujahideen.*[6]

As part of this effort, Saudi Arabia built and funded hundreds of *Madrassas* (Islamic schools) along the Pakistan-Afghanistan border. At these Islamic schools, young Afghani refugees and young Arab *Mujahideen* were taught the Quranic lessons of devotion and the Saudi *Wahhabi* creed's view of *Jihad* (holy war). More will be discussed about Wahhabism below. Suffice it to say that Mr. Bin Laden is a *Wahhabi* and that Wahhabism emphasizes *Jihad* as the lifeblood of Islam. Ironically, in prosecuting today's war against terrorism, the express policy of the United States has been to pressure the Pakistani government to temper the curricula of the *Madrassas*, which are now accused of continuing to churn out thousands of *Mujahideen* fighters ready to confront U.S. forces in the Gulf region and to participate in Islamic resistance movements worldwide.[7]

By 1984, Mr. Bin Laden had moved to Pakistan near the Afghani border. He brought with him much of the Bin Laden construction company's heavy equipment. He then entered Afghanistan and built roads and defensive fortifications to facilitate the delivery of equipment and fighters from Pakistan. He also participated in several combat engagements, and had a reputation for leadership and coolness under fire. It has been said that he never even flinched when artillery shells, bombs, and rockets exploded around him. There are anecdotes about his driving tractors while being targeted by Soviet aircraft. Apparently his men in Afghanistan would have followed him anywhere. They still do.

One final fact is worthy of mention regarding Mr. Bin Laden's activities in Afghanistan during the Soviet occupation. In 1988 he split with the organization he had first formed through which to funnel money and arms into Afghanistan - the *Maktab Al-Khadamat* (M.A.K., or "office of order" in English). The M.A.K. was supported by Saudi Arabia, Pakistan, and the United States, and nurtured by the I.S.I. His new organization was under his direct tutelage and was named, simply, *Al Qaeda*, or "the base."

When he returned to Saudi Arabia from Afghanistan in 1989, the year after the Soviet withdrawal, he was greeted as a hero. As expressed by the chief of staff of the director of Saudi Intelligence: "we were happy with him. He was our man. He was doing all of what we asked of him."[8] In fact, while he was in Afghanistan, Mr. Bin Laden had become the *Jihadi* "poster boy" for the Saudi regime.

After his return, one report states that Prince Turki asked him to organize a fundamentalist, religion-based resistance to the communist-style regime that was then in power in South Yemen. Mr. Bin Laden also continued to maintain contact with his organization of "Afghani" Arab fighters. When Kuwait was invaded by Iraq in 1990, he offered his men in defense of Saudi Arabia.[9]

The Saudi regime rejected his offer. Instead, it turned to the United States for military assistance against the perceived threat of invasion by Saddam Hussein's military forces in neighboring Kuwait. The estrangement between Osama bin Laden and the Saudi regime occurred the first moment that United States soldiers stepped onto the sands of Saudi Arabia.

From that moment to today, Mr. Bin Laden became a strident opponent of the Saudi regime. He was appalled that the regime would invite into the land of the Two Holy Places, i.e., the mosques at Mecca and Medina, the military forces of the Christian infidels. Never before had a Christian army set foot in the land of the Two Holy Places, the see of Islam. In Mr. Bin Laden's view, the Saudi royal family were now *Kufr*, (i.e., apostates non-believers), having left the fold of Islam by inviting the Christian army into the Holy Land. Although several Saudi religious scholars had issued *Fatwas* (religious decrees) justifying the presence of the Christian forces as a defensive necessity, Mr. Bin Laden rejected them as corrupt.

In Saudi Arabia, the *Ulema* (Islamic scholars) are all employed by the government and are closely controlled by the Ministry of Religious Affairs. Those who speak out against government policies are fired, or worse. Often they are called upon by the government to issue *Fatwas* supporting pet government policies. Thus, Mr. Bin Laden had little problem in rejecting the official *Fatwas* as corrupt.

In addition to the pending Persian Gulf War, there was much turmoil in Saudi Arabia in 1991. The regime's corruption and inefficiencies had reached such gigantic proportions that in February of that year 400 Islamic scholars, including Sheikh Abdel-Aziz ibn Baz, the chief scholar of the Saudi *Ulema* (who had also issued a *Fatwa* welcoming the Western military forces), wrote a letter to King Fahd calling for governmental reforms. Included in requested reforms were calls for an independent consultative assembly and the removal of corrupt government officials.[10] The letter also urged the protection of individual rights. No serious reforms resulted from the letter.

In the meantime, Mr. Bin Laden had become so vociferous in his criticisms of the regime that he was confined to the city of Jeddah. By early 1991 he was no longer welcome in Saudi Arabia. Early that year, his family slipped out of Saudi Arabia and made their way, first, to Pakistan, and then to Afghanistan. However, Saudi intelligence agents continued to shadow him there. Fortuitously for Mr. Bin Laden, in June of 1989 the National Islamic Front had seized power in Sudan. The new government opened its borders to any Muslim, with or without a travel visa. By the end of 1991, Mr. Bin Laden and his family were in Sudan.

While in Sudan, Mr. Bin Laden funded and administered several construction projects. Many of his *Mujahideen* (Islamic warriors) followers from Afghanistan also joined him in that venue. He also established legitimate businesses, including a tannery, two large farms, and a major road construction company. The Islamic Sudanese government was eager for the assistance of this rich Saudi benefactor.

Even though the Persian Gulf War drew to a quick and successful conclusion, the United States established permanent military bases in Saudi Arabia. The ostensible purpose of the bases was to enforce the northern and southern "no-fly zones" that had been created in Iraq in the aftermath of the War.

Mr. Bin Laden was furious with the Saudi regime for allowing United States military forces to remain in place. He believed that the Saudi regime's apostate leadership had allowed the permanent presence of the United States military forces in Saudi Arabia to protect themselves from their own people rather than to protect the country from attack by the decimated Iraqi army. He harbored similar feelings for the other Gulf States that welcomed United States military forces, e.g., Bahrain and Qatar.

In 1993, while building a highway to connect the village of Almatig to Khartoum and a motorway to connect Khartoum with Port Sudan, Mr. Bin Laden was interviewed by the British journalist Robert Fisk. Mr. Fisk described an almost evangelical Osama bin Laden, shaking the hands of the local villagers and receiving the adoration of the local sheikhs. At the time Egypt was accusing Mr. Bin Laden of sponsoring "terrorist training camps" in Sudan aimed at building resistance to Egyptian President Hosni Mubarak's neighboring secular regime, as well as to the regimes in Tunisia and Algeria. Mr. Bin Laden denied the charges, identifying himself as a busy construction engineer and agriculturalist.

According to Mr. Fisk, his interview with Mr. Bin Laden was the first the latter had granted to a Western journalist. Of his ventures in Afghanistan, Mr. Bin Laden told Mr. Fisk that the former had arrived in Afghanistan before the end of 1979, within days of the Soviet invasion (the Soviets invaded in late December). He acknowledged fighting there, but credited his fellow Muslims, especially those who had died in battle, with doing much more than he did. Mr. Bin Laden told of how he funneled thousands of *Mujahideen* (Islamic warriors) fighters from throughout the Middle East into Afghanistan. He supported them with weapons and his own construction company's equipment. Mr. Bin Laden was assisted in his Afghani construction efforts by Muhammad Saad, his Iraqi engineer. They constructed massive tunnels into the Zazi Mountains of Bakhtiar province for *Mujahideen* hospitals and arms dumps, and cut a *Mujahideen* trail across the country to within fifteen miles of Kabul. Mr. Bin Laden related to Mr. Fisk several incidents during which the former was under bombardment. He did not suffer a scratch. Mr. Bin Laden then acknowledged that some of his "comrades" from Afghanistan had accompanied him to Sudan, but demurred in giving any numbers to Mr. Fisk. The interview was then ended by one of Mr. Bin Laden's security officers.[11]

Mr. Bin Laden remained in Sudan between 1991 and 1996. It was during this period that Mr. Bin Laden first appeared on the United States intelligence communities' radar screens as a potential terrorist threat. According to a secret grand jury indictment issued against Mr. Bin Laden in June 1998, while in Sudan in 1992 Mr. Bin Laden and other members of Al Qaeda agreed that U.S. forces in Saudi Arabia, the Gulf States, and Somalia should be attacked. On December 29, 1992, a bomb exploded at a hotel in Aden, Yemen. The hotel had been a way-station for U.S. troops en route to Somalia as part of Operation Restore Hope. No U.S. soldiers were killed in the bombing because they had departed the hotel shortly before the bomb exploded. According to U.S. intelligence sources, this was the first attack mounted against American personnel by Mr. Bin Laden and his supporters. Then in 1993, the World Trade Center was bombed in New York City. Again, Mr. Bin Laden's organization was suspected of involvement. And when eighteen U.S. Army Rangers were killed in downtown Mogadishu, Somalia, on October 3-4, 1993, some, but not all, U.S. intelligence agents suspected Mr. Bin Laden's organization of involvement. In 1993, Sudan was placed on the U.S. State Department's list of countries supporting terrorism.[12]

Meanwhile, Mr. Bin Laden was increasing the intensity of his verbal and written attacks on the Saudi regime. In April of 1994 Mr. Bin Laden formed the Committee for Advice and Reform (aka Advice and Reform Committee) in London, England (a safe venue), to prosecute reform in Saudi Arabia. The Committee issued several communiqués critical of the Saudi regime.

On April 9, 1994, the Saudi government responded by stripping Mr. Bin Laden of his Saudi citizenship and freezing his substantial assets. Then in 1995, the Committee issued an open letter to King Fahd of Saudi Arabia expressing severe criticisms of the Kingdom's regime and demanding reform. The letter stated that the King and the Saudi leadership were "apostates" for inviting the "infidel forces" into the "land of the two Holy Places" and enacting man-made laws instead of abiding by the *Sharia* (Islamic law). The letter demanded that reforms be implemented, including the imposition of Islamic principles in all aspects of Saudi life and the removal of United States and Western military forces from the country. The letter also advocated guerilla attacks against U.S. military bases and personnel stationed on the Arbian Peninsula. Mr. Bin Laden openly signed the letter. It is reprinted *infra*.

Then on November 13, 1995, a truck bomb exploded in Riyadh, Saudi Arabia, killing five Americans and two Indians at a U.S.-operated Saudi National Guard training center. Mr. Bin Laden denied involvement but praised the attack.

In May, 1996, responding to pressure from the United States, Mr. Bin Laden was asked to leave Sudan. He immediately returned to Afghanistan. Meanwhile, on May 31, 1996, the Saudi government beheaded four men accused of complicity in the National Guard bombing. In confessions coerced from them before their deaths, they admitted having read Mr. Bin Laden's communiqués. In the spring of 1996, President Clinton issued a secret order authorizing the kidnapping or killing of Mr. Bin Laden and the destruction of his network. On June 25, 1996, a large truck bomb destroyed the U.S. military residence at the Khobar Towers in Dhahran, Saudi Arabia, killing nineteen U.S. service personnel. U.S. investigators are split on whether Mr. Bin Laden or his supporters were directly involved. But as the reader will see in this book, Mr. Bin Laden relishes the role of "inciter of *Jihad*" (holy war) and lauds this attack as well as others.

On August 23, 1996, Mr. Bin Laden became an official enemy of the United States of America. On that date he signed a "Declaration of War" against the United States (reprinted *infra*). The expressed goal of the war was the expulsion of U.S. military forces from the Arabian Peninsula, the toppling of the Saudi "apostate" regime, and the support of revolutionary Islamic movements worldwide. Mr. Bin Laden sought the establishment of a pan-Islamic state ruled by a "rightful" Caliph.

In February 1998, Mr. Bin Laden increased the ante by issuing a joint declaration (*Fatwa*) with the Islamic Group, *Al Jihad*, the *Jihad* Movement in Bangladesh, and the *Jamaat ul Ulema e Pakistan* under the common banner of the "World Islamic Front." In the declaration, or *Fatwa*, Muslims were authorized to kill Americans, military and civilian alike, anywhere in the world. The *Fatwa* is reprinted *infra*.

Thus, long before 9/11 Mr. Bin Laden had become a direct threat to the United States and to Americans everywhere. On June 8, 1998, the previously mentioned secret grand jury indictment was issued. It accused him of conspiracy to attack the United States and Americans. On August 7, 1998, the American Embassies in Tanzania and Kenya were bombed, killing over 200 people and wounding more than 4,500. Twelve U.S. nationals were among the dead. The United States believes that Mr. Bin Laden's supporters were directly involved in the bombings. On August 20, 1998, President Clinton retaliated for the bombings by launching cruise missile attacks on several of Mr. Bin Laden's bases in Afghanistan. It was a transparent attempt to kill Mr. Bin Laden, who claims he was hundreds of miles away at the time of the attacks. The United States then added Mr. Bin Laden's name to its list of terrorists whose funds are targets for seizure. On November 5, 1998, a superceding indictment was issued against Mr. Bin Laden, charging him with conspiracy in the embassy bombings. (The indictment is reprinted in the Appendix herein.) A reward of five million dollars (U.S.) was placed on his head.

The November indictment was itself superceded by an even more detailed indictment on January 16, 1999. Then on May 29, 2001, four followers of Mr. Bin Laden were found guilty of charges relating to the 1998 U.S. Embassy bombings.[13]

Mr. Bin Laden seemed oblivious to all of the U.S. efforts to kill or capture him. Between 1996 and 2001, he gave several interviews to Western journalists at his hideouts in Afghanistan. Though this book focuses on complete statements issued by Mr. Bin Laden himself, several of those later interviews contain information helpful to the reader.

In March of 1997, he told Peter Arnett of CNN that his *Jihad* (holy war) against America was aimed at U.S. military personnel in Saudi Arabia and not at civilians. Nonetheless, he warned U.S. civilians to leave Saudi Arabia. When discussing Ramzi Yousef (the convicted

World Trade Center bomber) later in the interview, Mr. Bin Laden warned that persistent U.S. provocation throughout the Middle East would result in the "transfer of the battle into the United States."[14]

In May of 1998, after the February 1998 *Fatwa* which called for the killing of Americans, he shared with ABC's John Miller the reasons for the *Fatwa*. Railing against the "Crusader" Western forces and their Jewish Zionist ally (Israel), Mr. Bin Laden recounted the worldwide "siege" against the Muslims, e.g., the post-Gulf War economic sanctions against Iraq that had resulted in the deaths of 1,000,000 Iraqi children; the chronic killing of Palestinian Muslims in the Occupied Territories by Israeli forces; the killing of Muslims in Kashmir, Chechnya, Bosnia, and the Horn of Africa; and the Western powers' support for the corrupt, secular, autocratic, and apostate regimes of the Middle East. He perceived himself and his forces as the vanguard of a defensive *Jihad* fighting the enemies of Islam everywhere. To him, Islam now faced a new Crusade, perhaps the most violent Crusade ever launched against it by the West. Accordingly, the American people were no longer innocents. Their expressions of sorrow at the deaths of Muslim children in Iraq and Palestine would not spare them from the consequences of those deaths. He stated that at that moment some Muslim groups harbored so much animosity toward the West, and the United States in particular, that they were ready to take the fight inside the United States. He stated that the Western governments themselves would be directly responsible for what might befall their populations. He warned the people of the West to elect new governments that would pursue more responsible policies toward Muslims, or else bear the consequences. The onus, then, was on the people of the West, not on Mr. Bin Laden and his sympathizers. They and their brother and sister Muslims were the real victims of a very real Crusade being mounted against them.[15]

On January 11, 1999, journalist Rahimullah Yusufzai, representing Time Magazine, interviewed Mr. Bin Laden. Mr. Bin Laden denied responsibility for the bombings of the U.S. embassies in Africa. He did admit his efforts to incite *Jihad* (holy war) against America. He stated that his job was to instigate and then let the people respond. Interestingly, Mr. Yusufzai asked Mr. Bin Laden whether he has been seeking weapons of mass destruction. Mr. Bin Laden responded that it was an Islamic duty to possess them in the defense of Islam and that it would be a sin not to attempt to possess such weapons to deter the infidels (i.e., the United States, the West, and Israel) from using them on Muslims.[16]

Later, on November 7, 2001, in an interview with Hamid Mir of the Dawn and AUSAF Group of newspapers, Mr. Bin Laden told Mr. Mir that he already possessed weapons of mass destruction as a deterrent. He refused to state where he had obtained them.[17]

Afghanistan had proved to Mr. Bin Laden that a technologically overwhelming superpower like the Soviet Union could be defeated by deeply pious *Mujahideen* (Islamic warriors) unhesitatingly carrying *Jihad* (holy war) to their enemy and happily dying in His Cause. In Mr. Bin Laden's mind, neither he nor his *Mujahideen* brothers defeated the Soviets. Rather, by God's Grace they were allowed to defeat the Soviets. It was God's Victory over the infidels; they were merely the instruments of God.

As a devout Muslim, that is how Mr. Bin Laden sees everything. All that happens in this world has been written in advance by God. In his mind he carries the same logic to the doorstep of the United States. Granted, this new Crusader is an overwhelming, technologically superior superpower. But this sort of enemy is familiar to Mr. Bin Laden. He is unafraid of it. He defeated one such enemy before in Afghanistan, and as he says, by God's Grace he will defeat this new one in the same way.

Immediately after 9/11, Mr. Bin Laden denied any involvement in the attack during several interviews that followed. Perhaps he was attempting to spare Afghanistan from the consequences of an American attack. However, in Afghanistan in November 2001, United States military forces captured a videotape of Mr. Bin Laden and several of his colleagues discussing 9/11. In December 2001 the United States government released the videotape for public broadcast. In the tape, Mr. Bin Laden admits his role in 9/11 and discusses some of the details of the attacks. The transcript of that videotape is reprinted *infra*. In later interviews and statements, he left no doubt that the 9/11 attacks were an Al Qaeda operation; and he identified Muhammad Atta as the commander. Several of these statements appear *infra*.

Having read all of this, the reader can easily conclude that 9/11 was merely a logical extension of all that had preceded it. The reader should be chagrined that America was kept so much in the dark about this dangerous man. The United States government should have done much more to bring the problem to the forefront of the public forum.

Where Mr. Bin Laden laments that the apostate leaders of the Middle East have disappointed the *Ummah* (Islamic nation), we here in the United States should lament that we have been disappointed by our own *elected* leaders. Not only were they not listening to Mr. Bin Laden's own words, they were not doing enough to catch him. If Peter Arnett, John Miller, and all of those other journalists could find Mr. Bin Laden and interview him between 1993 and 2001, why couldn't the Delta Force?

In addition to the Soviet invasion of Afghanistan, the 1979 toppling of the Shah of Iran by the Islamic revolutionary Ayatollah Khomeini also had a profound effect on Mr. Bin Laden. Ostensibly, Mr. Bin Laden was never enamored of the Shi'ite Ayatollah Khomeini. After the Prophet Muhammad (PBUH) died in 632, Islam suffered a profound schism. The vast majority of the Muslims became known as "Sunnis" and followed the elected Caliphs who succeeded the Prophet (PBUH). The Shi'ites, however, rejected any Caliph who was not a blood relative of the Prophet (PBUH). The schism persists to this day. Mr. Bin Laden is a *Wahhabi* Sunni Muslim. According to the *Wahhabi* creed, the Shi'ites are "non-believers." Even to this day, Shi'ites in Saudi Arabia face discrimination. Thus, Mr. Bin Laden could not be more than a benign supporter of the Iran Shi'ite revolution.

However, the example of the Iranian Shi'ite Islamic revolution taught Mr. Bin Laden two important lessons. First, it demonstrated to him that an Islamic state could be established in spite of the opposition of a superpower like the United States. Though the Shah of Iran was a close friend of the United States, it sat idly by as he was overthrown and exiled from his own country. This gave credibility to Mr. Bin Laden's view that a pan-Islamic state could be built even in the face of resistance from the Western powers. Second, and perhaps more important, during the chaos of the revolution, young radical students seized the United States Embassy in Tehran and held fifty-two Americans as hostages for 444 days. Throughout the crisis, the United States seemed impotent. Its only attempt at rescue in April 1980 ended in tragedy in the Iranian desert when rescue aircraft collided, killing eight American service personnel. To Mr. Bin Laden and many others in the Middle East, rather than a superpower, the United States seemed more like a "paper tiger."[18]

Thus, by the time the Soviets abandoned Afghanistan in 1988, Mr. Bin Laden had proof that Islam could overcome all that the West threw against it. He and his fellow *Mujahideen* (Islamic warriors) had driven the Soviet Union, one of the world's two superpowers, out of Afghanistan. In Iran the surrogate of the other superpower, the United States, had been overthrown and replaced by a fundamentalist Islamic regime. Where previous Islamic thinkers could only engage in wishful thinking about reform, Mr. Bin Laden could now cite actual Islamic accomplishments in propounding his own message.

Furthermore, Mr. Bin Laden comfortably fit into the tradition of Islamic reformist thinkers. He and they shared the common goal of establishing a pan-Islamic state. And they shared the common view that no matter the epoch, Islam's travails could always be attributed to the Muslims' failure to rigorously enforce the *Sharia* (Islamic law) and to live their lives according to the strictures of the *Holy Quran* and the *Sunnah* (the words, deeds, and example of the Prophet Muhammad [PBUH]). Thus, in order to fully understand Mr. Bin Laden's message, one must understand its historical and intellectual roots, especially regarding the perpetration of violence by Muslims against infidels and other Muslims.

Taqi al-Din Ahmed ibn Taymiya (1263 - 1328), known as "Ibn Taymiya," was the first Muslim scholar who rationalized violence against other Muslims. During his lifetime, the Mongols, who had sacked Baghdad in 1258, were still menacing the Muslim Empire (the Mamelukes stopped the last Mongol invasion of Syria in 1303). The Mameluke leaders of Egypt were having difficulty raising fighters to confront Mongols. The Mongols had converted to Islam, and it was forbidden for a Muslim to kill another Muslim. (*Holy Quran*, 4 (An-Nisa [The Women]):93.)[19] But because the Mongol rulers had corrupted the *Sharia* (Islamic law) by consolidating it with a Mongol code known as the *Yassa*, Ibn Taymiya declared the Mongols to be apostates, thus allowing violence against them. In branding the Saudi leaders as apostates, Osama bin Laden had borrowed Ibn Taymiya's logic to justify violence against them.

Ibn Taymiya's teachings are especially important to *Wahhabis* like Mr. Bin Laden. The founder of the *Wahhabi* creed, Sheikh Muhammad ibn Abd al-Wahhab (1703 - 1792) revived ibn Taymiya's teachings in the Arabian Peninsula. Sheikh Wahhab took to heart ibn Taymiya's Hanbali *Fiqh* (school of Islamic jurisprudence). Thus, Sheikh Wahhab insisted on the strict application of the *Sharia* (Islamic law) and rejected the other *Fiqh* as well as Sufism and Shi'ism.

The *Wahhabis*, also known as *Salafis*, call themselves *Muwahhidun* (Unitarians or Unifiers). Wahhabism is a more puritanical orientation within Salafism. The *Salafi* try as hard as humanly possible to imitate the Prophet Muhammad (PBUH) in every aspect of their lives. The *Wahhabis* differ in that they raise *Jihad* (holy war) to the level of a sixth pillar of Islam. The accepted Five Pillars of Islam are: 1) there is no god but God, and Muhammad (PBUH) was his Prophet; 2) *Salat* (prayer), 3) *Zakat* (charity), 4) *Saun* (fasting), and 5) *Haj* (the pilgrimage to Mecca in one's lifetime (if possible)). To the *Wahhabis*, *Jihad* is the life blood of Islam. *Jihad* at once protects Islam and also extends its reach.[20]

During the eighteenth century, Sheikh Wahhab became the religious guide for the Saud clan that controlled the Nejd province of the Arabian Peninsula. They offered each other mutual advantages: Sheikh Wahhab provided religious credibility to the Sauds during their efforts to conquer the Peninsula; and the Sauds provided him with protection and a political base. When the Saud family seized power in 1926, Wahhabism became the new Kingdom of Saudi Arabia's official creed.

Whereas Ibn Taymiya was concerned about an enemy from the East, by the nineteenth and twentieth centuries Islam faced new threats from the West. Napoleon's occupation of Egypt in the early 1800s was a temporary scare, but nothing compared to the shock of the destruction of the Ottoman Empire, the seat of the Islamic Caliphate, after World War I. In 1918, Islam quite literally found itself on the ropes, like a beaten and battered boxer. After the War, the Western powers proceeded to divide up the Arab provinces of the Ottoman Empire into respective spheres of influence. New countries were born of the new colonialism: Palestine and Trans-Jordan (Britain); the Kingdom of Iraq (Britain); the Levant (Syrian and Lebanon, under French rule); and by 1926 the new Kingdom of Saudi Arabia, protected by the British government, the patron of the Saud family.

By the 1920s and 1930s profound questions weighed heavily on the minds of the *Ulema* (Islamic scholars). Had Islam ceased to exist as a viable religion? Would it succumb to the Christian West after all? As is often the case during times of crisis, certain intellectuals stepped forward to foment an Islamic revolution aimed at saving Islam from the infidel West.

Jamal Ad-Din (1839 - 1897), also known as "Al Afghani,"

launched the first of the modern-era counterattacks. Preaching in Cairo, Egypt, Al Afghani called upon Muslims to turn the West's own weapons and techniques against itself. The Muslims had been defeated because their practice of Islam had been corrupted by worldly influences. To Al Afghani, rationalism was not to be shunned by Islam; rather, it lay at the core of uncorrupted Islam, the Islam practiced during the *Rashidoon*, i.e., the era of the first four "rightly guided" Caliphs.[21] A spiritual revival of Islam would result in the technological innovation necessary to overcome the advantages of the West.

The Ottomans did not view Al Afghani favorably. They opted instead for Prussian armaments and military advisors. The typically corrupt *Ulema* (Islamic scholars) on the Ottoman payroll condemned Al Afghani's teachings as un-Islamic. He was exiled to Paris.

The Ottomans found that they could exile the man but not his ideas. Al Afghani's leading student, Muhammad Abduh (1849 - 1905) followed his mentor to Paris. The two of them then published a journal called the *Indissoluble Bond*. The journal carried the message of Muslim unity in the face of Western power. Although some of Mr. Abduh's followers construed his call for rationalism as a call for secularism, the others chose a path that led, ultimately, to today's Al Qaeda.

These others were led by Rashid Ridha (1865 - 1935), Mr. Abduh's star pupil. Mr. Ridha emphasized his master's teaching of the idea of the pure Islam of the early era. To be pure Muslims meant to prosper, as in the era of the *Rashidoon*. Early Muslims were granted God's blessings and conquests because they were pure in their hearts and in their practice of Islam. An Islam cleansed of its corrupted elements would guarantee political success. Like Mr. Bin Laden, Mr. Ridha had no regard for the corrupted establishment *Ulema* (Islamic scholars) and sought to create a new cadre of scholars trained in reformist seminaries.[22]

Soon, the main targets for the reformist movements became the corrupt, secular regimes that had been installed by the Western colonial powers after World War I. Hassan al-Banna (1906 - 1949), a student of Mr. Ridha, launched the Muslim Brotherhood in Egypt in 1928. The Muslim Brotherhood sought to mobilize the Muslim world against the encroachments of the West. Mr. Al-Banna envisioned the toppling of the corrupt local regimes and the establishment of a pan-Islamic state across the Middle East. He was assassinated for his efforts.

The Muslim Brotherhood has been officially banned in Egypt

since 1954. However, it has tens of thousands of followers and is thought to be the most powerful opposition group in autocratic Egypt. Muslim Brotherhood leaders have oftentimes found themselves in hiding, in prison, or worse. As recently as March 27, 2005, the Egyptian government disrupted a rare Muslim Brotherhood-sponsored public demonstration demanding political reform and arrested several of its participants.[23]

Mr. Al-Banna's work was taken up by Sayyed Qutb (1906 - 1966). Recall that his brother was a professor of Mr. Bin Laden's while he matriculated at university in Jeddah. A strident member of the Muslim Brotherhood, Mr. Qutb warned of the Western influences on Islam during the 1940s and 1950s. It was the duty of Muslims to re-establish an era of pure Islam. Relying on ibn Taymiya's earlier teachings, Mr. Qutb singled out the Middle East's corrupt, secularized regimes as "apostates" and advocated their overthrow. They were the "near" enemies needing immediate treatment. The "far" enemies, the Western countries, could wait until later. Consistent with ibn Taymiya's teachings, violence against these Muslim apostates was permitted. In 1966, Egyptian President Nasser ordered Mr. Qutb to be hanged.[24]

The die was cast. Corrupt, secular regimes were fair game for revolutionary Islamic reformists. In 1981 President Anwar Sadat of Egypt was assassinated by just such a group, called *Jihad*, which had split off from the *al-Jamaa al-Islamiya* (The Islamic Group). (Note that as earlier discussed, both The Islamic Group and *Jihad* were signatories of Mr. Bin Laden's 1998 World Islamic Front declaration (*Fatwa*) calling for the killing of Americans everywhere.) The group's self-taught theologian, Abd al-Salam Faraj turned his trial into a forum on his ideology, publishing his manifesto, *The Neglected Duty*, from jail. The manifesto echoed Mr. Qutb's calls for attacks on the "near enemy," i.e., the corrupt, apostate regimes that suppress the Muslim population. The "far enemies," i.e., the United States and Israel, would be treated later. Mr. Faraj was executed for his role in the assassination of President Sadat.[25]

Next in line was Mr. Bin Laden. Interestingly, he himself has an acknowledged ideological mentor: Dr. Ayman al-Zawahiri, the Egyptian physician who is Mr. Bin Laden's number two, and probably the second most wanted man in the world. Originally, Dr. al-Zawahiri was a leader of one of the Egyptian *Jihadi* groups. He teamed up with Mr. Bin Laden in 1998. The two of them had first met when they were *Mujahideen* (Islamic warriors) fighting the Soviets in Afghanistan.

Though Mr. Bin Laden never credits Dr. Al-Zawahiri for ideological contributions to any of the former's published statements, Dr. Al-Zawahiri's writings are well known in the Muslim world. Both men share a common Islamist political philosophy. They want to establish a pure pan-Islamic state. Their *Jihad* (holy war) is a worldwide revolutionary movement to be waged by modern means, i.e., violence, propaganda, and political action. Historically, their primary targets had been the "near enemy," i.e., the corrupt, secular, apostate regimes of the Middle East.[26]

Obviously, 9/11 was the exception — an attack on the "far" enemy. Since then, and since the invasion of Iraq by the United States, the distinction between "near" and "far" enemies has been blurred. Iraq has become a new theater of operations not unlike Soviet-occupied Afghanistan. Messrs. Bin Laden's and Al-Zawahiri's revolutionary characters were forged in Afghanistan. New Bin Ladens and Al-Zawahiris are being forged in Iraq every day. It appears that the American invasion of Iraq has given Mr. Bin Laden deep traction throughout the Islamic world.

Moreover, the United States' invasion of Iraq facilitated Mr. Bin Laden's and Dr. Al-Zawahiri's goal to convert the character of the conflict from a localized campaign of guerilla attacks into a global *Jihad*. Like it or not, President Bush's use of the word "crusade" in describing the war on terrorism at a news conference on September 16, 2001, and his incursion into Iraq have placed the question of a modern-day Crusade against the Muslims on the radar screens of Islam's 1.2 billion followers. What shall the world do if one percent of the Muslims (12,000,000) opt for *Jihad*?

As the reader can see by now, Osama bin Laden has not just "fallen out of the sky." He has been well prepared for his role by the chain of Islamic reformers who preceded him and who espoused the same goals and raised the same criticisms of their own contemporaries. That is why he is such a formidable enemy.

In the Western media, and especially in the United States, the demonization of Osama bin Laden has been complete. Almost without exception, he is depicted as a maniacal terrorist who hates freedom and kills for the sake of killing. This is a lot of nonsense. Even Michael

Scheuer, whose job was to find Mr. Bin Laden, and who advocates Mr. Bin Laden's assassination to this day, could only describe Mr. Bin Laden with words of praise. Mr. Scheuer reached this conclusion by studying Mr. Bin Laden's own words. The reader now has the same opportunity as Mr. Scheuer: to study the enemy's own words in their proper historical and cultural context. Once the reader grasps the real Osama bin Laden, he or she will be able to formulate conclusions about Mr. Bin Laden; to understand his grievances and his goals, and how best to adopt strategies by which to win the war on terrorism before it morphs into a global holy war characterized by repetitive exchanges of weapons of mass destruction in locations predominantly inhabited by innocent civilians.

Forward

The Basics of Islam and Islamic History and Recurrent Themes

The Editor strongly recommends reading this Forward prefatory to reading Mr. Bin Laden's statements. This Forward details the basics of Islam, Islamic history, and Mr. Bin Laden's repetitive themes that are critical to a full understanding of Mr. Bin Laden's words.

Although the text and endnotes define the English meanings of each transliterated Arabic word, for the reader concerned about the correct pronunciation of the Arabic words themselves, a "speaking glossary" can be found at www.osama-bin-laden-book. com.

If Osama bin Laden is to win the new Crusade that he believes the United States, the West, and Israel have unleashed on Islam, he needs to recruit thousands, if not millions, of *Mujahideen* (Islamic warriors) to fight the global *Jihad* (holy war). As the reader will see in his statements that follow, in spreading his recruitment message he is a consummate propagandist. He stays "on message," he is optimistic, and he supports his view of current affairs with generous references to analogous incidents that occurred during the glorious days of the Seventh and Eighth Centuries A.D., when Islamic armies swept across the Middle and Near East, parts of Europe, and south Asia – conquering those in their paths. Mr. Bin Laden conveys his message with carefully chosen words spoken in especially eloquent Arabic. In doing so, he is following the tradition of the poets and sages who mesmerized the nomadic tribes of the pre-Islamic Arabian Peninsula with their oral histories and commentaries on the events of the time. Undeniably, his effect on today's Arabic-speaking Muslim audiences can be intoxicating, especially among young Arab Muslim men thirsting for contemporary Muslim heroes.

Unfortunately, for the most part Mr. Bin Laden's mass appeal in the Muslim world, especially to young Arab Muslim men, is lost on the Western reader who, until now, has been deprived of understandable English translations of his complete statements. The average Western reader usually has a limited knowledge of Islam and Islamic history.

Mr. Bin Laden has made the task of understanding his message somewhat easier because throughout his statements he repeats certain basic religious tenets and historical facts. In addition, where necessary to facilitate the reader's immediate understanding, the Editor will insert explanatory notes into the text of the statements themselves. Each of Mr. Bin Laden's statements are also annotated with extensive endnotes so that his words may be completely understood in their cultural and historical context.

Turning to the basics of *Islam*, a word about nomenclature is in order. *Islam* means "submission to God." A person who practices Islam is referred to as a *Muslim*, the Arabic meaning of which is "one who submits to God." Islam's God is a monotheistic being and Muslims believe that Muhammad (peace be upon him) was his Prophet.[1]

According to Islamic tradition, all oral and written references to the recognized prophets must be accompanied by the phrase, "peace be upon him (or her.)" Because Islam recognizes the line of Old Testament prophets and the New Testament's Jesus, such words of grace accompany any such references to these prophets as well as to Muhammad, e.g., *Issa* (Jesus) (peace be upon him). Through the book the phrase will be abbreviated "PBUH."[2]

The reader should also be familiar with the Islamic calendar because Mr. Bin Laden sometimes refers to dates according to that calendar. The first year of the Islamic calendar was 622 A.D., the year the Prophet Muhammad (PBUH) migrated from Mecca to Medina for reasons of personal safety. His migration is called the *Hijra* (sometimes, *Hegira*).[3] The Islamic calendar is a lunar calendar, unlike the Gregorian solar calendar. Year one of the Islamic calendar would be designated as 1 A.H., i.e., "*After Hijra*." 621 A.D. would be designated as 1 B.H., "*Before Hijra*." For the conversion of Gregorian dates to Islamic calendar dates, or vice versa, see www.rabiah.com/convert/. The Islamic calendar was adopted in 16 A.H./638 A.D. For the purposes of this book, unless otherwise indicated, all dates will be given according to the Gregorian solar calendar. Where necessary to avoid confusion, Gregorian dates will also be identified by the familiar designations "B.C." (Before Christ) and "A.D." (Latin: *Anno Domini*, the Year of Our Lord).[4]

Islam is a very straightforward monotheistic religion. Before 570, it did not exist. In that year, the Prophet Muhammad (PBUH) was born. By the time of his death in 632, Islam had become the dominant religion on the Arabian Peninsula.[5] Islam teaches that the angel *Jibreel* (Gabriel) revealed the divine words of the *Holy Quran* to the Prophet Muhammad. The Prophet (PBUH) was an illiterate man who suddenly began to recite eloquent Arabic verses about good and evil and one god, God the Creator.[6]

After the Prophet Muhammad's (PBUH) death in 632, Islamic scholars attempted to gather credible narrative evidence documenting the words, deeds, and the example (*Sunnah*) of the Prophet (PBUH) from those who had known him. These "traditions" (*Hadiths*) were then compiled into books called *Hadith* (as translated, the term can be either singular or plural). A credible *Hadith* reflects a chain of authenticity from narrator to narrator back to the Prophet (PBUH) and his Companions.[7]

Several Islamic scholars published versions of the *Hadith*. Imam Ahmad ibn Hanbal (780 - 855) published the well-known *Musnad*, an early scholarly work that contained over 29,000 individual *Hadiths*.[8] Later scholarship resulted in the publication of six "corrected" collections, each containing approximately 6,000 individual *Hadiths*. The scholars were Sahih al-Bukhari, (809 - 878) who was the most widely respected *Hadith* scholar, ; Sahih Muslim (878 - 882); Muwatta al-Imam Malik (725 - 800); Abu Dawud (824 - 897); Sahih al-Tirmidhi (831 - 901); Sahih An-Nis'I (836 - 925); and Sahih ibn Majah (831 -895).[9]

Islamic scholarship is important to Mr. Bin Laden, who fancies himself an Islamic cleric even though he has not been formally trained as such. For example, on February 16, 2003, he issued a sermon for the Feast of the Sacrifice, an Islamic holiday.[10] The sermon is reprinted *infra*. However, two Islamic scholars hold special significance to Mr. Bin Laden. Ibn Hanbal has already been mentioned in the previous paragraph, and will also be discussed below regarding the four *Fiqh* (schools of Islamic jurisprudence.) Also of note is Ibn Taymiya (1263 - 1328), a scholar of the *Hanbal Fiqh* who insisted on an Islamic society in which the *Sharia* (Islamic law) was strictly applied and who rejected other schools like Sufism and Shi'ism. Later, Muhammad Ibn Abd al-Wahhab, the founder of Wahhabism (see below) would revive Ibn Taymiya's teachings in the Arabian Peninsula in the 18th Century.[11]

Islam's message is simple. It is characterized by Five Pillars: 1) there is no god but God and Muhammad (P.B.U.H) was his Prophet; 2) *Salat* (prayer), 3) *Zakat* (charity), 4) *Saum* (fasting), and 5) *Haj* (the pilgrimage to Mecca in one's lifetime, if possible).[12] Islam's holy book is known as the *Holy Quran*, which has 114 chapters (*Suras*).[13] Muslims consider the *Holy Quran* to be the actual word of God as divinely revealed to the Prophet Muhammad (PBUH) in the Arabic language. Islam's God is "Allah," – the Creator. As previously discussed in the Introduction, Allah is synonymous with the word "God," and Islam's God is the God of *Ibrihim* (Abraham) – also the God of the Christians and the Jews. Muslims believe in the Afterlife. They accept *Issa* (Jesus) (PBUH) as one of the line of Prophets, his virgin birth, his miracles, his identity with the Messiah, and his anticipated return to adjudge humanity at the end of time – the Day of Judgment. However, Muslims do not accept the Christian Holy Trinity. For Muslims – the only god is God, the Creator. They also believe that Islam is the last word of God received on earth by mankind.[14]

The *Holy Quran* and the *Sunnah* (the words, deeds, and example of the Prophet Muhammad (PBUH)) form the basis of the system of Islamic jurisprudence known as the *Sharia*. It is an amalgam of four *Fiqh* (schools of jurisprudence): *Hanafi*, created by Abu Hanifah, is considered the most tolerant and is today the most influential school; *Maliki*, created by Malik Ibn Anas, a Medite, is more rooted in northern and western parts of Africa; *Shafi*, created by Ibn al-Shafi, bases its rationale on the Hadith and the use of analogy; and finally, *Hanbali*, created by Ahmad ibn Hanbal, an Islamic fundamentalist pioneer who stressed the Hadith over analogy, and whose school now dominates the Arabian Peninsula.[15]

There are ten "voiders" that can disqualify one from Islam. They are: 1) associating partners with God; 2) establishing intermediaries between oneself and God; 3) not considering polytheists as non-believers; 4) demeaning the perfection of the Prophet Muhammad's (PBUH) guidance, i.e., placing man-made law on a higher plane that Islamic law; 5) harboring hatred for any part of the Prophet's (PBUH) prohibitions; 6) ridicule of any aspect of Islam; 7) practicing magic; 8) aiding polytheists against Islam; 9) deviating from Islam; and 10) rejecting Islam.[16]

There are also seven major sins forbidden by Islam. They are: 1) associating anything [or anyone, i.e., partners] with Allah; 2) murder; 3) practicing magic; 4) abandoning *Salat* (prayer); 5) not paying *Zakat* (charity, tithe); 6) not fasting during the month of Ramadan [ninth month of the Islamic lunar calendar, the month named *Ramadan*] without excuse; 7) not performing *Haj* (pilgrimage to Mecca) while being able to do so.[17]

Today, Islam remains the fastest growing religion on the planet. Presently Muslims number between 1.2 billion and 2 billion. Their number is increasing annually at a rate of 2.9%, which is higher than the world's annual population growth rate of 2.3%. Christianity is estimated to be growing at an annual rate equal to the population growth rate of 2.3%. According to the U.S. Center for World Mission, Islam will surpass Christianity as the world's largest religion by 2025.[18]

Islam is also characterized by a schism between Sunni Muslims and Shi'ite Muslims. The schism arose after the Prophet Muhammad's (PBUH) death in 632.[19] By the consensus of the Prophet's (PBUH) followers, Abu Bakr was appointed as Caliph, the new leader of Islam. However, others believed that Islam should be led only by someone who bore a blood relationship to the Prophet (PBUH). Immediately after his death, such a person would have been *Imam* (cleric) Ali ibn Abdi Talib (born circa - 598), who was the Prophet's (PBUH) cousin and son-in-law. Ultimately Imam Ali became the fourth Caliph. However, he was assassinated, as was his son, Hussein. Their deaths caused a final divide between Sunnis and Shi'ites that persists to this day.[20] Shi'ite is an Anglicization of *Shaia*, literally "the followers of Ali."[21] Because Mr. Bin Laden is a Sunni, *Wahhabi* Muslim, this book will focus on Sunni Islam and leave Shiism to a future work.

Another basic element of Islam worthy of mention is the nature of the *Holy Quran* itself. Its reading in either the original Arabic or in English can pose a problem. The text can be fragmented and internally inconsistent due to the fact that it is a compilation of divine revelations that were communicated to the Prophet Muhammad (PBUH) in no specific order.[22] Therefore, explanatory comments usually accompany the original Quaranic text. Previously, the authoritative English translation was done by A. Yusif Ali in 1934. However, with the ascension of the Saud family to the leadership of Saudi Arabia in 1926, the *Wahhabi* creed of Islam became the dominant in the Saudi Arabian peninsula (see below). Today, contemporary *Holy Quran*s are usually published in Saudi Arabia under the auspices of the Saudi Ministry of Religious Affairs. The commentary to the text of these contemporary *Holy Quran*s usually reflects the official Saudi *Wahhabi* creed.

Today, one of the most widely accepted English translations of the *Holy Quran* is entitled *Interpretation of the Meanings of the Noble Qur'an in the English Language*, Dr. Muhammad Taqi-ud-Din al-Hilali and Dr. Muhammad Muhsin Khan, editors and commentators.[23] This version was chosen as a reference in *Osama Bin Laden: Americas's Enemy In His Own Words* for two reasons: first, for the most part, Osama bin Laden's Quranic references are consistent with this edition; and second, it also embodies more recent scholarship, including more citations to the *Hadith* (traditions of the Prophet Muhammad (PBUH)) to give depth to Quranic verse. In the endnotes herein, all Quranic references will be in this format: "*Holy Quran, Sura* [Chapter] Number:Verse.", e.g., 4 (An-Nisa [The Women]):129."

Mr. Bin Laden repetitively refers to certain landmark battles fought during the early years of Islam. The first was the Battle of Badr in 624. This battle was fought in Arabia against a Meccan army intent upon destroying the Prophet (PBUH) and his vastly outnumbered followers. The battle was won by the Muslims and marked the first Muslim victory over an enemy intent upon destroying Islam.[24] The *Holy Quran* celebrates the victory in Chapter 8 (Al-Anfal [The Spoils of War]) at verses 42-45.

A year later the Battle of Uhud in 625 saw the Muslims defeated by a superior Meccan army. The battle was the second battle in the history of Islam. The Meccan army was led by Khalid ibn al-Walid who later himself converted to Islam and became one of early Islam's most famous generals. The battle is of special significance to Islam because of the religious devotion and personal heroism of a few of the Prophet's

(PBUH) Companions who saved him from certain death.[25]

Next in chronological order was the Battle of the Trench (Ditch), which was fought in the year 627. In this battle, the city of Medina was occupied by the Prophet Muhammed (PBUH) and his followers. Medina was besieged by some 10,000 troops from the nearby city of Mecca. The besiegers were led by Abu Sufyan, who had become the Prophet's (PBUH) arch-enemy. A trench dug around Medina by the Prophet's (PBUH) forces prevented Abu Sufyan's army from gaining entry into Mecca; and after repeated failed attempts, Abu Sufyan and his army returned to Mecca.[26]

Lastly, Mr. Bin Laden often refers to the Battle of Yarmuk, which was fought in the year 636. This was one of the most important battles in Islamic history because it marked the first real Islamic victory outside Arabia. The great Muslim General Khalid ibn Walid faced a large Byzantine army at the Yarmuk River, a tributary of the Jordan River. Khalid's army was only half the size of the Byzantine force of approximately 40,000 troops, but Khalid prevailed.[27] Shortly after the Byzantine defeat, Damascus and Jerusalem fell to Khalid's forces.[28] Khalid died in 642.[29]

Turning now from these generalities to the specifics of Mr. Bin Laden's own *Wahhabi* belief structure, note that the *Wahhabis* are also known as *Salafis*. They are followers of the puritanical 18th Century Imam Muhammad Ibn Abd al Wahhab (1703 - 1792). [30] Ibn Taymiya (1263 - 1328) was an Islamic scholar of the Hanbal school who insisted on an Islamic society in which the *Sharia* (Islamic law) was strictly applied and who rejected other schools like Sufism and Shi'ism.[31] Ibn Abd al Wahhab would revive Ibn Taymiya's teachings in Saudi Arabia and found Wahhabism.[32] Both scholars emphasized the importance of *Jihad* in Islam.[33]

During the 18th Century, the Saud family of the Nejd province of Arabia fell under the sway of Imam Ibn Abd al Wahhab and adopted the *Wahhabi* creed as their own. It was a convenient, mutually beneficial mix of religion and politics. When the Sauds ascended to the leadership of all of Arabia in 1926, they declared Wahhabism to be the dominant creed of the renamed Kingdom of Saudi Arabia. To this day, the 18th Century *quid pro quo* between Ibn Abd al Wahhab and the Sauds continues in effect in Saudi Arabia: the Sauds take care of the politics and the *Wahhabi* clerics take care of the religion.

The members of the *Wahhabi/Salafi* creed also call themselves *Muwahhidun* (Unitarians or Unifiers). Wahhabism is noteworthy as a particularly puritanical orientation within Salafism. *Salafi* try as hard as humanly possible to imitate the Prophet (PBUH) in every aspect of life. They seek to recreate the Muslim *Ummah* (Islamic nation) and to build a global Islamic community in the likeness of the first three generations of Muslims: the *Sahabah* (Companions of the Prophet) (PBUH), the *Tabiun* (immediate followers), and the followers of the *Tabiun*.

The *Wahhabis* differ from the *Salafis* in one important respect: the *Wahhabis* raise *Jihad* to the level of a sixth pillar of Islam. As previously stated, the accepted Five Pillars of Islam are: 1) there is no God but God, and Muhammad (PBUH) was his Prophet; 2) *Salat* (prayer), 3) *Zakat* (charity), 4) *Saum* (fasting), and 5) *Haj* (the pilgrimage to Mecca in one's lifetime, if possible). The elevation of *Jihad* to such a high status distinguishes the *Wahhabis* from more mainstream Muslims, which construes the word *Jihad* to mean not only holy war but also a "struggle." An example of a more benign *Jihad* would be an inner struggle to be a good Muslim and abide by the *Sunnah* (the example of the Prophet (PBUH)). However, the *Wahhabis* distinguish themselves by viewing *Jihad* more in terms of aggressively applying force not only to defend but also to expand Islam.[34]

Certain Quranic verses noted in Mr. Bin Laden's statements are the lynchpins of the *Wahhabi* creed and of Mr. Bin Laden's call for *Jihad*, or holy war, against the West.[35] A complete understanding of the *Wahhabi* belief in *Jihad* can be seen from the commentary attending verse 190 of Chapter 2 (Al-Nisa [The Cow]) of the above referenced Saudi version of the *Holy Quran*.[36] That verse instructs the reader to fight in the way of God but not transgress the limits because God does not like transgressors. The reference to "limits" means the violation of the stringent conditions under which Muslims may wage war and under which Muslims must cease hostilities. For example, Muslims are forbidden from fighting during certain months and must also cease hostilities if their enemy surrenders.[37] In the footnote accompanying that version, the Saudi editors impart the *Wahhabi* creed to their readers. To them, fighting in God's cause is of the utmost importance in Islam and stands as one of its pillars. *Jihad* is the tool by which God's Word is established and made superior, i.e., there is no god but God and His Religion is Islam. The abandonment of *Jihad* would signal the destruction of Islam, and Muslims would become inferior, having lost their honor, lands, and authority to rule. *Jihad* is the duty of every Muslim, and any Muslim who evades this duty would die as a hypocrite. In support of these comments, the Saudi editors cite Sahih Al-Bukhari, *Hadith* No. 2782. In that *Hadith*, Mr. Al-Bukhari recites that the Prophet (PBUH) has said that *Jihad* is third in the line of good deeds behind prayer and respect of parents.

The commentary attending verse 190 is an excellent example of the *Wahhabi* viewpoint. In A. Yusuf Ali's authoritative 1934 English translation of this verse, his comments say nothing about elevating *Jihad* to a sixth pillar of Islam, they do not advocate the spread of Islam by *Jihad*, and they certainly do not predict the demise of Islam if offensive *Jihad* is abandoned by Muslim men.[38]

Moreover, the *Wahhabi* reliance on *Hadith* No. 2782 is suspect in that the *Hadith* does not distinguish between defensive and offensive *Jihad*.[39] The distinction is critical. Defensive *Jihad* arises when Islamic lands are invaded by non-believers and Muslims are called upon to defend against the invasion[40], e.g., the Crusades of the 11th through 13th Centuries. Offensive *Jihad* arises when the Caliph declares a *Jihad*. However, the Caliphate was dissolved in 1924 by Turkish President Mustafa Kemel Ataturk (the Republic of Turkey then being the successor of the Ottoman Empire, the old seat of the Caliphate).[41] Thus, because of the absence of a contemporary Caliph, offensive *Jihad* cannot be invoked. But the American invasions of Afghanistan and Iraq have given much traction to Mr. Bin Laden's view that ***defensive*** *Jihad* is necessary in response to the invading Crusader forces from the West.[42]

Since 1979 Saudi Arabia has sought to spread Wahhabism throughout the Islamic world. As part of that effort, it has funded the building of thousands of *Madrassas* (religious schools) in Muslim countries across the world, especially in Pakistan. These schools hew closely to the *Wahhabi* creed.[43]

Whenever he references Saudi Arabia, Mr. Bin Laden euphemistically refers to it as the "land of the Two Holy Places," or the "land of the Two Holy Mosques," meaning the mosques located in Mecca and Medina.[44] By using these euphemisms, he seeks to trivialize the importance of the Saud family, which renamed Arabia "Saudi Arabia" when it assumed control over the Arabian Peninsula in 1926.[45] And he also emphasizes the importance of the Arabian Peninsula to Islam. The

Masjid (mosque) *al-Haram* is located in Mecca, the holiest city in Islam. The mosque is the site of the *Kaba*, the small brick building which had housed Hubal, the Lord of the Kaba, the highest ranking of 360 gods worshipped by the pre-Islamic Arabs of the Arabian Peninsula.[46] In spreading the word of Islam, the Prophet Muhammad (PBUH) smashed the idols when his Islamic forces captured Mecca in 630. The ultimate destination of the annual *Haj*, or pilgrimage to Mecca, which every Muslim is obligated to complete during his or her lifetime, if possible, is the *Kaba*. The annual *Haj* to Mecca and the *Kaba* attracts approximately three million Muslims.[47]

The Prophet (PBUH) himself is buried in Medina at the *Masjid al-Nabawi* (the Mosque of the Prophet). Medina is the second holy city of Islam behind Mecca, not only because it is the burial site of the Prophet (PBUH) but because it was the destination to which the Prophet (PBUH) migrated from Mecca in 622. In the Arabic culture, the two mosques are often collectively referred to as the "*Al Haramain* ('twin cities')."[48]

Also frequently mentioned by Mr. Bin Laden is the *Al-Aqsa* mosque in *Al-Quds* (Jerusalem). This mosque is located in the Old City of East Jerusalem on the Temple Mount (*al-Haram ash-Sharif* —The Noble Sanctuary). It is the third holiest site in Islam. According to Islamic belief it is the site of the Prophet Muhammad's (PBUH) famous overnight journey from Mecca to Jerusalem (*Al-Quds*), from where he ascended to heaven on his Arabian steed, prayed with the prophets who preceded him, and returned to earth to complete his mission. The journey is believed to have occurred sometime between 617 and 624. Note that *Al Quds* was the original *Qibla* (the direction to which Muslims face when praying) but the Prophet (PBUH) changed the *Qibla* to Mecca after his return from Heaven. The Night Journey is recorded in the *Holy Quran* at 17 (Al-Isra [The Journey by Night]):1.[49]

Mr. Bin Laden also often urges a return to the era of the "rightly guided ones," or the era of the "*Rashidoon*." By this reference, he means the first four Sunni Caliphs (the era of the *Rashidoon*) — Abu Baker (632 – 634), Omar (634 – 644), Uthman (644 – 656), and Ali (656 – 661). Many Muslims believe that this was the true golden age of Islam during which the teachings of the Prophet Muhammad (PBUH) were fresh in the minds of his followers, who heeded those teachings closely. During this period, the Muslims were a unified community in which Islam flourished and spread throughout the Arabian Peninsula and its surroundings.[50] Mr. Bin Laden and his followers believe that contemporary Islam's woes are the direct result of a failure of Islam generally to emulate those early Muslims and their level of devotion to the teachings of the Prophet Muhammad (PBUH). Mr. Bin Laden and his followers hope to re-instill such devotion in today's Muslims so that once again Muslims can revisit the era of the *Rashidoon*.[51]

Reviving the era of the *Rashidoon* seems little more than fantasy. Presently, the Caliphate does not even exist. The Sunni based Umayyad Dynasty controlled the Caliphate from Damascus, Syria, between 661 and 750. Then the Abbasid wrested control of the Caliphate from the Umayyads and transferred it to Baghdad from 750-1258. The Abbasid Mamelukes then defeated the Umayyads for control of the Caliphate and transferred it to Cairo, Egypt between 1261 and 1517. Then it was finally taken over by the Turks of the Ottoman Empire between 1517 and 1924. In 1924, the Caliphate was dissolved by Kemel Ataturk, the then President of the Republic of Turkey, successor to the Ottoman Empire. Presently, no procedure exists by which to restore the Caliphate and appoint a Caliph.[52]

In the political arena, Mr. Bin Laden has a litany of recurring complaints. First, he views the colonization of the Middle East by the Western powers after the destruction of the Turkish Ottoman Empire during World War I as an extension of the original Crusades that began on November 25, 1095, when Pope Urban II called for a holy war against Islam and the recapture of the holy city of Jerusalem from the Muslims.[53] On July 15, 1099, the Crusaders seized Jerusalem from the Muslims and for the next two days proceeded to slaughter every Muslim or Jewish: man, woman, and child found in the city. An estimated 40,000 people were slain.[54] The Kurdish Sunni leader Saladin led a Muslim army in a defensive *Jihad* that recaptured Jerusalem on October 2, 1187.[55] Rather than to engage in the wholesale slaughter of Christians in the manner which the Christians had done to the Muslims in their conquest of Jerusalem, the Muslim Saladin placed a small ransom on the head of each Christian. Ultimately, most of the ransoms were never paid due to Muslims sparing the heads of Christians, and in an act of magnanimity, Saladin released the vast majority of the Christians from captivity. Most of them escaped with their lives and their wealth, taking up residence in the nearby city of Tyre on the southern coast of what is now Lebanon.[56]

Saladin's humanity ironically prolonged the inhumane Crusades. From Tyre and other strong points in the Holy Land, the West continued to launch a series of Crusades for the next one hundred years. The last of the series of original Crusades, the Eighth Crusade, was defeated at the hands of the Mameluke Sultan Baibars on August 25, 1270.[57]

The post-World War I colonization of the Middle East was accomplished according to the provisions of the Sykes-Picot Agreement (named after the chief British and French negotiators, respectively Sir Mark Sykes and Charles Francois Georges-Picot).[58] The Agreement resulted from negotiations between Britain, France, and Russia which met to discuss the dismembering of the Ottoman Empire and allocation of its territories to their respective geographic spheres of influence. Though Sykes-Picot envisioned an international administration of Palestine, on November 2, 1917, by letter, Sir Arthur James Balfour, British Foreign Secretary, declared Britain's favoring the creation of a home for the Jewish people in Palestine. This contradicted correspondence exchanged between 1915 and 1916 between the British High Commissioner, Sir Henry McMahon, and Sherif Hussein, the Emir of Mecca, in which the former endorsed the independence of the Arabs within what were then the boundaries of the Ottoman Empire.[59] The endorsement was intended to incite the Arabs to rise up against the Turks during World War I, which they did. The deceit of the British sowed the seeds for the enduring conflict between Israel's Jews, the Palestinian people, and the surrounding Arab states. In the eyes of Mr. Bin Laden and the majority of the Arab Middle East, the creation of the state of Israel was no more than a product of Western colonialism and mendacity.[60]

On November 29, 1947, the United Nations General Assembly adopted Resolution GA 181, partitioning Palestine into several cantons. The Jewish State and the Arab States each had three cantons that touched South of Nazareth and near Gaza. The partition was impractical at best and resulted in the 1948 Israeli-Arab War, which resulted in independence for the new state of Israel. The remainder of the Palestine mandate was divided between Egypt and Transjordan (now the Kingdom of Jordan).[61]

Mr. Bin Laden is also very angry about the situation in the province of Kashmir – located along the border between India and Pakistan. The two countries have been at odds over the province since the India-Pakistan partition of 1947. According to the partition plan, mostly Muslim Kashmir was free to accede either to India or Pakistan. The ruling *Maharaja* (local lord), Hari Singh, opted for India. Since then, India and Pakistan have fought two wars over the province, the first in 1947, and the second in 1965. Since 1989 an indigenous separatist movement has grown in intensity and ferocity. Pakistan's claims to the region are based on the population's Muslim majority.[62]

In discussing Kashmir, Mr. Bin Laden reminds his audience of the double standard in effect there in comparison to what transpired in East Timor. East Timor was an Indonesian province that was ninety percent Catholic. This province was the exception to Indonesia's overwhelmingly Muslim population. East Timor declared its independence on November 28, 1975. It was then invaded by Indonesian military forces, who brutally attempted to pacify the province. An estimated 250,000 - 600,000 people were killed during the violence that characterized Indonesia's twenty-seven year occupation. On August 30, 1999, in a United Nations-supervised referendum, the East Timorese voted for full independence from Indonesia. Independence was internationally recognized on May 20, 2002, and East Timor joined the U.N. on September 27, 2002.[63] Such an indigenous vote has never been allowed in Kashmir, to the detriment of that majority Muslim population.[64]

Next, Mr. Bin Laden cites a litany of Western interventions into Muslim countries that have taken thousands of Muslim lives. He cites the excesses perpetrated against Muslims during the Lebanese Civil War, which lasted between 1975 and 1989. Between September 16th and 18th, 1982, during the Israeli incursion into Lebanon, Christian Phalangist troops were allowed to massacre approximately 600 - 800 men, women, and children living in the Sabra and Shatilla Palestinian Refugee Camps, which were located in areas under control of the Israeli forces. Later, an investigating Israeli commission found Israel's local military leader, Ariel Sharon, to have been indirectly responsible for the massacres. The finding later led to his resignation as Israel's Defense Minister.[65]

The events in Bosnia-Herzegovina and Kosovo during the early 1990s also do not escape Mr. Bin Laden's attention. Between 1992 and 1995, Christian Orthodox Serbia, through the use of regular and irregular armed forces, committed genocide in the province of Bosnia by its campaign of "ethnic cleansing" by which its forces murdered hundreds of thousands of people in an attempt to cleanse the province of resident Muslims. In 1995, the Serbs overran the U.N. "safe haven" at

Srebrenica and massacred over 8,000 Muslim men and boys. Presently, a U.N. war-crimes tribunal is trying genocide suspects and meting out punishment of the guilty ones. Others are still on the run.[66]

1992 was also the year that saw the beginning of the Algerian Civil War when the army canceled parliamentary elections in the face of the imminent victory of the Islamic Salvation Front, an organization that intended to invoke the *Sharia* (Islamic law) in Algeria. The United States turned a blind eye towards the army's usurpation of the parliamentary elections. Throughout the Middle East, the double standard employed in the Algerian example continues to haunt United States policies in the region, and Mr. Bin Laden continually reminds his audience of the double standard in the region. The war persists at this writing. Between 1993 and 1998, an estimated 70,000 civilians were killed. In 2000, an amnesty program tempered the violence, but armed militants continue to confront the government.[67]

Similarly, Mr. Bin Laden negatively views Operation Restore Hope, the name of the United States' military incursion into mostly Muslim Somalia in 1993.[68] There, he claims that Western military forces killed over 13,000 Somali Muslims. By the fall of 1992, hundreds of thousands of Somalis had died from famine and hundreds of thousands more were at risk of death by famine or war. The country was rive with fighting between clans led by local warlords. The violence interfered with relief efforts, and President George H. W. Bush sent American troops in an operation entitled Restore Hope. The U.N.-approved, U.S.-led coalition's mission was to protect humanitarian operations. The U.S. Army participated between December 3, 1992, and May 4, 1993. Tragically, the U.S. mission lost sight of its humanitarian role and became embroiled in the local political machinations. In attempting to arrest a local warlord named General Muhammed Farah Aideed in Mogadishu, the capital of Somalia, on October 3, 1993, two U.S. Army Black Hawk helicopters were shot down by his forces, resulting in the death of 18 U.S. Army Rangers. This is the notorious "Black Hawk Down" incident from which a full-length cinematic film was made. It was a nasty firefight in which hundreds of Somalis were killed. General Aideed himself claimed that 315 people were killed and 812 wounded.[69]

Mr. Bin Laden also refers to the twenty-one year civil war fought between the government of Sudan and the Army of The Southern Sudan People's Liberation Movement. The Arab-Islamic government in

Khartoum was attempting to impose the *Sharia* (Islamic law) on the animist and Christian South. The war broke out in 1983 when southerners mounted a rebellion seeking autonomy. More than two million people were killed. On February 2, 2005, the Sudan Parliament ratified a comprehensive peace treaty effectively ending the war. However, a separate rebellion is ongoing in the western Darfur province.[70]

Mr. Bin Laden continuously rails at the Russian pillaging of Chechnya. The Russians first invaded oil-rich Chechnya, a Muslim country, in 1994, withdrew in 1996, and then invaded again in 1999. They remain there fighting a vicious war against Islamic rebels seeking independence. Both sides have committed and continue to commit atrocities.[71]

Mr. Bin Laden also repeatedly complains that over one million Iraqi children died as a result of the sanctions imposed on Iraq after the Persian Gulf War of 1991. Although his figure may be inflated, non-governmental organizations have estimated that approximately 500,000 Iraqi children died prematurely of malnutrition and lack of proper healthcare during the United Nation's sanctions period from 1991 to the United States' invasion of Iraq on March 20, 2003.[72] In the West, their deaths were either largely unnoticed or were attributed to Saddam Hussein's mismanagement of the humanitarian aid allowed during the sanctions period. However, the deaths of Iraqi children during the sanctions period received much treatment in the Middle East media and remain a sore subject in that part of the world.[73]

One of Mr. Bin Laden's more pronounced current complaints is the treatment of Palestinians in Israel and in the Occupied Territories, especially after the Palestinian *Intifada* (uprising). The *Intifada* refers to the *Al-Aqsa, or Second Intifada* that began on September 8, 2000, when the then Israeli opposition party leader Ariel Sharon and 1000 of his bodyguards provocatively visited the Temple Mount (called *Har Ha Bayt* in Hebrew and *al-Haram as-Sharif* in Arabic) in the Old Holy City of Jerusalem. As stated above, the site is the location of the *Al-Aqsa* mosque, the third holiest place in Islam. Mr. Sharon was warned that his visit might provoke a response, but he visited anyway. It did provoke a response: a general uprising (*Intifada*) by the Palestinians against Israel's occupation of Jerusalem, the West Bank of Palestine, and the Gaza Strip.[74]

The *Intifada* technically continues to this writing, though a truce is in effect to allow new Palestinian leadership an opportunity to seek peace with Israel. However, it has taken thousands of Arab and Jewish lives. Between 2000 and 2004, 3,500 Palestinians were killed outright and 52,500 were injured. 4,500 homes were demolished by Israeli forces and 28,000 Palestinians were detained. In comparison, 919 Israelis were killed, 635 of whom were civilians, and 6,709 were injured.[75]

Related to Mr. Bin Laden's professed empathy for the Palestinians is his rejection of the "road map for peace." The "road map" refers to a plan to achieve Israeli-Palestinian peace propounded by the "quartet" (the United States, the European Union, Russia, and the United Nations) and first outlined in a speech by President George W. Bush on June 24, 2002. In the speech, President Bush first expressed support for the establishment of an independent Palestinian state adjacent to the Israeli state.[76]

Likewise, Mr. Bin Laden has little regard for the 1993 Oslo Peace Accords by which the Palestinian Authority was created.[77] In the Accords, the Palestine Liberation Organization (P.L.O.) recognized Israel's right to exist. The Accords were first implemented by transfer of power and responsibilities over the Gaza Strip and Jericho pursuant to the Israeli-P.L.O., May 4, 1994, Cairo Agreement. The Accords were signed by Israeli Prime Minister Yitzak Rabin and P.L.O. Chairman Yasser Arafat, and were witnessed by representatives from the United States and the Russian Federation.[78] Ironically, Mr. Bin Laden views Yasser Arafat, the recently deceased President of the Palestinian Authority and Chairman of the P.L.O., as a corrupt, secular leader.[79]

Closer to home, Mr. Bin Laden does not spare the rod in his criticisms and disdain of the Saudi regime and for the Saud royal family as being *kufr* (apostate, non-believer.) He often reminds his listeners of the Saudi family's corruption and historic links to the British, even chastising Ibn Saud, the founder of Saudi Arabia, as having been an agent of the British government and a corrupt leader eager to receive his share of British gold. He often ridicules Ibn Saud for "wearing the cross on his chest," a reference to the knighting of Ibn Saud by the British monarchy on November 16, 1916.[80]

In April, 1994, Mr. Bin Laden formalized his disdain for the Saud royal family and the Saudi monarchy by forming The Committee for Advice and Reform (a.k.a. The Advice and Reform Committee) in London, England.[81] The Committee sought political reform in Saudi

Arabia and issued a number of communiqués to that effect. In 1994, probably in response to the formation of the Committee, the Saudi government stripped Mr. Bin Laden of his Saudi citizenship.[82] In 1995, the Committee issued "An Open Letter to King Fahd" of Saudi Arabia criticizing his regime and demanding reform. The demanded reforms included the imposition of Islamic principles in all aspects of Saudi life and the removal of United States and Western military forces from the country. Mr. Bin Laden personally signed the letter. It is reprinted infra.[83]

Presently, the Iraq War is highest on Mr. Bin Laden's list of complaints.[84] This complaint is a logical extension of his continuous vilification of Saudi Arabia and the other Gulf States for inviting American and Western military forces onto their soil during and after the Persian Gulf War of 1991. Their presence reached significant proportions with the 1991 Persian Gulf War and continues to this day, although since April 2003 the United States has reduced its military presence in Saudi Arabia. It was able to do so because of its seizure of permanent military bases in nearby Iraq. However, besides Iraq, it maintains significant forces throughout the remainder of the Middle East, including Saudi Arabia, Bahrain, Kuwait, and Qatar. At this writing, approximately 150,000 U.S. and coalition soldiers remain in Iraq, with many thousands more in logistical roles in Kuwait.[85]

Adding insult to injury in the eyes of Mr. Bin Laden, it has recently been revealed that the Iraq invasion actually was commanded by General Tommy Franks from the Prince Sultan Air Force base in Saudi Arabia and that immediately before the war began, Saudi Ambassador to the United States Prince Bandar was briefed on the American invasion plans by United States Secretary of Defense Donald Rumsfeld and senior American war planners.[86] As early as 1994 Mr. Bin Laden had predicted that the United States had designs on Iraq's oil and intended to invade that country for a second time as well as other Arab countries in the Middle East. Mr. Bin Laden feels that the current Iraq War is absolute proof of a Christian-Zionist Crusade against Islam. President George W. Bush's often changing rationales for the Iraqi invasion, from a search for weapons of mass destruction, to the conquering of the country in order to instill democracy in that venue, and to fighting a "global" war on terrorism (in a country which is less than twice as big as the land mass of the State of Idaho), play directly to Mr. Bin Laden's viewpoint of the West waging *Jihad* (holy war) on Islam and Muslims generally. Mr. Bin Laden's view about America's Crusader designs found even deeper support when United States Deputy Secretary of Defense Paul Wolfowitz commented that the singular rationale for waging war on Iraq — the supposed stockpiling of Weapons of Mass Destruction (W.M.D.) was used because it was — "convenient." This rationale was used for convincing the United Nations, the United States Congress and most importantly the citizens of the United States. Mothers and fathers have been asked to send their young men and women (their sons and daughters) to a foreign country to kill others, to risk being killed themselves and even to die — for the Bush administration's "convenient" rationale for war. Using the Iraq War as a catalyst, Mr. Bin Laden seeks to rally Muslims to fight American forces there and in other venues across the world. At this writing, thousands of *Mujahideen* (Islamic warriors) appear to be responding to his call and are flocking to Iraq to confront the new Crusaders.[87]

Finally, and tragically, in addition to 9/11 Mr. Bin Laden repeatedly lauds the results of several terrorist bombings suspected of having been committed by al-Qaeda or its sympathizers. On December 29, 1992, a hotel in Aden, Yemen, at which U.S. troops en route to Somalia were staying was bombed. The soldiers had already left. Two Austrian tourists were killed. U.S. intelligence believes that this was al-Qaeda's first terrorist attack[88]. On July 25, 1996, the Khobar Towers in Al-Khobar, Saudi Arabia were destroyed by a truck bomb. The Towers were being used to house foreign military personnel. 19 U.S. service persons were killed. The perpetrators are suspected of membership in Hezbollah.[89] On November 13, 1995, a car bomb exploded outside U.S. military headquarters in Riyadh, Saudi Arabia, killing five U.S. service personnel.[90] On August 7, 1998, the United States embassies in Dar es Salaam, Tanzania, and Nairobi, Kenya, were bombed. 157 people were killed and over 5,000 were wounded, of those killed twelve were Americans.[91] On October 12, 2000, in the Port of Aden, Yemen, the United States guided-missile destroyer The U.S.S. *Cole* was bombed and damaged by two suicide bombers who had drawn along side the ship on a rubber boat and detonated an explosive. Seventeen sailors died in the attack and thirty-nine were wounded.[92] On May 12, 2003, al-Qaeda suicide car bombs struck three expatriate compounds in Riyadh, Saudi Arabia.[93]

Mr. Bin Laden also often crows at the economic cost of 9/11. He brags that al-Qaeda invested $500,000 in the attacks, which cost the world one trillion dollars. In fact, the human and economic costs of the 9/11 attacks were enormous by any standard. 2,792 people were killed outright. In September, 2003, the world-wide cost of 9/11 was estimated to have been one trillion dollars in lost economic production, cleanup and reconstruction of damaged real estate. Of that sum, $500 billion was borne exclusively by the United States.[94] As of November 8, 2004, the families or loved ones of the civilians killed in the attacks had received total compensation in the sum of approximately thirty-eight billion dollars.[95]

The reader will also notice that throughout Mr. Bin Laden's statements this Editor offers translations of the transliterated Arabic words that appear in the text. However, certain words are so frequently used by Mr. Bin Laden that they merit preliminary treatment in this Forward. He repeatedly directs his entreaties to the *Ummah*, which means the "Islamic nation" of Muslims without regard to national borders.[96] By *Ummah*, he refers to the world's 1.2 billion Muslims, not just the 300 million Arab Muslims residing in the Middle East.

Ulema mean Islamic scholars of a higher status than the usual clerics (*Imams*) who might be in charge of a local mosque. (However, the title *Imam* should not be trivialized and in fact is shared by several of the more important figures in Islamic history.) Although there is no religious hierarchy in Sunni Islam, in actual practice the words of the *Ulema* are critical to the Sunni Muslims' understanding of what is or is not prohibited by Islam. The *Ulema* are educated at recognized Islamic institutions of learning like *Al Azhar* University in Cairo, Egypt, and issue their opinions through written religious decrees called *Fatwas*.[97] Mr. Bin Laden believes that the official *Ulema* of the autocratic Middle East countries have been corrupted because they are employed by the governments. Seeking to protect their jobs, if not their freedom and lives, he believes that they often corrupt their *Fatwas* to ensure consistency with governmental policies.[98] (As previously discussed, Shi'ite Islam is characterized by a hierarchy of Imams, or Ayatollahs. *Fatwas* issued by the higher-level Imams, or Ayatollahs, have much greater influence among the Shi'ite Muslims than the *Fatwas* issued by Sunni *Ulema*.)[99]

As previously discussed, the *Sharia* refers to the body of Islamic law, or jurisprudence. Mr. Bin Laden seeks to wage *Jihad* (holy war) by urging Muslims to become *Mujahideen*. *Mujahideen* are "Islamic warriors" who are actively engaged in *Jihad*. An individual warrior would be referred to as a *Mujahid*. (Note that in the Western press, *Mujahideen* are commonly referred to as "*Jihadists*" or "*Jihadi*" fighters. This is a misnomer. *Jihad* is a noun. *Jihadi* in Arabic is an adverb suggesting the state of *Jihad*. The correct term to describe fighters engaged in *Jihad* is *Mujahideen*.) Lastly, the reader is cautioned to avoid confusing *Imam* with *Iman*. *Imam* usually refers to a Muslim cleric; *Iman* means "belief."[100]

Having now been introduced to the basics of Islamic culture, the reader is ready to take a complete measure of Mr. Bin Laden. Hopefully the insights learned from his statements will enable the reader to more fully understand the true nature of Mr. Bin Laden's grievances. Armed with that information, the reader will then be better able not only to evaluate the current direction of the war on terrorism but also to seek necessary and immediate course changes to avoid transforming such a concise war into an indeterminate global holy war between Islam and Christianity. Although Mr. Bin Laden's statements appear in chronological order between 1994 and 2004, each may be read in any order.

Chapter 1

Peace, God's Mercy, and His Blessings be upon you.

We thank God who has revealed the *Holy Quran* as clear verses, has raised those who have given the Holy Word extra responsibilities, has contracted them to abide by right and declare the truth, and has warned them against hypocrisy and hiding truth. Prayers and peace be upon God's Messenger, our master, the Prophet Muhammad, (peace be upon him) [hereinafter "PBUH," words of grace that attend any oral or written reference to any of the Prophets recognized by Islam], who said "the best of *Jihad* [holy war] is a word of truth before a tyrant ruler."[2]

You know how God has blessed the *Ulema* [Islamic scholars] and has given them great position. No doubt they are the Prophet's (PBUH) inheritors. They have inherited this religion to protect it and to avoid its derailment by extreme falsehoods by ignorant interpreters and misrepresentations by oppressors. The *Ulema* stand as role models for the *Ummah* [Islamic nation], increasing the effort to spread the Truth [i.e., Islam] over all creation's beings.

The earlier, truthful scholars well fulfilled these tasks, notably, Said-Bin Jubair, who stood fast against Al-Hajaj's oppressive rulings;

1

and Ahmad-bin Hanbal, who defied the rulers with a great deal of patience during the *Fitna* [crises] of the *Holy Quran's* creation theory. Ibn Taymiya endured great suffering in prison for standing firm with the *Sunnah* (the words and deeds of the Prophet Muhammad [PBUH]). These famous scholars were examples who stood for the truth and to protect the religion, may God give them all mercy.[3]

Honorable Sheikh:

We mention the above to remind you of your sacred duty before Islam and to remind you of your great responsibility and of your obligations to the religion and to the *Ummah* [Islamic nation]. "Reminder benefits the believers."[4] We wanted to remind you now of your responsibility because falsehood has ballooned and its followers have aggressively suppressed truth, imprisoned the scholars, and silenced reformers.

Amazingly, this has happened not only with your knowledge, but also upon your *Fatwas*[5] and statements. We will mention some of these careless *Fatwas* and statements in which you degrade the *Ummah* [Islamic nation, and also Saudi Arabia] into deep misguidance.

In this way, you may contemplate the negative consequences and the grave danger presented by such *Fatwas*. Some examples follow:

1) The abject corruption that has affected all aspects of life [in Saudi Arabia] as a result of various and obvious *Munkars* [discredited narrations] cannot be hidden. This was detailed in the advisory memorandum propounded by the select *Ulema* [Islamic scholars] and the reform advocates. Some of their most ominous points were the *Shirk* [beliefs in idolatry, the sin of believing in any deity but for God] manifested by [the Saudi Arabian regime's] decreeing and adopting secular laws that legalize prohibited sins. One of these very ugly sins is dealing with *Riba* [usury, which in Islam includes interest on money lent] that has infected the country and has become the norm within the country's [commercial] institutions and banks, the towers of which outnumber the minarets of the Holy Mosques. It is well known that the usurious practices adopted by these banks and [commercial] institutions are authorized and approved by the governing regime. However, we did not hear any objection from you, except that "dealing with *Riba* [usury] is prohibited and un-Islamic." You did not care about how your statement

confused Muslims because you did not differentiate the legislator's responsibility from the one who practices usury. The difference is very clear: the usurer is a sinner but its legislator is considered *Murtad Kufr*. [*Murtad*: Muslim who rejects Islam, *Kufr*: non-believer, rejecter of Islam.] The *Murtad Kufr* is outside the *Ummah* [Islamic nation] because he has made himself God's partner in deciding what is permitted and prohibited. This will be detailed in a soon to be published separate letter, God willing.[6] Although, the usurer is warned of a "war with God and His Messenger (PBUH),"[7] we still hear your statements in favor of this regime, which has become addicted to usury and has legalized it.

The present economic and political crises afflicting the country and the rate of stoning crimes [i.e., Islam can prescribe stoning as a punishment for serious crimes] are our punishment for the war that The Almighty has declared against whoever insists dealing in usury and other prohibited sins.

2) When the smiling King [Ibn Aziz ibn-Saud, founder of Saudi Arabia] put a cross on his chest and then showed his happiness to the world, you justified it and sweetened this foul deed in spite of the fact that it was a flagrant act of apostasy.[8]

3) When the Judeo-Crusader coalition forces conspired with the regime to occupy the country [Saudi Arabia] in the First Gulf War [1991] under the pretext of liberating Kuwait, you sweetened it with your unfair *Fatwa* [religious decree] that justified the heinous act, which insulted the nation's glory and sullied its dignity and holiness. You did so by applying *Kufr* [non-believer] exceptions to God's Rules. You neglected the conditions under which such exceptions could only arise.[9]

4) When the Saudi ruling regime supported the Yemeni communist-socialist commanders against Muslim Yemenis during the last civil war [in that venue], you kept silent. Then, when the communists were losing, you declared, at the regime's orders, "advice" to all to reconcile and shake hands as Muslims, implying that the communists were Muslims who deserved to be spared. When did communists [i.e., *Kufr*, non-believers] become Muslims?[10]

Was it not you who originally decreed their [the communists'] *Ridda* [apostasy] and urged Muslims (i.e., *Mujahideen* — Islamic warriors) to fight them in Afghanistan?[11] Is there a difference between a Yemenite communist and an Afghani communist? Have the Islamic religious tenets become so confusing? This regime is still hosting *Kufr* leaders [i.e., non-believer Western military leaders and representatives] in several cities in the Kingdom of Saudi Arabia, but we do not hear any objection from you. The Prophet (PBUH) has said that: "God has cursed whoever hosts *Mohdith* [innovators]." [Narrated by Sahih Muslim.][12]

5) When the regime decided to persecute Sheikh Salman al-Ouda and Sheikh Safr al-Hawali, who have abided by the truth and endured suffering for God's sake, you decreed *Fatwas* to justify their persecution and the torture to which they were subjected. May God relieve their suffering and free them from oppression and captivity.[13]

This *Fatwa* [religious decree] has limited application; others, however, have wide effects. Take, for example, your *Fatwa* about peace with Jews. This is a real catastrophe for Muslims. You have surrendered to the regime's political will when it decided to publicize its hidden plan to surrender to the Jews. So, you decreed to have absolute and unconditional peace with the Jews. The enemy's Prime Minster and its Knesset have applauded it. The Saudi regime has followed it with intentions to go on with more normalization with the Jews.[14]

As though it was not enough to surrender the Land of the Two Holy Mosques[15] to the "Judeo-Crusader" occupation army, you surrendered the Third Holy Mosque by giving legitimacy to the agreements signed by the cowardly, tartar Mongol [a term of denigration in the Middle East] Arab dictators with the Jews.[16] Your saying is very dangerous and catastrophic because it misrepresents the truth in several aspects. Some examples:

1) The actual Jewish enemy is not an enemy who is settled on its original land and fighting outsider invaders. Thus, Islam prohibits treaty with it. Rather, it is an invader enemy who corrupts religion and life. Thus, Ibn Taymiya's description could be applied: "The invader enemy who corrupts religion and life must be resisted with no conditions and with all means," and that is the opinion of most scholars.[17]

The legal duty toward Palestine and our oppressed Palestinian brothers, sisters and children who have nothing is to call for *Jihad* [holy war][18] for God's sake until the whole land is liberated and returned to Islam. Palestine does not need *Fatwas* [religious decree] that reject *Jihad* and justify the enemy's occupation of one of our *Ummah's* [Islamic nation] most sacred lands. Such *Fatwas* give legitimacy to the occupation and support the enemy's plans to confront Islam's meager efforts to liberate Palestine by *Jihadi* ways. This was confirmed through the operation of the heroes with the stones [confronting Israeli tanks in the Occupied Territories with only stones for weapons] and the *Jihad* of young Muslims in Palestine as the only way to face the enemy and guarantee liberation by the Will of God. We remind you here about your previous *Fatwa* regarding this matter. When you were asked about the way to liberate Palestine, you have said that there was no solution to this matter but to deal with it as an Islamic matter with all Muslims' support until the return of all of the aggressor Jews to their original places.[19]

2) Suppose that this Jewish enemy is qualified and has the conditions for a peace treaty; can peace treaties, signed by those cowardly tyrant Arab regimes, be considered legitimate? All comprehend that such alleged peace is nothing except absolute treason that surrenders Jerusalem and the whole of Palestine and gives them [the Jews] the authority over it forever.

3) Those apostate rulers who fight God and his Messenger [PBUH] are not legitimate and have no authority over Muslims. They should not rule the *Ummah* [Islamic nation], but with your *Fatwas* you give these secular regimes legitimacy and accede to their authority over Muslims. This contradicts your earlier statements about apostate regimes. Some scholars have mentioned in their appeal to you not to give this *Fatwa*. We will forward copies as a reminder.

Your *Fatwa* was very confusing because of its misleading generalities. It is not useful for a just peace; rather it applies to the fake one with the Jews that rises to the level of absolute treason against Islam and Muslims. No ordinary Muslim would approve it, nor should a scholar like you who is supposed to care more for the *Ummah's* [Islamic nation] well-being.

The duty of whoever issues a *Fatwa* regarding the *Ummah's* [Islamic nation] significant and dangerous problems is to apply their knowledge to the panoply of dimensions and their consequences. Because this knowledge is one of the indispensable conditions to issuing *Fatwas*, Imam Ibnil Kayyem (Ibn Qayyim)[20] said:

No *Mufti* [Arabic scholar or judge] can issue a *Fatwa* unless he has two kinds of understanding:

1) Comprehension of the actual issue and deduction its elements by analyzing its circumstances and meanings; and

2) Understanding the reference from the divine decrees in the *Holy Quran* and *Sunnah* (words and deeds of the Prophet [PBUH])

then applying one or another.[21] Since these conditions are generally indispensable for any *Fatwa*, it is prerequisite for issues of *Jihad*, peace, etc.

Ibn Taymiya said: "In the *Jihad* issue, the opinion of those who have the two following skills:

- •The right religious knowledge; and
- •Real life experience,

is considered, and the opinion of those who have one only of the above components is disqualified." [22]

If the previous *Fatwas* have come from someone other than you, then it can be said that their falsehood is the responsibility of the other scholar, but these *Fatwas* are yours, and they do not lack the first component (the right religious knowledge). The anomaly then is in lacking the second component (real life experience). This should disqualify the *Fatwa*, and it should not stand; rather, it should be reviewed by specialized scholars who have the following two skills:

- •The right religious knowledge; and
- •Real life experience.

It is known that the Imam Ibn-Hanbal[23] has rejected many *Fatwas* and Imam Malik was referring all accent cases to Imam Nafee,[24] may God bless them all with mercy.

Honorable Sheikh: We remind you because of our grave concern over the country and because other of the *Ulema* [Islamic scholars] urge us to do so. We look up to you. The regime should not be able to use your statements and *Fatwas* to resist each reformer and silence the truth, as occurred with your reply to our "Advice Memorandum" and to the "Defense Committee of Legal Rights," and to others.[25]

Honorable Sheikh: you have long served Islam and are now very old. So, have piety and avoid those tyrant oppressors who have declared war against God and His Messenger (PBUH) and be with the truthful *Ulema* [Islamic scholars]. Good models for you are the examples of the early *Ulema* of the *Ummah* [Islamic nation]. The best example of their truthfulness was their detachment from the rulers. Imam Abu Hanifa[26] and others avoided working for their rulers despite the fact that they were good Muslims, especially in comparison to those of today, who have corrupted Islam and life.

In our era, when the scholar Abdurrahman Hamid realized the danger of the Saudi regime's policies, with all the dangerous and harmful consequences to the religious integrity of whoever associates with them, he resigned from his position as President of the Supreme Legal Council. The Imam al-Khatabi[27] has said to warn against mangling with rulers: "I wonder who can sit with them without approving their lies and who can be impartial with them and who can be an honest advisor to them."[28] And the authentic *Hadith* says, "Whoever comes to the ruler's doors is tested with *Fitna* [trouble]."[29]

So, be aware, Honorable Sheikh, do not rely on the sayings or deeds of the rulers. Instead, read Quranic verse: "do not rely on those oppressors so the hell touches you and you will not be protected then you get lost."[30]

Least of all, he who cannot say the truth and abide by it should at least be quiet and refrain from telling lies. Apply the *Hadith* (tradition of the Prophet [PBUH]): "Whoever believes in God the day after should say the truth or should stay silent."[31]

Lastly, we hope that you do not feel offended by these words and consider them to be beyond the usual ethic of private advice; but the issue is very serious, and the advice could not be conveyed in private. What we have mentioned was already known by the *Ulema* [Islamic scholars]. Previously, they have drawn your attention to the issues, and have made several appeals to you to refrain from giving such *Fatwas* [religious decrees] like those backing unjust peace treaties with the Jews. They explained that the required conditions of the alleged peace are incomplete. They also warned against the great danger to Islam and life. Among the previous appeal's signatories were the honorable Sheiks: Ibn Gebrin, Abdullah al-Kouod, Hamud al-Twaigeri, Hamud al-Shouaibi al-Barrak, Al-Ouda, Al-Khudairi, Al-Turairi, Al-Diban, Abdullah al-Towaijari, Abdullah al-Jalali, Ayed al-Qurani, and many others. [32]

In conclusion, we ask Almighty God to make us see truth as it is and help us to follow it, and to make us see falsehood as it is and help us to avoid it. And to install in this nation a regime that: glorifies those who obey God, humiliates sinners, enjoins goodness, forbids sins, rules with justice, abides by truth, and raises the *Jihad* [holy war] banner high. Thusly, the nation can recover its glory and dignity, and the monotheist banner can be raised again over all occupied Muslim lands, starting with Palestine and reaching the Andalusia [Spain] and the other lost Muslim lands that have been surrendered by some traitorous rulers and their oppressed Muslim populations.

We also ask Him Almighty to have the best amongst us as rulers and get the wrong doers away. And we ask His Help in saying and doing rightfully what He likes for us in this life and the Hereafter. He is Almighty and is capable of that, and our last invocation is thanks to God, the Lord of the Universe.

In conclusion, we pray to Almighty God to help us see the truth as it is and to work accordingly.

Hijra Date 27/07/1415
Gregorian Date: 29/12/1994
Advice and Reform Committee / London Office
Osama bin Muhammad bin Laden

This Page Left Intentionally Blank For Notes

Chapter 2

An Open Letter To King Fahd [1]
1994

Far removed from complimentary titles and words of glorification of the royal court, we send you this open letter. It is a frank manifesto to inform you of the violations you and those around you have committed against God and Islam, against the land of Islam [Saudi Arabia], against the Muslims, against the Sacred City [of Mecca], and against the *Ummah* [Islamic nation].

Hopefully our frankness in showing you the truth will tear through the barriers you have built between you and the truth.

Oh King, this letter responds to the criminality and deceptions that you and your toady princes practice on the people to suppress their anger toward you and their ways. Your marginal remedies are nothing but short-term sedative measures to ease the anger. An example would be the *Shura* [deliberative council] that you have established, for which the Muslim nation waited for so long.[2] Disappointingly, it was born dead. Now you have established this marginal ministerial change that has no effect on any of the evils, namely you, your Defense Minister, Internal Affairs Minister, Prince of Riyadh, and all of the rest of you.

The main reason for our writing your letter is not because of your oppression of the people – especially the scholars, the callers of righteousness, the businessmen, and the senior chiefs of the tribes – and their rights; it is not about your insulting our nation's dignity, your desecration of its sanctuaries, and your embezzlement of its resources and riches; it is not about the spread during your rein of bribery, forgery, and the disintegration of morals; it is not about the economic decline of the country almost to the point of bankruptcy.[3] These matters are important and will be discussed another time after we reveal the substance of our dispute with you. The substance of that dispute is that your regime has transgressed "*La ilaha ilia Allah.*" [There is no god but God. This phrase represents a Muslim's declaration of Faith.] That is the very basis on which the *Tawheed* [Islam's monotheism, belief in the oneness of God] distinguishes itself from disbelief. All of the earlier mentioned problems result from your transgressions against the basic tenets of the *Tawheed*. *Inshallah* [God Willing] we shall soon release detailed findings of our research of your transgressions. For now, we shall confine this letter to two main subjects:

1. Ruling and legislating by man-made laws [instead of the *Holy Quran* and the *Sharia* (Islamic law)]; and

2. Allying with the infidels

A recurrent theme in the *Holy Quran*, the *Sunnah* [the words and deeds of the Prophet Muhammad, peace be upon him, hereinafter "PBUH," words of grace that attend any oral or written reference to the Prophets recognized by Islam], and the writings of the *Ulema* [Islamic scholars] is that whoever follows man-made laws transgresses the laws of God and is, in fact, a *Kufr* [non-believer] outside of Islam.

God says:

"Have you seen those (hypocrites) who claim that they believe in that which has been sent down to you, and that which was sent down before you, and they wish to go for judgment (in their disputes) to the *Taghut* [false judges, etc.] while they have been ordered to reject them. But *Shaitan* [Satan] wishes to lead them far astray."[4]

In interpreting this verse, Sheikh Abdul-Rahmaan bin Hassan al-Shaykh — may God have mercy on him has said: "whoever turns for solutions other than to God and His Messenger [the Prophet Muhammad (PBUH)] has refuted their message, has assigned partners to God, and has violated the Prophet's (PBUH) lessons when God revealed the following verses to him:"

"And so judge between them by what God has revealed and follow not their vain desires, but beware of them lest they turn you far away from some of that which God has sent down to you. And if they turn away, then know that God's Will is to punish them for some sins of theirs. And truly, most men are *Fasiqun* (rebellious and disobedient to God)."[5]

"But no, by your Lord, they can have no Faith, until they make you the judge in all disputes between them, and find in themselves no resistance against your decisions, and accept [them] with full submission."[6]

Whoever contradicts God and his Messenger's (PBUH) commands and adjudicates between people by other than God's Word [the *Holy Quran*], or who seeks to sate his own desires, is a disbeliever and is expelled from the fold of Islam. In the verse cited above, God has disavowed feigned belief when he used the word "claim," referring to the false claim of belief, for they were "ordered to reject them." The disbelief in *Taghut* [false judges] is an essential foundation for believing in monotheism and the Oneness of God, as stated in the verse:

"Whoever disbelieves in *Taghut* and believes in God, then he has grasped the most trustworthy handhold that will never break."[7]

"If this pillar is not fulfilled, the person is not a monotheist, and monotheism is the base of the belief … and its absence hinders them."[8]

Sheikh Muhammad bin Ibraheem al-Shaykh said in the letter *Tahkeem al-Qawaneen* as regards to the interpretation [of the earlier cited verse 4:60]:[9]

"God disavows those hypocrites who profess belief but adjudicate between people by means other than the lessons of the Messenger (PBUH). Belief and arbitration by other than the lessons of the Messenger (PBUH) cannot be combined in the heart of a believer for they cancel each other."

God says: "Do they then seek the judgment of [the Days of] Ignorance? And who is better in judgment than God for a people who have firm Faith."[10]

In interpreting this verse, Ibn Katheer[11] says: "whoever disregards the laws of God that enjoin good and forbid evil and adopts man-made laws, views, and desires disregards the laws of God." This is like the Tartars who ruled by laws derived from their doctrine of the

"*Yassa*," implemented by their King Genghis Khan.[12] The *Yassa* was a collection of rules which Khan derived from Judaism, Christianity, Islam, and other creeds, as well as his own whims. The *Yassa* took priority over the *Holy Quran* and the *Sunnah* [the words and deeds] of his Messenger (PBUH). Such a person is a disbeliever deserving of death unless he returns to the laws of God and His Messenger (PBUH). Is not the *Yassa* an example of the rules that you, your regime, and those like you, follow? The legislation of man-made laws and adjudicating by them is a form of worship of the author of such laws and a form of distancing the adherents of the laws sent by God.

The Messenger (PBUH) clarified this to Abdy bin Haatim in the *Hadith* [traditions of the Prophet [PBUH]] related by Al-Tirmidhi and others:

While Abdy bin Haatim was still a Christian, he heard the Prophet (PBUH) reciting the verse:

"They [Jews and Christians] took their rabbis and their monks to be their lords besides God by obeying them in things they made lawful or unlawful according to their own desires without being ordered by God, and they also took as their Lord Messiah the son of *Maryam* [Mary]."[13]

He said: "O Messenger of God, we did not worship them." The Messenger (PBUH) said: "Did they not make forbidden that which God has made lawful for you, and so you forbade it? And they made lawful what God has forbidden, and you then legitimized it?" He said "They did." The Messenger (PBUH) replied: "That is a form of worshiping them."[14]

Abdy bin Haatim thought that worship was confined to religious rituals; and because Christians did not pray directly to their priests, he did not think they were worshipping them. But the Prophet (PBUH) rectified his misconception by noting that in obeying priests' admonitions as legitimate laws though contradictory of the Laws of God, they were themselves acting as gods besides God. This concept of monotheism is the concept that the *Ummah* [Islamic nation] has adopted, and it recurs in Islamic scholarship, as we mention below.

Ibn Hazm[15] says about the verse:

"They [Jews and Christians] took their rabbis and their monks to be their lords besides God by obeying them in things which they made lawful or unlawful according to their own desires without being ordered by God, and they also took as their Lord Messiah the son of *Maryam* [Mary]."[16]

Jews and Christians forbidding what their rabbis and priests forbade and adopting what the rabbis and priests enjoined as lawful was a form of worshipping the rabbis and priests. God has described this as taking gods besides Him, and that clearly is a form of ascribing partners to God.[17]

After mentioning the above *Hadith* [tradition of the Prophet (PBUH)] about Abdy bin Haatim, Sheikh Islam Ibn Taymiya, said: "And so has said Abu al-Bahktary: 'though they did not direct their prayers to them, they obeyed in legitimizing the unlawful and forbidding the lawful; thus they have taken them as lords besides God.'"[18] The Prophet (PBUH) has confirmed this view: obeying them is a form of associating partners with God. God says:

"...*La ilaha illa Ur'wa* [none has the right to be worshipped but Him]. Praise and glory be to Him, far above is He from having the partners they associate with Him."[19]

Sheikh Muhammad bin Abdul-Wahhab[20] quoted the aforementioned *Hadith* and said: "Whosoever obeys the Scholars and Princes in forbidding that which God has enjoined and in enjoying that which God has forbidden, has taken them as lords besides God."

The Sheikh al Islam Ibn Taymiya said: "It is known that whoever vindicates the adoption of a religion other than Islam, and a legislature other than the legislature brought by Muhammad (PBUH), is a disbeliever."[21]

He also said: "Islam encompasses submission to God alone. Whoever submits to God and someone else is therefore a *Mushrik* [a polytheist, one who ascribes partners to God]. And whoever does not submit to God, he is a *Mustakbir* [too proud to worship God]. So the *Mushrik* and *Mustakbir* are disbelievers. Submission to God requires that one submit fully and solely to the worship and obedience of Him alone." [22]

Sheikh Muhammad bin Ibrahim al-Sheikh [of Saudi Arabia] said: "It is major disbelief to put the vulgar laws on the same level of the laws that descended through the angel Gabriel [*Jibreel*] unto the heart of Muhammad (PBUH), who was sent, in a clear Arabic tongue, to judge between people and to serve as a guide and a reference for settling disputes."[23]

In a letter directed to the [Saudi Prince in charge of Riyadh], the Sheikh criticized man-made laws that were being applied to the commercial trading activities: "Considering or ruling by any man-made rule is undoubtedly a disrespect of the Rules of God and His Messenger (PBUH). And it reveals a person's belief that the Rules of God and His Messenger (PBUH) are inadequate for resolving matters, returning rights to people, and adjudicating justly between them. That belief is an apostasy that expels one from the Islamic creed. That is a serious matter that does not need clarification. Implementing God's Laws is the twin half of the worship of Him alone. The meaning of the Declaration of Faith is that the only deity worthy of worship is God alone, with no partners, and that His Messenger (PBUH) is the example to follow. The rules that have been revealed to the Prophet (PBUH) by God are the rules that are to be followed. Have the swords of *Jihad* [holy war] been put to action but for the cause of restoring the Laws of God among mankind?"[24]

The prominent scholar Sheikh Muhammad al-Ameen al-Shanqeetee[25] says in the book *Adwaa'al- Bayaan:* "Implementing a man-made system of adjudication between people is contradictory to the laws of the Creator of the heavens and earth and suggests disbelief in the Creator. It rebels against the divine system revealed [to the Prophet Muhammad (PBUH)] and the creation of the heavens and the earth. God knows best what is beneficial to His Creation. Exalted is He from ever having a competitor in legislating laws for His Creation. Say Oh Muhammad to these: 'Tell me, what provision God has sent down to you! And you have made it lawful and unlawful.' Say Oh Muhammad: 'Has God permitted you to do so, or do you invent a lie against God?'"[26]

In his commentary on the topic of man-made laws, Sheikh Muhammad Hamed al-Faqy says in his commentary on the book of *Tawheed* [the *Holy Quran*, the Book of monotheism]:

"Without doubt, he who enacts man-made laws and refuses to rule by that which God has sent down is a disbeliever and an apostate. His title as a Muslim and all his deeds, prayers and fasting shall not benefit him."[27]

Regarding man-made laws, Sheikh Ahmad Muhammad Shakir said: "This rebels against the rules of God and His Religion and demonstrates a preference for the Rules of the disbelievers over the Rules of God Almighty. No true Muslim doubts that this is an act of disbelief despite differences about whether such a person becomes an apostate."[28]

This evidence from the *Holy Quran* and quotations from Islamic scholars lie at the heart of the matter. This evidence is designed to end disagreement, bickering, and arrogance about the subject. Only a desire to be succinct deters us from citing further evidence regarding this principle theme of the *Holy Quran*. Nonetheless, we believe what we have thus far submitted is sufficient for anyone who respects the truth.

We now remind you [King Fahd] of what you and your regime are doing by enforcing these *Kufr* [non-believer] laws abrogating God's legitimate rulings. Neither the average Muslim nor the scholar will labor long to prove that you and your regime are enacting and enforcing secular laws on the people.

In fact, the regime's commercial-court statutes, usurious banking laws, employment laws, Saudi Army regulations, and similar *Kufr* [non-believer] laws underscore the extent to which these man-made laws have seized the country. Further, the Memorandum of Advice[29] mentioned the dozens of legal committees that adjudicate between people by applying the secular laws by which you rule the country and the people, apart from the laws that govern foreign relations.

An example of the latter is your submission to the jurisdiction of the Committee for Conflict Resolution of the Gulf Council for Cooperation.[30] Without doubt, this Council, the headquarters of which are located in Saudi Arabia, and of which you are the main member, is a secular, non-Islamic legislative organization. Article 9 of the Council's principal charter empowers the committee:

"The committee shall issue its recommendations and rulings in accordance with;

1) The provisions of the main constitution of the Council of Cooperation;

2) International law;

3) International norms; and

4) Principles of Islamic law.

Its reports shall then be submitted to the Supreme Council so that the latter may decide that which is appropriate."

What a mockery of Islam and what disdain of His Law!

You have placed *Sharia* [Islamic law] at the end of the list, after the human thoughts, norms, and traditions of disbelieving nations and regimes! In addition to all of your other disbelief and straying [from God's Law], you have now subjugated God's Law to the Supreme Council,[31] which is free to pick and choose which laws it will honor according to its whims.

What do the protectors of Islam, the guardians of the creed, and the callers to *Tawheed* [monotheism] say to such Committees and courts, "Oh Servant of *Al-Haramain* [the holy mosques located at Mecca and Medina, Saudi Arabia]?"[32] As we have previously indicated, the answer is as clear as the sun at high noon, admitting of no hesitancy, evasiveness, or appeasement. According to the *Holy Quran*, the *Sunnah* [words and deeds of the Prophet Muhammad (PBUH)], and the consensus of the *Ummah* [Islamic nation], *Kufr* [non-believer] has disqualified you from the fold of Islam.

We cite some statements by notable *Ulema* [Islamic scholars] who speak of *Kufr* and apply pertinent *Fatwas* [religious decrees].

Sheikh Muhammad bin Ibrahim [a past Justice Minister of Saudi Arabia], wrote in a letter he sent to Riyadh's Prince concerning the commercial courts: "We have received and reviewed half of a document entitled 'Charter of the Commercial Court of Saudi Arabia.' We found that it consisted of non-Islamic, secular systems. Implementing any of the … would be tantamount to expressing displeasure with the judgment of God and His Prophet (PBUH). That would be clear *Kufr* [non-believer] outside the realm of the *Ummah* [Islamic nation]."[33]

In a letter to the chair of the Supreme Court in Riyadh regarding the rules and regulations issued by the Office of Work and Workers and the duty of Islamic courts with respect to that office, the Sheikh said:

"From Muhammad bin Ibrahim to his Excellency, chair of the Supreme Council in Riyadh; *Assalamu Alaykum wa rahmatu Allah* [peace be upon you], we have received your memorandum regarding our responsibilities to the Office of Work and Workers. The appropriate procedures fall into two categories:

1) Regarding the transactions referred to the Supreme Court for final decision, the court should decide them because that is its core mission.

2) Regarding transactions submitted for temporary approval and return to the Office for final action through secular directives, they are unjust according to the *Sharia* [Islamic law], and the court must ignore them. Were the situation otherwise, then the action would be construed

as complicity in ruling on matters over which only the *Sharia* [Islamic law] has jurisdiction."[34]

Also, regarding the Charter of Work and Workers, Supreme Court Justice Abdallah bin Hamid wrote that application of the laws of the Charter would be *Kufr* [non-believer] outside Islam.

The aforementioned *Fatwas* demonstrate the adoption of discredited man-made laws. We need not elaborate any further.

Also, there is a clear distinction between those who commit such *Kabair* [aggravated offenses according to the *Sharia*, Islamic law] as *Riba*[35] [usury, which in Islam includeds interest on money lent] while knowing that it is prohibited, and those who enact laws that give license to all types of *Kabair*. He who commits *Riba*, though admitting it is prohibited, perpetrates one of the most egregious *Kabair*. Whereas, one who enacts laws that sanction *Riba* is an apostate. We need only point to the towers of the usurious banks that crowd the minarets of the Noble *Al-Haramain* [the cities of Mecca and Medina] that implement your [King Fahd's] regime's secular rulings.

As stated by God Most High,

"But no, by your Lord, they can have no Faith until they make you, Oh Muhammad (PBUH) judge in all disputes between them, and find in themselves no dislike against your decisions, and accept them with full submission."[36]

This verse asserts that he is a disbeliever who does not completely resign himself to the *Sharia* [Islamic law]. God stresses this truth in various modes, the foremost of which is an oath in His Exalted and Majestic Name that eliminates any misunderstandings, to wit: Adyy ibn Hatim: "They have appointed their rabbis and monks as gods besides God."[37]

In your foreign policy, the most striking example of *Kufr* [non-believer] is your partnership with the Western Crusaders and *Taghout* [*Kufr*, non-believers] regimes in the Muslim World. This truth is obvious to everyone familiar with the extent of these affiliations. In fact, how can your regime pretend to protect Islam and *Al-Haramain* [the holy mosques located in Mecca and Medina], when in 1991 it paid over four billion dollars to the Soviet Union while its hands were still wet with the blood of the Muslims of Afghanistan?[38]

"Oh guardian of the tolerant creed," your regime gave billions of dollars to the *Nusairis* [the Alawite creed of Shi'ite Islam, or *Alawain*, that controls Syria] in 1982 as a reward for their slaughter of tens of thousands of Muslims in Hamma [a city in Syria], as well as your support of the Christian Marronite Phalangist forces against the Muslims in southern Lebanon. Your regime lavished billions of Riyals on the *Taghout* [*Kufr*, non-believers] regime in Algeria while it was grinding the Muslims under its heels. And your regime supports the Christian rebels in southern Sudan with money and weapons.[39]

As numerous as are these crimes against Islam and the *Ummah* [Islamic nation], and despite your regime's diverting the people from the truth, God ensured their revelation during recent events in Yemen, where your duplicitous mask was torn away. Your political and military support for the communists nullified your Islamic credibility. You suffered a dreadful contradiction in Yemen that revealed that you supported the Afghani *Mujahideen* [Islamic warriors] not for the sake of Islam but rather to protect Western interests threatened by a Soviet victory there. Certainly an Afghani communist is no different than a Yemeni communist, just as the Muslim Afghanis do not differ from the Muslim Yemenis. How can you justify simultaneous support for Muslims against communists in Afghanistan and communists against Muslims in Yemen?[40]

Only those who are aware that your policies are dictated by the Western Crusaders can unravel this contradiction. Your sporadic support for some Muslim causes is driven by the motive to protect the interests of the Western *Kufr* [non-believer] countries — which sometimes support Islamic causes, such as in Afghanistan — rather than by the sincere embrace of Islamic causes generally.

In fact, to the detriment of the Muslims, you have always opposed Islamic causes which Western interests oppose. For example, with respect to the Muslims of Somalia[41], you worked in tandem with America, providing resources which you had robbed from the *Ummah* [Islamic nation.]

On top of all this lay the Palestinian cause. You have blessed the farce of a "peace" which is in fact forced submission and a march toward humiliation. Despite the economic hardship in Saudi Arabia, you volunteered 100 million dollars [U.S.][42] to Yasser Arafat's secular authority [the Palestinian Liberation Organization] that was formed to accomplish what the Jewish occupational forces had failed to accomplish — oppressing the Muslim Palestinians and waging of war on Islamic movements like Hamas and the Islamic Resistant Movement. You did not refrain from supporting Arafat's regime and greeted him in Riyadh, even after his opposition to the Gulf War and his obvious support for Saddam Hussein. In order to indulge America's sponsorship of this false "peace," you swallowed insult.[43]

None of this surprises us. Even if you yourself are dubious about the alleged "peace process," you will have no recourse but to submit to your American overseer. Did not the visiting President [William Jefferson] Clinton refuse to meet with you in Riyadh and insist that you come to him at the American military base in Hafr al Batin?[44]

The US president taught us two lessons:

1) His visit was primarily to see his troops stationed at those bases; and

2) To humiliate you and teach you that you are doomed to failure even inside your own kingdom without your true guardian, America — a kingdom that is no more than an American state subject to American jurisdiction.

The *Ulema* [Islamic scholars] harbor no doubt that taking *Kufr* [non-believers] as allies and supporting them against Muslims is an absolute voider of Islam. This was expounded by Sheikh al Islam Ibn Taymiyah, as well as Muhammad ibn Abdul Wahhab, in his "Ten Voiders of Islam."[45]

God Almighty says,

"O you who believe! Take not the Jews and the Christians as *Auliya* (allies, close friends, protectors, helpers, etc.); they are but *Auliya* to one another, and if any amongst you takes them as *Auliya*, then surely he is one of them. Verily, God guides not those people who are the wrongdoers."[46]

He also says:

"You will not find people who believe in God and on the Last Day befriending those who oppose God and his Prophet (PBUH), even if they are their fathers, progeny, brothers, or tribesmen."[47]

In fact, God informs us that taking *Kufr* [non-believers] as allies in order to gain power is the sign of the hypocrite:

"Give to the hypocrites the tidings that there is for them a painful torment. Those who take disbelievers for *Auliya* (allies, protectors, helpers or close friends) instead of believers, do they seek honor, power, and glory with them? Verily, then to God belongs all honor, power and glory."[48]

According to the *Ulema* [Islamic scholars], taking *Kufr* for *Auliya* means aiding them [against Muslims], sharing one's life with them, and not openly disassociating oneself from them. This is apostasy, and whoever engages in this behavior subjects himself to the *Fatwas* [religious decrees] applicable to apostates, as attested by the *Holy Quran*, the *Sunnah* [words and deeds of the Prophet Muhammad (PBUH)], and the statements of the *Ummah's* [Islamic nation] exemplary *Ulema* [Islamic scholars].

May God bless his heart, a poet wrote:

Whoever takes *Kufr* (non-believers) for *Auliya* is like them,

There's no doubt about his disbelief to the least sensible person.

And those who love, aid or support them,

And openly approve their actions,

Are like them as far as *Kufr* [non-believers] is concerned.[49]

This is the discourse of someone who can distinguish truth from error. What, then, can those pure of creed and monotheism say, Oh King, about your *Kufr* deeds? On what but false grounds could your defenders argue on your behalf?

"Lo! You are those who have argued for them in the life of this world, but who will argue for them on the Day of Resurrection against God, or who will then be their defender?"[50]

Having demonstrated that your regime violates monotheism [there is no god but God] and its tolerant creed, which you boast to protect, and having exposed your true nature according to Islam's criteria, let us now objectively evaluate your worldly achievements. We shall discuss the following points:

Undoubtedly, we all realize that our country sits astride a sea of oil that comprises one-fourth of the world's reserves. Its importance is no secret. On average, the country earns 100 million dollars a day [U.S.] from oil revenues, in addition to earnings of 140 million dollars per day when you assumed the throne. This surpassed the income of the United States, the United Kingdom, and France, combined, and our country produces one-third of OPEC's output.[51]

In past years the country witnessed an economic phenomenon that made a mockery of historic economic models. Nobody believed that a day would come when the economy would collapse and the country would be one of the most indebted in the world.

However, your self-destructive policies have proved otherwise. Within a decade of your assumption of power, the situation reversed. The country came to be indebted to a magnitude of eighty percent of its income, and the average citizen was transformed from the largest saver in the world to someone buried in debt.[52]

The weight of the collapsing economy has fallen on the lives of the people, whose shoulders bear much pressure because of taxes and fines. Their pocketbooks have been picked by the increasing prices of water, electricity, and food, which led to an insane inflation without precedent.

The educational system did not relieve the disaster because of immense overcrowding in classrooms, which affects students, teachers, and parents alike. The situation is made worse by the Ministry of Education's inability to maintain the classrooms and build new schools.

The hospital system is not much better off. The regime has failed to maintain it. It is transforming many hospital wings into what can only be described as human slaughterhouses without much need for medicine, treatment, and care. This problem is compounded by the Ministry of Health's inability to build new hospitals.

The situation is made even worse by the growing ranks of unemployed young university graduates. Over 150,000 of them cannot find jobs in our country, and the number grows annually. Because of the worsening economic crisis, the job market continues to shrink in front of their eyes.[53]

Aggravating the situation, neither you nor your governors hesitate to ask the people to conserve power at a time when your own extravagant behavior sets a horrible example that encourages even more extravagance. How can you ask people to save power when every day and night they can see your well-lighted palaces? And how can anyone accept your call to reduce spending when your own palaces and homes fill the land to the horizons and people hear much about your big offshore accounts containing the nation's wealth?

Estimates of your spending of the country's wealth on these palaces and homes world-wide range in the billions of dollars. The narrator hardly knows where to begin because of the magnitude of the situation. Shall the narrator begin with the enchanting industrial cities of Jeddah and Ajzar, where you have built your most grandiose palaces on the beachfronts? Or shall the narrator begin with the lands on which you built palaces underground? Or shall the narrator begin with your palaces in Mina, Taif, Huda, Shifa, Holy Mecca, Holy Medina, and the rest of the cities in the country? Or shall the narrator instead concentrate on the palaces you have built at various Western resorts and cities? These are palaces which you rarely, if ever, visit.

Were our words someone else, you probably would not believe them. But you know that they originate with the most knowledgeable people concerning these truths, which can no longer be hidden from the public, and who can warn you better than an expert?[54]

You, your loved ones, and your royal entourage have built palaces, committed avarice, and fought with each other. In fact, internal quarrels have consumed most of your time and effort. Your familial relations have been torn asunder and raised the anger of the people. Their anger is fueled by you and your material possessions.

The Prophet Muhammad (PBUH) was correct when he said:

"Miserable is indeed the slave of the *Dinar* [gold coin] and miserable is the slave of the *Dirham* [a silver coin, about one tenth the value of a *Dinar*], miserable is indeed the slave of the *Qutayfa* and the *Khumayla* [luxurious clothes], for he is pleased if these things are given to him, and if not, he is displeased! Let there be no one to help him in as much as pulling a thorn that he would step on."[55]

Indeed, your extravagance, excessive spending of the wealth of the nation, and jealously among your family are the main causes of the country being led to the precipice of bankruptcy under your "wise" policies. Indeed, the squanderers are the brothers of the devil!

The current crisis was the logical outcome of a series of fatal actions and policies implemented by you and your ruling family. The more serious are:

The Deterioration of Oil Prices

Though oil prices began their decline in the 1980s, they did not overtly affect the country's economy until the 1990s, when you repeatedly drew down the country's financial reserves to camouflage the effect of a budget that consumed the country's monetary reserves. Your policies do not contain any plan to solve the crisis, which worsens every day.[56]

As a reminder, recall your full supplication to the Western countries' instructions to back your old friend Saddam Hussein with twenty-five billion dollars [U.S.], combined with an increase in oil production to reduce prices in order to compensate for damages inflicted on him during the Iran-Iraq War. This played a large role in the decline of oil prices to their current levels, which prices serve the interests of the West's consumers. Though the West is careful not to kill the Saudi goose that lays eggs made of black gold, they are careful to ensure that the price of those eggs is the lowest possible.[57]

The Lack of Alternative Sources of Income

It is well known that the oil resource is being depleted and is subject to price fluctuations. Though there are numerous alternative sources of income available to the country, your regime has failed to develop them and has retained the country's exclusive dependence on oil.

The Exorbitant Spending on the Allied Forces During The Gulf War

Even with the financial distress pressing on the country during the 1991 Persian Gulf War, and with the destruction of the Muslims in Iraq as the goal of the Western powers, the Western powers found the opportunity of a lifetime by exploiting your cowardice in inviting them into our country and in blackmailing your regime. They insisted that you pay almost the whole cost of the War, approximately sixty billion dollars [U.S.], of which sum approximately thirty billion dollars lined the pockets of the Americans and approximately half of the remainder lined the pockets of the allies. The rest was spent on commissions, deals and local bribes.[58]

The costs did not stop there. Your solidarity with the allies has pushed you into more deals that benefited them after the War. These deals have cost more than forty billion dollars [U.S.], an unrealistic price for military and civilian contracts with the Americans alone. In addition, the purchase of Tornado fighter-bombers from the British as a compliment to former British Prime Minister John Major was accomplished even when the country lacked the manpower to utilize the aircraft. This was proved during the War. Further, the army's own engineering committee questioned the effectiveness of the aircraft, a point which will be discussed later.[59]

The Military Situation

For several decades, approximately one-third of the country's budget has been consumed by the armed forces. Note that France, a nuclear power, allocates only four percent of its annual budget to its armed forces. Despite our own country's massive military expenditures, the result has been a pile of weapons with no manpower to operate them.[60]

This is not surprising because the real purpose of the expenditures was to line the pockets of the Princes rather than to develop a strong army. Another reason was to compensate the Western powers for their assistance in defending your throne. Many of these transactions merely showed your appreciation to them for allowing you to be their loyal servants. For example, you purchased seventy F-15 fighter jets to help President George [H.W.] Bush's re-election campaign after the War. As favors to President [William Jefferson] Clinton, you purchased [Boeing] commercial aircraft for Saudi Airlines' fleet and you purchased equipment to expand the country's telephone network. The purchase of the 48 Tornados from the United Kingdom was another example of your largesse.

The Defense Ministry's embarrassing performance during the Gulf War reveals much about the real motivation of those weapons purchases. The [Saudi] Air Force possessed over 500 fighter jets, yet they only shot down two Iraqi warplanes that had no air cover. Despite the [Saudi] Navy's possession of thirty warships, twenty of them with missile-launching capability, not a single shot was fired by them during the War. The Army did not fare any better. Technical personnel from Pakistan had to be imported just to organize one armored infantry division. Hundreds of billions of dollars have been wasted.[61] Astonishingly, Prince Sultan, Minister of Defense for the past thirty-two years, accomplished nothing but failure during the War.

To put the magnitude of military spending into perspective, the financial burden on each Saudi citizen exceeds the financial burden on the individual citizens of America, Germany, Italy, Egypt, Romania, Poland, Spain, Ecuador, Uruguay, and Ireland. Some of these countries have nuclear capability, and some of them are active members of NATO.

It is also shocking to know that Saudi Arabia's expenditure on each of its military personnel exceeds what is spent in nine countries collectively: America, Germany, Belgium, Argentina, China, Iran, the Zionist enemy Israel, South Korea, and Tanzania.[62]

Do we not have the right to ask you, Oh King, where has all money gone? Do not bother to answer. Everybody knows how many bribes and commissions have lined your own pockets, Prince Sultan's pockets, and the pockets of those Princes in charge of arranging the deals with the arms dealers and construction companies. It is well known that you and your Princes pocketed between forty and sixty percent of the value of every transaction. Most of the remainder is devoted to the construction of military bases and facilities the size of which far exceeds the size and quality of the country's armed forces. Apparently, the facilities were built for use by America and the other Western armies. In many cities, American military personnel are indeed occupying those facilities.[63]

May we ask why foreign military forces with enormous fire power and equipment remain in our Holy Land? Does Iraq still pose a threat to your throne after the destruction of its armed forces and the starvation of its people? The presence of foreign powers in the Holy Land[64] is not to defend our country against a destroyed, starving Iraq. Rather, the truth is that the foreign powers are here to protect your throne from the growing threat of Islam. Praise be to God! The country is experiencing a blessed Islamic awakening that grows in many military and civilian sectors, causing you great concern.

The duty of the country's army is to protect the *Ummah* [Islamic nation] and to defend its interests everywhere, not merely to defend Saudi Arabia. Thus, nothing can justify the army's continued state of weakness. It is unconscionable to allow the country to become an American colony, with the filthy feet of American soldiers roaming everywhere, for no reason other than to protect your throne and the oil resources. The infidel Crusaders must not be allowed to remain in the Holy Land.

Does not the *Ummah* [Islamic nation] have the right to ask, "Who compromises our security? Who is the culprit behind the region's unrest?" Did not the regime itself allow the deterioration of military strength to the point of bringing the filth of the armies of the infidel Christians and Jews into our pure Holy Land? Or was it Osama bin

Laden, who calls for the spiritual and military preparation of the *Ummah* [Islamic nation] for the honor of defending it, its religion, its Holy Places, and its dignity?

In truth, you have no one to blame but yourself and your Minister of Defense. No one should blame the members of the armed forces or the National Guard, many of whom are honorable and brave. However, their hands are tied. You have marginalized many of them who may call for change. You even planted spies among their rank and file to abort any attempts at change. Furthermore, you forbade any coordination between the three branches of the armed forces even though such coordination is vital to any successful military campaign. However, protecting your throne was more important than the dignity of the *Ummah* [Islamic nation].

Conclusions

It has been proven that according to the *Sharia* [Islamic law] your regime has committed the types of violations that invalidate its legitimacy. The regime's wide-spread corruption and its total failure demand its ouster. You have enacted and ruled by man-made laws. You have forced people to be governed by man-made laws in total rejection of God's principles. God is the only law-giver. You have allied with *Kufr* [non-believers] against Muslims. Clearly you are an apostate who has invalidated your own system and rendered it subject to being overthrown. Even in the absence of the violation of any *Sharia* [Islamic law], your inability to implement sound economic and defense policies justifies your removal.

You have brought to our people the two worst calamities: blasphemy and poverty. Clearly, the disagreement between your regime and the *Ulema* [Islamic scholars], business leaders, and tribal leaders is not temporary or minor. Rather, it is fundamental and deeply rooted.

This is a struggle between God's Islamic system, which is based on complete submission to God's laws in all that we do, and a man-made system that serves only the interests of those who created it. God's system is beautifully illustrated in the following verse of the *Holy Quran*:

"Say, my prayer, religious act of worship, my life and death all belong to God, the Lord of all creation and creatures. That was what I was mandated to do and I am the first to declare being Muslim."[65]

God's system is the system of "There is no god but God and Muhammad (PBUH) was his Messenger," with all that entails regarding acceptable and forbidden conduct. The man-made system is also illustrated in the *Holy Quran*:

"Do you believe and accept some parts of the Holy Scripture and reject other parts? They (think to) deceive God and those who believe, while they only deceive themselves, and perceive it not!"[66]

Therefore, based on what we have described in this letter, any action taken by this *Ummah's* [Islamic nation] religious, business, and tribal leaders against your system does not constitute unlawful disobedience. It is your system that is unlawful. Furthermore, the consensus of the *Ummah* is that an apostate leader must be overthrown. Each stage on the road to change has unique means, and goals. In short, matters may not be decided in haste or unfairness. The decision to act is taken after full consultation with the faithful and trusted leaders of the *Ummah*, [Islamic nation] — those leaders who have proved worthy of managing this critical task through personal trial.

Oh King, in addition to what we have said here, it is incumbent on you to do all you can to end the suffering of this *Ummah* [Islamic nation]. Putting an end to all of the domestic and international problems that have beset our country is best for you, your family, and everyone around you. You are aged and your health is deteriorating. Your ability to maintain control is diminishing. Our best advice is that you resign so that the nation may appoint those who can lift it from the abyss in which you have cast it. You have no realistic chance of implementing needed changes, especially in view of your old age and ill health. Let me remind you of the words of a past poet:

"Once an old man becomes a fool, he will no longer be forbearing.

And a youth can only dream after becoming a fool."[67]

Recall that King Saud was removed[68] for less serious malfeasance than yours. At that time, you yourself were one of the strongest advocates of his removal. That was correct and justified. It is now time for a repeat performance. We hope not only that you resign but also that you call for the resignation of everyone in your regime who has participated in the current state of affairs.

It is only fair to ask you to rectify the damage you have done.

One example would be your Minister of Defense.[69] He has never succeeded at any political or administrative matter placed in his hands. He escalated the border problem with Qatar,[70] and he almost started a war with Yemen. This was in addition to his total failure in running the Ministry and the Saudi Airlines Company. I note that the airline went bankrupt as a result of his mismanagement.

Shuffling the positions in the various ministries has been useless. The new appointees are closely tied to the corrupt system. Therefore, they have a conflict of interest. Even should some of them mean to do what is right, your total control over them makes it impossible for them to implement any change. The shadow of a bent rod will never be straight. We remind you that we ask no more than what you demanded of King Saud. You were able to do it then; therefore, a repetition is not impossible.

Before we put down our pen, we ask you to think hard and search your soul in light of all that we have said herein. We hope that you will do that before acting arrogantly and rejecting our advice. Think hard before you decide to punish whoever attempts to deliver this letter, as you have done many times in the past. Time and again, faithful [i.e., uncorrupted] *Ulema* [Islamic scholars] have forwarded memoranda full of advice. Most famous is the one which identified all of the problems and provided a workable plan of remediation. It was organized in a format reflecting the highest level of care, respect, politeness, and sincere desire to do what is best for the nation. Not only have you rejected all attempts at corrective action, but you have punished those who tried to steer you in the right direction. You have used your agents, soldiers, supporters, and those fooled by you to punish and humiliate the sincere *Ulema* [Islamic scholars]. You went so far as to use your influence to have *Fatwas* [religious decrees] issued indicting these scholars. Though they remain in your jails, they have not lost patience. We ask God to set them free, facilitate their mission, and help us and them to stay the course — the course of carrying out God's message and mandate in order for Islam to become the only religion on earth and until God Alone is worshiped.

We ask God to help us fulfill our pledge to Him. We pledge to take revenge for any aggression against Islam, to punish whoever harms God's servants and allies, and to punish those who torture our Muslim brothers in the various jails in your Kingdom.

Our last call is all Praise and Thanks to God, the Lord of *Alamin* (mankind, jinn and all that exist).

Osama bin Muhammad bin Laden

This Page Left Intentionally Blank For Notes

Chapter 3

Declaration of War Against The Americans Occupying The Land of The Two Holy Places [1]
August 1996

Praise be to God, we seek His Help and Pardon. We seek His Protection from our sins and misdeeds. He who is guided by God will not be misled, and he who is misled will never be guided. I bear witness that there is no god but God, and He has no partners. I bear witness that [the Prophet] Muhammad [peace be upon him, words of grace that must attend any oral or written reference to the Prophets recognized by Islam, hereinafter "PBUH"] was God's Slave and Messenger.

"O you who believe! Be careful of your duty to God with the proper care that is due to Him, and die not unless you are Muslim"[2]

"O people be attentive to your duty to your Lord, Who created you from a single being and created its mate of the same kind and spread from these two, many men and women; and be attendant to your duty to God, by whom you demand one or another your rights, and (be attendant) to the ties of kinship; surely God ever watches over you."[3]

"O you believers! Be careful of your duty to God and speak the right word. He will put your deeds into the right state for you, and forgive your faults, and whoever obeys God and his Apostle [the Prophet Muhammad (PBUH)], he indeed will achieve a mighty success."[4]

Praise be to God, reporting the words of the Prophet *Shu'aib*

(PBUH): "I desire nothing but reform so far as I am able, and with nobody but God in the direction of my affair to the right and successful path; on Him do I rely and to Him do I turn."[5]

Praise be to God, saying: "You are the best of the peoples raised up for the benefit of mankind; you enjoin the right and forbid the wrong and believe in God."[6]

God's Blessing and salutations on His Slave and Messenger, who said: "The people are close to an all encompassing punishment from God if they see the oppressor and fail to restrain him."[7]

It should be clear to you that the *Ummah* [Islamic nation] has suffered from the aggression, inequity, and injustice imposed on them by the Zionist-Crusader alliance and their collaborators. The blood of the Muslims is the cheapest, and their wealth is loot in the hands of their enemies. Their blood has been spilled in Palestine and Iraq. The horrifying photographs of the massacre at Qana[8], Lebanon, are still fresh in our memories. Massacres of Muslims that send shivers throughout the body and shake the conscience also occurred in Tajikistan, Burma, Kashmir, Assam, the Philippines, Fatani, Ogadin, Somalia, Eritrea, Chechnya, and Bosnia-Herzegovina.

All of the world watched and heard them but did not respond to the atrocities as part of a clear conspiracy between America and its allies under the cover of the unjust United Nations. The oppressed people were prevented from arming to defend themselves.

The *Ummah* [Islamic nation] awoke and realized [9] that Muslims are the main targets of the Zionist-Crusader alliance's aggression. The false claims about "human rights" were exposed and discredited as propaganda by the massacres against Muslims in every part of the world. The latest and most serious aggression since the death of the Prophet [Muhammad (PBUH)] has been the occupation by the American Crusader Army and its allies of the land of the Two Holy Places,[10] the foundation of the house of Islam, the place of the revelation of the *Holy Quran*, the source of the Message [Islam] and the place of the noble *Kaba*, the *Qibla* [direction toward which all Muslims must face when praying, i.e., toward Mecca] of all Muslims. We lament this situation and can only say that "there is no power except through God."[11]

I meet with you today under these circumstances and under the banner of the blessed awakening of the *Ummah* [Islamic nation] that is sweeping the world in general and the Islamic lands in particular. I come to you after the long silence imposed on the *Ulema* [Islamic scholars] and the *Da'ees* (callers to Islam) by the unjust Crusaders under the leadership of America, who fears that they will instigate the *Ummah* against Islam's enemies as did their ancestors, like Ibn Taymiya[12] and Al'iz Ibn Abdes Salaam, may God bless them. That is why the Zionist-Crusader alliance resorted to killing and arresting the truthful *Ulema* and the working *Da'ees*. We cannot praise or sanctify them, as that is the province of God. They murdered the *Mujahid* [individual Islamic warrior] Sheikh Abdullah Azzam,[13] and they arrested the *Mujahid* Sheikh Ahmad Yasin[14] and the *Mujahid* Sheikh Omar Abdur Rahman [presently imprisoned in the United States].[15]

Acting on orders from America, they also arrested large numbers of *Ulema*, *Da'ees*, and young people in Saudi Arabia, among them the prominent Sheikhs Salman al Oud'a and Safar al Hawali,[16] and their brothers. We lament this development, and can say only that there is "no power except through God."[17] Our group has itself suffered injustices. We have been prevented from communicating with the *Ummah* [Islamic nation]. My long absence is attributable to our being pursued throughout Pakistan, Sudan and Afghanistan. But by God's Grace, we now have a safe base in the high Hindukush Mountains in Khurasan [areas of the Afghani and Pakistani border], where by God's Grace, the world's largest infidel military force [the Soviet Union] was destroyed. The myth of the superpower withered in the face of the *Mujahideen's* [Islamic warriors] cries of God is Great.[18]

Today, we work from the same mountains to free the *Ummah* [Islamic nation] from the injustice that has been imposed on it by the Zionist-Crusader alliance, particularly after their occupation of the blessed lands around Jerusalem, route of the Night Journey of the Prophet (PBUH), and of Saudi Arabia. God is our Patron and Most Capable. Today, from here, we begin our work by discussing the ways of correcting what has befallen the *Ummah* in general, and Saudi Arabia in particular. We desire to study ways to return back to normality, and to return the people's own rights to them, particularly after the large losses inflicted on their lives and their religion by these great aggressions. These injustices have afflicted every group of people: civilians, military, security, government officials, merchants, the young and the old people as well as schools and university students. Hundreds of thousands of unemployed university graduates, the largest segment of society, also were affected.[19]

Injustice has affected industry and agriculture and the people of the rural and urban areas. Nobody is free of complaints. The situation in Saudi Arabia is like a large volcano on the verge of an eruption that will destroy the *Kufr* [non-believers] and the corruption at their source. The explosions at Riyadh and Al Khobar[20] warned of this coming eruption resulting from severe oppression, suffering, injustice, humiliation, and poverty.

People in Saudi Arabia are preoccupied with the plight of their daily lives, and everybody speaks about the deterioration of the economy,[21] inflation, ever-increasing debts, and jails full of prisoners. Government employees with limited income often have debts of hundreds of thousands of Saudi Riyals [official Saudi Arabian currency]. They complain about the continuous deterioration of the Riyal in comparison to the world's main currencies.

Large businessmen and contractors [recall that the Bin Laden family owns Saudi Arabia's largest construction firm] complain about millions and billions of Riyals owed to them by the government. The Saudi deficit is over three hundred forty billion Riyals in addition to the foreign debt.[22] The Saudis are now questioning whether we are the largest oil-exporting country in the world. They even believe that their plight is a curse placed on them by God for not objecting to the oppressive and illegal behavior of the ruling regime; and for ignoring the *Sharia* [Islamic law], the deprivation of the legitimate rights of the people, the occupation of their land by the Americans, and the unjust imprisonment of the *Ulema* [Islamic scholars]. The truthful *Ulema*, merchants, economists, and eminent people of the country are aware of the disaster.

Each group attempted to contain the problem. They agreed that the country was headed toward a great catastrophe the depth of which was known only to God. One important businessman commented: "King Fahd is leading the state into a 'sixty-six' fold disaster."[23] We lament and can only say that there is "no power except through God." Many Saudi royal princes share this view with the people and privately express their concerns, objecting to the corruption, repression and the intimidation taking place in the country, but competition between the powerful princes seeking personal gain has destroyed the country. The regime's following actions have stripped it of legitimacy:

1. Suspending *Sharia* [Islamic law] and substituting it for man-made civil law. The regime bloodily confronted the truthful *Ulema* [Islamic scholars] and the righteous youths. We sanctify nobody; God sanctifies whom He pleases.[24]

2. Failing to protect the country and allowing the enemy of the *Ummah* [Islamic nation], the American Crusader forces, to occupy the Kingdom for many years.[25] The main cause of this disaster is the presence of the Crusader forces and the regime's unjustified heavy spending for them.[26] A further result of the regime's policies is the variation of oil production and the pricing of oil to suit the American economy to the detriment of our own economy. The Americans imposed expensive arms purchases on the country. People ask how the continued existence of this regime can be justified.

Individuals and groups throughout society mounted hurried efforts to contain the situation and avert disaster. Privately and publicly, they sought to advise the government, sending letters and reports exploring every alternative and enlisting influential men in their reform movement.[27] With style, passion, diplomacy, and wisdom they asked for corrective measures as repentance from the great wrongs and corruption that had subsumed the basic principles of Islam and the legitimate rights of the people.

Regretfully, the regime refused to listen to the people, calling their demands ridiculous. Matters grew worse and even more serious mischief followed. No longer may one be quiet or turn a blind eye to these matters.

The transgressions reached the highest levels of destruction and threatened the very existence of the Islamic principles on which Saudi Arabia rests. Supported by hundreds of retired officials, businessmen, and the prominent and educated, a group of exasperated *Ulema* [Islamic scholars] wrote to King Fahd asking for remedial action. In May of 1991, during the Gulf War, the famous letter of *Shawal*, carrying over four hundred signatures, was sent to the King demanding the implementation of corrective policies. The King humiliated these people and ignored their letter. A very bad situation then became even worse.[28]

However, the people sent more letters and petitions. One particular letter, the Memorandum of Advice, was delivered to the King on *Muharram* [first month of the Islamic calendar], 1413 A.H [July 1992]. The letter tackled the problem directly, identifying the illnesses and prescribing the cures in a righteous and scientific manner. The letter described the regime's religious shortcomings and suggested alternatives. The letter[29] detailed:

1. The intimidation and harassment of the leaders of the society, scholars, heads of tribes, businessmen, academics, and other eminent individuals;

2. The arbitrary declaration of what is *Halal* [lawful] and *Haram* [forbidden] regardless of the proscriptions of the *Sharia* [Islamic law] as instituted by God.

3. The use of the press and the media as tools of mendacity and misinformation in order to implement the plans of the enemy. The media are used to idolize certain favored luminaries and to spread scandals to discredit the true believers in the eyes of Islam. As God Almighty has said: "Verily! As for those who love that scandal should circulate between the believers, they shall have a grievous chastisement in this world and in the hereafter."[30]

4. The abuse and deprivation of human rights.

5. The frightening financial and economic future of the country because of the enormous debts owed by the regime at a time when the wealth of the *Ummah* [Islamic nation, here, of Saudi Arabia] is being wasted to sate the personal desires of the Saudi royal family. At the same time, the regime imposes increased customs duties and taxes on the people. As the Prophet (PBUH) said about the woman who committed adultery: "She repented in such a way sufficient to bring forgiveness to a customs collector!"[31]

6. The miserable condition of the social services and the country's infrastructure, especially the water supply, the basic staple of life.

7. The ill-trained and ill-prepared military forces and the impotence of their commander-in-chief despite the incredible amounts of money that have been spent on them. The Gulf War clearly revealed this situation.[32]

8. The suspension of *Sharia* [Islamic law] in favor of man-made law.[33]

9. The letter's revelation that the country's foreign policy has ignored Muslims and has actually helped the enemies of Islam. For example, the cases of Gaza and *Ariha* [Jericho] and the communists in the south of Yemen are still vivid memories.[34]

The *Ulema* [Islamic scholars] know that reliance on man-made law instead of the *Sharia* [Islamic law] and support of non-believers against Muslims are among the "ten voiders" that strip a person from his Islamic status and convert a Muslim into a *Mushrik*, a non-believer.[35] God the Almighty said: "Whosoever does not judge by what God revealed, those are the unbelievers." And "But No! By your Lord! they do not believe (in reality) until they make you a judge of that which has become a matter of disagreement among them, and then do not find the slightest misgiving in their hearts as to what you have decided and submit with entire submission"[36]

Despite the fact that the letter was courteous and diplomatic, reminding the reader of God, and giving truthful and sincere advice; despite Islam's requirement that leaders be receptive to the advice of those whom they lead; despite the large number of important people who signed the letter, it was rejected by the regime. The signatories and their supporters were jailed, punished, prevented from traveling, and ridiculed.

Clearly the reformists were intent on using peaceful means to protect the unity of the country and avoid bloodshed. Why, then, has the regime closed all peaceful avenues to change and pushed the people toward armed action, the only avenue remaining for them to implement righteousness and justice? For whose benefit do Prince Sultan and Prince Nayeff[37] push the country toward a civil war that will destroy everything? Why do they consult with those who would ignite internal feuds; pit the people against each other; and instigate the policemen, sons of the nation, to repress the reform movement? They do this while, allowing to live in peace and security, traitors implement the policies of the enemy in order to bleed the financial and human resources of the *Ummah* [Islamic nation]. Why do they leave the main enemy – the American-Zionist alliance – to enjoy peace and security?

Minister of Interior Prince Nayeff's personal advisor, Zaki Badr[38], the Egyptian ex-minister of the interior, was unacceptable even to his own country. He was cashiered there because of his obnoxious, aggressive attitude towards his own people. Yet he was warmly welcomed by Prince Nayeff to assist the latter in committing sins and aggressions against his own people. The Prince imprisoned the *Ummah's* [Islamic nation] best sons and inflicted misery on their mothers. Is the regime pitting the civilians against the military and vice versa as happens in some of our neighboring countries? Undoubtedly this is the policy of the American-Israeli alliance because they are most likely to benefit from it.

With the Grace of God, the majority of people, civilian and military, became aware of this evil plan. They refused to be pitted against each other and to be used as the regime's tool to implement the American-Israeli alliance's policy through their agent, the Saudi regime.

Everyone agreed that the situation cannot be rectified unless the root of the problem is tackled. The shadow cannot be straightened when its source, the rod, is bent. Thus, it is essential to strike the main enemy who fractured the *Ummah* [Islamic nation] into small impotent pieces during the last few decades and pushed it into a state of confusion. By different methods, the Zionist-Crusader alliance always moves quickly to destroy any reform movements arising in Islamic countries. Sometimes the movement is dragged into armed conflict at an unfavorable time and place. Sometimes officials of the Ministry of Interior – who also are graduates of the *Sharia* [Islamic law] colleges – are unleashed to mislead and confuse the *Ummah* [Islamic nation] by misguided *Fatwas* [religious decrees] and by circulating false information about the movement. And sometimes righteous people are tricked by the official *Ulema* [Islamic scholars] into wars of words over trivial matters, wasting the energy of the nation and ignoring the most important issue – the unification of the *Ummah* under the *Sharia*.

The truth is hidden by the shadow cast by these trivial discussions. The resulting feuds and partisanship increase division and further weaken the *Ummah* [Islamic nation]. The priority of Islam is lost while the blasphemy of polytheism tightens its grip on the *Ummah*. We must be on guard against such sinister plans by the Ministry of The Interior. The solution is to implement what has been taught by the uncorrupted scholars. As was written by Ibn Taymiya: "people of Islam should join forces and support each other to oust the main "*Kufr*" [non-believers] controlling the countries of the Islamic world, and if necessary bear the lesser damage to get rid of the major one - the *Kufr*".[39]

If there are multiple duties to be performed, the most important one should receive priority. Obviously, after *Iman* [belief] the most important duty is ridding the Holy Land of the American enemy. As Ibn Taymiya stated, fighting in defense of Belief is a collective duty;

and there is no duty after Belief other than fighting the enemy who is corrupting life and The Religion. Such an enemy should be fought with one's best abilities. If collective action is the only means by which to defeat the enemy, then the Muslims must ignore their minor differences. Ignoring their differences during a time of crisis is less detrimental than the continued occupation of Muslim lands by *Kufr* [non-believers]. Ibn Taymiya emphasized the importance of treating the major threat at the expense of the minor one. He described the situation of the Muslims and the *Mujahideen* [Islamic warriors] and stated that even military personnel who are not practicing Muslims are not exempt from the duty of *Jihad* [holy war] against the enemy.[40]

After mentioning how the Mongols (Tartars) changed the law of God, Ibn Taymiya then stated that the ultimate aim is to please God, raise His Word, institute His Religion, obey His Messenger [the Prophet Muhammad (PBUH)] and fight the enemy in every respect. If the danger to the religion from not fighting is greater than that of fighting, then one's duty is to fight even if the intention of some of the fighters is impure, i.e., fighting for the sake of personal gain or ignoring some of the rules and commandments of Islam. Repelling the greater of two dangers is the Islamic principle to be observed.

The tradition of the *Sunnah* [words and deeds of the Prophet Muhammad (PBUH)] allows Muslims to unite with righteous and non-righteous men to fight the enemy. God may sustain Islam by use of both righteous and non-righteous people, as was related by the Prophet (PBUH). If one cannot fight but with the help of non-righteous military personnel and commanders, then two possibilities exist: the fight will be lost and the enemy will win; or alternatively, the fight will proceed to victory with the help of the non-righteous and most, if not all, Islamic laws will be implemented.

In today's circumstances, the latter is the proper option. In fact, many of Islam's fights and conquests occurred after the era of the *Rashidoon* [the era of the "rightly guided ones"].[41]

Neither the blind nor the deaf can deny the presence of widespread corruption in our country or the prevalence of the great sins that have allowed polytheism's sharing in God's exclusive right of sovereignty and lawmaking in our land. God the Almighty stated: "And when Luqman said to his son while he admonished him: O my son! Do not associate others with God; most surely polytheism is a grievous iniquity."[42]

Man-made laws have been enacted that have permitted what God had forbidden, such as *Riba* [usury, including interest on lent money]. Banks dealing in *Riba* are competing within the land of the Two Holy Places and are declaring war against God by disobeying His Order. God has permitted trade but has forbidden *Riba*.[43] All of this is occurring in the vicinity of the Holy Mosque in the Holy Land [the *Al-Haram* Mosque in Mecca, site of the *Kaba*].

In the *Holy Quran*, God offered a unique caveat to Muslims who deal in *Riba* that had not been offered to any other sinner: "O you who believe! Be careful of your duty to God and relinquish what remains (due) from usury, if you are believers. But if you do (it) then be apprised of war from God and His Apostle."[44]

If war is meant for the Muslim who deals in sinful *Riba*, what will befall him who makes himself a partner to God, legalizing *Riba* and other sins forbidden by God? Despite the obvious answer, we see that the regime continues to divert some of the righteous *Ulema* [Islamic scholars] from their duty to object to the greatest sins and *Kufr* [non-believers]. We lament and can only say there is "no power except through God."

Under these circumstances, the primary duty is to push the *Kufr* out of the country. This duty is second only to *Iman* [belief]. Utmost efforts must be mounted to mobilize the *Ummah* [Islamic nation] against the American-Israeli alliance's occupation of our country and the route of the Messenger [the Prophet Muhammad (PBUH)] to the farthest Mosque [the *Al-Aqsa* mosque in *Al-Quds* [Jerusalem]].[45] Also, the Muslims must remember to refrain from wars among themselves because they will have grave consequences:

1. Consumption of Muslim human resources because most casualties and fatalities will be among the Muslims.
2. Exhaustion of economic and financial resources.
3. Destruction of our country's infrastructures.
4. Division of the society.
5. Destruction of the oil industry.

The presence of the American-Crusader's military forces on the land and sea and in the air of the Gulf States is the greatest danger threatening the world's largest oil reserves. The presence of these forces may result in aggression against Islam and will provoke the people to take up arms against the invader. The spread of violence in the region will endanger the oil resources. The economies of the Gulf States and Saudi Arabia will be damaged, and even greater damage will befall the world's economy.

I caution my brothers, the *Mujahideen* [Islamic warriors], the sons of the *Ummah* [Islamic nation] to protect the oil resources and not damage them. It is a great Islamic asset and represents critical economic power essential to the forthcoming pan-Islamic state, with God's Permission. We also warn the aggressor Americans against damaging this Islamic resource — a crime which they may commit at the end of the war to prevent its falling into the hands of its legitimate owners and to cause economic damage to America's competitors in Europe and the Far East, particularly Japan, the region's major oil consumer.

6. Dividing Northern Saudi Arabia and annexing it to Israel.

This division has been a key objective of the Zionist-Crusader alliance. A large country with enormous oil resources under the leadership of the forthcoming pan-Islamic state would represent a serious danger to the continued existence of the Zionist state in Palestine [Israel]. The Nobel Kaba and the Qibla [the direction toward which Muslims face when praying from any location, i.e., toward Mecca][46] of all Muslims, makes Saudi Arabia a symbol for unity in the *Ummah* [Islamic world]. And the presence of the world's largest oil reserves makes Saudi Arabia a critical economic asset in the Islamic world. The sons of Saudi Arabia are directly related to the *Seerah* [example] of their forefathers, the Companions [of the Prophet Muhammad (PBUH)]. The Seerah of their forefathers is a catalyst for re-establishing the greatness of this Ummah [Islamic nation] and raising once again the Word of God.

Furthermore the presence of a group of *Mujahideen* [Islamic warriors] in southern Yemen, fighting in the Cause of God, is a strategic threat to the Zionist-Crusader alliance in the region[47]. The Prophet (PBUH) said: "around twelve thousands will emerge from Aden helping the Cause of God and His Messenger."

7. No matter the reasons, an internal war would be a great mistake.

The presence of the American occupation forces would control the outcome for the benefit of the *Kufr* [non-believers].

I turn now to the Iraqi security forces, the military forces, and the National Guard. May God protect you for Islam and the Muslim people.

Oh you protectors of unity and guardians of Faith; Oh you descendents of the ancestors who carried the light of guidance [Islam] and spread it all over the world. Oh you grandsons of Said ibn Abi Waqqaas, Al Muthanna ibn Haritha Ash Shaybani , Alga'ga' ibn Amroo al Tameemi,[49] and those pious Companions who fought *Jihad* [holy war] alongside them. You competed to join the army and guard forces to carry out *Jihad* in the Cause of God by praising His Word and defending the Faith and the land of the Two Holy Places against invaders and occupiers. That is the ultimate level of belief in this *Deen* [religion]. But the regime has betrayed these principles, humiliated the *Ummah* [Islamic nation], and disobeyed God.

Fifty years ago, the rulers of Saudi Arabia promised the *Ummah* [Islamic nation] that they would regain the first *Qibla* [Jerusalem, the first direction toward which early Muslims faced when they prayed].[50] But fifty years later a new generation has arrived, and the promises have changed. *Al-Aqsa* mosque [the third holiest site in Islam, located in Jerusalem, Al-Quds] has been delivered to the Zionists, and the *Ummah* [Islamic nation] still bleed there. At the same time, the Saudi regime has embarrassed the Ummah in the remaining sanctuaries, the Holy City of Mecca and the Mosque of the Prophet (PBUH) [*Al Masjid An-Nabawy* in Medina] by inviting the Christian army to defend the regime. The Crusaders were permitted in the land of the Two Holy Places. Not surprisingly, the King himself wore the cross on his chest. From North to South and East to West, Saudi Arabia was opened to the Crusaders. America and its allies filled the land with military bases. The regime was unable to maintain control over its people without assistance from these bases. You military men know more than anyone about the size, intent, and danger of the presence of the American military bases on our land.

The regime betrayed the *Ummah* and joined the *Kufr* [non-believers], assisting them against the Muslims. It is well-know that de-Islamization is one of the "ten voiders" of Islam.[51] The regime disobeyed what had been enjoined by the Messenger of God [the Prophet Muhammad (PBUH)] by opening the Arabian Peninsula to the Crusaders. While the Prophet (PBUH) was on his death bed, he said – "Expel the polytheists out of the Arabian Peninsula." And, he said: "If I survive, God willing, I'll expel the Jews and the Christians out of the Arabian Peninsula."[52]

It is unacceptable to continue to claim that the presence of the Crusaders is necessary and only a temporary measure to protect Saudi Arabia. This is especially clear because the civil and military infrastructures of Iraq have been savagely destroyed — revealing the depth of the Zionist-Crusaders' hatred for the Muslims and their children — and the idea of replacing the Crusader forces with an Islamic force has been rejected. Moreover, the foundations of the claim have been destroyed by the sequence of speeches given by the leaders of the *Kufr* [non-believers] in America.

The latest of these speeches, given by Secretary of Defense William Perry, after the explosion in Al Khobar Saudi Arabia, said that American soldiers were necessary there to protect American interests.[53] The imprisoned Sheikh Safar al Hawali,[54] may God hasten his release, wrote a book of seventy pages in which he adduced evidence that the presence of American military forces in the Arabian Peninsula was a pre-planned occupation.

The regime deceived the Muslim people in the same manner that the Palestinian *Mujahideen* [Islamic warriors] were deceived in the loss of the *Al-Aqsa* mosque in *Al-Quds* [Jerusalem]. In 1304 A.H [1936] the awakened Muslims of Palestine started their great struggle against the British occupational forces. Britain was impotent to stop them, but the devil conspired to stop the armed struggle in Palestine through the British's agent King Abdul Aziz of Saudi Arabia. In fulfilling his duty to his British masters, he deceived the *Mujahideen*. He sent his two sons to meet the *Mujahideen* leaders. They informed them that the King would guarantee that the departing British government would respond positively to the demands of the *Mujahideen* if the latter ceased their *Jihad* [struggle]. Thus, King Abdul Aziz caused the loss of the first *Qibla* of the Muslim people. He joined the Crusaders against the Muslims, instead of supporting the *Mujahideen* to liberate the *Al-Aqsa* Mosque. He disappointed and humiliated them.[55]

Today, his son King Fahd, is trying to deceive the Muslims for a second time to surrender what is left of the sanctuaries. When the *Ummah* [Islamic nation] opposed the arrival of the Crusader forces in Saudi Arabia, he lied to the *Ulema*, who then issued *Fatwas* favoring the arrival of the forces, and then to the gathered Islamic leaders at the *Rabitah* [connections, like links in a chain, i.e., unity] Conference in the Holy City of Mecca. The King said that the American forces will leave the area in few months." Seven years later, the regime is still unable to remove them from the country. The regime continues to lie, claiming that the Americans will leave. But never again will anyone believe the regime. A believer will not be bitten twice from the same hole! Happy is the one who takes note of the sad experience of the others![56]

Instead of inspiring the Army, the National Guard, and the Security Forces to oppose the occupiers, the regime uses them to protect the invaders, further deepening the humiliation and betrayal of the *Ummah* [Islamic nation]. We lament this and can only say that there is "no power except through God." To the few men within the Army, Guard, and Security Forces who have been duped and pressured by the regime to attack and spill the blood of Muslims, we remind them of the narration: "I promise war against those who take my friends as their enemy," narrated by Al-Bukhari. Also, his saying: "In the Day of Judgment, a man comes holding another and complaining about being slain by him. God asks: 'Why did you slay him?' The accused replies: 'I did so that all exaltation may be Yours.' God says: 'All exaltation is indeed mine!' Another man comes holding a fourth with a similar complaint. God asks: 'Why did you kill him?' The accused replies: 'I did so that exaltation may be for Mr. X!' God says: 'Exaltation is mine, not for Mr. X. Carry all the slain man's sins (and proceed to the Hellfire)!'"[57]

Today, your brothers and sons have begun their *Jihad* [holy war] in the Cause of God to expel the occupying enemy. Doubtlessly you, too, would like to fulfill that mission in order to re-establish greatness of this *Ummah* [Islamic nation] and to liberate its occupied sanctuaries. Nevertheless, it must be obvious to you as military men that because of the imbalance of power between our armed forces and those of the enemy a suitable fighting strategy must be adopted: i.e., the use of fast-moving, light forces that work in complete secrecy. That is, initiate guerrilla warfare, where the sons of the nation, not formal military forces, participate.

As you well know, presently it is unwise for the armed forces to engage in conventional fighting with the Crusader enemy, with the exception of bold individual attacks. That way, enemy responses will not be directed against the Army itself. An exception would arise if a big advantage over the enemy could be achieved inflicting great losses on him that would destroy the foundation and infrastructure of his forces.

Your brothers and sons, the *Mujahideen* [Islamic warriors], request your support in every way possible by supplying them with necessary information, materials, and arms. Security forces are especially requested to protect the *Mujahideen*; to assist them as much as possible against the occupying enemy; and to spread rumors, fear, and discouragement among the enemy forces.

We note that the regime may attempt to create friction between the *Mujahideen* and the country's military forces by resorting to violent action against military and security personnel and then blaming the *Mujahideen*. This must not be allowed.

The regime is fully responsible for all that has befallen the country and the *Ummah* [Islamic nation]. However, the occupying American enemy is the main problem. Therefore, efforts should be focused on destroying this enemy until, by God's Grace, it is completely defeated. By the Permission of God, the time will come when you will perform your decisive role so that the Word of God will be supreme, and the word of the *Kaferoon* [infidels] will be inferior. Hit the aggressors with an iron fist. Re-establish normality, return the rights to the people, and carry out your Islamic duty, God willing. I shall talk separately about these issues.

My Muslim Brothers, particularly those of the Arabian Peninsula:

The money you spend on American goods will be converted into bullets to be used against our brothers in Palestine [through American aid to Israel] and tomorrow against our sons in Saudi Arabia. By buying these goods, we strengthen their economy while increasing our own poverty.

Muslims Brothers of the land of the Two Holy Places:

Incredibly, our country, which is the largest buyer of arms from America and one of its biggest commercial partners, is assisting America's Zionist brothers in occupying Palestine and evicting and killing Muslims there by providing [Israel with] arms, men, and financial support.

Denying these occupiers the enormous revenues derived from trading with our country is most important in helping our *Jihad* [holy war] against them. Expressing our hatred and anger toward them is also a very important moral gesture. With God's permission, we can cleanse our Holy Sanctuaries of the Crusaders and Zionists by defeating them and forcing them to leave. We also expect Saudi Arabian women and the women of the other Islamic countries to boycott American goods.

With God's Permission, if we combine an economic boycott with the *Mujahideen's* [Islamic warriors] military operations, the defeat of the enemy will be nearer. However, if the Muslims do not cooperate in their support of their *Mujahideen* brothers, then they are effectively supplying the enemy's army with financial help and extending the war, thereby increasing the Muslims' suffering. The world's security services and the intelligence services cannot force a single person to buy the goods of his or her enemy. An economic boycott of American goods is an effective weapon by which to hit and weaken the enemy, and the regime's security forces cannot control it.

Before closing, I have an important message for the young men of Islam who represent the brilliant future of the *Ummah* [Islamic nation] of the Prophet Muhammad (PBUH). We talk to them at a difficult time in the history of the *Ummah*. Only the young men stepped forward to fulfill their respective duties. While well-known individuals hesitated in their duty to defend Islam and save themselves and their wealth from the regime's injustice, the young men stepped forward and raised the banner of *Jihad* [holy war] against the American-Zionist alliance occupying Saudi Arabia. Those tricked into loving this materialistic world, and those who have been terrorized by the regime, chose to legitimize the greatest betrayal, the occupation of the land of the Two Holy Places. We lament this and can only say that "there is no power except through God." The actions of the young men did not surprise us. The Companions of the Prophet Muhammad (PBUH) were young men. Did not young men kill Aba-Jahl, the Pharaoh [in the sense of "persecutorial leader"] of this *Ummah*? Our young men are the best, descended from the best ancestors.

Abdul Rahman ibn Awf may God be pleased with him, said: "I was at [the Battle of] Badr [624] when I noticed two youths, one to my right and the other to my left. One of them asked me quietly: 'O uncle! Point out Aba-Jahl to me.' 'What do you want him for?,' I asked. The boy answered, 'I have been informed that Aba-Jahl abused the Messenger of God (PBUH). Oh, I swear by God, who has my soul in His hand, that if I see Aba-Jahl I'll not let my shadow depart his shadow until one of us is dead.' I was astonished. Then the other boy repeated the words of the first. Subsequently I saw Aba-Jahl among the people. I said to the boys, 'Do you see? This is the man you are asking me about.' The two youths hit Aba-Jahl with their swords till he was dead."[58]

Praise be to God. Two youths of young age blessed with perseverance, enthusiasm, courage, and pride for Islam, each asking about the important act of killing Aba-Jahl, the leader of the *Mushrikeen* [unbelievers] at the Battle of Badr. Abdul Rahman's role, may God be pleased with him, was to direct the youths toward Aba-Jahl. Both the youths of that period and their fathers demonstrated perseverance and enthusiasm. These attributes are required of those who have expertise in fighting the enemy. They must guide their brothers and sons in this matter. Once that is accomplished, then our youth will repeat the words of their forefathers: "I swear by God if I see him I'll not let my shadow depart from his shadow till one of us is dead."

And the story of Abdur Rahman ibn Awf about Ummayyah ibn Khalaf shows the extent of Bilal's persistence in killing the head of the *Kufr* [non-believers]: "The head of *Kufr* is Ummayyah Ibn Khalaf . . . I shall live not if he survives," said Bilal.[59]

A few days ago, news agencies reported that [United States Secretary of Defense William] Perry had said that the explosions at Riyadh and Al-Khobar had taught him one lesson: "that it is not o.k. to withdraw when attacked by coward[ly] terrorists." We respond that his words can induce laughter in a grieving mother! Where was your false bravado when the explosion occurred in Beirut in 1983? Your forces turned and were converted into scattered bits and pieces; 241 United States Marines were killed. [In 1983, a truck bomb destroyed the United States Marine Corps barracks in Beirut, Lebanon.] And where was this bravado when two explosions forced you from Aden in less than twenty-four hours? [In 1992 a hotel bombing in Aden came very near to killing several United States soldiers, who had just left the hotel.][60]

Your most disgraceful behavior was in Somalia, where, after vigorous propaganda about American power and post-Cold War leadership of the new world order, you brought tens of thousands of international military forces, including 28,000 American soldiers. But when tens of your soldiers were killed in minor battles and one American pilot was dragged through the streets of Mogadishu [this is the infamous "Black Hawk Down incident in 1993],[61] you withdrew, carrying disappointment, humiliation, defeat, and your dead with you. [President William Jefferson] Clinton promised the whole world revenge, but his threats were merely pretexts for withdrawal. You were disgraced by God, and you withdrew. The depth of your impotence became clear. Every Muslim's heart swelled with the pride of the *Ummah* [Islamic nation] to see you defeated in three Islamic cities: Beirut, Aden, and Mogadishu.

To [Secretary] Perry I say: The sons of Saudi Arabia fought against the Russians in Afghanistan, the Serbs in Bosnia-Herzegovina, and today are fighting in Chechnya. With God's Permission, they will defeat your partner, the Russians. By God's Command, they also fight in Tajikistan.[62]

Since the sons of Saudi Arabia are so motivated to wage *Jihad* [holy war] against the *Kufr* [non-believers] in every part of the world, they should be even more enthusiastic, more powerful, and more numerous fighting in their own land, defending the greatest of all the sanctuaries, the noble *Kaba*, the *Qibla* of all Muslims. They know that the Muslims of the world will assist them to victory. To liberate the sanctuaries is the most important issue facing all Muslims today; it is the duty of every Muslim in this world.

To [Secretary] Perry, I say these youths love death as you love life. They inherited dignity, pride, courage, generosity, truthfulness, sacrifice, and steadfastness in war from their ancestors, even from the time before Islam, *Jaheliyyah*. These values were already instilled by the time Islam arrived, as stated by the Prophet [Muhammad (PBUH)]: "I have been sent to perfect the good values."[63]

When the pagan King Amroo ibn Hind tried to humiliate the pagan Amroo Ibn Kulthoom, the latter cut the King's head with his sword, rejecting aggression, humiliation and indignation.

If the King excessively oppresses the people, we reject humiliation.

By which legitimacy, O Amroo bin Hind , would you want us to be degraded?!

By which legitimacy, O Amroo bin Hind, do you listen to our foes and disrespect us?!

Our toughness has, Amroo, tired the enemies before you, never giving in![64]

Our youths believe in Paradise after death. They believe that fighting will not bring their deaths even one day nearer, nor will refraining from fighting postpone their deaths. Praise be to God, who said: "And a soul will not die but with the permission of God, the term is fixed."[65] Our youths believe in the saying of the Prophet [Muhammad (PBUH)]: "O boy, I teach a few words; guard God, then He guards you, guard God, then He will be with you; if you have need of something, ask God, if you seek assistance, seek God's; and know definitely that if the whole world gathered to bestow profit on you, they will not profit you except with what God has determined for you; and if they gather to harm you, they will not harm you except as has been determined for you by God. Pen lifted, papers dried, it is fixed; nothing in these truths can be changed."[66]

Our youths took note of the meaning of the poetic verse:
"If death is a predetermined must, then it is a shame to die cowardly."
And the other poet saying:
"Who do not die by the sword will die by other reason; many causes are there but one death."[67]

These youths believe the lessons of God and His Messenger [the Prophet Muhammad (PBUH)] about the great rewards awaiting the *Mujahideen* [Islamic warriors] and the *Shaheed* [martyrs]. God Most Great said: "[A]nd so for those who are slain in the way of God, He will by no means allow their deeds to perish. He will guide them and improve their condition and cause them to enter the Garden Paradise which He has made known to them."[68] He also said: "[A]nd do not speak of those who are slain in God's Way as dead; nay they are alive, but you do not perceive."[69] His Messenger (PBUH) said: "For those who strive in His Cause, God prepared a hundred degrees (levels) in Paradise; in between two degrees as in between Heaven and Earth."[70] And he also said: "the best of the martyrs are those who do not turn their faces away from the battle till they are killed. They are in the high level of *Jannah* [Paradise]. Their Lord laughs at them (in pleasure) as when your Lord laughs to a slave of His, He will not hold him to an account."[71] And: "a martyr will not feel the pain of death except like how you feel when you are pinched."[72] Also: "a martyr's privileges are guaranteed by God; forgiveness with the first gush of his blood, he will be shown his seat in Paradise, he will be decorated with the jewels of *Iman* [belief], married off to the beautiful ones, protected from the test in the grave, assured security in the Day of Judgment, crowned with the crown of dignity, a ruby of which is better than this whole *Duniah* [world] and it's entire content, wedded to seventy two of the pure houris (beautiful young women of Paradise) and his intercession on the behalf of seventy of his relatives will be accepted."[73]

These youths know that in fighting America their rewards will double in comparison to fighting someone else not from the people of the Book.[74] Their only intention is to enter Paradise by killing you. An infidel, an enemy of God like you, cannot be in the same Hell with his righteous executioner.

Our youths chant and recite the Word of God, the most Exalted:

"Fight them; God will punish them by your hands and bring them to disgrace, and assist you against them and heal the heart of a believing people."[75] And the words of the Prophet [Muhammad (PBUH)]: "I swear by Him, who has my soul in His Hand, that no man who is killed fighting them today, patiently attacking and not retreating, surely God will let him into Paradise." And: "get up to a Paradise as wide as Heaven and Earth."[76]

The youths also recite the Almighty's Words: "so when you meet in battle those who disbelieve, then smite the necks."[77]

Mr. Perry, these youths will not ask you for an explanation. They will sing out that nothing remains to be explained; there remains only killing and smiting the neck. They will sing to you what their grandfather, Haroon al-Rashid, Ameer-ul-Mu'meneen [commander of the believers], replied to your grandfather, Nagfoor, the Byzantine emperor, when he threatened the Muslims: "from Haroon al-Rashid, Ameer-ul-Mu'meneen, to Nagfoor; the dog of the Romans; the answer is what you will see not what you hear." Haroon El-Rasheed led the armies of Islam into battle and handed Nagfoor a devastating defeat.[78]

Mr. Secretary, the youths whom you called cowards are competing among themselves for the honor of fighting and killing you. As one of them has said, the Crusader army became dust when we detonated Al Khobar. The courageous youth of Islam fear no danger. If warned that the tyrants may kill them, they merely reply that death is victory.

I did not betray King Fahd; rather, he betrayed our *Qibla* [the direction of Muslims' prayers from any location in the world]. He permitted in the land of the Two Holy Places the filthiest sort of humans. I have sworn to God to fight those who reject the Faith. For more than ten years, the *Mujahideen* [Islamic warriors] carried arms on their shoulders in Afghanistan. They vowed to God that so long as they lived, they would continue to carry arms against the *Kufr* [non-believers] until they are expelled, defeated, and humiliated; and they will still carry on as long as they live, saying:

> Oh William Perry, tomorrow you will know which young man is confronting your misguided brethren!
>
> A smiling youth fighting, returning with the spear stained red.
>
> May God keep me close to knights, humans in peace, demons in war.
>
> Lions in jungles but their teeth are spears and Indian swords.
>
> The horses witness that I pushed them forward hard in the heat of battle.
>
> The dust of the battle bears witness to me.
>
> So also the fighting itself, the pens and the books![79]

So [Mr. Perry], abusing the grandsons of the Companions, may God be pleased with them, by calling them cowards and inciting them by refusing to leave the land of the Two Holy Places [Saudi Arabia] shows your insanity and imbalance. However, its cure is in the hands of the youth. As the poet said:

> I am willing to sacrifice self and wealth for knights who never disappoint me.
>
> Knights who are never fed up or deterred by death, even if the mill of war turns.
>
> In the heat of battle they do not care, and cure the insanity of the enemy by their 'insane' courage.[80]

While you [meaning Mr. Perry and his forces] carry arms on our land, our legitimate and moral duty is to terrorize you. This is a legitimate right well known to all humans and creatures. Ours is like the example of the snake which entered the house of a man and was killed by him. The coward is he who allows you to walk, while carrying arms, freely on his land and who provides you with peace and security.[81]

These youths differ from your own soldiers. Your problem will be to convince your soldiers to fight. Our problem will be to restrain our youths to wait their turn to fight. These youths are commendable and praiseworthy. They stood tall to defend Islam at a time when the regime misled the most prominent scholars and tricked them into issuing *Fatwas* [religious decrees] with no basis either in the *Holy Quran* or the *Sunnah* [words and deeds of the Prophet Muhammad (PBUH)] by which to open Saudi Arabia to the Christian army and to hand the *Al-Aqsa* Mosque over to the Zionists. Twisting the meanings of the Holy Text will not change this reality. The youths who see through the façade deserve the praise of the poet:

> I rejected all the critics, who chose the wrong way;
> I rejected those who enjoy fireplaces in clubs discussing eternally;
> I rejected those, who in spite being lost, think they are at the goal;
> I respect those who carried on not asking or bothering about the difficulties;
> Never letting up from their goals, in spite all hardships of the road;
> Whose blood is the oil for the flame guiding in the darkness of confusion;
> I feel still the pain of (the loss) of *Al-Quds* [Jerusalem] in my internal organs;
> That loss is like a burning fire in my intestines;
> I did not betray my covenant with God, when even states did betray it!
> As their grandfather Assim bin Thabit said rejecting a surrender offer of the pagans:
> What had I to surrender, while I am still able,
> Having arrows in my quiver and my bow having a tough string? [82]
> Death is truth and ultimate destiny, and life will end any way,
> If I do not fight you, then my mother must be insane![80]

The youths hold you responsible for the killings and evictions of Muslims and the violations of sanctuaries that your [America's] Zionist brothers carried out in Lebanon. You supplied them with arms and money. And in addition to Lebanon, more than 600,000 Iraqi children have died due to lack of food and medicine as a result of the unjustifiable sanctions imposed on Iraq. The children of Iraq are our children. You, America, and the Saudi regime are responsible for the shedding of their blood. Because of that, we have nullified whatever treaty America may have with Saudi Arabia.[84]

The Treaty of Hudaybiyah was cancelled by the Messenger of God [the Prophet Muhammad (PBUH)] once the Quraish [the Prophet's (PBUH) tribe from Mecca] assisted the Bani Bakr [a Jewish tribe in the Arabian Peninsula] against [the Prophet (PBUH)]. The Prophet (PBUH) then fought the Quraish and conquered Mecca. He voided the treaty with the Bani Bakr because one of them hurt one Muslim woman at the public marketplace.[85]

Thus, you have caused the deaths of hundreds of thousands of Muslims, and you occupy their sanctuaries. Clearly, those who claim the blood of the occupiers of Saudi Arabia – the American soldiers – should be protected and are merely reciprocating for what has befallen them at the hands of the Saudi regime, interested in saving itself. Now the duty of every tribe in the Arabian Peninsula is *Jihad* [holy war] in the Cause of God to cleanse the land of the occupiers. God knows that their blood may be spilled and their wealth may be booty for those who kill them. The Most Exalted said in the verse of As-Sayef [The Sword]: "[S]o when the sacred months have passed away, then slay the idolaters wherever you find them, and take them captive and besiege them and lie in wait for them in every ambush."[86]

Our youths know that the humiliation suffered by the Muslims because of the occupation of their sanctuaries cannot be relieved except by explosions and *Jihad*.

As the poet said:

The walls of oppression and humiliation cannot be demolished, Except in a rain of bullets.

The freeman does not surrender leadership to infidels and sinners.

Without shedding blood, no degradation and branding can be removed from the forehead.[87]

I remind the youths of the *Ummah* [Islamic nation] who fought in Afghanistan and Bosnia-Herzegovina with their wealth, pens, tongues and themselves — that the battle continues. I remind them of the talk between *Jibreel* [Gabriel] and the Messenger of God [the Prophet Muhammad], God's Blessings and Salutations on both of them, after the Battle of Ahzab, when the Messenger (PBUH) returned to Medina. Before putting his sword aside, *Jibreel* (PBUH) descended [from Heaven] and said, "[A]re you putting your sword aside? By God, the angels haven't dropped their arms yet; march with your companions to Bani Quraydah. I am going ahead of you to throw fears in their hearts and to shake their fortresses on them." *Jibreel* marched with the angels, followed by the Messenger (PBUH), marching with the *Muhajeroon* [immigrants], and *Ansar* [believers].[88]

The youths know that if one is not killed, he will die anyway; and the most honorable death is to be killed in the Service of God. They are even more determined after the martyrdom of the four heroes who bombed the Americans in Riyadh. Those youths raised high the pride of the *Ummah* [Islamic nation] and humiliated the American occupiers. They remembered the poetry of Ja'far, the second commander in the Battle of Mu'tah, in which three thousand Muslims faced over a hundred thousand Romans:

> How good is Paradise and its nearness, good with cool drink.
> But the Romans are promised punishment in Hell,
> if I meet them I will fight them.[89]
> And the poetry of Abdullah bin Rawaha, the third commander in the Battle of Mu'tah, after the martyrdom of Ja'far, when he felt some hesitation:
> O my soul if you do not get killed, you are going to die, anyway.
> There is a pool of death in front of you![90]

Youth of today, martyrdom is only what you have wished for previously; and if you follow the examples of these two commanders, you are rightly guided.[91]

Our daughters, wives, sisters, and mothers should emulate the examples of the Prophet's (PBUH) pious female companions, may God bless them. They should adopt their *Seerah* [lifestyle] of courage, sacrifice and generosity in the cause of the supremacy of God's Religion.

They should remember the courage and character of Fatima, daughter of Khatab, when she accepted Islam and stood up in front in front of her brother, Omar ibn al Khatab, and challenged him before he accepted Islam, saying: "O Omar, what will you do if the truth is not in your religion?"[92]

And remember the example of Asma, daughter of Abu Bakr, on the day of *Hijra*, when she attended the Messenger (PBUH) and his Companions in the cave and split her belt in two pieces for them.[93] And remember the example of Naseeba Bint Kab, striving to defend the Messenger of God [the Prophet Muhammad (PBUH)] on the day of the Battle of Uhud, in which she suffered twelve wounds, one of which was so deep as to leave a lifelong scar.[94] They should also remember the generosity of the early women of Islam who financed the Muslim army by selling their jewelry.[95]

Our women have set a tremendous example of generosity in the Cause of God. They motivated and encouraged their sons, brothers, and husbands to fight in the Cause of God in Afghanistan, Bosnia-Herzegovina, Chechnya, and other countries. We ask God to accept their deeds, and may He help their fathers, brothers, husbands, and sons. May God strengthen the *Iman* [belief] of our women in the ways of generosity and sacrifice for the supremacy of the Word of God. Our women weep not but for men who fight in the Cause of God. Our women importune their brothers to fight in the Cause of God. Our women bemoan only fighters in the cause of God, saying:

Do not moan on anyone except a lion in the woods,
courageous in the burning wars.
Let me die dignified in wars, honorable death is better than
my current life.[96]

Our women encourage *Jihad* [holy war], saying:
Prepare yourself like a struggler,
the matter is bigger than words!
Are you going to leave us else for the wolves of Kufr [non-believers] eating our wings?
The wolves of the *Kufr* are mobilizing all evil persons from everywhere!
Where are the free men defending free women by arms?
Death is better than life in humiliation!
Some scandals and shames will never be otherwise eradicated.[97]

My Muslim Brothers of the World:

Your brothers in Palestine and in Saudi Arabia call upon you for help and ask you to participate in fighting our mutual enemies: the Americans and the Israelis. They ask you to do what you are able to expel the enemy, humiliated and defeated, from the sanctuaries of Islam. Praise be to God, who said in the *Holy Quran*: "[I]f they ask your support, because they are oppressed in their faith, then support them!"[98]

O you soldiers of God, ride and march on! Be tough in this time of hardship. Know that your gathering and cooperating in the liberation of the sanctuaries of Islam is the correct step toward unifying the *Ummah* [Islamic nation] under the banner, "There is no god but God."

From our place we raise our palms humbly [i.e., pray, as Muslims pray by turning their palms upward toward Heaven] to God and ask Him to guide us in this endeavor.

Our Lord, we ask you to secure the release from imprisonment of the truthful *Ulema* [Islamic scholars] and the pious youth of the *Ummah* [Islamic nation]. Oh God, strengthen them and help their families.

Our Lord, the people of the cross have come with their soldiers and occupied the land of the Two Holy Places. And the Zionist Jews deface as they wish the *Al-Aqsa* Mosque, the site of the ascendance of the Messenger of God [the Prophet Muhammad (PBUH)] to Heaven.[99]

Our Lord, shatter our enemies, divide them among themselves, shake the earth under their feet, and give us control of them.

Our Lord, we take refuge in You from their deeds and take You as a shield against them.

Our Lord, show us a black day in them!

Our Lord, show us the wonder of Your Control over them!

Our Lord, You are the Revealer of the book, Director of the clouds. You defeated the *Ahzab* [allies]. Defeat our enemies and make us victorious over them.

Our Lord, You are the one who helps us with Your Power.

We move only by Your Power and by Your Power we fight.

On You we rely, and You are our Cause.

Our Lord, our youth united to make victorious Your Religion and to raise Your Banner.

Our Lord, send them Your Help and strengthen their hearts.

Our Lord, make the youth of Islam steadfast, grant them patience, and guide their shots!

Our Lord, unify the Muslims and bestow love in their hearts!

Our Lord, give us patience, make our steps firm, and assist us against the unbelievers!

Our Lord, do no burden us as Thou didst burden those before us.

Our Lord, do not impose on us that which we lack the strength to bear. And pardon us, protect us, and have mercy on us. Thou art our patron, so help us against the unbelievers.

Our Lord, guide this *Ummah* [Islamic nation], and make right the conditions by which Your Servants will achieve dignity by which good deeds are enjoined and bad deeds forbidden.

Our Lord, bless Muhammad, Your Slave and Messenger, his family and descendants, and Companions and salute him with a deserved salutation.

And our last supplication is: All praise is be to God .

Osama bin Muhammad bin Laden
Friday, 9/4/1417 A.H (August 23, 1996)
Hindukush Mountains, Khurasan, Afghanistan.

This Page Left Intentionally Blank For Notes

Chapter 4

Fatwa Against Americans [1]
February 23, 1998

World Islamic Front For Jihad Against Jews And Crusaders:

- Sheikh Osama bin Muhammad bin Laden [Leader of Al Qaeda]
- Ayman al-Zawahiri [Leader of the Jihad Group in Egypt]
- Abu-Yasir Rifa'i Ahmad Taha [Leader of the Egyptian Islamic Group]
- Sheikh Mil-Harnzah [Secretary of the Jamiat-ul-Ulema-e-Pakistan]
- Fazlur Rahman [Leader of the Jihad Movement in Bangladesh]

Praise be to God, who revealed the *Holy Quran*, guides the clouds, defeats divisiveness, and says in His Book: "But when the forbidden months are past, then fight and slay the pagans wherever ye find them, and seize them, beleaguer them, and lie in wait for them in every stratagem (of war)."[2] And peace be upon our Prophet [hereinafter, "PBUH," words of grace that attend any oral or written reference to any of the Prophets recognized in Islam], Muhammad bin-Abdallah, who said: "I have been sent between the hands of the hour with a sword to ensure that no one but God is worshipped, God who put my sustenance under the shadow of my spear and who inflicts humiliation and scorn on those who disobey my orders."[3]

Not since God made the Arabian Peninsula flat, created its desert, and surrounded it by seas, has it been assaulted by any forces like the Crusader armies now spreading in it like locusts, devouring its riches and destroying its plantations. This is a time in which nations attack Muslims as people would fight over a plate of food. In light of the present grave situation, all of us are obligated to discuss these matters and agree on how to solve them.

Today, nobody can deny three incontrovertible facts,[4] which we list in order as a reminder to everyone:

First, for more than seven years the United States has been occupying the land of the Two Holy Places, the Arabian Peninsula,[5] plundering its riches, dictating to its rulers, humiliating its people, terrorizing its neighbors, and turning Peninsula bases into spearheads through which to attack neighboring Muslims. Those in the past who questioned the existence of the occupation now agree with all of the people of the Peninsula that it is fact. America's use of the Peninsula as a staging area for its continuing aggression against Iraq is the strongest proof of it. Even though the Peninsula's rulers are opposed to their lands being used for such purpose, they are powerless to prevent it.[6]

Second, in spite of the great devastation suffered by the Iraqis at the hands of the Crusader-Zionist alliance [during the 1991 Persian Gulf War], and in spite of the large number killed, which exceeds one million, the Americans continue to repeat these horrific massacres, not content with the protracted economic sanctions imposed on Iraq after the ferocious war of fragmentation and devastation.[7] Now they come to annihilate those who are left and to humiliate their Muslim neighbors.

Third, in addition to the economic and religious aims behind these wars, America's aim is also to serve the Jews' petty state [Israel] by diverting attention from its occupation of *Al-Quds* [Jerusalem] and its murder of Muslims there. The strongest proof of this lay in America's eagerness to destroy Iraq, the strongest Arab state neighboring Israel, and its goal to fragment all of the nations of the region, such as Iraq, Saudi Arabia, Egypt, and Sudan into paper fragments, and through their disunity and weakness, to guarantee Israel's survival and the continuation of the Crusaders' brutal occupation of the Peninsula.

All of these crimes and sins committed by America clearly demonstrate a declaration of war on God, his Messenger [the Prophet

Muhammad] (PBUH), and Muslims. *Ulema* (Islamic scholars) throughout Islamic history have unanimously agreed that *Jihad* (holy war)[8] is an individual duty if an enemy destroys Muslim countries. This was revealed by Imam bin-Qadamahin in Al-Mughni, Imam Al-Kisai in Al-Badai, Al-Qurtubi in his interpretation, and Sheikh Al-Isam in his books, where he said: "As for fighting to repulse (an enemy), it is aimed at defending sanctity and religion, and it is a duty as agreed (by the *Ulema*). Nothing is more sacred than Belief except repulsing an enemy who is attacking religion and life."[9]

On that basis, and in compliance with God's order, we issue the following Fatwa to all Muslims:

By the ruling, it is an individual duty for every Muslim who can do it to kill Americans and their allies – civilian and military – in any country where it is possible to do so, in order to liberate the Al-Aqsa mosque [the third holiest site in Islam, located in *Al-Quds* (Jerusalem)][10] and the Holy Mosque [the *Al Haram* mosque in Mecca, home of the *Kaba*][11] from their grip, and in order to remove their armies from the lands of Islam, defeated and unable to threaten any Muslim. This is in accordance with the words of Almighty God: "and fight the pagans all together as they fight you all together," and "fight them until there is no more tumult or oppression, and justice and faith in God prevail."[12]

These words are in addition to the words of Almighty God: "And why should ye not fight in the Cause of God and of those who, being weak, are ill-treated, oppressed women and children, whose cry is: 'Our Lord, rescue us from this town, whose people are oppressors; and raise for us from thee one who will help!'"[13]

With God's Help, we call upon every Muslim who believes in God and wishes to be rewarded to comply with God's Order to kill the Americans and plunder their money wherever and whenever they find it. We also call on the Muslim *Ulema* [Islamic scholars], leaders, youth, and soldiers to launch raids on Satan's American troops and Satan's supporters allying with them in order to displace their leaders so that they may learn a lesson.

Almighty God said: "O ye who believe, give your response to God and His Apostle, when He calleth you to that which will give you life. And know that God cometh between a man and his heart, and that it is He to whom ye shall all be gathered."[14]

Almighty God also says: "O ye who believe, what is the matter with you, that when ye are asked to go forth in the Cause of God, ye cling so heavily to the Earth! Do ye prefer the life of this world to the hereafter? But little is the comfort of this life, as compared with the hereafter. Unless ye go forth, He will punish you with a grievous penalty, and put others in your place; but Him ye would not harm in the least. For God hath power over all things."[15]

Almighty God also says: "So lose not heart, nor fall into despair. For ye must gain mastery if ye are true in faith." [16]

Chapter 5

Praise be to God. We ask for His Help and Forgiveness.

He whom God guides is rightly guided, but he whom God leaves to stray, for him wilt thou find no protector to lead him to the right way.[2]

There is no god but God and Muhammad was his Prophet, (peace be upon him) [hereinafter "PBUH," words of grace that attend any oral or written reference to any of the Prophets recognized by Islam].

There is America, struck by God in its most vulnerable spots. Thanks be to God, He destroyed its greatest buildings. America was full of fear from north to south and east to west. Thanks be to God for that.

What America now tastes is insignificant compared to what we have tasted for scores of years. Our *Ummah* [Islamic nation] has been tasting humiliation and contempt for more than 80 years. [Mr. Bin Laden refers to the colonization of the Middle East after the conclusion of World War I in 1918.][3] Its sons are killed, its blood is shed, its sanctuaries are attacked, and it is not ruled according to what God has declared. Nobody hears or heeds.

When God blessed the vanguards of Islam [on 9/11], He allowed them to destroy America. I pray that God bless them and grant

64

them Paradise. Only He can do so. When these young men [on 9/11] defended the oppressed sons, brothers, and sisters in Palestine and in many other Islamic countries, the world cried out. The infidels shouted first, followed by the hypocrites.

As I speak, millions of innocent children are being killed. They are dying in Iraq even though they have committed no sins. [Mr. Bin Laden refers to Iraqi children dying of malnutrition and lack of medicines because of the economic sanctions imposed on Iraq after the conclusion of the Persian Gulf War in 1991.][4] We do not hear any condemnations or *Fatwas* [religious decrees] from the [Middle East] rulers' *Ulema* [Islamic scholars]. Israeli tanks invade Palestine – in Jenin, Ramallah, Rafah, Beit Jala, and other places in Islamic lands, and we hear no voices raised or action taken.[5]

After 80 years, the sword now fell on America, and hypocrisy raised its ugly head, lamenting for the killers [meaning the casualties of 9/11] who have abused the blood, honor, and holy places of the Muslims. Such lamenters are morally debased. They support falsehood and support the butcher over the victim, the oppressor over the innocent child. May God show them the punishment they deserve.

I submit that the situation is clear. In the aftermath of the event [9/11], senior officials have spoken in America, beginning with the head of the infidels and his supporters, [President George W.] Bush. They arrogantly came in force with their men and horses and even made countries that belong to Islam part of their treachery. They show their tail to God and fight Islam to suppress the *Ummah* [Islamic nation]. In the name of [the war against] terrorism, they fight those who declared their faith in God and who refused to abandon Islam.

By the hundreds of thousands, people young and old were killed in Japan, the end of the Earth. [Mr. Bin Laden refers to the atomic bombing of Hiroshima and Nagasaki, Japan, by the United States in 1945.][6] It was not then considered a war crime, but rather an action that was justified. But millions of children dying in Iraq today has justification. But when dozens are killed in Nairobi and Dar es Salaam [Mr. Bin Laden refers to the 1998 bombings of the United States Embassies in those cities.],[7] Iraq and Afghanistan were bombed. The hypocrites stood behind the head of the world's infidels, behind the Hubal [pre-Islamic god of the Arabian Peninsula][8] of the age – America and its supporters.

These events divided the world into two sides – the side of Faith free of hypocrisy, and the side of the infidels. May God protect us from the infidels. Each Muslim must rise to make Islam victorious. The winds of change have come to eradicate oppression from the Peninsula of the Prophet Muhammad (PBUH) [Saudi Arabia]. I swear by God, who has raised the sky without pillars that neither America nor its people will know security before we see its reality in Palestine and before the infidel armies leave the land of Muhammad (PBUH).

God is great. Praise be to Islam. May God's blessings and mercy be upon you.

This Page Left Intentionally Blank For Notes

Chapter 6

Second Statement Regarding Afghanistan[1]
Novemeber 3, 2001

We praise God, seek His Help, and ask His Forgiveness.

In God we seek protection from the evils of our souls and our bad deeds.

One who is guided by God will never be misguided, and anyone who is misguided by God can never be guided by anyone else.

I bear witness that there is no god but God, Who has no partner.[2]

Among the significant developments in the wake of the great attacks against America in its most important venues of New York City and Washington, D.C., a huge upheaval has arisen in the media's opinions about these events. People divided into two parts. One part supported the attacks against the tyrannical America, and the second denounced the attacks.

After America launched its unjust campaign against Islamic Afghanistan [on October 7, 2001, the United States invaded Afghanistan][3], people again split into two parts. The first supported the invasion; the second denounced it.

These tremendous events are of great interest to Muslims because they involve them. These events are also closely linked to Islam and to acts that corrupt a person's Islam. Muslims must comprehend the nature and the truth of the conflict so they can easily decide where they stand.

In truth, worldwide opinion polls have revealed that in the United States and elsewhere, more than eighty percent of the Westerners and Christians were saddened by the [9/11] attacks. The polls also revealed that the vast majority of Muslims were happy about the attacks because they believed them to be reactions to the criminality practiced by Israel and the United States on Palestine and other Muslim countries.[4]

After the attacks began in Afghanistan, positions changed. Those who were happy about striking America were saddened when Afghanistan was attacked, and those who were saddened when America was attacked were happy when it struck Afghanistan. Millions of people comprise these groups.

With few countries excepting, the entire West supports the inhumane campaign in Afghanistan, even though there is no evidence that the people of Afghanistan were involved in what befell America. The people of Afghanistan had nothing to do with it. America's unjust campaign, however, continues to annihilate villages and innocent women and children.

The positions of the two groups are very clear. Mass demonstrations have spread across the Islamic world from east to west, including Indonesia, the Philippines, Bangladesh, India, Pakistan, the Arab world, Nigeria and Mauritania. This clearly proves the fundamentally religious nature of the war. The people of the East are Muslims. They sympathize with the Muslims against the people of the West, who are the new Crusaders.[5]

Those who try to deny this fact, which the whole world has admitted, are deceiving the *Ummah* [Islamic nation]. They are trying to divert the *Ummah* from the truth about this conflict. This is proved in the *Holy Quran* and in the teachings of our Messenger [the Prophet Muhammad], may God's peace and blessings be upon him. [Hereinafter, these words of grace will be abbreviated "PBUH." These words always attend any oral or written reference to the Prophets recognized by Islam.] Under no circumstances should we ever forget the hostility between Muslims and Christians because the hostility is based on creed.

We must be loyal to those who believe that there is no god but God [the first pillar of Islamic monotheism]. We should also renounce atheists and infidels. I need only seek God's help against them. God has said:

"Never will the Jews or the Christians be satisfied with thee unless thou follow their form of religion."[6] The question is one of faith, not one of war against terrorism, as [President George W.] Bush and [British Prime Minister Tony] Blair describe it.[7]

In the past, many thieves belonging to the West were captured, but nobody cared.[8] The masses now awakened in the East and West are not awake because of Osama; rather, they have awakened for the sake of their religion. They know that they are right and that they are resisting the most ferocious and violent Crusade against Islam since the Message was revealed to Muhammad (PBUH) [in the Seventh Century].[9] Once this becomes clear, every Muslim must know where he stands in relation to this war.

After American political leaders spoke, and after the media filled Americans with crusading hatred to mobilize the West against Islam, [President] Bush left no room for doubt because before the whole world he clearly described this as a crusader war. [At a news conference convened on September 16, 2001, President Bush described the war on terrorism as a "Crusade."][10]

Those who allege that this is a war against terrorism have little proof. How can they speak of terrorism when the *Ummah* [Islamic nation] has been slaughtered for scores of years without their raising their voices or taking any action? But when the victim starts to exact revenge for the deaths of the innocent children in Palestine, Iraq, southern Sudan, Somalia, Kashmir and the Philippines, the rulers' *Ulema* [Islamic scholars] and the hypocrites defend the obvious blasphemy. It is enough for me to seek God's help against them.[11]

The common people understand the issue. But there remain those who conspire with nonbelievers to sedate the *Ummanh* [Islamic nation] in order to prevent it from carrying out *Jihad* [holy war] so that God's Word will be supreme.

In truth, [President George W.] Bush carries the cross, raises its banner high, and stands at the front of the line. Anyone who supports his campaign has committed one of the "ten voiders" that disqualify one from Islam. Islamic scholars are unanimous that allegiance to and support for infidels against the true believers [Muslims] is a major violation of Islam.[12]

There is no power but in God. Let us ask whether the (recent) War in Afghanistan is a unique event or is linked to a long series of Crusader wars against the Islamic world.

After World War I, which ended more than 83 years ago, the *Ummah* [Islamic nation] fell to the Crusader banners – [flown by] the British, French, and Italian governments. They divided the world, and Palestine was occupied by the British.[13]

Since then, and for more than 83 years, our brothers, sons, and sisters in Palestine have suffered grievously. Hundreds of thousands of them have been killed, and hundreds of thousands of them have been imprisoned or maimed.[14]

In looking at the more recent developments, take Chechnya as an example. The Chechens are Muslims who have been attacked by the Russian bear, which adheres to the Christian Orthodox faith. The Russians have annihilated the Chechens and have forced them to flee to the mountains, where they are afflicted by snow, poverty, and disease.

Nonetheless, nobody tried to help them. There is no strength but in God.[15]

Then came the genocidal war in Bosnia, in the heart of Europe, within sight and hearing of the entire world. For several years, our brothers have been killed, our women raped, and our children massacred, even in the safe havens, with the knowledge and cooperation of the United Nations.[16]

Those who would refer our tragedies to the United Nations for resolution are hypocrites who deceive God, His Prophet [Muhammad (PBUH)], and the believers. Were not the tragedies caused by the United Nations? Who passed the Partition Resolution in 1947 and surrendered Muslim land to the Jews? [Mr. Bin Laden refers to the U.N. Resolution creating Israel in 1948.] It was the United Nations.[17] Those claiming to be Arab leaders who still appeal to the United Nations have disavowed what was revealed to the Prophet (PBUH). In seeking international legitimacy, they have disavowed the legitimacy of the Holy Book and the tradition of Prophet Muhammad (PBUH). The United Nations has caused us much suffering. Under no circumstances should any Muslim or sane person support it. It is no more than a tool of crime. Each day we are massacred while the United Nations does nothing.[18]

For over fifty years our brothers and sisters in Kashmir have been subjected to the worst forms of abuse. They have been massacred, killed, raped, their blood shed, and their houses trespassed upon. Yet, the United Nations continues to do nothing.[19]

Without any evidence, the United Nations today enacts resolutions supporting unjust and tyrannical America, which oppresses the helpless people of Afghanistan who have just emerged from a merciless war with the Soviet Union. Again, we must look at Chechnya, where a second war is still underway. [The Russians first invaded resource-rich Chechnya in 1994, withdrew in 1996, and re-invaded in 1999, where they remain.] Once again, the Chechen people are being engaged by the Russian bear. Humanitarian agencies, even in America, demanded that President [William Jefferson] Clinton stop supporting Russia. He said stopping support for Russia would be contrary to American interests. Last year, [Russian President Vladimir] Putin demanded that the cross and the Jews stand by him. He told them that they must support the Russians because they were warring against Muslim fundamentalism.[20] The enemies of Islam are speaking very clearly while the leaders of the region [the Middle East] hide and are ashamed to support their Muslim brothers.

Let us examine the positions of the West and the United Nations toward [Muslim] Indonesia when they acted to divide the Islamic world's largest country [in terms of population]. The criminal, Kofi Annan [General Secretary of the United Nations], publicly put pressure on the Indonesian government, giving it twenty-four hours to divide [the heavily Christian province of] East Timor from the rest of Indonesia. Otherwise, he would send military forces to divide it by force. Crusader Australian forces were already on Indonesian shores. In fact, they landed to separate East Timor, which is part of the *Ummah* [Islamic nation].[21]

Thus, we should view these events as linked to a long series of conspiracies, a war of annihilation in the true sense. In Somalia, 13,000 of our brothers were killed on the excuse of restoring hope. [The 1993 aid mission to Somalia was known as "Operation Restore Hope."] In the South of Sudan, hundreds of thousands have been killed. [Mr. Bin Laden refers to the Sudanese Civil War, which was ended by a peace treaty on February 2, 2005.] [22] But when we turn to Palestine and Iraq, there are no limits to what we can say. Over one million children have been killed in Iraq.[23] The killing continues. As for what is occurring in Palestine these days, I can only say we have nowhere to turn to complain but to God.[24]

What is occurring cannot be tolerated by any nation. Not just the nations of the human race, but also those of the other creatures, the animals. Not even they would tolerate what is occurring. A close friend told me he saw a butcher slaughtering a camel in front of another camel. The other camel got agitated on seeing the blood spurt from the other camel and struck out with rage, biting the man's hand and breaking it.

How can the powerless mothers in Palestine endure the killing of their children in front of their eyes by the unjust Jewish executioners relying on American support and American aircraft and tanks? Those who differentiate between America and Israel are the real enemies of the *Ummah* [Islamic nation]. They are traitors who betrayed God and His prophet (PBUH), and who betrayed the *Ummah* and the trust placed in them. They sedate the *Ummah*.

These battles cannot be viewed in any respect as isolated. Rather, they are part of a chain of the long, fierce, and ugly Crusader war. Every Muslim must stand under the banner of "There is no god but God, and Muhammad (PBUH) was His Prophet." [This is the First Pillar of Islam: monotheism.]

I remind you of what our Prophet (PBUH) told Ibn Abbas. He told him: "Boy, I am going to teach you a few words. Obey God. He will protect you. Obey Him. You will find Him on your side. If you ask for something, ask God. If you seek help, seek the Help of God. You should know that if all the people cooperate to help you, they can only help you as far as God has preordained for you. And if they assemble to harm you, they can only harm you insofar as God has preordained for you. God wrote man's fate, and it will never change."[25]

I tell the Muslims who performed their best during these past weeks: you must continue on the same march. Your support for us will strengthen us and your brothers in Afghanistan. Try harder to combat this unprecedented war crime.

Fear God, Oh Muslims, and rise in support of your religion. Islam calls you. Oh Muslims! Oh Muslims! Oh Muslims!

God bears witness that I have conveyed the message. God bear witness that I have conveyed the message. God bear witness that I have conveyed the message.

God's peace and blessings be upon you.

Chapter 7

The "Smoking Gun" Video Tape
December 13, 2001

* The following three paragraphs are the Editor's notes to the transcript and videotaped statements. The following is a transcript prepared by the United States' State Department from a videotape transcript provided by the Department of Defense ["DOD"]. The videotape is believed to have been made in the vicinity of the city of Qandahar in Southern Afghanistan in mid-November, 2001. The videotape is commonly referred to as "the smoking gun" because of the candid discussion of 9/11 attacks, including several incriminating statements by Mr. Bin Laden himself. He is surrounded by several unidentified individuals, including a visiting Saudi Arabian paraplegic Sheikh who was paying a courtesy visit to Mr. Bin Laden. The sheikh was later identified as Ali Bin Said al-Ghandi a veteran of the Afghanistan resistance to the Soviet invasion and a resident of Mecca, Saudi Arabia. Also on the videotape are Al Qaeda spokesperson Suleiman Abu Ghaith and Mr. Bin Laden's ideological mentor, Dr. Ayman al-Zawahiri, the world's second most wanted man after Mr. Bin Laden himself.[1] The tape and an English-language transcript were released by the DoD on December 13, 2001. Because of its poor quality, the transcription is not verbatim; but Mr. Bin Laden makes several extremely incriminating

74

statements. They are embolden and italicized below.

Accompanying the December 13th release of the videotape and transcript was a DOD news release that stated that the videotape had been discovered by U.S. military forces in the vicinity of Jalalabad, Afghanistan, in late November, 2001. The one-hour tape is in three segments: a twelve-minute segment of a visit by some people to the site of a downed U.S. helicopter in the Ghazni Province; and two segments documenting the Sheikh's courtesy visit with Mr. Bin Laden and some of his aides. On the original tape, the helicopter segment bifurcates the two other segments. The transcription appearing below begins with the approximately forty-minute first visit.

According to the Pentagon news release, "The tape was released with an English translation and English subtitling, prepared independently by George Michael, translator, Diplomatic Language Services; and Kassem M. Wahba, Arabic language program coordinator, School of Advanced International Studies, Johns Hopkins University. They collaborated on their translation and compared it with translations done by the U.S. government for consistency. There were no inconsistencies in the translations." The transcript may be viewed at:

http://usembassy-australia.state.gov/hyper/2001/1213/epf405.htm.

Transcript of Videotape

Sheikh: (...inaudible...) You have given us weapons, you have given us hope and we thank God for you. We don't want to take much of your time, but this is the arrangement of the brothers. People now are supporting us more, even those ones who did not support us in the past, support us more now. I did not want to take that much of your time. We praise God, we praise God. We came from Kabul. We were very pleased to visit. May God bless you both at home and [at] the camp. We asked the driver to take us, it was a night with a full moon, thanks be to God. Believe me it is not in the country side. The elderly...everybody praises what you did, the great action you did, which was first and foremost by the grace of God. This is the guidance of God and the blessed fruit of *Jihad* [holy war].

OBL: Thanks to God. What is the stand of the Mosques there (in Saudi Arabia)?

Sheikh: Honestly, they are very positive. Sheikh al-Bahraini [phonetic spelling][2] gave a good sermon in his class after the sunset prayers. It was videotaped and I was supposed to carry it with me, but unfortunately, I had to leave immediately.

OBL: The day of the events?

Sheikh: At the exact time of the attack on America, precisely at the time. He (Bahraini) gave a very impressive sermon. Thanks be to God for His blessings. He (Bahraini) was the first one to write at war time. I visited him twice in Al-Qasim [a province in Saudi Arabia].

OBL: Thanks be to God.

Sheikh: This is what I asked from God. He (Bahraini) told the youth: "You are asking for martyrdom and wonder where you should go (for martyrdom)?" God was inciting them to go. I asked God to grant me to witness the truth in front of the unjust ruler. We ask God to protect him and give him the martyrdom, after he issued the first *Fatwa* [religious decree].[3] He was detained for interrogation, as you know. When he was called in and asked to sign, he told them, "don't waste my time, I have another *Fatwa*. If you want me, I can sign both at the same time."[4]

OBL: Thanks be to God.

Sheikh: His position is really very encouraging. When I paid him the first visit about a year and [a] half ago, he asked me, "How is Sheikh Bin-Laden?" He sends you his special regards. As far as Sheikh Sulayman 'Ulwan[5] is concerned, he gave a beautiful *Fatwa*, may God bless him. Miraculously, I heard it on the *Quran Radio Station*. It was strange because he ('Ulwan) sacrificed his position — which is equivalent to a director. It was transcribed word-by-word. The brothers listened to it in detail. I briefly heard it before the noon prayers. He ('Ulwan) said this was *Jihad* [holy war] and those people were not innocent people (World Trade Center and Pentagon victims). He swore to God. This was transmitted to Sheikh Sulayman al 'Omar, God bless him.[6]

OBL: What about Sheikh al-Rayan?[7]

Sheikh: Honestly, I did not meet with him. My movements were truly limited.

OBL: God bless you. You are welcome.

Sheikh: (Describing the trip to the meeting) They smuggled us and then I thought that we would be in different caves inside the mountains so I was surprised at the guest house and that it is very clean and comfortable. Thanks be to God, we also learned that this location is safe, by God's Blessings. The place is clean and we are very comfortable.

OBL: (…Inaudible…) when people see a strong horse and a weak horse, by nature, they will like the strong horse. This is only one goal; those who want people to worship the lord of the people, without following that doctrine, will be following the doctrine of Muhammad, peace be upon him [hereinafter, "PBUH," words of grace that attend any oral or written reference to the Prophets recognized by Islam].

(OBL quotes several short and incomplete Hadith[8] verses, as follows):

"I was ordered to fight the people until they say there is no god but God, and his Prophet is Muhammad [PBUH]."[9]

"Some people may ask: why do you want to fight us?"

"There is an association between those who say: I believe in one God and Muhammad is his Prophet [PBUH], and those who don't (… inaudible…)"

"Those who do not follow the true *Fiqh* [Islamic school of jurisprudence].[10] The *Fiqh* of Muhammad [Hanbal], the real *Fiqh*. They are just accepting what is being said at face value."

OBL: Those youth who conducted the operations did not accept any *Fiqh* in the popular terms, but they accepted the *Fiqh* that the Prophet Muhammad [PBUH] brought. Those young men (…inaudible…) said in deeds, in New York and Washington, speeches that overshadowed all other speeches made everywhere else in the world. The speeches are understood by both Arabs and non-Arabs-even by Chinese. Some of them said that in Holland, at one of the centers, the number of people who accepted Islam during the days that followed the operations were more than the people who accepted Islam in the last eleven years. I heard someone on Islamic radio who owns a school in America say: "We don't have time to keep up with the demands of those who are asking about Islamic books to learn about Islam." This event made people think (about true Islam) which benefited Islam greatly.[11]

Sheikh: Hundreds of people used to doubt you and few only would follow you until this huge event happened. Now hundreds of people are coming out to join you. I remember a vision by Sheikh Salih al-Shuaybi.[12] He said: "There will be a great hit and people will go out by hundreds to Afghanistan." I asked him (Salih): "To Afghanistan?" He replied, "Yes." According to him, the only ones who stay behind will be the mentally impotent and the liars (hypocrites). I remembered him saying that hundreds of people will go out to Afghanistan. He had this vision a year ago. This event discriminated between the different types of followers.

OBL: (…Inaudible…) *we calculated in advance the number of casualties from the enemy, who would be killed based on the position of the tower. We calculated that the floors that would be hit would be three or four floors. I was the most optimistic of them all. (…Inaudible…) due to my experience in this field, I was thinking that the fire from the gas in the plane would melt the iron structure of the building and collapse the area where the plane hit and all the floors above it only. This is all that we had hoped for.*

Sheikh: God be praised.

OBL: *We were at (…inaudible…) when the event took place. We had notification since the previous Thursday that the event would take place that day. We had finished our work that day and had the radio on. It was 5:30 p.m. our time. I was sitting with Dr. Ahmad Abu-al-Khair.[13] Immediately, we heard the news that a plane had hit the World Trade Center. We turned the radio station to the news from Washington. The news continued and no mention of the attack until the end. At the end of the newscast, they reported that a plane just hit the World Trade Center.*

Sheikh: God be praised.

OBL: After a little while, they announced that another plane had hit the

World Trade Center. The brothers who heard the news were overjoyed by it.

Sheikh: I listened to the news and I was sitting. We didn't…we were not-thinking about anything, and all of a sudden, God willing, we were talking about how come we didn't have anything, and all of a sudden the news came and everyone was overjoyed and everyone until the next day, in the morning, was talking about what was happening and we stayed until four o'clock, listening to the news every time a little bit different, everyone was very joyous and saying "God is Great," "God is Great," "We are thankful to God," "Praise God." And I was happy for the happiness of my brothers. That day the congratulations were coming on the phone non-stop. The mother was receiving phone calls continuously. Thank God. God is great, praise be to God.

(Quoting the verse from the *Holy Quran*)

Sheikh: "Fight them, God will torture them, with your hands, he will torture them. He will deceive them and he will give you victory. God will forgive the believers, he is knowledgeable about everything."[14]

Sheikh: No doubt it is a clear victory. God has bestowed on us…honor on us…and he will give us blessings and more victory during this holy month of Ramadan. And this is what everyone is hoping for. Thank God America came out of its caves. We hit her with the first hit and the next one will hit her with the hands of the believers, the good believers, the strong believers. By God it is a great work. God prepares for you a great reward for this work. I'm sorry to speak in your presence, but it is just thoughts, just thoughts. By God, there is no god but Him. I live in happiness, happiness…I have not experienced, or felt, in a long time. I remember, the words of [Burhannudin] al-Rabbani [ex-President of Afghanistan, ousted by the Taliban in 1996],[15] he said they made a coalition against us in the winter with the infidels like the Turks, and others, and some other Arabs. And they surrounded us like the days…in the days of the Prophet Muhammad [PBUH]. Exactly like what's happening right now. But he comforted his followers and said, "This is going to turn and hit them back."[16] And it is a mercy for us. And a blessing to us. And it will bring people back. Look how wise he was. And God will give him blessing. And the day will come when the symbols of Islam will rise up and it will be similar to the early days of *al-Mujahideen* [Islamic warriors] and *Al-Ansar* [helpers, believers, usually those who first followed the Prophet Muhammad (PBUH)] (similar to the early years of Islam).[17] And victory to those who follow God. Finally said, if it is the same, like the old days, such as Abu Bakr and Othman and Ali[18] and others. In these days, in our times, that it will be the greatest *Jihad* [holy war] in the history of Islam and the resistance of the wicked people.

Sheikh: By God my Sheikh. We congratulate you for the great work. Thank God.

Tape ends here

The Second segment of the Bin Laden visit, shows up at the front of the tape:

OBL: *Abdallah Azzam[19], God bless his soul, told me not to record anything (...inaudible...) so I thought that was a good omen, and God will bless us (...inaudible...). Abu-al-Hasan al-Masri[20], who appeared on Al-Jazeera TV a couple of days ago and addressed the Americans saying: "If you are true men, come down here and face us." (...inaudible...) He told me a year ago: "I saw in a dream, we were playing a soccer game against the Americans. When our team showed up on the field, they were all pilots!" He said: "So I wondered if that was a soccer game or a pilot game? Our players were pilots." He (Abu-al-Hasan) didn't know anything about the operation until he heard it on the radio. He said the game went on and we defeated them. That was a good omen for us.*

Sheikh: May God be blessed.

Unidentified Man Off Camera: Abd al Rahman al-Gharnri said he saw a vision, before the operation, a plane crashed into a tall building. He knew nothing about it.

Sheikh: May God be Blessed!

Sulayman Abu Gaith: I was sitting with the Sheikh [OBL] in a room, then I left to go to another room where there was a TV set. The TV broadcasted the big event. The scene was showing an Egyptian family sitting in their living room, they exploded with joy. Do you know when there is a soccer game and your team wins, it was the same expression of joy. There was a subtitle that read: "In revenge for the children of *Al-Aqsa*, Osama Bin Laden executes an operation against America." So I went back to the Sheikh [meaning Mr. Bin Laden] who was sitting in a room with 50 to 60 people. I tried to tell him about what I saw, but he made gesture with his hands, meaning: "I know, I know."

OBL: He did not know about the operation. Not everybody knew (…inaudible…). Muhammad Atta[21] from the Egyptian family (meaning the Al Qaeda Egyptian group), was in charge of the group.

Sheikh: A plane crashing into a tall building was out of anyone's imagination. This was a great job. He was one of the pious men in the organization. He became a martyr. God bless his soul.

Sheikh (Referring to dreams and visions): The plane that he saw crashing into the building was seen before by more than one person. One of the good religious people has left everything and come here. He told me, "I saw a vision; I was in a huge plane, long and wide. I was carrying it on my shoulders and I walked from the road to the desert for half a kilometer. I was dragging the plane." I listened to him and I prayed to God to help him. Another person told me that last year he saw, but I didn't understand and I told him I don't understand. He said, "I saw people who left for *Jihad* [holy war]…and they found themselves in New York…in Washington and New York." I said, "What is this?" He told me the plane hit the building. That was last year. We haven"t thought much about it. But, when the incidents happened he came to me and said, "Did you see…this is strange." I have another man… "my god"… he said and swore by God that his wife had seen the incident a week earlier. She saw the plane crashing into a building…that was unbelievable, my God.

OBL: *The brothers, who conducted the operation, all they knew was that they have a martyrdom operation and we asked each of them to go to America but they didn't know anything about the operation, not even one letter. But they were trained and we did not reveal the operation to them until they were there and just before they boarded the planes.*

OBL: (…inaudible…) then he said: *Those who were trained to fly didn't know the others. One group of people did not know the other group. (…inaudible…)*

(Someone in the crowd asks OBL to tell the Sheikh about the dream of Abu-Da'ud.

OBL: We were at a camp of one of the brother's guards in Qandahar. This brother belonged to the majority of the group. He came close and told me that he saw, in a dream, a tall building in America, and in the same dream he saw Mukhtar teaching them how to play karate. At that point, I was worried that maybe the secret would be revealed if everyone starts seeing it in their dream. So I closed the subject. I told him if he sees another dream, not to tell anybody, because people will be upset with him.

(Another person's voice can be heard recounting his dream about two planes hitting a big building).

OBL: They were overjoyed when the first plane hit the building, so I said to them: be patient.

OBL: The difference between the first and the second plane hitting the towers was twenty minutes. And the difference between the first plane and the plane that hit the Pentagon was one hour.

Sheikh: They (the Americans) were terrified thinking there was a coup.

[Note: Ayman al-Zawahiri says first he informed Mr. Bin Laden of what the media was saying. Then he says it was the first time for them (Americans) to feel danger coming at them.]

OBL: (reciting a poem):

I witness that against the sharp blade
They always faced difficulties and stood together…
When the darkness comes upon us
and we are bit by a sharp tooth, I say…
"Our homes are flooded with blood and the tyrant is freely wandering in our homes"…And from the battlefield vanished the brightness of swords and the horses…

And over weeping sounds now we hear the beats of drums and rhythm...
They are storming his forts...
And shouting: "We will not stop our raids until you free our lands."[22]

Bin Laden visit footage complete. Footage of the visit to the helicopter site follows the poem.

(End transcript)

(Distributed by the Office of International Information Programs, U.S. Department of State. Web site: http://usinfo.state.gov) [See also] http://usembassy-australia.state.gov/hyper/2001/1213/epf405.htm

Chapter 8

Third Statement Regarding Afghanistan[1]
December 27, 2001

All praise is for God. We ask His Help and Forgiveness and His Protection from the mischief of our souls and the results of our bad deeds. God guides and those whom He Declares misguided none can guide to the right path. I testify that there is none worthy of worship but God, who is Alone and without partners.[2]

Three months after the blessed [9/11] attacks on the worldwide evil's leader, America — and approximately two months since the ferocious Crusader attack on Islam [the United States invasion of Afghanistan on October 7, 2001] — we are pleased to explain these events.[3] They have clarified many important matters for Muslims.

It is now crystal clear that the West, and in particular, the United States, harbor a Crusader's implacable hatred against Islam. Is it is impossible to plumb the depth of this hatred. Those who have lived these months under air-attack by various types of U.S. warplanes know this fact is self-evident. How many villages of innocents have been destroyed? If we count them, millions of innocent people have been exposed to severe cold. These are the weak and oppressed men, women, and children[4] who today seek refuge in tents in Pakistan. They did nothing wrong. On mere suspicion, America ferociously attacks them.

Even if the U.S. had irrefutable evidence that the perpetrators [of 9/11] were Europeans, for example, the I.R.A. [Irish Republican Army], [5] they would have pursued avenues other than war to resolve the matter. But when suspicion falls on the Islamic world, America's ugly face is revealed; and the Crusaders' hatred of Islam comes to the forefront.

In this statement, I describe the conflict between us and America. It has important consequences for Muslims and affects the whole world. America has no proof of its accusations against this group that strives in the Way of God; rather, it relies on oppression, injustice, and aggression.[6]

By God's Grace, the history of the Arab *Mujahideen* [Islamic warriors] is written on a snow-white slate. Twenty years ago, they set out against the Soviet Union's terrorism against the innocent children and civilians of Afghanistan. These Arab *Mujahid* [individual *Mujahideen*] left their work, their schools, their families and their friends in search of God's Pleasure to support the Faith [Islam] by helping the weak and oppressed Muslims.

It is illogical that such men would start killing innocents, of which they are accused. America's own history records that it helped these men fight Russia, but when God directed them to the opportunity to help the weak and oppressed Palestinians and their innocent children, America railed against all of them who had fought in Afghanistan.

The crimes in today's Palestine[7] have been clear to humanity since the Prophet Adam [peace be upon him, hereinafter "PBUH," words of grace which must attend any oral or written reference to any of the Prophets recognized by Islam]. Although it is human nature to disagree on many matters, God has insulated some matters from disagreement because they are so fundamental. One such matter is that all humans agree that they may not kill innocent children.

What has happened in Palestine and what is happening today is the deliberate murder of innocent Palestinian children. It is utterly revolting, unjust, oppressive, and threatens all humanity.

Through the ages, one rarely finds instances of the deliberate killing of children. One such instance occurred during the reign of the Pharaoh. In that situation, God was benevolent to the Israelis and saved them from the Pharaoh. As the *Holy Quran* says, "And remember the time when We delivered you from Pharaoh's people who afflicted you with grievous torment, slaying your sons and sparing your women."[8]

But these same Israelites now use the same unjust and evil tactics of the Pharaoh against our sons in Palestine. The whole world watched Israeli troops kill Muhammad al-Durra [a twelve-year-old Palestinian boy whose death by Israeli bullets was captured on videotape and shown worldwide on September 30, 2000][9] and many others like him.

The whole world, in all directions, regardless of religion, unanimously condemned this act. But America unjustly continues to aid and abet these attackers on our sons in Palestine. God provides guidance in this matter: it is hideous when a person who rebels reaches the point where his attacks kill without justification; but it is even more repulsive when he slays innocent children. God says that "whosoever killed a person — unless it be for killing a person for creating disorder in the land — it shall be as if he killed all mankind; and whosoever saved a life, it shall be as if he had saved the life of all mankind."[10]

Thusly Israel and America kill the children of the world. Who will prevent Israel from killing our sons tomorrow in Tabook or in Jauf,[11] or in the surrounding areas of Palestine? What will the rulers [of the Middle East] do if Israel begins expanding its false and unjust settlements — as depicted by our rulers — beyond their current boundaries [in Palestine] and, for example, extends them to Medina [in Saudi Arabia]?[12] They will merely yield to the American Zionist lobby.

As always, rational people will awake and realize that what befell Muhammad al-Durra will happen to their own sons and daughters tomorrow. There is no power and force but from God. The grave fact is that America practices vicious terrorism in its most repulsive form in Palestine and Iraq. The ill-fated [President George Herbert Walker] Bush the Father [of President George W. Bush] caused the deaths of over a million Iraqi children, not including the others killed.[13] [Mr. Bin Laden refers to the deaths of thousands of Iraqi children from malnutrition and lack of medicines because of the sanctions imposed on Iraq after the conclusion of the Persian Gulf War in 1991.]

September 11th was but a reaction to the continuing injustice and oppression practiced against our sons in Palestine, Iraq, Somalia, southern Sudan, Kashmir and Assam. It is incumbent on the *Ummah* [Islamic nation] to wake the people from their slumber and quickly solve this disastrous problem.

Those who condemned the [9/11] attacks viewed them in isolation and failed to connect them to past events. They looked at the result, not the causes. Those who did look at the causes did not approach them from legal and rational perspectives; rather, they saw America and the media criticizing the acts and they stood behind the criticism.

They are like the story of the wolf that saw a newborn lamb: "Are you the one who dirtied the water last year?" the wolf asks. The lamb replies,"It was not I. It was you," the wolf said. The lamb replied, "I was only born this year." The wolf said, "It must have been your mother," and then proceeded to eat the lamb. What was the mother to do when she saw her son between the wolf's teeth? In a fit of rage, she butted the wolf. The wolf was unaffected and cried out, "Look at this terrorist!" The parrots joined in, parroting what the wolf had said and adding, "We saw the ewe butt the wolf!" But where were you when the wolf ate her son?

The blessed and successful strikes [on 9/11] were but reactions to what has happened in our lands — in Palestine and in Iraq, and in other places. With the arrival of [President George W.] Bush the Son, America continued these policies. His administration began with a series of violent attacks on Iraq.[14] He also subscribes to the same policies of injustice and oppression, and to him, Muslim blood is cheap.

By the grace of God, 9/11 was the response. These laudable strikes attest that although America is an arrogant and haughty power because of its economic strength — the Hubal[15] of the Age — it is very fragile and its fragility will hurry its fall.

Nineteen Arab countries did not carry out the attacks— no armies were mobilized. Nor were they the Arab government departments that submit to the West and accept the injustices we suffer in Palestine and in other areas. There were nineteen ordinary post-secondary students (may God accept their sacrifice). They rattled the throne of American power and hit the American economy in the center of its heart and penetrated the heart of the greatest military force on earth. All this they did with God's Grace.

The blow was struck against the global, interest-based economy supported by American military force. The blow will accelerate America's fall. By America's own admission, this blow caused losses in the markets of New York City and elsewhere of upwards of a trillion dollars.[16] The goal was achieved by simplicity — using enemy planes and studying in the enemy's schools. The *Mujahideen* [Islamic warriors] did not need any training camps. God Himself helped them and taught a hard lesson to the arrogant nations who know nothing of freedom unless it applies to the white race. Other nations in the Middle East realize that they are submissive slaves, but they do not lift a finger to help us when we are attacked; rather, through their leaders, they applaud, as happened in Iraq.[17]

Through its show of force in Afghanistan, where it vented its extreme anger on the weak and oppressed people — America taught us great lessons in the methods of resisting them, by God's grace. For example, if the front line facing the enemy is 100 kilometers long, it also should be deep. 100, 200, or even 300 meters is unsatisfactory. The depth must be many kilometers, and trenches must be dug along the length and breadth of the area. In this fashion, the bulk of the American bombardment is dissipated before it reaches the front line. Deploy light and mobile forces so they may move from line to line, from one bunker to another.

We learned this from the dense American bombardment of the front lines north of Kabul. By employing such methods, with God's Permission, America will not be able to breach the front lines of the *Mujahideen* [Islamic warriors] even after years have passed.

To the contrary, it is well known that war cannot escape its two basic constituents: the lives of the soldiers and money with which to purchase weapons. This is emphasized in the *Holy Quran*. Many verses teach this. For example: "Surely God has bought of the believers their persons and their property for this, that they shall have the garden."[18]

One possibility of prevailing in spite of the gap between us and the American military establishment, which is very wide, is the use of wide defensive lines to absorb the air attacks. The other possibility is to attack the economic base at the foundation of the military establishment. When their financial reserves are spent, they will bicker among themselves and refrain from enslaving the weaker nations.

I submit that it is critical to concentrate on striking the American economy by every possible means.[19] With our own eyes, we have witnessed the true crimes of those who preach humanity and freedom. A sliver of munitions is more than enough to kill a man — a sliver weighing seven grams is more than enough! Out of hatred for the Taliban and Muslims at large, America rained down on our front lines seven-ton bombs. Do the calculations: 7,000 kilos which is seven million grams, and seven grams are more than enough to kill a man.

When the youths in Nairobi [Mr. Bin Laden refers to the bombing of the United States Embassy in Kenya in 1998] [20] (we beseech God to accept their martyrdom) detonated a bomb weighing less that two tons, America declared it a terrorist strike. But when America uses these weapons of mass destruction — bombs weighing more than 7 million grams each — there is no harm!

And Secretary of Defense Donald M. Rumsfeld said after his forces had attacked whole villages without cause, "It is to save people from terrorism and to make them fear hosting terrorists." He continued: "It is our right to do so." By what right do they exterminate foreign nations that do not submit to America? These are the clear crimes of which we accuse them. Whatever they say about mistakes is clearly a lie.

A few days ago they attacked suspected Al Qaeda locations in Khost [a province in Afghanistan] and directed a precision bomb into a mosque. Then they said it was a mistake. An investigation revealed that Islamic scholars in Khost were conducting the nightly Ramadan prayer and were hosting a post-prayer meeting with the *Mujahid* [an individual *Mujahideen* warrior] hero, Sheikh Jalaluddin Haqqani. [21] He was one of the foremost leaders of the *Jihad* [holy war] against the Soviet Union — and one of those who condemned the American occupation of Afghanistan. The hit on the mosque killed 150 praying Muslims. There is no power or force except God. The Sheikh was all right. We beseech God to Bless him.

This demonstrates the hatred of the Crusaders. Hiding their true intent, they keep repeating that they are after "terrorists." Our terrorism against America is praiseworthy — to repel the injustice of the oppressor so that America will withdraw its support for Israel, who kills our sons. The matter is clear. Why do you not understand?

Repeatedly, American and Western leaders declare Hamas, *Al-Jihad*, and other militias in other areas, to be terrorist organizations. Nothing can be legal if self-defense is terrorism. Our defending ourselves is no different than their doing so. Our battle is no different from the battle fought by our brothers in Palestine like Hamas. We fight for the sake of the Muslim creed, "There is no god but God." God's Word is supreme, and the words of the disbelievers are debased. We also fight to relieve the injustice practiced upon the weak and oppressed people in Palestine and elsewhere. [22]

No rational Muslim can sit on the fence under the guise of

"many religious interpretations of the situation." The matter is crystal clear. This is the most dangerous, severe, and ferocious of the Crusades waged against Islam thus far. God willing, America's end is near and is not dependent on the continued existence of this poor slave of God. By God's Grace, whether Osama lives or dies, the awakening has begun. This is one of the fruits of our operations. We beseech God to accept the youths [of 9/11] as martyrs and bring them to the company of the Prophets (PBUH), the truthful, the other martyrs, and the good; the best of company are they![23]

These youths carried out a great mission, a gracious mission, and may God reward them with the best of rewards. We beseech God that He grants blessings for their fathers and mothers. God willing, the youths have raised high the heads of the Muslims and have taught America a lesson that it will never forget.

In a previous interview with the ABC TV Channel, I warned that America has picked a fight with the sons of the Two Holy Places and will forget the travails of Vietnam in comparison. This has happened, thanks to God's Grace. With God's Permission, what is yet to happen will be even greater.

From the lands of the Two Holy Places came fifteen young men [Mr. Bin Laden refers to the nineteen 9/11 hijackers, fifteen of whom came from Saudi Arabia][24] — we beseech God to accept them as martyrs. From the land of Islam, the greatest treasure of the Muslims, where our Prophet Muhammad (PBUH) planted and perfected the Faith as he migrated to Medina. These youth came as a cobra from its burrow. Two of them also came from the eastern Arabian Peninsula — from the [United Arab Emirates] — and one other from the *Sham* [Syria], Ziyad al-Jarrah. We beseech God to accept him among the martyrs. The last one came from the land of Canaan [Egypt], Muhammad Atta. We beseech God to accept all of them as martyrs.[25]

In carrying out their complicated operation, they demonstrated that they were motivated by the Faith in their hearts and were inspired by the Muslim creed, "There is no god but God." They opened the floodgates of goodness and truth. Those who criticize martyrdom operations parrot the voices of the media and repeat the tyrannical words and desires of America and its clients.

Every day, from east to west, the *Ummah* [Islamic nation] of 1.2 billion Muslims experiences slaughter in Palestine, Iraq, Somalia, southern Sudan, Kashmir, the Philippines, Bosnia, Chechnya, and Assam. We do not hear a whisper of outcry. But when the victim rises up and protects himself for the sake of his Faith, they scream. They do not feel the slaughter of 1.2 billion Muslims when a man stands to defend Islam. They merely repeat the favorite phrases of the tyrants — that the defenders are unintelligent and uncivilized.

The *Hadith* [story, i.e., tradition of the Prophet Muhammad (PBUH)] of the boy, the king, the magician and the monk is a good example of Faith's [Islam] priority over one's life. Though the story also supports the success [of 9/11], its fundamental lesson must not be forgotten.

The people of *Uhud* (the Pit) are mentioned and immortalized by God's Praise for their perseverance in their Faith in the *Holy Quran* at *Sura* [Chapter] 85, [verses] 4 – 11 [the *Hadith* is reprinted in a footnote to these verses]. They had to choose between their Faith and death by fire pit, and they refused to disbelieve God and were cast into the fire. Near the end of the story, after the unjust king had ordered that they be thrown into the fire pit, a frail mother came toward the pit carrying her baby and then hesitated, fearful for her life and the life of her baby. Then the baby cried out, "be steadfast, Mother — for you are right,"[26] whereupon she threw herself and her baby into the fire.

No true Muslim would suggest that the [9/11] *Mujahideen* [Islamic warriors] profited or wasted their lives. Only an idiot would say so. They earned God's Grace and the Paradise He promised them. Victory is not measured merely by material gains, but rather by adherence to principles.

In the *Hadith* mentioned earlier,[27] an uneducated boy shuttled between a sorcerer and a monk. One time an animal blocked the road, and the boy said he would know how to identify the better Muslim, the monk or the magician. Because of his own lack of knowledge, he could not decide for himself, so he asked God to show him. If the monk were nearer to God, then God would kill the animal. The boy then flung a stone at the animal and killed it. Then the monk came to him and said, "My son, today you are better than I."[28] In spite of the monk's knowledge and the boy's ignorance, God filled the boy's heart with the light of Faith. The boy then started to sacrifice for God's Sake.

The youth of Islam expect such words from their scholars. They demand that they tell them of those who carried their heads high for the Sake of God, words like those of the monk. They expect today's scholars to tell them, "You are now better than us." This is the truth.

According to the Prophet's (PBUH) example, Muslims differ based on the extent of their Faith in God. Both knowledge of Islam and the use of such knowledge are important. As the Prophet (PBUH) said, he who struggles against *Kufr* [non-believers] with his hand is a believer, he who struggles against them with his tongue is a believer, and he who struggles against them with his heart is a believer.[29] Whoever fails to do any of these has not a grain of faith. [The youth of 9/11] struggled against the biggest infidel [the United States] with their hands and hearts. We pray that God will accept them as martyrs.

As recorded in *Al-Jami Sahi* by Sahih Bukhari [the most respected *Hadith* scholar], the best of all the martyrs was Hamzah Bin Abd al Muttalib[30], a simple man whose heart was filled with Faith by God. He stood up to rebuke an unjust *Imam* [a ruler rather than a cleric] and was then killed by him. Hamzah achieved a great victory. He was not a contemporary either of the Followers or of the esteemed Companions,[31] but God elevated him to the status of the best of all martyrs. We did as our Prophet (PBUH) urged. How could any sane Muslim say we benefited from this? This is manifest misguidance. We ask God to spare us such misguidance.

These young men [of 9/11] faced the head of the world's infidels, America and its allies, and told them, "You are wrong and misguided." They sacrificed themselves for the sake of "There is no god but God."

Much more can be said about these profound events, but I shall concentrate on the need to continue *Jihad* [holy war], militarily and economically, against the United States. Praise be to God, the United States has declined. Its economy is hemorrhaging, but further attacks are necessary. The young warriors must look for the key pillars of the U.S. economy and attack them, God willing.

Before concluding, I want to mention the heroes, the great young men who removed the *Ummah's* [Islamic nation's] disgrace. I shall recite some poetry praising them and all who follow the path of the Prophet Muhammad (PBUH). Before I do so, I emphasize the point that today's around-the-clock battles against the Arab *Mujahideen* [holy warriors] and the Taliban in Afghanistan have revealed the weaknesses of U.S. power and the fragility of the U.S. soldier.

In spite of its overwhelming military technology, the U.S. was dependent on the renegades and hypocrites. [Mr. Bin Laden refers to the Northern Alliance indigenous forces in Afghanistan relied upon by the U.S. in place of American soldiers.] There was no difference between Babrak Karman, who invited the Russians to occupy Afghanistan and deposed [Afghani] President Rabbini.[32] President Rabbini had no *Deen* [religion]. The former brought the Russians to occupy the land of Islam, and the latter brought the Americans to occupy the land of Islam. As I have said, this shows the weakness of the American soldier, Praise be to God. Therefore, the young people should take the chance and continue *Jihad* [holy war] against the Americans.

I conclude by reciting a poem about [the 9/11] heroes, who came from the land of the Hijaz [Saudi Arabia][33], from the land of the Faith — from Ghamid, Zahran, Bani-Shihr, Harb, and Najd.[34] We pray to God to accept them all as martyrs. There are also those who came from Holy Mecca: Salim and Nawwaf al-Hazmi and Khalid al-Mihdar.[35] There are those who left the Holy City of Medina. They renounced life and its pleasures for the sake of, "There is no god but God."

I witness that against the sharp blade
They always faced difficulties and stood together...
When the darkness comes upon us and we are bitten by a
Sharp tooth, I say...
Our homes are flooded with blood and the tyrant
Is freely wandering in our homes...
And from the battlefield vanished
The brightness of swords and the horses...
And over weeping sounds now
We hear the beats of drums and rhythm ...
And shouting: 'We will not stop our raids
Until you free our lands'[36]

May God's blessings be upon you.

Chapter 9

In the Name of God, the Most Gracious, the Most Merciful.
"Permission to fight [against disbelievers] is given to those [believers] who are fought against, because they have been wronged; and surely, God is Able to give them [believers] victory."[2]

"Those who believe, fight in the Cause of God, and those who disbelieve, fight in the cause of *Taghut* [anything worshipped other than God e.g. Satan]. So fight against the friends of Satan; ever feeble is indeed the plot of Satan."[3]

Some writers in America have written articles speculating about why we fight."[4] The articles generated a number of responses. Some were true and based on Islamic law, and others were false. Seeking God's Reward, and success and support from Him, here we now reveal the truth as both a warning and an explanation.

While seeking God's Help, we reply with two questions directed to the Americans: why do we fight you, and what do we want from you?

As for the first question, the answer is very simple: we fight you because you attacked us and continue to attack us. You attacked us in Palestine, which has drowned under eighty years of military occupation. With your support, the British handed Palestine[5] over to the Jews, who have occupied it for more than fifty years — years marked by repression, tyranny, crimes, killings, expulsions, destruction, and devastation. The creation and continuation of Israel is one of the greatest crimes. You direct its criminal rulers. Of course, we need not explain the magnitude of American support for Israel. Israel's creation is a crime that must be erased. Each person whose hands have been sullied by contributing to the crime must pay a heavy price.

We continue to laugh to tears on hearing that you have not tired of professing your fabrication that the Jews have a historical right to Palestine as promised in the Torah. Anyone who disputes this claim is branded anti-Semitic. This is one of the most widely-circulated fabrications in history. The Palestinian people are pure Arabs and original Semites. The Muslims are the heirs of *Musa* [Moses] [peace be upon him, hereinafter "PBUH," words of grace which must attend any oral or written reference to the Prophets recognized by Islam] and the heirs of the real unchanged *Torah* [*the Holy Quran*]. Muslims believe in all of the Prophets, including *Ibrahim* [Abraham], *Musa* [Moses], *Issa* [Jesus], and Muhammad, peace and blessings of God upon all of them. If *Musa's* followers have been promised Palestine in the *Torah*, then the Muslims are the most worthy recipients. When the Muslims ousted the Romans and conquered Palestine, [6] *Al-Quds* (Jerusalem) returned to Islam, the religion of all the Prophets, peace be upon them. Therefore, the call to a historical right to Palestine cannot be raised against the *Ummah* (Islamic nation) that believes in all of the Prophets, peace and blessings be upon them. We do not distinguish between them.

The blood spilling from Palestine must be reciprocated. Know that the Palestinians do not cry alone, their women are not widowed alone, and their sons are not orphaned alone.

You [the United States] also attacked us in Somalia. You supported Russian atrocities against us in Chechnya, the Indian oppression against us in Kashmir, and the Jewish aggression against us in Lebanon. [7]

The governments of other countries attack us daily as your agents with your supervision, consent, and directions. Using violence and lies, these governments prevent our people from enacting the *Sharia* [Islamic law]. These governments place us in a large prison of fear and humiliate us. They steal our *Ummah's* [Islamic nation] resources and sell them to you at a paltry price. [Mr. Bin Laden is referring to what he considers to be the depressed price of the only resource of the Middle

East — oil.][8] These governments have surrendered to the Jews, and handed them most of Palestine, acknowledging the existence of their state over the dismembered limbs of their own people.[9]

Removing these governments is our obligation and is necessary to free the *Ummah* [Islamic nation] in order to make the *Sharia* [Islamic law] supreme and to regain Palestine. Our fight against these governments is the same as our fight against America.

Because of your international influence and military power, you can steal our oil at paltry prices. This is one of the biggest thefts ever witnessed in the history of mankind.

Your military forces occupy our countries and spread military bases throughout them. You corrupt our lands and besiege our sanctuaries in order to protect the Jews and ensure the continuing pillaging of our treasures.[10]

In Iraq, you have starved Muslims and children die every day. No wonder that more than 1.5 million Iraqi children have died as a result of your sanctions. [Mr. Bin Laden is referring to the effects of the economic sanctions imposed on Iraq after the conclusion of the Persian Gulf War in 1991.] And you show no concern. But when 3,000 of your people died [on 9/11], the entire world rose up and has yet to sit down.[11]

You have supported the Jewish idea that Jerusalem is their eternal capital. You agreed to move your embassy there. With your help and protection, the Israelis are planning to destroy the *Al-Aqsa* Mosque [the third holiest site in Islam, located in *Al-Quds* (Jerusalem)]. Under the protection of your weapons, [Israeli Prime Minister Ariel] Sharon entered the *Al-Aqsa* mosque in order to soil it in preparation for its destruction. [Mr. Bin Laden is referring to Mr. Sharon's provocative visit to the mosque in September, 2000, accompanied by one thousand bodyguards. The visit provoked the Palestinian uprising known as the *Intifada*, which has claimed thousands of Palestinian lives, hundreds of Jewish lives and continues to this day.][12]

These calamities are only a few examples of your aggression against us. Our religion and our intellect command that the oppressed have the right to reciprocate. All you will receive from us is *Jihad* [holy war][13] resistance, and revenge. Is it logical to assume that we will leave America in security and peace after she has attacked us for more than a half century?

You dispute that this does not justify aggression against civilians for crimes they did not commit. This argument contradicts your continuous contention that America is the land of freedom. The American people freely chose their government — a choice that demonstrates agreement with its policies. Thus the American people have consented to and affirmed their support for the Israeli oppression of the Palestinians; the occupation and confiscation of Palestinian lands; and the continuous killing, torture, punishment, and expulsion of Palestinians. The American people can reject or change their government's policies if they want.

The American people also pay the taxes that fund the planes that bomb us in Afghanistan, the tanks that destroy our homes in Palestine, the armies that occupy our lands in the Arabian Gulf, and the fleets that blockade Iraq. Tax dollars are given to Israel so it can continue to attack us and confiscate our lands. Thus, the American people fund the attacks against us; and through their elected officials they oversee the expenditure of their monies according to their wishes.

Also, the American Army is comprised of the American people, the same people who shamelessly help the Jews fight us. The American people employ their men and women in the American forces that attack us. This is why the American people are not innocent of the crimes committed against us by America's military forces and by the Jews.

Almighty God Legislated permission for us to take revenge. If we are attacked, then we have the right to respond. We have the right to destroy the villages and towns of whoever has destroyed our own villages and towns. We have the right to destroy the economy of whoever has stolen our wealth. And we have the right to kill the civilians of whoever has killed our civilians.

The American government and press still have not answered the question: Why did they attack us in New York and Washington? If in [President George W.] Bush's eyes [Israeli Prime Minister] Sharon is a man of peace, then we are also men of peace![14] America does not comprehend the language of manners and principles, so we must address it in language that it understands.

In answer to the second question — What do we want from you? First, we invite you into the fold of Islam. Islam is the religion that unifies God; frees Him of partners; loves Him completely; submits to His Laws completely; and discards all opinions, orders, theories, and beliefs that contradict the Faith that He Sent down to His Prophet

Muhammad (PHUH). Islam is the religion of all the Prophets, peace be upon them all, and does not distinguish between them.

To Islam we invite you; the seal of all previous religions; the Religion of the unification of God; of sincerity, manners, righteousness, mercy, honor, purity, and piety. It is the Religion of kindness to others, granting people their rights, and defending the oppressed and the persecuted. It is the Religion that enjoins good and forbids evil with the hand, tongue, and heart. It is the Religion of *Jihad* [holy war] in the Path of God so that God's Word, the *Holy Quran*, and Islam reign supreme. It is the religion that unifies and agrees on obedience to God and the equality of all people without regard to color, sex, or language. It is the Religion whose book — the *Holy Quran* — remains immutable after the other Divine Books and messages have been changed. The *Holy Quran* remains a miracle to the Day of Judgment. God challenges anyone to bring another book — or even ten verses — like it.

Second, we ask you to stop your oppression, lies, immorality and debauchery that are widespread among you. We ask you to become a people of manners, principles, honor, and purity. We ask you to reject the immoral acts of fornication, homosexuality, intoxicants, gambling, and trading with *Riba* [usury, including interest on money lent].[15] We ask you to do these things in order to free you from the lie that you are a great nation — a lie that your leaders spread among you to conceal your despicable state. Sadly, we must tell you that you are the worst civilization in the history of mankind.

Rather than to incorporate the *Sharia* [Islamic law] of God into your Constitution and laws, you choose to make laws as you desire. You separate religion from your government, which contradicts the affirmation of absolute authority in God and your Creator. You evade the embarrassing question: How can God create you, grant you power over all creatures and the land, grant you the amenities of life, and then deny you that which you need most: knowledge of the laws necessary to govern your lives?[16]

Your nation permits *Riba* [usury, including interest on money lent], which has been forbidden by all religions. You build your economy on *Riba*. As a result, Jews have taken control of your economy; and in turn, they have taken control of your media. Now they control all aspects of your lives, making you their servants and achieving their aims at your expense. This is precisely what Benjamin Franklin warned you against.[17]

[Editor's Note: Mr. Bin Laden refers to an alleged prophecy shared by Ben Franklin during the Constitutional Convention of 1787. The prophecy was allegedly made in a "chit chat around the table during intermission" and was recorded in the diary of Charles Cotesworth Pinckney, a delegate from South Carolina. Franklin allegedly wanted to protect the nation against Jews, whom he viewed as morally decadent, anti-Christian, and intent on building a state within a state. The Anti-Defamation League believes the prophecy was a fraud. See "The Franklin 'Prophecy:' Modern Anti-Semitic Myth Making," at http://www.adk. org/special_reports/franklin_prophecy/franklin_documenting_fraud. asp. What is most intriguing about this statement by OBL is that he even knew about the alleged Franklin Prophecy. The statement suggests an eclectic and intimate knowledge of the United States.]

Your nation permits the production, trading and usage of intoxicants. You also permit drugs. You forbid trade in illegal drugs, but your nation is the world's largest consumer of them.[18]

Your nation permits immorality as a pillar of personal freedom. You have continued to sink down in the abyss from level to level until incest has become widespread and neither your sense of honor nor your laws object. You did not hold him to account, other than to say that he had erred, and the incident passed without punishment. Can there be a worse event by which your nation's name will be remembered in history by the other nations? [The Editor believes that Mr. Bin Laden is referring to President William Jefferson Clinton's tryst with former, but then current White House intern, Monica Lewinsky, for which he was impeached but not convicted.]

Your nation permits gambling in all its forms. The corporations also gamble, resulting in inflated investments and criminals becoming rich.

Your nation exploits women as consumer products and advertising tools, enticing customers to purchase them. You use women to serve passengers, visitors, and strangers in order to increase your profit margins. Then you rant in support of the liberation of women.

Your nation allows giant corporations to practice sex in all its forms under the guises of art, entertainment, tourism, freedom, and other such deceptions, and because of this, history records that you are a nation that spreads diseases that were previously unknown to man.

Go ahead, boast to the nations of man that you brought them AIDS as a Satanic American invention.

Your nation destroys the environment by emitting more industrial waste and gases than any other nation in history. Despite this, you refused to sign the Kyoto Agreement so your greedy companies and industries can continue to profit.[19]

Your laws are the laws of the rich and wealthy, who control the political parties and fund the election campaigns with their gifts. Standing behind them are the Jews, who control your policies, media, and economy.

In the history of mankind, you are noted for using force to destroy mankind more than any other nation in history in order to protect your interests and profits rather than to defend principles and values. You dropped nuclear bombs on Japan, even though Japan was ready to negotiate an end to the war. How many acts of oppression, tyranny, and injustice have you carried out?

Let us not forget one of your major characteristics: hypocrisy in manners and principles. Your manners, principles, and values have two scales: one for you and one for all others. Your call for freedom and democracy is only for yourselves and the white race.

You impose your monstrous and destructive policies — and favored governments that you call "American friends" — on the rest of the world while you prevent the people from establishing democracies. When the Islamic Party in Algeria practiced democracy and won the election, you unleashed your agents in the Algerian Army to attack them with tanks and guns and to imprison them and torture them — a new lesson taken from the "American book of democracy!" [Mr. Bin Laden refers to the 1992 Algerian Parliamentary elections, which were won by the Islamic Salvation Front. The Front intended to adopt the *Sharia* [Islamic law] as the law of the land. Instead, the Algerian army interceded and voided the elections, sparking a civil war that continues to this day. The United States turned a blind eye to the Army's intervention.][20]

You only apply your policy prohibiting weapons of mass destruction to certain countries which you do not permit to possess them. Other countries like Israel have your consent to maintain and use such weapons to defend their security. Other nations whom you suspect of manufacturing or maintaining these kinds of weapons are branded as criminals and are threatened with military action.

You claim the right to punish anyone who violates the policies and conventions of international law, yet you are the last to respect them. For the past fifty years, Israel has ignored United Nations resolutions with impunity with America's support. [Since 1967, Israel has defied more than 138 U.N. resolutions concerning its behavior in the Middle East.][21]

Regarding the war criminals whom you censure and for whom you convene criminal courts, you shamelessly ask that your own nationals be granted immunity! [The Bush administration has refused to recognize the jurisdiction of the International Criminal Court and has pressured other countries to exempt United States military personnel and civilian contractors from its jurisdiction.][22] However, history will not forget the war crimes that you committed against the Muslims and the rest of the world. Those whom you have killed in Japan [with nuclear weapons], Afghanistan, Somalia, Lebanon and Iraq will remain a blot that you will never be able to erase. Suffice it to remind you of your latest war crimes in Afghanistan, where you destroyed villages densely populated with innocent civilians, and where you bombed mosques, causing the roofs to crash down on the heads of the Muslims praying inside. You broke your agreement with the *Mujahideen* [Islamic warriors] when they left Qunduz, bombing them in the Jangi Fort. And you killed more than 1,000 prisoners through suffocation and thirst.[23] Only God alone knows how many people have died by torture at the hands of you and your agents. Your planes remain in the Afghani skies, looking for anyone remotely suspicious.

You claim to be the vanguards of human rights, and your State Department issues annual reports containing data regarding countries that violate human rights.[24] However, this all vanished when the *Mujahideen* [Islamic warriors] struck you [on 9/11]. You then implemented the methods of the repressive countries you used to criticize. In America, you arrested thousands of Muslims and Arabs, held them in secret custody without reason or trial, and did not even disclose their names. You also enacted newer, harsher laws.[25] What happens in Guatanamo Bay, Cuba, is a historical embarrassment to America and its values. It screams "hypocrites" in your faces. What is the value of your signature on any agreement or treaty?[26]

Third, we call upon you to assume an honest view of yourselves — which I doubt you will do — to learn that you are a nation without principles or manners and that the values and principles you demand of others do not apply to you.

Fourth, we advise you to stop supporting Israel, end your support of the Indians in Kashmir, the Russians against the Chechens, and cease supporting the Manilla Government against the Muslims in the southern Philippines.[27]

Fifth, we also advise you to pack your luggage and get out of our lands. For you, we desire goodness, guidance, and righteousness; so, do not force us to send you back in coffins as cargo.

Sixth, we call upon you to stop supporting the corrupt leaders in our countries. Do not interfere in our politics or our methods of education.[28] Leave us alone, or else expect us again in New York City and Washington, D.C.

Seventh, we invite you to deal with us on the basis of mutual interests and benefits rather than by policies of subversion, theft, and occupation, and to discontinue your policy of supporting the Jews because this will lead to further disasters for you.

If you fail to respond to all of these conditions, then be prepared to fight the *Ummah* [Islamic nation]. The nation of monotheism puts complete trust in God and fears none other than Him. The *Ummah* which is addressed in the *Holy Quran* with the words: "Do you fear them? God has more right that you should fear Him if you are believers. Fight against them so that God will punish them by your hands and disgrace them and give you victory over them and heal the breasts of believing people. And remove the anger of their (believers') hearts. God accepts the repentance of whom He wills. God is All-Knowing, All-Wise."[29]

"But honor, power and glory belong to God, and to His Messenger (Muhammad — peace be upon him) and to the believers."[30]

"So do not become weak (against your enemy), nor be sad, and you will be superior (in victory) if you are indeed (true) believers."[31]

The *Ummah* [Islamic nation] of martyrdom; the *Ummah* that desires death more than you desire life:

"Think not of those who are killed in the way of God as dead. Nay, they are alive with their Lord, and they are being provided for. They rejoice in what God has bestowed upon them from His Bounty and rejoice for the sake of those who have not yet joined them, but are left behind (not yet martyred) that on them no fear shall come, nor shall they grieve. They rejoice in a grace and a bounty from God, and that God will not waste the reward of the believers."[32]

The *Ummah* [Islamic nation] to whom God has promised victory and success:

"It is He Who has sent His Messenger (Muhammad peace be upon him) with guidance and the Religion of truth (Islam), to make it victorious over all other religions even though the polytheists hate it."[33]

"God has decreed that 'Verily it is I and My Messengers who shall be victorious.' Verily God is All-Powerful, All-Mighty."[34]

The *Ummah* [Islamic nation] dismissed and destroyed previous evil empires like you. The *Ummah* repels your attacks, wishes to remove your evils, and prepares to fight you. You well know that to the very core of its soul, the *Ummah* despises your haughtiness and arrogance.

If the Americans refuse to heed our advice and the goodness, guidance and righteousness to which we have invited them, then be assured that they will lose this Crusade that [President George W.] Bush began, just like the previous Crusades in which you were humiliated at the hands of the *Mujahideen* [Islamic fighters], fleeing back to your homes in silence and disgrace. If the Americans do not respond, their fate will be that of the Soviets, who fled from Afghanistan to face military defeat, political breakup, ideological downfall, and economic bankruptcy.[35]

This is our answer to the message of the Americans. Do they now know why we fight them and why we shall be victorious over their form of ignorance?

Chapter 10

Call To Jihad[1]
November 12, 2002

In the name of God, the Merciful, the Compassionate, from His Servant, Osama bin Laden, to the people of the allies of the tyrant government of the United States.

May God grace those who choose the right path, Islam. Ending aggression begins the path to safety. Reciprocity is part of justice. Since the [9/11] raids on New York City and Washington, D.C., reciprocal reactions here and there have occurred — the killing of Germans in Tunisia; the killing of French in Karachi; the bombing of the French supertanker in Yemen; the killing of U.S. Marines in Failaka [Failaka Island, fifty kilometers east of Kuwait City]; the killing of British and Australians by explosions in Bali; and the recent operation in Moscow.[2] Responding to the mandate of God and his Prophet [Muhammad (peace be upon him, hereinafter "PBUH," words of grace that must attend any oral or written reference to the Prophets recognized by Islam)], zealous sons of Islam carried out these actions in defense of their religion.

Today's pharaoh [President George W.] Bush is killing our sons in Iraq, and Israel — the ally of the United States — is bombing the homes of the elderly, women, and children with U.S.-made aircraft in Palestine, prompted the sane among your rulers [meaning the rulers of the Islamic nation, the *Ummah*] to distance themselves from this criminal gang.

Our relatives in Palestine have been slain and severely tortured for nearly a century. If we defend the Palestinians, then the world becomes angry and lines up against the Muslims under the false pretense of fighting terrorism. What do your governments want by allying with the criminal gang in the White House against the Muslims? Are your governments unaware that the gangsters in the White House are the biggest butchers of this age? [Secretary of Defense Donald M.] Rumsfeld, the butcher of Vietnam, killed more than two million people, not to mention the wounded.[3] [Vice President Dick] Cheney and [Secretary of State Colin] Powell killed and destroyed more in Baghdad than Hulegu [1217 – 1265, grandson of Genghis Khan] of the Mongols.[4] What do your governments want from their alliance with the United States, particularly Britain, France, Italy, Canada, Germany and Australia, in attacking us in Afghanistan?[5].

We previously warned Australia against participating in the war in Afghanistan and about its despicable efforts to separate East Timor.[6] It ignored the warning until it awakened to the sounds of explosions in Bali. The Australian government falsely claimed that Australians were not targeted.

If you were upset by the deaths of your own men and those of your allies in Tunisia, Karachi, Failaka Island, Bali, and Amman [Jordan][7], remember our children are killed in Palestine and Iraq everyday; remember our deaths in the Khowst mosque [in Afghanistan]; and remember the premeditated killing of people in weddings in Afghanistan.[8] If you were upset by the killings of your people in Moscow, I remember our people in Chechnya.[9]

Why should fear, killing, destruction, displacement, orphaning and widowing plague us while you enjoy stability and happiness? This is unjust. It is time to get even. You will be killed just as you kill, and you will be bombed just as you bomb.

You can expect more distress. Thanks be to God, The *Ummah* [Islamic nation] has started attacking you with the hands of its beloved sons, who pledged to God to continue *Jihad* [holy war] through words and weapons as long as they live to establish right and expose falsehood.

In conclusion, I ask God to help us champion His Religion and to continue *Jihad* for His Sake until we meet Him when He is satisfied with us. Praise be to Almighty God.

This Page Left Intentionally Blank For Notes

Chapter 11

Statement To Iraqis[1]
February 11, 2003

In the name of God, the Most Gracious, the Most Merciful:

I have a message for our Muslim brothers in Iraq. May God's Peace and Blessings be upon you.

Oh believers, fear God as he should be feared by doing what he instructs and abstaining from what is forbidden.

Remember Him, thank Him and obey Him. When you die, die as a Muslim completely submitting to God.[2]

We are greatly concerned about the Crusaders' preparations for war to occupy Baghdad, the former capitol of Islam [between the years of 750 and 1258 Baghdad was the seat of the Abbasid Caliphate],[3] loot Muslims' wealth, and install a puppet government obedient to its masters in Washington, D.C., and Tel Aviv, like all the other treasonous Arab governments.

This is preparation for the establishment of Greater Israel.[4] [In Zionist literature, a "greater" Israel is envisioned extending from the Euphrates River in Iraq to the Nile River in Egypt.]

"God is Sufficient for us and He is the Best Disposer of affairs."[5]

In the midst of this unjust war waged by infidels and debauchers led by America and its allies, we stress these important values:

First, fight for the sake of the one God, not to champion ethnic groups or the non-Islamic Arab regimes, including Iraq.

God says: "Those who believe fight in the Cause of God, and those who reject Faith fight in the cause of evil. So fight ye against the friends of Satan; feeble indeed is the cunning of Satan."[6]

Second, victory only comes from God, and we must prepare for *Jihad* [holy war].[7]

God says: "Oh ye who believe! If ye will help the Cause of God, He will help you and plant your feet firmly."[8]

We must hurry to seek God's Forgiveness from our sins [in preparation for *Jihad*].

Prophet Muhammad [peace be upon him, hereinafter "PBUH," words of grace that must attend any oral or written reference to the Prophets recognized by Islam] said: "Avoid the seven destructive sins; polytheism, sorcery, killing, (unless permitted by God), usury, taking the money of orphans, fleeing from combat, and slandering innocent faithful women."[9]

Other grave sins are consuming alcohol, committing adultery, disobeying parents, and committing perjury. Generally, obey God, and in particular, mention His Name before combat.

Abu-al-Darda, said: "Before an attack, perform a good deed because you fight with your deeds."[10]

Third, we have learned from fighting Americans that they primarily depend on psychological warfare because of their massive media machine. They also use massive air attacks to mask their major weakness: cowardice and the lack of morale among their soldiers.

These soldiers have accepted the lies and injustices of their government. They also do not have a cause to defend. They fight for capitalists, usurers, and the merchants of arms and oil, including the criminals at the White House, including the personal grudges borne by [ex-President George H.W.] Bush, [father of President George W. Bush].[11]

We have learned that a most effective defense against air attacks by the Crusader air force is the construction of numbers of covered and camouflaged trenches. I previously referred to this in a statement last year during the Battle of Tora Bora.[12] There, Faith trumped the materialistic forces of an evil people, thanks to God.

I will tell you about part of that battle to demonstrate the cowardice of the American soldiers and the effectiveness of the trenches. About 300 of us *Mujahideen* [Islamic warriors] dug about 100 trenches in an area no bigger than a square mile. Three brothers occupied each trench to avoid high casualties from the bombardment. From the first moment of the United States attack on Afghanistan on October 7, 2001, our main forces were exposed to concentrated bombardment. The bombardment continued until mid-Ramadan. [The annual Islamic thirty-day fasting period that occurred between November 17th and December 17th in the year 2001. The dates of Ramadan vary each year because they are based on a lunar calendar.] On the seventeenth day of Ramadan there occurred a particularly fierce bombardment because the United States commanders were convinced that remnants of Al Qaeda, including me and brother *Mujahid* [individual Islamic warrior] Dr. Ayman al-Zawahiri, were still in Tora Bora.[13] The bombardment was nonstop day and night. The U.S. Pentagon worked ferociously to destroy this small parcel. Fire fell from all of the planes in the sky, especially after they completed their other missions in Afghanistan. We were attacked with smart bombs, cluster bombs, bunker-blaster bombs, and bombs that weighted thousands of pounds. B-52 bombers used to fly overhead for two hours or more and drop twenty to thirty bombs at a time. Modified C-130 [Specter gun-ships] kept carpet-bombing us at night. Despite the unprecedented intensity of these attacks and the massive propaganda, the U.S. forces themselves did not dare attempt to seize our positions. But for fifteen days they cajoled the hypocrite forces [Northern Alliance indigenous forces, the surrogate United States forces in Afghanistan] into fighting us non-stop. But every time the hypocrites attacked, we repelled them. Can there any clearer evidence of the cowardice of the American and the lies regarding their alleged powers?

In sum, the international alliance of evil lost the battle. All of its might could not dislodge a small number of *Mujahideen* [Islamic warriors] — 300 — dug into trenches over a square-mile area with an ambient temperature of negative 10 degrees Celsius. The battle claimed only six percent of our forces. We pray God will accept their martyrdom. Only two percent of our trenches were damaged. If the world's forces of evil could not destroy their targets in a single square mile of land against such a small number of *Mujahideen* with very limited capabilities, how can they triumph over the *Ummah* [Islamic nation]? This will be impossible if, God Willing, people follow Islam and insist on *Jihad* [holy war].

Mujahideen brothers in Iraq, do not be afraid of United States propaganda about its power and its smart missiles and bombs. They will have no material effect in the hills and trenches or in the plains or forests. They must have clear targets. Well-camouflaged trenches and targets are immune to either smart or dumb missiles and bombs. Limit yourselves to haphazard strikes to dissipate the enemy's ammunition and waste its money. Dig many trenches!

The early Muslim Caliph Omar [who served from 634 – 644],[14] may God be pleased with him, stated: "Take the ground as a shield." This will ensure the exhaustion of the enemy's weapons within months. Their daily production is too little and can be managed, God Willing.[15]

We also recommend luring the enemy forces into close-quarter, exhausting fighting, using camouflaged defensive positions in plains, farms, mountains, and cities. They fear urban warfare the most — warfare in which they anticipate grave casualties.

We also stress the importance of martyrdom operations — operations that have inflicted unprecedented harm on the United States and Israel, all thanks to God.

We note that whoever supported the United States, including the hypocrites inside Iraq and the Arab rulers who approved its actions and participated in this Crusader war by fighting or by providing bases or any form of support, including words, by which to kill Muslims in Iraq, are apostates and outside the *Ummah* [Islamic nation]. Their blood may be spilled and their property confiscated.

God says: "O ye who believe! Take not the Jews and the Christians for your friends and protectors; they are but friends and protectors to each other. And he amongst you that turns to them [for friendship] is of them. Verily, God guideth not a people unjust."[16]

We emphasize that in the midst of such grave events as these, true Muslims should incite and mobilize the *Ummah* [Islamic nation] in order to liberate themselves from the renegade ruling regimes — which themselves are enslaved by the United States — and establish the rule of God on Earth. The countries most in need of liberation are Egypt, Jordan, Morocco, Nigeria, Pakistan, the land of the Two Holy Places [Saudi Arabia],[17] and Yemen.

Suffice it to say that this Crusader war is primarily aimed at the *Ummah* [Islamic nation]. Irrespective of the survival or removal of the socialist Baathist Party in Iraq or of Saddam Hussein, Muslims in general, and Iraqis in particular, must brace for *Jihad* [holy war] and obtain weapons and ammunition. God says: "And let them pray with thee taking all precautions and bearing arms: the unbelievers wish if ye were negligent of your arms and your baggage, to assault you in a single rush."[18] It is God's Prescription that we do this. And fighting under non-Islamic banners is prohibited. However, he who fights to spread Islam fights for God's Sake fights under a clear [religious] banner. Under such circumstances no harm will result if Muslims conflate with the socialists to fight against the Crusaders in spite of our belief that the socialists are infidels.[19] The legitimacy of socialists and their rulers was lost long ago. They are infidels wherever they are, even in Baghdad or Aden.[20]

The fighting which will be waged is like that which characterized the fighting between the Muslims and Byzantium in the ancient past. The confluence of Islamic and non-Islamic interests is not harmful. In the fighting with Byzantium, the interests of the Muslims converged with those of the Persians. [Between 627 and 1453, the Muslims fought both the Persian and the Byzantine Empires, at times united with the Persians against the Byzantines. By the end of this time period, the Muslims had conquered both Empires.] This did not harm the Prophet's [PBUH] Companions.[21]

Before concluding I repeat the importance of maintaining high morale and I caution against the spread of false rumors, defeatism, uncertainty, and discouragement.

The prophet said: "Bring good omens and do not discourage people."[22]

He also said: "The voice of Abu-Tal'hah [one of the Prophet's Companions] in the army is better than 100 men."[23]

During the Al-Yarmuk Battle, a man told Khalid bin-al-Walid [an Islamic commander]: "The Byzantine soldiers are too many and the Muslims are few."

So, Khalid told him: "Shame on you. Armies do not triumph with large numbers but are defeated if the spirit of defeatism prevails."[24]

Remember this saying: "It is not fitting for a Prophet that he should have prisoners of war until he hath thoroughly subdued the land. Therefore, when ye meet the unbelievers (in fight), smite at their necks."[25]

You should refer the new Crusader to this verse of poetry: "The only language between you and us is the sword that will strike your necks."[26]

Finally, I advise us to fear God and be patient in *Jihad* [holy war]. Patience will achieve victory.

I also advise both myself and you to pray more.

"O ye who believe! When ye meet a force, be firm, and call God in remembrance much (and often); That ye may prosper."[27]

"God, Who sent the book unto the Prophet [PBUH], who drives the clouds, and who defeated the enemy parties, defeat them and make us victorious over them."

"Our Lord! Give us good in this world and good in the Hereafter and save us from the torment of the Fire!"[28]

May God's Peace and Blessings be upon Prophet Muhammad [PBUH] and his house.

Chapter 12

Sermon For The Feast of The Sacrifice[1]
February 16, 2003

[Editor's note: the Muslim Feast of The Sacrifice celebrates Abraham's offer to sacrifice one of his sons to demonstrate his devotion to the One God and then being allowed instead to sacrifice a sheep. The incident is revealed in the *Holy Quran* at 37 (As-Saffat [The Arrangers]):83–111.]

Praise be to God, Who revealed the Verse of the Sword to His servant and His Messenger [the Prophet Muhammad, peace be upon him, hereinafter "PBUH," words of grace that must attend any oral or written reference to the Prophets recognized by Islam] to establish truth and eradicate falsehood. Praise be to God, Who says:

"Then when the Sacred Months have passed, then kill the polytheists wherever you find them and capture them and besiege them, and prepare for them each and every ambush. But if they repent and perform *Salat* [prayer] and give *Zakat* [charity], then leave their way free. Verily, God is Oft-Forgiving, Most Merciful."[2]

Praise be to God, who says:

"Fight them and God will punish them by your hands and disgrace them and give you victory over them and heal the hearts of a believing people."[3]

114

Peace and blessings be upon our Prophet Muhammad [PBUH], who said:

"I was sent with the sword in the waning hour until God Alone is worshipped without any partners, and He placed my sustenance beneath the shadow of my spear and He placed disgraced and belittlement on he who opposes my orders and he who imitates a people, then he is one of them." And He also said: "Expel the polytheists from the Arabian Peninsula."[4]

At this time, the blood of the Muslims continues to flow in Palestine, Chechnya, the Philippines, Kashmir and Sudan, and children are dying because of the American sanctions on Iraq [economic sanctions imposed on Iraq after the conclusion of the 1991 Persian Gulf War].[5] Our wounds are still healing from the Crusader Wars against the Islamic world waged in the last century. [Mr. Bin Laden refers to the fall of the Islamic Ottoman Empire after the conclusion of World War I.][6] Because of the Sykes-Picot Agreement in 1916 between France and Britain, which led to the division of the Islamic World and the continuing rule of the Crusaders to this very day, we are witnessing another Sykes-Picot Agreement. [By this treaty, after the conclusion of World War I the victorious Allied Powers colonized the Middle East provinces of the defeated Ottoman Empire.] This time the agreement is between President George W. Bush and British Prime Minister Tony Blair. The new agreement has the same nature and purpose: the destruction of the *Ummah* [Islamic nation] of our beloved Prophet (PBUH).[7]

Though the Bush-Blair Agreement proclaims to eradicate terrorism, its real purpose is to destroy Islam. The rulers of the region [the Middle East countries, including the Gulf States] speak in support of the Bush War on Terror, which is in fact a War on Islam. This is a clear betrayal and treachery against the *Ummah* [Islamic nation], reinforced by corrupt government scholars and ministers.[8] It is no secret that the recent deployment of forces to attack Iraq is but another link in the chain of continuing attacks on the countries of the region, including Egypt, Syria, Iran and Sudan. However, the new Crusader's real intention is to divide and conquer the Land of the Two Holy Sanctuaries [Saudi Arabia, home to Mecca and Media, the two holiest places in Islam]. Sixty years ago, they realized the strategic value of this target when Britain passed this goal to the United States. [The United States and Saudi Arabia established a special relationship on February 14, 1945, during a meeting between President Franklin [Delanor] Roosevelt and King Abdul Aziz of Saudi Arabia.][9]

America tried to achieve this goal thirty years ago during the War of the 10th of Ramadan [The Arab-Israeli War of 1973], when then President [Richard] Nixon threatened to invade the land of the Two Holy Sanctuaries. However, he was unable to do so at the time. But since the beginning of the Second Gulf War [The Persian Gulf War of 1991], America has built powerful military bases in the Land of the Two Holy Sanctuaries, especially close to its capitol, Riyadh. All that remains is the division of the Land of the Two Holy Sanctuaries, and the time of division appears close. Thus, the American buildup in the region is not a transient summer cloud that will bring peace to the World; rather, it is aimed at a strategic target of immense value that will never be ignored by the cunning American foreign policy at any cost. God is Sufficient for us and what an Excellent Guardian is He![10]

Have the governments in the region done anything to counteract this enemy objective? They have done nothing but increase their support for the Crusaders. They have unified their interior ministers to fight against the *Mujahideen* [Islamic warriors], and repressed the righteous scholars who were trying to warn the *Ummah* [Islamic nation] to protect itself.

The establishment of a Jewish super-state is one of the objects of this latest Crusade. The super-state will include all of Palestine and parts of Iraq, Egypt, Syria, Lebanon, Jordan, and a huge part of the Land of the Two Holy Sanctuaries. You cannot imagine the harm and suffering that this Greater Israel will bring to this region. [Zionist literature envisioned a "greater Israel" extending from the Euphrates River in Iraq to the Nile River in Egypt.][11]

The events in Palestine are a small sample of what awaits the region: killing of men, women and children; imprisonment; terrorism; destruction of houses; pillaging of the land; razing of factories; and creation of a perpetual state of fear where the people can expect death at any moment from a rocket or shell destroying their homes and killing their women. Even a strong man finds it difficult to absorb what is happening in Palestine. What about an oppressed mother watching her child die in her very hands?[12]

To God we belong and to Him we return.[13] God is an Excellent Guardian for us. Oh, God! Before You I distance myself from what these

Jews, Christians, treacherous rulers, and their supporters are doing. I apologize to You for those who are sitting idly by and not working for the victory of Islam. The creation of Greater Israel will lead to the total domination of our lands by the Jews.

What did you tell us about the Jews? These are the same Jews who lied and tried to trick the Creator. They killed the Prophets and broke their promises.

As God said: "Is it not (the case) that every time they make a covenant, some party among them throws it aside? Nay! The truth is most of them are faithless."[14] The Jews are the lords of usury and the leaders of treachery. They will leave you neither Religion nor anything else.

God said about them: "Or have they a share in the dominion? Then in that case they would not give mankind even a *Niqira* (speck on the back of a date-stone [date pit]."[15] Jews, whose religion teaches them that mankind is enslaved to them, and whoever refuses to serve them deserves to be killed. [In the Old Testament, the Jews were given license by God to apply the "ban" or "anathema" to conquered peoples, meaning the killing of all of them. Deuteronomy 20:16–18, etc.][16]

God said about them: "… they say: 'there is no blame on us to betray and to take the properties of the illiterates (Arabs).' But they tell a lie against God while they know it."[17] These are some of their characteristics, so be aware of them.

These are the intentions behind the Crusader plan. Understand them well. How can we protect ourselves from the evil of the disbelievers and save our lands? My answer is what the righteous servant Prophet Shuaib (PBUH) said: "I only desire reform so far as I am able, to the best of my power, and my guidance cannot come except from God, in Him I trust and unto Him I repent."[18]

Therefore, the way to protect ourselves from the evil of the disbelievers is *Jihad* [holy war] in the Path of God. As God said: "Then fight (O Muhammad [PBUH]) in the Cause of God, you are not responsible except for yourself, and incite the believers (to fight along with you), it may be that God will restrain the evil might of the disbelievers, and God is Stronger in Might and Stronger in Punishing."[19]

Let me tell you the good news first. With God's Blessings, today's *Ummah* [Islamic nation] possesses great capabilities and powers to rescue Palestine and the other lands of the Muslims. But the *Ummah* has been restrained. We must work hard to unleash its capabilities. I can also tell you that God has promised our *Ummah* victory. Only our own sins and retrenchment from Islam delays victory. God said: "If you help (in the cause of) God, He will help you, and make your foothold firm."[20] Furthermore, our *Ummah* has been promised victory over the Jews. As the Prophet (PBUH) informed us: "The Day of Judgment will not be until the Muslims fight against the Jews and the Muslims will kill them until the Jews hide behind trees and rocks, and the trees and rocks will speak, saying, 'O Muslim! O Servant of God! There is a Jew behind me so come and kill him, except for the Gharqad tree [a thorny tree], for it is the tree of the Jews.'"[21]

This *Hadith* [authenticated tradition of the Prophet Muhammad (PBUH)] informs us that the confrontation will be face-to-face battle, not the long-term depletion of the *Ummah*'s [Islamic nation] resources by using the guise of democracy and other such tricks. I will tell you about other Muslim victories during the past twenty years as examples that, God Willing, will assist our *Jihad* [holy war] and raise the morale of the sons of the *Ummah*. It is critical to inspire them so the *Ummah* can protect itself from this latest Crusade. Verily, the *Ummah* is the greatest human power on the face of the Earth if it roots in Islam properly. Only then will it be able to face the so-called "superpowers."

Let me tell you about a previous confrontation between Muslims and a superpower. The scholars of history said that Al-Muthanna Ash-Shaibani[22] came to Medina seeking help in fighting the Persians. The Caliph Omar bin-al Khattab [the second Caliph, 634 - 644] called a mobilization for three days, but nobody volunteered. Omar [bin-al Khattab] realized the extent of the Muslims' inflated fear of the Persians' power, so he asked Al-Muthanna [Ash-Shaibani] to tell them about his victories against the Persians to ameliorate their fears. This excited the people. Abu Ubaidah Ath-Thaqafi[23] stood up and Omar [bin-al Khattab] gave him the banner of the Muslims. He then marched to battle, with the people following him, may God be pleased with them.

Imitate these great people; do not let the force of America and its army intimidate you. By the grace of God, we have struck them many times and have routed them repeatedly. They are cowardly. We learned during our fighting in Afghanistan that they rely heavily on psychological warfare through their large media apparatus and their indiscriminate bombing, which hides the cowardice and lack of fighting spirit of their soldiers. I do not have sufficient time to tell you about some unbelievable incidents that happened in our encounters with them at Tora Bora and Shani-Kot.[24]

I also remind you of the *Mujahideen*'s [Islamic warriors] defeat, with God's Grace, of the world's largest superpower, the Soviet Union, after ten years of fierce fighting by the sons of the Afghanis and their allies from the sons of the Muslims. [Mr. Bin Laden refers to the Soviet occupation of Afghanistan between 1979 and 1988, when the defeated Soviets withdrew.][25] Similarly, I remind you of the defeat of the Russians in Chechnya, when the Chechen *Mujahideen* and their Arab and foreign brothers smashed the arrogant Russians, inflicting defeat after defeat upon them. The Russians withdrew from Chechnya after the first war, only to return a second time with American support. Nonetheless, they continue to suffer heavy defeats at the hands of a small group of believers, and we ask God to make them strong and grant them victory. [Russia invaded Chechnya in 1994, withdrew in 1996, and re-invaded in 1999.][26]

Let me also remind you of the defeat of the American forces in Beirut in 1983, soon after the Israeli invasion of Lebanon. The Lebanese resistance was personified by the truck laden with explosives that struck the main military base of the U.S. Marines in Beirut, killing 242 soldiers — Hell was their final destination, and what an evil destination that is.[27]

Then, after the Second Gulf War [The Persian Gulf War of 1991], America deployed her forces to Somalia and killed over thirteen thousand sons of the Muslims. Then the lions of Islam from amongst the "Arab Afghans" and their brothers from that region pounced upon America's military forces and rubbed her arrogance into the dust, killing scores of them, destroying their tanks, and downing their aircraft. [Mr. Bin Laden refers to the notorious Black Hawk Down incident in Mogadishu, Somalia, that occurred on October 3, 1993.][28] Then America and her allies secretly fled under the cover of darkness. Praise and Glory be to God for this.

At the same time, *Mujahideen* [Islamic warriors] detonated explosives near the Americans in Aden; and in less than twenty-four hours the cowardly Americans fled the country.[29]

Next, in 1995 an explosion in Riyadh killed four Americans, a clear message from the people demonstrating their rejection of the American policy of bankrolling the Jews and occupying the land of the Two Holy Sanctuaries. The following year, another explosion at Al-Khobar killed 19 Americans and wounded more than 400 of them, prompting them to move their bases from the cities to the desert.[30]

In 1998 the *Mujahideen* (Islamic warriors) warned America to cease its support for the Jews and to leave the Land of the Two Holy Sanctuaries. But the enemy refused. So, with God's grace, the *Mujahideen* smashed them with two mighty hits in eastern Africa. [Mr. Bin Laden refers to the bombings of the United States Embassies in Tanzania and Kenya.] Later, though America was warned again, she refused to heed the warnings. So, the *Mujahideen* launched a martyrdom operation that destroyed the American warship the U.S.S. *Cole* in the port of Aden, striking a solid blow to the face of the American military and simultaneously exposed the Yemeni government as American agents, just like all the other countries in the region.[31]

Then the gang of thugs in the White House hid the truth. Their stupid and foolish leader [President George W. Bush], who is elected and supported by the [American] people, denied reality and proclaimed that the *Mujahideen* [Islamic warriors] attacked them because we were jealous of them. In reality, we are attacking them because of the evil and injustice they commit against the whole of the *Ummah* [Islamic nation], especially in Iraq, Palestine, and their occupation of the land of the Two Holy Sanctuaries. In return, the *Mujahideen* decided to teach them a lesson and to take the war to [America's] heartland. On the blessed Tuesday, September 11, 2001, we attacked America while the Zionist-American alliance was attacking our children and our people in the blessed land of the *Al-Aqsa* mosque [the third holiest site in Islam located in *Al-Quds* [Jerusalem, Palestine]] with American-made tanks and planes operated by the Jews, while our people in Iraq were suffering from America's sanctions upon them, and while the *Ummah* was a long way from properly rooting in Islam.[32]

Because of all this, the Muslims were very disheartened, except for those upon whom God had Mercy. While America was carrying out all this without concern, there came forward the [nineteen 9/11] youths with disheveled hair and dusty feet, who were wanted and pursued all over the world. They believed in their Lord, so God Provided them with Guidance. He put constancy in their tongues and *Iman* [belief] in their hearts, so they stopped fearing for the Sake of God. They poured out the water of their lives but not the water of their dignity. They launched their airborne attacks [on 9/11] in a magnificent feat of heroism, unmatched by any before them.

They destroyed the idols of America; they struck at the very heart of the United States' Department of Defense; and they hit the black heart of the U.S. economy, rubbing America's nose in the dust and rolling her hubris into the mud. Accompanying the destruction of the Twin Towers in New York City was an even greater destruction: that of the great American dream and the legacy of democracy. American dignity and values are at the lowest lever ever. The legend of being the land of freedom, of being the safest and most secure place on earth, and the legend of the C.I.A., have all been destroyed with the Help of God. Praise and Glory be to God.

One of the many positive results of the retaliatory attacks on New York City and Washington, D.C., was that they revealed the true characteristics of the Crusaders and the extent of their hatred of Muslims. The attacks skinned the American wolf and left it standing in its naked, filthy reality. The whole world awakened, and the *Ummah* [Islamic nation] realized the importance of loving and hating for the Sake of God. The ties of brotherhood between Muslims strengthened, which is an excellent step toward unity and the re-establishment of the Righteous [pan-] Islamic Caliphate, God willing.[33] Now it is clear that America, this great, oppressive power, can be struck and disgraced. The American public now knows what is happening in Palestine and that what happened in Manhattan was because of the policies of its elected leaders.

Obviously America is a great power with unbelievable military strength and a vibrant economy. But all of this is built on a weak and hollow foundation. Therefore, it is easy to target the flimsy base and concentrate on its weak points. If we are able to target even one-tenth of the weak points, we will be able to crush America and prevent it from conquering the world.

This small group of Muslims, facing an international coalition against them and Islam, proved that it is possible to fight militarily against this superpower. They protected Islam and benefited the *Ummah* [Islamic nation] much more than have the fifty-odd Islamic countries because this small group chose the path of *Jihad* [holy war] to achieve victory for Islam. As Abu Hialah[34] said:

"There are reasons for victory and for defeat as well,

And every method that generates eternity is successful.

The ways towards dignity are many but the shortest one is the one that puts forward one's blood around its difficult path."

By the Grace of God, there have been many such champions in the *Ummah* [Islamic nation], but most of them have been restrained by present circumstances; so, we have to unify to release them so they can engage in *Jihad* [holy war] in the Path of God because *Jihad* is the way to honor the *Ummah* and secure it.

Regarding the many restrictions preventing our youth from marching toward *Jihad*, we shall discuss only the more important ones. I begin with a *Hadith* [authenticated tradition of the Prophet Muhammad (PBUH)]. If you take guidance from it, you will benefit; if you deviate from it, you will be destroyed. The Prophet (PBUH) said: "Nations before you were destroyed because when a noble person amongst them stole, they would leave him alone, and when a poor, weak person amongst them stole, they would establish the penal punishment against him."[35]

Those of you with insight, learn from this. And let me tell you about the story of Khalid bin al-Walid's conversion to Islam.[36] Imam Ahmad[37] said: "From a lack of understanding, a man blindly follows his religion from other men [instead of from God]."

Thus, the first of the restrictions [on the *Ummah* (Islamic nation)] comes from the present rulers and the naysayers among their corrupt governments' scholars, ministers, salaried writers, and their ilk. The people already know about the treachery and weaknesses of their leaders. To those who ask us to pledge ourselves to those leaders, we merely ask, "When did the masses ever pledge their allegiance to these leaders in the first place so that they can now be advised to renew their pledge to them?" In truth, they never pledged allegiance to them, and the result has been our oppression by disbelievers. It is said: "Those who betray in their affairs when the situation is easy, then they will never be able to rectify their affairs when the situation is difficult."[38]

Ours is not a minor difference with the leaders that can be easily resolved; rather, we are talking about the root of Islam: there is no god but God.[39] These leaders destroyed this root and allied with the disbelievers, ruled by their own man-made laws, and supported the atheist United Nations. The *Sharia* [Islamic law] prohibits pledging allegiance to such leaders, but we need not delve more deeply into this matter because we already informed the people about it in the previous 17th Declaration of the Advice of the Reform Committee.[40]

How, then, is it possible for a Muslim to ask other Muslims to pledge themselves to the likes of Hamid Karzai [President of Afghanistan][41] and cooperate with him to lift the oppression of the Afghani people and also to stop America in its tracks? This is impossible because Karzai is an American agent. Supporting him against the Muslims takes a person outside of the *Ummah* [Islamic nation]. We have to ask whether Karzai differs from the Karzai-like Arab rulers. Who enthroned the rulers of the Arabian Gulf? None other than the Crusaders, who also appointed the Karzai of Kabul, the Karzai of Pakistan [President-General Pervez Musharraf], the Karzai of Kuwait [Emir Sheikh Jaber al-Ahmad al-Sabah], the Karzai of Bahrain [Emir Sheikh Issa bin Sulman al-Khalifa], the Karzai of Qatar [Emir Sheikh Hamad bin Khalifa al-Thani], and the others. Who appointed the Karzai of Riyadh [Mr. Bin Laden refers to Abdul Aziz ibn Saud, founder of the Saud dynasty] and brought him [to Saudi Arabia] from Kuwait where he was a bandit in order to fight against the Ottoman Empire and its leader, Ibn Rasheed [Turkish governor of Arabia during the last days of the Ottoman Empire.] [Mr. Bin Laden refers to British patronage of Abdul Aziz, the founder of Saudi Arabia, between 1916 and 1926, when he seized the Arabian Peninsula and declared himself to be King of the Kingdom of Saudi Arabia.][42] None other than the Crusaders, who continue to enslave us to this very day.

God said: "Are your disbelievers (O Quarish!) better than these (previous destroyed nations)? Or have you an immunity (against Our Torment) in the Divine Scriptures?"[43]

Those traitors would solve our *Ummah*'s [Islamic nation] problems, including one of the most important, Palestine, according to the rules and regulations of the United Nations or the dictates of America. This is similar to the initiative launched by Crown Prince Abdullah [of Saudi Arabia] in Beirut, in which he sold out the blood of our martyrs and the Palestinian cause in order to help the Jews and Americans against the Muslims. These leaders have betrayed God and His Messenger (PBUH), left the fold of Islam, and betrayed the *Ummah*. [In 2002, Crown Prince Abdullah of Saudi Arabia proposed recognizing Israel in return for her withdrawal from the Occupied Territories.][44]

Those who want to solve these problems by relying on such traitors only trick themselves and fool the *Ummah*. They are the ones who lead toward the oppressors and who have gone astray. This is a clear deviation. At best, these Muslims are weak evil-doers. It is incumbent on Muslims first to advise them of their errors, and then if they do not accept the advice, to warn them and be warned of them.[45]

Muslims must declare themselves free of the tyrannical leaders. Distancing oneself from the tyrant is one of the two pillars of *Tawheed* [monotheism], and *Iman* [belief]. Islam cannot root in the absence of either. God said: "Whoever disbelieves in false deities and believes in God, then he has grasped the most trustworthy hand-hold that will never break. God is All-Hearer, All-Knower."[46]

Regarding the corrupt governments' scholars, ministers, salaried writers, etc., it has been said that in every era there will be states with followers who distort the truth and speak evil even within the Sacred House and during the Sacred Months.[47] They tell the people that the treacherous rules are righteous and that they must be supported in order to maintain our nation. These people deviate from the true Path of Islam. Muslims are obliged to shun them and warn others of them.

The government displays these scholars on religious television programs where they issue *Fatwas* [religious decrees] supporting the system just like the day when King Fahd allowed the Americans to enter this land.[48] He instructed the scholars to issue a favorable *Fatwa* even though it was against Islam. These scholars corrupted the minds of the public, and because of this traitorous king, the *Ummah* [Islamic nation] today suffers because he opened the land of the Two Holy Sanctuaries to the forces of the non-believers.

Whoever studies the biographies of the righteous scholars of past difficult times - such as the life of Imam Ahmad bin Hanbal - will find vast differences between the true scholars and those who compromise. We find such stories in the *Siyar A'laam An-Nubalaa* by Imam Adh-Dhahabi:[49]

"We raise our worldly life by tearing and ripping our religion. Eventually neither our religion nor what we are raising will remain."

The second obstacle consists of those scholars who love the truth and hate falsehood but refrain from *Jihad* [holy war]. At first, these scholars saw falsehood spreading and attempted to revive the truth by enjoining good and forbidding evil. Multitudes of people were nourished by them by God's Guidance, and naturally, falsehood felt the discomfort of the truth. Then the oppressors restrained the scholars, banned them from giving sermons, removed them from their jobs, and imprisoned some of them. But for some on whom God had mercy, the remainder deviated from the truth. A person cannot make correct decisions under extreme pressure, especially when his safety is threatened. As said by the Prophet (PBUH): "A judge cannot pass judgment between two people when he is angry."[50] What happens when he is frightened? Thus, the government's policy of repression has destroyed every aspect of life, including religion. Religion requires sincere advice, but there can be none without personal security.

Fear has now divided the people into factions. One faction sides with the leaders and gives their loyalty to the corrupt states. Another faction struck an evil compromise with the leaders to protect their learning institutions, homes, families, and themselves. They let themselves stray and led others astray. God protected the third faction from the threats of the treacherous leaders. They did not compromise and remained steadfast in enjoining truth and forbidding evil in their callings to God. Because of the extreme repression, they hesitated because they were ill-prepared for the pains of *Hijra* [migration] and *Jihad* [holy war];[51] and they suffered anyway. Moreover, twenty years ago there was an excellent opportunity to rectify the situation but they failed to act because they could not make the correct decision under the difficult situation of the time.[52] That is why some of them still refrain from *Jihad* and resistance to the enemy.

Islam's ultimate victory must overcome many difficulties. This is clear from the Book of God and in the Life of His Messenger (PBUH) and his Noble Companions, may God be pleased with them. Whoever fails to follow in their footsteps will not be able to achieve the real victory of Islam because the path demands the biting of swords and the carrying of heads in the hands on the Path of God. These are the descriptions mentioned by God in the *Holy Quran*:

"O you who believe! Whoever from among you turns back from his religion, God will bring a people whom He will love and they will love Him; humble towards the believers, stern towards the disbelievers, fighting the Way of God, and never afraid of the blame of the blamers. That is the Grace of God which He Bestows on whom He Wills. God is All-Sufficient for His Creatures' needs, All-Knower."[53]

And in the incident that took place when the Prophet (PBUH) met Waraqah bin Nawfal,[54] who said to him: "Woe be to me, would that I be alive when the time comes when your people will turn against you and expel you!" So the Prophet (PBUH) replied to him: "Will they really turn against me and expel me?" Waraqah replied, "Yes, as there has never before come a man with the likes of you, except that he evokes hostility. If I live to witness that day, then I will surely stand by you and support you."

The condition of one who carries the Word of Islam is enmity from the people of falsehood; and the condition of the one who desires to establish Islam is to exert himself to the utmost with his own life and the lives of others. As Waraqah said: "If I live to witness that day, then I will surely stand by you and support you."

Such was the state of the believers on the day they made their historic pledge at Aqaba. [Mr. Bin Laden refers to the acceptance of Islam by the first twelve followers of the Prophet Muhammad (PBUH) between 620 and 624 on a hill called Aqaba outside Mina, outside Mecca.] [55]

Thus, Islam cannot be victorious merely by giving lectures. We must sacrifice our time and our wealth because the Currency of God [Paradise] is expensive. When *Jihad* [holy war] is compulsory, a vast difference exists between giving lectures and sacrificing lives and heads for Islam. That is why Al-Abbas bin Abdul-Muttalib,[56] despite following the religion of his forefathers, wanted to satisfy himself that his nephew, the Prophet (PBUH), was safe before [the latter] migrated to Medina. Al-Abbas the *Ansar* [the Prophet Muhammad's (PBUH) helpers] said,

"If you really are a people of strength ... you will realize the hostility of the Arabs and that they will ... (unite to fight you) if you accept this man into your fold."[57]

Thus, I say that because these characteristics were necessary for the people of *Iman* [belief] to protect the Messenger of God (PBUH), they are necessary today to protect the religion of the Messenger of God (PBUH).

When Al-Abbas finished his address, Al-Baraa bin Maroor said: "We have understood your words if there was any doubt in our hearts, by God we would have said it, but we have been chosen to be loyal and true to protect the Messenger (PBUH) despite the consequences."[58]

Thus, I say that Islam is the True Religion and can be established by loyalty and truth despite the consequences. Then the people of Medina stood up to pledge their allegiance.

This is exactly what the *Mujahideen* [Islamic warriors] are saying to the scholars who love the truth and do not compromise with falsehood: You have raised the banner of Islam and you know that the Religion of the Messenger of God (PBUH) is true, so your adopting Islam means opposition to the corrupt governments of the Arabs and the non-Arabs in the entire world; the sacrificing of the best of you; and the biting of swords. If you are able to bear that patiently, then protect the banner; and your reward will be with God. If you harbor even an iota of weakness in yourselves, then leave the banner of fighting and defending and refrain from interfering with the youths of the *Ummah* [Islamic nation] engaged in *Jihad* [holy war] in the Path of God. That will be more excusable before God.

What, then, are the obligations of the Muslims facing this new Zionist-Crusader war against the *Ummah*? God said: "Then fight (O Muhammad [PBUH]) in the Cause of God, you are not held responsible except for yourself, and incite the believers (to fight along with you), it may be that God will restrain the evil might of the disbelievers, and God is Stronger in Might and Stronger in Punishing."[59]

Today, the first obligation after *Iman* [belief] is defending and fighting against the enemy aggressor. Sheikh-al-Islam ibn Taymiya[60] said: "As for defending against the enemy aggressor who spoils the religion and the worldly affairs, then there is nothing more obligatory after *Iman* then repelling him and there are no conditions for this ruling."

Thus, today *Jihad* [holy war] is compulsory on the entire *Ummah* [Islamic nation]; and she will remain sinful until she produces her sons, her wealth and her power, to the extent of being able, to wage *Jihad* and defend against the evil of the disbelievers waging war on Muslims in Palestine and elsewhere. It is obligatory upon Muslims to wage *Jihad* to the utmost of their abilities in order to establish truth and eradicate falsehood. According to Sahih Muslim, the Messenger of God (PBUH): "So, whoever strives against them with his hand is a believer, and whoever strives against them by his heart is a believer, and whoever strives against them by his tongue is a believer, and beyond that there is not a mustard-seed's amount of faith."[61]

This great *Hadith* [authenticated tradition of the Prophet Muhammad (PBUH)] categorizes all of the believers as *Mujahideen* [Islamic warriors] for the victory of Islam in the Path of God. To a believer who refrains from *Jihad* [holy war] with his hand or his tongue, he is obliged to engage in *Jihad* with his heart, hating the enemies of God and working against them. He must support the believers and the *Mujahideen* and enable them to feel the brotherhood of *Iman* [belief] that connects Muslims from East to West. Only wishing to wage *Jihad* by hand and tongue is the weakest action in the Path of God. He also is obliged to boycott American products and those of her allies, and he must be especially vigilant against assisting falsehood in any way that might support the non-believers against Muslims. As stated by the scholars, this is clearly *Kufr* [non-believers]. Also, he must avoid being among those about whom God said: "Those who are miserly and enjoin miserliness on other men;"[62] or from among those about whom God said: "God already knows those among you who keep back (men) from fighting in God's Cause, and those who say to their brethren, 'Come here towards us,' while they themselves come not to the battle except a little."[63] Therefore, he must not conflate the major sin of refraining from *Jihad* [holy war] with the major sin of betrayal. Although *Jihad* is obligatory on the entire *Ummah* [Islamic nation], it is even more obligatory on the wealthy Muslims.

By God's Grace, many of the *Ummah* [Islamic nation] have opened their breasts to *Jihad* [holy war] in His Way and in the protection of Islam and the protection of His Servants. They are obliged to assist them, encourage them, and facilitate their efforts so they can repel any oppression, betrayal, or sin against the *Ummah*. They are also obliged to protect the *Jihad* and lend it support with every means at their disposal. This *Jihad* is a very valuable asset to us, as in the examples of Palestine, Chechnya, Afghanistan, Kashmir, Indonesia, the Philippines, and the other Muslim lands. In spite of vicious attacks by their enemies, the banner of *Jihad* in these places remains aloft only by the Grace of God. For those *Mujahideen* [Islamic warriors] who have made the extreme sacrifice of their blood and bones, we ask God to accept them amongst the martyrs.

I also inform you that, by the Grace of God, the *Jihad* [holy war] in Afghanistan currently is in good shape and the conditions there are very favorable to the *Mujahideen* [Islamic warriors]. We are now in the second year of our fight against the Americans; and until now, America has been unable to fulfill her objectives. To the contrary, she is now trapped in the Afghan swamp. Regarding the early victories of the Americans in which they captured the cities after the *Mujahideen* withdrew, any military expert or specialist in Afghanistan can attest that these were tactical withdrawals by the Taliban consistent with the history of the Afghans, long experienced in guerilla warfare. At the time, there existed no organized Taliban army that could have defended the cities.

Now, with God's Grace, the Afghans have re-organized and have dug in for a long guerilla war to be fought from the deep, rugged and harsh mountains of Afghanistan. They are using against the Americans the same tactics that they employed against the Soviet Union. Their rate of operations has reached two per day. This is problematic for the Americans, for they cannot protect their forces or bring stability to the country or protect President Karzai or the Afghan people.

Since last year, the *Mujahideen* [Islamic warriors] have united. They are extremely enthusiastic because they realize that they are obliged to wage *Jihad* [holy war] against the Americans. If not for a lack of resources, they would have increased their rate of operations to ten per day, the number they had mounted against the Soviets. The Americans would never be able to tolerate this. Therefore, the *Ummah* [Islamic nation] is obliged to assist the Afghanistan *Jihad* because it is one of the most important arenas of *Jihad*. Moreover, we must concentrate on Afghanistan, for defeating the Americans there will be the beginning of the end of America, God Willing. With God's Permission, neither we nor our Afghan *Mujahideen* brothers will attack you. We hope that we are not attacked by you.[64]

Today's *Ummah* [Islamic nation] finds itself in one of God's Epochs in which the *Ummah* must not tire or transgress. To the contrary, it must unite against the ranks of the disbelievers and must seek repentance from its minor and major sins. Equally important, it must shun a life of play, amusement, and extravagance and prepare for the reality of killing, fighting, attacking and destroying. Think about what Sheikh Islam Ibn Taymiya said in a similar situation: "Know, may God reform you, that it has been confirmed from many sources that the Prophet (PBUH) said: 'There will never cease to exist a group from my *Ummah* [Islamic nation], fighting for the Decree of God, overpowering their enemy, that will not be harmed by those who oppose them, until the hour approaches them and they are upon it (i.e. fighting for the truth).'"[65]

This situation, then, divides the *Ummah* into three parts: first, the victorious, who are the *Mujahideen* [Islamic warriors] against the evil ones; second the Opposing Party, who are clear in their opposition to Islam; and third the Treacherous Party, who refrain from *Jihad* [holy war] even though they practice Islam. Let every man choose his party; there is no fourth choice.

Sheikh Islam Ibn Taymiya continued: "By God, even if the Foremost Vanguard of the Muslims from amongst the Emigrants and the Helpers, like Abu Bakr, Omar, Uthman, Ali [the first four Caliphs, the "rightly guided ones"] and others, were present with us at this time, the best of their actions would be to wage *Jihad* [holy war] against this nation of criminals, and no one misses an opportunity like this, except that this activity incurs losses, self is humiliated, and he is deprived of a good portion of both his worldly life and his Hereafter."[66]

Therefore, I advise the youth to acclimate their minds to *Jihad* [holy war] because they are the first ones upon whom *Jihad* is obligatory, just as Ash-Shatibi[67] pointed out. They must know that targeting Americans and Jews and killing them in any corner on Earth is the greatest of their obligations and the most expedient method by which to gain nearness to God. I also advise them to be smart and to kill secretly.

Congratulations to you and particularly to our brothers in Palestine whose *Mujahideen* [Islamic warriors] brothers are continuing to follow the path of *Jihad* targeting Jews and Americans. We will never abandon or forsake you, so continue your efforts with the Blessings of God. We are with you. Before concluding, I incite myself and my believing brothers to *Jihad* by these words:

And most surely this year will I lead my steed and hurl it and my soul at one of the targets.

So O my Lord if my demise has come, then let it not be upon a bier draped with green mantles.

But let my grave be an eagle's belly, its resting place in the sky's atmosphere amongst perched eagles.

And I become a martyr, dwelling amongst a band, attacked in a level mountain pass of the Earth.

Knights of Qahtaan: devoutness to God has joined them together, they descend when the armies meet.

When they depart from their worldly life, they depart from the harm and reach the appointment found in the scriptures."[68]

In conclusion, I advise myself and my Muslim brothers to

increase supplications and humble ourselves before God. Perhaps God will accept our repentance, relieve our calamity, and release our imprisoned brothers from the hands of the Americans and their agents, especially Sheikhs Omar Abdur Rahman and Said bin Zuair, and our brothers in Guantanamo Bay, Cuba.[69] May God make resolute the *Mujahideen* [Islamic warriors] in Palestine and in the other Muslim lands. May He Help us against our enemies. I also advise you to increase prayer and ponder and recite *The Holy Quran*; for it is a reminder, a cure, a guide, and a source of mercy. God says: "O mankind! There has come to you good advice from your Lord (*The Holy Quran*) and a healing for that (disease of ignorance, etc.) in your breasts — a guidance and a mercy for the believers."[70]

Our Lord, give us the good in this life, the good in the Hereafter, and save us from the Fire of Hell. "And God will overcome with all His Affairs, but most of men know not."[71]

And the last of our prayers is Praise to God, Lord of the Worlds.

Chapter 13

Comments On Jihad[1]
July 2003

Since the fall of the Islamic Caliphate [Turkish President Kemel Ataturk abolished the Islamic Caliphate in 1924],[2] governments that rule in violation of the *Holy Quran* have arisen in the Middle East. In truth, these governments are fighting against the Law of God. In spite of numerous universities, schools, books, *Imams* [clerics], mosques, and reciters of the *Holy Quran*, Islam is in retreat because the people are straying from the path of the Prophet Muhammad [peace be upon him, hereinafter "PBUH," words of grace that must attend any oral or written reference to any of the Prophets recognized by Islam].

The *Ummah* [Islamic nation] can only be established if five conditions are met: a gathering of Muslims, a hearing, obedience to God, *Hijra* [a migration to a friendly venue] and *Jihad* [holy war].[3] Without *Hijra* and *Jihad*, the Path of God cannot be understood.

We no longer have a reputable Islamic country to which to migrate. A rare opportunity existed, but since the fall of the Caliphate, the Crusaders have prevented a true Islamic state. The Crusaders temporarily relinquished their opposition to an Islamic state when the Russians invaded Afghanistan in 1979 because they feared Russia. They attempted to repel the Russians by any means, including the use of the

Mujahideen [Islamic warriors] and the *Jihadi* [individuals engaged in *Jihad*] warriors of Islam.[4]

The opportunity arose in Afghanistan; but ten years later, the *Ummah* [Islamic nation][5] failed its obligation, especially the clerics and Islamic universities. Only a few youth came to Afghanistan to help the *Mujahideen* [Islamic warriors], and some funds were contributed by some businessmen. But these efforts could not overcome local tribal loyalties.[6] Our Afghani brothers could have established an Islamic state, but the opportunity was lost. Since then, matters have worsened.

With God's Help, the Taliban reconciled the warring Afghanis and established the Taliban state. They stayed in power for six years but succumbed to a people resistant to their ways and subject to the influence of the slanders of the world's media toward the Taliban.[7]

Though only a few hours from Islamic countries, the Taliban state disappeared.[8] No Islamic country tried to help. Now the *Ummah* [Islamic nation] has the power to re-establish the Islamic state and the Caliphate. The people must be taught this, and the forces of opposition must learn that they are sinners because of their resistance.

Those who say that *Jihad* [holy war] does not require the entire *Ummah* [Islamic nation] are correct. Actual resistance to the *Kufr* [non-believer] enemy is carried on by only a small portion of the *Ummah*. However, *Jihad* is every Muslim's obligation. Our opponents claim that even if they were to send a few thousand *Mujahideen* [Islamic warriors], we could not absorb them; or that it is illogical for all of us to engage in *Jihad*.[9] But *Jihad* is the top priority because it is a personal obligation. As stated by Sheikh al-Islam, only Faith itself is more important than repelling the aggressors who corrupt Islam and the world.[10]

Once there are sufficient numbers of *Mujahideen* [holy warriors] to repel the enemy, then the personal obligation of *Jihad* [holy war] transforms into a collective obligation. Anybody who claims that *Jihad* is eclipsed by other rituals is misinformed of [the Prophet] Muhammad's (PBUH) true path.

The young who have the capacity to sacrifice themselves for Islam hurt themselves by obeying clerics who refrain from *Jihad*. Such clerics must be ignored.

They prevent the young from carrying out their individual and collective obligations. Even in a world of clerics, there can be no religious revival without the five conditions.

Great evil is being spread through the *Ummah* [Islamic nation] by official clerics who stand at the sides of the corrupt rulers of the region, adopting non-Islamic ideas and man-made laws and propagating them through the media and their own networks. Such clerics are calling the *Ummah* to the gates of Hell.

This heresy against God and His Prophet (PBUH) is publicized in the newspapers, television, radio, and symposiums; but nobody opposes it. In such a scenario, besides Faith itself, only *Jihad* [holy war] takes precedence. Yet the official clerics ignore it, but for the few of them who have God's mercy [i.e., who are uncorrupted]. Most of them are too busy praising the despotic rulers of the region who ignore God and his Prophet (PBUH). In turn, the rulers reciprocate by praising the corrupt clerics, congratulating the latter for deceiving the *Ummah* [Islamic nation].

Today the *Ummah* [Islamic nation] faces its greatest catastrophe. Past crises were localized, but today's crisis touches the entire *Ummah* because of the communications revolution in which the media enters every home. No home in the city or in the desert will be spared from *Fitna* [internal strife].

The official clerics are the prisoners and hostages of the despot leaders of the region. The young understand that a civil servant is a civil servant. Ironically, some of them object to our connecting the official clerics to the tyrannical rulers in spite of their obvious connection.[11]

The true role of some civil servants is to spread falsehoods. For example, the Minister of Information usually bears false witness. He and his ministry deceive the people every day, portraying the country in the best light and the ruler as an unrivaled genius. Likewise, the Defense Minister says that our situation is good and our armed forces are good, though we have been occupied for more than ten years. [Mr. Bin Laden refers to the continuing presence of United States military forces in Saudi Arabia and in the Gulf States after the conclusion of the 1991 Persian Gulf War.][12] Everybody in the world knows that we are occupied and that American aircraft can take off day or night without prior notification to the regime; then the Defense Minister tells us we are independent. That is a falsehood.

But the danger does not really arise from such Ministers because they cannot really mislead anyone; the people already know that they are deceiving them. The real danger comes from the official clerics who bear false witness every morning and evening and lead the *Ummah* [Islamic nation] astray. The situation is made even worse when the falsehood comes from the venues of *Al-Haram* [the mosque in Mecca that houses the *Kaba*, the holiest site in Islam] and the *Kaba* [a small building in which the Prophet Muhammad (PBUH) destroyed the pre-Islamic idols].[13]

Falsehood is one of the gravest sins, and it is even graver every Friday in the house of *Al-Haram*,[14] and every time the corrupt clerics lead the *Ummah* astray for a handful of coins. [The reference to Friday refers to the Muslim Sabbath.] These clerics are civil servants to whom no reasonable person can turn for advice about religious matters. As Sheikh Muhammad bin Abd al-Wahhab[15] said, the least you can say about them is that they are corrupt. The people must boycott and banish them.

It is error to say that Islam can exist in Saudi Arabia even though the rulers rejected God and His Prophet (PBUH) a hundred years ago, when they [i.e., the Saud royal family] rose to power through English strength, English support, English weapons, and English gold. [Mr. Bin Laden is noting that the Sauds received money and support from Britain during their rise to power, which culminated in the patriarch Abdul Aziz declaring himself to be the King of the new Kingdom of Saudi Arabia in 1926.[16] There can be no Faith or Islamic rule if the ruler is a non-believer. Only a credible Muslim can assume the position of ruler [of a Muslim country].

The rulers of the Arabian Gulf States deceive us and support non-believers while claiming to cling to Islam. Their deceit is compounded by their creation of entities studying Islamic law and jurisprudence that are actually intended to lead the people astray. Their aim is to enable their official *Ulema* [Islamic scholars] to utilize satellite television and radio stations to broadcast *Fatwas* [religious decrees][17] issued for the rulers' own advantage, not to spread the Faith. If they truly wanted to spread the Faith, they would allow faithful [i.e., uncorrupted] *Ulema* on television and radio.

For example, when the Saudi Arabian government decided to invite American Crusader [military] forces into the land of the Two Holy Places,[18] and the youth angrily opposed the decision, the Saudi official clerics issued *Fatwas* praising the ruler, whom they referred to as *Wali Amir* [a blessed person to be respected].[19] In truth, he was no *Wali Amir*.

[The Saudi government invited American forces into their country in August 1990 for fear of invasion by Iraqi forces that had just conquered Kuwait.]

People may wonder and ask how it is possible for an anonymous *Sheikh* [also, *Imam*, or cleric][20] who is a respected elder to betray the Religion for a small worldly sum of money. I respond that nobody is immune from error. Over the past centuries, the history of the *Ummah* [Islamic nation] is characterized by recurring errors. Many times, clerics have misled because of threats, beatings, imprisonment, or perhaps even death. Few of them have remained steadfast; and as you know, one of these was Ahmad ibn Hanbal.[21]

The corrupt regime usually appropriates vast sums of money for these corrupt clerics whose role is to legitimize the regime.[22] For example, in Saudi Arabia, the offices of the Clerics Authority are adjacent to the royal palace. In Egypt, the building of the *Fatwa* Authority of *Al Azhar* [University] is adjacent to [Egyptian President] Hosni Mubarak's Palace.[23] How can it be possible to ask such a civil servant for an objective ruling regarding the king and whether the king is supporting non-believers?

Clerics who wear robes and grand titles are still civil servants. Their own books tell us that one of the "ten voiders" of Islam is supporting non-believers.[24] Privately, they speak candidly, but openly they are afraid and skew their interpretations in favor of the regimes.

The survival of Islam and our resistance to any domestic or foreign attempt to distort it lay in the strength of martyrdom as our weapon. *Jihad* [holy war] attains truth and demolishes falsehood. Therefore, the youth who would sacrifice themselves for God and their love for Islam must pay no heed to those civil servants who refrain from *Jihad*. Because of the communications revolution, young people learn from a young age that certain *Imams* [clerics] sit by the side of the ruler every Monday.[25] The people are misled into believing that if the ruler were no good the *Imams* would not be with him. They disregard the fact that the *Imams* are civil servants employed by the Royal Offices or the Interior Ministry.

The Prophet Muhammad's (PBUH) laws are nowhere found among the religious laws of the official clerics and rulers. They do not understand the path of God. We must acknowledge that Islam requires us to reject the people who speak falsehoods.[26]

Faithful clerics bear the characteristics described in the *Holy Quran*, the most important of which are Faith and *Jihad* [holy war] for the Sake of God. Embarking on *Hijra* [migration], supporting God and his Prophet (PBUH), and waging *Jihad* mark the faithful ones. Contrariwise, the other clerics are silent when the rulers support non-believers and do not rule in accordance with the laws sent down by God. They praise despots and ignore the towers of the banks that charge *Riba* [usury, including interest on money lent] next to the *Al-Haram* Mosque in Mecca. No faithful cleric can deny that *Riba* is a great sin.[27]

The reality is that Saudi Arabia is occupied by non-believers. The greatest obligation after Faith is repelling the aggressive enemy. The Saudi rulers' own statements attest to the situation. In a press interview with several agencies of the world press, Prince Talal bin Abd al-Aziz[28] said that if the Saudis told the Americans to leave, they would not. That is candor. The land is occupied, but the people are preoccupied with rituals. We must focus on making *Jihad* [holy war] for the Sake of God. We are obliged to establish truth and eradicate falsehood.[29]

Chapter 14

Commentary On The 9/11 Attacks[1]

September 11, 2003

Those youths inflicted heavy losses on the enemy's morale and materials. They also disrupted the enemy's hostile plans. Documents have now shown that the enemy planned to occupy and partition the region [the Middle East and south Asia] six months ahead of the two conquests. [Mr. Bin Laden is referring to the United States' invasions of Afghanistan and Iraq.][2]

The disruption (i.e., the 9/11 attacks) awoke the Muslim people from their slumber and caused them to rise up in *Jihad* [holy war][3] in the name of God.

I had the honor of knowing these youths. God has honored them and allowed them to champion the cause of Islam. I see them only as seeds planted in the Faith by God and grown in obedience to Him. May God Bless them.

"These are my forefathers; get me men like them if we are to meet again, O Jarir."[4]

To learn faithfulness, honesty, generosity, and courage in support of religion, one must emulate the examples of Said al-Ghamidi, Muhammad Atta, Khalid al-Mihdhar, Ziad al-Jarrahi, Marwan al-Shehhi, and their brothers, may God have mercy on them. [Mr. Bin Laden names some of the 9/11 hijackers.][5]

These persons learned from the *Hadiths* [traditions] of our Prophet Muhammad, may God's Peace, Mercy, and Blessings be upon him [hereinafter "PBUH," words of grace that must attend any oral or written reference to the Prophets recognized by Islam], who is the most honest, courageous, and generous man.[6] He said: "You will never find me to be stingy, a coward, or a liar."[7] These traits cannot sustain Islam. Whoever has these traits cannot champion the Faith.

I say to those who have these traits or who have failed to carry out *Jihad*, "He who is not convinced of killing should go away and not influence those who are convinced (of killing)."[8] I say to them: "he who fears climbing mountains will always live among holes."[9]

Mankind is judged by the smallest parts of his body: his tongue and his heart.[10] However, the faithful youth are men with big minds and great resolve. They repeatedly protected themselves from succumbing to the deceptions of the agent governments [i.e., agents of the West] and their institutions, which paint vice as virtue, virtue as vice, falsehood as right, and enemies as friends.[11]

This is because these young men were true believers; and believers are not bitten twice from the same hole, as our Prophet (PBUH) says.[12]

These youths knew that the road to eternal damnation is opposition to the *Sharia* [Islamic law].[13] They refused to lick the boots of even princes and *Ulema* [Islamic scholars][14] over this subject. They believe in the preeminence of the *Sharia* over the safety of men, regardless of their greatness.

In God's Faith [Islam], people are treated as equals. They are guided by the saying of the Prophet (PBUH): "By God, if Fatima Bint-Muhammad [daughter of the Prophet Muhammad (PBUH)] were to steal, I would chop off her hand."[15]

These young men have understood the core phrase of Islam: "There is no god but God."[16] It must control our actions and guide us in all aspects of our life.

However, on Earth reality is otherwise. The rulers' whims now prevail over the people's wishes. Even though the rulers allow the people to perform some religious rituals, these young men knew that the rulers were wrong.[17] In fact, the rulers are apostates, even if they pray, fast, and claim to be Muslims.

These young men refused to stay behind and engage in mundane matters. They set out on *Jihad* [holy war] and hurried to champion the Cause of God and Islam's call for monotheism: "There is no god but God. Muhammad (PBUH) is the Prophet of God."

They waged *Jihad* against the non-believers. Their situation was like that of Muaz bin al-Jamuh, when he asked Abdur Rahman bin-Awf, the following question:

"'O Uncle, do you know Abu-Jahl?'[18]

Bin-Awf said: 'What, my nephew?'

Bin al-Jamuh said: 'I have been told that he called the Messenger of God by names. By God, if I see him, I will engage him in a fight until the one who is predestined to die before the other is killed.'"

This is honesty and faith. Each and every matter has its own reality.

The reality of the present hero, Saeed al-Ghamidi, and his brothers is that they showed the veracity of their Faith by offering themselves and their souls for the Sake of God. Thus, they gained a status that has greatly angered the infidels and will continue to anger them for a long time, God Willing.

This occurred because they chose practical solutions to champion the cause of Islam and rejected the unjust and atheistic solutions offered by the United Nations, parliaments, and the tyrannical rulers, who have turned themselves into demigods who legislate and reject God's Rulings.

Moreover, they did not heed the futile solutions of the prevaricators — the Arabs of the desert [the Arabs of the Arabian Peninsula] — who failed to join the *Mujahideen* [Islamic warriors], who were preoccupied with their wealth, and who deceived themselves for dozens of years into thinking that they were too busy for such matters.[19] They are different from the *Mujahideen* because they view *Jihad* [holy war] as hardship, resulting in separation of fathers from sons and risking one's life and wealth. Thus, Satan prevents such a man from embarking on *Jihad* just like the others who failed to join the *Mujahideen*.

And regarding him who views *Jihad* as the marketplace of Paradise with its doors open, and who fears that the doors will close if he displeases God by being even one hour late, the opponents of *Jihad* will make him lag behind.

God says: "And if they had intended to march out, certainly, they would have made some preparation for it; but God was averse to their being sent forth, so he made them lag behind, and it was said to them: 'Sit you among those who sit (at home).'"[20]

If he does not respond to God's Call and fails to embark on *Jihad* by obeying the Arabs of the desert who failed to join the *Mujahideen* [Islamic warriors], God will not come between him and his heart, and thus he will stray from the Right Path and be one of the sinful ones.

God says: "O you who believe! Answer God and his Messenger (PBUH), when he calls you to that which will give you life, and know that God comes between a person and his heart. And verily, to Him you shall be gathered."[21]

God says: "Say: If your fathers, your sons, your brothers, your wives, your kindred, the wealth that you have gained, the commerce in which you fear a decline, and the dwellings in which you delight are dearer to you than God and His Messenger (PBUH), and striving hard and fighting in His Cause, then wait until God brings about His Decision. And God does not guide the people who are *Al-Fasiqun* [the rebellious, disobedient to God]."[22]

Chapter 15

Praise be to God, who says: "O Prophet! Strive hard against the non-believers and the hypocrites, and stand firm against them. Their abode is Hell — an evil refuge indeed."[2]

Prayers and peace upon our Prophet Muhammad, peace be upon him [hereinafter "PBUH," words of grace that must attend any oral or written reference to any of the Prophets recognized by Islam], who says: "He who is killed for his money is a martyr, he who is killed for his blood is a martyr, he who is killed for his Religion is a martyr and he who is killed for his family is a martyr."[3]

This is our second letter to our Muslim brethren in Iraq. You are the grandsons of Saad, Al-Muthanna, Khalid and Al-Muanna, and Saladin. Peace, Mercy and Blessings of God be upon you.[4]

I congratulate you on your blessed *Jihad* [holy war].[5] Indeed, you have slaughtered the enemy and have pleased the hearts of all Muslims, particularly the Palestinian people. You will be rewarded by Almighty God. Thank you for your *Jihad*, and may God help you.

Be glad of the good news: America is mired in the swamps of the Tigress and Euphrates rivers. Because of Iraq and its oil, [President George W.] Bush is easy prey. He is now in an embarrassing situation,

142

and today America is being ruined before the eyes of the whole world.

Thanks to God, who answered America's malicious deeds, which forced it to seek assistance from criminals and beg for mercenaries from East and West. Your extraordinary punishment of America is no surprise; you are the sons of those great kings who took Islam to the East until they reached China.[6]

Be warned that the Iraq War is a new Crusade against the *Ummah* [Islamic nation]. It is a decisive war for the *Ummah*. For the uninitiated, its repercussions are dangerous and wicked for Islam and for Muslims. Oh, youth of Islam everywhere, especially in Iraq's neighboring countries and in Yemen, *Jihad* [holy war][7] is your duty and righteousness is your path. Never be followers of those who act to satisfy their material desires or those who have allied themselves with tyrants in order to discourage you from *Jihad*.

As before in Palestine, Egypt, Jordan, Yemen and elsewhere, voices have arisen in Iraq calling for a peaceful, democratic solution in dealing with the apostate governments, or with the Jewish and Crusader invaders, instead of fighting in the name of God. Hence, it is necessary to warn against the danger of these deceptive words that contradict God's Teachings to fight in the name of God.

How can you obey those who have never fought for God? Have you never imagined that it was they who followed their material desires and disassembled the *Ummah's* [Islamic nation][8] stock of faithful men? These men have chosen democracy, the faith of the ignorant, by becoming members of legislative councils. They have gone astray[9] and have misled many people.

Why do they become members of the councils of polytheism? Islam has rejected such representative councils. Those who obey their leaders or *Ulema* [Islamic scholars] in permitting what God has prohibited, such as becoming members of the legislative councils, or in prohibiting what God has permitted, such as *Jihad* [holy war] for the Sake of God, have made the kings and corrupt scholars their lords rather than to obey God.

I call upon Muslims in general, and the Iraqi people in particular, to warn the collaborators to refrain from supporting the American Crusaders and their supporters. Whatever their official titles, those who assist the United States and the coalition forces are renegades and infidels. This also applies to those who support infidel parties like the

Baathist Party, the Kurdish parties and the like.[10]

It is also obvious that any government organized by America will be a puppet government and a traitorous regime, as are the other governments of the region, such as Karzai's and Mahmoud Abbas's governments, which were formed to avert *Jihad* [holy war]. [Mr. Bin Laden refers to President Hamid Karzai of Afghanistan and President Mahmoud Abbas of the Palestinian Authority.][11]

The "road map" peace plan is only a new link in the chain of conspiracies to stop the blessed *Intifada* [uprising, referring to the Palestinian uprising in the Occupied Territories that has been continuing, with temporary truces, since September of 2000]. Hence, *Jihad* [holy war] must continue until a Muslim government is established on the basis of the *Sharia* [Islamic law].[12]

Fellow Muslims! This is no joking matter. This is the time for those who can contribute assistance, energy or money to the *Jihad*. Under such circumstances, people will be adjudged to separate the honest from the mendacious and the altruistic from the selfish. Our prudent Muslim women also must play their role.[13]

I inform my *Mujahideen* [Islamic warriors][14] brothers in Iraq that I share their concerns. I feel what they feel, and I envy them in their *Jihad* [holy war]. As God is my witness, if I had the opportunity to join you, I would not delay. How could I not join you when our Prophet [Muhammad (PBUH)] said that were it too hard for the other Muslims, he himself would join every battle for the Sake of God? He also said that he wished he could join a battle, be killed, battle again and be killed, and battle again and be killed.[15]

This is the path of our Prophet Muhammad (PBUH), the path that leads us to the triumph of our Faith and the establishment of the *Ummah* [Islamic nation]. You Muslims have to follow this path. You are the descendents of Rabiaa, Mudar, and the Kurdish clans. You must hoist your flags. Never be scared of the infidels and their weaponry, for God has weakened their cunning.[16]

Never be afraid of their numbers because their hearts are empty. Their strength has begun to weaken, militarily and economically. This was particularly true after the blessed day of New York City [9/11], by the grace of God, when their losses following the attack and its aftermath reached more than one trillion dollars.[17] Moreover, America has had a budget deficit for the third consecutive year. This year, the deficit reached a record peak of more than U.S. $450 billion. Praise be to God.[18]

In conclusion, I compliment my brothers the *Mujahideen* [Islamic warriors] in Iraq; the heroes in Baghdad, the center of the Caliphate; the supporters of Islam, the descendents of Saladin [the Muslim leader who seized back Jerusalem from the Christian Crusaders in 1187]; the free people of Baquba, Mawsil, and Anbar;[19]and those who have traveled to Iraq to fight for the sake of God so that they may be killed for the sake of their Religion. To those who have left their parents, sons, relatives and homes, I convey my salutations.

I also tell you that you are the soldiers of God, the arrows of Islam and the first line of defense for the *Ummah* [Islamic nation]. The Romans have gathered under the banner of the Christian cross[20] to fight against the Nation of Muhammad (PBUH). So, maintain the *Jihad* [holy war]. I hope Islam will not be disappointed by you. God is blessing your efforts. After God, we are pinning our hopes on you. So do not disappoint the *Ummah* [Islamic nation] — follow the example of Saad (may God be pleased with him) who said on the day of the Battle of Al-Khandaq[21] that death is welcome when one is destined to die anyway.

I call upon all of us to obey God, implicitly and explicitly; to recite the *Holy Quran*, contemplate its meaning; and to follow its teachings, particularly Chapters Eight and Nine.[22]...You must glorify and pray to God. May God grant us virtue in this world and in the Afterlife and protect us from Hell. May God lead the hearts of our youth to the path of *Jihad* [holy war], strengthen their hearts, encourage them, help them to reach their targets, and link their hearts together in fidelity and unity.

May God bestow His Triumph upon the *Mujahideen* [Islamic warriors] in Palestine, Iraq, Chechnya, Kashmir, the Philippines and Afghanistan, and everywhere.[23]

Chapter 16

Message To Americans[1]
October 18, 2003

Oppression only oppresses the oppressors.

This message to the American people concerns their aggression in Iraq. Peace be upon those who follow the righteous path.

Some believe that you are a reasonable people. But the majority of you are vulgar and lack ethics and good manners. You elect from among you evil people — the greatest liars and the most indecent — to be your leaders. You are enslaved by the richest and most influential among you, especially the Jews, who use the lie of a democratic Israel to entice you to support the Israelis, their schemes, and their abject antagonism toward Islam.[2] The cost of these schemes is paid for in our blood and land and now in your blood and economy.

Recent events have proved this: the war in Iraq has nothing to do with you. With heavy clubs and hard hearts, [President George W.] Bush and his gang are an evil to all mankind. In the eyes of the world, they have stabbed the truth until they killed it. Their behavior has encouraged hypocrisy and has shamelessly spread vice and political bribes among the heads of state of the Middle East.

This gang and their leader enjoy lying, war, and looting to serve their own ambitions. The blood of the children of Vietnam, Somalia,

146

Afghanistan, and Iraq is still dripping from their teeth. They have fooled you and deceived you into invading Iraq a second time, and in doing so they have lied to you and the whole world.

Nations consist of no more than their ethics and morals. If these disappear, then the nation disappears. Claiming he was defending international peace and American security, Bush has sent your sons into a lion's den, to slaughter and be slaughtered.

On the one hand, regardless of the harm that will befall your people and your economy, he is carrying out the demands of the Zionist lobby that helped him into the White House. These demands are to destroy the military strength of Iraq because of its proximity to the Jews in occupied Palestine.[3] On the other hand, Bush is concealing the Zionist lobbying and his own ambitions for oil. He is still following the mentality of his ancestors who killed the Native Americans and stole their land and wealth. This time, he thought the task would be easy and that his lies would not be exposed.

But God sent him to Baghdad, the seat of the Caliphate [the seat of the Abbasid Caliphate was in Baghdad from 750 – 1258],[4] the homeland of people who prefer death to honey. So the Iraqis have turned his profits into losses, his joy into sadness, and now he is merely looking for a way back home.[5]

Thanks be to God Almighty who has exposed Bush's lies and made his term as president a continuous catastrophe.

To Bush I note that you are begging the world to come to your aid and begging for mercenaries from every corner of the world, even the small states. The begging has destroyed your pride and has revealed how trivial and weak you are, even though you claim to be defending the world.[6] Now you are like the knight who tried to protect the people from the Sword of Malik, and ended up begging someone to protect him.[7]

We reserve the right to retaliate, at the appropriate time and place, against all of the countries involved: the United Kingdom, Spain, Australia, Poland, Japan, and Italy; and those Muslim states that took part, especially the Gulf States, and in particular Kuwait, which has become a launching pad for the crusading forces.[8]

Now that all of the lies and the greatest liar Bush have been exposed, I say to the American forces in Iraq that your presence there compounds the oppression and is a great folly.[9] It demonstrates that you are selling your own lives and spilling your blood to swell the bank accounts of the White House gang, their fellow arms dealers, and the proprietors of great corporations. The greatest folly in life is to sell your life for the lives of others.

In conclusion, I say to the American people that we will continue to fight you and continue to conduct martyrdom operations inside and outside the United States until you depart from your oppressive course, abandon your folly, and rein in your fools. You know that we are counting our dead, may God Bless them, especially in Palestine, who are killed by your allies, the Jews. We are going to take revenge for them from your blood, God willing, as we did on the day of New York City [9/11].[10] Remember what I said to you on that day about our security and your security. [Mr. Bin Laden described 9/11 as "blowback" for American policies injurious to Muslims.][11] Baghdad, the seat of the Caliphate, will not fall to you, God willing, and we will fight you as long as we carry our guns. And if we fall, our sons will take our place.

May our mothers become childless if we leave any of you alive on our soil.[12]

This Page Left Intentionally Blank For Notes

Chapter 17

Statement To The Entire Islamic Nation[1]
January 4, 2004

May God's Peace, Mercy, and Blessings be upon you.

My message is about urging *Jihad* [holy war][2] to repel the great plots against our *Ummah* [Islamic nation],[3] particularly the more obvious ones like the Crusaders'[4] occupation of Baghdad, the court of the Caliphate [the seat of the Abbasid Caliphate was located in Baghdad from 750– 1258],[5] with the help of apostates, under the false pretense of searching for weapons of mass destruction.[6] Also, I note the vicious attempt to destroy the *Al-Aqsa* Mosque [the third holiest site in Islam, located in *Al-Quds* (Jerusalem)],[7] and the *Mujahideen* [Islamic warriors] in beloved Palestine under the false pretense of the "road map" peace plan and the Geneva Peace Initiative.[8]

America has clarified its intentions in its recent statements about changing the beliefs, curricula, and morals of the Muslims so they can become more tolerant. Clearly, this is a religio-economic war. Iraq's occupation is but another link in the Zionist-Crusader chain of evil. The complete occupation of the remaining Gulf States[9] will be the opening to the attempt at control and domination of the whole world. The great powers believe that the key to controlling the world is to control the Gulf States, because of their large oil reserves and the [strategic value] of the Arabian Gulf.

O Muslims! The situation is critical and the crisis momentous. By God, I intend to safeguard Islam and your lives in this world. Lend me your ears and open your hearts so we may analyze these dark misfortunes and find a way to avert calamity.

The West's occupation of our countries is not new. The struggle with the West began centuries ago [the eight original Crusades began in 1095 and continued until 1270],[10] and will continue because right and falsehood will clash until Judgment Day. Note this fundamental rule: there can be no dialogue with occupiers except through arms. This rule applies today, and it is what we need. In the past, Islamic countries were liberated from the Crusaders' military occupation only by *Jihad* [holy war] in the Cause of God.

Using the pretext of fighting terrorism, the West is doing its best to discredit *Jihad* and kill *Mujahideen* [Islamic warriors]. The region's hypocrites are supporting the West in this attempt because they know that *Jihad* is a threat to their own regimes and conspiracies. *Jihad* is the right path; therefore, seek it. If we attempt to defeat the West by any means other than Islam, then we would merely be going in circles. We would also be like our forefathers, the *Al-Ghasasinah*.[11] Their elders were concerned about those among their number being appointed officers and local governors in the Arabian Peninsula by the Romans because they would be required to protect Roman interests by killing Arabs. Such is the character of the new *Al-Ghasasinah*: today's Arab rulers.

O Muslims! If you do not punish the occupiers for their sins in Jerusalem and Iraq[12], they shall defeat you. They will also rob you of the land of *Al-Haramain* [Mecca and Medina, the two holiest places in Islam].[13] Today they robbed you of Baghdad, and tomorrow they will rob you of Riyadh [Saudi Arabia], and so on, unless God deems otherwise. Sufficient for us is God.

How can we stop this tremendous onslaught? In dark times, some *Ulema* [Islamic scholars] call for uniting all of the governments with the people. Everyone must do what is required to repel the Zionist-Crusader onslaught. The question arises whether the governments of the Islamic world are capable of renouncing their relations with the United States and defending the Faith in unity with the *Ummah* [Islamic nation].

Others strangely claim that the path to righteousness lay only in defending the individual country itself. In response, I submit that even if you have an excuse to refrain from *Jihad* [holy war], you do not have the right to rely on the unjust ones, e.g., the United States, the West and the hypocrites. To do so makes you responsible not only for your own sins but also for the sins of those whom you misguide.

Fear God for your sake and for the sake of the *Ummah* [Islamic nation]. The welfare of Islam does not justify flattering dictators.[14]

The Gulf States were totally vulnerable to the Iraqi invasion in 1990. They sought help from the Crusaders, led by the United States.[15] How can these States now stand up to the United States?

In short, these States helped the United States attack Iraq, which had previously allied with them through mutual defense agreements. Those mutual defense covenants were reiterated by the Arab League only a few days before the American attack on Iraq. The Gulf States completely violated them. They betrayed the *Ummah* [Islamic nation].[16]

These regimes vacillated before deciding to attack Iraq. Sometimes they rejected participation in the pending war, and sometimes they joined in the U.N. resolutions. In fact, their populations opposed participation. However, the governments finally submitted to U.S. pressure. They opened their air, land, and sea bases to American use during the military campaign despite the tremendous implications of their decision.[17]

The most important implication was that it was a sin against Islamic tenets.[18] To them, the most dangerous development was their fear that the Iraq invasion had opened the door to the toppling of their own regimes by the intervention of foreign armed forces from abroad, especially after they saw Saddam Hussein under arrest.[19] He was their former comrade in treason and an agent of the United States when it ordered him to provoke the first Gulf War between Iraq and Iran. [The Iran-Iraq War lasted from 1980 to 1988. The United States provided support for Iraq throughout the War.][20]

That war consumed everything and plunged the region into an abyss from which it has not recovered to this day. The region's leaders know that their turn will come. They do not have the will to confront the aggressor. In addition, they believe that they lack the necessary material resources. In reality, they were prevented from establishing their own credible military forces when long ago they were forced to sign secret pledges.[21]

In short, such a ruler cannot defend the country. Those who

support the infidels over the Muslims and who, in order to remain safe, leave the blood, honor, and property of their brothers to the enemy — claiming that they really love their brothers but are forced into this path — are apt to do likewise against each other in the Gulf States, or even within their own states.

Those who read and understand the history of kings know that they are capable of committing even more serious transgressions. Indeed, the region's rulers have betrayed the sons of the land by persecuting and imprisoning them, unjustly accusing them of becoming like the *Al-Khawarji*[22] sect, who declared Muslims to be infidels and killed them. We hold the victims of the rulers to be martyrs and God will judge them. The campaign of the rulers against the sons of the land was intended to win favor with the United States and implement its orders. All this happened before the Riyadh explosions in Rabi al-Awwal in [May 2003].[23]

The above has clarified the extent of the danger to the region. Clearly, the rulers are not qualified to carry the banner of Islam and defend the Muslims. In fact, they have proved that they are implementing the schemes of the enemies of the *Ummah* [Islamic nation] and that they are capable of abandoning their countries and people.

Having exposed the rulers, we now examine their policies. Anyone who does so will quickly see that they harbor Crusader loyalties and follow their own whims, desires, and personal interests. The problem is not one of secondary importance, like personal corruption confined to the palace. Rather, the flaw lay in the approach: the spread through all social levels of belief in the absolute supremacy of the rulers and in absolute obedience to them instead of to Islam. In other countries, they use the guise of parliaments and democracy.

Thus, in all walks of life, the people of the Arab countries have suffered great decline in religious and worldly matters. We are in this miserable situation because many of us lack a correct and comprehensive understanding of Islam. Many of us understand Islam as meaning only the performance of some rituals of worship, like praying and fasting. Despite the great importance of these rituals, Islam encompasses all aspects of life. It includes economic, military, and political affairs, as well as the scales by which we weigh the actions of men — rulers, *Ulema* [Islamic scholars] and others. Islam teaches us how to deal with the ruler according to prohibitions set by God that the ruler cannot violate. We believe that the clear solution lay tightly holding onto Islam, through which God granted us pride in past centuries, and in installing a strong and faithful leadership that applies the *Holy Quran* to us and raises the true banner of *Jihad* [holy war].

The honest people who are concerned about this situation, such as the uncorrupted *Ulema* [Islamic scholars], respected leaders, dignitaries, notables, and businessmen, should meet in a safe place away from the shadow of these repressive regimes and form a council for *Ahl al-Hal wa al-Aqd* [literally, "those who loose and tie," meaning righteous people qualified to remove leaders][24] to fill the vacuum caused by the religious disqualification of these regimes and the rulers' deficiencies. The *Ummah* [Islamic nation] has the right to appoint an *Imam* [leader]. The *Ummah* also has the right to compel him to correct his course if he deviates from Islam and to remove him if warranted, e.g., for apostasy and treason.

This temporary council should be made up of the minimum number of people available without involving the rest of the people, unless the Religion allows otherwise.

The number can increase as the situation improves, God Willing. The council's policy should be based on the Book of God and the *Sunnah* [words and deeds][25] the Prophet Muhammad (PBUH). They should begin by directing Muslims to the priorities of the moment and by leading them to a safe haven. However, their first priorities should be uniting the Muslims under the word of monotheism; defending Islam, its people, and its countries; and declaring a general mobilization of the *Ummah* [Islamic nation] to repel the raid of the Romans, which started in Iraq. Nobody knows where it will end.[26]

God is Sufficient for us and He is the best support.

This Page Left Intentionally Blank For Notes

Chapter 18

Offer of Peace Treaty With Europe[1]

April 15, 2004

This message is addressed to our neighbors north of the Mediterranean Sea in which we propose a peace treaty in response to positive developments that have emerged there.

What happened on September 11th and March 11th [Mr. Bin Laden, of course, refers to the attacks on New York City and Washington, D.C., on 9/11, and the bombings of commuter trains in Madrid, Spain, on March 11, 2004,[2] are your own deeds coming back to haunt you. We note that your defining us as terrorists actually defines yourselves since we have reacted in kind to your actions towards us. Our actions react to your actions, like the killing of our people in Afghanistan, Iraq, and Palestine.

Suffice it to say that the killing of the old man in the wheelchair, Ahmad Yassin [the founder and spiritual leader of Hamas, who was assassinated in the occupied Gaza Strip of Palestine by a missile launched from an Israeli attack helicopter on March 22, 2004[3] — God's mercy upon him — shocked the world. God willing, we pledge to take vengeance on the United States for what happened to him.

By what compassion can you measure your dead as innocents while ours are considered worthless? By what logic is your blood

156

considered blood while ours is considered water?

Justice demands a response in kind, and those who begin the cycle of violence are more blameworthy.

When you witness what has happened and what continues to happen, the killings in your countries and in ours, a critical fact emerges: oppression is forced both on us and on you by your politicians, who, against your wishes, send your sons to Iraq to kill and be killed. Therefore, both sides share a common interest to thwart those who shed the blood of our respective peoples for their own narrow interests: i.e., to thwart our enslavement to the White House gang.

The Iraq War generates billions of dollars for big corporations, either munitions makers or those working in reconstruction, such as Halliburton[4] and its sister companies.

It is obvious who benefits from this War and the bloodshed: the merchants of war and the bloodsuckers who control the world from behind the scenes.

President [George W.] Bush and his kind, the media giants, and the United Nations are mortal dangers to the world, and the Zionist lobby is their most dangerous member. God willing, we will continue to fight them.

Therefore, in order to deprive the merchants of war of further opportunities, and responding to the recent positive developments seen in recent public opinion polls,[5] which indicated that most Europeans want peace, I urge the establishment of a permanent commission to develop European awareness of the justness of our causes, especially the cause of Palestine, and I propose that the [West's] vast media resources be used toward this end.

I hereby offer the Europeans a peace treaty, the substance of which is our commitment to halt any further actions against any country that commits itself to refraining from attacking Muslims or intervening in their affairs, including the American conspiracy against the *Ummah* [Islamic nation]. If both sides agree, this peace treaty may be renewed on expiration of the term of one government and the rise of the next one. The peace treaty will take effect immediately upon the exit of the last soldier of any European country from our land.

The door of peace will remain open for three months following the broadcast of this statement. Whoever rejects the peace treaty and opts for war should know that we are the *Mujahideen* [Islamic warriors].

We will abide by this peace treaty with whoever wants it and signs it.

Stop shedding our blood to protect your own blood. The solution to this not-so-difficult equation is in your hands. Know that the longer you delay, the worse the situation will become. Do not blame us for what next happens; blame yourselves.

As for those liars who say that we hate freedom and kill for the sake of killing, reality proves that we speak the truth and that they lie. They lie because the killing of the Russians occurred only after they invaded Afghanistan and Chechnya.[6] The killing of Europeans occurred only after the invasion of Iraq and Afghanistan.[7] The killing of the Americans in the Battle of New York City [9/11] occurred only after they supported the Jews in Palestine and after their invasion of the Arabian Peninsula. [Mr. Bin Laden refers to the United States' historic support for Israel and to the introduction of American military forces in Saudi Arabia and the Arabian Gulf in 1990.[8] The killings in Somalia only occurred after Operation Restore Hope [the 1993 United States mission to Somalia that ended with the tragic Black Hawk Down incident].[9] By the grace of God, we restored them without hope.[10]

This Page Left Intentionally Blank For Notes

Chapter 19

Second Statement To The American People[1]
October 29, 2004

During the month of Ramadan [the ninth month of the Islamic lunar calendar, the month of fasting and meditation], for all things prohibited there is the law of reciprocity. If then anyone transgresses the prohibition against you, you may transgress likewise against him. But fear God, and know that God is with those who restrain themselves. Praise be to God who created Creation for His Worship and commanded mankind to be just and permitted the wronged one to retaliate against the oppressor in kind.[2]

To begin, peace be upon he who follows the Guidance [Islam].

People of America, I direct this statement to you. It concerns how to prevent another Manhattan [9/11] and deals with the causes and effects of the war against America. Before I begin, I say to you that, contrary to [President George W.] Bush's claim that we hate freedom,[3] security is an indispensable pillar of human life. Free men do not forfeit their security. If we hate freedom, then let him explain why we did not strike, for example, Sweden. We know that those who hate freedom do not possess defiant spirits like those of the nineteen [the 9/11 hijackers].[4] May God have mercy upon them.[5]

No, we fight you because we are free men who do not sleep

under oppression. We want to restore freedom to our *Ummah* [Islamic nation].[6] Just as you lay waste to our *Ummah,* so shall we lay waste to yours. Only a dumb thief jeopardizes the security of others and then makes himself believe that he will be secure. Contrariwise, when disaster strikes rational people, their first priority is to look for its causes in order to prevent its recurrence. Even though it has been over three years since September 11th, I remain amazed at you. Bush still engages in distortion and deception and hides the real causes [of 9/11] from you. Thus, circumstances are still ripe for a repetition. So I shall talk to you about the story behind those events [9/11]; and for your edification, I shall tell you truthfully about the moment in which the decision was taken [to launch the attacks].

I say to you that God knows that it had never occurred to us to strike the towers [of the World Trade Center] until the oppression and the tyranny of the American-Israeli coalition against our people in Palestine became unbearable. Then, Lebanon came to my mind.

The events that directly affected my soul started in 1982,[7] when America permitted the Israelis to invade Lebanon, and the American Sixth Fleet helped assisted them. The bombardment [of Lebanon] began and many were killed and injured, and others were terrorized and displaced. [In 1983, United States warships bombarded a variety of Arab Muslim positions in Lebanon.] I couldn't forget those moving scenes: blood, severed limbs, women and children sprawled everywhere. Houses were destroyed along with their occupants, and high-rise buildings demolished on the heads of their residents. Rockets rained down on our homes without mercy. The situation was like a crocodile meeting a helpless child who is powerless to defend himself except for his screams. Does the crocodile understand a conversation that does not include a weapon? The whole world saw and heard what was occurring in Lebanon but did not respond.

In those most difficult moments, many indescribable ideas arose in my soul, but ultimately they produced an intense desire to reject tyranny and gave birth to a strong resolve to punish the oppressors. As I looked at those demolished towers in Lebanon, it entered my mind that we should punish the oppressor in kind. We should destroy towers in America so that Americans could taste some of what we have tasted, and to deter them from the further killing of our women and children. On that day, I concluded that oppression and the intentional killing of innocent women and children was a deliberate American policy.

In the vocabulary of the United States, freedom and democracy mean destruction while resistance means terrorism and intolerance. Freedom and democracy mean oppressing and embargoing to death of millions of people, as Bush Sr. [President George H.W. Bush] did in Iraq, perpetrating the greatest mass slaughter of children mankind has ever known. [Mr. Bin Laden is speaking of the deaths of hundreds of thousands of Iraqi children from malnutrition and lack of medicine due to the economic sanctions imposed on Iraq after the conclusion of the Persian Gulf War of 1991.][8] Freedom and democracy also mean the dropping of millions of pounds of bombs and explosives on millions of children – also in Iraq – as [President George W.] Bush Jr. did in order to remove an old agent of the United States, Saddam Hussein,[9] and replace him with a new puppet to assist in pilfering Iraq's oil.

So with these images as a background, the events of September 11th came as a reply to those great wrongs. Should a man be blamed for defending his sanctuary? Is defending oneself and punishing the aggressor in kind objectionable terrorism? If it is such, then it is unavoidable for us.

This is the message which I had sought to communicate to you in word and deed repeatedly for many years before September 11th. If you wish, you can read this in my interview with Scott in *Time Magazine* in 1996,[10] with Peter Arnett on *CNN* in 1997,[11] or my meeting with John Weiner in 1998.[12] If you wish, you can observe it in Kenya, Tanzania,[13] and Aden. [Venues were terrorist attacks were carried out against Americans.][14] And you can also read about it in my interview with Abdul Bari Atwan [editor of *Al-Quds al Arabi*, an Arabic-language newspaper published in London, England],[15] as well as my interviews with [British journalist] Robert Fisk.[16] The latter is one of your compatriots and co-religionists, and I consider him to be neutral. [Mr. Fisk maintains a website that contains many of Mr. Bin Laden's interviews not only by Mr. Fisk but also by other noted journalists. See robert-fisk.com.]

I dare the White House and the media controlled by them to broadcast an interview with him so that he may relay to the American people what he has understood from us to be the causes of our fight against you. If you Americans eliminate those causes, then you will have taken the correct path that will restore you to the pre-9/11 level of security.

Having addressed the causes of the war, I turn now to the results. By the Grace of God, they have been positive and enormous. By all measures they have exceeded all of our expectations. This is due to many factors. Chief among them is our facility in dealing with the Bush administration because it resembles the regimes in our own countries, half of which are ruled by the military and the other half of which are ruled by the sons of kings and presidents. Our experience with them is lengthy, and both types are characterized by pride, arrogance, greed, and misappropriation of wealth.

The resemblance rooted after the visit of [President George H. W.] Bush to the region at a time when some of our compatriots were being mesmerized by America. They had hoped that his visits would positively affect our countries. Suddenly, he was enamored with these monarchies and military regimes. He envied their ability to remain in power for decades so they could embezzle the public wealth of the *Ummah* [Islamic nation] without accountability. So, under the pretense of fighting terrorism, he taught his son dictatorship and the suppression of freedoms, and they called it the Patriot Act.[17] In addition, [President George H. W.] Bush [Sr.] sanctioned the installing of his sons as state governors[18] and did not forget to import from the Middle East regimes, into Florida, the expertise in election fraud to be used in moments of difficulty.[19]

All that we have mentioned makes it easy for us to bait this administration. All that we have to do is send *Mujahideen* [Islamic warriors] to the farthest point East to raise a piece of cloth on which is written "Al Qaeda" in order to cause the American generals to race there, causing America to suffer economic and political losses without its achieving anything other than some financial benefits for their private companies. This is in addition to our experience in guerilla warfare and war of attrition to fight tyrannical superpowers. Along side the *Mujahideen* [Islamic warriors] in Afghanistan we bled Russia for ten years until it went bankrupt and was forced to withdraw in defeat.[20] All Praise is due to God.

Thus, we are continuing this policy to bleed America to the point of bankruptcy. God is Willing, and nothing is too great for God.

Those who say that Al Qaeda has won or the [Bush] administration has lost this war against terrorism are both incorrect. When one scrutinizes the results, one cannot say that Al Qaeda was solely responsible for these spectacular gains. Rather, White House policy that demands the opening of new war fronts to occupy their various corporations — whether in the fields of arms manufacturing, oil production, or reconstruction — has helped Al Qaeda to achieve these enormous results.

Some analysts and diplomats have said that we and the White House are playing on the same team in fulfilling the economic goals of the United States even though our respective motivations differ. British diplomats and others referred to this notion in their lectures at the Royal Institute of International Affairs when, for example, they pointed out that Al Qaeda spent $500,000 on [9/11][21] while the incident and its aftermath have cost America more than half a trillion dollars. This meant that, by the Grace of God, every dollar Al Qaeda spent cost America a million dollars and a huge number of jobs. As for the size of America's economic deficit, it has reached record-high, astronomical numbers estimated to total more than a trillion dollars.[22] Even more dangerous and bitter-tasting to America is the fact that the *Mujahideen* [Islamic warriors] recently forced Bush to resort to emergency funds[23] to continue the fight in Afghanistan and Iraq. With God's Permission, this demonstrates the success of the bleed-until-bankruptcy plan.

True, this reflects Al Qaeda gains; but on the other hand it shows that the Bush administration has also gained something. One need only look at the magnitude of the contracts acquired by the corrupt administration-linked mega-corporations like Haliburton. This all demonstrates that the real losers are you: the American people and their economy.

And for the record, we had agreed with the Commander, Muhammad Atta,[24] may God have mercy on him, that the [9/11] operations would be carried out within twenty minutes before Bush and his administration noticed. [Mr. Atta was the acknowledged ring-leader of the 9/11 hijackers.] It never occurred to us that the Commander-in-Chief of the American Armed Forces [President George W. Bush] would abandon 50,000 of his citizens in the twin towers to face those great horrors alone at the time when they most needed him. To him, occupying himself by talking to the little girl about the goat and its butting was more important than occupying himself with the aircraft and their butting of skyscrapers. We were given three times the time period necessary to execute the operations.[25] All Praise is due to God. And it's no secret that American intellectuals and perceptive people warned Bush [about 9/11] before the attack.[26]

The nations of the world sympathized with you in your desire for security [after 9/11] and in conducting inspections [in Iraq] aimed at the removal of weapons of mass destruction – assuming they existed. So, it was in America's interest that it not be thrust into an unjustified war with an unknown outcome. But the darkness of the black gold [oil] blurred [President George W.] Bush's vision and insight, and he gave priority to private interests over the national interests of America. So, the Iraq War proceeded, the death toll rose, the American economy bled, and Bush became embroiled in the swamps of Iraq that now threaten his future. [President]Bush fits the saying: "Like the naughty she-goat who used her hoof to dig up a knife from under the earth [and cut herself]."

So I say to you [that in Iraq] over 15,000 Iraqis have been killed and tens of thousands injured, while more than a thousand of you have been killed and more than 10,000 injured.[27] Bush's hands are stained with the blood of all of those killed from both sides, all for the sake of oil and keeping America's private companies in business. Be aware that it is the same nation that punishes the weak man when he kills one of its citizens for money while letting the powerful escape liability when, also for money [i.e., oil], he causes the killing of more than one thousand of its sons.[28]

The same is true of your ally [Israel] in Palestine. It terrorizes women and children and kills and captures [its targeted] individuals while they lie sleeping with their families.[29] Recall that for every action, there is a reaction.

Finally, it behooves you to reflect on the last wills and testaments of the thousands who departed [on 9/11] as they lamented in despair. They are important testaments that should be studied. Among the most important of those that I have read were the lamentations in which they say, "How mistaken we were to have allowed the White House to implement its aggressive foreign policies against the weak without supervision." It is as if they were telling you, "The people of America hold to account those who have caused us to be killed and happy is he who learns from others mistakes." Among that which I read was a verse of poetry.[30]

Injustice chases its people
And how unhealthy the bed of tyranny.
As has been said,

An ounce of prevention is better than a pound of cure.

And know that

It is better to return to the truth than persist in error,

And that the wise man doesn't squander his security, wealth, and children,

for the sake of the liar in the White House.

In conclusion, I tell you truthfully that your security is not in the hands of [Senator John] Kerry or Bush or Al Qaeda. No, your security is in your own hands, and every state that doesn't menace our own security is automatically guaranteed its own security.

God is our Guardian and Helper, while you have no guardian or helper.

This Page Left Intentionally Blank For Notes

Chapter 20

Message To The Islamic World[1]
December 16, 2004

Praise be to God, the Cherisher and Sustainer of the worlds. Peace be upon Prophet Muhammad and his Companions. ["Peace be upon him" are words of grace that must attend any oral or written reference to the Prophets recognized by Islam. Hereinafter, "PBUH."]

This message is directed to all Muslims everywhere, and in particular, those of the land of the Two Holy Places [the mosques located in Mecca and Medina, Saudi Arabia].[2] It addresses the conflict between the Kingdom [of Saudi Arabia] and its people.[3]

Security and the need to spare Muslim blood have been discussed extensively [in Saudi Arabia]. The importance of unity and the dangers of polarization and internal fighting have also been much discussed. The Kingdom claims that the *Mujahideen* [Islamic warriors][4] are responsible for the country's deteriorating state of affairs. Truthfully, the blame falls on the rulers themselves. They have abdicated their responsibility to attain security, promote unity, and avoid bloodshed. They have disobeyed God and have committed such major sins as to subject the country to God's Wrath. In the *Holy Quran*, God has warned us by telling us the stories of the wrong-doers and their punishments.

In the *Holy Quran*, God relates a parable: A quiet, secure city, abundantly supplied with sustenance from everywhere; yet, it was ungrateful of God's Bounty. So, God subjected it to hunger and terror in the extreme because of the evil of its people.[5]

"(All) these transgressed beyond bounds in the land, and heaped therein mischief. Therefore did the Lord pour on them a scourge of diverse chastisements: For the Lord is Watchful."[6]

Those who support the legitimacy of the Saudi Kingdom, obey its rulers, implement its man-made laws, and refrain from forbidding that which is prohibited by God's Laws are responsible for what has happened and for what shall come by way of God's Punishment.

"Curses were pronounced on those among the children of Israel who rejected Faith, by the tongue of *Dawud* [David] and of *Issa* [Jesus] (PBUH) the son of *Maryam* [Mary] because they disobeyed and persisted in excesses. Nor did they forbid one another the inequities which they committed: Evil indeed were the deeds which they did."[7]

Our Prophet [Muhammad (PBUH)], in a *Hadith* [tradition of the Prophet] cited by Al-Hakim, has said: "Whenever the nation's *Imams* [meaning rulers, not clerics] refuse to govern by God's Guidance from God's Revelations in the *Holy Quran*, God will turn their force and power against each other instead of against their enemies."[8]

Also, in a *Hadith* by Abu Dawood, the Prophet (PBUH) said: "If people do not rise up and stop the transgressor, God might punish everyone."[9]

"Beware those who resist the Messenger's (PBUH) enjoinders, else some trial or grievous chastisement will befall them."[10]

Among the words of wisdom:

"If you are blessed with good things, let it be known: sins wipe out all the blessings."[11]

The regime's violations of the *Sharia* [Islamic law] are far beyond the most serious sins.[12] The rulers' sins have removed them from Islam. They have oppressed and humiliated the people, made a mockery of the people's intelligence, and have mismanaged the country's wealth. Today [in Saudi Arabia], millions suffer poverty so that the ruling family can deposit millions of SRs, [i.e., Saudi Riyals, the official currency of Saudi Arabia] into their personal bank accounts.

Additionally, public services have deteriorated, private property has been unlawfully seized by force, members of the ruling family have forced themselves on unwilling business owners as partners, and many other serious transgressions characterize the royal regime. The rulers have even gone beyond that which disqualifies them from Islam by allying with *Kufr* [non-believers][13] America and supporting America against the Muslims — all acts which sealed the fate of the rulers. They have become apostates. The ruling regime has elevated itself to the status of a partner with God by authoring laws and *Fatwas* [religious decrees] that legitimize and forbid acts according to their whims, regardless of God's Laws. The alliance with infidels itself is one of the ten violations ["voiders," in the parlance of Islam][14] that disqualify the offender from Islam.

More information about the vast array of violations committed by the ruling family can be found in our previous Communiqué # 17. [Mr. Bin Laden refers to The Committee on Advice and Reform, which he founded in the safe venue of London, England, in 1994 to pursue political reform in Saudi Arabia.][15] If the ruler is willing to do what is necessary to effect change, correcting past mistakes is simple. Further, the ruler need not originate any solutions; rather, he need merely turn to Islam, which has all of the solutions. God knows that we want nothing more than to reconcile the Kingdom's internal and foreign policies with what God's Messenger [the Prophet Muhammad (PBUH)] has mandated.

We have abandoned our homes and lands [as exiled members of The Committee and as *Mujahideen* (Islamic warriors)] solely to establish *La Ilaha Ilia Allah – Muhammad Rasoulu Allah* [There is no god but God]."[16] Everyone knows that we already possessed all of the material things that this life can provide, so we did not abandon our homes and lands to seek materialistic pleasure or social status. Nor have we left the land of the Two Holy Places [Saudi Arabia] seeking another land closer to our hearts. In fact, we have been away for a long time, and we miss it and its hardships. But in the Cause of God, our present hardship is easy and a small price to pay.

The love of Hijaz [Saudi Arabia] is deep in my heart
But the rulers are wolves.
In Afghanistan, I have a home and companions
And from God comes a door for sustenance.
Like friends, horses are few,
Even if they appear many, in the eyes of the inexperienced.
And anyone who appreciates kindness is loved

And any place where glory is home-grown is blessed.

[Mr. Bin Laden notes that he has a home and sympathetic companions in Afghanistan, but like a good horse to an equestrian, they are few and far between. Obviously, he finds it to be more Islamic than Saudi Arabia.]

He who trusts God needs only God. The wise one is he who will not be misled and will not grow prideful by this life's materialistic offerings. Only life according to God's Laws is meaningful. Therefore, we ask God for steadfastness and a happy ending to our lives.

In short, the only way to ensure a happy ending is to embark on the Straight Paths of God and His Messenger (PBUH). "Therefore stand firm as you are commanded — you and those who with you turn (unto God); and transgress not — for He well sees all that you do."[17]

"Nor would the Lord destroy the towns unjustly while their people are righteous."[18]

The Messenger of God [the Prophet Muhammad (PBUH)] also said: "Say! I believe in God, and then stand firm."[19]

In order for the *Ummah* [Islamic nation] to find the correct path, it must follow the example of its ancestors fourteen centuries ago. At that time, the Arabian Peninsula was a lawless land. Killing, oppression, total ignorance, and a lack of wisdom [i.e., religion] prevailed.

However, when God sent Prophet Muhammad (PBUH) to reveal the Holy Quran, the people followed that guiding light and stood firm with the Messenger (PBUH) of God. Their lives changed for the better. From their state of humiliation, God graced them with Islam. Between them they now shared affection and unity rather than the animosity and divisiveness of the past. God replaced hunger with bounty, and fear with security, and He put affection between their hearts:

"Not if you had spent all that is in the Earth, could you have produced that affection, but God has done it, for He is exalted in might and wise."[20]

"If the people of the towns had only believed and feared God, He should indeed have opened for them blessings from Heaven and Earth; but they rejected the Messenger (PBUH), and He brought them to account for their misdeeds."[21]

Resolution of the dispute between the Ruler and the ruled lies in what the first Caliph, [22] Abu Bakr, said to his successor, the second Caliph, Omar ibn al-Khattab: "Stand firm in the Path of God, so your people will stand firm with you and for you." Those words of wisdom came from the rightly guided ones. [The term "rightly guided ones" refers to *Rashidoon* [the first four Caliphs] — Abu Baker (Caliph 632 – 634, Omar (Caliph 634 – 644), Uthman (Caliph 644 – 656), and Ali (Caliph 656 – 661)][23] They drew their guiding light from the clear light [*the Holy Quran*] that God revealed to them. If the *Emir* [ruler] precisely follows the straight path, the people will follow; and they will be obligated to obey him. But in accordance with God's Commands, if the ruler deviates from God's Path and becomes an apostate, the people are obliged to disobey him and remove him from power.

In Islam, obedience to the ruler is not absolute; it is conditioned on implementing the Laws of God. The *Ulema* [Islamic scholars] agree that unity and affection are partners with obeying God.

Sheikh al-Islam, Ibn Taymiya,[24] said: "The reason for togetherness, unity and affection between Muslims is simply knowing and practicing the whole *Deen* [Religion, i.e., Islam]; and the simple reason for divisions and disputes is ignoring any part of the Religion." He also added: "Narrowing and marginalizing the Religion by the rulers and the *Ulema* [Islamic scholars] of the *Ummah* [Islamic nation] gives the enemies of the *Ummah* the advantage. Muslims' disobedience to God and any of His Commands, major or minor, will result in the imposition of the enemies' ideology [read theology] on the Muslims."

As practiced by our rightly guided earlier generations, unity means conducting oneself in the example of the Messenger of God [the Prophet Muhammad (PBUH)] and his Companions.[25] Only in this way can one be among those to be saved on Judgment Day. Unity must be for righteous purposes, even if one is alone. Clearly, whenever Muslims abandon any portion of God's Commands, hatred and animosity will afflict them; and their enemies will exploit their weakness. That is our current state of affairs.

Can the rulers [of Saudi Arabia] stand firm in the straight Path of God so the people will stand with them and enjoy the best Religion and the best life? Some say yes, noting that they have already begun the process. They have begun a national dialogue and municipal elections. But that really changed nothing because it did not address the core problem. At best, the rulers will repeat the election "games" previously played by the rulers of Yemen, Jordan, and Egypt.[26] For decades they will go in circles and accomplish nothing. Participating in legislative bodies is *Haram* [forbidden] because they legislate for people [i.e., enact man-made laws], which is equivalent to *Shirk* [the sin of taking partners with God] because God is the only law-giver.

Therefore, to resolve the conflict between the rulers and the ruled, we must lay our hand on the root cause of the problem. The conflict is partly regional, but it is also a greater struggle between two camps: one camp is America, representing the global *Kufr* [non-believers] and accompanied by all of the apostates. The other camp is the *Ummah* [Islamic nation], headed by its *Mujahideen* [Islamic warriors] brigades.

The current members of the ruling family in Saudi Arabia are agents of the *Kufr* infidels. They oppress the masses, quash any attempts at reform, and impose policies that contradict Islam. They are members of the same family that allied with the Crusaders against Muslims a century ago. [Mr. Bin Laden refers to British support for Abdul Aziz ibn Saud, the patriarch of the Saud family and the founder of the Kingdom of Saudi Arabia in 1926.][27] They do so now as agents of America and its allies, and their betrayal is merely an extension of the last original Crusader war against Islam [i.e., the machinations of the British and the Western powers in the post-World War I Middle East, especially in Arabia and Mesopotamia [Iraq], which in turn are viewed in the Middle East as but further extensions of the original Crusades of the 11th through 13th Centuries].

An analysis of [Saudi Arabia's] internal policies reveals the extent of the control of the Zionists and the "Cross Worshippers." For example, according to a long-standing agreement between America and past monarchs, America must approve the appointment of a King or his Crown Prince.[28]

The current disgraceful state of the government of Saudi Arabia is according to American plans. The country is being ruled in a manner not previously seen in human history. Governing a nation for a few hours after the death of a ruler may be expected; but governing for a decade after the ruler has lost his mental capacity is unheard of; indeed, it is one of the wonders of the world. [Mr. Bin Laden refers to the fact that since King Fahd's stroke in 1995, Crown Prince Abdullah has been acting as de facto regent.][29] Based on Islamic principles, King Fahd lost not only his right to rule because of his religious transgressions but also because of the deterioration of his mental capacity to the point of his inability to carry out basis tasks. How can he be expected to carry out the affairs of the entire country? King Fahd's sons keep him at the helm because they oppose the ascension of Crown Prince Abdullah to the throne. Were that to occur, he would reduce the influence of the other brothers.

Crown Prince Abdullah knows that he cannot afford to alienate the other brothers, especially because they control the powerful ministries of interior and defense. In addition, his brothers control the security apparatus [i.e., intelligence, military, and National Guard forces], and more importantly, the Royal Executive Office. Control of the Royal Executive Office enables them to issue royal edicts in the name of King Fahd, relieve Prince Abdullah of his duties, and appoint a replacement.[30]

This sharp conflict within the royal family allowed America a golden opportunity to extort the competing princes, especially Prince Abdullah. He knows that were he to disobey America in any way, at the least his brothers would remove him [as Crown Prince], just as they had removed King Saud before him. [King Saud was removed from power in 1958 for his profligate ways and for bringing financial crisis to the Kingdom.][31] He also knows that his competitors are well experienced in the games of power and politics and that they are quite capable of doing more than merely removing him should the need arise.

An obvious reminder of America's role in the decisions to fire royal family members [in the Middle East] is found in the case of Prince Hassan bin Talal of Jordan. After serving as Crown Prince for decades, he was removed [in 1999] by his brother King Hussein, who had come to America [for medical treatment] and returned to Jordan with the decision to fire his brother. That incident weighs heavily on the mind of Prince Abdullah. He knows that should he disobey his masters in Washington [D.C.], his fate would be similar to Prince Hassan. Therefore, it is no secret that the decision-makers for Saudi Arabian policies reside in the White House, not Riyadh.[32]

The Arab rulers' response to the Crusaders' demands to change the educational curricula in Islamic countries demonstrates the extent of the Crusaders' control over our lands. The change is intended to erase the Islamic identity of the *Ummah* [Islamic nation]. As yet, their agents in the region have disobeyed their master's order. The demand is not new; it begun several decades ago at *Al Azhar* University in Egypt. After that, America demanded changes from the rest of their puppets in the area to dry the roots of uprising or *Jihad* [holy war]. America first asked

Yemen to close down religious institutions twenty years ago.[33]

America demanded educational changes from the rulers of Saudi Arabia, and they changed the curricula. That occurred fifteen years before [9/11]. Then the regime's rulers gave the Americans even more than they had requested. Recently they implemented additional changes and fired many *Imams* [Islamic clerics] and *Ulema* [Islamic scholars].[34] The interference of the Worshippers of the Cross on our educational programs is most dangerous because it has resulted in a change of Islam, and Islam cannot be divided; it must be accepted and practiced intact. Anyone who believes in part of the *Holy Quran* and rejects other parts is indeed a *Kufr* [non-believer]. Infidels are infidels; their hearts are alike.

"But when our clear signs are recited unto them, those who hope not for their meeting with us, say: 'Bring us a *Quran* other than this, or change this.' Say: 'It is not for me of my own accord, to change it: I follow only what is revealed to me: if I were to disobey my Lord, I should myself fear the Chastisement of a Great Day [to come].'"[35]

Fearful of America, the [Saudi] rulers changed the educational curricula. The detrimental impact on Islam and our culture is obvious. Regarding the impact on Islam, it is apostasy. The result will be manifested in the new graduates, who will be friends and allies of America. They will learn to sell the national interest for personal gain; and smile in the face of any American even though he occupies their land, steals their wealth, erases their identity, and imposes Western customs under the excuse of equal rights and the United Nations Charter. This truly is a model for interfering with our domestic policies.

The other ruling families in the region also have responded positively to America's agenda, betraying the Muslim masses to please their masters in Washington [D.C.]. For example, King Hussein of Jordan betrayed the Palestinians as he followed the same path as his father and grandfather.

And now his son, Abdullah II, is carrying out his role in the grand mission against Palestine and the rest of the Muslims, and Muhammad V, King of Morocco, also follows his father's and grandfather's footsteps.[36] Neither time nor space allows a proper listing and discussion of all of the ruling families' transgressions against Islam. Thus, we shall focus on some of the more important ones.

The Saudi government has joined the global Crusader alliance, headed by [President George W.] Bush against Islam and against the

Muslims of Afghanistan and Iraq. They have allowed American military forces to use bases in Saudi Arabia from which to invade Iraq with ease. The Saudi Defense Minister insulted all Muslims and their religion when he claimed that his government had permitted the Americans to use [Saudi] airports for humanitarian reasons.[37] If that were not enough, recently they performed a new episode for everyone to see in their series of continuing plots against Muslims. They authored an initiative to send Arabic and Islamic troops to maintain peace in Iraq. Thus, not only did they join the forces of the *Kufr* [non-believers] against Muslims, they proposed the initiative in order to legitimize the American occupation of Iraq.[38] God is Sufficient to protect us against them, and we place our full trust in God.

Matters worsened when Crown Prince Abdullah assumed power. People hoped that he would rid the country of corruption and mismanagement in the areas of finance, public relations, media, and civics. People also hoped that he would put an end to the disgraceful master-slave relationship with America. The people were expecting good news; instead, what they got were calamities.

While America was deploying troops to the [Arabian or Persian] Gulf in preparation for the invasion of Iraq, the [Saudi] government was lying to the *Ummah* [Islamic nation] by publicizing false statements declaring their objection to the use of force against Iraq.[39] A few days before the invasion begun, Prince Abdullah proposed what he called a humanitarian initiative. He called on Saddam [Hussein] to leave Iraq and go into exile in order to spare the blood of many Muslims. His initiative was nothing more than an attempt to deliver Iraq to America on a gold platter.[40] Imagine that one day you were on your way home and suddenly a big bully appeared in the middle of the road and prevented you from going anywhere. While you were wondering what was wrong, one of the bully's comrades walked up to you and said: "My advice to you is to think about your family, your home, and your money and to leave town. The only way to save your life is to leave town and let this man take your land." This scenario illustrates Prince Abdullah's initiative: Abdullah simply wanted to facilitate the American theft of Iraq's wealth, land, and oil — with the help and advice of the Arabian Prince himself. Of course, Saddam himself was a thief and an apostate. But the solution to Iraq's problems should never have been removing Iraq from the hands of a local thief and putting it in the hands of a global thief. This act by

Abdullah to pave the way for the *Kufr* [non-believers] to take Muslim lands and control the Muslims in their own land constitutes one of the ten causes of apostasy.[41]

Prior to the invasion of Iraq, Prince Abdullah convened a press conference to assure his people that the massive deployment of American troops to the Gulf was not for the purpose of invading Iraq. Less than a year later, before the eyes of millions of people, God exposed his lies, his betrayal, and his state of apostasy. This was accomplished with irrefutable fact, not circumstantial evidence. Just as Prince Talal ibn Abdul Aziz[42] admitted publicly that his father used to collect money from the British, confirming what documents had previously demonstrated, i.e., that his father was an agent of the British government, now along comes his nephew, Prince Bandar, to make his own admission. Prince Bandar, the Ambassador of Saudi Arabia to the United States, has admitted that he met with the U.S. Vice President [Dick Cheney], the U.S. Defense Secretary [Donald Rumsfeld], and the Chairman of the Joint Chiefs of Staff [Richard Myers], who shared with him the top-secret plans for the impending invasion of Iraq. His admission closely followed on the heels of the publication of a book exposing Prince Abdullah's enticing America to forge ahead with the invasion of Iraq and promising to help logistically.[43]

Obviously Prince Abdullah's previous statement that the U.S. deployment of troops was not for the purpose of war was nothing less than misleading. On behalf of the United States, Prince Abdullah took the first hostile step: psychological warfare. He attempted to deceive the *Ummah* [Islamic nation] and the Iraqi Army into thinking that war was not on the table and thus there was no need for them to mobilize their forces. The ultimate goal was to eliminate any meaningful resistance to American troops. His actions were a shame, an apostasy, and a betrayal.

People still remember the day when Iraqi envoys came to Beirut[44] and met with their Saudi counterparts. A truce was called [between Iraq and Saudi Arabia], but Prince Abdullah then made a secret agreement with America to invade Iraq and pledged one billion dollars (U.S.) towards the cost of the war.[45] How far will the Saudi rulers go in service to their master? After all of their transgressions, they still claim to be the guardians of the *Ummah* [Islamic nation].

For a meager price, they deceive and lie to the *Ummah*. May God give them their just rewards.

May God give them what they deserve.

Because of the immense damage to the *Ummah* [Islamic nation], it is time for all rational people to pause and evaluate the rulers' action. No Muslim should be led by such corrupt, apostate rulers. To those who believe they can persuade the rulers to change by talking them into implementing reforms, I pose the following question: how can you expect reform while the ship navigates through a stormy, high sea full of offensive and awful characters? It is not possible because the ship invariably sinks.

We also have seen that the rulers change their ostensible approaches without substantively changing their policies. They vacillate between lies and delay tactics, or between enticing and trapping, or between imprisonment and exile. But nothing will change their loyalty to the Crusaders. Whenever the rulers agree to a dialogue with any reformist group, their only goal is to destroy the group, no matter how long it takes. Ask me! I myself have experienced that.[46]

Two decades ago, through grand *Ulema* [Islamic scholars] I offered my advice to the rulers; but nothing changed. I also addressed the problem directly with the Deputy Interior Minister. I outlined for him all of the major violations of the *Sharia* [Islamic law] that must be rectified. I received no response. I then met with the Assistant to the Deputy Minister for Security Affairs. He scolded me for addressing the issues with him and the Deputy Interior Minister. He recited all of the violations of which I had complained to the both of them. Then he informed me that the regime was fully aware of the violations and their relationship to the *Sharia* [Islamic law] and did not need anyone to lecture them about what is *Halal* [legal] and what is forbidden *Haram* [forbidden]. This meant that despite the conflict between man-made laws and God's Laws, the power to legislate remains in the hands of the King; and people must obey him.

"He could not take his brother by the law of the King except that God willed it (so). We raise to the degree (of wisdom) whom we please: but over all endowed with knowledge is one, the All-Knowing."[47]

Anyone with vision and perception can see the applicability of that verse to the rulers. According to the rulers, loyalty and obedience is to be to the King and not to God. Whatever the King makes legal becomes legal and whatever the King forbids becomes forbidden.

Riba [usury, including interest on lent money] is an example.

We know that Islam forbids *Riba*. "But God has permitted trade and forbidden usury."[48] But the [Saudi] regime has enacted laws allowing the use of interest and punishing anyone who tries to forbid it.[49] Once more, legalizing what God has forbidden is a cause for disqualification from Islam.

The second example is the alliance with the *Kufr* [non-believers]. The government of Jordan is pagan and *Kufr*, but nonetheless the Saudi regime allied with [Jordanian] King Hussein. Because of the alliance, the Saudi regime prohibited any criticisms of King Hussein or accusations of his being a Jewish agent [because his efforts at Israeli-Palestinian peace on terms slanted toward Israel]. But when King Hussein sided with Saddam [Hussein] when the latter invaded Kuwait, King Fahd disavowed him. As a result of the King's new position, Saudi Arabia was awash with documentary and photographic evidence depicting King Hussein as a traitor and a Jewish agent. That was true. Likewise, Jordan's newspapers wasted no time in filling their pages with documents and photographs proving that the Saudi rulers were British agents before they became American agents. That was also true.[50]

Shortly thereafter, America suggested to King Fahd that he invite King Hussein to Saudi Arabia for an official state visit. King Fahd let the disputes between them evaporate [and invited him]. When King Hussein died, Saudi princes attended his funeral, alongside the Israeli and American delegations. King Fahd also ordered an absentee prayer for him in the Holy Mosque of Mecca.

What a shame! *Wala'a wa Albara'a* [love and hate for God's Sake] are the strongest and most important bonds of *Iman* [faith]. We are required to love who God loves, and hate those whom God hates. We take allies and protectors only from among those whom God loves.[51]

But the [Saudi] hypocrites, slaves to the dollar, follow their King, right or wrong. They love and ally with whomever the King loves; and they hate and reject whomever the King hates.

How can a human being remain decent if he changes his mind like a pendulum? Must the Muslim set aside his Religion and intellect in order to be a good citizen?

[Ex-Egyptian President Gamal] Abdel Nasser, [Ex-Egyptian President Anwar] Sadat, and [Colonel Muammar] Qaddafi [dictator of Libya][52] exemplify the flip-flop rulers of [Saudi Arabia]. Nasser had a dispute [with the Saudi regime]. They pronounced him a *Kufr* [non-believer], and he actually was; but later they resolved their differences, and he then became a Muslim. As regards to Qaddafi, for thirty years whenever he disagreed [with the Saudi regime], he was a *Kufr*; but whenever they were cordial, he was a Muslim. And do not forget Sadat. When he signed the surrender agreement with the Jewish state [Israel], they accused him of being a traitor and a [Jewish] agent; and he was cursed in every newspaper in Saudi Arabia. When Prince Abdullah did the same thing when he proposed his peace initiative in Beirut, he was hailed by all of the [Saudi] hypocrites and the corrupt *Ulema* [Islamic scholars].

One can thus see that the ruler has his own *Deen* [religion]. Knowing what the Saudi rulers, in particular, and the other rulers in the region have done, one can see that the dispute is actually a dispute between two distinctly different paths: one is the Path of God. This is the complete Path on which all affairs of life are handled with complete submission to the Will of God.

"Say: Truly, my prayer and my service of sacrifice, my life and my death, are all for God, The Cherisher of the worlds: No partners has He: This am I commanded, and I am the first of those who submit to His Will."[53]

La Ilaha Ilia Allah - Muhammad Rasoulu Allah [There is No god but God and Muhammad (PBUH) was His Prophet — the primary tenet of Islam] is the True Path of Islam, with all of its meanings and obligations. The other path is the secular path.

"They think they deceive God those who believe, but they only deceive themselves, and realize it not!"[54]

It is the path on whose behalf God says:

"When it is said to them: 'Come to what God has revealed to the Messenger (PBUH):' You see the Hypocrites avert their faces from you in disgust."[55]

The only path to corrective action is to remove the ruler, as commanded by the *Sharia* [Islamic law]. If he refuses to step down voluntarily, the Muslims are obligated to remove him by force. This is mandated by God and his Messenger (PBUH). All that the rulers have offered the reformers is to accept the King's laws without condition. However, the correct action for the King and for the Muslims is to implement God's Laws without conditions.

Saudi Arabia's Interior Minister [Prince Naif bin Abdul Aziz] made it abundantly clear to the reformers that if they did not accept the King's laws and policies, then their only dialogue with Saudi Arabia would be with the sword and the rifle. It is common knowledge that anyone who practices a religion must possess weapons to protect his religion. How could any rational person believe reform is possible by peaceful means when the security agents of the apostate [Saudi] ruler are deployed in full battle gear at every corner?[56]

To believe that an apostate ruler would entertain ideas of reform by peaceful means is to embark on a falsehood that hinders the establishment of the *Haq* [Right Path]. Recall that we are not discussing a ruler who has committed only minor sins; rather, we are discussing a ruler who has committed *Kufr* [apostasy] and who has betrayed the entire *Ummah* [Islamic nation].

In implementing the American policies and agenda for the [Middle East] region, there is no difference between [Paul] Bremer [the former Administrator of the Iraq Coalition Provisional Authority] and [Iyad] Allawi, the [interim] Prime Minister of Iraq. By the same token, there is no difference between Bremer and the rest of the rulers of the entire region.

The consensus of the *Ulema* [Islamic scholars] is that the right to govern, rule, or lead cannot be given to a *Kufr* [non-believers], and if a ruler becomes *Kufr,* he falls from the fold of Islam, and his right to govern follows him. Alqadi Ayad[57], a respected classic scholar has said: "If a ruler becomes *Kufr* and begins to change what God has legislated, he loses the pledge given to him by Muslims, and he should be removed and replaced by a just *Imam* [ruler]."

We did not originate the *Fatwa* [religious decree] for disobeying or removing a *Kufr* ruler. This has long been the consensus of the *Ulema* [Islamic scholars] and is what *Sharia* [Islamic law] mandates.

Accordingly, I now call upon all Muslims to mobilize to effect the needed changes. The level of the commitment must be commensurate with the magnitude of the conflict, and they must consider that the current [Saudi] rulers and their infrastructure are no less than extensions of the global *Kufr* [non-believers] system. Reform must be sought from the Straight Path of God. Otherwise, it would be a deviation from the Straight Path, wasting time and energy, and ultimately would result in a state of disarray. The attempt to effect reforms must be with good intentions; and the absence of good intentions will result in lies and deception.

Those who disdain armed, as opposed to peaceful, dialogue with the present regime to restore justice are deluding themselves. When the ruler becomes apostate and refuses to step down, he can only be removed by force. Those who disdain armed dialogue share the same boat with two other groups: one group openly declared the rulers committed *Kufr* [non-believers] when they assisted the Crusaders against Muslims; but they did so only to deceive the *Ummah* [Islamic nation] into believing they were restoring justice. The other group mixes righteousness with falsehood. On the one hand, they reject helping the *Kufr* to occupy Muslim land, and that is a form of righteousness; yet they refuse to use force to remove the apostate ruler, and that is a form of falsehood. Despite the disparate views of all three groups, their results are the same.

The path followed by these groups is extremely dangerous for two reasons.

Because they allowed their own desires to interfere with implementing God's Laws, they themselves are in serious trouble. "It is not fitting for a believer, man or woman, when a matter has been decided by God and his Messenger (PBUH), to have a choice about their decision."[58]

They obstruct people from the Path of God by preventing them from taking back their rights by means God has declared to be lawful. This could enable the hypocrites and the ignorant to adopt systems such as that of the Northern Alliance [forces opposed to the Taliban rule in Afghanistan before the United States invasion in 2001],[59] or a similar secular system like the one adopted by Iraqi [Interim] Prime Minister Alawi and his team. Such practice is absolutely forbidden.

At this juncture, we respond to certain frequent accusations leveled at us for the past two years by the regime. It has accused the *Mujahideen* [Islamic warriors] of being *Khawarji* [those who secede],[60] but they know we are not. Our letters and actions clearly testify that we are not what they accuse us of being. Is it not true that those who attacked our house [i.e., attempted to assassinate Mr. Bin Laden] in Sudan were *Khawarji*?[61] We firmly believe that sins less than *Kufr* [non-believers] do not disqualify one from Islam. If someone committed major sins like murder or drinking wine and died before repenting, then his fate would be exclusively in God's Hands. God may decide to punish him or to forgive him. But ultimately, his final destination will be Paradise. Further, we do not declare a general *Taqfir* [condemning an entire group, people, or country as *Kufr*], and we do not spill the blood of Muslims carelessly. It is permitted to [shed Muslim blood] if it is unavoidable in reaching the *Kufr*, as is killing by mistake or accident. In all such instances, we ask God's Forgiveness and take full responsibility for our deeds. However, allow me to enlighten the Saudi rulers about those who kill Muslims and pronounce general *Taqfir*.

Your father, Abdul Aziz [founder of Saudi Arabia] sided with the British against the [Muslim] Ottoman Government and its governor in Hael. You yourself initiated an armed confrontation against your brother King Saud. If it were not for God, a bloodbath would have ensued. Your *Ulema* [Islamic scholars] never called either you or your father deviant. What about the slaughter at Taif?[62] Do not those deeds inform you who is making general *Taqfir*? Did not your father [Abdul Aziz] deceive his soldiers by telling them that the people of the Hijaz [Taif and Mecca are part of the portion of the Arabia Peninsula known as the Hijaz] were *Kufr* [non-believers] and that they were fighting them in *Jihad* [holy war] in the Cause of God? Didn't he lie to his soldiers? Do we really want to talk about the details of this horrific onslaught? Opponents must exercise self-discipline and adhere to the rules of honor during their disputes and restrain themselves and their mouths from lying.

You well know that no matter how much you lie about us, we shall never lie about you. Had I thought you needed reassurance about that, I would have done so. I shall never lie to you or about you unless you inquire about a Muslim for whom you are searching in order to do him an injustice and he is hiding in my abode. In that case, lying to save that innocent Muslim is permitted.

You are accusing the *Mujahideen* [Islamic warriors] of violations that you yourselves have perpetrated. Let me direct your attention to what the great scholar of Islam, Al-Nawawi[63] said in this regard: "If we are speaking about the well-known duties such as prayer and fasting, and if we are speaking about the well-known unlawful acts such as adultery and wine, and others, all Muslims are fully aware of them." Now, are you aware of any Muslim who does not know that allying with a *Kufr* [non-believers] is forbidden? Is there a Muslim who is unaware of the prohibition against *Riba* [usury, including interest on money lent]? Does anyone dispute God's Verdict with respect to such transgressions?

Perhaps you seek to assemble a committee of *Ulema* [Islamic scholars] who are loyal to you, just like some Christians are. Do you seek to alter Islam to legalize the forbidden and forbid the legal to suit your own agenda? Why do you accuse good Muslim youth [i.e., young *Mujahideen* (Islamic warriors)] of being misguided?

Just who are those misguided youths? Are they not the same as those who answered the Call of the Messenger of God [the Prophet Muhammad (PBUH)] to expel the Jews and Christians from the Arabian Peninsula, in a true *Hadith* [tradition] documented by Bukhari?[64]

The Messenger of God (PBUH) also said: "No two religions should coexist in the Arabian Peninsula." He also said: "I will expel the Jews and the Christians from the Arabian Peninsula until no one remains but for Muslims."[65]

Or, are they the ones who took the *Hadiths* of the Messenger of God (PBUH) in jest? Or are they like the ones who sought to evade the Messenger's (PBUH) direct order, just like the people on the Sabbath?[66]

Crown Prince Abdullah said the legal basis on which we wage *Jihad* [holy war] against the infidels [in Saudi Arabia] is flawed. He said that they [the infidels] came to help. But in response we say that our legal basis is as strong as possible because it is founded on undisputed *Hadiths* that oblige the Muslims to expel the infidels; there are no exceptions. It makes no difference whether the infidels are here to help or to receive help.

Are we really the advocates of misguided and faulty ideologies? What about those [like yourselves] who betrayed the entire *Ummah* [Islamic nation] by opening the [Arabian] Peninsula of the Prophet Muhammad (PBUH) to the Jews and Christians. Those who did that are the real traitors.

The Prophet Muhammad (PBUH) said: "Every traitor comes on Judgment Day with a banner as big and as high as the level of his crime." The worst traitor is a general *Emir* [a ruler].[67]

Are the misguided those who enjoin the right and forbid the wrong, and believe in God; or are those who corrupt Muslims with their policies and propaganda, even in the sacred months [the first, seventh, eleventh, and twelfth months of the Islamic calendar] and in the sacred Mosque [*Masjid Al-Haram* in Mecca] the misguided ones? "And any whose purpose therein is profanity or wrongdoing He causes to taste of a most grievous chastisement."[68] She [the Queen of Sheba] said: "Kings, when they enter a country, despoil it, and make the noblest of its people its meanest thus do they behave."[69]

Are those who defend Muslims, Muslim wealth, Muslim dignity, and Muslim honor in Iraq, Afghanistan, Palestine, Chechnya, Kashmir, and elsewhere, misguided? Or are the misguided those who join the alliance of global *Kufr* [non-believers] against Muslims, in addition to robbing and wasting public treasures?

Do you remember the large [Saudi Arabian] arms deal? Or should we call it the large robbery? It is called "The *Yamamah* [dove] Accord,"[70] in which you paid thirty billion dollars [U.S.] for arms five years before the [1991] Gulf War. Why did we not see any use of the purchased arms during the Gulf War? At the time of that huge arms deal, the jobless rate [in Saudi Arabia] was very low. Assume there were 100,000 jobless persons at the time. Dividing thirty billion dollars by 100,000, results in over one million dollars per unemployed person. Why was this money not invested in projects that could have provided work for the jobless, money for the poor, the needy, the debtors, the sick, etc.?

Should we talk about the unlawful confiscation of private property and the [Saudi] rulers' obsession with building palaces? King Fahd has ordered the building of the Salam Palace, which will cost four billion [Saudi] Riyals [approximately one billion dollars (U.S.)]. What about the [cost of the] Thahaban Palace? This one is on the Red Sea coast, 40 kilometers from Jeddah. Were they to place the country of Bahrain in the [Palace's] atrium, the guests would not even notice the presence of Bahrain. Realizing that Bahrain encompasses 100 million square meters with a population of one million people, one can only imagine how big the Thahaban Palace is. Does history know of a more foolish example of wasted resources than this one?[71]

No matter the transgressions of the [Saudi] ruler, the hypocrites [i.e., the corrupt *Ulema* (Islamic scholars)] find ways to describe his actions as wise and just. When he confiscated private property from its rightful owner, a stone's throw away from the Holy Mosque [*Masjid Al-Haram*] in Mecca, to build his Palace, none of the *Imams* [clerics] of the Holy Mosque said anything publicly or privately. How many times have they recited the following verse: "For there was after them a certain king who seized every boat by force." [72]

Just who are the real misguided ones? Are they those who violate the Sacred City of Mecca and kill Muslims there? Are they Khalid al-Mihdhar, Nawaf al-Hazmi, and his brother Salem, who, together left Mecca and hit the homeland of America to defend Islam in Mecca and its surrounding? [These were 9/11 hijackers.][73]

Or, is it [King] Fahd ibn Abdul Aziz, who violated the sacred status of the Holy Mosque in Mecca [the *Masjid Al-Haram*, site of the Kaba, when it was seized by protesters in 1979]?[74] Level-headed people at the time believed that the incident could have been resolved without bloodshed. All that was necessary was time, especially knowing that there were only a few dozen inside the Mosque, who were surrounded and were mostly armed with hunting rifles and had only limited supplies of ammunition. But King Fahd, the enemy of God, did what Hajjaj did not do.[75] He arrogantly refused to listen to any advice and ordered tanks and armored vehicles to enter the Sacred Mosque. The sight of scores of dead Muslims and the destruction of minarets, waifs, and pavement of a mosque that is supposed to be sacred is unforgivable.

Who then violated the sacred status of the Mosque and the sacred status of the Muslim's life? Was it you, Fahd, or is it [today's] *Mujahideen* [Islamic warriors]? Or was it your security forces who killed a number of poor and weak people in the Al-Rasifah neighborhood of Mecca and evicted by force those who escaped so your *Emir* [meaning local leader] could have their land? Did nobody object to that act because the victims were poor and weak?

Who are the misguided ones, then? Are they the *Mujahideen* [Islamic warriors] or are they those who cooperated with America in the killing of one million [Iraqi] children, the biggest slaughter of children in history during the unjust sanctions imposed on Iraq? [Non-Governmental Organization's estimate that approximately 500,000 Iraqi children died from malnutrition and lack of medicines during the sanctions period.][76] The Messenger of God (PBUH) said: "A woman was sent to hellfire on account of a cat. She tied the cat to a leash. She neither fed the cat nor did she let the cat go free to eat from whatever was on the streets. The cat died."[77]

Those who support this regime are equally responsible for all the crimes committed by it. The Messenger of God (PBUH) said: "If the inhabitants of the skies and the earth join hands to kill one Muslim, God will throw all of them into hellfire."[78]

"Should a man intentionally kill a believer, his recompense is Hell, to abide therein forever. The Wrath and Curse of God are upon him, and a dreadful chastisement is prepared for him."[79]

The Messenger of God (PBUH) said: "The first crimes God will adjudge on Judgment Day are those which ended in spilling blood."[80]

He (PBUH) also said: "Wiping out this Earth is more palatable to God than killing one Muslim."[81]

He also said: "On Judgment Day, the person who had been killed will come carrying his head with one hand and blood will be seen pouring out of his arteries, and he will bring with him his killer, dragging him along and asking God: 'My Lord, ask this person why did he kill me?' He will repeat this until God will bring him close to His Throne."[82]

This is what happens when just one person has been killed unjustly. What do you think will transpire on Judgment Day when one million children step forward, each one is carrying his head, dragging his killer behind, and saying "Oh Lord, ask why they killed us?" That was a very grave crime. All Muslims should repent, show remorse, and disassociate themselves from the *Kufr* [non-believers] governments that participated in that crime.

"And Abraham prayed for his father's forgiveness because of a promise he made to him, but when it became clear [that his father was an enemy] to God, he disassociated himself from him."[83]

There is an excellent example in *Ibrahim* [Abraham] and those with him, when they said to their people: "We are free of you and whatever you worship besides God. We have rejected you, and there has arisen, between you and us, enmity and hatred forever unless you believe in God and Him alone."[84]

While this onslaught against the children of Iraq continued for several years, we heard nothing from [the Saudi regime's] Grand *Imams* [top clerics employed by the regime] or official *Ulema* [Islamic scholars] about the sacred status of Muslim blood. But when our *Mujahideen* [Islamic warriors] youth killed one Cross Worshiper[85] whose work was directly related to killing Muslims, your paid *Imams* and writers filled the air waves and loudspeakers across the country and across the world with condemnations of that act. Your paid *Imams* and so-called *Ulema* falsely claimed that he was under covenant [i.e., protection] and he should not have been killed; but they know better than that.[86] Here again, Islam, the Religion of God, not only permitted but mandated the slaughter of God's and the Muslims' enemies. But the *Deen* [religion] of the King calls for sparing the lives of those enemies.

How could the killing of one million children be justified while the killing of one Cross-Worshiper is an unforgivable crime? God will protect me from all of you.

The most incredible accusation against us is accusing the *Mujahideen* [Islamic warriors] of being Zionist agents. What kind of a lie is this? What kind of deception is this? What kind of insult to people's intellect is this? It does not take a genius to see that the Zionist's worst enemy is the *Mujahideen*. But the rulers want to shift the blame of their own crimes to the *Mujahideen* by accusing them of wrongdoing. "But if anyone earns a fault or a sin and throws it to one that is innocent, he burdens himself with falsehood and flagrant sin."[87]

At this point I want to ask the rulers [of Saudi Arabia] the following questions:

• Who contributed 100 million dollars [U.S.] to [Chairman Yasser] Arafat in order to quash the first Palestinian uprising against the Jews?[88]

• In 1969, who was allied with the Jews against the weak in Sharm al-Sheikh?[89]

• Who made [Saudi Arabian] military bases available for use in the invasion of Iraq?[90]

• Who pledged to pay the cost of training of the Iraqi police force so that they can fight and kill the *Mujahideen* there?[91]

• Are you not the proud owners of the Beirut Initiative,[92] in which you legitimized Israel and its occupation of Palestine?

• Were you out of your minds?

• Have you lost all dignity and honor as human beings?

The Messenger of God (PBUH) said: "On the Day of Judgment, three types of people will not be spoken to, purified, or looked at by God: A wicked sheikh, a king who lies, and an arrogant guardian."[93] You have gone so far as to order the *Imams* [clerics] in all the mosques to refrain from asking God to help the *Mujahideen* [Islamic warriors] in Chechnya and elsewhere. You further ordered them to ask God to punish the *Mujahideen* in the land of the Two Holy Places [Mecca and Medina] because you allege that they are Zionist agents. You know you are lying about those *Mujahideen*, and you ordered the *Imams* to participate in the lies and deception campaign with you. Your *Imams* know that you are liars and traitors, but unfortunately they lie with you. However, the Messenger of God (PBUH) has foretold the *Ummah* [Islamic nation] about the time we live in:

"The time will come when deception will be widespread. The truth teller will not be believable, and the liar will be seen as telling the truth. The traitor will be considered trustworthy, and the trustworthy will be accused of betrayal, and the *Rowaibidah* will speak. The Companions asked: 'What is the meaning of *Rowaibidah*?' He said: 'It is the worthless, good-for-nothing man who debates great issues of public importance.'"[94]

I now appeal to all Muslims to call on God to reveal the Zionists and their agents. If you [the Saudi rulers] are sincere in your [allegations that the *Mujahideen* [Islamic warriors] are Zionist agents], I appeal to you to make the following personal *Dua'a* [personal prayer as opposed to required prayers] from both Holy Mosques and instruct your subordinates to do likewise:

"Oh God, use Your Might against the Zionist-American coalition and all those who support and assist them. Oh God, destroy their establishment, break their backs, take away their dominion, make their hearts divided, undo their unity, cause their women to become widows, make their fighting spirit strong only to fight among themselves, expose their private parts in disgrace as they are doing to the *Mujahideen*, disgrace them before the entire world, and punish them more as you will."

I want especially to address my *Mujahideen* [Islamic warriors] brothers. You stood up to defend Islam when very few stood with you. You have sought *Jihad* [holy war] when *Imams* [clerics] and *Ulema* [Islamic scholars] chose to stay behind. You have made known your stand for righteousness when the fearful and selfish remained silent. They said what the sorcerers said before they became believers: "So there came the sorcerers to Pharaoh: They said, 'Of course we shall have a reward if we win!' He said; 'yes, in that case you shall be nearest (to me).'"[95] [Mr. Bin Laden means those who seek protection from the worldly Pharaoh rather than from God.]

But as far as you *Mujahideen* [Islamic warriors] are concerned, your goal is to achieve reward from and be nearest to God, the Most Gracious. You have tasted the sweetness of *Iman* [faith]; and therefore, you have not been deceived by the sweetness of life in this world. That is my thought, but ultimate judgment rests in the Hands of God. May God give you the best rewards for what you have done.

You stood tall, and he who stands tall does not doubt death. You have erased any misconceptions. You have been swimming in the sea of death, and he who does not fear death does not turn back.[96]

You have shattered the myths that have surrounded the tyrants for decades through their lies and deceptions. Congratulations on a job well done! Your blood has provided a guiding light for many generations to come to find the Straight Path of God and stand firmly on it, and to avoid the crooked paths of the tyrants and transgressors. The Messenger of God (PBUH) has said: "I swear by God, if you put one man on the Straight Path, this will benefit you more than owning an unlimited number of red camels."[97]

May God's Mercy be upon our martyred brothers in Palestine, Iraq, Saudi Arabia, Morocco, Kashmir, Afghanistan, Chechnya, Nigeria, Indonesia, the Philippines, Thailand, and everywhere.

May God's Mercy also be upon Sheikhs Yusuf al-Ari, Abu Ali al-Harthy, Khalid al-Haj, Abdel Aziz al-Moqrin, Issa al-Aushan, and all of their brothers. May God also give mercy to the *Mujahideen* [Islamic warriors] who stormed the American Consulate in Jeddah. [Gunman attacked the United States consulate in Jeddah, Saudi Arabia, on December 6, 2004. Several people were killed.][98]

How could the Americans expect to have security if they continuously rain destruction and murder down on our brothers and sisters in Palestine and Iraq? They are not entitled to any level of security any place in the world. According to God's and His Messenger's [the Prophet Muhammad, (PBUH)] Commands, their presence in the Holy Land [Mecca and Medina, the sites of the two Holy Places] and in the entire Arabian Peninsula is forbidden.[99] We hope that God will accept as martyrs our brothers who were killed in the storming of the consulate. I would like to say to our brothers and their parents that God takes what he gives and everything ends at a time predetermined by God. Therefore, be patient, seek God's Best Judgment, and remember what God says: "No misfortune can happen on Earth or in your souls but which is recorded in a book before we bring it into existence. That is truly easy for God."[100]

How could a Muslim not be patient? Here is God, who is the Creator of All Creatures and Things, directing [the Prophet Muhammad (PBUH)] in the mission of which we are a part: "Now await in patience the Command of your Lord. Verily, you are in our eyes, and celebrate the praises of your Lord while you stand forth."[101]

After the end of the Battle of The Trench[102] and the horror which accompanied it, God said: "You have, indeed, in the Messenger of God an excellent example for him who believes in God and the Final Day, and who remembers God much. When the believers saw the Confederate [enemy] forces, they said: 'This is what God and His Messenger (PBUH) have promised us, and God and His Messenger told us what was true.' And it only added to their faith and their zeal in obedience."[103]

The Messenger of God (PBUH) said: "The greater the trial, the greater the reward. And if God comes to Love someone, He will test them with trials. God will then be pleased with those who accepted the tests, and He will not be pleased with those who resented the tests," [In the Quranic verse reproduced in the endnote, the sentence actually ends with a comma.][104]

For what is inflicted on me, I am in a state of perseverance.

Is it not sufficient that God praises perseverance?

And I will not seek pleasures and wealth

If the state of glory happens to be associated with poverty.[105]

So, continue on the Path of God. Do not fear hardship. Cleanse the Arabian Peninsula of infidels and perverts, and do not slacken.

"And slacken not in following up the enemy: If you are suffering hardships, they are suffering similar hardships: but you hope from God what they have not. And God is full of knowledge and wisdom."[106]

Do not let the cowards and wicked deceive you. Our Messenger of God (PBUH) said: "There will always be a part of my *Ummah* [Islamic nation] who will stay steadfast in fighting in the Cause of God and in achieving victory over the enemy. They will not be harmed by those who disagree with them, until Judgment Day."[107]

To the tyrant [King Fahd] we repeat the words of the believers: "They said: 'Never shall we prefer you to what has come to us of the clear signs of Him who created us. Whatever you decree, you can only decree regarding the life of this world.'"[108]

Oh you *Mujahideen* [Islamic warriors], persevere in patience and constancy; and know that God Will Suffice. This is the road of the Prophets, migration and blood, fighting, and scattering [the weak enemies]. You terrify your enemy and your enemy terrifies you. It is no secret that the hottest challenges facing our *Ummah* [Islamic nation] now are the *Jihads* [holy wars] in Palestine and Iraq. So, try your best to support them because you have a golden opportunity to weaken America by attrition. In Iraq, you can weaken America militarily, economically and morally. Lest you regret it, do not waste this opportunity.

You must realize that our enemy's biggest incentive is to control our land and steal its oil. So, do not spare any effort to stop the greatest robbery in history. The oil is the treasure of the current and future generations. The West plots with its allies and puppets in the region to buy our oil at a very low price. All [other] products have increased in price several fold except for oil, which is the basic component of all industry. Oil prices do not reflect market reality. Oil was sold for $40.00 per barrel [U.S.] two decades ago, but sold for [only] $9.00 per barrel a decade ago. The fair price for a barrel of today's oil is $100.00 [U.S.]. Oh you *Mujahideen* [Islamic warriors] do your best to prevent their stealing it. Focus your operations on it, especially in Iraq and the Gulf. This will choke them.

In closing, I send a brief message to the rulers [of Saudi Arabia], and another one to the prominent people among the respected *Ulema* [Islamic scholars], leaders, and businessmen.

Here is my message to the rulers:

Governing is a contract between the *Imam* [ruler] and the people governed. This contract contains rights and obligations for both parties. It also has provisions for cancellation and for making it null and void. One of the provisions which nullifies the contract is betraying the *Deen* [Religion] of the *Ummah* [Islamic nation]. And that is exactly what you have done. Of course, this assumes the contract was valid in the first instance. But we all know that you [the Saudi rulers] have forced yourselves on the people without their consultation or acceptance. You enlisted the help of the British to appoint yourselves the rulers and guardians of the land. The people [now] have awakened from their slumber and have become aware of [your] enormous transgressions, corruption, and encroachment on their property and money. The Muslims [of Saudi Arabia] are determined to reclaim their rights no matter how high the price.

Therefore, you have two choices:

1. Peacefully return to the rightful owners what you have unlawfully taken from them, and allow the people to choose a new Muslim ruler who will govern by the *Holy Quran* and the *Sunnah* [example] of his Messenger (PBUH).

2. Or, refuse the first choice and continue to oppress the people, transgress their rights, and corrupt some members of the general public to beat and kill their brothers and kin who reject your right to govern.

However, by now you must realize that matters are beyond tolerance. You must also know that when the people move to reclaim their rights, no one will be able to stop them, not even the best security apparatus anywhere. Remember what happened to the Shah of Iran, despite the infamous experience and power of his security agencies.[109] Recall the fate of [Nicolae] Ceausescu [110] and his family in Romania.

Thus, you are well advised to consider seriously the first choice. You well know that we at Al Qaeda are not condemning you for anything in this world but for your violations of the *Sharia* [Islamic law]. Your failure to govern by God's Commands and siding with the *Kufr* [non-believers] against Muslims especially must be stopped.

My message to the respected *Ulema* [Islamic scholars, i.e., those who have not been corrupted of the truth], prominent people in key leadership positions, and businessmen is this: realize the seriousness of the situation before it is too late. Events are occurring and matters are changing at incredible speeds. Do your best to defuse the problem. Know that the *Mujahideen* [Islamic warriors] in Saudi Arabia have not yet begun the fight against the government. Should they start, they would undoubtedly begin with the head of the *Kufr* [non-believers], the rulers of Saudi Arabia. What is now occurring there is merely an extension of the war against the Crusader coalition, headed by America, that wages war against us everywhere, as we do likewise. That includes [Saudi Arabia], and we intend to expel them from there, God Willing.

Oh you uncorrupted, prominent *Ulema* [Islamic scholars], respected Islamic leaders, businessmen, and anyone in a position of influence, fear God for your own sake and for the sake of your *Ummah* [Islamic nation]. Those of you who can leave the country must do so in order to fulfill your duty in leading the *Ummah* to a place that is free from the persecution of the tyrant rulers. [Mr. Bin Laden evokes the Islamic notion of *Hijra*, or migration, to a friendly Muslim venue. In his view, Taliban-led Afghanistan was such a venue.]

The longer you hesitate, the worse the problem will become. Matters will get more complicated and will open the door for the *Mujahideen* [Islamic warriors] to act without you. The *Mujahideen* may start their armed operations against the rulers [of Saudi Arabia] the moment that they conclude that they are prepared for the mission of overthrowing the tyrants, and the mission has a reasonable chance of success. However, such a noble and great mission should be carried out using all the efforts of all the believers, lovers, and protectors of the truth. But if some groups are cowardly, that does not relieve the others from the obligation to remove the *Kufr* [non-believers] rulers.

I have advised you about this in the past, but to no avail. Remember that fighting almost erupted at the time of the dispute between the current rulers of Riyadh and their brother, King Saud, but mediation succeeded in averting violence and convincing King Saud to step down.[111] You can do likewise this time. You can try to convince these tyrants to step down without the need for bloodshed.

And finally I call on God with this *Dua'a* [personal prayer]:

Oh God, bless us in this life and in the Hereafter. Give us salvation form the Hellfire.

Oh God, show us the Right Path and guide us to it. Oh God, show us the wrong paths and guide us to avert them.

Oh God, put affection between the hearts of the Muslims, unify their hearts and their bodies [i.e., unite them as one], have mercy on them for their weakness, and cure their ills.

Oh God, bless our *Ummah* [Islamic nation] with a destiny in which those who obey you are glorified and those who disobey you are disgraced — a destiny characterized by enjoining the right and forbidding the wrong.

Oh God, fill our hearts with love for *Iman* [faith] and fill our hearts with hate for *Kufr* [non-believers], disobedience, and deviance.

Oh God, open the hearts of our young men and women to hold tightly Your Commands. Give us the means for piety.

Oh God, hold our feet firm [i.e., steadfastness] at a time in which many feet will slip.

Oh God, help us and the *Mujahideen* [Islamic Warriors] everywhere to stand firm on your Path, especially in Palestine, Iraq, Kashmir, Afghanistan, Chechnya, and the land of the two Holy Mosques [Saudi Arabia].

Oh God, help the *Mujahideen* to strike their targets, fill their hearts with calmness and courage, give them Divine Support, and give them victory over Your Enemy and their enemy. For no one can help or give victory to us or to them but for You, the Exalted and Most Powerful. God has full power and control over His Affairs; but most among mankind know it not.

Oh God, may Your Prayer and Blessings be upon [the Prophet] Muhammad (PBUH), his household, and his Companions.

And our last call is: Praise be to God the Cherisher and Sustainer of the Worlds.

Epilogue

Lessons Learned For America

Having now read Osama bin Laden's own words, you have learned two important lessons about him. First, he does not hate us because we are free. He hates us because he claims that the United States is engaged in a Christian Crusade against Islam. As evidence of this Crusade, he points to six policies of the United States: 1) support for Israel; 2) support for the autocratic regimes of the Middle East; 3) support for non-Muslim countries outside the Middle East who are either repressing Muslims or battling Muslim insurgencies; 4) stationing of military forces in Saudi Arabia and the Gulf States; 5) invasions of Afghanistan and Iraq; and 6) exploitation of Middle East oil resources by pressuring the producing countries to depress oil prices below their real market value.

Second, he is neither a nihilist nor a madman. He is a brilliant and formidable foe who eloquently appeals to the world's 1.2 billion Muslims, especially the 300 million Muslim Arabs who live in the Middle East. What makes him so dangerous is that his complaints about our policies and the autocratic regimes of the Middle East mirror the Muslim Arabs' own complaints. The repressive governments of the region prevent them from freely expressing themselves. However, whenever Mr. Bin Laden releases a new video or audiotape criticizing the regimes, he is acting as a conduit for their own grievances. Ironically, even though he is a fugitive, he is living more freely than they are.

Immediately after 9/11, many Muslims condemned the attacks as un-Islamic. Also, many Muslims empathized with the United States because of the grievous loss of life. However, today much of that empathy has dissolved. The United States is now hated throughout the Muslim world, and Mr. Bin Laden is perceived as the new Robin Hood.[1]

Tragically, we have brought this situation upon ourselves. Since 9/11, the Bush administration has alienated a good portion of the Islamic world because of its mistreatment of Muslim detainees in Afghanistan, Iraq, and Guantanamo Bay, Cuba. The administration's "rendition policy" (by which it seizes perceived terrorist suspects and spirits them away to third-world countries like Uzbekistan for brutal interrogation) and its invasion of Iraq have also given deep traction to Mr. Bin Laden's warning about a new Christian Crusade having been unleashed on the Islamic world. If we do not reverse course, our self-declared war on terrorism will soon degenerate into a long and bitter holy war against the world's 1.2 billion Muslims — a war that we cannot win. If we do not act soon, it will be too late for many of us. In this era of proliferating weapons of mass destruction, it is not a question of whether we will be attacked with weapons of mass destruction; rather it is a question of the number of such attacks we shall have to endure. That number will dramatically increase during a prolonged holy war on Islam.

Ironically, President George W. Bush jump-started the risk of holy war by his use of one word. On September 16, 2001, he described the war on terrorism as a "crusade." (See Preface, endnote 8.) Though the White House later retracted his statement, the damage had been done. His use of the word "crusade" has been broadcast repeatedly in the media throughout the Middle East and the Islamic world. Since 1991, Mr. Bin Laden had been warning the Islamic world that the United States was engaged in a new Crusade against Islam that began with its introduction of military forces into Saudi Arabia in August 1990. Now President Bush was conveying the same message.

The United States provided tangible proof of the new Crusade on March 20, 2003, when it invaded Iraq. Whereas the West focused on the sight of Saddam Hussein's statute being toppled in downtown Iraq a few days after the invasion, the Muslim world focused on the humiliating sight of Christian soldiers occupying Baghdad, which had been the seat of the Abbasid Caliphate.[2] Osama bin Laden could not have been happier when American troops began pouring into Iraq. The United States had vindicated him and his message.

Muslims everywhere are now beginning to ask themselves whether the Iraq invasion and the continuing attacks on Muslims in Palestine, China, Chechnya, Kashmir, India, and the Philippines are being driven by a new Crusade. If their answer is in the affirmative, Mr. Bin Laden has told them what to do: their duty is to engage in *Jihad* (holy war) and defend Islam wherever it is under attack. He has reminded them that according to the *Holy Quran* and the *Hadith* (traditions of the Prophet Muhammad [peace be upon him, hereinafter "PBUH"]), they have three weapons from which to choose: their hands, their tongues, and their hearts.[3] In the Arab Middle East, seventy percent of the population is younger than the age of twenty-five.[4] The young people who answer his call to *Jihad* will choose their "hands." Tongues and hearts are the weapons of the elderly.

Mr. Bin Laden has also shown them the way to ultimate victory. He and his devout *Mujahideen* (Islamic warriors) defeated the two greatest "infidel" superpowers in the West with the simplest of weapons and plans. Between 1979 and 1988, they shot the Soviet Union's military forces out of Afghanistan; and on 9/11, he and his co-conspirators successfully attacked the continental United States and inflicted mass casualties. In his statements in the preceding pages, he has mocked U.S. military technology and has imparted tactical lessons of warfare that he learned while evading U.S. forces in Afghanistan after 9/11. He reminds the new *Mujahideen* that if they stay on good terms with the Lord, they can accomplish anything. In his *Fatwa* (religious decree) of 1998, he identified their targets. They are authorized to kill Americans and their collaborators, military or civilian, wherever they are found.

President Mubarak of Egypt predicted that the American invasion of Iraq would create "a hundred Bin Ladens."[5] More likely it has created thousands. In an Islamic world thirsty for modern heroes, poems will be written about Mr. Bin Laden, millions will adore him, and most worrisome of all, millions will emulate him. 9/11 was the "Big Bang." A resulting holy war against the world's 1.2 billion Muslims will create an inflationary and inflamatory universe full of religious hatred with unimaginable losses of human life. A focused, secular war on terrorism will create a finite universe in which we can achieve victory in the foreseeable future. The outcome will depend on whether the United States can shed its Crusader image by revising its flawed policies and fighting strategies.

We can begin by redefining the war on terrorism itself. Terrorism is a tactic, not a target. The Congress of the United States should have declared war on Osama bin Laden and Al Qaeda rather than to give the president carte blanche to engage in worldwide preemptive wars against Muslim countries. As you have read in the previous pages, Mr. Bin Laden had declared war on the United States in 1996. We should have reciprocated, if not in 1996, then certainly in 2001. Targeting him would have engaged us in a focused war with an end in sight. We could have brought all of our resources to bear on our main targets, Mr. Bin Laden and Al Qaeda. Had we put more troops on the ground in Afghanistan in 2001, the war would have been over by now.

Instead, President Bush launched a global war against the tactic of terrorism that too easily translates into a war on Islam. At this writing, the United States has invaded and occupies Afghanistan and Iraq, both Muslim countries. Today, we are training Philippine government military forces in counterinsurgency tactics so that they can face a Muslim separatist movement in the southern islands that has been raging, on and off, since 1521! We are training Georgian military forces so that they can confront Muslim Chechen insurgents who are hiding out in the adjoining Pankisi Gorge. We have built military bases in Kyrgyzstan, Uzbekistan, and Tajikistan and have an agreement for "landing rights" in Kazakhistan. Besides protecting the Caspian Sea oil pool's estimated 200 billion barrels of reserves, these bases also help to deter attacks against these repressive regimes by indigenous Muslim separatist movements.[6]

The above listed activities have hurt the war on terrorism in two distinct ways. First, they have given the war an overwhelmingly anti-Islamic flavor. Second, they have diluted and diverted our resources away from the important targets. For example, in December 2001 we should have been concentrating our attention and our forces on the capture or killing of Osama bin Laden, who was hiding out in Tora Bora, Afghanistan. Instead, General Tommy Franks was already preparing for the invasion of Iraq.[7] Mr. Bin Laden escaped, and his whereabouts remain unknown at this writing.

In spite of our military's engagement of Islam on multiple fronts worldwide, the Bush administration continues to try to convince Muslims that Islam is not the enemy. Since his use of the word "crusade" in 2001, President Bush has sought to restore his credibility in the Islamic world by referring to Islam as a religion of peace. He has even invited Muslim leaders to the White House to share in feasts celebrating Muslim holidays. His efforts have failed thus far because he, his administration, and his supporters have been sending mixed messages to the Islamic world.

Since 9/11, the Reverends Jerry Farwell, Franklin Graham, Pat Robertson, and Jerry Vines, the leaders of the Christian Right, President Bush's political base, have repeatedly and publicly blasphemed Islam and the Prophet Muhammad (PBUH). They have called the Prophet (PBUH) a terrorist, a pedophile, and an outlaw. They have branded Islam as a religion of violence. President Bush has yet to criticize these leaders by name. To the contrary, over the protests of Islamic groups across the country, his administration allowed Reverend Graham to deliver the homily at the Pentagon breakfast on Good Friday 2003.[8]

Similarly, Lt. General William Boykin, the Pentagon's Deputy Undersecretary of Defense for Intelligence, addresses evangelical Christian church audiences while dressed in full military uniform and claims that his God is "bigger" than Islam's and that Islam's God is an "idol." For all intents and purposes, General Boykin perceives himself to be a Crusader. Rather than to punish him for his inflammatory rhetoric, Defense Secretary Donald Rumsfeld commended the General as a fine officer.[9]

In addition, the atrocities committed by United States military and civilian personnel against detainees in Afghanistan, Iraq, and Guantanamo Bay, Cuba demonstrate to the Islamic world that the administration is long on words about respecting Islam but short on deeds. The physical abuse and sexual humiliation of Muslim detainees at the notorious Abu Ghraib prison in Baghdad were documented by photographs taken by their guards. The infamous photograph of a smiling female guard pointedly mocking the genitals of a naked male Muslim prisoner set back the cause of women's rights in the Islamic world a hundred years. And in an Islamic world where dogs are considered filthy, the photographs of naked Muslim detainees on their hands and knees wearing dog collars and leashed to their guards will never disappear from the media. Because of these photographs, millions of Muslims around the world will not need Osama bin Laden to convince them that a new Crusade has been unleashed on Islam.

Proof of this occurred during the week of May 9, 2005, when violent anti-U.S. protests at which several people were killed broke out across the Islamic world. They began in Afghanistan on May 11th and by May 14th had spread to Gaza, Palestine, Pakistan, and Indonesia. The catalyst was an article in the May 9th issue of *Newsweek Magazine* which reported that American guards had desecrated a prisoner's *Holy Quran* by flushing it down a toilet. The Islamic world is so inflamed at the United States that just thirteen words in one English-language magazine launched thousands of angry Muslim demonstrators into streets across the Islamic world.

Though the Bush administration has publicly announced that it is investigating the incident, the Islamic world knows that this is the same administration that authored the infamous "torture memoranda" in 2001 that gave the green light to interrogators in Afghanistan, Iraq and other venues to physically and psychologically abuse Muslim detainees in violation of the Geneva Convention. Only in December, 2004, after many protests from human rights groups across the world and after the publication of the photographs of the atrocities at the Abu Ghraib prison, did the administration recant the memoranda. Nor has the administration punished any high echelon military officers or civilian leaders as a result of the revelations about the abuse of the Muslim detainees. Rather, lower-echelon guards have been made the scapegoats. They have been court-martialed and reprimanded in what appears to the Islamic world to be a whitewash of the decision-makers responsible for the abuses. Note also that White House Counsel Alberto R. Gonzalez, who approved the "torture memoranda" in 2001 and passed them on to President Bush for action, has been promoted by the President to the position of Attorney General of the United States. Thus, the Bush administration does not have much currency in the Islamic world when it says that it will investigate the alleged abuses of Muslim detainees and punish the perpetrators.

The Islamic world also well knows that the administration has been kidnapping or capturing dozens of Muslims across the world as "terrorist suspects" and secretly spiriting them away to third world countries for brutal interrogation that certainly includes physical torture. Ironically, several of the destinations of these "renditions," as they are officially known, are to Middle East countries like Syria and Egypt. Muslim Arabs across the Middle East are very familiar with those repressive regimes' inhumane interrogation techniques.[10]

Frankly, the Islamic world is aflame with anti-American hatred because America lit the match. Before President Bush can credibly convince the Islamic world that he is not actually engaged in a Crusade against Islam, he first has to get his own house in order. Instead of doing so, he has made matters even worse by recently implementing a new program that is certain to alienate the Islamic world even further.

The Muslim World Outreach Program is an outgrowth of a 2003 White House National Strategy for Combating Terrorism. The administration has now decided that the United States is "radioactive" in the Islamic world not because of its policies but rather because of Islam. In spite of American's Constitutional guarantee of freedom of religion, the government is embarking upon a program to change the practice of Islam itself. Opting for Cold War strategies successfully employed against the godless Soviet Union, the United States now seeks to provide covert financial assistance to Islamic "moderates" (whatever those are) in an effort to promote the shared values of democracy, women's rights, and tolerance. (All of this presupposes that Islam contravenes democracy, represses women, and is intolerant. Muslims respectfully disagree with this depiction.[11]) The Central Intelligence Agency (C.I.A.) is also authorized to target Islamic media, Muslim clerics and scholars, and Muslim political parties. This very well could involve the assassination of offending Muslim religious and political leaders. Pentagon money is already pouring into at least two dozen Muslim countries across the world, directed to Islamic radio and television shows, coursework in Islamic schools, the building of such schools, Islamic think tanks, political workshops, and programs promoting our version of Islamic moderation. A listing of those countries and programs was recently published in *U.S. News and World Report.*

The Muslim World Outreach Program is a provocation of the Islamic world. First, no Christian country should be attempting to redefine Islam. This is sacrilege and gives deep traction to Mr. Bin Laden's contention that the United States is a crusading power intent on destroying Islam. Second, the revelation of the financial ties between "moderates" and the United States will likely discredit all Islamic moderates as perceived agents of the United States government. They will be afraid to speak out for fear of their personal safety. Third, the program completely misapprehends Islam. I respectfully submit that the Muslim World Outreach Program failed the moment it was exposed in the public forum.[12]

The elements of the Program also demonstrate how deeply Islam is misunderstood by America's leaders and by Americans themselves. Even the much vaunted 9/11 Commission's recent report on terrorism completely misapprehends Islam and the nature of the war on terrorism. Its simplistic and superficial treatment of Islam and the roots of terrorism resulted from its failure to draw on insights from Islamic scholars. Its errors of omission are almost as injurious as its errors of commission.

For example, the report never addresses the need to change the specific policies of the United States in the Islamic world that have been the main catalysts of Islamic fundamentalism. Rather, the report perceives Islam as the threat and offers strategies to bring Islamic moderates to the forefront. Conceivably, the report could result in our government's formulating a "good-Muslim, bad-Muslim policy." Perhaps the Muslim World Outreach Program is just such a policy.[13]

The Program also plays right into Mr. Bin Laden's hands. The Islamic world will not tolerate this effort by the United States to redefine its religion. The *Holy Quran* teaches Muslims to respect the holy books of Christians and Jews because they are monotheists. However, it also teaches them to protect their Faith against the non-believers who would corrupt it. As you have read in the preceding pages, Mr. Bin Laden concentrates on these latter verses to galvanize his supporters. President Bush must retract the Muslim Outreach Program immediately. He and his administration must realize that they cannot tinker with Islam. In spite of Christianity's 622-year head start, Islam remains the world's fastest growing religion because its hallmarks are the spread of the faith, economic and social justice, and tolerance.[14]

Having demonstrated that Islam is not the problem, I now return to the specific American policies which Mr. Bin Laden cites as proof of the new Crusade: 1) support for Israel; 2) support for the autocratic regimes of the Middle East; 3) support for non-Muslim countries outside the Middle East who are either repressing Muslims or are battling Muslim insurgencies; 4) stationing of American military forces in Saudi Arabia and the Gulf States; 5) the American invasions of Afghanistan and Iraq; and 6) exploitation of Middle East oil resources. I shall discuss them in order. The reader will soon understand that, indeed, they have directly contributed to America's radioactivity in the Islamic world, especially in the Middle East. In discussing the policies, I shall suggest corrections that will neutralize Mr. Bin Laden's message. If the corrections are not implemented, then religious hatred will overwhelm reason and we will have chosen the inflationary and inflammatory universe that I described a few paragraphs back.

Preliminarily, I note that in criticizing our support for Israel, Mr. Bin Laden seizes upon the *political* division between Arabs and Jews in Palestine and transmutes it into a *religious* division. Putting aside the fact that a significant percentage of the Palestinian Arabs are Christian, Mr. Bin Laden portrays the dispute in entirely religious terms as a fight between Muslims and Jews. He selects snippets of Quranic verse and the *Hadith* (traditions of the Prophet [PBUH]) in urging his followers to wrest control of Jerusalem (*Al Quds*) and the *Al-Aqsa* mosque from their Jewish masters. But he ignores the *Holy Quran's* admonishment that Muslims must respect Jews because they are monotheists.[15]

Furthermore, he ignores the positive common history shared by the Arabs (Muslim and Christian alike) and the Jews in the Middle East. Before 1948, the Arabs and the Jews got along much better than they do now. Israel was created in that year. After that, small fissures between them became crevasses. But the point to recognize is that since 1948 the divide between the Arabs and the Jews has been political, not religious. The dispute is about land and sovereignty, not about who has the better God. After all, Abraham's God is the God of both peoples. Perhaps if more Jews and Arabs focused on their earlier, glorious history together, they would be more disposed to make peace now. Therefore, I begin my discussion of America's support for contemporary Israel by harkening back to the 8th Century A.D.

When the Muslim Arabs conquered the Byzantine Empire (the remnant of the Roman Empire) and seized Constantinople (Turkey), in the 8th Century, the Jews living in the Empire fared much better than they had under the rule of the Christian Byzantines.

Between the 8th and 12th Centuries the Jews and the Arabs of the Middle East shared in the remarkable achievements of that period of Islamic history. For example, in Muslim Babylonia (Iraq) Jewish academies were instrumental in establishing the Babylonian Talmud as the authoritative text of Judaism.

However, earlier tolerance for the Jews in Christian Europe declined precipitously with the coming of the Crusades in 1095. The passion of the Crusaders and their attendant hostility toward non-Christians was first directed toward the Jews of the Rhineland. The Christian Crusaders massacred them while they traveled to the Holy Land. When the Crusaders seized Jerusalem in 1099 they slaughtered every Muslim *and* Jewish man, woman, and child in the city. It is said that the blood reached the knees and bridle reins of the Crusaders' horses as they rode through the Temple Mount.[16]

Between the 11th and 14th Centuries, the Jews found themselves living precariously under the crusading Christians' rule. In the 13th Century, they were the victims of the infamous "blood libel," which accused them of kidnapping and killing Christian children so that they could use their blood in religious rituals. Catholic councils in 1179 and 1215 prohibited Jews from employing Christians, prohibited Christians from living in Jewish neighborhoods, and insisted that Jews wear special badges of identification. European countries also began to expel the Jews. England expelled them in 1290, France in 1306, and Germany through to the 15th Century. Christian hostility towards the Jews also increased during the Black Death Plague between 1347 and 1351, when the Christians accused them of having caused the Plague by poisoning the water wells.

Throughout this period, the Jews were best treated and flourished in southern Spain, controlled by Muslim Arabs. Northern Spain was still under Christian rule. In southern Spain the Jews and the Arabs together achieved a cultural golden age between the 12th and 13th Centuries. Many of Spain's Jewish intellectuals were educated in philosophy, science, poetry, Hebrew grammar, and history. Many of the Jews spoke Arabic and occupied important administrative positions in the government. Because of their language skills, they intermediated between the Spanish-speaking and Arabic-speaking populations.

But by the 14th Century Roman Catholic monastic orders in northern Spain had become increasingly powerful. They routinely preached against the Jews. In 1391 northern Spain was racked by Christian attacks on the Jews. The Jews had three choices: escape to the Muslim South, convert to Christianity, or die.

In 1492, the Christian Spaniards re-conquered southern Spain from the Muslim Arabs. In the same year, King Ferdinand V and Queen

Isabel I expelled all non-converted Jews and Arabs from Spain. The converts who remained became the targets of the notorious Spanish Inquisition. After the expulsion, many Jews migrated to the lands of the Ottoman Empire, including Greece, northern Africa, Palestine, and Turkey. There they were granted sanctuary by the Muslims.

Beginning in the 16th Century, Jews began to migrate back to European venues. For a short period they benefited from the increased religious tolerance of the Scientific Revolution of the 17th Century and the coming Industrial Revolution. In 1791 France became the first country to grant them emancipation. Germany followed suit in 1871. By the 19th Century such grants proliferated throughout much of Europe. Russia, however, hesitated.

After emancipation, the Jews began to enjoy prominence in many areas of Christian Europe's educational, mercantile, and cultural endeavors. Their numbers in the universities and the professions rose to levels beyond their proportion in the population. They became successful entrepreneurs and bankers.

However, success bred jealousy. By the 1870s, European hatred of the Jews was expressed in a new form: Anti-Semitism, which asserted that Jews were a distinct, inferior race that represented a clear and present danger to Christian Europe. After the assassination of Tsar Alexander II in 1881, the Russians organized Anti-Semitic massacres of Jews called Pogroms. Pogroms swept across the southern part of the Russian empire and parts of Europe. During recurrent Pogroms Jews were killed in large numbers. Just as they had done after the Spanish expulsion, many Jews fled to the lands of the Ottoman Empire. Again they were granted sanctuary by the Muslims. Tragically, however, the worst was yet to come for the Jews of Europe: the Nazi Holocaust of 1933-1945.[17]

Thus, with their shared history of mutual benefit during the heyday of the Islamic empire and mutual victimization by the Christians, Jews and Muslim Arabs had more in common than divided them. That all changed with the creation of Israel in 1948. Between 1915 and 1916, British High Commissioner Sir Henry McMahon had promised Sherif Hussein, the Emir of Mecca, independence for the Arabs if they rose up against the Ottoman Turks, Britain's enemy during World War I. They did so and expected the British to fulfill their promise. However, by a secret declaration in 1917, British Foreign Secretary Sir Arthur James

Balfour promised support for an independent Jewish state in Palestine, contradicting the McMahon-Hussein correspondence. Thus, the British effectively promised Palestine to both the Arabs (Muslim and Christian) and the Jews.[18]

British deceit provoked violence between the Arabs and the Jews, especially Jewish Zionists who had gravitated to Palestine. Ironically, Theodore Hertzl had founded the Zionist movement in the late 1800s in response to European Pogroms and Anti-Semitism. Zionism sought a secure Jewish state in Palestine. Finally in 1947, under the auspices of the United Nations, Palestine was partitioned into Jewish and Arab sections. The Palestinians rejected the plan and war broke out. Neighboring Arab countries joined in, but Israel's forces prevailed.

The positives of the shared history of the Jews and Arabs were quickly forgotten in the flames of the 1948 war. The Arab Middle East viewed Israel's creation as the product of Western colonialism. Of course, the Jews viewed Israel's creation as a rightful return to their Biblical land. After 1948, Jews and Arabs fought four wars between themselves: the 1948 war, the 1967 war, the 1973 war (which led to a peace treaty with Egypt), the 1982 war (when Israel invaded Lebanon), and the Palestinian *Intifada* (2000 to the present). During most of this period, the Arabs saw the United States giving generous military and financial aid to Israel while at the same time attempting to broker peace between the warring parties whenever the opportunity arose.

The outcome of the 1967 war exacerbated the tensions between the Jews and the Arabs (Muslim and Christian). Now Israel found itself an occupying power, having seized the West Bank of the Jordan River and the Gaza Strip to the south. Millions of Palestinians lived under the occupation of the Israeli Defense Forces (I.D.F.). Since then, over forty years of occupation have brutalized both the occupiers and the occupied.

During the occupation, and especially after the beginning of the Palestinian *Intifada* in 2000, Palestinian resistance was met with harsh responses. Collective punishment was commonly meted out to hundreds of thousands of Palestinians; thousands of Palestinian homes were bulldozed in the name of security; thousands of Palestinians and hundreds of Jews were killed and wounded; and thousands of Palestinian men were imprisoned, often without charges. At this writing, 8,000 of them remain in Israeli prisons.[19]

Lacking arms comparable to those of the IDF, Palestinian desperation led to a rash of suicide bombings in the Occupied Territories and Israel proper. Hamas, the Al-Aqsa Martyrs Brigade, and Islamic Jihad claimed responsibility for many of the bombings. Though many Christians are counted among Palestinian Arabs, today's Palestinian resistance has assumed a definite Islamic flavor.

President George W. Bush assumed office in 2000 and made matters worse. Whereas Presidents Jimmy Carter and William Jefferson Clinton had taken a proactive approach to the Israeli-Palestinian peace process in which they desperately tried to reconcile the warring parties, President Bush and his administration remained on the sidelines. The timing could not have been worse. In September 2000, Ariel Sharon, then the Likud Party leader, insisted on visiting the Nobel Sanctuary (Temple Mount) and the *Al-Aqsa* mosque (Islam's third holiest site) with approximately 1,000 bodyguards. He was warned that it would provoke a response by the Palestinian Muslims. The response was the *Intifada*, originally referred to as the "*Al-Aqsa Intifada.*"

In 2002, President Bush added fuel to the fire when he referred to Prime Minister Ariel Sharon as a "man of peace." His comment inflamed the Arab Middle East almost as much as his "crusader" comment of 2001. Most of the Middle East views Mr. Sharon as a war criminal for his complicity in the 1982 massacre of Palestinian men, women, and children by Christian Phalangist militia in the Sabra and Shatila refugee camps in Beirut, Lebanon, during the Lebanese Civil War. Then General Sharon had led Israel's military forces into Lebanon that same year. His forces were in control of the sector of Beirut in which the massacres occurred. Later, an Israeli investigative commission found him to be indirectly responsible for the massacres for failure to prevent them. The allegation ultimately resulted in his resignation as Defense Minister.[20]

President Bush's policy of benign neglect had the effect of giving Prime Minister Ariel Sharon free rein to deal with the Palestinians as he saw fit. At this writing, Mr. Sharon seeks to impose a unilateral peace with the Palestinians. He is building a massive barrier the length of Israel to divide Israel from the Palestinians. The barrier reaches deeply into the land promised to the Palestinians according to the 1993 Oslo Accords in order to protect Jewish settlements and ensure that the Palestinian state will be no more than a cluster of Palestinian Bantustans. He also intends to withdraw unilaterally from Gaza and leave it isolated from other

Palestinian areas. Though President Bush has said that he favors the creation of a Palestinian state, he has done nothing to deter Mr. Sharon's destructive plans.

All of this has played right into Osama bin Laden's hands. He rails about the deaths of the Palestinians at the hands of the Israelis. He rails about Israel's control of the Noble Sanctuary-Temple Mount and the *Al-Aqsa* mosque. He speaks of the Palestinian resistance as a Muslim resistance to the "Zionist-Christian Crusaders." He even rejects the now-deceased Chairman Arafat and the Palestinian Authority as un-Islamic. In his eyes and in the eyes of millions of Muslims in the Islamic world, Israel's repressive measures in the Occupied Territories are being practiced on Muslims, not necessarily Palestinians. Because high-profile Islamic insurgent groups like Hamas and the *Al-Aqsa* Martyrs Brigade (deemed terrorist organizations by the United States) are leading the fight against Israel in the Occupied Territories, the resistance has taken on an Islamic hue to the advantage of Mr. Bin Laden.

The Editor fully believes that were the United States to resume the role of neutral arbiter and work hard to achieve a fair peace agreement that resulted in a viable Palestinian state, much of Mr. Bin Laden's appeal would disappear almost overnight. The Islamic template with which he has overwritten the Palestinian resistance would lose its traction in the Islamic world.

Moreover, in spite of Mr. Bin Laden's inflammatory rhetoric about Israel's continued existence, no reasonable person in the Middle East or the Islamic world advocates the "destruction" of the state of Israel. Even as radical a group as Hamas has declared a ceasefire in Palestine in order to give newly elected Palestinian Authority President Mahmoud Abbas an opportunity to negotiate a peace agreement with Israel.

It is also an opportune time to achieve peace because even Prime Minister Ariel Sharon realizes that Israel has no choice but to withdraw from the Occupied Territories. Five million Jews live in Israel's pre-1967 borders along with one million Israeli Arabs. 3.5 million Palestinians live in the Occupied Territories. The high Palestinian birth rate is a ticking time bomb ready to explode Israel's national identity as a Jewish state. Some Palestinian political thinkers are even discussing the withdrawal of their demand for an independent Palestinian state and allowing the Palestinian birth rate to decide Israel's ultimate fate. By the year 2020, there will be 6.5 million Jews in Israel proper and 8.5 million Arabs in Israel and the Occupied Territories, plus another one million non-Jews of other origins.[21]

In all respects, the direct interests of Israel and the Palestinians, and the national security interests of the United States, demand the achievement of a viable peace agreement between Israel and the Palestinians. That means the creation of a viable Palestinian state that controls its borders, its air space, and its water rights, and the question of control over the Noble Sanctuary-Temple Mount must be answered to the satisfaction of all concerned. The Muslims of the world must be able to visit and pray at the *Al-Aqsa* mosque at any time; and the Jews of the world must be able to visit and pray at the Wailing Wall at any time.

It is no wonder, then, that the United States finds itself so "radioactive" in the Middle East and the Islamic world. If President Bush continues to pursue his policy of benign neglect while Prime Minister Sharon imposes his unilateral and unjust peace on the Palestinians, Mr. Bin Laden's message about the "Christian-Zionist Crusade" against Islam will root deeply. The Islamic character of the Palestinian cause will assume exponential proportions and attract thousands, if not millions, of new *Mujahideen* (Islamic warriors) to Mr. Bin Laden's cause.

Mr. Bin Laden next points to American support for the corrupt, autocratic regimes of the Middle East as another facet of the new Crusade against Islam. This has as much, if not more, traction than his complaint about American support for Israel. After all, these repressive regimes directly affect their populations. In one important respect the two contentions are interrelated. Through their controlled media, the regimes continue to stir the caldron of hatred toward Israel in order to divert attention away from themselves. Though impotent in the face of Israel's overwhelming military strength, they depict themselves as "front-line" states facing the Islamic world's archenemy. It is better to allow them to continue to rule than to allow instability to weaken them in the face of the enemy. Ironically, one of the greatest perpetrators of this fraud is Egypt, which signed a peace treaty with Israel in 1979 and receives 1.3 billion dollars a year in financial aid from the United States for having done so.[22]

Any discussion of America's support for the corrupt, autocratic regimes of the Middle East must begin with a discussion of American hypocrisy in the region. Having found no weapons of mass destruction in Iraq, President Bush now says that he invaded that country to create a democracy as a catalyst for democratic regime change throughout the Middle East.[23] However, the Bush administration has done nothing to encourage true democratic reform in the countries of the Middle East other than Iraq. To the contrary, its policy seems to be one of expounding democratic platitudes while conducting business as usual. The record is replete with examples of the administration's doublespeak.

On April 25, 2005, President Bush hosted a visit by Saudi Arabian Crown Prince Abdullah at the former's ranch in Crawford, Texas. The media were treated to a photo opportunity session at which they captured the president holding the hand of the Crown Prince as he led the latter into his home.[24] Crown Prince Abdullah heads the most corrupt, autocratic, and repressive regime in the Middle East. Saudi Arabia's internal issues were specifically not discussed at the meeting; rather the main subject was oil prices.[25]

In addition to the president's intimacy with the Crown Prince, during the same week Egyptian President Hosni Mubarak's government disrupted pro-democracy demonstrations mounted by the popular Muslim Brotherhood political party. Ironically, the demonstrations were in response to President Bush's call for democratic reform in the region. Large numbers of demonstrators and Muslim Brotherhood leaders were arrested. At this writing, the cycle continues to repeat itself in autocratic Egypt. Yet the Bush administration has done nothing to punish the Egyptian government for its repressive actions.[26]

Moreover, during her visit to the Middle East in late June 2005, Secretary of State Condolezza Rice clearly signaled that the Bush Administration is emphasizing stability over the aggressive pursuit of democracy in the region. Miss Rice refused to meet with representatives of the Muslim Brotherhood. Throughout her trip she barely nudged the autocrats of Egypt, Jordan and Saudi Arabia towards democracy demurring to each nation's finding its "own pace" towards democracy. The wait may, indeed, be very lengthy as none of the autocratic regimes expressed a willingness to surrender their absolute power.[27]

President Bush has also commended Saudi Arabia's recent elections for municipal councils, but he did not mention that women were not allowed to vote in the elections; the municipal councils have no power; and fifty percent of their membership will be appointed by the Saudi government. That Islamic fundamentalists dominated the elections did not bother President Bush because he knows that the councils are powerless.[28]

Similarly, he commended Egyptian President Mubarak's announcement that the coming Egyptian presidential election will be opened to other candidates. But viable opposition candidates are ineligible to run for the office. The presidential election will be as much of a sham as have been past elections. The United States has done nothing to prevent this fraud on the Egyptian electorate. Nor has President Bush criticized President Mubarak's intention to run for a highly unpopular fifth term of office. Perhaps this is the quid pro quo for Egypt's interrogation and torture of the dozens of "rendered" detainees sent to that venue by the United States.[29]

Recently, President Bush welcomed Libyan dictator Colonel Mohammar Qaddafi back into the fold of the Western powers because he had confessed to possessing uranium-enrichment equipment when he was about to be confronted with evidence that he possessed it. Although Colonel Qaddafi's prisons are overflowing with thousands of political prisoners, President Bush has not mentioned democracy or free elections to the Colonel.[30]

The Bush administration also lauds Lebanon's recent demonstrations against the presence of Syrian troops after the assassination of Prime Minister Rafiq Hariri on February 14, 2005, as emblematic of the new democracy sweeping across the Middle East. Under pressure from the United States and the United Nations, the Syrians withdrew their troops. The only problem with President Bush's view is that Lebanon was already a democracy with a viable constitution. The Syrians were invited into Lebanon as a peace keeping force after the conclusion of the Lebanon Civil War in 1990. With their departure in 2005, it remains to be seen whether the cultural and religious hatreds that drove the Civil War will be revisited on the Lebanese people.[31]

The Islamic world also sees a prime example of American hypocrisy toward Islam in its position regarding Muslim Iran's development of nuclear power technology. (Ironically, though a theocracy, Iran actually has an elected President and an active Parliament with many women members.) Without pause, the United States rails against Iran's uranium enrichment program as masking a secret ambition to develop nuclear weapons. However, the United States remains stonily silent about Israel's possession of approximately 200 nuclear weapons.

Though the Iranians deny any ambition to develop nuclear weapons and claim that their enrichment program is intended for peaceful purposes, the United States disbelieves them. However, even if the United States is correct about Iran's nuclear ambitions, the Islamic world views Israel's possession of nuclear weapons as provoking her neighbors to develop such weapons for their own protection. If the United States wants to gain currency in the Islamic world on the issue of the proliferation of nuclear weapons, then it is better advised to begin speaking of a "nuclear free" Middle East. That would include Israel.[32]

Thus, the Muslims of the Middle East and the Islamic world do not subscribe to the Bush administrations charade of substantive, democratic change in the Middle East. They view the Iraq invasion as a grab at Iraq's oil. To their eyes, the United States is building a pliant Iraqi government that will grant her long-term agreements for the basing of American military forces in that venue. They also believe that the United States will continue to coddle the region's existing corrupt, autocratic, and repressive regimes because it fears what may result from true democracy in the region. They may be correct.

Since the 1979 Iran Revolution, the United States has apparently opted for the lesser of two perceived evils, choosing to support the mostly secular, autocratic regimes of the Middle East over their "illiberal" populations.[33] For example, in 1992 it gave tacit support to the Algerian Army's seizure of power when free elections were about to transfer control of the government to the Islamic Salvation Front, which had promised to adopt the *Sharia* (Islamic law). The coup provoked a bitter, bloody civil war that persists to this writing.[34] America's continued coddling of the Egyptian and Saudi regimes suggests that America's perception of the local populations remains unchanged.

Ironically, American support for the pro-American theocratic Saudi regime has facilitated Osama bin Laden's popularity. Provoked by its own fear of the spread of Shi'ism after the 1979 Iranian Revolution, the Saudi government has spent approximately 75 billion dollars (U.S.) spreading their own *Wahhabi* brand of Islam.[35] Mr. Bin Laden is a *Wahhabi*. As you learned from the preceding pages, *Jihad* (holy war) is the lifeblood of Wahhabism and the Saudi-sponsored *Madrassas* (Islamic schools) along the Pakistan-Afghanistan border are churning out thousands of *Mujahideen* (Islamic warriors) ready to confront the new Crusader — the United States.

Moreover, by allowing the corrupt, autocratic and repressive regimes of the Middle East to deprive their populations of sufficient "political space" to develop the domestic foundations necessary for democracy, i.e., independent courts, a free press and mainstream political parties, America has indirectly cultivated the rise of fundamentalist Islamist political parties. At the mosques the repressed populations interact and tacitly organize opposition to the repressive regimes. Underground Islamist parties form and enjoy a ready supply of members from among the congregations. Their leaders learn organizational skills and often provide social services that the governments are either unwilling or unable to supply. Should an opportunity for free elections arise, these Islamist parties are usually the best organized and have the best chance at victory because there are no viable, experienced "moderate" parties to oppose them. That is what happened in Algeria in 1992.

The result has been that in today's world sixty-three percent of the governments are democratic. Of the twenty-two members of the Arab League, none is an electoral democracy.[36] Outside of Iraq none of these regimes seems interested in effecting serious democratic reforms. President Mubarak continues to arrest Muslim Brotherhood demonstrators by the hundreds, having refused entreaties from his people to revoke the emergency laws he invoked twenty-four years ago in order to assume dictatorial power.[37] He does not seem too worried about President Bush's call for regime change. Neither are the Saudis, still aglow over the presidential hand-hold, and neither are the other autocratic leaders in the Middle East. They know that the United States does not want real democratic reform in the Middle East countries because it secretly fears their "illiberal" populations.

This has had a devastating effect on the war on terrorism. The continued repression of Islamists by the Middle East's secular regimes gives deep credibility to Osama bin Laden's message that these "apostate" regimes are merely the agents of the New Crusader, the United States. This is especially true of Saudi Arabia, whose leaders invited the Christian Army to occupy the land of the Two Holy Places (more about that below) and administer one of the most profligate "kleptocracies" in the history of the modern world. If we sincerely want to make any progress in defeating Mr. Bin Laden *and* his message of a new Crusade, then America has to get serious about democracy in the Middle East.

America needs to reverse course immediately and encourage

actual democratic reform in that part of the world, even if it leads to Islamists assuming power. America needs to force President Mubarak and his ilk to open up the "political space" necessary to root democratic institutions. America needs to withhold aid and impose trade sanctions on any regime that does not join the democracy bandwagon. It can also motivate the oil-rich states by limiting our own consumption of their oil so that they will have less money to spend on royal palaces and the Bin Ladens of the world. A 55 mile per hour (M.P.H.) speed limit and a substantial increase in the fuel-efficiency requirements of manufactured automobiles would go far in staunching the flow of Saudi Arabian money to Mr. Bin Laden. If America's military forces are actually being used to protect regimes that will not engage in true democratic reform, then it should withdraw those forces and let the people decide the fate of their corrupt and autocratic rulers.

If America does all of this, then it can discredit Mr. Bin Laden's vision of the New Crusade in two very important ways. First, it can assist in rooting necessary democratic institutions like a free press and independent political parties in the countries whose repressive, autocratic regimes have caused much of the problem. Second, and more important, it can demonstrate that it has weaned itself from its phobic fear of Islamist regimes. It can allow democracy to take itself where it will, including toward the Islamic fold.

Ironically, most of the world's Muslims already live in democracies: India, Indonesia and Turkey. This fact totally discredits the popular view that Islam is incompatible with democracy. In Indonesia and Turkey, Islamist political parties control the governments and pose no strategic threats to the United States. By definition, politics demands compromise. Whenever an Islamist party rises to political power, it must make compromises in order to put bread on the tables of its constituents. This happened in Indonesia and Turkey. It can also happen in Algeria, Egypt, Saudi Arabia and the rest of the Middle East.[38] Were Osama bin Laden to be elected to power in any Muslim country, he would soon find that pious Islamic platitudes have to take second seat to the pragmatic needs and demands of his constituents.

Mr. Bin Laden next cites American support for non-Islamic countries outside the Middle East who repress Muslims as evidence of the new Crusade. Against the backdrop of the Iraq War, the massive loss of Muslim lives in places like Kosovo, Bosnia-Herzegovina,

Chechnya, China, Kashmir, India, and the Philippines give traction to his contention that there exists a worldwide Crusade against Islam. In Kosovo and Bosnia-Herzegovina, thousands of Muslims were murdered before the Western powers took action. In Chechnya, China, Kashmir, and the Philippines, Muslims are seeking independence from repressive, non-Islamic regimes. Yet the United States persists in supporting these regimes even though its national security interests are not in play. For example, it has gratuitously designated the East Turkistan Islamic Movement (E.T.I.M.) as a foreign terrorist organization and froze its assets. The E.T.I.M. consists of ethnic Uighurs, a nomadic Turkic group of Muslims that occupy an area of northwestern China known as Xingjian. They represent no strategic threat to the United States. Perhaps the designation was influenced by China's overwhelming importance to the U.S. economy and its large reserves of U.S. dollars. But actions such as these in the name of the war on terrorism give that war a distinct religious flavor that Muslims worldwide find distasteful. In this very blatant example America is seen as persecuting Muslims on behalf of the godless Chinese Communist government.[39]

The same scenario plays out in Chechnya. Russia portrays its occupation of that country as a facet of the global war on terrorism rather than as a naked attempt to seize Chechnya's natural resources. The Russians unilaterally invaded Chechnya in 1994, withdrew in 1996, and re-invaded in 1999.[40] They are waging a vicious, no-holds-barred total war against the indigenous Muslim population not unlike the war the old Soviet Union waged against Afghanistan. Neither side pays much attention to human rights. The city of Grozny is no more than a shell of bombed-out buildings. The Chechens are merely seeking the independence enjoyed by many of the old Soviet satellite states. But when they take their bitter fight into neighboring Russian provinces and engage in deplorable tactics commensurate with those befalling their families in Chechnya, they are branded as terrorists. Unfortunately, the United States has given Russia its leash in Chechnya. To Muslim eyes, this seems more like a conspiracy against Islam.

Similarly, America does not press India to convene free elections in Kashmir. India has been resisting elections in Kashmir since the partition of India and Pakistan in 1947. India knows that the vast majority of the people in Kashmir are Muslims who would vote to join Pakistan. Nuclear armed India and nuclear armed Pakistan have fought three wars over the resource-rich province. Yet, in East Timor America pressured the Muslim Indonesian government to convene a referendum in the heavily Christian province. The predictable result was that the Christians voted overwhelmingly for independence, which was granted with the assistance of the United Nations. The Islamic world is well aware of the double standard applied to Kashmir and to East Timor.

In India, large-scale massacres of Muslims have occurred in the province of Gujarat, with the complicity of the nationalistic Hindu government.[41] Even in the non-Christian venue of India, the crusading United States is careful not to alienate the Indian government. Thousands of American jobs have been outsourced to India, and that country's importance to the U.S. economy is rapidly growing.[42]

In the Philippines, the Muslims of the southern islands have been fighting intermittently for their independence from the Christian North since 1521, when Ferdinand de Magellan first claimed the Archipelago on behalf of Spain. Most recently they have mounted an active insurgency since 1978. Now, their efforts at independence are being labeled as "terrorism" by both the Philippine and the United States governments. The United States is maintaining an unpopular military presence in the southern Philippines in order to train the Christian government's counterinsurgency forces.[43]

Sadly, the United States has painted with too broad a brush in its war on terrorism. It brands indigenous Muslims as terrorists when they are either defending themselves from repressive regimes or are fighting for their independence just as America fought the British for its own independence. None of these movements represents a strategic threat to the national security of America. But its support for the regimes fighting them casts it in the role of the crusading force that Mr. Bin Laden has scripted for it. If America's strategic interests are not in play, then perhaps its policies are driven by a faith-based president whose evangelical Christian supporters and subordinates see themselves as the new Crusaders. Millions of Muslims across the Islamic world are ready to agree with this view and answer Mr. Bin Laden's call to *Jihad* (holy war).

Mr. Bin Laden's remaining three examples of the new Crusade, i.e., the presence of United States military forces in the Arabian (Persian) Gulf, the American invasions of Afghanistan and Iraq, and the pressures upon Middle East oil-producing countries to maintain artificially low oil prices, will now be treated. Logic does not support his contentions about the suppression of oil prices and the invasion of Afghanistan. They will be discussed first.

Paraphrasing the Shah of Iran in a rare moment of profundity, "oil is too precious to burn."[44] He was right. It is a non-renewable resource that is the life-blood of the Western economies. They demand cheap oil, and the producing countries are expected to provide it. Because of Saudi Arabia's vast oil resources and production capacity, it has the market power to increase or decrease worldwide oil prices either by increasing or decreasing its daily production. Of the total global oil production per day of approximately eighty million barrels, the Oil Producing and Exporting Countries (O.P.E.C.) producing countries, led by Saudi Arabia, produce 30.4 million barrels. Saudi daily production hovers between 9.5 million barrels and a maximum of 11 million barrels. The Saudis have announced plans to increase production to 12.5 million barrels per day by 2009. On April 1, 2005, crude oil hit a high of $57.00 per barrel. After the Crown Prince's April 25th visit with President Bush, the Saudis announced that they would tap spare oil production capacity if necessary. By May 3, 2005, a week after President Bush's April 25th visit with Crown Prince Abdullah, June futures contracts were at $49.50 per barrel. As previously discussed, the primary purpose of the April 25th meeting was to discuss oil prices. Obviously President Bush succeeded in pressuring the Saudis to lower the prices.[45] Again, it was business as usual between the Saudis and the United States.

Americans consume over 20 million barrels of the world's daily consumption of eighty million barrels. They drive a fleet of 210 million vehicles, including light trucks and SUVs.[46] Unlike any other country in the world, Americans are still in love with large vehicles and take cheap energy prices for granted.

This latest accommodation by the Saudis of America's gluttonous appetite for cheap oil gives some traction to Mr. Bin Laden's view that artificially depressed oil prices are the result of the new Crusade. However, most Muslims see cheap oil more as a matter of economics rather than religion. O.P.E.C.'s other members include the non-Arab venues of Venezuela and Nigeria. Mr. Bin Laden is correct when he contends that the consuming nations of the Christian West pressure producing nations to lower oil prices. As a trained economist he should know that compared to other commodities used to produce goods and services, high oil prices are very inflationary and destructive of Western economies. If the Western economies fail, then the economies of the producing countries will soon follow suit for lack of markets in which to sell their oil at inflated prices, or at any price for that matter.

Mr. Bin Laden also overlooks China's surging demand for oil. In 2003, China surpassed Japan to become the second largest consumer of oil — second only to the United States. By 2030, China will be consuming ten million barrels of imported oil per day, equal to the U.S. consumption total today. China's demand is nudging oil prices toward $60.00 per barrel.[47] China is not a Christian country, but it is certainly interested in cheap oil prices. As much as Mr. Bin Laden would like us to believe the contrary, it is economics — not religion — that drives the price of oil.

Putting aside the price of oil, if America were to substantially curtail, or else eliminate altogether, its dependence on foreign oil, the Saudis would have a lot less discretionary money to spend on exporting Wahhabism and tacitly giving financial aid to Mr. Bin Laden and his ilk.[48] Thus, in the name of our own national security, we should immediately reduce our highway speed limit to 55 M.P.H. and dramatically increase the fuel efficiency requirements of our manufactured automobiles.[49] Likewise, in the longer term we can take a more serious look at nuclear power and alternative forms of energy such as wind, solar, biodiesel, biomass, hydroelectric, and fuel cells, to name a few.

Unfortunately, both President Bush and Vice President Dick Cheney are "oil men" who are reluctant to do anything that would hurt domestic oil companies, even to the detriment of our national security. Precipitous reductions in the importation of foreign oil would hurt the earnings of U.S. companies like Exxon Mobil Corporation. Its Mobil Division is one of the partners of Saudi Arabian oil giant, the Aramco Corporation. Aramco is the latest iteration of the consortium of oil companies that first contracted with the Saudi government seventy-two years ago to develop the Kingdom's oil fields.[50]

Moreover, instead of taking immediate action, the Bush administration's answer to the problem of our dependence on foreign oil is to develop domestic resources by opening up more areas to exploration. This is a long-term solution that hurts the war on terrorism, which demands immediate action. It is also impractical because our oil production actually peaked in 1970. We just do not have enough oil resources to sate our gluttonous appetite. Even if we were to proceed with the administration's controversial plan to open the Artic National Wildlife Refuge to oil exploration and production, we would have to wait ten years to begin extracting the estimated 4.3 – 11.8 billion barrels of recoverable oil under the Refuge. Assuming our present consumption rate of 20-million-barrels-per-day remains unchanged (it will not due to more people, more big vehicles, rates of highway speeds, and other factors), and assuming 10 billion barrels of recoverable oil, that results in a mere 1.36 year supply of oil. Thus, domestic reserves are not the answer to reducing our dependence on foreign oil.[51] In the name of the war on terrorism, rather than to wait ten years, the Bush administration should act now to reduce Saudi Arabia's discretionary spending.

Mr. Bin Laden's objection to the American invasion of Afghanistan as proof of the new Crusade is also easily dismissed. The attacks that he and his co-conspirators mounted on 9/11 provoked the invasion. As coy as was Mr. Bin Laden in denying any responsibility for the attacks in several interviews between October and November 2001, the United States had plenty of evidence implicating him and Al Qaeda in the attacks. President Bush had no choice but to go after them. The president gave Afghani leader Mullah Omar ample opportunity to deliver Mr. Bin Laden to American authorities, or alternatively, to expel him from Afghanistan. The Mullah chose to defy President Bush. At the time, America was not in a particularly tolerant mood. President Bush already had warned the world during his speech to the Joint Session of Congress on September 21, 2001 that either you were with us or you were with the terrorists. On October 7, 2001, as the bombs began to fall on Afghanistan, Osama bin Laden, Mullah Omar, and the Afghani people began to pay the price for 9/11.

Turning to the stationing of American military forces in Saudi Arabia and the Gulf States and the invasion of Iraq, one sees that they are interrelated and have given deep traction to Mr. Bin Laden's message about a new Crusade. When the first American troops set foot on Saudi soil in August, 1990, Mr. Bin Laden became the self-declared archenemy of the Saudi regime. In his eyes, the Saudi leaders committed apostasy by inviting a Christian army into the land of Islam's Two Holy Places, the mosques at Mecca and Medina.[52] The Saudi leaders justified their invitation because they feared invasion by the Iraqi forces that had just invaded and occupied neighboring Kuwait.

After the quick conclusion of the 1991 Gulf War, Mr. Bin Laden was chagrined to see American military forces remain in Saudi Arabia and the Gulf region. The U.S. built permanent bases in Saudi Arabia, Kuwait, Qatar, and Bahrain. The ostensible purpose was to enforce the no-fly zones over Iraq and to keep an eye on Saddam Hussein. However, Mr. Bin Laden and many others believed that the forces were there to protect the unpopular Saudi regime and to launch a new Crusade against Islam. As you read in the preceding pages, in his 1998 *Fatwa* (religious decree) Mr. Bin Laden predicted that the United States had established bases in Saudi Arabia partly to further its Crusader designs on Iraqi oil. The Crusading army was there to seize the Middle East oil fields and later to seize Saudi Arabia itself and dedicate part of its lands to the creation of Greater Israel.

Initially the mainstream Islamic world did not subscribe to Mr. Bin Laden's view that the American military bases in Saudi Arabia and the Gulf States were the vanguards of the new Crusade.[53] Saddam Hussein had invaded Kuwait, a Muslim country, and had refused to leave after being given the chance to do so. In addition, Muslim countries like Egypt, Saudi Arabia, Syria, Turkey, and the United Arab Emirates had joined the coalition of countries that freed Kuwait. But they were careful to resist any inclination to invade Iraq proper, as was President George H. W. Bush. After the conclusion of the 1991 Persian Gulf War, the bases, indeed, appeared necessary to enforce the "no-fly" zones created over northern and southern Iraq. The Middle East media was more outraged by the catastrophic effects of the Iraq sanctions on Iraqi children than by the presence of the military bases.

Furthermore, in order to defuse Mr. Bin Laden's criticisms about the presence of Christian military forces in Saudi Arabia, the Saudi government called upon its official *Ulema* (Islamic scholars) to issue *Fatwas* (religious decrees) validating the presence of the forces as necessary to the survival of Islam. Of course, Mr. Bin Laden and his sympathizers, including many Saudis, rejected the *Fatwas* as corrupt.

However, the Islamic world's perceptions about the bases changed dramatically after the American invasion of Iraq on March 20, 2003. On that date, President George W. Bush assumed the mantle of the new Crusader. Just as Mr. Bin Laden had predicted in his 1998 *Fatwa*, American bases in the Middle East had been used to plan, stage, and control the forces invading Iraq, once the seat of the Caliphate. General

Tommy Franks had commanded the military forces invading Iraq from the Prince Sultan Air Force Base in Saudi Arabia.[54] Not only was the United States engaged in a new Crusade against Islam, but the Saudi regime had helped this new Crusader to occupy Baghdad, the old seat of the Caliphate. Millions of Muslims now began to see the world through Mr. Bin Laden's eyes.

Even if the Islamic world were to give President Bush the benefit of the doubt and acknowledge that, indeed, he is attempting to build democracy in Iraq, it would still reject the final result as non-Islamic. For example, in spite of what the Iraqi people themselves may prefer, Coalition Provisional Authority Administrator Paul Bremer stated that the United States would never accept an Iraqi Islamic state.[55] Before Mr. Bremer departed Iraq in June 2004, his administration had enacted a body of laws that assured the privatization of Iraq's resources, the implementation of capitalism at all levels of the economy, and the equality of women. He was endeavoring to create a democracy on the model of that of the United States. However, before the invasion, Iraq's economy had been socialist. No vote will be taken on the implementation of capitalism. Moreover, Iraq's banking industry will be required to apply Western commercial laws and charge interest. As we have seen from the preceding pages, *Riba* (usury or interest on lent money) violates basic Islamic tenets. This is exactly what Mr. Bin Laden has been complaining about: the adoption of "man-made laws" that run afoul of the *Sharia* (Islamic law).[56]

Moreover, sixty percent of the Iraqis are Shi'ite Muslims whose religious leaders exercise close control over their flock. Sooner or later, they will insist on a theocratic Iraq that adopts the *Sharia* and the "tenets of Islam." Already they have inserted language into the Iraqi interim constitution that declares Islam to be the state religion and proscribes any law that violates the "tenets of Islam." This provision directly conflicts with another provision that prohibits discrimination against other religions.[57] Because the "tenets of Islam" are not defined, this language certainly will lead to problems later. Note also that at the time of this writing, and as will be further discussed below, American and coalition forces cannot suppress the growing insurgency by the **minority** Sunnis. How can they expect to suppress a widespread Shi'ite insurgency should Shi'ite leaders like Imam Muqtada al-Sadr (whose "Mahdi Army" militia viciously fought the Americans in April 2004) decide that they are not happy with the government we are creating for them in Iraq?[58]

Because of its preoccupation with the Iraq War, the war on terrorism is almost an afterthought to the Bush administration. We need only to look to its own statements for proof of this contention. President Bush has been notably silent about Mr. Bin Laden, publicly mentioning his name only once during the last year.[59] Since Mr. Bin Laden's trail grew cold in December 2001, the Bush administration has also downplayed his significance to the global war on terrorism. Today, the "terrorist of the moment" seems to be Abu Musab al-Zarqawi, who is one of the leaders of the Iraqi insurgency.

I respectfully submit that Mr. Al-Zarqawi is a localized insurgent who in no fashion can compare to the importance of Mr. Bin Laden in the war on terrorism. The Bush administration's de-emphasis of Mr. Bin Laden disserves the American people and attests to the diversion of valuable resources away from the war on terrorism. Granted, Mr. Al-Zarqawi is an immediate threat to American and Iraqi lives. But he is operating in a theater populated by over 140,000 U.S. and Coalition troops. He will fall sooner rather than later; but the point is that in fighting the war on terrorism, it is Mr. Bin Laden, not Mr. Al-Zarqawi, who should be trying to evade 140,000 U.S. and coalition troops. Instead, Mr. Bin Laden plays tag with only 17,000 American troops assigned to Afghanistan's harsh environs. And none of these troops is allowed into Pakistan, where he might well be hiding. After all, Ramzi Binalshibh and Khalid Shaikh Muhammad, the 9/11 masterminds, were captured in Pakistan, not Afghanistan.

Thus, on a practical level, the Iraq invasion has benefited Osama bin Laden enormously. It has diverted valuable resources away from the war on terrorism[60] and away from the search for him. As mentioned earlier, even autocratic Egyptian President Hosni Mubarak had predicted that the Iraq invasion would create "a hundred Bin Ladens." Mr. Al-Zarqawi is one such example. Perhaps 100,000 Iraqi civilians have been killed since the invasion.[61] Baghdad, once the seat of the Caliphate, and the Iraqi venues of Shi'ite Islam's holiest shrines, are all under Christian occupation. *Mujahideen* (Islamic warriors) fighters from all corners of the Islamic world are flocking to Iraq to fight the new Crusader. Mr. Bin Laden could not be happier at these developments.

America is not winning in Iraq, which bodes ill for its future.

On October 16, 2003, Secretary of Defense Donald Rumsfeld wondered in his now well-known memorandum whether "we [are] capturing or killing or deterring and dissuading more terrorists every day than the madarassas and the radical clerics are recruiting, training and deploying against us?"[62] The simple answer is, "no!" Contrary to the wishful thinking of the Pentagon planners (who failed to envision the insurgency in the first instance), the minority Sunni insurgency is growing. Each week hundreds of Iraqis are killed or wounded by car bombs, suicide bombers, ambushes, and the whole panoply of guerilla tactics. American soldiers are dying, too, but at a lesser rate because they have stepped back in the hope that the Iraqi security forces can protect the population. The insurgents have responded by specifically targeting Iraqi forces. According to the authoritative Brookings Institute, the insurgents killed approximately 1,800 Iraqi soldiers and police officers between June 4, 2004, and April 27, 2005, The security forces cannot even protect themselves.[63]

What America is learning from the carnage in Iraq is that the war is a microcosm of any future holy war on Islam. *Mujahideen* (Islamic warriors) are not flocking to that venue to restore Saddam Hussein to power. They are flocking there to fight American soldiers, the New Crusaders.

But what makes Iraq so dangerous to America's future is that if it insists on remaining in that country, it shall have to invoke "scorched earth" tactics to suppress the insurgency. If it does that, then it shall permanently alienate the Islamic world and evoke an irreversible holy war on Islam. *Jihad* (holy war) will become the rule rather than the exception among the majority of Islam's 1.2 billion members. What we did in the Iraqi city of Fallujah is a case on point. Some pundits believe that it almost evoked the holy war there. Others believe that at the very least it triggered the broader insurgency that it now faces.[64]

Fallujah's 300,000 people were living in relative peace until April 28, 2003, when U.S. Marines occupied the local secondary school. Local Iraqis angry about the occupation demonstrated outside the school. The Marines fired on the crowd, killing thirteen civilians. Two days later there was a repetition in which two Iraqi civilians were killed. No Marines were killed or injured in either instance. Of course, the locals and the Marines disagree about the circumstances surrounding the killings. Nonetheless, they triggered an increasing cycle of violence.

Locals felt hurt and humiliated. As one cleric stated at the time, "The future is *Jihad*."[65]

For the next year, the Marines were unable to pacify Fallujah. In April 2004, they finally entered the city in force to root out the growing insurgency. However, our military leaders grew worried about civilian casualties and withdrew them. Then they gave the city's 300,000 residents time to flee. Many, but not all, fled. The Marines re-entered in November 2004 and brought heavy fire power to bear inside the city. When they finished, 71 Marines had died and 623 were wounded. They estimated that they had killed between 1000 and 6000 insurgents. The world does not know the civilian death toll because as a matter of official policy the American military does not count civilian casualties. Estimates of the destruction of buildings have ranged as high as 36,000 homes and 8,400 shops. After the Marines were finished, Fallujah resembled the bombed-out Chechen city of Grozny. At the time of this writing in early July 2005, less than a third of Fallujah's 300,000 residents have returned to the devastation that used to be their homes. For all intents and purposes, the shell of Fallujah is now pacified. That is how you defeat insurgents.[66]

But that did not go far enough. America must also destroy the insurgents' supportive infrastructure wherever they operate in Iraq. That means teaching the lesson of Fallujah to the Anbar Province, the infamous Sunni Triangle (a 100 mile swath north from Baghdad to Tikrit), Ramadi, and the growing number of other restive areas. If the Shi'ites do not like the new paradigm in Iraq and rise up in rebellion, then they will have to suffer the same fate. Farms, crops, homes, buildings, and even hospitals must be destroyed. Note that on May 6, 2005, the media in Iraq reported that Abu Musab Al-Zarqawi had visited a hospital in Ramadi for treatment.[67] If there had been no hospital in Ramadi, Mr. Al-Zarqawi would have been hard pressed to find medical aid.

Moreover, infrastructure destruction is of paramount importance in Iraq because the insurgents enjoy easy access to an inexhaustible supply of arms and ammunition. Saddam Hussein's regime left behind a stockpile of at least 600,000 tons of arms and ammunition in 10,000 munitions dumps spread across Iraq. (As a measure of the magnitude of that stockpile for a country as small as Iraq [population twenty-five million people], that sum represented one-third of the total munitions reserves of the United States military at the start of the Iraq War.) They are within easy reach of the insurgents. Using our best efforts, we have been able to control or destroy approximately 414,000 tons of Iraqi munitions. However, our work is far from over because the 600,000 ton figure is a "low" estimate. Before the Iraq War, our military commanders estimated that it would require five years of effort to destroy the entire stockpile.[68] Thus, infrastructure destruction is of paramount importance in suppressing the Iraqi insurgency.

Moreover, just as America did in Fallujah, it will have to relocate the civilian populations in every venue in which the insurgents operate. Iraqi society revolves around clan and tribal affiliations. Insurgents routinely seek protection from accommodating fellow clan and tribal members. If the insurgency is to be defeated, then this network of clan and tribal support must be disrupted.

Clearly, then, America shall have to destroy Iraq in order to save it. But if it does that to a Muslim country that once was the seat of Sunni Islam's Caliphate and is the venue of Shi'ite Islam's most holy sites, we shall earn the undying enmity of the entire Islamic world, Sunni and Shi'ite alike. America shall find itself fighting an indeterminate global holy war that it cannot possibly win.

To begin with, sheer numbers militate against our ultimate victory. 1.2 billion Muslims comprise the Islamic world. If America adopts the conservative figure of one percent as reflecting the number of *Mujahideen* (Islamic warriors) created by its flawed policies and fighting strategies, it shall find itself facing 12,000,000 *Mujahideen* worldwide, including, 3,000,000 Muslim Arabs in the Middle East itself. But if America applies "scorched earth" tactics to Iraq, the number of *Mujahids* will increase exponentially. It does not have enough bombs to kill them all.

From a practical military standpoint, America is already so overextended in Iraq and Afghanistan that it is unable to deal with armed conflicts that may arise in other dangerous venues, such as the Korean Peninsula, for example.[69] America simply lacks the resources to invade, defeat, and occupy, all of the Muslim venues of the Islamic world.

Long supply lines and manpower shortages haunted the Christian Crusaders of the 11th through 13th Centuries. Those concerns still haunt America today and certainly will haunt it were it to find itself engaged in a global holy war against Islam.

Already some political pundits are calling for the reenactment of the draft. By conscripting its young men and women, the pundits believe that the United States can fill the fighting ranks of its crusading army and loose it upon the Islamic world.[70] But The Editor submits that Americans are not ready to accept national conscription and send the flower of America's youth on a global Crusade against Islam.

At the time of this writing, America is in a dangerous situation. Because of the Iraq War, its military is facing severe manpower and equipment shortages. The lack of armored Humvees and trucks has cost hundreds of American lives. The reserve forces are at the breaking point. Much of its equipment is being utilized far beyond its design criteria and is failing. All branches of the armed forces are unable to fulfill their 2005 recruitment goals and the predictions for 2006 are even grimmer.[71] Frankly, were the North Koreans to provoke a war on the Korean Peninsula, America would be hard pressed to do anything about it other than to mount air strikes and pray that the North Koreans do not use their nuclear weapons. The American people must ask themselves whether the Iraq War is worth the risk to the national security that it has engendered.

Thus, if America hopes to shed its Crusader image, refocus on Osama bin Laden, and restore the operational integrity of the armed forces, it has no choice but to withdraw from Iraq immediately. Those who say that by remaining in Iraq America is "fighting the terrorists there instead of here [in the United States]" are oblivious to two important facts. First, not all *Mujahids* are killed in Iraq. Rather, many of them are trained and blooded there and then sent elsewhere to confront Americans in other venues.[72] This is exactly how Mr. Bin Laden got his start in Soviet occupied Afghanistan in the 1980s. Second, for every *Mujahid* American troops kill in Iraq, probably a hundred new ones are created to take his place. That multiplier would increase exponentially were it to implement the earlier discussed "scorched earth" tactics.

Nor would it be dishonorable for America to depart from Iraq immediately. The "peace with honor" slogan of President Richard Nixon's 1968 presidential campaign caused thousands of needless deaths in the Vietnam War.[73] In Iraq, America has not lost its honor because it achieved the stated mission: the toppling of Saddam Hussein's regime. America is free to withdraw at any time and leave United Nations peacekeepers in its wake. An international peacekeeping force comprised of peacekeepers from countries that did not participate in the Iraq invasion would becalm the insurgency. Thousands of Iraqi and American lives would be saved.

In this way, America can restore its credibility in the Islamic world and be ready to face more serious threats to its national security.

In addition to withdrawing from Iraq, it can also seek to avoid a holy war against Islam by pursuing an alternative suggested by Osama bin Laden himself. In his statement of July 2003, *infra*, Mr. Bin Laden depicted the *Ummah* (Islamic nation) as divided and led by disparate governments that have left the fold of Islam. He claimed that the *Ummah* could only be restored on the satisfaction of five conditions: a convention, or meeting, of Muslims; a hearing of their grievances; obedience to God; migration (*Hijra*) to a friendly venue; and *Jihad* (holy war). He claims *Jihad* is already a reality. However, since the Taliban's fall, he sees no viable Muslim country to which to migrate. But why not try to short-circuit the looming holy war by convening a worldwide Islamic peace conference? Perhaps through the efforts of a pan-Islamic group like the Muslim Brotherhood, such a conference could be convened. Muslims and Islamists of all persuasions would be invited to attend. All participants would enjoy temporary immunity while traveling to and from and participating in the conference. The corrupt regimes of the Middle East would be barred from participation. After all, they are part of the problem. This would be a conference primarily of repressed Islamic political parties and uncorrupted *Ulema* (Islamic scholars) at which candid views could be aired and decisions about Islam's future could be made.

More interestingly, Mr. Bin Laden has previously indicated that under the appropriate circumstances, he would allow himself to be tried for his alleged crimes by the *Sharia* (Islamic law).[74] Islamic law does not countenance the killing of innocents and non-combatants. If a bona fide Islamic tribunal could be fashioned from the conference, Mr. Bin Laden would have no choice but to surrender to its jurisdiction. After all, he himself suggested it. In this world of clashing civilizations, this would be a golden opportunity for the United States to win back the respect of the world's Muslims by letting them adjudge and punish their own. Moreover, Islam countenances the death penalty that most of the world disdains. If Mr. Bin Laden were to be found guilty of mass murder by the tribunal, the *Sharia* would call for his execution. In that way, he would die as a convicted murderer, not as a *Shaheed* (martyr) at the hands of the new Christian Crusader.

In conclusion, America must apply the lessons learned in this book from Mr. Bin Laden's own words and from its own mistakes since 9/11. Time is running out. The Iraq War is morphing into a global holy war against Islam that we cannot win. The war on terrorism must be redirected away from Islam and re-focused on the specific targets of Osama bin Laden and Al Qaeda. 2,400 years ago Sun Tzu warned of the dangers of a protracted war. Today a protracted holy war against Islam would exponentially increase the risk of multiple uses of weapons of mass destruction on United States population centers. The time is now to redefine the war on terrorism in secular terms and focus on winnable goals.

Glossary

*** At the website osama-bin-laden-book.com, the verbal pronunciation of each the vocabulary words appearing in the Glossary may be heard.

Ahzab – parties, allies

Al Ahzab – describes the different tribes that fought the Muslims in the Battle of the Ditch, 5 A.H./627 A.D

Al Ansar – The supporters, the residents of Medina who received the Prophet Muhammad (PBUH).

Al Aqsa – holy mosque at *Al-Quds* (Jerusalem), site of the Night Journey

Al Haramain – collectively referring to the holy mosques at Mecca and Medina

Al Masri – the Egyptian, Egypt

Al Muhsinun – doers of good

Al Munkar – wrong, evildoing

Al Mushrikun – polytheists, pagans

Al Quds – Jerusalem

Al Yamamah – dove

Alawain – Alawites, a Shi'ite sect

Al-Haram As-Sharif – Noble Sanctuary, *Al Quds*, site of *Al Aqsa* mosque

Allah – God, the Creator

Auliya – allies, protectors, helpers

Ayat – proofs

Ayyub – Job

Da'ees – callers to prayer

Dajjal – false Messiah

Dawud – David

Deen – religion

Dinar – gold coin

Duniah – whole world

Dunya – this world or life as opposed to the Hereafter (*Akhira*).

Fatwa – a religious decree issued by *Ulema*

Fiqh – Literally, "understanding," this term refers to the body of knowledge and legal opinions developed by Muslim jurists and scholars from the primary sources in Islam, the Quran and the *Sunnah* (way) of the Prophet Muhammad (PBUH). *Fiqh* is an interpretation and application of *Sharia* (Islamic law) to specific circumstances. It usually refers to one of the Islamic schools of jurisprudence, Hanbali, Hanifi, Maliki, and Shafi

Fitna – crisis

Ghasasinah – Arab tribe in north Arabian Peninsula near Syrian border

Hadith – also, "*Alhadith*,"authenticated words and deeds, or tradition, of the Prophet Muhammad (PBUH)

Haj – annual Islamic pilgrimage to Mecca

Halal – permitted by Islam

Haram – forbidden by Islam, sinful

Harun – Aaron

Hegira – migration

Hijra – migration

Ilah – a god

Imam – leader, if a cleric, a leader of a mosque

Iman – belief, not to be confused with *Imam*

Injeel – Gospel

Intifada – uprising, specifically Palestinian uprising beginning in September 2000

Issa – Jesus (PBUH)

Ishaq – Isaac

Isnad – chain of narration, usually of *Hadith*

Istawa – throne

Jahiliya – the time of ignorance before Islam, polytheistic religions

Jebreel – Gabriel

Jihad – literally, a "struggle," but in the lexicon of the West, holy war

Jizyah – Islamic head tax on Christians and Jews

Kaba – stone building in Mecca, destination of the Haj

Kabair – aggravated violations of the *Sharia*

Kaferoon – infidels

Khawarji (also, Kharijites) – those who seceded, Shi'ite sect

Khumayla – luxurious clothes

Kufr – literally, a non-believer in Islam or apostate

La ilaha Allah – none to be worshipped but God

Madrasa – Now in the English lexicon, an Islamic religious school

Mahdi – the guided one

Majid – mosque

Malik – gatekeeper of Hell

Maryam – Mary

Masjid – mosque

Mohdith – innovators who would seek to amend Islam with prohibited innovation

Muhajirun – immigrants who traveled to Medina with the Prophet Muhammad (PBUH)

Mujahideen – literally, Islamic warriors; *Mujahid*, singular.

Munhars – discredited narration

Musa – Moses (PBUH)

Muwahhidun – unifiers, i.e., *Wahhbis*.

Nejd – central Arabia, original home of the Saud royal family

Night Journey – overnight journey of Prophet Muhammad (PBUH) to heaven and back

Nusairis – Alawites, a Shi'ite sect

Qibla – the direction to which Muslims worldwide face when praying, toward Mecca

Rabitah – a chain, a connection between us

Rashidoon – era of the first four Caliphs, the "rightly-guided ones," 7th Century A.D., in order: Abu Baker (Caliph 632 A.D. – 634 A.D., Omar (Caliph 634 A.D. – 644 A.D.) , Uthman (Caliph 644 A.D. –656 A.D.), and Ali (Caliph 656 A.D. – 661 A.D.)

Riba – usury, including interest on money lent according to Islamic doctrine

Ridda – apostasy

Ruh – proofs, true guidance, light

Sabaullah – qualities of God

Sahabah – Companions of the Prophet Muhammad (PBUH)

Saheeh (also *Sahih*) – authenticated, e.g., Sahih Bukhari

Saitan – Satan

Salafi – Islamic creed emulating example of Prophet Muhammad (PBUH)

Salat (also, al-Salat) – prayer

Saum - fasting

Seerah – example of forefathers

Shaheed - martyr

Sharia – Islamic law

Shirk – polytheism

Sulaiman – Solomon

Sunnah – the example of the Prophet Muhammad (PBUH) through his words and deeds

Sura – chapter, usually of Holy Quran

Ta'til – ignoring them

Tazeer – punishment greater than merited by the crime

Tabuin – followers of the Companions of the Prophet Muhammad (PBUH)

Tafseer (also Tafsir) – Quranic exegesis

Taghout – false judges, disbelievers

Tahannuth – worship for a number of nights

Taliban – students

Taqfir – condemnation of a whole group or country, especially as nonbelievers

Taqlid – precedents

Tashbih – giving similarity to any of the creatures

Taurat – Jewish Torah

Tawheed – monotheism

Tawheed – oneness of God, fundamental pillar of Islam: there is no god but God

Tawil – interpreting meanings into different things

Ulema – Islamic scholars, often clerics

Ummah – Islamic nation without regard to national borders

Usool – fundamentals of Islamic jurisprudence

Wahhabi – Islamic creed originating in 18th Century Arabian Peninsula

Wala'a wa albara'a – love/hate for God's sake

Wali – guiding friend

Yaqub – Jacob

Yassa (also, *Yassiq*) – Genghis Khan's moral-legal code of conduct

Yusuf – Joseph

Zakat – charity

Zalimun – polytheists, wrongdoers

Zulm – wrong

This Page Left Intentionally Blank For Notes

Appendix

Federal Indictment of Osama Bin Laden

11/06/98

http://www.usembassy.it/file9801/alia/98110621.htm

TEXT: US GRAND JURY INDICTMENT AGAINST USAMA BIN LADEN

UNITED STATES DISTRICT COURT

SOUTHERN DISTRICT OF NEW YORK

UNITED STATES OF AMERICA

- V-

USAMA BIN LADEN,

a/k/a "Usamah Bin-Muhammad Bin-Laden,"

a/k/a "Shaykh Usamah Bin-Laden,"

a/k/a "Mujahid Shaykh,"

a/k/a "Abu Abdallah,"

a/k/a "Qa Qa,"

Defendant

COUNT ONE

Conspiracy to Attack Defense Utilities of the United States

The Grand Jury charges:

Background: Al Qaeda

1. At all relevant times from in or about 1989 until the date of the filing of this Indictment, an international terrorist group existed which was dedicated to opposing non-Islamic governments with force and violence. This organization grew out of the "mekhtab al Khidemat" (the "Services Office") organization which had maintained (and continues to maintain) offices in various parts of the world, including Afghanistan, Pakistan (particularly in Peshawar) and the United States, particularly at the Alkifah Refugee Center - in Brooklyn. From in or about 1989 until the present, the group called itself "Al Qaeda" ("the Base"). From 1989 until in or about 1991, the group was headquartered in Afghanistan and Peshawar, Pakistan. In or about 1992, the leadership of Al Qaeda, including its "emir" (or prince) USAMA BIN LADEN the defendant, and its military command relocated to the Sudan. From in or about 1991 until the present, the group also called itself the "Islamic Army." The international terrorist group (hereafter referred to as "Al Qaeda") was headquartered in the Sudan from approximately 1992 until approximately 1996 but still maintained offices in various parts of the world. In 1996, USAMA BIN LADEN and Al Qaeda relocated to Afghanistan. At all relevant times, Al Qaeda was led by its "emir," USAMA BIN LADEN. Members of Al Qaeda pledged an oath of allegiance to USAMA BIN LADEN and Al Qaeda.

2. Al Qaeda opposed the United States for several reasons. First, the United States was regarded as "infidel" because it was not governed in

a manner consistent with the group's extremist interpretation of Islam. Second, the United States was viewed as providing essential support for other "infidel" governments and institutions, particularly the governments of Saudi Arabia and Egypt, the nation of Israel and the United Nations, which were regarded as enemies of the group. Third, Al Qaeda opposed the involvement of the United states armed forces in the Gulf War in 1991 and in Operation Restore Hope in Somalia in 1992 and 1993. In particular, Al Qaeda opposed the continued presence of American military forces in Saudi Arabia (and elsewhere on the Saudi Arabian peninsula) following the Gulf war. Fourth, Al Qaeda opposed the United States Government because of the arrest, conviction and imprisonment of persons belonging to Al Qaeda or its affiliated terrorist groups, including Sheik Omar Abdel Rahman.

3. Al Qaeda has functioned both on its own and through some of the terrorist organizations that have operated under its umbrella, including: the Islamic Group (also known as "al Gamaa Islamia" or simply "Gamaa't"), led by co-conspirator Sheik Oxar Abdal Rahman; the al Jihad group based in Egypt; the "Talah e Fatah" ("Vanguards of conquest") faction of al Jibad, which was also based in Egypt, Which faction was led by co-conspirator Ayman al Zawahiri ("al Jibad"); Palestinian Islamic Jihad and a number of Jihad groups in other countries, including Egypt, the Sudan, Saudi Arabia, Yemen, Somalia, Eritrea, Kenya, Pakistan, Bosnia, Croatia, Algeria, Tunisia, Lebanon, the Philippines, Tajikistan, Chechnya, Bangladesh, Kashmir and Azerbaijan. In February 1998, Al Qaeda joined forces with Gamaa't, Al Jihad, the Jihad Movement in Bangladesh and the "Jamaat ul Ulema e Pakistan" to issue a fatwah (an Islamic religious ruling) declaring war against American civilians worldwide under the banner of the "International Islamic Front for Jibad on the Jews and Crusaders."

4. Al Qaeda also forged alliances with the National Islamic Front in the Sudan and with the government of Iran and its associated terrorist group Hezballah for the purpose of working together against their perceived common enemies in the West, particularly the United States. In addition, al Qaeda reached an understanding with the government of Iraq that al Qaeda would not work against that government and that on particular projects, specifically including weapons development, al

Qaeda would work cooperatively with the Government of Iraq.

5. Al Qaeda had a command and control structure which included a majlis al shura (or consultation council) which discussed and approved major undertakings, including terrorist operations.

6. Al Qaeda also conducted internal investigations of its members and their associates in an effort to detect informants and killed those suspected of collaborating with enemies of Al Qaeda.

7. From at least 1991 until the date of the filing of this Indictment, in the Sudan, Afghanistan and elsewhere out of the jurisdiction of any particular state or district, USAMA BIN LADEN, a/k/a "Usamah Bin-Muhammad Bin-Laden," a/k/a "Shaykh Usamah Bin-Laden," a/k/a "Mujahid Shaykh," a/k/a "Abu Abdallah," a/k/a "Qa Qa," the defendant, and a co-conspirator not named as a defendant herein (hereafter "Co-conspirator") who was first brought to and arrested in the Southern District of New York, and others known and unknown to the grand jury, unlawfully, willfully and knowingly combined conspired, confederated and agreed together and with each other to injure and destroy, and attempt to injure and destroy, national-defense material, national-defense premises and national-defense utilities of the United States with the intent to injure, interfere with and obstruct the national defense of the United states.

Overt Acts

8. In furtherance of the said conspiracy, and to effect the illegal object thereof, the following overt acts, among others, were committed:

a. At various times from at least as early as 1991 until at least in or about February 1998, USAMA BIN LADEN, the defendant, met with Co-conspirator and other members of Al Qaeda in the Sudan, Afghanistan and elsewhere;

b. At various times from at least as early as 1991, USAMA BIN LADEN, and others known and unknown, made efforts to obtain weapons, including firearms and explosives, for Al Qaeda and its affiliated terrorist groups;

c. At various times from at least as early as 1991 USAMA BIN LADEN, and others known and unknown, provided training camps and guest houses in various areas, including Afghanistan and the Sudan, for the use of Al Qaeda and its affiliated terrorist groups;

d. At various times from at least as early as 1991, USAMA BIN LADEN, and others known and unknown, made efforts to produce counterfeit passports purporting to be issued by various countries and also obtained official passports from the Government of the Sudan for use by Al Qaeda and its affiliated groups;

e. At various times from at least as early as 1991, USAMA BIN LADEN, and others known and unknown, made efforts to recruit United States citizens to Al Qaeda in order to utilize the American citizens for travel throughout the Western world to deliver messages and engage in financial transactions for the benefit of Al Qaeda and its affiliated groups;

f. At various times from at least as early as 1991, USAMA BIN LADEN, and others known and unknown, made efforts to utilize non-Government organizations which purported to be engaged in humanitarian work as conduits for transmitting funds for the benefit of Al Qaeda and its affiliated groups;

g. At various times from at least as early as 1991, Co-conspirator and others known and unknown to the grand jury engaged in financial and business transactions on behalf of defendant USAMA BIN LADEN and Al Qaeda, including, but not limited to: purchasing land for training camps; purchasing warehouses for storage of items, including explosives; transferring funds between bank accounts opened in various names, obtaining various communications equipment, including satellite telephones and transporting currency and weapons to members of Al Qaeda and its associated terrorist organizations in various countries throughout the world;

h. At various times from in or about 1992 until the date of the filing of this Indictment, USAMA BIN LADEN and other ranking members of Al Qaeda stated privately to other members of Al Qaeda that Al Qaeda should put aside its differences with Shiite Muslim terrorist organizations, including the Government of Iran and its affiliated terrorist group Hezballah, to cooperate against the perceived common enemy, the United States and its allies;

i. At various times from in or about 1992 until the date of the filing of this Indictment, USAMA BIN LADEN and other ranking members of Al Qaeda stated privately to other members of Al Qaeda that the United States forces stationed on the Saudi Arabian peninsula, including both Saudi Arabia and Yemen, should be Attacked;

j. At various times from in or about 1992 until the date of the filing of this Indictment, USAMA BIN LADEN and other ranking members of Al Qaeda stated privately to other members of Al Qaeda that the United States forces stationed in the Horn of Africa, including Somalia, should be attacked;

k. Beginning in or about early spring 1993, Al Qaeda members began to provide training and assistance to Somali tribes opposed to the United Nations intervention in Somalia;

l. On October 3 and 4, 1993, members of Al Qaeda participated with Somali tribesmen in an attack on United States military personnel serving in Somalia as part of Operation Restore Hope, which attack killed a total of 18 United States soldiers and wounded 73 others in Mogadishu;

m. On two occasions in the period from in or about 1992 until in or about 1995, Co-conspirator helped transport weapons and explosives from Khartoum to Port Sudan for transshipment to the Saudi Arabian peninsula;

n. At various times from at least as early as 1993, USAMA BIN LADEN and others known and unknown, made efforts to obtain the components of nuclear weapons;

o. At various times from at least as early as 1993 USAMA BIN LADEN and others known and unknown, made efforts to produce chemical weapons;

p. On or about August 23, 1996, USAMA BIN LADEN signed and

issued a declaration of Jihad entitled "Message from Usamah Bin-Muhammad Bin-Laden to His Muslim Brothers in the Whole World and Especially in the Arabian Peninsula: Declaration of Jihad Against the Americans Occupying the Land of the Two Holy Mosques; Expel the Heretics from the Arabian Peninsula" (hereafter the "Declaration of Jihad) from the Hindu Kush mountains in Afghanistan. The Declaration of Jihad included statements that efforts should be pooled to kill Americans and encouraged other persons to join the jihad against the American enemy";

q. In or about late August 1996, USAMA BIN LADEN read aloud the Declaration of Jihad and made an audiotape recording of such reading for worldwide distribution; and

r. In February 1998, USAMA BIN LADEN issued a joint declaration in the name of Gamaa't, Al Jihad, the Jihad movement in Bangladesh and the "Jamaat ul Ulema e Pakistan" under the banner of the "International Islamic Front for Jihad on the Jews and Crusaders," which stated that Muslims should kill Americans -- including civilians -- anywhere in the world where they can be found.

(Title 18, United States code, Section 2155(b).)

This Page Left Intentionally Blank For Notes

ENDNOTES

PREFACE

1. Richard W. Stevenson, "Bush Acknowledges Difficulties, Insisting on Fight to the End," *New York Times*, June 29, 2005.

2. Michael Jansen, "Growing Muslim Hostility to Britain Linked to Iraq War," *AlJazeerah. info*, at www.aljazeerah.info; see also, Frank Gregory and Paul Wilkinson, "Riding Pillion for Tackling Terrorism Is a High-Risk Policy," *Security, Terrorism, and the UK*, Chatham House, ISP/NSC Briefing Paper 05/01, July 2005; Alan Cowell, "Britain Assails Critical Report on Iraq Role," *New York Times*, July 19, 2005; and Elaine Sciolino and Don Van Natta, Jr., "June Report Led Britain to Lower Its Terror Alert," *New York Times*, July 19, 2005.

3. Sun Tzu, *The Art of War*, p. 84, translated by Samual B. Griffith (Oxford University Press 1963).

4. Patrick Quinn and Katherine Shrader, "Officials: Most Suicide Attackers Not Iraqis," *Associated Press, San Diego Union Tribune*, July 1, 2005.

5. Douglas Jehl, "Iraq May Be Prime Place for Training of Militants, C.I.A. Report Concludes," *The New York Times*, June 22, 2005.

6. Anonymous (Michael Scheuer), *Imperial Hubris: Why the West Is Losing the War on Terrorism*, pp. 106 and 110 (Brassey's Inc. 2004).

7. See endnote 3 of OBL's statement of October 29, 2004.

8. Philip Kennicott, "An About Face On America," *Washington Post*, August 24, 2004.

9. Dan Eggen and Walter Pincus, "Ex-Aide Recounts Terror Warnings: Clarke Says Bush Didn't Consider Al Qaeda Threat a Priority Before 9/11," *Washington Post*, March 25, 2004.

10. Sun Tzu, *The Art of War, supra*, at pp. 73 and 84.

11. See "Bush Clarifies View on War against Terrorism," *MSNBC.com*, August 31, 2004, in which the president clarifies his earlier statements that he did not think that the war on terrorism can be won.

12. Andrew Gray, "London Mayor Says West Fueled Islamic Radicalism," *Washington Post,* July 20, 2005.

INTRODUCTION

1. Information about Mr. Bin Laden's early life comes from several sources: an interview that Mr. Bin Laden gave to *Al-Jazeera Television* in 1998 (see an English transcript available at www.robert-fisk.com/usama_interview_aljazeera.htm); also a document given to *PBS* by a source close to Mr. Bin Laden and found at "Osama bin Laden," *PBS*, reprinted at www.angelfire.com/home/pearly/htmls1/osama-bio.html; "Osama bin Laden," *Wikipedia: the Free Encyclopedia*, see www.en.wikipedia.org/wiki/Osama_bin_Laden; Mary Ann Weaver, "The Real bin Laden," *The New Yorker*, January 24, 2000, posted at *The New Yorker* archive on September 13, 2001, found at www.newyorker.com/archive/content/?010924fr_archive03; and Benjamin Orbach, "Usama Bin Ladin and Al-Qa'ida: Origins and Doctrines," *Middle East Review of International Affairs,* Vol. 5, No. 4 (December 2001).

2. The term "political Islam" means the use of the Islamic religion to effect governmental change in Islamic regimes of the Middle East and thereafter to administer the newly constituted regimes according to the dictates of Islam, i.e., the *Holy Quran*, the *Sunnah* (the example of the Prophet Muhammad [PBUH], and the *Sharia* (Islamic law based on the *Holy Quran* and the *Sunnah*).

3. See "Abdullah Azzam: The Godfather of Jihad," *Perspectives on World History and*

Current Events: Middle East Peace Project, at www.pwhce.org/azzam.html. Professor Azzam was a Palestinian jihadist who would become the spiritual leader of Hamas, the Palestinian branch of the Muslim Brotherhood, which seeks to establish a pan-Islamic state throughout the Middle East. See also Steve Coll, *Ghost Wars,* at p. 85 (The Penguin Press 2004). For an example of Professor Azzam's work, see *Sheikh Abdullah Azzam,* "Chapter 1: Defense of Muslim Lands: The First Obligation After Iman [Belief]," *Islamistwatch.org,* at www.islamistwatch.org/texts/azzam/defense/chap1.html.

4. Coll, *Ghost Wars,* supra, at pp. 84-85.

5. See "9/11 Commission Report Confirms Key Fahrenheit 9/11 Facts," *MichaelMoore.com,* August 2, 2004, at www.michaelmoore.com/warroom/index.php?id=24.

6. See Coll., at 84-87. Also, see Richard Clark, *Against All Enemies,* pp. 47-54 (Free Press 2004).

7. See "Two U.S. Allies Review Islamic Curricula at Schools, Mosques," *World Tribune.com,* May 21, 2003, at www.216.26.163.62/2003/me_egypt_05_21.html.

8. See Coll, at p. 88.

9. Clarke, *Against All Enemies,* supra, p. 59.

10. See Nasser Momayezi, "Islamic Revivalism and the Quest for Political Power," *The Journal of Conflict Studies,* University of New Brunswick, Vol. XVII, No. 2, Fall 1997, at www.lib.unb.ca/Texts/JCS/bin/get.cgi?directory=FALL97/articles/&filename=MOMAYEZI.html.

11. See "Usama Bin Laden: Account of an Interview He Gave to the *Independent Newspaper's* Robert Fisk – 6th December 1996," at www.robert-fisk.com/usama_bin_ladin_in_sudan1996.htm.

12. On December 29, 1992, a hotel at which U.S. troops en route to Somalia were staying was bombed. The soldiers had already left. Two Austrian tourists were killed. U.S. intelligence believes that this was Al Qaeda's first terrorist attack. On October 12, 2000, the United States guided-missile destroyer U.S.S. *Cole* (DDG 67) was bombed and damaged by two suicide bombers who had drawn along side the ship on a rubber boat in the port of Aden, Yemen. Seventeen sailors died in the attack and thirty-nine were wounded. See www.pbs.org/wgbh/pages/frontline/shows/binladen/etc/cron.html; and "USS Cole," *Wikipedia,the Free Encyclopedia; at* www.en.wikipedia.org/wiki/USS_Cole_bombing. Operation Restore Hope was the name of the United States military incursion into Somalia in 1993. On October 3, 1993, militia loyal to Somali warlord Farah Aideed shot down two U.S. Blackhawk helicopters over downtown Mogadishu, killing 18 U.S. Rangers. The U.S. withdrew its forces from Somalia shortly after the incident. See Clarke, *Against All Enemies, supra* pp. 84-89; and "Somalia," *Military.com,* at www.military.com/Resources/HistorySubmittedFileView?file=history_somalia.htm.

13. For a comprehensive chronology of these events, see "Osama bin Laden: A Chronology of His Political Life," *PBS:Frontline,* at www.pbs.org/wgbh/pages/frontline/shows/binladen/etc/cron.html.

14. "Transcript of Osama bin Laden Interview by Peter Arnett," *CNN,* March 1997, at www.robert-fisk.com/usama_interview_cnn.htm.

15. "Interview of Usama Bin Laden by John Miller – May 1998," *ABC News,* at www.robert-fisk.com/usama_interview_john_millerabc.htm.

16. Time Magazine printed an interview with OBL on January 11, 1999, vol. 153, no. 1. Rahimullah Yusufzai, a journalist who worked for Pakistan's *The News* conducted the interview. No interview by anyone named Scott representing *Time Magazine* occurred in 1996. The Time interview may be seen at www.robert-fisk.com/usama_interview_timemagazine.htm.

17. Mir, Hamid, interviewer, *"Dawn" and "AUSAF" Group of Newspapers,* November 7, 2001, at www.robert-fisk.com/usama_interview_hamid_mir_ausaf.htm.

18. "1981: Tehran Frees US Hostages After 444 Days," *BBC News*: On This Day, Stories From January 21, 1981, at www.news.bbc.co.uk/onthisday/hi/dates/stories/january/21/newsid_

2506000/2506807.stm.

19. "And whoever kills a believer intentionally, his recompense is Hell to abide therein; and the Wrath and the Curse of Allah* are upon him, and a great punishment is prepared for him."

* "Allah" means "the Creator." Muslims pray to the "Creator," or "God," the God of Abraham. The Muslim God is indistinguishable from the "God" of the Christians and the Jews, who are also the children of Abraham. Throughout the remainder of the book, all religious references will be to "God," rather than to the Arabized "Allah." Two reasons dictate this format. First, the book is addressed to the Western reader, who is accustomed to the term "God" to denote the Higher Being. Second, and more important, recent attacks on Islam by the Christian right suggest that Christianity's "God" is somehow different than Islam's "Allah." See for example the religious musings of Lt. General William Boykin, Deputy Secretary of Defense for Intelligence, distinguishing his "God," Jesus, from that of Islam, and blaspheming Islam's God as an "idol." According to the fundamental tenet of Islam, "There is no god but God, and Muhammad was his Prophet." Any right thinking Muslim is comfortable with using the English word "God" interchangeably with "Allah." Therefore, the word "God" will be utilized throughout the remainder of this book. See Mustafa Abdel-Halim, "Top Brass Under Fire for Calling Allah 'Idol,'" *IslamOnline.com*, October 17, 2003, at www.islamonline.net/English/News/2003-10/17/article06.shtml.

20. Regarding Wahhabism, see www.globalsecurity.org/military/intro/islam.htm and /islam-kharijite.htm and /islam-salafi.htm. See also See Stephen Schwartz, *The Two Faces of Islam*, pp. 54-56 and 71 (Doubleday November 2002). Regarding Ibn Taymiya, see Christopher Henzel, "The Origins of Al-Qaeda Ideology," *National Defense University, National War College*, pp. 5-6, April 20, 2004.

21. The term "rightly guided ones" refers to the first four Caliphs [the *Rashidoon*] – Abu Baker (Caliph 632 - 634, Omar (Caliph 634 – 644), Uthman (Caliph 644 – 656), and Ali (Caliph 656 – 661)

22. For discussions of Al Afghani, Abduh, and Ridha, see Henzel, *Id.*, at pp. 7-9; also, Andrew Wheatcroft, *Infidels*, p. 299 (Random House 2003, 2004).

23. "Egypt Frees Muslim Brotherhood Men," *Aljazeera.net*, April 10, 2005, at www.english.aljazeera.net/NR/exeres/0B8D1B0E-E2AA-42FD-83AC-4E79EA9E0C92.htm.

24. Henzel, "The Origins of Al-Qaeda Ideology," *National Defense University, National War College*, supra, pp. 11-12.

FORWARD

1. See *Answers.com*, "Islam" and "Muslim."

2. "Muhammad," *Wikipedia, the Free Encyclopedia*, www.en.wikipedia.org/wiki/Muhammad.

3. See "Hijra (Islam)," *Wikipedia, the Free Encyclopedia*, at http://en.wikipedia.org/wiki/Hijra_%28Islam%29.

4. "Calendar," *Wikipedia, the Free Encyclopedia* see http://en.wikipedia.org/wiki/Anno_Domini, http://en.wikipedia.org/wiki/Before_the_Common_Era, http://en.wikipedia.org/wiki/A.H.

5. "Islam," *Wikipedia, the Free Encyclopedia*, www.en.wikipedia.org/wiki/Islam

6. "Muhammad," *Wikipedia, the Free Encyclopedia*, www.en.wikipedia.org/wiki/Muhammad.

7. "Hadith," *Wikipedia, the Free Encyclopedia*, at http://en.wikipedia.org/wiki/Hadith.

8. See generally, Dr. G. F. Haddad, "Imam Ahmad [Hanbal]," http://www.sunnah.org/publication/khulafa_rashideen/hanbal.htm; Fazlur Rahman, "Hadith, General Information," http://mb-soft.com/believe/txw/hadith.htm; "Ilm of Hadiths," at http://www.geocities.com/~abdulwahid/hadith/ilm_hadith.html. The University of Southern California maintains a data base of the collections of the works of Bukhari, Muslim, Abu-Dawud, and Malik Muwatta in English

at http://www.usc.edu/dept/MSA/reference/searchhadith.html.

9. See the previous endnote.

10. See Mr. Bin Laden's statement of February 16, 2003. The feast celebrates Abraham's offer to sacrifice his son as a testament to his belief in the one God. The event is depicted in the *Holy Quran* at Sura (Chapter) 37 (As-Saffat [The Arrangers]), verses 83-111.

11. See Schwartz, *The Two Faces of Islam*, *supra*, pp. 54-56 and 71 (Doubleday November 2002).

12. "Five Pillars of Islam," see http://en.wikipedia.org/wiki/Five_pillars_of_Islam.

13. "Quran," *Wikipedia, the Free Encyclopedia*, at http://en.wikipedia.org/wiki/Qur%27an. Also, for an online Quran, see http://www.islamicity.com.

14. See generally, "Islam," *GlobalSecurity.Org*, at www.globalsecurity.org/military/intro/islam.htm and the materials that follow. Also, "Islam," *Wikipedia, the Free Encyclopedia*, at http://en.wikipedia.org/wiki/Islam.

15. Stephen Schwartz, *The Two Faces of Islam*, *supra*, p. 41

16. See "Violations of Islam," *IdrisMosque.com*, at www.idrismosque.com/vio.html.

17. See "Major Sins," http://www.themodernreligion.com/misc/hh/major_sins.htm; "Fatwa Bank, Details of Fatwa, What Are the Major Sins?," October 21, 2003, *IslamOnline.net*, at http://islamonline.net/fatwa/english/FatwaDisplay.asp?hFatwaID=106447; and "Islamic Holidays and Observances," see http://www.colostate.edu/Orgs/MSA/events/Ramadan.html.

18. "Growth Rate of Christianity & Islam," ReligiousTolerance.org at www.religioustolerance.org/growth_isl_chr.htm.

19. See "Islam," *Wikipedia, the Free Encyclopedia*, at http://en.wikipedia.org/wiki/Islam.

20. "Shia Islam," *Wikipedia, the Free Encyclopedia*, at http://en.wikipedia.org/wiki/Shia_islam.

21. "Muhammad," *Wikipedia, the Free Encyclopedia*, http://.en.wikipedia.org/wiki/Muhammad.

22. "Quran," *Wikipedia, the Free Encyclopedia*, at http://en.wikipedia.org/wiki/Qur%27an.

23. Dr. Muhammad Taqi-ud-Din Al-Hilali and Dr. Muhammad Muhsin Khan, translators/editors, *Interpretation of the Meanings of The Noble Quran in the English Language*, Islamic University, Al-Madinah Al-Munawwarah (Darussalam Publishers & Distributors 17th Ed. Revised 1997). Note that these editors provide commentary to the Quranic verse, as is often the practice in rendering the free flowing verse of the Quran understandable to the reader. See generally, "Quran," *Wikipedia, the Free Encyclopedia*, at http://en.wikipedia.org/wiki/Qur%27an.

24. See "Battle of Badr," *Wikipedia, the Free Encyclopedia*, at http://en.wikipedia.org/wiki/Battle_of_Badr. See also "Abu Jahl," Comparative Index to Islam, http://answering-islam.org.uk/Index/J/abu_jahl.html; also, "The Avowed Enemy – The Devout Mujahid," originally published in the 20th issue of *Nida/ul Islam Magazine*, September-October 1997, at http:www.islam.org.au/articles/20/ikrimah.htm.

25. "Battle of Uhud," Muslim American Society, Minnesota Chapter, at www.masmn.org/documents/Books/Safiur_Rahman_Mubarakpuri/Raheeq_Al_Maktoom/408.htm, see also "Battle of Uhud," *Wikipedia, the Free Encyclopedia* at http://en.wikipedia.org/wiki/Battle_of_Uhud.

26. "Battle of the Trench" *Wikipedia, the Free Encyclopedia* at http://en.wikipedia.org/wiki/Battle_of_the_Trench

27. "Battle of Yarmuk," *Wikipedia, the Free Encyclopedia* at http://en.wikipedia.org/wiki/Battle_of_Yarmuk.

28. See previous endnote.

29. See previous endnote.

30. For a discussion of Wahhabism, see "Wahhabism," *Wikipedia, the Free Encyclopedia*, at http://en.wikipedia.org/wiki/Wahhabism.

31. "Ibn Taymiya," *Wikipedia, the Free Encyclopedia* at http://en.wikipedia.org/wiki/Ibn_

Taymiya.

32. Ibn Abd al Wahhab revives Ibn Taymiya's teachings in modern day Saudi Arabia. See Stephen Schwartz, *The Two Faces of Islam, supra,* pp. 54-56 and 68-71. Regarding Ibn Taymiya, see Henzel, "The Origins of Al-Qaeda Ideology," *National Defense University, National War College, supra,* pp. 5-6.

33. See previous endnote.

34. Regarding Wahhabism, see http://www.globalsecurity.org/military/intro/islam.htm and /islam-kharijite.htm and */islam-salafi.htm.* See also Schwartz, *The Two Faces of Islam, supra,* pp. 54-56 and 71. Regarding Ibn Taymiya, see Christopher Henzel, "The Origins of Al-Qaeda Ideology," *National Defense University, National War College, supra,* pp. 5-6.

35. See, Sheikh Abdullah bin Muhammad bin Humain, Chief Justice of Saudi Arabia, "The Call to Jihad," Appendix III, appearing in Al-Hilali and Khan, *The Interpretation of the Meaning of the Noble Quran in English,* at p. 960. Some of the verses cited by the Sheikh: *Holy Quran,* 2 (Al-Baqarah [The Cow]):216, 9 (At-Taubah [The Repentance]):41, and 61 (Surat As-Saff [The Row or the Rank]):10-13. The Appendix is a must read for those interested in understanding the importance of *Jihad* to the Wahhabis.

36. Al-Hilali and Khan, *The Interpretation of the Meaning of the Noble Quran in English, supra,* at p. 51. The *Wahhabi* influence on these editors is manifested in their comments to this verse.

37. See for example, *Holy Quran,* 2 (Al-Baqarah [The Cow]):217, and *Holy Quran,* 9 (At-Taubah [The Repentance]):5.

38. A Yusuf Ali, The *Holy Quran,* Verse 190, and comments, at p. 75 (1934 Ed. Copyright 1946, Khalil Al-Rawaf).

39. Al-Hilali and Khan, *The Interpretation of the Meaning of the Noble Quran in English, supra,* at p. 51. The *Wahhabi* influence on these editors is manifested in their comments to this verse. For a general discussion of defensive and offensive *Jihad,* see Stephen Schwartz, *The Two Faces of Islam, supra,* pp. 54-56 and 71 (Doubleday November 2002).]

40. See "Jihad," *Wikipedia, the Free Encyclopedia,* at http://en.wikipedia.org/wiki/Jihad.

41. See generally, "Caliph," *Wikipedia, the Free Encyclopedia,* http://en.wikipedia.org/wiki/Caliph.

42. See, for example, Mr. Bin Laden's *1996 Declaration of War Against The United States,* and the 1998 *Fatwa* authorizing the killing of Americans, reprinted *infra.* Also, his statements following the United States' invasions of Afghanistan (October 7, 2001) and Iraq (March 20, 2003). All reprinted infra.

43. Since 9/11 the United States has pressured Islamic countries, mainly Saudi Arabia, Pakistan, Yemen, and Egypt, to moderate and modernize the curricula taught at the *Madrassas,* or, religious schools in those venues. For example, on January 1, 2004, Kuwaiti lawmakers rejected religious pressures from the United States and other Western governments to change their schools' curricula, refusing to "'Americanize'" their educational institutions. In May, 2003, Egypt and Saudi Arabia promised to review their schools' curricula with a view toward tempering religious extremism. The Saudis attempted to temper their curricula by limiting references to battles and *jihad.* The proposals have been met with serious opposition in *Wahhabi* Saudi Arabia. Recently, 156 Saudi religious scholars attacked the proposals as undermining the principles of the *Wahhabi* creed, which legitimizes the Saud family's rule in the kingdom. See endnote 23 of OBL's statement of July 2003, *infra,* for a discussion of Al Azhar. See "Two U.S. Allies Review Islamic Curricula at Schools, Mosques," *World Tribune.com,* May 21, 2003, at http://216.26.163.62/2003/me_egypt_05_21.html; "Kuwait Will Not 'Americanize' Textbooks," *Jihad Watch,* January 2, 2004, at www.jihadwatch.org/archives/000542.php; and Abdul Raheem Ali, "Argument Over Saudi Curricula 'Reform,'" *IslamOnline.net,* January 3, 2004, at http://www.islamonline.net/

English/News/2004-01/03/article08.shtml.

44. See Naseem ul-Haq, "Al-Saud: The West's Custodians of the Haramain [holy cities of Mecca and Medinah]," *MuslimMedia.com*, at http://www.muslimmedia.com/archives/special-edition/hajj/hajj2.htm.

45. See previous endnote See also Craig Unger, *House of Bush, House of Saud*, pp. 85-86 (Scribner 2004).

46. See "Hubal, the Moon God of the Kaba," *Islam: Truth or Myth*, at http://www.bible.ca/islam/islam-moon-god-hubal.htm; and "Kaaba," *Wikipedia, the Free Encyclopedia*, at http://en.wikipedia.org/wiki/Kaaba.

47. "Haj," see *Wikipedia, the Free Encyclopedia*, at http://en.wikipedia.org/wiki/Hajj.

48. Nadeem ul-Haq, "Al-Saud: the West's Custodians of the Haramain," *Muslimmedia.com*, at Naeem ul-Haq, at http://www.muslimmedia.com/archives/special-edition/hajj/hajj2.htm.

49. See generally, *noblesanctuary.com* for a layout of the Holy Site, and Kais Al-Kalby with Emad J. Meerza, "History of Al Aqsa Mosque," at http://www.stanford.edu/~jamila/Aqsa.html.
See also, "Hijra (Islam)," *Wikipedia, the Free Encyclopedia*, at http://en.wikipedia.org.

50. Reza Aslan, *No god but God*, p. 114 (Random House 2005); see also, "Four Righteously Guided Caliphs," *Wikipedia, the Free Encyclopedia*, at http://en.wikipedia.org.

51. Many of OBL's speeches have text that states that OBL wants to reinstate the times of the *Rashidoon*.

52. See generally, "Caliph," *Wikipedia, the Free Encyclopedia*, http://en.wikipedia.org/wiki/Caliph.

53. Karen Armstrong, *Holy War*, p. 3 (Second Anchor Books Edition 2001).

54. Armstrong, *Holy War, supra*, pp. 178-179.

55. Armstrong, *Holy War, supra*, pp. 258-259.

56. Armstrong, *Holy War, supra*, pp. 258-259.

57. Armstrong, *Holy War, supra*, pp. 448-450.

58. "Sykes-Picot Agreement," *Wikipedia, the Free Encyclopedia* at http://en.wikipedia.org/wiki/Sykes-Picot_Agreement.

59. See "The Arab Israeli Conflict: History Palestine, Jordan, etc., at *Arab2.com*, http://www.arab2.com/biography/Arab-Israeli-Conflict-mid.htm.

60. See the previous endnote.

61. See "Mid East Maps: Map of UN Partition Plan for Palestine – 1947," at http://www.mideastweb.org/unpartition.htm; and "1948 Arab-Israeli War," *Wikipedia, the Free Encyclopedia*, at http://en.wikipedia.org/wiki/1948_Arab-Israeli_War.

62. See "Q & A: Kashmir Dispute," *BBC News*, November 25, 2002, at http://news.bbc.co.uk/1/hi/world/353352.stm.

63. See "East Timor," *Wikipedia, the Free Encyclopedia*, at http://en.wikipedia.org/wiki/East_Timor.

64. See previous endnote.

65. Ted Thornton, "Civil War in Lebanon," *History of the Middle East Database*, http://www.nmhschool.org/tthornton/mehistorydatabase/civil_war_in_lebanon.htm; and "Lebanese Civil War," *Wikipedia, the Free Encyclopedia*, at http://en.wikipedia.org/wiki/Lebanese_Civil_War.

66. "Serbs Sorry for Srebrenica Deaths," *BBC News World Edition*, November 10, 2004, at www.news.bbc.co.uk/2/hi/europe/3999985.stm.

67. See "Armed Conflict Events Data, Algerian Civil War, 1992-Present," at http://www.onwar.com/aced/data/alpha/falgeria1992.htm.

68. See Richard A. Clarke, *Against All Enemies, supra*, pp. 84-89; and "Somalia," at *Wikipedia, the Free Encyclopedia* at http://en.wikipedia.org/wiki/Somalia; "Operation Restore Hope," *GlobalSecurity.org*, at http://www.globalsecurity.org/military/ops/restore_hope.htm;

"Somalia: Human Rights Developments," *Human Rights Watch*, 2004, at "Somalia: Human Rights Developments," *Human Rights Watch*, 2004, at www.hrw.org/reports/1994/WR94/Africa-08.htm.

69. See the previous endnote.

70. "Sudanese Celebrate Peace Treaty," *ABC News*, January 9, 2005, at http://abcnews. go.com/International/wireStory?id=398719.

71. See "Chechnya Goes to Polls in Wake of Airline Terror Claim," *Sunday Herald*, August 29, 2004, at http://www.sundayherald.com/print44391.

72. See "2003 Invasion of Iraq," *Wikipedia, the Free Encyclopedia*, at http://en.wikipedia. org/wiki/2003_invasion_of_Iraq.

73. "Iraq Surveys Show 'Humanitarian Emergency,'" *UNICEF Information Newsline*, August 12, 1999, http://www.unicef.org/newsline/99pr29.htm; Kate Randall, "Iraqi Child Deaths Have Doubled Under UN-Imposed Sanctions," *World Socialist Web Site*, August 14, 1999, http://www.wsws.org/articles/1999/aug1999/iraq-a14.shtml; Paul Craig Roberts, "A Country Destroyed," April 20, 2004, http://www.lewrockwell.com/roberts/roberts38.html; Matthew McAllester, "Doctors Tell How Children's Deaths Became Propaganda," *Newsday*, May 24, 2003, http://www.smh.com.au; Michael Rubin, "Sanctions on Iraq: A Valid Anti-American Grievance?," *Middle East Review of International Affairs (MERIA)*, vol. 5, no. 4, December 2001, www.meria. idc.ac.il/journal/2001/issue4/jv5n4a6.htm.

74. See "Road Map for Peace," *Wikipedia, the Free Encyclopedia*, http://en.wikipeida. org/wiki/Road_map_for_peace and /wiki/Al-Asqa_Intifada. See also "Intifada Timeline," *Al-Ahram Weekly Online*, Issue No. 710, 30 September to 6 October, at http://weekly.ahram.org. eg/print/2004/710/fo5.htm; and Paul de Rooij, "Palestinian Misery in Perspective," *Arabic Media Internet Network*, June 1, 2004, at http://www.amin.org/eng/paul_de_rooij/2004/jun01.html.

75. See "Road Map for Peace," *Wikipedia, the Free Encyclopedia*, http://en.wikipedia. org/wiki/Road_map_for_peace and /wiki/Al-Asqa_Intifada. See also "Intifada Timeline," *Al-AhramWeeklyOnline*, Issue No. 710, 30 September to 6 October, at http://weekly.ahram.org. eg/print/2004/710/fo5.htm; and Paul de Rooij, "Palestinian Misery in Perspective," *Arabic Media Internet Network*, June 1, 2004, at http://www.amin.org/eng/paul_de_rooij/2004/jun01.html.

76. Road Map for Peace," *Wikipedia, the Free Encyclopedia*, at http://en.wikipedia.org/ wiki/Road_map_for_peace; "Geneva Peace Initiative Set to Take Off," see www.aljazeerah.info, December 1, 2003.

77. See "What is the Palestinian Authority and How Did It Originate?," *Palestine Facts, Israel 1991 to Present PA Origins*, at http://www.palestinefacts.org/pf_1991to_now_pa_origin. php.

78. See previous endnote.

79. See Mr. Bin Laden's 1995 Open Letter to King Fahd and his statement of December 16, 2004, reprinted *infra*.

80. It is common knowledge that Abdul Aziz accepted British financial aid during his uprising against the Turkish Ottoman Empire before and during World War I, and afterward, during his post-war battles for control of the Arabian Peninsula. See generally, "Commanding Heights, Saudi Arabia, Overview," *PBS*, at http://www.pbs.org/wgbh/commandingheights/lo/ countries/sa/sa_overview.html. Regarding knighthood for Ibn Saud, the investure occurred on November 16, 1916, and was performed by Sir Percy Cox, the High British Gulf Resident. The King's new title would be that of Knight Commander of the Most Eminent Order of the Indian Empire (KCIE). The King proudly wore his new title and the bright British sash and jeweled star and was photographed wearing them. See Sindi, Dr. Abdullah Mohammed, "The Direct Instruments of Western Control Over the Arabs: The Shining Example of the House of Saud," at http://www.kaananonline.org/readings/read7.pdf.

81. See generally, Joshua Teitelbaum, "Holier than Thou, Saudi Arabia's Islamic Opposition," *The Washington Institute for Near East Policy, Executive Summary*, 2000, at www.

washingtoninstitute.org/templateC04.php?CID=53; "Britain Gets Tough," *Al-Ahram Weekly Online*, Issue No. 397, October 1-7, 1998, at http://weekly.ahram.org.eg/1998/397/eg9.htm; and "Saudi Arabia Plagued by Dissent, Economic Instability," *Jewish Institute for National Security Affairs*, September 1, 1996, at http://www.jinsa.org.

82. See previous endnote. See also "A Biography of Osama Bin Laden," *Frontline, PBS.org*, at http://www.pbs.org/wgbh/pages/frontline/shows/binladen/who/bio.html.

83. See endnote 81.

84. See, *infra*, Mr. Bin Laden's statements after March 20, 2003, the date of the United States' invasion of Iraq, especially his statements of October 29, 2004, and December 16, 2004.

85. See generally, Stephen J. Hedges, "Military to Leave Saudi Arabia," *Chicago Tribune*, April 30, 2003, http://www.globalsecurity.org/org/news/2003/030430-psab01.htm; "US Pulls Out of Saudi Arabia," *BBC News*, April 29, 2003, http://www.news.bbc.co.uk/2/hi/middle_east/2984547.stm; "Most of U.S. Forces Withdrawn From Saudi Arabia," *USA Today*, August 28, 2003, www.usatoday.com/news/washington/2003-08-28-ustroops-saudiarabia_x.htm; Christine Spolar, "14 'Enduring Bases' Set in Iraq," *Chicago Tribune*, March 23, 2004, http://www.globalsecurity.org/org/news/2004/040323-enduring-bases.htm; "Military Forces in the Middle East," *The Houston Chronicle*, March 18, 2003, http://www.globalsecurity.org/org/news/2003/030318-military02.htm; and "U.S. Forces Order of Battle of December 2004," http://www.globalsecurity.org/military/ops/iraq_orbat.htm.

86. Bob Woodward, *Plan of Attack*, pp. 263-266 (Simon & Schuster 2004). In unleashing the Iraq War, the United States gained tacit permission from Saudi Arabia, Jordan, Kuwait, Qatar, and Bahrain to use bases located in their countries from which to conduct military activities in support of the War. *Plan of Attack*, at pp. 112, 136, 230,264, and 330. General Tommy Franks actually commanded the War from the Prince Sultan Air Base in Saudi Arabia. *Id.* at p. 378.

87. The Bush administration's primary stated rationale for the Iraq War was Iraq's possession of weapons of mass destruction. None were found after the conclusion of the War. Controversy continues to swirl around the question whether the administration "wagged the dog" in declaring war on Iraq. See generally, Byron York, "The Trudh About Bush's 'Lies,'" *National Review Online*, June 16, 2003, www.nationalreview.com/york/york060303.asp; Bill Nichols, "U.N.: Iraq Had No WMD After 1994," *USA Today*, March 2, 2003, at http://www.usatoday.com/news/world/iraq/2004-03-02-un-wmd_x.htm; Tom Raum, "Bush Shifts War Rationale From Iraqi Arms, *KansasCity.com*, *The Kansas City Star*, September 8, 2003, at www.kansascity.com/mld/kansascity/news/breaking_news/6722744.htm; Mark Sandalow, "News Analysis: Record Shows Bush Shifting on Iraq War – President's Rationale for the Invasion Continues to Evolve," *San Francisco Chronicle*, September 29, 2004, www.sfgate.com/cgi-bin/article.cgi?file=/c/a/2004/09/29/MNGE590O711.DTL. For Deputy Secretary of Defense Paul Wolfowitz's comment in an interview appearing in the July, 2003, issue of *Vanity Fair* (published on June 16, 2003) that the administration seized on the WMD rationale to justify the Iraq invasion because that was the only rationale that "everybody could agree on," see "Iraq WMD Report Enters Political Fray," *CNN.com*, October 4, 2004, at http://edition.cnn.com/2004/ALLPOLITICS/10/07/wmd.iraq/; "Wolfowitz Comments Revive Doubts Over Iraq's WMD," *USA Today*, May 30, 2003, at http://www.usatoday.com/news/world/iraq/2003-05-30-wolfowitz-iraq_x.htm; and Cliff Kincaid, "Another Media Scandal," *Accuracy in Media*, June 17, 2003, at http://www.aim.org/media_monitor/A328_0_2_0_C/. For the growing insurgency in Iraq, see Jim Landers, "Iraq's Unsecured Ammo Dumps Providing Explosives for Insurgency," *The Dallas Morning News*, December 22, 2004, at http://www.duluthsuperior.com; John Diamond, "Small Weapons Prove the Real Threat in Iraq," *USA Today*, September 29, 2003, at www.usatoday.com/news/world/iraq/2003-05-30-wolfowitz-iraq_x.htm; and Douglas Jehl, "Iraq May Be Prime Place for Training of Militants, C.I.A. Report Concludes," *New York Times*, June 22, 2005.

88. "Aden, Yemen Car Bomb Attack by al-Qaeda," see *Wikipedia, the Free Encyclopedia*,

http://en.wikipedia.org/wiki/Car-bomb.

89."Khobar Towers Bombing," *Wikipedia, the Free Encyclopedia*, http://en.wikipedia.org/wiki/Khobar_Towers_bombing.

90. "Car bombing," see *Wikipedia, the Free Encyclopedia* at http://en.wikipedia.org/wiki/Car_bombing.

91. "Embassy Bombings" *Wikipedia, the Free Encyclopedia* see http://en.wikipedia.org/wiki/1998_U.S._embassy_bombings.

92. "USS *Cole*," *Wikipedia, the Free Encyclopedia*, at www.en.wikipedia.org/wiki/USS_Cole_bombing.

93. "Expatriots Compound Bombed," *Wikipedia, the Free Encyclopedia*, at http://en.wikipedia.org/wiki/Car_bombing.

94. Business Staff, "Sept. 11 Economic Toll: $1 Trillion," *The Oakland Press, Online Edition*, September 7, 2003.

95. David W. Chen, "New Study Puts Sept. 11 Payout at $38 Billion, *New York Times, November 8, 2004; Business Staff,* "Sept. 11 Economic Toll: $1 Trillion, " *The Oakland Press*, Online Edition, September 7, 2003.

96. OBL's referencing in his speeches about the *Ummah* not only in the Middle East but the whole world. For *Ummah's* definition, see: "List of Islamic Terms in Arabic," *Wikipedia, the Free Encyclopedia*, at http://en.wikipedia.org.

97. "Education of the Ulema," see *Wikipedia, the Free Encyclopedia;* at http://en.wikipedia.org/wiki/Ulema. see also endnote 1 of OBL's 1998 Fatwa, *infra*.

98. See generally, "Egypt Fights Terror with Imams and Newsprint," *Christian Science Monitor*, July 16, 2002 edition, http://www.csmonitor.com/20020716/p01s03-wome.htm; and "Report on International Religious Freedom: United Arab Emirates," *Jewish Virtual Library*, http://www.jewishvirtuallibrary.org/jsource/anti-semitism/relunitedarabemirates00.html. See also, "Encyclopedia: Ulema," *Nationmaster.com*, at http://www.nationmaster.com/encyclopedia/Ulema also "In the name of Allah, the Merciful, the Compassionate the permissibility of celebrating the meelad-un nabi (sallal laahu alaihi wasallam) in refutation of the fatwa of sheikh Abdul Aziz bin Baaz of Saudi Arabia," *IslamicSupremeCouncil.com*, at http://www.islamicsupremecouncil.com/fatwabinbaz.htm.

99. See "Encyclopedia: Shia," *Nationmaster.com*, at http://www.nationmaster.com/encyclopedia/Shi'a; also, "Shiite," *Answers.com*, at http://www.answers.com/topic/shiite. Regarding the heightened influence of Shi'ite clerics in comparison to Sunni clerics, see: Uwe Siemon-Netto, UPI, "Analysis: Sistani – Dean, Ruler, Pope?," *The Washington Times*, September 2, 2004 (Grand Ayatollah Sayyid Ali Hussaini Sistani), "one of the Prophet's [PBUH] descendents, as his title, sayyid, and his black turban indicate ...)"; also, Judith S. Yaphe, "Turbulent Transition in Iraq: Can It Succeed?," *Strategic Forum*, No. 208, June, 2004, Note 4 ("Unlike Sunnis, Shi'a Muslims must follow a living mujtahid (religious scholar such as Khomeini or Sistani) who can interpret the *Quran*, collect tithes, and issue fatwas. While clerics in both sects [Shi'a and Sunni] can issue fatwas, Shi'a authorities have more latitude to interpret the law and tradition."), at http://www.ndu.edu/inss/strforum/SF208/sf208.htm.

100. For further definitions and pronunciations, please see the Glossary at www.osama-bin-laden-book.com.

CHAPTER 1

1. Sheikh Abdel-Aziz ibn Baz was Saudi Arabia's most eminent Islamic scholar. Ironically, in 1991 he and 400 other scholars wrote a letter to King Fahd of Saudi Arabia calling for governmental reforms. Included in requested reforms were calls for an independent consultative assembly and the removal of corrupt government officials. The letter also urged the protection of individual rights. See Nasser Momayezi, "Islamic Revivalism and the Quest for Political Power,"

The Journal of Conflict Studies, University of New Brunswick, Vol. XVII, No. 2, Fall 1997, at www.lib.unb.ca/Texts/JCS/bin/get.cgi?directory=FALL97/articles/&filename=MOMAYEZI.html.

2. OBL refers to Ahmad ibn Muhammad Hanbal, more about Hanbal can be found in the Forward.

3. Said Bin Jubiar, was a Companion of the Prophet Muhammad (PBUH) (570 – 632) and is commonly cited as a narrator of *Hadiths* by noted *Hadith* scholars like Bukhari. See www.usc.edu/dept/MSA/.Ahmad ibn Muhammad Hanbal is addressed in the Forward. Ibn Taymiya is addressed in the Forward.

4. *Holy Quran*, 51 (Adh-Dhariyat [The Winds that Scatter]:55.

5. *Fatwa*: a religious decree of an Islamic scholar which is followed by those who follow his *Taqlid* (precedents). See "List of Islamic Terms in Arabic," *Wikipedia, the Free Encyclopedia*, at www.answers.com/topic/list-of-islamic-terms-in-arabic.

6. See OBL's 1995 *An Open Letter to King Fahd of Saudi Arabia*, reprinted *infra*.

7. *Holy Quran*, 2 (Al-Baqarah [The Cow]):278-279.

The "Holy Mosques," OBL refers to the mosques located in Mecca and Medina. Please see the Forward for more about Mecca and Medina and the Two Holy Mosques.

8. It is common knowledge that Abdul Aziz accepted British financial aid during his uprising against the Turkish Ottoman Empire before and during World War I, and afterward, during his post-war battles for control of the Arabian Peninsula. See generally, "Commanding Heights, Saudi Arabia, Overview," *PBS*, at http://www.pbs.org/wgbh/commandingheights/lo/countries/sa/sa_overview.html; regarding knighthood for Ibn Saud, the investure occurred on November 16, 1916, and was performed by Sir Percy Cox, the High British Gulf Resident. The King's new title would be that of Knight Commander of the Most Eminent Order of the Indian Empire (KCIE). The King proudly wore his new title and the bright British sash and jeweled star and was photographed wearing them. See Sindi, Dr. Abdullah Mohammed, "The Direct Instruments of Western Control Over the Arabs: The Shining Example of the House of Saud," at http://www.kaananonline.org/readings/read7.pdf; and generally, "Commanding Heights, Saudi Arabia, Overview," *PBS*, at http://www.pbs.org/wgbh/commandingheights/lo/countries/sa/sa_overview.html.

9. As the grand Mufti, the most respected religious scholar in Saudi Arabia at the time, Sheikh Abd al Aziz Bin Baz endorsed the introduction of United States military forces into Saudi Arabia in August, 1990, in response to Saddam Hussein's invasion of neighboring Kuwait. The Sheikh's *Fatwa* stated: "Even though the Americans are, in the conservative religious view, equivalent to non-believers as they are not Muslims, they deserve support because they are here to defend Islam." Quoted in "The Power of Saudi Arabia's Islamic Leaders," *Middle East Quarterly*, September 1999, quoting in turn Abir, *Saudi Arabia: Government, Society, and the Gulf Crisis*, p. 178. See www.meforum.org/article/482.

10. OBL refers to Saudi Arabia's support of Ali Salim al-Baidh, ex-President of the former Marxist Peoples Democratic Republic of Yemen (unified), who in 1994 launched a breakaway movement of the area previously known as South Yemen. Hostilities lasted from April to July, 1994, and the movement failed. However, Saudi Arabia and the Gulf States did give tacit support to al-Baidh. The Saudi government is upset with the Yemeni government because in 1991, while serving as chair of the United Nations Security Council, Yemen voted against the resolution that authorized the use of force to liberate Kuwait. Saudi Arabia and Yemen harbor historic differences, including border disputes. For an especially enlightening discussion of their checkered relationship, see John Duke Anthony, "Saudi Arabian-Yemeni Relations: Implications for U.S. Policy," *ArabiaLink.com*, June 28, 2000, at www.arabialink.com/Archive/GWDigests/GWD2000/GWD_2000_06_19.htm#GWP1.

11. In 1980, after the Soviet invasion of Afghanistan in 1979, Sheikh Baz issued a *Fatwa* (religious decree) urging Muslims to fight the Soviet "infidel" invaders of that Muslim country.

Today's Saudi dissident clerics like Salman al-Odeh and Safar al-Hawali claim that Baz's *Fatwa* also applies to present-day Iraq, occupied by United States and "coalition" military forces. See Lothar, "The Axis of Evil: US, Pakistan, Israel, & Saudi Arabia," January 29, 2005, at www. matrix.bangkokpost.co.th/forums/print.php?Message_ID=7919. These two clerics are in good steed in today's Saudi Arabia. For example, on March 7, 2003, immediately before the United States invasion of Iraq, Sheikh Ouda issued a *Fatwa* forbidding Muslims from attacking Iraq or supporting an attack on Iraq. Most recently, on November 7, 2004, Sheikh Hawali, Sheikh Ouda, and twenty-four other Saudi Sheiks issued a message to the Iraqi people urging them to wage *Jihad* (holy war) against the U.S.-led coalition forces. None of these sheikhs has been jailed by the Saudi authorities. See Susan Schmidt, "Spreading Saudi Fundamentalism in U.S.: Network of Wahhabi Mosques, Schools, Web Sites Probed by FBI," *Washington Post*, October 2, 2003; "Saudi Scholar Forbids Taking Part in Attacking Iraq," *ArabicNews.com*, March 7, 2003 at www.arabicnews.com/ansub/Daily/Day/030307/2003030714.html; "26 Saudi Scholars Address Message to the Iraqi People," *Site Institute (The Search for International Terrorist Entites), Site Publications*, November 7, 2004, at www.siteinstitute.org/bin/articles.cgi?ID=publications105 04&Category=publications&Subcategory=0; and "Saudis Confront Extremist Ideologies: Anti-Terror Forum Is Latest Sign of Changing Attitudes," *Washington Post*, February 6, 2005.

12. One who attempts to change Islam, or innovate contrary to Islam.
Sahih Muslim, *Hadith*, Book 007, Number 3166: see: www.usc.edu/dept/MSA/.
Book 009, Number 3601: see www.usc.edu/dept/MSA/.
Book 022, Number 4876: see www.usc.edu/dept/MSA/.
Book 022, Number 4877: see www.usc.edu/dept/MSA/.
Book 022, Number 4878: see www.usc.edu/dept/MSA/

13. See endnote 11, *infra*. At various times in the 1990's, these two clerics were jailed by the Saudi government.

14. On September 13, 1993, the *al-Hayat Newspaper* in Saudi Arabia published a *Fatwa* (religious decree) by Sheikh Baz in which he pronounced support for the concept of peace with Israel and the transfer of some Muslim land to Israel. "Saudi Arabia Is Not An Islamic State – Saudi Arabia Decides Laws on the Basis of Self-Interest, Rather Than Halal and Haram," *Islamic-State.org*, at www.islamic-state.org/saudi/selfinterest.shtml. His *Fatwa* was issued in the milieu of the 1994 Jordan-Israel peace treaty and the 1993 Oslo Accords between the Palestinians and Israel.

15. See the discussion of the Two Holy Mosques in the Forward.

16. The *Al-Aqsa* Mosque is discussed in the Forward.
More about the creation of the Palestinian Liberation Organization can be found in the Forward.
The Editor believes that OBL's reference to the "cowardly tartars" arises either from the participation of the Russian Federation in the Oslo Accords, or alternatively, because Genghis Khan (also known as Temujin or Temucin) (ca. 1155, 1162 or 1167 – 1227) (whose grandson Hulego conquered the Baghdad Caliphate in 1258), incorporated the *Sharia* (Islamic law) into his own legal system in a code of laws called the *Yassa* and demanded that his subjects adhere to its prohibitions. This was perceived as anti-Islamic because Khan essentially set himself up as a partner of God. See "Genghis Khan," *Wikipedia, the Free Encyclopedia*, see www.en.wikipedia. org/wiki/Genghis_Khan. See the text pertinent to, and endnote 12 of, OBL's 1995 Letter to King Fahd, *infra*, for a discussion of OBL's negative view of Khan.

17. Al-Ikhtiarat Alfiqhia, page 309.

18. See the Forward for a discussion of *Jihad* in the *Wahhabism.*.

19. *Fatwa* of Sheikh Bin Baz, 281/1.

20. Ibn Qayyim al-Jawziyyah (1290 - 1350), a *Hadith, Tafseer* (Quranic exegesis), *Usool* (fundamentals of jurisprudence), and *Fiqh* (jurisprudence) scholar. He was a student of Sheikh

Ibn Taymiya, under whom he studied for sixteen years. AKA "Imam Ibnul-Qayyim," he authored over sixty works, including the cited *I'llamul-Muwaqqi'een*, in the fields of *Fiqh* and *Usool*.

21. *Ielam al-Mouwakien*, 87/1.

22. *Al-Ikhtiarat Al-Fiqhia*, p. 311.

23. Please see the Forward for more information regarding Imam Ahmad ibn Hanbal's most famous work the *Musnad*.

24. Imam Nafe Madani, an early Islamic scholar of the recitation of the *Holy Quran* and the permitted forms of recital (*Qira'at*) of the *Holy Quran*. Imam Nafe obviously was a contemporary of Imam Malik to whom the latter referred questions of the proper accenting of Arabic words attributed to the *Holy Quran*. Arabic is a sensitive language in which even a slight variation in pronunciation can change the meaning of a word. See generally, "Qira'at," *Tajweedul Quran: 7 Ways of Qira'at*, at www.tajweedulquran.com/qirat.asp. See also endnote 6 of OBL's 1998 Fatwa, *infra*.

25. Please see the Forward for more information about the Committee for Advice and Reform (a.k.a. Advice and Reform Committee.)

26. Please see the Forward for more information regarding Imam al Azam Abu Hanifa.

27. Abu Sulaiman Ham bin Muhammad al-Khatabi, died in 998, a *Hadith* scholar who authored *Ma'alim As-Sunan*, collected by al-Da'as. Writings of Hadith Early Misrepresentations of Scholars' Statements, Muslimtents.com, at www.muslimtents.com/aminahsworld/Writing_hadith.html.

28. Al-Uzla

29. This is a famous *Hadith* narrated by Abu Huraira, a contemporary of the Prophet Muhammad (PBUH) – "Whoever lives in the desert becomes rough; whoever follows the game becomes careless; and whoever comes to the doors of the rulers falls into *Fitnah* (trouble); and a slave does not come nearer to the ruler, except that he becomes farther from God." *Musnad Ahmad*, Sheikh Ahmad Shakir saying that its *Isnad* (chain of narration) is *Saheeh* (authentic). "Let the Scholars Beware," *Islamicweb.com*, at www.islamicweb.com/beliefs/creed/sultan_scholars. htm. See also, "Abu Huraira: The Beloved Narrator," at http:www.islam.org.au/articles/16/ hurairah.htm.

30. *Holy Quran*, 11 (Hud [Prophet]):113.

31. OBL attributes this *Hadith* to Al-Bukhari. However, this famous *Hadith* was published not by Al Buhkari but rather by Imam Tirmidhi (824 – 894). More information about Tirmidhi can be found in the Forward.

32. The Editor believes OBL is referring to the signatories of the 1991 letter to King Fahd. Not all of these gentlemen can be found in Western sources searched by "Google," but several of them are clerics who continue to be held in good steed by the Saudi government, e.g., a reference to Mu'jab Ayed Al Qurani is found in "Saudis Divided Over Foreign Troops Presence in Riyadh," February 19, 2001, *Saudi Arabia: An NCO Reports* [sic], August 15, 2001, at www.d-n-i.net/fcs/ comments/c424.htm; Abdul Rahman Al Turairi was dean of education at King Saud University in 2002 (see "Two U.S. Allies Review Islamic Curricula at Schools, Mosques," *WorldTribune.com*, May 21, 2003, at www.216.26.163.62/2003/me_egypt_05_21.html; as recently as 2004, Sheikh Ibrahim Al-Khudairi was a cleric and judge in Riyadh, Saudi Arabia (see "SAUDI ARABIA: Saudi Clerics Forbid Muslims to Watch US Arabic Channel [Al Hurra]," *The Straits Times*, March 8, 2004, reproduced in *Asia Media: The Asia Pacific Media Network*, UCLA Asia Institute, at www.asiamedia.ucla.edu/article.asp?parentid=8702); and finally, regarding Sheikh Ouda, see endnote 11, *infra*.

CHAPTER 2

1. This letter was communicated to King Fahd of Saudi Arabia by the Committee for Advice and Reform, which OBL founded in London, England, in 1994, the same year Saudi Arabia

stripped him of his citizenship. The stated purpose of the Committee was to seek reform in Saudi Arabia. The Committee was based in London because Saudi Arabia was not a friendly venue to anyone seeking to reform the government. See the Forward.

2. In 1992, the Saudi government elected to revive the *Shura* Council, an advisory council originally contemplated by Abdul ibn Aziz al Saud (1880. – 1953), founder of Saudi Arabia. The Council was formed in 1993 and vested with powers to propose laws in the interest of the state and the people. Its edicts have been effectively ignored by the regime. Recently, the government has forbidden the signing of petitions by government employees or criticizing the government to the press. And on January 13, 2005, the government ordered the flogging and imprisonment of fifteen demonstrators who had been arrested for peacefully demonstrating for reform. The Council of Ministers, and especially the Ministry of the Interior, have the upper hand in Saudi Arabia. "About Gulf-Co-Operation: Saudi Arabia Kingdom: Locomotive of the GCC Co-Operation Drive," *Qatar News Agency*, at www.ips.org/QNA/Arabia.htm; Faiza Saleh Ambah, "Moves Toward Reform Wane in Saudi Arabia," *Christian Science Monitor*, October 4, 2004, at www.csmonitor.com/2004/1004/p06s01-wome.html; and endnote 30 of OBL's December 16, 2004, speech, *infra*.

3. Per capita income in Saudi Arabia has fallen from $25,000 dollars (U.S.) in 1983 to $8,000 in 2003. See "Saudi Arabia," *Wikipedia, the Free Encyclopedia*, at www.en.wikipedia. org/wiki/Saudi_Arabia.

4. *Holy Quran*, 4 (An Nisa [The Women]:60.

5. *Holy Quran*, 5 (Al Maidah [The Table Spread with Food]):49.

6. *Holy Quran*, 4 (Al Nisa [The Women]):65.

7. *Holy Quran*, 2 (Al Baqarah [The Cow]):256.

8. The citation is to Abdur-Rahman ibn Hassan al-Sheikh's *Fath al-Majeed*, which can be purchased at Online-Islamic-Store.com, at www.store.talkislam.com/b8246.html.

9. From the the book *Fat-h ai-Majeed, Sharh Kitaab al-Tawheed*, pg. 392-393.

10. *Holy Quran*, 5 (Al Ma'idah [The Table Spread with Food]):50
    Sahih al-Bukhari, Hadith No. 6882.

11. Imad Ad-Deen Isma ibn Omar ibn Katheer al Basri Al-Dimashqi was born in 1322. He was well known for his work in the field of exegesis of the *Holy Quran*. "Biography of Ibn Katheer (700-774 A.H.)," *IslamBasics.com*, see www.islambasics.com/view. php?bkID=80&chapter=3. His mentor was Ibn Taymiya. For more on Ibn Taymiya, see the Forward.

12. Genghis Khan, original name (Temujin/Temucin), (ca. 1155, 1162 or 1167 – 1227), the first great Khan of the Mongol Empire, who led Mongol and Tartar hordes in conquering Northern China, Western Xia, Central Asia, Persia, and Mongolia, his namesake. By 1202 he had conquered the Tartars, a neighboring people, melded them into his own forces and began his series of amazing conquests that cut a swath across the civilized world, reaching from the Yellow Sea to the Caspian Sea by the time of his death. He created a code of laws, properly called the *Yassa* and demanded that his subjects adhere to its prohibitions. See "Genghis Khan," *Wikipedia, the Free Encyclopedia*, www.en.wikipedia.org/wiki/Genghis_Khan.

13. Abdi bin Haatim, (d. 686); At-Tirmidhee, (d. 896). See generally, "Thoughts on the Ten Commandments," www.etori.tripod.com/commandments.html; Shaykh Muhammad bin Saalih al-Uthaaymeen, "Ruling by Other Than the Law of Allaah, Taken from *Al-Qawl al-Mufeed 'alaa Kitaab at-Tawheed* [2/263-269]," *The Reign of Islaamic Da'Wah*, at www.tripod.org/.
    Holy Quran, 9 (At-Taubah [The Repentence]):31.

14. See the previous endnote.

15. Ibn Hazm (456 – 1064), a Muslim scholar, philosopher, and author, whose full name was Abu Muhammad Ali ibn Ahmad ibn Said ibn Hazm. He was born in Cordova, Spain, and is best known for literary works delving into human psychology. In his work, *Al-ihkam fi usul*

al-ahkam (Judgment on the Principles of *Ahkam*), he established five judicial categories (*Ahkam*) by which to judge human acts: obligatory, recommended, disapproved, forbidden, and lawful. Any action falling within the first four must find its source in either Quranic text or an authentic *Hadith* tradition. He expanded on this methodology in this voluminous treatise, *Kitab al-muhalla* (The Book of Ornaments). See Roger Arnaldz "Ibn Hazm," (translated from French by Miriam Rosen), *Islamic Philosophy Online Project*, April 28, 2003, at www.muslimphilosophy.com/

16. See endnote 12, *infra*.

17. The reference is to Ibn Rushd (Averroes), (1126 – 1198), Islamic philosopher whose best known work is *Kitab Fasl al-Maqal* (On the Harmony of Religion and Philosophy). See generally "Ibn Rushd (Averroes), 1126-1198 CE," *Islamic Philosophy Online Project*, at www. muslimphilosophy.com/ir/art/ir100.htm; and George F. Hourani, translator, "Averroes," *Islamic Philosophy Online Project*, at www.muslimphilosophy.com/ir/fasl.htm. The quoted verse is found at 3-66 of the *Kitab*.

18. More information about Ibn Taymiya (1263 - 1328) can be found in the Forward. OBL quotes from Sahih al-Bukhari, *Hadith*, Al-Tarikh al-Kabir, p. 533.

19. See endnotes 12 and 14, *infra*. *Fatawa* is plural for *Fatwa* and means Islamic religious decrees. This is at *Fatawa* 7-67, according to *JihadUnspun.com*.

20. See endnote 16, *infra*. *Tawheed* means Islamic monotheism. For the *Kitaab At-Tawheed* by Sheikh Imam Muhammad Abdul-Wahhab, see the "Book of *Tawheed*," translated by Sameh Strauch, published by the Islamic Publishing House, online at www.usc.edu/dept/MSA/fundamentals/tawheed/abduhwahab/.

21. *Fatawa* part 12/524 Taymiya; accord: *JihadUnspun*.

22. *Fatawa* 3/91 Taymiya; accord: *JihadUnspun*.

23. Sheikh letter as quoted; accord: *JihadUnspun*.

24. *Fatawa*, 12/251; accord: *JihadUnspun*.

25. Scholar Sheikh Muhammad al-Ameen al-Shanqeetee,a prominent Islamic Scholar 1907 - 1973.

26. *Holy Quran*, 10 (*Yunus* [Jonah]):59.
Adwaa' al-Bayaan 4/84, Muhammad Alamin al-Shanqiti, also Jamharet al-Ansab.

27. See endnote 18, *infra*. Fath al-Majeed by Abdur-Raman ibn Hassan Aal-Sheiky, with commentary by Bin Baz, at *Online-Islamic-Store*.com at www.onlineislamicstore.com/b8246. html.
Fath al-Majeed was written by Abdul-Rahman bin Hasan al-N ajdi al-Wahhabi, the explanation of the book of *Tawheed*.

28. Ahmad Muhammad Shakir, Egyptian judge, 1892 - 1958. See Ron Shaham, "An Egyptian Judge in a Period of Change: Qadi Ahmad Muhammad Shakir, 1892- 1958," *The Journal of the American Oriental Society*, July 1, 1999.
From *Omdal al-Tasfeer*, 4/157; accord: *JihadUnspun*. Shakir bin Ahmad bin Abd al-Qadir was born in 1866 in a city in Upper Egypt. He studied at Al Azhar University in Cairo, Egypt. In 1900 he was appointed Chief Justice in Sudan for four years. He was then appointed as Wakil of Al Azhar. He was a member of Al Azhar Corps of High Scholars and a member of the Legislative Society (Al-Jam'iyaa Al-Tashri'iyya) in 1913. He died in 1939 in Cairo. Among his works are: *Al-Durus al-Awwaliyya fi al-'Aqa'it al-Diniyya, al-Qaw al-Fasi fi Tarjamat al-Quran al-Karim*, and *al-Sira al-Nabawiyya*. His son, Sheikh Ahmad Muhammad Shakir wrote his biography in a treatise entitled *Muhammad Shakir'Alam min A'lam al-Asr*. For further information see: *Khayr al-Din al-Zirikli, Al-A'lam, Dar al-illm lil-Malayin*, Beirut, N.D., Vol. 6, pp. 156-157; cf. *Daghr*, op. cit., Vol. 2, p. 466.

29. OBL refers to his Committee for Advice and Reform. See the Forward. See generally, Joshua Teitelbaum, "Holier than Thou, Saudi Arabia's Islamic Opposition," *The Washington Institute for Near East Policy*, Executive Summary, 2000, at www.washingtoninstitute.org/

templateC04.php?CID=53; "Britain Gets Tough," *Al-Ahram, Weekly Online,* Issue No. 397, October 1-7, 1998, at www.weekly.ahram.org.eg/1998/397/eg9.htm; and "Saudi Arabia Plagued by Dissent, Economic Instability," *Jewish Institute for National Security Affairs,* September 1, 1996, at www.jinsa.org/articles/articles.html/function/view/categoryid/111/documentid/297/history/3,2359,947,653,111,297 etc.

30. Saudi Arabia was a prime mover in the establishment of the Gulf Cooperation Council in 1981 in response to the outbreak of the Iran-Iraq War. The Council also included Bahrain, Kuwait, Oman, Qatar, and the United Arab Emirates (UAE). The purpose of the Council was to deter outside intervention in the Gulf. The Council is headquartered in Riyadh, Saudi Arabia. See "Gulf Cooperation Council – GCC," Arab German Consulting, at www.arab.de/arabinfo/gcc.htm.

31. For a listing of the Closing Statements of the GCC since its formation, see www.gcc-sg.org/closingsessions.html.

32. *Al-Haramain* means "twin cities" in Arabic, i.e., Mecca and Medina, the two holiest cities in Islam. In order, the three holiest places in Islam are Mecca, home of the *Masjid* (Mosque) *Al-Haram* that houses the Kaba; Medina, the city to which the Prophet Muhammad migrated from Mecca in 622, and which houses his tomb at the Mosque of the Prophet (*Masjid Al Nabawi*); and the *Masjid Al-Aqsa* on the *Al-Haram Ash-Sharif* (The Noble Sanctuary) in Jerusalem (Al-Quds). Nadeem ul-Haq, "Al-Saud: the West's Custodians of the Haramain," *Muslimedia.com,* at Naeem ul-Haq, at www.muslimedia.com/archives/special-edition/hajj/hajj2.htm. For a discussion of these Mosques, please see the Forward.

33. Excerpt from the *Fatawa* of the Sheikh, 12/251; accord: *JihadUnspun.*

34. April 20, 1960, excerpted from the *Fatawa* of the Sheikh 12/251; accord: *JihadUnspun.* For further information about Saudi secular laws, especially in the labor arena, see endnote 33 of OBL's 1996 Declaration of War on the United States, *infra.*

35. *Holy Quran,* 2 (Al-Baqarah [The Cow]):275.

36. *Holy Quran,* 4 (An Nisa [The Women]):65.

37. See endnote 12, *infra.*

38. OBL refers to one billion dollars (U.S.) in grants and four billion dollars (U.S.) in loan guaranties paid by the Saudi Regime to the Soviet Union for its support for the Persian Gulf War and the liberation of Kuwait from its Iraqi occupiers. See "Contemporary Chronology of Iraq," at www.firethistime.org/contempchrono.htm.

39. OBL refers to a litany of complaints. Saudi Arabia began giving aid to Syria upon the latter's intervention against leftist Muslim forces in the Lebanon Civil War in 1976, resulting in a strain in Soviet-Syrian relations. Saudi Arabia then made regular payments to Syria in return for the latter's September 1978 rejection of the Camp David accords. After the outbreak of the Iran-Iraq War (1980-1988), Syria received generous financial aid from Saudi Arabia in the hope of tempering the regimes leftist policies. Syria aligned with Iran because the Iraq Baathist Party was a bitter rival of the Syrian Baathist Party. In February, 1982, the Muslim Brotherhood fought Syrian government forces in the city of Hamah, Syria. Estimates of the dead range from 10,000 to 25,000, and the city lay in waste. The minority Alawite Muslim (a small Shi'ite sect) President Hafez Assad and his Alawite army leadership showed the Sunni Muslims of Hamah no mercy, and the slaughter remains a bitter memory in Sunni history. See generally, "Milnet: Country Studies, Syria, Syrian Military," *Milnet,* www.milnet.com/pentagon/mideast/syria/syrmil.htm; and "The Assad Era," *Country Studies,* at www.country-studies.com/syria/the-assad-era.html.

The Algerian Civil War began in 1992 when the army canceled parliamentary elections in the face of the imminent victory of the Islamic Salvation Front, an organization that intended to invoke Islamic law (*the Sharia*) in Algeria. The War persists at this writing. Between 1993 and 1998, an estimated 70,000 civilians were killed. In 2000, an amnesty program tempered the violence, but armed militants continue to confront the government. See "Armed Conflict Events Data, Algerian Civil War, 1992-Present," at www.onwar.com/aced/data/alpha/falgeria1992.htm.

A twenty-one year civil war was fought between the government of Sudan and the Southern Sudan People's Liberation Movement/Army. The war broke out in 1983 when southerners rebelled in an effort to seek autonomy. More than two million people were killed. On February 2, 2005, the Sudan Parliament ratified a comprehensive peace treaty effectively ending the war. However, a separate rebellion is ongoing in the Western, Darfur province. See "Sudanese Celebrate Peace Treaty," *ABC News*, January 9, 2005, at www.abcnews.go.com/International/wireStory?id=398719.

40. OBL refers to Saudi Arabia's support of Ali Salim al-Baidh, ex-President of the former Marxist Peoples Democratic Republic of Yemen (unified), discussed in endnote 10 of OBL's 1994 Letter to Sheikh Baz, *infra*.

41. For a discussion of the U.S. intervention in Somalia in order to protect Saudi Arabia from the threat of continued instability in Somalia and Islamic fundamentalists in that venue, see Christopher Whalen, "In Somalia, the Saudi Connection," *The Washington Post*, October 17, 1993.

42. Saudi Arabian contributions to the Palestine Liberation Organization were on the magnitude of $85 million (U.S.) per year between 1979 and 1989. The funding dried up in 1990 after Yasser Arafat sided with Saddam Hussein during the latter's occupation of Kuwait in 1990. See Karin Lamb, "Worries Arise About Fate of Arafat Financial Empire," *Seattle Times*, December 11, 2004.

43. In the continuing saga of the Middle East "peace process," 1995 was characterized by a faltering process brought about by the assassination of Israeli Prime Minister Yitzhak Rabin in 1995. See "Struggle for Peace: Special Section," *CNN.com*, www.cnn.com/WORLD/struggle_for_peace/.

44. A city in Saudi Arabia. See *TripAdvisor.com* at www.tripadvisor.com/Hotels-g298549-Hafr_Al_Batin-Hotels.html.

45. *Kitaab At-Tawheed (The Book of Tawheed [Oneness of God])*, found at www.islamicweb.com/beliefs/creed/abdulwahab/.

More information about the "ten 'voiders' that disqualify one from Islam" can be found in the Forward.

46. *Holy Quran*, 5 (Al-Ma'idah [The Table Spread with Food]):51.

47. *Holy Quran*, 58 (Al-Mujadilah [The Woman Who Disputes]):22.

48. *Holy Quran*, 4 (An-Nisa [The Women]):138-139.

49. No such poet has been found, but the *Holy Quran* contains the same words:
Holy Quran, 3 (Al-Imran [The Family of Imran]):28.

50.*Holy Quran*, 4 (An-Nisa [The Women]):139-140.
 Holy Quran, 4 (An-Nisa [The Women]):109.

51. Indeed, Saudi Arabia sits on approximately 261.9 billion barrels of proven oil reserves (including 2.5 billion barrels in the Saudi-Kuwaiti Neutral Zone) – around one-fourth of proven, conventional world oil reserves – Saudi Arabia is the world's leading oil producer and exporter. Between January and October, 2004, Saudi Arabia supplied the United States with 1.5 million barrels of oil per day, 15% of its crude oil imports for such period. See "Saudi Arabia, Country Analysis Briefs," *Energy Information Agency, United States Department of Energy*, at www.eia.doe.gov/emeu/cabs/saudi.html.

52. For the decline of the Saudi Arabian economy, see endnote 3, *infra*.

53. In fact, Saudi Arabia has experienced a slowing economy attributable to a rising birth rate, continuing dependence on foreign workers, and fluctuating oil prices. Up to 20% of Saudis are jobless. See Shaheen Chughtai, "Profile: Kingdom of Saudi Arabia," *Aljazeera.net*, October 14, 2003, at www.english.aljazeera.net, and "Gulf States Face Unemployment Problems," *Migration News*, February, 1995, at www.migration.ucdavis.edu/mn/.

54   In an indirect, and starkly effective, way OBL reminds the reader, i.e., King Fahd, that

the Bin Laden family owns the largest construction company in Saudi Arabia and has constructed many of the edifices about which OBL now complains. The point would not be lost on any reader in Saudi Arabia. How can the King deny the statements of his own contractor? See generally, "A Biography of Osama bin Laden," *PBS: Frontline*, at www.pbs.org/wgbh/pages/frontline/shows/binladen/who/bio.html.

55. Sahih Bukhari, *Hadith*, Vol. 4, Book 52, No. 137 at www.usc.edu/dept/MSA/.

56. Between 1986 and 2000, the average per-barrel price of oil was less than nineteen dollars. Betweem 1971 and 2001, oil prices vacillated from a low of fifteen dollars (2003 dollars) per barrel in 1971 to a high of seventy-nine dollars per barrel in 1980, down to a low of eighteen dollars per barrel in 1998. See "Prince Faisal bin Turki's Speech in U.K on Saudi Energy Industry," Royal Embassy of Saudi Arabia, Washington, D.C., December 2, 2000, at www.saudiembassy.net/2000News/Statements/SpeechDetail.asp?cIndex=347

1044 Andrew McKillop, "Per Capita Oil Demand and World Oil Demand Growth," September 20, 2004, at www.archives.econ.utah.edu/archives/a-list/2004w38/msg00011.htm.

57. Throughout the Iran-Iraq War, the Saudis were aligned with Saddam Hussein and gave him approximately one hundred million dollars (U.S.) in aid. They became estranged from his regime when he invaded Kuwait in 1990. See "Saudi Cash Joins Forces with Nuclear Pakistan," *Financial Times*, August 4, 2004, at www.inn.globalfreepress.com/modules/news/article.php?storyid=645; and "Saudi Arabia: History and Culture," *U.K. Travel Guide*, at www.uk.holidaysguide.yahoo.com/g-middle_east-saudi_arabia-hisotry_culture.html.

58. As of March, 1992, Saudi Arabia had contributed approximately fifteen billion dollars (U.S.) to the Gulf War expenses incurred by the United States. Ultimately, the War cost the United States a paltry seven billion dollars of the estimated sixty-one billion dollar cost of the War. See "How Much Did the Gulf War Cost the US?," *Conduct of the Persian Gulf War, The Final Report to the U.S. Congress by the U.S. Department of Defense*, April, 1992, Appendix P, at www.people.psych.cornell.edu/~fhoran/gulf/GW_cost/GW_payments.html.

59. In January, 1993, Saudi Arabia placed its *al Yamamah II* order for 48 Tornado Interdictor Strike aircraft from Britain. See endnote 70 of OBL's statement of December 16, 2004, *infra*, regarding the *al Yamamah* (the dove) purchases. Richard Aboulafia, "The End of the Saudi Aircraft Market?," *Industry Insights: Aerospace America*, November, 2003, at www.aiaa.org/aerospace/Article.cfm?issutocid=424&ArchiveIssueID=44. The article also discusses Saudi purchases of F-15 aircraft from the United States, saving the assembly line from a shutdown.

60. In fiscal 2003, Saudi Arabia allocated 21.3 billion dollars (U.S.) to military spending. It's annual budget for 1994 was 40 billion dollars (U.S.) on income of 35 billion dollars, and approximately 12 percent of its GDP (gross domestic product) was allocated to military spending. Its total GNP (gross national product) in 2002 was approximately 187 billion dollars (U.S.), resulting in a per capita income of $8,530 (U.S.). See "U.S. Military Budget for FY 2003," *International Institute for Strategic Studies*, U.S. Department of Defense, at the Center for Arms Control and Non-Proliferation, at www.armscontrolcenter.org/archives/000568.php; and "Saudi Arabia," *Encarta Encyclopedia*, see www.uk.encarta.msn.com/encnet/refpages/RefArticle.aspx?refid=761575422&pn=2.

OBL appears to have inflated French military spending. In February, 1996, the French devoted 2% of their GNP to military spending. See "What Are the Trade-Offs?," *Feminist Budget, Feminist Majority Foundation*, February 1996, at www.feminist.org/other/budget/budget5.html; in 1995, the figure was 2.5%, "France: Facts and Figures, Military," *World Sites Atlas*, adopted from *CIA World Fact Book 1998*, at www.sitesatlas.com/Europe/France/frastats.htm.

61. For a discussion of the poor performance of the Saudi Arabian military forces during the Gulf War, see Kenneth M. Pollack, *Arabs at War: Military Effectiveness*, 1948-1991 (University of Nebraska Press 2002).

62. Astoundingly, in 1995 Saudi Arabia spent $919 per capita on military expenditures,

ranking it fifth behind Kuwait, Israel, Singapore, and the United States. For a listing of the ranking of countries by variables including per capita military spending, percentage of GNP military spending, see "World Military Expenditures and Arms Transfers (WMEAT) 1996," U.S. *Arms Control and Disarmament Agency*, at www.fas.org/man/docs/wmeat96/.

63. For a fascinating treatment of Saudi royal family corruption, see Seymour Hersh, "King's Ransom," *New Yorker*, October 22, 2002. In the article, Mr. Hersh quotes from an October 9, 2001, "Frontline" PBS interview of Saudi Prince Bandar, Saudi Arabia's ambassador to the United States, in which he states when asked about corruption in the royal family: "If you tell me that building this whole country [Saudi Arabia]... we misused or got corrupted with fifty billion, I'll tell you, 'Yes,... So what?' We did not invent corruption, nor did those dissidents, who are so genius, discover it.'"

Though this letter was written in 1995, OBL was prescient: On March 8, 2003, shortly before the Iraq War began (March 19, 2003), Saudi Defense Minister Prince Sultan bin Abdul Aziz actually denied that Saudi Arabia was allowing the United States to use Saudi bases for war preparations, depicting the U.S. presence as for "humanitarian and technical assistance." General Tommy Franks actually commanded the Iraq War from the Prince Bin Sultan Air Force Base in Saudi Arabia. See "Bombs Defused in Jeddah, Saudis Deny Facilities to U.S.," *IslamOnline.net*, March 9, 2003, at www.islam-online.net/english/News/2003-03/09/article02.shtml; and Patrick Martin, "US Accelerates Preparations for Invasion of Iraq," *World Socialist Web Site*, January 4, 2003, at www.wsws.org/articles/2003/jan2003/iraq-j04.shtml.

64. OBL refers to the presence of United States and Western military forces in Saudi Arabia.

65. *Holy Quran*, 6 (Al-An'am [The Cattle]):162-163.

66. *Holy Quran*, 2 (Al-Baqarah [The Cow]):8-9.

67. The Editor is unable to find this poet.

68. See endnote 31 of OBL's statement of December 16, 2004, *infra*, regarding the removal of King Ibn Saud from power.

69. Prince Sultan Bin Abdul Aziz is Second Deputy Prime Minister and Minister of Defense and Aviation and Inspector General. See "Al Sudairi Clan," GlobalSecurity.org, www.globalsecurity.org/military/world/gulf/sudairi.htm.

70. Beginning in 1992, Saudi Arabia and Qatar had a border dispute concerning sixty kilometers of sea and land border. Armed clashes intermittently characterized the dispute. The dispute was resolved by written agreement in 2001. See "Qatar, Saudi Arabia Sign Border Agreement," *People's Daily*, March 22, 2001, at www.english.people.com.cn/english/200103/22/eng20010322_65657.html.

CHAPTER 3

1. This is the text of the *Fatwa* (religious decree) in which Osama bin Laden declared war against the United States of America. It was first published by *Al-Quds Al Arabi*, a London-based Arabic-language newspaper in August, 1996.

2. *Holy Quran*, 3 (Al-Imran [The Family]): 102.

3. *Holy Quran*, 4 (An-Nisa [The Women]):1.

4. *Holy Quran*, 33 (Al-Ahzab [The Confederates]):70-71.

5. *Holy Quran*, 11 (Hud [Prophet]):88.

6. *Holy Quran*, 3 (Al-Imran [The Family of Imran]):110.

7. Sahih Bukhari, *Hadith*, Vol. 3, Book 43, No. 624: see: www.usc.edu/dept/MSA/. See also, Dr. Muhammad Shafi, "Notes on the Quran and Hadith," *Dar Al Islam*, at www.daralislam.org/programs/reach/notes_on_the_Quran.html.

8. On April 18, 1996, Israeli military forces bombarded a United Nations military base near Tyre, in Southern Lebanon. The base was populated by Lebanese civilian refugees who had fled to the base seeking sanctuary from Israel's air, sea, and artillery attacks against suspected

Hezbollah positions in the vicinity of the base. More than 90 civilians were killed in the attack. See "Lebanon Mourns U.N. Camp Victims," *CNNineractive World News*, April 30, 1996, at www. cnnstudentnews.cnn.com/WORLD/9604/30/lebanon.funerals/index.html. For an eyewitness account of the attack, see Robert Fisk, "Massacre in Sanctuary; Eyewitness," at www.robert-fisk. com/articles18.htm. The other venues that follow the reference to Qana are more familiar sites where Muslims were massacred, e.g., Chechnya and Bosnia-Herzegovina.

9. The Editor will use American spelling and syntax.

10. OBL refers to the *Kaba,* more information about the *Kaba*, Medina and the *Qibla* can be found in the Forward.

11. OBL rails against the presence of United States and Western, and by definition, Christian, military forces in Saudi Arabia, venue of the Two Holy Places. See the previous endnote for a discussion of the Kaba and Medina. By *Qibla*, OBL means the *Kaba* as the ultimate destination of the pilgrims during their *Haj* (pilgrimage) to Mecca.

Regarding the quoted language:

This phrase is commonly recited during the required prayers, or *Salat*. It derives from the *Holy Quran*, 18 (Al-Kahf [The Cave]):39-40:

12. More information about Ibn Taymiya can be found in the Forward. Al'Izz ibn Abdus-Salaam was an Islamic *Hadith* scholar, d. 1282. See Uthmaan Alee Hasan, "The Aahaad Narration, Does the Aahaad Narration Amount to Knowledge?" at www.troid.org/articles/hadeeth/additionalinfo/aahaadnarration.htm.

13. OBL refers to Dr. Abdullah Yusuf Azzam (1941 - 1989), an Islamic scholar and early contributor to the development of political Islam. More information about Mr. Azzam can be found in the Introduction.

14. More information about Ahmad Yassin can be found in the Forward.

15. Sheikh Omar Abdel Rahman was arrested in Egypt, transported to New York for trial, and convicted of conspiracy in the 1993 bombing of the World Trade Center. His attorney, Lynn Stewart, was tried on federal charges that she aided and abetted the Sheikh in communicating with his sympathizers outside of his prison. See Barbara Ferguson, "Lawyer Accused of Aiding Sheikh Omar," *Aljazeerah.Info*, June 26, 2004, at www.aljazeerah.info ; "Sheikh Omar Abdul Rahman," at www.islam.co.za/saiin/abdulrahman.html On February 10, 2005, she was convicted of all counts. She is appealing the decision. Julia Preston, "Civil Rights Lawyer Is Convicted of Aiding Terrorists," *New York Times*, February 10, 2005.

16. OBL refers to two radical, Wahhabi sheiks in Saudi Arabia who were jailed in Saudi Arabia in the 1990's for radical activities. They are in good steed in today's Saudi Arabia. For example, on March 7, 2003, Sheikh Ouda issued a *Fatwa* (religious instruction) forbidding Muslims from attacking Iraq or supporting an attack on Iraq. Most recently, Sheikh Ouda, Sheikh Hawali, and twenty-four other Saudi Sheiks, issued a message to the Iraqi people on November 7, 2004, urging them to wage holy war against the U.S.-led coalition forces. None of these sheiks has been jailed by the Saudi authorities. See Susan Schmidt, "Spreading Saudi Fundamentalism in U.S.: Network of Wahhabi Mosques, Schools, Web Sites Probed by FBI," *Washington Post*, October 2, 2003; "Saudi Scholar Forbids Taking Part in Attacking Iraq," *ArabicNews.com*, March 7, 2003, at www.arabicnews.com/ansub/Daily/Day/030307/2003030714.html; "26 Saudi Scholars Address Message to the Iraqi People," *Site Institute (The Search for International Terrorist Entitles), Site Publications*, November 7, 2004, at www.siteinstitute.org/bin/articles.cgi?ID=p ublications10504&Category=publications&Subcategory=0; and "Saudis Confront Extremist Ideologies: Anti-Terror Forum Is Latest Sign of Changing Attitudes," *Washington Post*, February 6, 2005.

17. See endnote 11, *infra*, for a discussion of the quoted language.

18. OBL means the destruction and withdrawal of the then superpower Soviet Union's military forces from Afghanistan in 1988.

19. OBL is actually referring to the overall economic plight of the Middle East. He is trained as an economist. The actual statistics give his message much traction, to wit:

- The combined GDP of the 22 Arab League countries is less than that of Spain.

- Approximately 40 percent of adult Arabs – 65 million people – are illiterate, two thirds of whom are women.

- Over 50 million young people will enter the labor market by 2010, 100 million will enter by 2020 - a minimum of 6 million new jobs need to be created each year to absorb these new entrants.

- If current unemployment rates persist, regional unemployment will reach 25 million by 2010.

- One-third of the region lives on less than two dollars a day. To improve standards of living, economic growth in the region must more than double from below 3 percent currently to at least 6 percent.

- Only 1.6 percent of the population has access to the Internet, a figure lower than that in any other region of the world, including sub-Saharan Africa.

- Women occupy just 3.5 percent of parliamentary seats in Arab countries, compared with, for example, 8.4 percent in sub-Saharan Africa.

- Fifty-one percent of older Arab youths expressed a desire to emigrate to other countries, according to the 2002 United Nations Arab Human Development Report, with European countries the favorite destination.

See "G-8 Greater Middle East Partnership Working Paper," *Al-Hayat*, February 13, 2004, at *Middle East Intelligence Bulletin, Greater Middle East Initiative Working Paper (4 February 2004)*, at www.meib.org/documentfile/040213.htm.

20. On July 25, 1996, the Khobar Towers in Al-Khobar, Saudi Arabia were destroyed by a truck bomb. The Towers were being used to house foreign military personnel. 19 U.S. service persons were killed. The perpetrators are suspected of membership in Hezbollah. "Khobar Towers Bombing," *Wikipedia, the Free Encyclopedia*, www.en.wikipedia.org/wiki/Khobar_Towers_ bombing. On November 13, 1995, a car bomb exploded outside U.S. military headquarters in Riyadh, Saudi Arabia, killing five U.S. service personnel. "Terrorist Attacks," Infoplease, December 15, 2004, at www.infoplease.com/pa/A0001454.html; and "Car Bomb," *Wikipedia, the Free Encyclopedia*, www.en.wikipedia.org/wiki/Car-bomb. *Wikipedia* reports a total of seven deaths, including U.S. personnel.

21. Per capital income in Saudi Arabia has fallen from $25,000 dollars (U.S.) in 1983 to approximately $8,000 in 2003. See "Saudi Arabia," *Wikipedia, the Free Encyclopedia*, at www. en.wikipedia.org/wiki/Saudi_Arabia. See also endnotes 19 and 26, *infra*.

22. Saudi Arabia's annual budget for 1994 was 40 billion dollars (U.S.) (on an income of 35 billion dollars [U.S.]), and approximately 12 percent of its GDP (gross domestic product) was allocated to military spending. Its total GNP (gross national product) in 2002 was approximately 187 billion dollars (U.S.), resulting in a per capita income of $8,530 (U.S.). See "U.S. Military Budget for FY 2003," International Institute for Strategic Studies, U.S. Department of Defense, at the Center for Arms Control and Non-Proliferation, at www.armscontrolcenter. org/archives/000568.php; and "Saudi Arabia," *Encarta Encyclopedia*, www.uk.encarta.msn.com/

encnet/refpages/RefArticle.aspx?refid=761575422&pn=2.

23. The Editor cannot find this quoted language in any English-language source. With respect to the quoted language, see endnote 11, *infra*.

24. OBL refers to reform efforts in Saudi Arabia. The Committee for Advice and Reform (a.k.a. Advice and Reform Committee) was organized in London, England, in 1994 by OBL through his surrogate, Khalid al-Fawwaz, to express criticisms of the Saudi regime and seek reform. More about the Committee can be found in the Forward.

25. These forces were first invited into Saudi Arabia in numbers in 1990 upon Saddam Hussein's invasion of Kuwait and his perceived threat to Saudi Arabia.

26. Saudi United States dollar surpluses disappeared in 1986, with the collapse of oil prices that year. Saudi Arabia, Kuwait, and the other Gulf States paid the United States 36 billion dollars (U.S.) as reimbursement for the cost of the 1991 Gulf War. Since then, Saudi Arabia has maintained high levels of defense spending, forcing the government to slash its national budget by 20 percent between 1990 and 1995. See "Saudi Arabia and the United States: Parting of the Ways?." *Center for Defense Information*, January 23, 2002, at www.cdi.org. Also, Saudi Arabia's annual budget for 1994 was 40 billion dollars (U.S.) (on income of 35 billion dollars [U.S.]), and approximately 12 percent of its GDP (gross domestic product) was allocated to military spending. Its total GNP (gross national product) in 2002 was approximately 187 billion dollars (U.S.), resulting in a per capita income of $8,530 (U.S.), down from $25,000 in the early 1980s. See "U.S. Military Budget for FY 2003," *International Institute for Strategic Studies*, U.S. Department of Defense, at the Center for Arms Control and Non-Proliferation, at www.armscontrolcenter. org/archives/000568.php; and "Saudi Arabia," *Encarta Encylopedia*, www.encarta.msn.com/ encyclopedia_761575422/Saudi_Arabia.html.

27. See endnote 24, *infra*.

28. February 1991 marks the year that 400 Islamic scholars, including Sheikh Abdel-Aziz ibn Baz, Saudi Arabia's then most eminent Islamic scholar, wrote a letter to King Fahd calling for governmental reforms. Included in requested reforms was a call for an independent consultative assembly and a call for the removal of corrupt government officials. The letter also urged the protection of individual rights. See Nasser Momayezi, "Islamic Revivalism and the Quest for Political Power," *The Journal of Conflict Studies*, University of New Brunswick, Vol. XVII, No. 2, Fall 1997, at www.lib.unb.ca/Texts/JCS/bin/get.cgi?directory=FALL97/articles/ &filename=MOMAYEZI.html.

29. See previous endnote; this report issued in 1992, and consisting of 45 pages. It boldly attacked the Saudi government's paid clerics for supporting the regime's domestic and international policies.

30. *Holy Quran*, 24 (An-Nur [The Light]):19.

31. Sahih Muslim, *Hadith*, Book 17, No. 4206: see www.usc.edu/dept/MSA/.

32. See endnotes 58 and 61 of OBL's letter to King Fahd, *infra*, which address the poor performance of Saudi forces during the Gulf War and the magnitude of Saudi military expenditures.

33. Ostensibly, the Saudi legal system is based on the *Sharia* [Islamic law]. However, by royal decree special courts and secular tribunals have been created outside the *Sharia* to deal with commercial issues, security matters, and motor vehicles. Arbitration and appeal boards exist by which to settle commercial disputes, especially involving foreign businesses. The Ministry of Labor and Social Affairs issues decrees pertaining to labor matters, and those decrees, in turn, are enforced by special committees within the Ministry. See "Saudi Arabia: The Legal System," *Country Studies*, U.S. Department of State, 1993, maintained by the U.S. Library of Congress and found at www.countrystudies.us/saudi-arabia/51.htm. See also, "Saudi Arabia: Legal Review," *Info-Prod Research (Middle East) Ltd.*, 1999, at www.infoprod.co.il/article/24.

34. OBL refers to Saudi Arabia's failures to come to the aid of Muslim groups in Palestine

and instead render assistance to the secular Palestinian Liberation Organization/Palestinian Authority then led by Yasser Arafat. The Authority was created by the 1993 Oslo Accords, which were first implemented by transfer of power and responsibilities over the Gaza Strip and Jericho pursuant to the Israel-P.L.O. May 4, 1994, Cairo Agreement on the Gaza Strip and the Jericho Area. See "What is the Palestinian Authority and How Did It Originate?" *Palestine Facts, Israel 1991 to Present PA Origins*, at www.palestinefacts.org/pf_1991to_now_pa_origin.php.

OBL also refers to the Saudi's support of Ali Salim al-Baidh, ex-President of the former Marxist Peoples Democratic Republic of Yemen (unified), who in 1994 launched a breakaway movement of the area previously known as South Yemen. Hostilities lasted from April to July, 1994, and the movement failed. However, Saudi Arabia and the GCC (Gulf Cooperation Council) countries did give tacit support to Al-Baidh. The Saudi government is piqued at the Yemeni government because in 1991, while serving as chair of the U.N. Security Council, Yemen voted against the resolution that authorized the use of force to liberate Kuwait. Saudi Arabia and Yemen harbor historic differences, including border disputes. For an especially enlightening discussion of their checkered relationship, see John Duke Anthony, "Saudi Arabian-Yemeni Relations: Implications for U.S. Policy," *ArabiaLink.com*, June 28, 2000, at www.arabialink.com/ Archive/GWSpecials/GWS2000/GWS_2000_20.htm.

35. More about the "ten 'voiders' that disqualify one from Islam" can be found in the Forward.

36. *Holy Quran*, 5 (Al-Ma'idah [The Table Spread With Food]):44.

Holy Quran, 4 (An Nisa [The Women]):65.

37. Prince Sultan bin Abdul Aziz is Second Deputy Prime Deputy Prime Minister and Minister of Defense and Aviation and Inspector General. Saudi Defense Minister Prince Sultan bin Abdul Aziz; Saudi Interior Minister Prince Naif Bil Abdulaziz. See "Al Sudairi Clan," *GlobalSecurity.org*, www.globalsecurity.org/military/world/gulf/sudairi.htm.

38. General Zaki Bakr was Egypt's Interior Minister. He arrested an estimated 20,000 persons as dissidents during his four-year tenure. He was relieved by Egyptian President Mubarak in January, 1990. See "Introduction: Egypt," *Country Studies, U.S.*, at www.countrystudies.us/ egypt/3.htm.

39. At least one scholar, Rosalind Gwynne of the Department of Religious Affairs, University of Tennessee has expressed an inability to find this quote. See her work, "Draft: Al-Qaida and Al-Qur'an: The 'Tafsir' of Usamah bin Ladin, footnote 31," September 18, 2001, at www.web.utk.edu/~warda/bin_ladin_and_quran.htm.

However, this Editor believes that the quoted language does not exist in Ibn Taymiya's *Fatawa*. To the contrary, in his *Minhaj Us Sunnah* (4/527), Ibn Taymiya contended just the opposite, to wit: that the overthrow is a corruption greater than the resulting benefit and that and even greater evil would result. Instead of revolt, he counseled the *Ummah* (Islamic nation) to be patient. See quoted 4/527 at the YM [an acronym for *Iman*, belief] *Online Discussion Forum*, "We Get the Rulers We Deserve," quotation submitted by "ia43" on December 20, 2003, at www. forum.ymuk.net/archive/index.php/t-6132.html.

40. See Ms. Gwynne's excellent treatment of this paragraph and the following paragraph in footnotes 36 – 39, inclusive, of her Draft, cited in the previous endnote herein. In her footnotes, Ms. Gwynne observes that the term "collective duty" appears as a mistranslation of the word "*imja'an*." She also notes that the phrase beginning with "to fight in defense of religion" and ending "*Fatawa*" is actually *Kitab al-Ikhtiyarat al-Ilmiyyah fi Ikhtiyarat Shaykh al-Islam ibn Taymiyyah*, in *Al-Fatawa al-Kubra*, both compiled by Ala al-Din Abu al-Hasan Ali al-Ba'li, Beirut, Dar al-Ma'rifah, 1988, vol. 4, p. 319-559, the paraphrased quotation appearing at page 520. Ibn Taymiya (1263 - 1328) was an Islamic scholar of the Hanbal *fiqh* (Islamic school of jurisprudence) who insisted on an Islamic society in which the *Sharia* (Islamic law) was strictly applied and who rejected other schools like Sufism and Shi'ism. Later, Muhammad ibn Abd al-

Wahhab (b. 1703) would revive Ibn Taymiya's teachings in Saudi Arabia and found Wahhabism, now the dominant creed in Saudi Arabia. See the Forward for a discussion of Wahhabism.

And when OBL proceeds to discuss Ibn Taymiya's admonition that "if the danger to the religion from not fighting is greater than that of fighting," Ms. Gwynne points out that OBL's reference actually is to Ibn Taymiya's *Majmu al-Tatawa*, vol. 26, p. 506, or possibly due to a misprint, actually appearing at vol. 28 at p. 506.

Lastly, she points out at page 15 of her Draft that OBL is paraphrasing Ibn Taymiyah and is invoking a logical conclusion arising from an amalgam of "Islamist arguments," to wit: Sayyed Qutb's denial of purely "defensive *Jihad*" in preference to the view that *Jihad* (holy war) fulfills a right and duty of Islam to abolish all "man-made *Jahili* political and religious systems;" and Muhammad Abd al-Salam Faraj's work, entitled *Neglected Duty*, in which he proposes that the establishment of an Islamic state as the Muslim's solemn duty, even at the price of war.

Though her work is a draft, it is well worth a complete reading to any reader interested in plumbing the depths of Islamic scholarship.

41. More about the first four Caliphs and the Era of the *Rashidoon* can be found in the Forward.

42. *Holy Quran*, 31 (Luqman [Luqman]):13.

43. *Holy Quran*, 2 (Al-Baqarah [The Cow]):275.

44. *Holy Quran*, 2 (Al-Baqarah [The Cow]):278-279.

Al-Mushrikun: polytheists, pagans, idolaters, and disbelievers in the Oneness of God and in His Messenger Muhammad (PBUH)."

45. More information about the *Al Aqsa* Mosque an be found in the Forward.

46. In spreading the word of Islam, the Prophet Muhammad (PBUH) conquered Mecca in 630, smashed the idols at the *Kaba* and directed the "desert Arabs" of the Arabian Peninsula toward Islam's monotheism. See the Forward for a further discussion of the *Kaba*.

47. See endnote 34, *infra*, for a discussion of the Yemeni insurgency in 1994.

48. OBL refers to the *Hadith* of Riyad-us-Saliheen, Book 7, The Book of the Etiquette of Traveling, Chapter 167, "The Desirability of Undertaking a Journey in a Group and Appointing a Leader," No. 961: "Ibn Abbas (May God be pleased with them) reported: The Prophet (PBUH) said, 'The best number of companions is four, the best detachment if four hundred and the best army is four thousand; and twelve thousand men will not be defeated as a result of smallness of number. [At-Trimidhi and Abu Dawud]." See Muslim American Society, Minnesota Chapter, "Study the Hadith," at http:www.masmn.org/.

49. Sa'd ibn Abi Waqqaas (d. 676), was one of the companions of the Prophet (PBUH). Al Muthanna ibn Haritha Ash Shaybani (d. 635), was the Muslim general who defeated the Persians at the Battle of Babylon in the summer of 634. Alga'ga' ibn Amroo Al Tameemi (d. 660), was the son-in-law of Hamzah [Hamzah bin Abdul Muttalib], the Prophet's (PBUH) uncle. Al Tameemi has been called the "Lion of God" and the "Lion of the Messenger of God" for his prowess in battle. He did much to spread the message of Islam. See William Muir, K.C.S.I., *The Caliphate: It's Rise, Decline, and Fall*, "Chapter X, Campaign in Al-Iraq – Need of Reinforcements." Also, "Al-Muthanna Finds Abu Bakr on His Deathbed. First Half of March-August 634," *Answering Islam*, at www.answering-islam.org. "Sa'd ibn Abi Waqqas," *IslamOnline.com*, July 29, 2004, at http://www.islamonline.com; and "Druze: Introduction," *Crescentlife.com*, www.geocities.com/defender_of_the_truth/druze.html?200517; and "Good Manners at Home," *Crescentlife.com*, at www.crescentlife.com/family%20matters/good_manners_at_home.htm.

50. More information about "*Al-Quds*," can be found in the Forward.

51. Seediscussion of "voiders" in the Forward.

52. Sahih Bukhari, *Hadith*, Vol. 3, Book 39, No. 531: at www.usc.edu/dept/MSA/. See also, "Appendix I, Jihad and Expulsion of Non-Muslims from Islamic Countries," at www.bharatvani. org/books/jihad/app1.htm.

53. At page 21 of her Draft (see endnote 39 *infra*), Ms. Gwynne points out that OBL himself offered to defend Saudi Arabia from the 1990 Iraqi onslaught into Kuwait by marshalling thousands of *Mujahideen* to protect the land of the Two Holy Places. See also footnote 53 of her work. On July 25, 1996, the Khobar Towers in Al-Khobar, Saudi Arabia were destroyed by a truck bomb. The Towers were being used to house foreign military personnel. 19 U.S. service persons were killed. The perpetrators are suspected of membership in Hezbollah. More information regarding the "Khobar Towers Bombing," can be found in the Forward and at *Wikipedia, the Free Encyclopedia*, at www.en.wikipedia.org/wiki/Khobar_Towers_bombing.

54. See endnote 16, *infra*.

55. The *Qibla* is the direction to which Muslims prayer no matter their location in the world: toward Mecca, home of the *Kaba*. Originally, during the Prophet Muhammad's (PBUH) lifetime, the Muslims prayed toward Jerusalem until the Prophet (PBUH) changed the *Qibla* to Mecca. Between 1936 and 1939, the Palestinians revolted against increased Jewish immigration and land acquisition during the British mandate. The Palestinian rebellion was led by Hajj Amin Al Husayni and the Arab Higher Authority, a loose coalition of Arab political parties. Their demands included the cessation of Jewish immigration and the establishment of an Arab national government. The British owed fealty to the 1917 Balfour Declaration, which had promised the Jews a national home in Palestine. The post-WW I British Mandate in Palestine had the establishment of a Jewish homeland as one of its goals. By 1936, some 400,000 Jews had resettled in Palestine. In 1937, the British and their local ally, King Abdul Aziz ibn Saud of Saudi Arabia, mediated a temporary end to the revolt pending the report of a Royal commission appointed to study the problem. The commission's report was issued in July 1937. It saw no alternative but the partitioning of Palestine into Arab and Jewish states. The Twentieth Zionist Congress agreed to partition in principle; the Arabs rejected partition. In the autumn of 1937, the Palestinians again revolted and were met with a heavy hand by the British military forces. The intervention of King Abdul Aziz has been construed as destructive of the Palestinian effort because it resulted in the fractionalizing of the AHA. See "Israel: The Palestinian Revolt, 1936-1939," *Ask Jeeves*, at www.kalabhavanshow.info/world_ref/20f3/il0026.htm; and Ghassan Kanafani, "The 1936-1939 Revolt," originally published by the *Tricontinental Society*, London, 1980; and "The 1936-1939 Revolt in Palestine," published originally by the *Committee for a Democratic Palestine*, New York, 1972, at www.newjerseysolidarity.org/resources/kanafani/kanafanicover.html.

56. More information regarding *Hadith*s can be found in the Forward. "A believer is not bitten from the same hole twice." Reported by Al-Bukhari, Muslim, Ahmad, Abu Dawood, and Ibn Majah [*Hadith* scholars]. See "Certain Qualities of Believers," *Al-Jazeerah.info*, www.english.aljazeera.net/HomePage; also, Abdullah Jibrit Oyekan, "Accommodating *Kufr* [apostates, non-believers]," *Salaam*, www.salaam.co.uk/knowledge/kufr.php. Initially, King Fahd assured the Saudi Arabians that American forces would remain only for a few months.

57. Imam al-Nisa, *Hadith*, (ca. 900) See www.quran-Hadith-index.com. "The murdered man will come on the Day of Judgment with the murderer and say, 'Ask him why I was killed?' The murdered will say I killed him during the reign of so and so. The reporter Junab says, 'Guard yourself against it.'"

58. Aba Jahl* was an outspoken Meccan opponent of the Prophet Muhammad (PBUH). The Battle of Badr, 624, marked the first military victory of the Muslim forces under the leadership of the Prophet (PBUH). In the Muslim attack on the Meccan caravan, Aba Jahl was killed. His real name was Aba Hakam (judge), so named by his people for his wisdom. The Muslims assigned him the derogatory name Aba Jahl (ignorance) because of his refutation of Islam. As related by Sahih Bukhari, *Hadith*, Vol. 4, Book 53, No. 369: See www.usc.edu/dept/MSA/.

*"Aba" is used interchangeably with "Abu" and means "the father of." See also, "Life of Mohamet: The Biography of Mohamet," and "Rise of Islam: The Battle of Badr, Ramadan,

January, 624," Vol. 3, Chapter 12, at www.bible.ca/islam/library/Muir/Life3/chap12.htm.

    59. Sahih Bukhari, *Hadith*, Vol. 3, Book 38, No. 498: see www.usc.edu/dept/MSA/.

    60. On October 26, 1983, the United States Marines Corps barracks in Beirut, Lebanon, was blown up by a truck bomb. 241 Marines were killed. At approximately the same time, the French Multi-National Forces barracks was also bombed, killing 58 soldiers. For an excellent chronology of the Lebanese Civil War, see Ted Thornton, *Civil War in Lebanon, History of the Middle East Database*, at www.nmhschool.org/tthornton/mehistorydatabase/civil_war_in_lebanon.htm

    OBL next refers to the December 29, 1992, bombing of a hotel in Aden at which U.S. troops en route to Somalia were staying. Two Australian tourists were killed. The soldiers had left before the bomb exploded. U.S. intelligence believes that this was Al Qaeda's first terrorist attack aimed at U.S. forces. See the Forward.

    61. OBL refers to the 1993 United States incursion into Somalia and to the famous Black Hawk Down incident in Mogadishu. More information regarding the incident can be found in the Forward.

    62. After the fall of the Soviet Union, a civil war erupted in Tajikistan between Islamists and pro-democracy forces and the repressive Soviet-style government. Eventually, 20,000 lives were lost and 600,000 people were displaced. In 1994 a ceasefire was achieved, only to see war again erupt in 1995. In 1997 a peace accord was signed. See "Timeline: Tajikistan: A Chronology of Key Events," *BBC News*, March 1, 2005, at www.news.bbc.co.uk/2/hi/asia-pacific/country_profiles/1297913.stm.

    63. Malik's Muwatta (*Hadith*), Book 47, Number 47.1.8: at www.usc.edu/dept/MSA/fundamentals/hadithsunnah/muwatta/047.mmt.html.

    64. King of Al-Hirah Amr III ibn Hind al-Hirahi was patron of the pre-Islamic Arabic poetry of Tarafah and others associated with Al-Mu'allaqat ('The Suspended Odes'). He was born circa 525. He was the son of King of Al-Hirah Al-Mundhir III ibn al-Nu'man al-Hirahi and Hind bin Harith Banu Kinda. He avenged the death of his father, by a fierce and instant attack upon the Ghassanide kingdom in 562. King of Al-Hirah in Mesene, Iraq, between 562 and 574. He was dissatisfied at the discontinuance of a pension previously received by his father, sent an embassy of complaint to Constantinople; he was mortified by the incivility with which it was received, and again overran Syria with his armies. He also waged bloody wars with the Bani Tay and Bani Tamim, the latter of whom had murdered his brother. He died in 574. Traditionally held to have been killed by Amr ibn Kulthum, pre-Islamic Arab poet whose qasidah ('ode') is one of the seven that comprise the celebrated anthology of pre-Islamic verse Al- Mu'allaqat, supposedly for an insult addressed to the poet's mother. 'He met with his death, in a singular mode, highly illustrative of Arab manners. He had vaingloriously sworn that his own mother should be served by the mother of the haughtiest Arab in the land. At an appointed festival, the mother of Amr a warrior-poet of the Bani Taghlib, was invited into the tent of the prince's mother, who sought to entrap her into the apparently insignificant act of handing to her a dish. But the proud spirit of the Arab lady spurned the office, and resenting the affront she screamed aloud for help. Amr the poet sprang forward at his mother's call, and struck Amr the prince dead upon the spot.' at www.homepages.rootsweb.com/~cousin/html/p174.htm#i10851; see also "Amr ibn Kulthum," at www.britannica.com.

    65. *Holy Quran*, 3 (Al-Imran [The Family of Imran]):145.

    66. *Holy Quran*, 57 (Al-Hadid [Iron]):22.

    Sahih Al-Tirmidhi (831 - 901) was an Islamic scholar who studied under Imam Bukhari, Imam Muslim, and Imam Abu Dawd. He was known for his remarkable memory, gathered a large number of students under his tutelage in the Islamic world, and compiled his own book of *Hadiths* entitled *Al-Jami*. He pointed out discrepancies between the narrators of the *Hadiths* of the other mentioned scholars. See "Iman Tirmidhi" *Wikipedia, the Free Encyclopedia*, at www.en.wikipedia.org/wiki/Al-Tirmidhi.

67. The poet is Ibn-Alsaadi. Ref. Amuhibbi in "Khulaset al-Athar Fi Aeyan Alquarn Alhadi Ashar, pp. 1186

68. *Holy Quran*, 45 (Muhammad):4-6.

See the Forward for a discussion of how this verse of the *Holy Quran* and its attendant commentary reflect the deep roots of *Jihad* in the *Wahhabi* creed.

69. *Holy Quran*, 2 (Al-Baqarah [The Cow]:154.

70. Ibin Manzhur, *Mukhtasar Tarikh Dimashq*, p 3106.

71. Ibin Hazem, *Almuhalla*, pp 849 *Al-Nawawi, Riyadhussaliheen* pp. 9, Alqurtoubi, *Tafseer Alqurtoubi,* pp 2721-2722 and Al-Shafe-e, Al-Oumm, pp 972.

72. Almuttaqi Alhindi, *Kanzul-Ommal*, pp 567, Al-Nawawi, *Riyadhussaliheen* pp 145.

73. "Tahzeeb Altahzeeb" by "Ibin Hajar al-Asqalani" – page 1701.

74. Neither this Editor nor Ms. Gwynne can find any authority for this reward of "doubling."

75. *Holy Quran*, 9 (At-Taubah [The Repentance]:14.

76. *Holy Quran*, 3(Al-Imran [The Family of Imran]), Verse 133.

77. *Holy Quran*, 45 (Muhammad):4-6.

78. Harun al-Rashid aka Haroon Al Rasheed (ca. 763 - 809) was the fifth Abbasid Caliph, who ruled from 786 to 809. He held sway over the wondrous Baghdad court immortalized in *The Book of One Thousand and One Nights*. A patron of the arts, he encouraged learning, poetry, and music. As the leader of a 95,000-soldier army loosed on the Byzantine (Eastern Roman) Empire by his father, the Caliph al-Mahdi, the Third Abbasid Caliph, Harun defeated the Byzantine Empress' army led by General Nicetas in 782 and marched on Constantinople, the Byzantine capitol. In return for an annual ransom of 70,000 pieces of gold, Harun spared Constantinople and led his victorious army back to Baghdad. In 802, the Eastern throne was usurped by one Necephorus, who then refused to pay the tribute. This is the prelude to the famous exchange between Harun and Necephorus. The latter wrote Harun: "The weak and faint-hearted Irene submitted to pay you tribute. She ought to have made you pay tribute to her. Return to me all that she paid you; else the matter must be settled by the sword." Accompanying the message delivered by Necephorus's ambassadors was a bundle of Roman swords, which was then tossed at Harun's feet. With one swipe of his Arab scimitar, Harun cut the Roman swords in half, and sent his reply to Necephorus: "Harun-al-Rashid, Commander of the Faithful, to Necephorus, the Roman dog: I have read thy letter. Thou shalt not hear, thou shalt see my reply." Harun then set out that very day in the lead of a large army that proceeded to ravage the Eastern Roman territories, sacking Heraclea on the Black Sea. Necephorus, too, found himself paying a tribute to Harun, who returned to Baghdad. Shortly after Harun returned to Baghdad, Necephorus again refused to pay the tribute. Harun mounted a force of 15,000 and advanced into Roman territory at Phrygia, in Asia Minor, where Necephorus met him with a force of 125,000 men. The battle was joined, Necephorus was wounded, 40,000 of his men were killed outright, and he again promised to pay tribute. But again, he failed to pay as promised. This time, Harun vowed to kill Necephorus, but illness and death overtook Harun before he could fulfill his vow. See "Harun al-Radhid," *Wikipedia, the Free Encyclopedia*, at www.en.wikipedia.org/wiki/Haroun_Al_Raschid. Note also, the Harun's tactics comported themselves with the *Holy Quran*'s Verse 45:4 (see endnote 68, *infra*) which commands magnanimity to the victorious Muslim commander, either freeing of the prisoners or ransoming them, after the fighting has subsided.

OBL's reference to these events has a twofold effect: first, it harkens back to the glorious times of the Islamic empire; and second, it challenges today's young Muslims to rise to the level of bravery and proficiency of men like Harun. It is an intoxicating invitation to the young Middle Eastern Muslim male. And it is highly effective in light of the fact that over seventy-five percent of the 280 million people populating the 20 Middle Eastern countries are under the age of twenty-five. Recruiting *Mujahideen* fighters will be no problem for OBL, his sympathizers, and their long-term successors, especially after the United States' invasion of Iraq and its continued hostility to Muslim countries like Iran and Syria. Continued American pressure on Iran's nuclear program has little traction in the Middle East, where the panoply of Islamic countries are threatened by nuclear-armed Israel. See generally, "U.S. Uses Diplomacy to Pressure Iran on Nuclear Program," U.S. Policy and Issues, U.S. Embassy, Tokyo, Japan, August 19, 2004, at www.tokyo.usembassy.gov/e/p/tp-20040819-12.html.

79. Almoutanabbi in al-Mountazam, *Ibn-Aljawzi*, pp 1713.

80. The poet is Abu-al-Ghoul al-Tahawi, in *Samtul-La-Alee, Almaimani*, pp 168 and in Alhayawan, Al-Jahez,, pp 215

81. Poetry is *the* art form in the Arabic-speaking Middle East because of the oral tradition of the Arabic language. In English, these words are eloquent. In Arabic, they are even more embellished, exaggerated, and eloquent. For an excellent treatment of the subject, see Linda Clarke, University of Toronto, from Al-Serat, Vol. XII (1986)- *Elegy (Marthiya) on Husayn: Arabic and Persian*, at www.al-Islam.org/al-serat/Elegy.htm.

82. OBL refers to the Battle of Uhud (625). More information regarding the battle can be found in the Forward.

83. The poet is Al-Laythi, in Oyoun al-Akhbar, Ibin Qutayba al-Dainouri, pp 72

84. OBL refers to the post-1991 Gulf War sanctions against Iraq, which resulted in the premature deaths of an estimated 500,000 Iraqi children for lack of nutrition and medications. See the Forward. Also, he generally refers to the suffering of the Palestinian Arabs under Israeli occupation and Israel's costly incursion into Lebanon between 1982 and 1984, which included the horrible massacres at the Sabra and Shatilla Palestinian refugee camps in Beirut, for which Ariel Sharon bore responsibility as the local Israeli military commander. For information about the Lebanese incursion and Sharon's responsibility, see the treatment and links found at *The Palestine Monitor*, "Israeli Politics: Information Regarding Sabra and Shatilla," at www.palestinemonitor. org/israelipoli/sabra_shatilla_links.htm.

85. After the Prophet's (PBUH) migration [*Hijra*] to Medina in 622, the members of the Quraish tribe controlling Mecca continued to war on the Muslims in Medina. The Prophet (PBUH) and his followers desired to perform the annual migration to the Kaba in Mecca. In the sixth year of the *Hijra* (628), he and approximately 1,400 of his followers proceeded to Mecca. At a place called *Al-Hudaibiyah* (the English spellings vary), they were confronted by Quraish forces. Emissaries were exchanged, and negotiations ensued. Upon seeing the devoutness of the Muslims and their unwavering desire to make the pilgrimage, the Quraish relented. A peace treaty ensued: the Muslims could return annually but not stay in Mecca for more than three days; they may bring to Mecca only sheathed swords kept in bags; hostilities between the two sides would be suspended for ten years; Quraish men who might seek to join the Muslims without their guardians' consent would be returned to Mecca (the provision did not address women), but Muslims who might return to Mecca and the Quraish would not be returned; and neither side would interfere with anyone wanting to leave one side and join the other. Although the treaty was criticized by companions of the Prophet (PBUH), especially the one-sided repatriation provision, he declared it a victory, as would the Quran: "Verily, We have given you (O Muhammed Sallahah alaihi wa sallam) a manifest victory." *Holy Quran*, 48 (Al-Fath [The Victory]):1. However, the Quraish soon violated the treaty by supporting the Bani Bakr tribe against the Khaz'ah tribe, which had allied with the Muslims. Although a peace treaty had been previously negotiated between the Muslims and the Bani Bakr, the Prophet (PBUH) declared that treaty abrogated when the Bani Bakr had assisted the Quraish at the Battle of the Trench in the year 627 in which the city of Medina, occupied by the Prophet Muhammad (PBUH) and his followers, was besieged by some 10,000 Quraish troops from the city of Mecca. The besiegers were led by Abu Sufyan, the Prophet's (PBUH) arch-enemy. A trench dug around Medina by the Muslims forces prevented Abu Sufyan's army from gaining entry into Medina, and after repeated failed attempts, Abu Sufyan and his army returned to Mecca. www.angelfire.com/ny/dawahpage/

hist3.html; "Muhammad," *Wikipedia, the Free Encyclopedia*, at www.en.wikipedia.org/wiki/ Muhammad. Similarly, the Prophet (PBUH) declared the Treaty of Hudaybiyyah abrogated and set out to conquer Mecca in the eighth year of Hijra (630) The Muslim force of over 10,000 men entered the city unmolested. By the ninth year of the Hijra, the Muslims had united the whole of the Arabian peninsula under their protection. See Sh. Safi ur-Rahman al-Mubarakfuri, "Al Hudaibiyah Treaty," *Islaam.com: Sunnah*, at www.islaam.com/; and "Chapter 4: Madina and the Holy Wars," *TheMuslimHistory.Net*, at www.themuslimhistory.net/INenglish/The%20holy%wars/ Ch4print.htm.

86. *Holy Quran*, 9 (At-Taubah [The Repentance]:5.

87. At pp. 25-29 of her Draft (see endnote 39 *infra*), Ms. Gwynne engages in an enlightened discussion of how OBL has cobbled Quranic Verses 47:4 and 9:5 together to move from the notion of offensive *Jihad* seemingly countenanced by them to the concept of defensive *Jihad*. Her discussion details Islamic scholarship about the sequence of revelation of Quranic verses and whether earlier revelations were abrogated by later ones. OBL confidently holds the view that neither verse was ever abrogated and each requires every Muslim man to engage in offensive *Jihad* on pain of being branded a hypocrite, or worse. And in response to those Muslims who might contend that the verses have been abrogated or that they do not support broad-brush offensive *Jihad*, OBL turns to his trump card: defensive *Jihad*. Citing the panoply of attacks against Muslims across the world and the occupation of Saudi Arabia, the seat of the Two Holy Places, by United States and Western (read Christian and "non-believer) military forces, OBL invokes the obligation of every Muslim to engage in defensive *Jihad* to protect the lands of Islam. OBL's arguments are as sophisticated as is Ms. Gwynne's analysis of them. He is a formidable enemy and a first-rate Islamic scholar. Note that he was raising these rationales in 1996, long before the United States's invasion of Iraq, where the Caliphate once sat. If anything, at this writing in the year 2005, his rationales play to a wider and even more receptive young audience across spectrum of Muslim countries in the Middle East and South Asia.

The poet is Al-Mouyanabbi, in Khass Alkhass, Al-Tha-alibi, pp. 46.

88. OBL paraphrases a *Hadith*. See Sahih Bukhari, *Hadith*, Vol. 5, Book 59, No. 448, at www.usc.edu/dept/MSA/.

89. In "Sharh Nahjul-Balagha" by "Ibin Abi-Hadeed, p 1578.

90. The port is Abdullah ibn Rawahah, in "Arrawdul-Mietar Fi-Khabar al-Aqtar" by "Al-Hameeri" page 203.

91. In the year 630, Jafar ibn Abi Talib, a companion of the Prophet Muhammad (PBUH), was among an army mustered by the Prophet (PBUH) to confront Byzantine forces marshaled in Syria. The Byzantines had mercilessly killed the peace emissary sent by the Prophet. Zayd ibn Harithah was appointed the army's commander. Second in command was Jafar ibn Abi Talib. Abdullah ibn Rawahah was third in command. The Muslim army of approximately 3,000 found itself confronting approximately 100,000 men at Mutah, a small village in Jordan. The Muslims attacked with typical Islamic fervor. Zayd, Jafar, and Abdullah were killed, each fighting to his glorious end. Khalid ibn al-Walid was hastily chosen as the new commander. He tactically withdrew, regrouped, and then mounted counterattacks against the Byzantines from several different directions. The Byzantine forces ultimately fled the field in disarray. See "Jafar ibn Abi Talib," *Anwary-Islam.com*, at www.anwary-islam.com/companion/s_jafar-ibn-abi-talib.htm.

In "Sharh Nahjul-Balagha" by "Ibin Abi-Hadeed, p 1578.

92. Ref. "Ibin Hisham" in *Seerat Ibin Hisham*, pp 99.

93. Ref. "Ibn-al-Athir" in *Al-Kamel fi Tarikh*, page 676.

94. Ref. "Al-Surkhusi" in *Shareh Kitab al-Siar Alkabeer* page 461.

95. Islamic lore is replete with activist women who directly and indirectly participated in the propagation of Islam and its defense in the many battles that marked its early years. OBL invites women to support his contemporary endeavors. For a short treatment of women in Islamic history,

see "Women's Role in the Islamic Civilization," at *Swipnet.se*, at www.home.swipnet.se/islam/books/hijab/07.htm.

96. In *Al-Amali* by Abu-Ali Alqali, page 80

97. In *Ala-Aghani*, Abu AlFaraj al-Asfahani 2648

98. *Holy Quran*, 8 (Al-Anfal [The Spoils of War]):72.

99. See endnote 45, *infra*.

CHAPTER 4

1. This purported *Fatwa* (religious decree) was issued by the above named individuals on February 23, 1998. The Arabic text of the *Fatwa* was faxed to the London, England, daily Arabic-language newspaper, *Al-Quds al'Arabi*. According to *Usul al-Fiqh* (Islamic jurisprudence), a *Fatwa* is binding when it agrees with relevant legal proofs deduced from Quranic verses and *Hadiths* (authenticated traditions of the Prophet Muhammad (PBUH) recorded by reputable Islamic scholars); it is issued by a duly qualified religious scholar or group of scholars; it is free of individual opportunism and outside influence; and it fits the needs of the contemporary world. See editor's note of the translation hosted by the Emergency Response and Research Institute at www.emergency.com/bladen98.htm. The actual Arabic text reprinted from the *Al-Quds Newspaper* is found at www.library.cornell.edu/colldev/mideast/fatw2.htm.

2. See the Forward for a discussion of the English translation of the *Holy Quran* selected for use in this book and *Wahhabi* influence on that translation. Also, see the Forward for an explanation of *Hadith*, which are authenticated "traditions" of the Prophet Muhammad (PBUH).

3. The Prophet (PBUH) said in a *Sahih Hadith* narrated by Ahmad and Tabarani: "I have been raised between the hands of the Hour with the sword, until God the Exalted is worshipped alone with no associates. He has provided sustenance from beneath the shadow of spears and has decreed humiliation and belittlement for those who oppose my order. And whoever resembles a people, he is of them." See Sheikh Abdullah Azzam, "Chapter 1: Defense of Muslim Lands: The First Obligation After Iman (belief)," *Islamistwatch.org*, at www.islamistwatch.org/texts/azzam/defense/chap1.html.

4. In calling upon the Muslim reader to remember three facts, OBL is referring to the *Holy Quran*'s treatment of the Battle of Badr, the first great victory of Islam, to wit:

Holy Quran, 8 (Al-Anfal [The Spoils of War]):42 – 45.

See Rosalind Gwynne of the Department of Religious Affairs, University of Tennessee, "Draft: Al-Qaida and Al-Qur'an: The 'Tafsir' of Usamah bin Ladin," September 18, 2001, at www.web.utk.edu/~warda/bin_ladin_and_quran.htm.

5. The United States first sent military forces to Saudi Arabia in 1990 after the Iraqi invasion of Kuwait. They have remained there ever since at various force levels. OBL's reference to "holy places" usually means the two most holy places in Islam, the cities of Mecca and Medina. More information about The Two Holy Places (Medina and Mecca) and the Qibla can be found in the Forward.

6. After conclusion of the 1991 Gulf War the United States and allied air forces continually bombed Iraq in the Northern and Southern "no-fly" zones (North and South of Baghdad) from bases in Kuwait and Saudi Arabia. The pace of the bombing quickened after 2001, and reached a crescendo during the year before the beginning of the Iraq War on March 19, 2003. For a *detailed* daily summary of those bombing missions, see "U.S. Bombing Watch: Archive of U.S. Bombings, Invasions, and Occupations of Iraq (Methodology History of U.S. Bombing Watch)," *Colorado Campaign for Middle East Peace*, December 31, 2004, at www.ccmep.org/usbombingwatch/2003.htm.

7. For more information regarding the Gulf War casualties, please see the Forward.

8. OBL refers to defensive *Jihad*, a pillar of *Wahhabi* creed. See the Forward.

9. Sheikh ibn Qudama (d. 1134) and Islamic scholar of the Hanbali school (*Fiqh*) of Islamic

jurisprudence, best known for his work *Al-Mughni*. See the Advanced Legal Studies Institute, "Islamic Classical Legal Texts," at www.nyazee.com/islaw/alsi%20Islamic%20Law%20Series. html; and *Al-Mugni*, at www.mac.abc.se/home/onesr/h/58.html. Imam al-Kila'I (d. 904), an Islamic scholar and reciter of the Quran and author of one of the seven bona fide modes of recitation of the Quran. Aisha Bewley, "The Seven Qira'at of the Qur'an," at www.ourworld. compuserve.com/homepages/ABewley/Page6.html. Al-Qurtubi (d. 1273) is known for his twenty-one volume *Tafsir* (interpretation) of the Quran, entitled *Al-Jami li-Ahkan Al-Qur'an*. See Gwynne, "Draft," cited in endnote 4, *infra*. Sheikh al-Islam refers to Ibn Taymiya (1263 - 1328), who was an Islamic scholar of the Hanbal school who insisted on a Islamic society in which the Islamic *Sharia* (law) was strictly applied and who rejected other schools like Sufism and Shi'ism. OBL refers to his writings found in "Kitab al-Ikhty-iyharat al-Ilmiyyah fi Ikhiyarat Shaykh al-Islam Ibn Taymiyyah," in "Al-Fatawa al-Kubra," both compiled by Ala al-Din Abu al-Hasan Ali al-Ba'li, Beirut, Dar al-Ma'rifah, 1409/1988, vol. 4, p. 319-559. The quotation is from page 520. See Gwynne, "Draft," footnote 72 and accompanying text. Later, Muhammad ibn Abd al-Wahhab (b. 1703) would revive Ibn Taymiya's teachings and found *Wahhabism*, the dominant school in Saudi Arabia. Both scholars emphasized the importance of *Jihad* (holy war) in Islam. *Wahhabism* is an especially puritanical and intolerant brand of Islam. As previously stated, OBL is a *Wahhabi*. See the Forward for more information regarding Wahhabism.

10. More information regarding the *Al-Aqsa* Mosque can be found in the Forward.

11. OBL refers to Mecca's *Masjid al Haram*, site of the *Kaba*. See the Forward.

12. *Holy Quran*, 2 (Al-Baqarah [The Cow]):193.

13. *Holy Quran*, 4 (An-Nisa [The Women]):75.

14. *Holy Quran*, 8 (Al-Anfal [The Spoils of War]):24.

15. *Holy Quran*, 9 (At-Taubah [The Repentance]):38-39.

16. *Holy Quran*, 3 (Al-Imran [The Family of Imran]):139.

CHAPTER 5

1. Videotape statement by OBL broadcast by *Al-Jazeera Television* on October 7, 2001. That is the same date on which the United States began its invasion of Afghanistan. It is unclear whether the videotape was made before, after, or during the attacks.

2. *Holy Quran*, 18 (Al-Khaf [The Cave]):17.

3. OBL refers to the post WW I mandates that arose from the partitioning of the Turkish-Ottoman Empire after the defeat of Turkey and its allies during WW I. More specifically, after WW I the British and the French were given mandates by the League of Nations over portions of the Middle East according to the Versailles Peace Treaty of 1919 and secret agreements negotiated in the infamous Sykes-Picot agreement of 1916. Britain's mandate encompassed Egypt, Iraq, and Palestine; and France's included what was then known as the Levant, which included present-day Syria and Lebanon. See generally, "World War I," at www.countrystudies.us/syria/8. htm; and "The Arab Israeli Conflict: History Palestine, Jordan, etc., at *Arab2.com*, www.arab2. com/biography/Arab-Israeli-Conflict-mid.htm. See also the Forward for a further discussion of the Sykes-Picot agreement.

4.Please see the Forward for more information regarding the post 1991 Gulf War sanctions against Iraq.

5. For a history of Israel's destructive incursions into Palestinian lands and cities, see "A History of the Israeli-Palestinian Conflict: 1991-2001," *Promises* (Justine Shapiro, B.Z. Goldberg, and Carlos Bolado), *PBS*, at www.pbs.org/pov/pov2001/promises/timeline.html.

6. Interestingly, OBL refers to Japan in the terms of the feudal ages as an "end" of the earth. He refers to the hundreds of thousands of Japanese men, women, and children killed by the United States when its air force dropped atomic bombs on the Japanese cities of Hiroshima and Nagasaki in August, 1945.

7. On August 7, 1998, the United States embassies in Dar es Salaam, Tanzania, and Nairobi, Kenya, were bombed. 157 people were killed and 5,000 were wounded. Twelve Americans died. See the Forward.

8. OBL refers to the moon god Hubal. For more information regarding Hubal, please see the Forward.

CHAPTER 6

1. Videotaped statement by OBL broadcast by *Al-Jazeera Television* in Arabic on November, 3, 2001.

2. The fundamental tenet of Islam is that there is no god but God and that Muhammad (PBUH) was his Prophet. See: *Holy Quran*, 7 (Al-A'raf [The Heights or the Wall with Elevations]):158.

3. The United States invaded Afghanistan on October 7, 2001.

4. Actually, apart from the United States, Israel, and India, a majority of people in thirty-seven countries surveyed by Gallop International in late September, 2001, preferred the extradition and trial of the perpetrators of 9/11 rather than military attacks. See Dr. David Miller, "World Opinion Opposes the Attack on Afghanistan," *Global Issues*, November 21, 2001, at www. globalissues.org/Geopolitics/MiddleEast/TerrorInUSA/Polls.asp. However, the United States suffers from an abject lack of popularity in the Middle East both then and now. See "Middle East: Attitudes Towards the United States," *Congressional Research Service*, CRS Report for Congress, the Library of Congress, December 31, 2001, at www.fpc.state.gov/documents/ organization/7858.pdf. Also, see Bob Deans, "America's Popularity Plunges Worldwide, *Seattle Post-Intelligencer*, December 5, 2002 (true dislike and hatred for America concentrated in Muslim nations of Middle East and Central Asia, e.g., Pakistan, a key partner in the war on terrorism; only 10% of the people favorably view the United States, and in Turkey only 30%) at www.seattlepi.nwsource.com/national/98525_poll05.shtml. Likewise, Eric Marquardt, "Losing the Hearts and Minds," *Power and Interest News Report*, June 22, 2003, at www.pinr.com/report. php?ac=view_report&report_id=60&language_id=1. For a viewpoint directly from the Middle East, see Muqtedar Khan, "Clear and Present Danger," *Al-Ahram Weekly,* Issue No. 643, June 19-25, 2003, at www.globalpolicy.org/empire/analysis/2003/0619danger.htm. Finally, the best source of polling in the Middle East is the Pew Research Center. See "A Year After Iraq War," Pew Research Center, March 16, 2004, at www.people-press.org/reports/display.php3?ReportID=206. Ironically, it is OBL, not the United States, who is winning over the hearts and minds of the people of the Middle East by means of the policies of the United States meant to neutralize him. "While Al-Qa'eda posed grave threats in the short term, the Al Qa'eda phenomenon – the rise of anti-Americanism in the Muslim world that attracted recruits to the organization and similar groups – posed a more severe long-term challenge." Muqtedar Khan, *Id.*

5. In fact, global demonstrations were organized protesting the United States' invasion of Afghanistan. See, for example, "International Day of Action," *The Guardian*, October 17, 2001, documenting demonstrations in Britain, Germany, India, Nigeria, Pakistan, and many other countries on October 13, 2001, declared to be an International Day of Action against the Afghanistan War. See www.cpa.org.au/garchve4/1067day.html.

The Crusades are a common theme in OBL's statements. For more information regarding the Crusades, please see the Forward.

6. *Holy Quran*, 2 (Al-Baqarah [The Cow]:120.

7. At a news conference convened on September 16, 2001, President Bush launched his war against terrorism by describing it as a "crusade" in response to a question. The use of the word inflamed public opinion in the Middle East and even evoked protests from the despotic regimes of the region. A few days later, the administration retracted the word, but the damage had been done and still haunts United States policy in the region. Obviously, OBL has not forgotten President

Bush's use of the word. See Philip Kennicott, "An About-Face on America," *Washington Post*, August 24, 2004, p. C1.

8. The Editor has no idea what OBL means when he refers to captured thieves.

9. The divine revelations that became the *Holy Quran* began probably in the year 13 B.H.*/610 A.D. and ended with the Prophet Muhammad's death in 632. Scholars believe that the first verses revealed to the Prophet (PBUH) are found in the ninety-sixth *Surah* (chapter) of the *Holy Quran*, Surah al-Alaq (The Clot). See

Muhammad Asad, "The Message of the Quran, Al-Alaq (The Germ Cell), the Ninth-Sixth Surah," at www.geocities.com/masad02/096.html?200512.

10. See endnote 7, *infra*.

11. In all of these venues, Muslims are being slaughtered. Please see the Forward for more information regarding the venues in which Muslims are being slaughtered and the *Al-Aqsa Intifada*.

12. More information about the "ten 'voiders' that disqualify one from Islam" can be found in the Forward.

13. OBL refers to the partitioning of the Middle East after World War I. The problems relating to Palestine arose with the Sykes-Picot agreement, a secret exchange of notes in 1916 between Britain, France and Russia relating to the partitioning of the Ottoman Empire after its impending defeat in World War I. More information regarding the Sykes-Picot Agreement can be found in the Forward.

14. The casualty rate among Palestinians in the Occupied Territories (the West Bank and the Gaza Strip) at the hands of Israel Defense Forces reached a plateau during the *intifada* [see endnote 24, *infra*]. Form more information about the Intifada, please see the Forward.

15. For more information about Chechnya, please see the Forward.

16. Between 1992 and 1995, Christian Orthodox Serbia, through the use of regular and irregular armed forces, committed genocide in the province of Bosnia by its campaign of "ethnic cleansing" by which is murdered hundreds of thousands of people in an attempt to cleanse the province of Muslims. In 1995, the Serbs overran the U.N. "safe haven" at Srebrenica and massacred over 8,000 Muslim men and boys. Presently, U.N. war crime tribunals are trying genocide suspects and meting out punishment of the guilty ones. Others are still on the run. See "Bosnian Serbs Apologize for Srebrenica Massacre," at www.freerepublic.com/focus/f-news/1276830/posts. See also, "Serbs Sorry for Srebrenica Deaths," *BBC News World Edition*, November 10, 2004, at www.news.bbc.co.uk/2/hi/europe/3999985.stm.

17. On November 29, 1947, the United Nations General Assembly adopted Resolution GA 181, partitioning Palestine into several cantons. The Jewish State and the Arab state each had three cantons that touched South of Nazareth and near Gaza. The partition was impractical at best and resulted in the 1948 Israeli-Arab War, which resulted in independence for the new state of Israel. The remainder of the Palestine mandate was divided between Egypt and Transjordan (now the Kingdom of Jordan). See "Mid-East Maps: Map of UN Partition Plan for Palestine – 1947," at www.mideastweb.org/unpartition.htm; and "1948 Arab-Israeli War," *Wikipedia, the Free Encyclopedia*, at www.en.wikipedia.org/wiki/1948_Arab-Israeli_War.

18. OBL is not alone in his rejection of the United Nations. The 1947 partitioning of Palestine and the resulting creation of the Jewish state of Israel are sore subjects in the Middle East. Whereas the West looks favorably on the United Nations, the indigenous people of the Middle East often view it as but an extension of colonialism.

19. India and Pakistan have been at odds over the province of Kashmir since the India-Pakistan partition of 1947. For more information regarding Kashmir, please see the Forward.

20. For more information about Chechnya, please see the Forward.

21. For more information regarding East Timor, please see the Forward.

22. For more information regarding Somalia, please see the Forward.

For more information regarding the twenty-one year civil war, please see the Forward.

23. For more information regarding the deaths associated with the "U.N. Iraq Sanctions," please see the Forward.

24. For more information regarding the *Al-Aqsa Inifada*, please see the Forward.

25. OBL refers to a *Hadith* by Imam Tirmidhi (824 - 894), whose best-known work is *Al-Jami 'ut-Tirmidhi,* in which he repeated only eighty-three *Hadiths*. He was known for his incomparable memory. See "Imam Tirmidhi (209-279 H)," at *Wikipedia, the Free Encyclopedia,* at www.en.wikipedia.org/wiki/Al-Tirmidhi. See the Forward for a discussion of *Hadith* scholarship. Suffice it to say here that a *Hadith* is an authenticated "tradition" of the Prophet Muhammad (PBUH) capturing his words or example.

The complete *Hadith* recited by OBL is as follows:

"Narrated Ibn Abbas: 'O boy, I will teach you a few words: Be loyal and obedient to God, remember Him always, obey His Orders. He will save you from every evil and will take care of you in all parts of life. Be loyal and obedient to God, and you will find him near. If you ask, ask God. If you seek help, seek help from God. Know that if all the people gather in order to benefit you with something, they will not be able to benefit you in anything except what God has decreed for you. And if they gather in order to harm you, they will not be able to harm you except as God has decreed for you. The pens have stopped writing, and the papers have dried." (Sahih al-Tirmidhi) Hashi al-Eritre, *Islamic Forum*, December 20, 2004, at www.gawaher.com/forum/index.php?act=ST&f=53&t=4567&.

CHAPTER 7

1. The visiting Sheikh is identified as Ali bin Said al-Ghandi, a radical Islamic Saudi cleric who was a professor of theology in Saudi Arabia. In 1995, he was suspended from his teaching position and briefly detained by the Saudi government. John Diamond and Michael A. Levy, "U.S. Keeps Up Pressure," *Chicago Tribune*, December 15, 2001, at www.chicagotribune.com/news/nationworld/chi-0112150129dec15,1,3039875.story?ctrack=1&cst=true. See also Khaled Dawoud, "Caught on Camera," *Al-Ahram Weekly Online*, Issue No. 565, December 20-26, 2001, re Mr. Ghaith at www.weekly.ahram.org.eg/2001/565/7war1.htm. See also endnote 12, *infra*.

2. Fawzee al-Atharee al-Bahraini, a Saudi cleric. See also, Barry Rubin and Judith Culp Rubin, *Anti-American Terrorism And The Middle East* (Oxford University Press June 2004), at pp. 243-244.

3. For a discussion regarding *Fatwas*, please see the Forward.

4. It is unclear to what *Fatwa* of Sheikh Bahreini (see endnote 2 infra) the speaker refers.

5. See citation in endnote 2 above.

6. Dr. Nasir bin Sulayman al-Omar, former Professor of Quranic Studies, Al-Imam University, Saudi Arabia. See "Signatories to 'How We Can Coexist," *Islamtoday.com*, at www.islamtoday.com/showme2.cfm?cat_id=29&sub_cat_id=472.

7. Al Rayan is a common popular name in Saudi Arabia, adorning companies, oil fields, to schools, to streets, to districts. The Editor can find no reference to a Sheikh al-Rayan.

8. For a discussion of *Hadiths*, please see the Forward.

9. Sahih Muslim, *Hadith*, Book 001, No. 0032: and [*Holy Quran*, 88 (Al Ghashiyah [The Overwhelming]):22.] and Sahih Muslim, *Hadith*, Book 001, No. 0033: see www.usc.edu/dept/MSA/. The next three quoted *Hadiths* cannot be found by the Editor. OBL tends to paraphrase to the point that the original source cannot be identified.

10. For a discussion of *Fiqh*, please see the Forward.

11. Ironically, after 9/11 there occurred in the West a surge of interest in Islam. See "News Watch: A Post 9/11 Look At Islam," *Christian Research Journal*, Vol. 25, No. 1 (2002), published by the Christian Research Institute, and available at www.equip.org/free/DI911.htm.

12. Sheikh Hammud al-Shuaybi, a radical Islamic cleric who was released from Saudi

government custody in 1995. See Ron Fournier, "Bush Mocks bin Laden As Evil Man," *Associated Press*, December 14, 2001, at www.multimedia.belointeractive.com/attack/response/ 1214bushvideo.html.

13. The Editor is unable to find any references to this man other than OBL's.

14. The Sheikh has corrupted Quranic verse, as no English translation of the *Holy Quran* contains the word "torture." See the Forward for a discussion of the selection of the English translation of the *Holy Quran* used for this book. Suffice it to say here that the selected translation's annotations and commentary will be slanted toward the *Wahhabi* creed.

Turning to the Sheikh's corrupted Quranic verse, the Editor believes that he is referring to two possible verses: *Holy Quran*, 9 (At-Taubah [The Repentance]):5. The second verse to which the Sheikh might have been referring is as follows: *Holy Quran*, 9 (At-Taubah [The Repentance]):52.

15. OBL refers to Professor Burhannudin Rabbani, a fundamentalist cleric. He was the first holder of the rotating office of the presidency of the Afghani constitution of 1992. The Taliban militia ousted him from Kabul on September 27, 1996, and set up its own Islamic regime. See "Afghanistan," *People in Power*, January 1, 2001, at www.circa-uk.demon.co.uk/x.html; and "'Barbak Karmal," *Wikipedia, the Free Encylcopedia*, www.en.wikipedia.org/wiki/Barbrak_ Karmal. See also, "Glossary of Search Terms – Afghan & Arabic Terms," Georgia Southwestern State University Library, at www.gsw.edu/~libraryref/911/searchterms.html.

16. Again, a corrupted verse from the Sheikh. The Editor believes he meant as follows: *Holy Quran*, 8 (Al-Anfal [The Spoils of War]):15.

17. He refers to the early Islamic warriors (*Mujahideen*) and to the early believers (*Ansar*).

18. Abu Bakr al-Saddiiq (d. 635), Omar ibn al-Khattab (d. 645), Uthman ibn Affan (d. 657), and Ali ibn Abdu Taalib (d. 662) were the first four Caliphs who succeeded the Prophet Muhammad (PBUH). This was the era of the *Rashidoon*, the era in Islam known as the period of the four "rightly guided" Caliphs, all of whom were actual Companions of the Prophet Muhammad (PBUH). For more information about this era, please see the Forward.

19. OBL refers to Dr. Abdullah Yusuf Azzam (1941-1989), an Islamic scholar and early contributor to the development of political Islam. For more information regarding Mr. Azzam, please see the Introduction.

20. OBL erroneously refers to the radical London-based Islamic cleric Abu Hamza al-Masri [*al-Masri* – "the Egyptian," born in Egypt and a British citizen until his British citizenship was stripped in 2004] as "Abu-al-Hassan." Al-Masri is wanted in Yemen on charges of sabotage. He is the former Imam of the Finsbury Park Mosque in North London, which has been linked to Richard Reid, the infamous "shoe bomber" who tried to explode a U.S. airliner by means of a bomb in his shoe, and Zacarias Moussaoui, on trial for his life in Alexandria, Virginia, for Al Qaeda membership and conspiracy in the 9/11 attacks. On October 20, 2004, the British government arrested al-Masri and charged him with sixteen offenses of encouraging murder, stirring up racial hatred, and possessing a terrorist document. He also faces potential extradition to the United States to face criminal charges of links to Al Qaeda. See Beth Gardner, "A Cleric Who Stuck to His Guns," *Associated Press – MSNBC*, May 27, 2004, at www.msnbc.msn. com/id/5078153/; and Stewart Tandler, "Abu Hamza Accused of Inciting Hate and Murder," *Timesonline*, October 20, 2004, at www.timesonline.co.uk/printFriendly/0,,1-2-1319188-2,00. html.

21. A complete list of their names follows: From Boston: American Flight 11 - Muhammad Atta, Abdul Aziz Omari, Satam al Suqami, Wail al Shehri, and Waleed al Shehri; United Flight 175: Marwan al Shehhi, Fayez Banihammad, Mohand al Shehri, Ahmed alGhamdi, and Hamza al Ghamdi; From Washington Dulles: American Flight 77 – Khalid al Mihdar, Majed Moqed, Hani Hanjour, Nawaf al Hazmi, and Salem al Hazmi (brothers); Newark, New Jersey: United Flight 93: Saeed al Ghamdi, Ahmed al Nami, Ahmad al Haznawi, and Ziad Jarrah. *The 9/11 Commission*

Report, pp. 1-4 (Authorized Edition 2004).

22. This poem was written by Yousef Abu-Helaleh, a lecturer of Islamic studies at King Hussein University in Jordan. Abu-Helaleh regards OBL as a holy warrior. Abu-Helaleh met OBL when the former taught Islamic studies at the Islamic University of Al-Imam bin Saud in Riyadh, Saudia Arabia in the early 1990s. Abu-Helaleh also corresponded with OBL when the latter moved to Sudan in 1992. Abu-Helaleh denies further contact with OBL after the former moved back to Jordan, which considers OBL to be a terrorist. The subject poem was published in 1997 in an anthology of poems entitled *Poems in the Time of Oppression*. The poem "The Fighting Eagle" was dedicated to OBL. On the videotape, OBL recites Abu-Helaleh's poem, "The Believers." That poem in its entirety follows.

"I witness that against the sharp blade
They always faced difficulties and stood together…
When the darkness comes upon us and we are bitten by a
Sharp tooth, I say…
'Our homes are flooded with blood and the tyrant
Is freely wandering in our homes'…
And from the battlefield vanished
The brightness of swords and the horses …
And over weeping sounds now
We hear the beats of drums and rhythm …
And shouting: 'We will not stop our raids
Until you free our lands.'"

See "Poet Flattered by Bin Laden's Attention," *FoxNews.com*, January 6, 2002, at www.foxnews.com/story/0,2933,42314,00.html.

CHAPTER 8

1. This statement was first broadcast by *Al-Jazeera Television* on December 27, 2001.

2. OBL recites the beginning of the Arabic sermon delivered upon the solemnization of a Muslim marriage. See Ata Ullah Kaleem, "Marriage in Islam," *The Review of Religions*, November 1992, appearing at Ahmadiyya Muslim Community, at www.alislam.org/library/links/00000137.html.

3. OBL refers to the September 11, 2001, attacks on the World Trade Center and the Pentagon and to the October 7, 2001, U.S. military invasion of Afghanistan.

4. OBL refers to the *Holy Quran*, 4 (An-Nisa [Women]):75.

In 2001, approximately 200,000 refugees fled Afghanistan and another 511,000 were displaced internally. See "UNHRC Releases 2001 Global Refugee Statistics," *EuropaWorld*, June 21, 2001, at www.europaworld.org/week87/unhcr21602.htm.

5. OBL refers to the Irish Republican Army.

6. OBL refers to Al Qaeda, and himself, as "immigrants" to Afghanistan. He and others like him, commonly known as the *Mujahideen* [Islamic warriors] traveled to Afghanistan and Pakistan beginning in 1979 to fight the "godless" Soviet invaders.

7. OBL refers to the Israeli occupation of the West Bank and the Gaza Strip, lands commonly referred to as Palestine throughout the world.

8. *Holy Quran*, 2 (Al-Baqarah [The Heifer]):49.

9. OBL refers to a 12-year-old Palestinian boy killed by a barrage of bullets in Gaza's Bureij Refugee Camp on September 30, 2000. A French news agency's television crew tragically videotaped Muhammad's untimely death for the world to witness. The Israeli Army at first denied, then accepted, then denied responsibility for his death. The Palestinians and the Arab world place responsibility at the feet of the Israelis. Master al-Durra is now a well-known martyr in the Arab Muslim world. See Matt Rees, "Muhammad al-Durra," *Time Magazine Pacific*, No. 51,

December 25, 2000, at www.time.com/time/pacific/magazine/20001225/poy_mohammed.html.

10. *Holy Quran*, 5 (Al-Ma'idah [The Feast]):32.

11. OBL refers to two cities in Northern Saudi Arabia. The Muslim invasion and peaceful conquest of Tabook (the Roman army thought better of a fight and withdrew) in 631, and secured the remainder of the Arabian peninsula for the Muslims. See "March on Tabook, Rajab 9 A.H.," at www.inter-islam.org/Seerah/MarchonTabookL2P1.html.

12. OBL refers to the holy city of Medina, Saudi Arabia, the city to which the Prophet Muhammad (PBUH) migrated from Mecca in the year 622 for reasons of personal safety.

13. OBL refers to the effects of the economic sanctions imposed on Iraq after the 1991 Gulf War. His figure may be inflated. For more information regarding the Gulf War Sanctions please see the Forward.

14. After conclusion of the 1991 Gulf War the United States and allied air forces continued to bomb Iraq in the Northern and Southern "no-fly" zones. The pace of the bombing quickened after 2001, and reached a crescendo during the year before the beginning of the Iraq War on March 19, 2003. For a detailed daily summary of those bombing missions, see "U.S. Bombing Watch: Archive of U.S. Bombings, Invasions, and Occupations of Iraq (Methodology History of U.S. Bombing Watch)," *Colorado Campaign for Middle East Peace*, December 31, 2004, at www.ccmep.org/usbombingwatch/2003.htm.

15. OBL refers to the moon god Hubal. For more information about Hubal, please see the Forward.

16. The human and economic costs of 9/11 were enormous by any standard. For more information regarding the costs, please see the Forward.

17. OBL refers to the failure of the Middle East countries to raise an outcry about the consistent bombing of Iraq after the end of the 1991 Gulf War. See the Forward and endnote 14 *infra.*.

18. *Holy Quran*, 9 (At-Taubah [Ultimatum]:111.

19. OBL is trained as an economist. Note the repetitive references to America's economy and to the need to attack its economy. In the West, the media all too often portrays OBL as a psychopathic terrorist intent on mass murder. Quite to the contrary, he is a formidable foe who understands that his proper target is the American economy. See generally, Anonymous, *Imperial Hubris: Why the West Is Losing the War on Terror*, pp. 105-115, 168-170 (Brassey's, Inc., 1st Ed. 2004).

20. OBL refers to the bombing of the United States embassies in Nairobi, Kenya, and Dar 'es Salaam, Tanzania, on August 8, 1998. 157 people were killed and 5,000 were wounded. See the Forward.

21. Mullah Jalaluddin Haqqani has been described as the most prominent *Mujahideen* [Islamic warriors] commander who sided with the Taliban after the Soviets were driven from Afghanistan. His stronghold was Khost, on the Eastern border that separates Afghanistan from Pakistan. Pravda reported on December 27, 2001, that in bombing Khost, United States warplanes might have wounded Mr. Haqqani. Apparently he was – and remains - a high-profile target in Afghanistan. See "One Member of the Taliban Has Been Wounded," *Pravda*, December 27, 2001, at www.english.pravda.ru/world/2001/12/27/24530_.html; Marc W. Harold, "The Failing Campaign to Kill Jalaluddin Haqqani," *Cursor,* January 18, 2002, at www.cursor.org/stories/jalaluddin.htm.

22. *Holy Quran*, 9 (At-Taubah [Ultimatum]:40.

23. *Holy Quran*, 4 (An-Nisa [Women]):69.

24. Fifteen of the nineteen young men participating in the 9/11 attacks were from Saudi Arabia.

25. See endnote 21 of OBL's statement of December 13, 2001, *infra*, for a complete listing of the names of the participants and their home countries.

26. *Holy Quran*, 85 (Al-Inshiqaq [The Rapture]:4-11.

For the story of the Boy and the King, see endnote 28, *infra*.

27. A *Hadith* is an authenticated "tradition" of the Prophet Muhammad (PBUH) that exemplifies his words or his deeds. See the discussion of *Hadith* scholarship in the Forward.

28. Sahih Muslim, *Hadith*, Book 42, No. 7148, at www.usc.edu/dept/MSA/.

29. Sahih Muslim, *Hadith*, Book 001, No. 0081: at www.usc.edu/dept/MSA/fundamentals/.

30. Hamzah is considered the first of the Muslim martyrs. Sahih Bukhari, *Hadith*, Vol. 5, Book 59, No. 399, see www.usc.edu/dept/MSA/.

31. Islam holds in highest regard the Prophet Muhammad's (PBUH) immediate Companions; next in regard are his followers who were his contemporaries; and then their followers. See "Who Were His Friends," IslamOnline.net, August 8, 2003, at www.islamonline. net/English/introducingislam/Prophet/Companions/article01.shtml.

32.Also, see "The Best Generations," *Islam and New Zealand Muslim Community*, May 14, year unknown, at www.nzmuslim.net/article101.html.

Babrak Karmal (1929 - 1996) was the third President of Afghanistan between 1980 - 1986 during the communist Democratic Republic of Afghanistan. The Soviets invaded Afghanistan in December of 1979 and installed Karmal as President. The Soviets replaced him in 1986 Burhannuddin Rabbini was the first holder of the rotating office of the presidency of the constitution of 1992. The Taliban militia ousted him from Kabul on September 27, 1996, and set up its own Islamic regime. See "Afghanistan," *People in Power*, January 1, 2001, at www. circa-uk.demon.co.uk/x.html; and '"Barbak Karmal," *Wikipedia, the Free Encyclopedia*, www. en.wikipedia.org/wiki/Barbrak_Karmal.

33. The Hijaz is a province of northwestern Saudi Arabia in which is located the Holy City of Mecca.

34. OBL speaks of other provinces and regions of Saudi Arabia, often designated by their tribal affiliation, e.g., Bani Harb is a tribe.

35. These were three of the participants in the 9/11 attack. All of them were on the aircraft that struck the Pentagon. The Al-Hazmis were brothers.

36. This poem was written by Yousef Abu-Helaleh, a lecturer of Islamic studies at King Hussein University in Jordan. Abu-Helaleh regards OBL as a holy warrior. Abu-Helaleh met OBL when the former taught Islamic studies at the Islamic University of Al-Imam bin Saud in Riyadh, Saudi Arabia in the early 1990s. Abu-Helaleh also corresponded with OBL when the latter moved to Sudan in 1992. Abu-Helaleh denies further contact with OBL after the former moved back to Jordan, which considers OBL to be a terrorist. The subject poem was published in 1997 in an anthology of poems entitled *Poems in the Time of Oppression*. The poem "The Fighting Eagle" was dedicated to OBL. OBL also recited the poem in his statement of December 13, 2001, *infra*, and discussed therein at endnote 22. See "Poet Flattered by Bin Laden's Attention,"

FoxNews.com, January 6, 2002, at www.foxnews.com/story/0,2933,42314,00.html.

CHAPTER 9

1. First broadcast on Arabic Internet websites on October 26, 2002.

2. *Holy Quran*, 22 (Al-Hajj [The Pilgrimage]):39.

3. *Holy Quran*, 4 (An-Nisa [The Women]):76.

4. Rather than to a specific title or article, OBL refers to the general subject of the basis for the fighting, as he implies in the next sentence.

5. The problems related to Palestine arose with the Sykes-Picot agreement, a secret exchange of notes in 1916 between Britain, France and Russia relating to the partitioning of the Ottoman Empire after its defeat in World War I. For more information regarding the Sykes-Picot Agreement please see the Forward.

6. Muslim forces achieved victory over Palestine in 634 and conquered Jerusalem in 638.

See "Arabic Timeline," at www.princeton.edu/~batke/itl/scroll/600tx.html.

7. For more information OBL's complaints regarding Somalia, Chechnya, Kashmir, Lebanon and please see the Forward.

8. OBL always rails at the low price of the oil sold to Western countries by Saudi Arabia and the other Middle East suppliers.

9. On March 27, 2002, the Arab League announced a peace plan for the Middle East that had been floated by then Saudi Crown Prince Abdullah. The plan called for the withdrawal of Israeli forces to the 1967 borders in return for recognition of Israel by the Arab states. See "The Arab Peace Initiative," *Middle East Web*, March 28, 2002, at www.mideastweb.org/saudipeace. htm; and "The Arab League 'Peace Plan,'" *Jewish Virtual Library*, March 27, 2002, at www. jewishvirtuallibrary.org/jsource/Peace/arabplan.html.

10. Even before the Iraq War of 2003, the United States maintained military forces in Saudi Arabia, Qatar, and Bahrain, and continues to do so at this writing, having added to the list bases in Kuwait and Iraq. For a discussion of U.S. military bases in the Middle East, see Chalmers Johnson, *The Sorrows of Empire: Militarism, Secrecy, and the End of the Republic*, at pp. 226-253 (Metropolitan Books, 1ˢᵗ Ed. 2004).

11. Thus far, the best available data indicate that the post-1991 Gulf War sanctions against Iraq resulted in the premature deaths of an estimated 500,000 Iraqi children for lack of nutrition and medications. For more information on the sanctions, please see the Forward.

12. For more information regarding the history of *the Al-Aqsa Mosque*, please see the Forward.

13. By *Jihad*, OBL means a defensive *Jihad* in defense of Islamic lands under attack by non-believers. For a comprehensive discussion of the meaning of *Jihad*, see the Forward.

14. On April 18, 2002, President George W. Bush referred to Israeli Prime Minister Ariel Sharon as a "man of peace" as he tilted United States policy even more toward Israel to the detriment of the Palestinians. See Peter Slevin and Mike Allen, "Bush: Sharon a Man of Peace," *Washington Post*, April 19, 2002.

For more information about Mr. Sharon please see the Forward.

15. Islam forbids interest, which it equates with usury. *Holy Quran*, 2 (Al-Baqarah [The cow]):275.

16. This passage is especially important and must be weighed against the rationale finally seized upon by the Bush administration to justify its invasion of Iraq when no weapons of mass destruction were found: establishing democracy in Iraq and throughout the Middle East. The democracy conceived of by the Bush administration envisions a secular democracy separating church and state. That is almost a non-starter in the Islamic Middle East, where religion is viewed as a pillar of the existing government. Even in secularized, autocratic Egypt the state maintains two systems of justice: secular courts and religious courts attending to family matters like marriage and inheritance. Saudi Arabia and Iran maintain exclusively religious courts. See the Forward regarding the Bush administration's changing rationales for the Iraq War. See also, Andrew Grossman, "Finding the Law: Islamic Law (Sharia)," *LLRX.com*, August 1, 2002, updated August 11, 2002, at www.llrx.com/features/islamiclaw.htm.

17. OBL refers to an alleged prophecy shared by Ben Franklin during the Constitutional Convention of 1787. The prophecy was allegedly made in a "chit chat around the table during intermission" and was recorded in the diary of Charles Cotesworth Pinckney, a delegate from South Carolina. Franklin allegedly wanted to protect the nation against Jews, whom he viewed as morally decadent, anti-Christian, and intent on building a state within a state. The Anti-Defamation League believes the prophecy was a fraud. See "The Franklin 'Prophecy:' Modern Anti-Semitic Myth Making," at www.adl.org/special_reports/franklin_prophecy/franklin_intro. asp. What is most intriguing about this statement by OBL is that he even knew about the alleged Franklin Prophecy. The statement suggests an eclectic and intimate knowledge of the United

States.

18. In fact, the United States consumes more than 350 metric tons of cocaine per year, over one-third of that consumed in the entire world. The U.S. is the largest drug-consuming country in the world. See "Anti-Drug Idea: More Tests in US," *Miami Herald*, November 28, 2002.

19. In 2002 President George W. Bush rejected the Kyoto Protocol to reduce greenhouse gases that has been ratified by thirty-four other industrialized nations. The United States itself is the world's largest polluter of greenhouse gases, contributing approximately thirty-six percent of total emissions. See "Campaigners Target US Over Kyoto," *BBC News*, February 13, 2005, at www.news.bbc.co.uk/2/hi/uk_news/4259569.stm; and "Historic Kyoto Treaty Inked Without the World's Biggest Polluter the US," *Agence France Presse*, February 16, 2005, at www. commondreams.org/headlines05/0216-12.htm.

20. More information about The Algerian Civil War can be found in the Forward.

21. Since 1967 Israel has defied more than 138 United Nations resolutions concerning its behavior in the Middle East, including its occupation of Palestinian lands and its treatment of the Palestinian people. See Michael S. Ladah & Suleiman I. Ajlouni, "Mr. Bush, What About Israel's Defiance of UN Resolutions: An Open Letter to George W. Bush," *Media Monitors*, September 29, 2002, at www.mediamonitors.net/michaelsladah&suleimaniajlouni1.html. In comparison, there had been only 69 resolutions concerning Iraq between 1967 and 2000.

22. On July 17, 1998, an international conference adopted the statute creating the International Criminal Court to investigate and prosecute those accused of crimes against humanity and genocide. 120 countries voted to adopt the treaty; seven voted against it, including the United States, Israel, and China. By December 31, 2000, sixty-six countries (six more than necessary) ratified the treaty, which became effective on April 11, 2002. The tribunal came into force on July 1, 2002, and its jurisdiction also commenced on that date. Since the inception of the Court, the United States has attempted to undermine it by negotiating bilateral treaties with numerous countries exempting United States military and civilian personnel from its jurisdiction. With ongoing military activities in Afghanistan and Iraq, and in light of the documented abuse, torture, and murder of prisoners by U.S. military and civilian personnel in those venues and Guantanamo Bay, Cuba (see endnote 23, *infra*), one can infer very practical reasons why the United States opposes the Court. See "International Criminal Court," *Human Rights Watch*, www. hrw.org/campaigns/icc; "United States Efforts to Undermine the International Criminal Court: Legal Analysis of Impunity Agreements," *Human Rights Watch*, www.hrw.org/campaigns/ icc/docs/art98analysis.htm; and "US and the ICC," Coalition for the ICC, at www.iccnow.org/ documents/usandtheicc.html.

23. In the summer of 2002, hundreds of Afghani prisoners of war were crowded into sealed, windowless metal cargo containers and allowed to suffocate to death at the hands of the forces of the Afghani warlord (and U.S. ally) General Abdul Rashid Dostum, recently appointed chief of staff of Afghani President Hamid Karzai. See "Rights Groups Dismayed by Afghan Strongman's Post," *ABC Online*, March 3, 2005, at www.abc.net.au; and Eric Jaffa, "The Mistreatment of Iraqi Prisoners: More Than Six People Involved," *MoveLeftMedia*, at www.moveleft.com/moveleft_ essay_2004_05_03_the_mistreatment_of_iraqui_prisoners_more_than_six.asp.

24. OBL refers to the United States State Department's "Country Reports." Issued annually in March by the Department's Bureau of Democracy, Human Rights and Labor, each report adjudges the subject country's human rights record. After the United States' incursions into Afghanistan and Iraq, and the human rights abuses that have attended those incursions, many countries in the world are turning the tables on the U.S. and issuing their own evaluations of America's human rights records. For example, the *South Africa Sunday Times* faulted the March 2005 State Department report concerning South Africa as "presumptuous." And for the past several years, China, usually the subject of severe criticisms in the State Department report, has responded by issuing its own report: "The Human Rights Record of the United States in 2004,"

issued by China's State Council on March 3, 2005. China's report is replete with references to prisoner abuse in Iraq, Afghanistan, and Guantanamo Bay, Cuba, as well as a broad-based documentation of racial and ethnic discrimination in the U.S., overcrowded prisons, and elections bought and sold by special-interest-group money, etc. The Chinese report makes for interesting reading. As the *Holy Bible* says, "Let him who is without sin cast the first stone," John 8:7. See Donaly Pressly, "US Country Report Presumptuous," *SundayTimes.Co.Za*, March 3, 2005, at www.sundaytimes.co.za; and "Full Text of Human Rights Record of US in 2004," *People's Daily Online*, March 3, 2005, at www.english.people.com.cn/200503/03/print20050303_175406.html.

25. In the aftermath of 9/11, the United States rounded up over 1,200 Arab and Muslim men and held them in secret custody. Many of them were not allowed to see a lawyer, many were arbitrarily deported, and none of them was ever charged with participation in 9/11 or with plotting a terrorist act here in the United States. Three of them were this Editor's clients. In October, 2001, the Congress also passed the Patriot Act, intended to expand law enforcement tools in the war against terrorism. Many people in the United States believe that the Act goes too far, e.g., allowing secret searches of homes and offices and of personal information like library and bank records, and thus must be reconsidered in calmer times. Also, a bill has been introduced in Congress intended to prohibit the kinds of excesses that occurred after 9/11: The Civil Liberties Restoration Act of 2004. See "U.S.: Restore Rights Undercut by Post 9-11 Policies: Congress Should Act on Legislation to Protect Basic Rights in the United States," *Human Rights Watch*, June 16, 2004, at www.hrw.org/english/docs/2004/06/16/usdom8773_txt.htm. See also, Eric Lichtblau, "Coalition Forms to Oppose Parts of Antiterrorism Law, *The New York Times*, March 23, 2005.

26. In a series of memoranda originating in the Department of Justice and the Office of White House counsel in the aftermath of 9/11, the Bush administration concluded that the Geneva Convention would not apply to its activities in Afghanistan, and later, Iraq. In treating detainees seized in those venues, it chose to ignore that Convention and other treaties and protocols applicable to the humane treatment of detainees and combatants. For a chronological listing of these notorious "torture memos," see "Bush Administration's Legal Debate Over Torture, Interrogation Policies, Treatment of Enemy Combatants and Detainees, and the Applicability of Prisoner of War Status," *FindLaw.Com*, at www.news.lp.findlaw.com/hdocs/docs/torture/powtorturememos.html; and "Timeline on Terror Prisoners' Treatment," *Newsday. com*, January 6, 2005, at www.newsday.com/news/nationworld/world/wire/sns-ap-prisoner-abuse-timeline,0,7785463.story. Several of these memoranda were penned by Professor John C. Yoo, a Justice Department attorney and now a professor at the University of California, Berkeley, School of Law. As recently as February 2, 2005, he and a colleague from his Justice Department days, Robert J. Delahunty, after acknowledging their authorship of the Justice Department memoranda, wrote in an Op Ed column for the San Francisco Chronicle, entitled "The Geneva Convention Isn't the Last Word," www.sfgate.com. See also "International Law and the War on Terrorism," John C. Yoo & James C. Ho, *YOO NYU Combatants.Doc*, August 1, 2003. If one talks to John Yoo, one would wonder whether the U.S. ever would be bound by any international treaty. For the opposing view, see Professor Jordan Paust, "The Common Plan to Violate the Geneva Conventions," *Jurist: Legal Intelligence*, University of Pittsburg School of Law, May 25, 2004, at www.jurist.law.pitt.edu/forum/paust2.php. In December, 2004, after a public outcry, the Bush administration backtracked. The Department of Justice issued a new memorandum refuting Professor Yoo's rejection of the Geneva Convention's protections and reaffirming its protections and those of various other international conventions prohibiting the mistreatment of prisoners. See "New U.S. Memo Backs Off Torture Arguments," *Associated Press, The New York Times*, December 31, 2004.

27. With the acquisition of the Philippines in 1898 as a result of its victory in the Spanish-American War, the United States inherited the Philippine Insurrection from Spain. The

Insurrection was mounted against Spain in 1896 by Philippine nationalist Emilio Aguinaldo. During the brief Spanish American War, the United States briefly allied with Aguinaldo, who laid siege to Manila while Admiral Perry destroyed the Spanish fleet in Manila Bay. However, the American victory over Spain soon became American occupation. The promise of independence never materialized; and fighting between Aguinaldo's forces and U.S. forces began on February 4, 1899, and continued until 1902, when President Theodore Roosevelt declared the Insurrection at an end.

Mindanao and the Southern Philippines were another story. The Muslims of the Southern island of Mindanao (the second largest Philippine island, about the size of the state of Indiana), the Sulu Archipelago, and the Palawan, Basilan and Jolo islands, had begun their struggle against the Spanish-Christian rule with Ferdinand de Magellan's arrival in 1521. Even after the officially declared end of the Philippine Insurrection in 1902, the Southern Muslims, known by their Spanish moniker, "the Moros," continued their struggle against even the victorious American forces. Moro resistance was characterized by especially brutal tactics on both sides, and pacification to a degree was finally achieved by American forces in 1915.

But the story did not end there. Reacting against physical and cultural incursions from the Manila government, the insurgent Moro Liberation Front was formed in the late 1960's under the leadership of Nur Misuari. By 1972, he had recast his organization as the Moro National Liberation Front ("MNLF"). After a failed cease-fire and referendum in 1977, the Front splintered into various factions. One was the Moro Islamic Liberation Front ("MILF"), led by Hashim Salamat. An active insurgency has continued since 1978.

In 1986, the MNLF signed an accord with the Manila government relinquishing its demand for independence and accepting an offer of autonomy. The MILF refused the offer and continues its resistance to the Manila government. It maintains a website at www.luwaran.com and demands an autonomous Muslim state in the Southern Philippines. The MILF is not on the U.S. State Department's list of terrorist organizations and denies affiliation with the Abu Sayaf separatist group that is on the list and based primarily in Mindanao, Jolo, and Basilan. See Cherilyn A. Walley, "A Century of Turmoil: America's Relationship with the Philippines, *Special Warfare*, September 2004, at www.findarticles.com/p/articles/mi_m0HZY/is_1_17/ai_n8573960; "Fighting Islam's Fierce Moro Warriors – America's First War with Suicidal Islamic Warriors," *Military History Magazine*, April 2002, at www.freerepublic.com/focus/news/654540/posts; "Moro National Liberation Front (MNLF) - Terrorist Group Profile," *MIPT-Terrorism Knowledge Base*, at www.tkb.org/Group.jsp?groupID=202; "Moro Islamic Liberation Front," *Wikipedia, the Free Encyclopedia*, at www.en.wikipedia.org/wiki/Moro_Islamic_Liberation_Front; "Moro Islamic Liberation Front," Federation of American Scientists: Intelligence Resource Program, at www. fas.org/irp/world/para/milf.htm.; *Luwaran.com* at www.luwaran.com; "Abu Sayyaf," *Wikipedia, the Free Encyclopedia*, www.en.wikipedia.org/wiki/Abu_Sayyaf; and "Appendix B: Background Information on Terrorist Groups, Patterns of Global Terrorism – 2000," Released by the Office of the Coordinator for Counterterrorism, U.S. State Department, April 30, 2001, at www.state.gov/s/ct/rls/pgtrpt/2000/2450.htm.

28. Since 9/11 the United States has pressured Islamic countries, mainly Saudi Arabia, Pakistan, Yemen, and Egypt, to moderate and modernize the curricula taught at the *Madrassas*, or religious schools, in those venues. For example, on January 1, 2004, Kuwaiti lawmakers rejected pressures from U.S. and Western governments to change their schools' curricula, refusing to "Americanize" their educational institutions. And in May, 2003, Egypt and Saudi Arabia promised to review their schools' curricula with a view toward tempering religious extremism. The Saudis attempted to temper their curricula by limiting references to battles and *Jihad* (holy war). The proposals have met with serious opposition in Wahhabist Saudi Arabia. Recently, 156 Saudi religious scholars attacked the proposals as undermining the principles of the Wahhabi Doctrine, which legitimizes the Saud family's rule in the kingdom. See "Two U.S. Allies Review Islamic

Curricula at Schools, Mosques," *World Tribune.com*, May 21, 2003, at www.216.26.163.62/2003/ me_egypt_05_21.html; "Kuwait Will Not 'Americanize' Textbooks," *Jihad Watch*, January 2, 2004, at www.jihadwatch.org/archives/000542.php; and Abdul Raheem Ali, "Argument Over Saudi Curricula 'Reform,'" *IslamOnline.net*, January 3, 2004, at www.islamonline.net/English/ News/2004-01/03/article08.shtml.

29. *Holy Quran*, 9 (At-Taubah [The Repentance]):13-15.

30. *Holy Quran*, 63 (Al-Munafiqun [The Hypocrites]):8.

31. *Holy Quran*, 3 (Al-Imran [The Family of Imran]:139.

32. *Holy Quran*, 3 (Al-Imran [The Family of Imran]):169-171.

33. *Holy Quran*, 61 (As-Saff [The Row or the Rank]:9.

34. *Holy Quran*, 58 (Al-Mujadilah [The Disputation]):21.

35. OBL refers to the Soviet invasion in Afghanistan, which began in the winter of 1979 and ended in the Spring of 1988, after the signing of the Geneva Accords on April 14, 1988. The Soviet Union ceased to exist on December 25, 1991. See Professor Archie Brown, "Reform, Coup, Collapse: The End of the Soviet State," *BBC*, December 10, 2001, at www.bbc.co.uk/ history/war/coldwar/soviet_end_01.shtml.

CHAPTER 10

1. OBL audiotape broadcast in Arabic on *Al-Jazeera Television* on Tuesday, November 12, 2002.

2. OBL refers to several bloody and violent acts that occurred in 2002. On April 11, 2002, a natural gas truck exploded adjacent to the Ghriba Synagogue on the Tunisian resort island of Djerba. A group linked to Al Qaeda claimed responsibility. Seventeen people, including eleven German tourists, were killed. See Mitchell Bard, "The Jews of Tunisia," citing the April 17 and 23, 2002, issues of the *Washington Post*, *Jewish Virtual Library*, at www.jewishvirtuallibrary. org/jsource/anti-semitism/tunisjews.html.

On May 8, 2002, a car bomb exploded outside the Karachi, Pakistan, Sheraton Hotel, killing fourteen people, including eleven French engineers. Islamic militants were suspected of having perpetrated the bombing. "Pakistan Arrests Militant Wanted for Killing French," *Reuters Foundation*, March 2, 2005, reporting the arrest of an Islamic militant suspected of a role in the bombing. See www.alertnet.org. On October 6, 2002, the French supertanker Limburg was attacked by and explosive-laden small boat off the coast of Yemen. The blast caused a hole in the hull and killed a Bulgarian sailor. Islamic militants were suspected as having perpetrated the bombing. "Yemen Admits 'Terrorist Act' Behind Tanker Blast," *IslamOnline.net*, October 17, 2002, at www.islamonline.net/English/News/2002-10/17/article12.shtml.

On October 8 and 14, 2002, United States Marines training in Kuwait came under fire from civilian vehicles and from an ambush laid by two Kuwaitis who had trained with the Marines. One Marine was killed in the attacks. Fifteen men arrested in connection with the October 8th attack have confessed. The Kuwaiti government refers to the incidents as terrorist attacks. One of the leaders of the group, who was killed in the October 8th attack, had pledged loyalty to Osama bin Laden. See "U.S. Troops in Kuwait Attacked Again," *CBSNEWS.com*, October 14, 2002, at www.cbsnews.com/stories/2002/10/17/attack/main525967.shtml.

On October 12, 2002, car bombs caused the deaths of approximately 190 people, mainly Australians, on the Indonesian resort island of Bali. Islamic militants were suspected of the bombings. See "12 October 2002: Dozens Killed in Bali Nightclub Explosion," *BBC - On This Day, bbc.co.uk*, at www.news.bbc.co.uk/onthisday/hi/dates/stories/october/12/newsid_ 2543000/2543731.stm.

On October 23, 2002, Chechen rebels seized approximately 800 hostages at a Moscow theater. Russian special forces troops used a gas to immobilize the rebels; however, the gas did not discriminate between hostage and rebel and the death toll among the hostages reached 120, all but two of whom died from the gas. All fifty rebels were killed. See *The World Almanac E-Newsletter*, Vol. 2, No. 11 – November 2002, Chronology, International, at *www.worldalmanac.com/200211WAE-Newsletter.html*.

3. Apparently OBL has mistaken Donald Rumsfeld for Robert McNamara, President Kennedy's and President Johnson's Secretary of Defense during the Vietnam War between 1961 and 1968. During the Vietnam War, Donald Rumsfeld served in the Nixon administration (1968-1974) on the White House staff, and later as Chief of Staff. See James Mann, *Rise of the Vulcans – The History of Bush's War Cabinet*, pp. 1-4 (Viking-The Penguin Group – 2004). In the Vietnam War, the United States military suffered 58,202 killed and 304,704 wounded. On April 4, 1995, the Vietnamese government revealed that approximately 2,000,000 Vietnamese civilians were killed in North Vietnam, and 2,000,000 Vietnamese civilians were killed in South Vietnam. North Vietnamese military casualties were 1.1 million killed and 600,000 wounded in twenty-one years of war. See "Casualties – US vs. NVA/VC," recommended by the History Channel, at www.rjsmith.com/kia_tbl.html.

4. Hulegu (1217 - 1265), the Mongol grandson of Genghis Khan, conquered the Baghdad Caliphate in1258. Gregory Guzman, "Christian Europe and Mongol Asia," *Essays in Medieval Studies 2,* at www.illinoismedieval.org/ems/VOL2/2ch13.html.

5. The United States and its allies invaded Afghanistan on October 7, 2001.

6. OBL rails against Australia's role in East Timor's (90% Catholic) secession from Indonesia (90% Muslim). For more information about East Timor, please see the Forward.

7. On October 28, 2002, Laurence Foley, an employee of the U.S. Agency for International Development, was gunned down outside his home in Amman, Jordan. His was the first known killing of a Western envoy in the Jordanian capital. Islamic militants were suspected. See "U.S. Official Gunned Down in Jordan," *CBS News*, October 29, 2002, at www.cbsnews.com/stories/2002/10/29/world/main527289.shtml.

8. On November 16, 2001, two United States Air Force jets bombed a mosque in Khowst, Afghanistan. Casualties were unknown. See "U.S. Bomb Damages Mosque," *CNN.com*, November 16, 2001, at www.archives.cnn.com/2001/WORLD/asiapcf/central/11/16/ret.mosque. On July 1, 2002, United States military forces attacked a wedding party in Afghanistan's Uruzgan province. Approximately dozens of people were killed when an AC-130 gunship fired on them. The U.S. military alleges the wedding party was standing near an anti-aircraft site that was the intended target of the gunship. See "Afghans Protest Over Wedding Party Bombing," *CNN. com*, July 4, 2002, at www.archives.cnn.com/2002/WORLD/asiapcf/central/07/04/afghanistan. bombing.

9. The Russians first invaded oil-rich Chechnya in 1994, withdrew in 1996, and then invaded again in 1999. For more information about Chechnya, please see the Forward.

CHAPTER 11

1. Broadcast on *Al-Jazeera Television* on February 11, 2003.

2. *Holy Quran*, 3 (Al-Imran [The Family of Imran]):102.

3. For more information about the Caliphate, please see the Forward.

4. In Zionist literature, Greater Israel envisions a reconstituted land of Israel that extends from the Euphrates River in Iraq to the Nile River in Egypt. This view would be consistent with Genesis 15:18: "I give unto them the land where they have sown their seed, from the river of Egypt unto the great river of Euphrates." The term can also mean Eretz Israel, which would encompass the land from the Mediterranean Sea to the Jordan River, encompassing today's Israel, the occupied West Bank, the Gaza Strip, and parts of Jordan. Ariel Sharon and Israel's present Likud Party leadership envision Greater Israel as including the lands between the Mediterranean and the Jordan River, comprising the ancient kingdoms of Judea and Samaria. See Comment, "Why Greater Israel Vision Has Perished," *The Observer/Guardian Unlimited*, January 11, 2004,

at www.observer.guardian.co.uk/comment/story/0,6903,1120533,00.html; John Mitchell Henshaw, "Israel's Grand Design: Leaders Crave Area from Egypt to Iraq," *Media Monitor*, reprinting an article that first appeared in the *American Mercury* magazine in the spring of 1968, at www.mediamonitors.net/johnhenshaw1.html; *"Land of Israel," Wikipedia, the Free Encyclopedia*, www.en.wikipedia.org/wiki/Eretz_Yisrael.

5. *Holy Quran*, 3 (Al-Imran [The Family of Imran]):173.

(*Sahih al-Bukhari, Hadith* No. 4563).

(Sahih al-Bukhari, Hadith No. 4564).

6. *Holy Quran*, 4 (An-Nisa [The Women]):76.

7. *"Jihad"* as OBL employs the term means a defensive war to protect Islam. See the Forward for a discussion of *Jihad*.

8. *Holy Quran*, 47 (Muhammad):7.

9. For more information about major and minor sins, please see the Forward.

10. Abu-al-Darda (died 652), a companion and contemporary of the Prophet (PBUH) who is a well-known narrator in many *Hadiths*. See

www.dictionary.al-islam.com/Arb/Dicts/SelDict.asp?TL=1&DI=26&Theme=26.

11. George H.W. Bush, 41st President of the United States, who led the 1991 international coalition that wrestled Kuwait from Iraqi control after Iraq's invasion of that country in 1990.

12. During the first ten days of December 2001, the United States surrogate forces had OBL and several hundred of his fighters cornered in an area of Eastern Afghanistan known as Tora Bora. The area was a *Mujahideen* (Islamic fighter) stronghold during the war against the Soviet invaders (1979 – 1988) and was laced with caves and defensive positions. OBL and many of his fighters were able to slip away, probably into Pakistan. Western military analysts ascribe his escape to the failure of the United States to commit its own ground troops to the battle. The analysts surmise that the surrogate forces either failed to seal off escape routes or else colluded in the escape. Barton Gellman and Thomas E. Ricks, "U.S. Concludes Bin Laden Escaped at Tora Bora Fight," *Washington Post*, April 17, 2002; Richard Bernstein, "Bin Laden Bribed Afghan Militias, German Official Says," New York Times, April 12, 2005 (August Hanning, head of German intelligence reported that Bin Laden bribed his way to freedom).

13. Dr. Ayman al-Zawahiri, a physician, founded Egyptian Islamic Jihad in the 1980s, described as a "radical *Jihadi*/rejectionist group." Since that time, he has merged his organization with al-Qaeda and has become OBL's "right-hand-man." See "Dr. Ayman al-Zawahiri," *Perspectives on World History and Current Events: Middle East Project*, at www.pwhce.org/zawahiri.html.

14. OBL refers to Omar, the second Caliph (634 - 644), and companion of the Prophet [PBUH].

15. In fact, OBL might have believed that the U.S. lacked adequate supplies of cruise missiles. See Dave Eberhart, "Cruise Missile Gap May Help Explain Iraq Bypass," *NewsMax.com*, January 11, 2002, at www.papillonsartpalace.com/clintCons.htm. In his article, Mr. Eberhart notes that the Department of Defense budget for cruise missiles for FY 2001 and FY 2002 noted a shortage of conventionally armed, air-launched missiles.

16. *Holy Quran*, 5 (Al-Ma'idah [The Table Spread with Food]):51.

17. By the land of the Two Holy Places, OBL refers to Saudi Arabia, the cities of Mecca and Medina, Islam's two most holy places. See the Forward for a discussion of Mecca and Medina.

18. *Holy Quran*, 4 (An-Nisa [The Women]):102.

19. OBL refers to the socialist Baathist party in Iraq, soon to be invaded by the United States on March 20, 2003.

20. See endnote 10 of OBL's October 12, 2003, statement, *infra*, for a discussion of the Baathist Socialist Party in Iraq; and endnote 10 of OBL's 1994 Letter to Sheikh Baz, *infra*, for a discussion of the Saudis' support for Marxist-socialist movements in Yemen.

21. After a long history of warfare, the decisive battle between the Byzantines (Eastern Romans) and the Persians was fought at Nineveh in 627. The Byzantines unexpectedly defeated the Persians and regained territory lost in earlier wars. Thereafter, the Muslims conquered southern Mesopotamia in 633, achieved a victory over the Byzantines in Palestine at Ajnadayn in 634, and between 633 - 644, under the Caliph Omar Ibn al-Khattab, conquered Persia. Thereafter, Muslim forces continually engaged the Byzantines on land and at sea until the latter's ultimate conquest by the Muslim Ottoman Turks in 1453, marking the end of the Eastern Byzantine (Roman) Empire. See "The Ottoman Empire: A Chronological Outline," at www.turizm.net/turkey/history/ottoman.html; and "Arabic Timeline," at www.princeton.edu/~batke/itl/scroll/600tx.html.

22. Sunan Abu Dawud, *Hadith*, Book 29, No. 3909.

23. Talhah Ibn Ubaydullah, hero of the Battle of Uhud (625) in which a force from Mecca defeated the Prophet (PBUH) and his band of followers. The battle was the second battle in the history of Islam. The Meccan army was led by Khalid Ibn al-Walid who later himself converted to Islam and became one of early Islam's most famous generals. See "The Battle of Uhud," *Muslim American Society, Minnesota Chapter*, at www.masmn.org.

Talhah exemplified bravery in protecting the injured Prophet from further harm in spite of extensive wounds to himself. He was later killed at the Battle of the Camel (656), fought between the forces loyal to Ali Abdi Talib, the fourth Caliph, and followers of Aisha, the Prophet's (PBUH) widow, who was upset at Ali's ascension to the Caliphate on the Caliph Uthman's assassination. Aisha had hoped that either Talhah or Zubayer Ibn al-Awwam, her brothers-in-law, would succeed Uthman. Unfortunately, this battle marked the first time that Muslims had fought each other. Of course, the ultimate result of resistance to Ali's ascension to the Caliphate resulted in the schism in Islam between Sunnis and Shi'ites (followers of Ali) that exists to this day. Zubayer was also killed in the Battle. See "Biography of a Companion (*Sahabah*): Talhah Ibn Ubaydullah," www.usc.edu/dept/MSA/; "Ali Ibn Abi Talib," see *Wikipedia, the Free Encyclopedia;* at www.en.wikipedia.org/wiki/Ali_ibn_Abi_Talib ; and "The Battle of Jamal (Camel)," *Islamic Occasions Network*, at www.ezsoftech.com/islamic/jamal.asp.

24. The Battle of Yarmuk occurred in the year 636, and is one of the most important in Islamic history because it marked the first real Islamic victory outside Arabia. More information about the battle can be found in the Forward.

25. OBL is paraphrasing Quranic verse. See: *Holy Quran*, 8 (Al-Anfal [The Spoils of War]):67.

Holy Quran, 45 (Muhammad):4-6.

26. The Editor is unable to find any source for this poem other than OBL himself.

27. *Holy Quran*, 8 (Al-Anfal [The Spoils of War]):45.

28. *Holy Quran*, 2 (Al-Baqarah [The Cow]):201.

CHAPTER 12

1. This statement was first broadcast on February 16, 2003, on *Al-Jazeera Television* and several Islamic websites; excerpts were published in the London-based *Al-Hayat* Arabic-language newspaper on February 16, 2003, though the newspaper omitted OBL'S criticisms of Arab regimes in general and the Saudi regime in particular. A version with limited footnotes appears at *JihadUnspun.com.*

The feast celebrates Abraham's act of offering to sacrifice his son to the one God if requested to do so and in then being allowed to sacrifice a sheep instead of his son. The event is depicted in the *Holy Quran* at Sura (Chapter) 37 (As-Saffat [The Arrangers]), Verses 83-111.

2. *Holy Quran*, 9 (At-Taubah [Ultimatum]):5.

3. *Holy Quran* 9 (At-Taubah [Ultimatum]):14.

4. In Islam, after the Prophet Muhammad's (PBUH) death in 632, scholars gathered his

words and examples from those who had known him and compiled them into books referred to as the *Hadith*, or traditions, of the Prophet (PBUH). For more information regarding Hadiths, please see the Forward.

See Sahih Bukhari, *Hadith*, Vol. 4, Book 52, No. 288: see www.usc.edu/dept/MSA/.

See Sahih Muslim, *Hadith*, Book 19, No. 4366: see www.usc.edu/dept/MSA/.

Also, refer to Bukhari, Vol. 4, Book 53, No. 393, narrated by Said bin Jubair; Bukhari; Vol. 5, Book 59, No. 716, narrated by Ibn Abbas; and Malik Muwatta, another *Hadith* scholar, at Book 45, No. 45.5.18. See the *Hadith* collection at the University of Southern California, at www.usc.edu/dept/MSA/.

5. For more information regarding the Gulf War sanctions, please refer to the Forward. See also Richard Hooker, "Islam: The Abbasid Dynasty," www.wsu.edu/~dee/ISLAM/ABASSID.HTM.

6. OBL refers to World War I and World War II, during which Western warring states fought each other in venues in the Middle East. During World War I, the British fought the Turkish forces in Palestine, Saudi Arabia, and other venues of the Middle East. After WWI, the British and the French were given mandates over portions of the Middle East according to the Versailles Peace Treaty of 1919 and secret agreements among them negotiated in the infamous Sykes-Picot treaty of 1916 (see the Forward). For example, Britain's mandate encompassed Egypt and Palestine, and France's included what was then known as the Levant, which included present-day Syria and Lebanon. OBL refers to these wars as Crusader Wars because Christian military forces invaded Islamic lands and remained there in control Islamic lands. See generally, "World War I," at www.countrystudies.us/syria/8.htm; and "The Arab Israeli Conflict: History Palestine, Jordan, etc.," at *Arab2.com*, www.arab2.com/biography/Arab-Israeli-Conflict-mid.htm.

7. For more information regarding The Sykes-Picot Agreement, please see the Forward.

8. For ore information regarding the use of the word "Crusade" by George W. Bush, please see endnote 8 of the Preface.

9. The reference to the "Two Holy Sanctuaries" refers to the cities of Mecca and Medina, located in Saudi Arabia. More information regarding the Two Holy Sanctuaries can be found in the Forward.

OBL refers to the meeting between the Saudi Arabian King Abdul Aziz and President Roosevelt that occurred on the United States cruiser *U.S.S. Quincy* on February 14, 1945, in the Suez Canal. During that meeting, the Saudi King established a special relationship with the United States that continues to this day. The King was quick to realize that in the post-World War II world, previous colonial powers like Great Britain had been exhausted by the war and had been eclipsed by the superpower, the United States. On November 30, 1967, Great Britain withdrew the last of its troops from Aden/Yemen, leaving the security of the Arabian and Red Seas to the United States and surrendering its last colonial vestige in the Middle East. See "Saudi-U.S. Relations: A Future of Steady Growth," *The Washington Times, A Special International Report*, September 22, 2000, at www.internationalspecialreports.com/middleeast/00/saudiarabia/2.html; and www.infopedia.ruv.net/19/1967.html.

10. OBL refers to the Arab-Israeli War of 1973 when President Nixon, worried about possible Soviet intervention on the side of the Arabs, threatened United States military intervention and provided to the Israelis advanced M-60 tanks that were impervious to the Soviet-supplied anti-tank missiles then utilized by the Egyptian army. For more information on the use of Saudi bases by U.S. forces, please see the Forward. See also "Israel, Military Cooperation with the United States," at www.country-data.com/cgi-bin/query/r-6860.html. Regarding U.S. military presence in the Middle East, see generally, Stephen J. Heges, "Military to Leave Saudi Arabia," *Chicago Tribune*, April 30, 2003, www.globalsecurity.org/org/news/2003/030430-psab01.htm; "US Pulls Out of Saudi Arabia," *BBC News*, April 29, 2003, www.news.bbc.co.uk/2/hi/middle_east/2984547.stm; "Most of US Forces Withdrawn From Saudi Arabia," *USA Today*, August 28,

2003, www.usatoday.com/news/washington/2003-08-28-ustroop-saudiarabia_x.htm; Christine Spolar, "14 'Enduring Bases' Set in Iraq," *Chicago Tribune*, March 23, 2004, www.usatoday.com/news/washington/2003-08-28-ustroops-saudiarabia_x.htm; "Military Forces in the Middle East," *Houston Chronicle*, March 18, 2003, also see "U.S. Forces Order of Battle 21 October 2004, at www.globalsecurity.org/military/ops/iraq_orbat.htm.

11. OBL refers to the January 13, 2003, meeting of the Arab internal affairs ministers in Tunis, Tunisia. The ostensible purpose of the meeting was to resolve to assist in the international war against terrorism. See "Middle East and North Africa: Information and Interior Ministers Must Tackle Clampdown on Freedom of Expression," *Amnesty International*, January 17, 2003, at www.web.amnesty.org/library/Index/ENGMDE010012003?open&of=ENG-300. See also "Prince Naif ibn Abdul Aziz Reiterates the Keeness of the Council of Arab Interior Ministers to Enhance Security and Stability in the Arab World," *Ain-al-Yaqeen*, January 24, 2003, at www.ain-al-yaqeen.com/issues/20030124/feat5en.htm; and "Saudi Arabia Calls for Internal Arab Reforms," *Al-Jazeera Information*, January 14, 2003, at www.aljazeerah.info/; "Riyadh Urges Diplomatic Efforts to Resolve Crisis," *Id.*, January 14, 2003; and "Naif Condemns Move to Frame Arab Nation," *Id.*, January 14, 2003.

In Zionist literature, Greater Israel envisions a reconstituted land of Israel that extends from the Euphrates River in Iraq to the Nile River in Egypt. This view would be consistent with Genesis 15:18: "I give unto them the land where they have sown their seed, from the river of Egypt unto the great river of Euphrates." The term can also mean Eretz Israel, which would encompass the land from the Mediterranean Sea to the Jordan River, encompassing today's Israel, the occupied West Bank, the Gaza Strip, and parts of Jordan. Israeli Prime Minister Ariel Sharon and Israel's present leadership envision Greater Israel as including the lands between the Mediterranean and the Jordan, comprising the ancient kingdoms of Judea and Samaria. See Comment, "Why Greater Israel Vision Has Perished," *The Observer/Guardian Unlimited*, January 11, 2004, at www.observer.guardian.co.uk/comment/story/0,6903,1120533,00.html; John Mitchell Henshaw, "Israel's Grand Design: Leaders Crave Area from Egypt to Iraq," *Media Monitor*, reprinting an article that first appeared in the *American Mercury* magazine in the spring of 1968, at www.mediamonitors.net/johnhenshaw1.html; "Land of Israel," *Wikipedia, the Free Encyclopedia*, www.en.wikipedia.org/wiki/Eretz_Yisrael.

12. OBL refers to Israel's well-known occupation of the Gaza Strip and the West Bank and generally to its practices of arbitrary arrests, killings, collective punishment of Palestinians, and extrajudicial execution of its perceived enemies in these Occupied Territories by helicopter-launched missiles that often result in the killing of innocent Palestinian bystanders.

13. *Holy Quran*, 2 (Al-Baqarah [The Cow]:156.

14. *Holy Quran*, 2: (Al-Baqarah [The Cow]):100.

15. *Holy Quran*, 4 (An-Nisa [The Women]):53.

16. In the *Old Testament*, Jews were given license to practice the "ban" or "anathema" on all conquered peoples, meaning killing all of them: "In the cities of the nations the Lord your God is giving you as an inheritance, do not leave alive anything that breathes. Completely destroy them – the Hittites, Amorites, Canaanites, Perizzites, Hivites and Jebusites – as the Lord your God has commanded you. Otherwise, they will teach you to follow all the detestable things they do in worshipping their gods, and you will sin against the Lord your God." See Deut.20:16-18.

"When the Lord your God has delivered them over to you and you have defeated them, then you must destroy them totally (according to the law of anathema). Make no treaty with them, and show them no mercy." See Deut.7:2-5, 2:34, Num.25:1-5, 31:14-17, Ex.23:33, Joshua 6:17, 8:26.

17. *Holy Quran*, 3 (Al-Imran [The Family of Imran]):75.

18. *Holy Quran*, 11 (Hud [Prophet]):88.

19. *Holy Quran*, 4 (An Nisa [The Women]):84.

20. *Holy Quran*, 47 (Muhammad):7.

21. The reference is to a thorny tree. OBL somewhat paraphrases the *Hadith*. See Sahih Muslim, *Hadith*, Book 41, No. 6985: at www.usc.edu/dept/MSA/.

22. Al Muthanna ibn Harithah (d. 635), chief of Banu Shayban, a clan of Banu Bakr, had distinguished himself in the battle of Dhu Qar against the Persians. He was responsible for reconciling the clans of Banu Bakr when Khalid ibn al Walid, the most famous of the Muslim generals, entered the clan's territories. Al Muthanna and his men were allowed to join the Muslim army, which then defeated the Persians in the battle which was joined in present-day Kuwait. See endnote 4 of OBL's statement of October 12, 2003, *infra*.

23. See the previous endnote. Abu Uaidah Ath-Thaqafi, a contemporary of Al Muthanna, was a prominent Muslim general who took part in the battle after being motivated by Caliph Omar's sermon. See also, "Omar (R.A.)," *Al-Islaah Publications,* at www.alislaah2.tripod.com/caliphs/id2.html.

24. OBL refers to the United States' invasion of Afghanistan on October 7, 2001, and the battles at Tora Bora and Shahi-Kot in December 2001, when OBL and his al-Qaeda fighters were supposedly surrounded by American and Northern Alliance forces.

25. OBL refers to the Soviet invasion of Afghanistan on December 26, 1979, and its withdrawal in May of 1988, having been defeated by *Mujahideen* insurgents, including Osama bin Laden, who were then supported and funded mainly by Saudi Arabia and the United States Central Intelligence Agency. See generally, Steve Coll, *Ghost Wars*, pp. 176-177 (The Penguin Press 2004).

26. The Russians first invaded Chechnya in 1994 and then withdrew in 1996. For more information regarding Chechnya, please see the Forward.

27. OBL refers to the Lebanese Civil War, which lasted from 1975 to 1989. More information regarding the Lebanese Civil War can be found in the Forward.

28. OBL refers to the 1993 United States incursion into Somalia and to the famous "Black Hawk Down" incident in Mogadishu, the Somali capitol. More information regarding Somalia can be found in the Forward.

29. OBL refers to a December 29, 1992, bombing of a hotel in the port city of Aden, Yemen, at which U.S. troops en route Somalia were staying. More information about the bombing can be found in the Forward.

30. On July 25, 1996, the Khobar Towers in Al-Khobar, Saudi Arabia, were destroyed by a truck bomb. More information regarding the Towers can be found in the Forward.

31. On August 7, 1998, the United States embassies in Dar es Salaam, Tanzania, and Nairobi, Kenya, were bombed. More information regarding the bombings can be found in the Forward.

32. OBL himself has said that he is not opposed to freedom and democracy. See OBL's speech of October 29, 2004, *infra*. Rather, he is opposed to United States policies in the Middle East, including its favoritism of Israel in the Israeli-Palestinian conflict and the stationing of United States and Western military forces throughout the Middle East, including especially Saudi Arabia, the venue of the "Two Holy Places," i.e., Mecca and Medina. See endnote 12 of OBL's October 18, 2003, statement, *infra*. Also, endnote 8 of OBL's September 11, 2003, statement, *infra*; and endnotes 13 and 18 of OBL's July, 2003, statement, *infra*. See also Anonymous, *Imperial Hubris: Why the West Is Losing the War on Terror*, pp. x, 16-17, 105-126 (Brassey's, Inc., 1st Ed. 2004).

The *Al-Aqsa* Mosque is the third holiest site in Islam, located on the *Haram al Sheik*, or Temple Mount, in Jerusalem. More about the *Al-Aqsa Mosque* can be found in the Forward.

33. The Islamic Caliphate, or leader of Islam, especially Sunni Islam see "Caliphate," *Wikipedia, the Free Encyclopedia* at www.wikipedia.org.

34. More about this poem can be found in the Forward.

35. Sahih Bukhari, *Hadith*, Vol. 5, Book 59, No. 597: www.usc.edu/dept/MSA/.

36. Khalid ibn al-Walid was the most famous Muslim general during the early Muslim

conquests in the middle to late seventh centuries. Before becoming a Muslim, he actually led the Meccan army that defeated the Prophet Muhammad (PBUH) and his followers at the battle of *Uhud*. OBL is referring to Walid's admiration for the leaders of the Quraish, the tribe of the Prophet (PBUH). The Battle of *Uhud* occurred in 625. See "The Battle of *Uhud*," Muslim American Society, Minnesota Chapter, at www.masmn.org.

37. Imam Ahmad ibn Hanbal (702 - 772), is discussed in the Forward.

38. This verse appears in OBL's 1995 letter to King Fahd of Saudi Arabia, reprinted *infra*. In the letter, OBL chastises the Saudi regime and advocated a guerilla war against U.S. forces based in Saudi Arabia.

39. "There is no god but God," the fundamental pillar of monotheistic Islam.

40. OBL fled to the Sudan in 1991. The Saudi government revoked his citizenship in 1994. His status as an enemy of the state was later cemented by his August 3, 1995, letter to King Fahd, and a car bombing in Riyadh in November 1995, that killed five Americans. See "Osama bin Laden, A Chronology of his Political Life," *Frontline*, at www.pbs.org/wgbh/pages/frontline/shows/binladen/etc/cron.html ; and Najla al Rostamani, "At the Crossroads: Saudi Arabia in Transition," *Gulf News Online Edition*, November 25, 2003, at www.gulf-news.com/Articles/opinion.asp?ArticleID=103790. In 1994 OBL, through his London-based surrogate, Khalid al-Fawwaz, had formed the Committee for Advice and Reform to seek reforms of the Saudi government. The Saudi government rejected the Committee's suggestions. See Douglas Davis, "Mossad Warned CIA of Attacks – Reports," *The Internet Jerusalem Post*, September 17, 2001, at www.cgis.jpost.com.; and "When Suspicion is Mistaken as Proof – The Sorry Tale of Khalid al-Fawwaz," *Salaam.com*, March 6, 2003, reprinted from the February 20, 2003, edition of the *Financial Times*, at www.salaam.co.uk/themeofthemonth/january03_index.php?l=29%82%22=0.

41. In February, 2003, Karzai was the titular head of Afghanistan's interim government. A favorite son of the United States government, he was elected President of Afghanistan on October 26, 2004, and remains in Kabul guarded by American Special Forces troops and private American security contractors. See "Karzai Aborts Visit After Blast," *BBC News*, September 16, 2004, at www.news.bbc.co.uk/2/hi/in_depth/3662352.stm.

42. OBL refers to the patriarch of the Saud family, Abdel Aziz ibn Saud, who conquered Saudi Arabia and founded the Saudi dynasty in 1926. Ibn Rasheed was the Turkish governor of the Arabian province of the Ottoman Empire. See endnote 80 of the Forward.

43. *Holy Quran*, 54 (Al-Qamar [The Moon]):43.

44. Between 1995 and 2005, Crown Prince Abdullah was the titular head of Saudi Arabia, surrogate for the infirm King Fahd. On March 27, 2002, the Arab League announced a peace plan for the Middle East that had been floated by Saudi Crown Prince Abdullah. The plan called for the withdrawal of Israeli forces to the 1967 borders in return for recognition by the Arab states. See "The Arab Peace Initiative," *Middle East Web*, March 28, 2002, at www.mideastweb.org/saudipeace.htm; and "The Arab League 'Peace Plan,'" *Jewish Virtual Library*, March 27, 2002, at www.jewishvirtuallibrary.org/jsource/Peace/arabplan.html.

45. The use of the term "astray" is significant in that it suggests apostasy, as the first Sura (chapter) of the *Holy Quran* prays to God that the Muslims not go astray in their beliefs. The Sura is the most recited prayer in Islam. In the Islamic tradition, the perceived violators are first advised and then warned.

46. *Holy Quran*, 2 (Al-Baqarah [The Cow]):256.

Regarding the two pillars of the *Taweed*, See "Chapter 2: The Islamic Concept of *Tawheed (Monotheism)," Tawheed al-Ibaadah*, at www.ahya.org/tjonline/eng/02/2tawheed.html.

47. The references are to the *Al-Haram* Mosque in Mecca, site of the *Kaba*. The months of *Muharram, Rajab, Dhul Qadah* and *Dhul Hijja* are considered to be sacred according to the *Holy Quran*, 9 (Al-Taubah [The Repentance]):36 (the 1st, 7th, 11th and 12th months of the Islamic lunar calendar). Fighting is prohibited during these months. See "Islamic Calendar," *Islam.com*,

at www.islam.com/IslamCalen.htm; however, the cited source refers to Sura 5 of the *Holy Quran* instead of Sura 9.

48. King Fahd, through his surrogate Crown Prince Abdullah allowed the United States to base military forces in Saudi Arabia shortly after the Iraqi invasion of Kuwait on August 2, 1990. The Saudis feared that Iraqi forces would also invade Saudi Arabia.

49. Ahmad ibn bin Muhammad Hanbal (780 - 855) was the Muslim theologian who founded the Hanbal school of theology, or *Fiqh*. More information about Hanbal can be found in the Forward.

50. Sahih Bukhari, *Hadith*, Vol. 9, Book 89, No. 272: at www.usc.edu/dept/MSA/.

51. More information about *Hijra* can be found in the Forward.

52. OBL seems to be referring to February 1991, when 400 Islamic scholars, including Sheikh Abdel-Aziz ibn Baz, Saudi Arabia's most eminent Islamic scholar, wrote a letter to King Fahd calling for governmental reforms. Included in requested reforms was a call for an independent consultative assembly and a call for the removal of corrupt government officials. The letter also urged the protection of individual rights. See Nasser Momayezi, "Islamic Revivalism and the Quest for Political Power," *The Journal of Conflict Studies*, University of New Brunswick, Vol. XVII, No. 2, Fall 1997, at www.lib.unb.ca/Texts/JCS/bin/get.cgi?directory=FALL97/articles/&filename=MOMAYEZI.html.

53. *Holy Quran*, 5 (Al-Ma'ida [The Table Spread With Food]):54.

54. Sahih Muslim, *Hadith*, Book 001, No. 0301: see www.usc.edu/dept/MSA/.

55. On a hill named Aqaba outside Mina, near Mecca, six men of the Khazraj tribe of Medina accepted Islam in 620. Then, in 621, at the same location, seven more men of the Khazraj converted, including two men of the other leading tribe of Medina, the Aws. The twelve pledged their loyalty to the Prophet Muhammad (PBUH). This event was known as the "First Aqaba." Then in 622, seventy-three men and two women swore fealty to the Prophet (PBUH). This became known as the "Second Aqaba." That same year, the Prophet (PBUH) and his followers migrated from Mecca to Medina. See Ted Thornton, "Muhammad and Early Islamic Period 50-632 C.E.," at www.nmhschool.org/tthornton/mehistorydatabase/muhammad_and_early_islamic_perio.htm.

For an interesting perspective on the "*Shababa*," meaning those who knew the Prophet (PBUH) and the levels of fealty to Him and to Islam, see "The Shahaba According to 'Ahl al-Sunnah wal Jama'a," at www.al-shia.com/html/eng/books/shia-real/40.htm.

56. Al-Abbas ibn Abd al-Muttalib, father of the Abbasid dynasty, was the Prophet Muhammad's (PBUH) paternal uncle. For further information on Al-Abbas, see www.dictionary.al-islam.com/Arb/Dicts/SelDict.asp?TL=1&DI=25&Theme=42; "Some Significant Instances of Devotion," *Allaahuakbar.net*, at www.allaahuakbar.net/muhammad/some_significant_instances_of_devotion.htm; and "Glimpses of Hope," at www.home.swipnet/islam/A_Personality/The_Apostle/7hope.htm.

57. See endnote 55 *infra*. Al-Abbas is said to have informed the *Ansar* (helpers) at the Second Aqaba: "People of Khazraj, do you know what you are committing yourselves to, swearing allegiance to this man? You are committing yourselves to war with men of all races... But if you think you will be able to keep your promises, however much loss you incur, and however many of your leaders are killed, then take him with you to Medina. This will be better for you in both this world and the next." See "Allegiance of the Madinites to the Prophet," *A Probe Into the History of Ashura*, Chapter 40, at www.al-islam.org/ashura/41.htm; "Prophet's Love and Tolerance for Mankind," at www.alrisala.org/Articles/Prophet/Seerah%20As%20Movement.htm; and "Glimpses of Hope," Light of Islam, at www.home.swipnet.se/islam/A_Personality/The_Apostle/7hope.htm, citing Al-Wafa bi-Ahwal al-Mustafa, vol. 1, p. 334. Al-Mizan Exegesis, vol. 9, Surah of Al-Anfal.

58. See previous endnote.

59. *Holy Quran*, 4 (An Nisa [Women]):84.

60. More information about Ibn Taymiya (1263 - 1328) can be found in the Forward. More information about the *Sharia* can be found in the Forward.

61. Again, OBL paraphrases the *Hadith*. Sahih Muslim, *Hadith*, Book 001, No. 0081: see www.usc.edu/dept/MSA/.

62. *Holy Quran*, 4 (An-Nisa [The Women]):37.

63. *Holy Quran*, 33 (Al-Ahzab [The Confederates]):18.

64. OBL seems to be giving assurances to the *Ummah* (Islamic nation) that it has nothing to fear from OBL or his *Mujahideen* [Islamic warriors], unless they are attacked first. This scenario changed on May 12, 2003, when Al Qaeda-linked suicide bombers attacked two compounds housing foreign workers and killed 35 people and wounded 200. See "Saudi-US Relations Information Service Newsletter Special Supplement: Terrorists Strike Multiple Targets in Riyadh," May 13, 2003, at www.saudi-us-relations.org/newsletter/saudi-relations-supplement-5-13.html. This was the opening round of Saudi Arabia's battle with indigenous terrorists, and Saudi society continues to be peppered with bombings and gunfights.

65. See the Forward for a discussion of Ibn Taymiya.

66. *Muhajirun* are the Emigrants who migrated with the Prophet Muhammad (PBUH) from Mecca to Medina in the year 622. *Ansar* are the Helpers, his early supporters in Medina. Abu Bakr, Omar, Uthman, and Ali refer to the first four Caliphs, the era of Islam known as the period of the four "rightly guided" (the era of the *Rashidoon*) Caliphs, all of whom were actual companions of the Prophet Muhammad (PBUH). Schwartz, *The Two Faces of Islam*, pp. 27, 28, 33 (1st Ed. Doubleday Nov. 2002).

67. Abu Ishaq al-Shatibi (d. 1378) was a legal scholar. The full name of his work is *Al-Muwafaqat fi usul al-Fiqh*.

68. Poem by Al-Tirrimah ibn al-Hakim al-Tal (660 - 743).

69. Sheikh Omar Abdel Rahman was arrested and convicted of conspiracy in the 1993 bombing of the World Trade Center. His attorney, Lynn Stewart, was tried and convicted of federal charges that she aided and abetted the Sheikh in communicating with his sympathizers outside of his prison. She is appealing her conviction. See Barbara Ferguson, "Lawyer Accused of Aiding Sheikh Omar," *Aljazeera.Info*, June 26, 2004, at www.aljazeera.com/me.asp?service_ ID=7163, "Sheikh Omar Abdul Rahman," at www.islam.co.za/saiin/abdulrahman.html.

Sheikh Saeed bin Zuair is known as Saudi Arabia's longest-serving political prisoner who was released from custody without comment on March 25, 2003, shortly after this OBL speech aired. However, the Sheikh later was re-arrested and has been sentenced to prison for five years for "instigating sedition." See "Leading Saudi Dissident 'Freed,'" *BBC News*, March 25, 2003, at www.news.bbc.co.uk/1/hi/world/middle_east/2885647.stm, and "Saudi Sentences Reformist to 5 Years," *DefenseSupplier.com*, reprinting UPI press release dated September 14, 2004, at www. defensesupplier.com/defense/defensenews/crime-news/crime-news-p-9272.html. OBL refers to the Guantanamo Bay, Cuba, detention facility in which the United States detains hundreds of suspected "enemy combatants" seized in Afghanistan, Iraq, and other parts of the world in its continuing "war on terrorism."

70. *Holy Quran*, 10 (Yunus [Johah]):57.

71. *Holy Quran*, 12 (Yusuf [Joseph]):21.

CHAPTER 13

1. OBL statement posted in segments on various Islamic websites in July, 2003.

2. More about Kemak Ataturk, President of Turkey, can be found in the Forward.

3. See the Forward for a discussion the English translation of the *Holy Quran* chosen for use in this book as well a discussion of Wahhabism, the Sunni Islamic creed that dominates Saudi Arabia.

4. OBL perceives the modern Western military forces in the Arabian (Persian) Gulf countries, Afghanistan, and Iraq to be modern-day Christian Crusaders. He suggests that the West's fear of the Soviet Union and godless communism prompted them to forego their disdain for Muslims and use the latter against the U.S.S.R. when it invaded Afghanistan in 1979. Between 1979 and the Soviets' withdrawal in 1988, the United States provided vital financing and materiel to the Afghani and Arab *Mujahideen* (Islamic warriors) fighting the Soviet forces. In opposing the Soviet presence in Afghanistan, by 1987 the United States had provided the *Mujahideen* with approximately 600 million dollars in arms, including Stinger anti-aircraft, shoulder-fired missiles. The consequences of the arming and training of thousands of fanatical non-Afghani *Mujahideen* after the end of the Soviet occupation were not thought through until September 11, 2001. See generally, Richard A. Clark, *Against All Enemies*, pp. 47-54 (A Free Press 2004). Interestingly, ironically, and finally, tragically, the young Osama bin Laden was one of the early *Mujahideen* funded by the Central Intelligence Agency and Saudi Arabian intelligence agencies to wage holy war against the godless forces of the U.S.S.R. See also, Steve Koll, *Ghost Wars*, pp. 84-87.

5. OBL speaks of the *Ummah*, the Islamic Nation of Muslims throughout the world without regard to physical boundaries.

6. OBL refers to the chaos that beset Afghanistan after the departure of the Soviet Union. The several warlords and tribal factions began fighting among themselves in a bloody civil war. Chaos prevailed until the Pashtun "Taliban" (literally, "religious students") rose up in 1994 in the province of Kandahar along the Pakistani border, led by their supreme leader, the puritanical Mullah Muhammad Omar. The Taliban are fundamentalist Muslims who "preach for a re-born alliance of Islamic piety and Pashtun might." Tired of the chaos of internecine warfare, most Afghani people accepted the Taliban because in addition to strict Islamic law, they also imposed order in areas under their control. See Steve Coll, *Ghost Wars, supra* pp. 283-284 (The Penguin Press 2004). Though the Taliban were Islamic fundamentalists, the Afghani people opted for order, a small price to pay to eliminate the carnage and chaos that had been afflicting them after the Soviets' departure in May of 1988. *Id.* at pp. 176-177. The Taliban seized Kabul, the capital of Afghanistan on September 26, 1996. (*Id.* at p. 333). A few weeks later the remnants of the coalition government that had fled Kabul was reorganized by Ahmed Shah Massoud into the United Front, more commonly called the Northern Alliance. The Alliance under Massoud's leadership was able to hold positions in the Panjshir Valley in the northernmost portion of the country. *Id.*, at pp. 344-345. On October 7, 2001, the Northern Alliance forces became the spear point of the United States invasion of Afghanistan and provided most of the ground forces used to dislodge the Taliban from the population centers of Afghanistan.

7. OBL probably refers to the world-wide outcry against the Taliban when they very publicly demolished the large Buddhist statutes located in central Afghanistan on March 1, 2001. They had been constructed by a thriving Buddhist community between the third and fifth centuries. Steve Coll, *Ghost Wars, supra*, at p. 548. The Western world recoiled at this destruction of these religious icons. However, Buddhism is not a monotheistic religion. Its religious idols do not stand much chance in any truly devout Muslim country. Islam began when the Prophet Muhammad (PBUH) destroyed the idols in the *Kaba* in Mecca in the year 630. See "The Story of the Ka'Ba," *Daily News*, March 4, 2001, at www.geocities.com/mforumsl/kaaba.htm. To this day, Muslims recoil at the sight of idols and idolatry. To allow the continued existence of such statutes in a pious Muslim state was anathema to the fundamentalist Taliban.

8. Only Saudi Arabia and Pakistan had formally recognized the Taliban regime. Steve Coll, *Ghost Wars, supra*, p. 349.

9. OBL is responding to differing interpretations of *Jihad* offered by *Ulema* (Islamic scholars) loyal to the despotic Middle East regimes that he perceives as corrupt and apostate.

10. OBL refers to the scholar known as Ibn Taymiya (1263 - 1328). More about Taymiya can be found in the Forward.

11. The Middle East regimes without exception maintain tight control over the Muslim clerics by making them civil servants and putting them on government payrolls. Further, each government keeps a close eye on the words and deeds of their servant *Ulema* (Islamic scholars). See generally, "Egypt Fights Terror with Imams and Newsprint," *Christian Science Monitor*, July 16, 2002 edition, www.csmonitor.com/2002/0716/p01s03-wome.html; and "Report on International Religious Freedom: United Arab Emirates," *Jewish Virtual Library*, www.jewishvirtuallibrary.org/jsource/anti-semitism/relunitedarabemirates00.html.

12. OBL refers to the continuing presence of Western, and especially, United States military forces in the Arabian (Persian) Gulf States. For more information regarding this subject matter, please see the Forward.

13. OBL refers to the holiest place in Islam, the *Masjid (Mosque) Al-Haram* in Mecca, the final destination of the annual pilgrimage (*Haj*) to Mecca that every Muslim is expected to complete at least once during his or her life. For more information about the Haj, please see the Forward.

14. Friday is the Muslim Sabbath. After the midday prayer, the highpoint of the celebration of the Sabbath, the Imam delivers the *Kutbah*, or lecture, to the assembled congregation. This is the most important address of the week, reaches the largest number of congregants, and may treat any subject matter within the context of religious relevance.

15. See the Forward for Ibn Taymiya.

16. It is common knowledge that King Abdul Aziz ibn Saud, the founder of Saudi Arabia, accepted British financial aid before during and after World War I. For more information regarding the financing, please see endnote 80 of the Forward.

17. In Islam, a *Fatwa* is a religious edict issued by credible Islamic clerics on the religious view or requirements of any subject. For more information regarding *Fatwas*, please see the Forward.

18. OBL refers to Saudi Arabia, the venue of the cities of Mecca and Medina, the two holiest sites in Islam. Mecca is the site of the *Masjid (Mosque) Al-Haram*, discussed in the Forward, *infra*. Medina, of course, was the Prophet Muhammad (PBUH) destination when he migrated from Mecca in 622. Medina also is the site of the Mosque of the Prophet (*Masjid Al Nabawi*), where the Prophet is buried. Upon Saddam Hussein's invasion of Kuwait in 1990, the Saudi Arabian government invited the United States to base military forces in Saudi Arabia to defend the Kingdom against possible invasion by Iraqi forces. From Saudi Arabia, the United States and the then coalition of Western and Middle Eastern countries launched the Persian Gulf War to liberate Kuwait. Thereafter, United States military forces remained in Saudi Arabia. The command center for the Iraq War was located at the Prince Sultan Air Force Base in Saudi Arabia, and United States forces remain in Saudi Arabia today. As stated in the Forward, in April of 2003, the Saudi government tacitly asked the United States to reduce its forces in Saudi Arabia, possibly to mollify Bin Laden supporters in Saudi Arabia. But the reduction was little more than form over substance because United States military command facilities still exist in Saudi Arabia as well as an undetermined number of combat forces based away from population centers. See also endnote 10 of OBL's statement of February 16, 2003.

19. "Tenth Hadith: On Desire and Hope, Forty Hadiths," *Al-Islam.com*, at www.al-islam.org/fortyhadith/10.htm.

20. "Sheikh" is a euphemism for "Imam," or cleric, and also is used to address a local leader, such as the head of a tribe or clan.

21. Ahmad Ibn bin Muhammad Hanbal is discussed in the Forward.

22. The Saudi Arabian government allocates approximately $530 million dollars annually to the Ministry of Islamic Affairs. David B. Ottaway, "U.S. Eyes Money Trails of Saudi-Backed Charities," *Washington Post*, August 19, 2004, www.washingtonpost.com/wp-dyn/articles/A13266-2004Aug18.html.

23. The "Clerics Authority" refers to the Saudi Ministry of Islamic Affairs. Because Sunni Islam lacks the clerical hierarchy that characterizes the Shi'ite clergy, most Sunni Muslims look to the scholars of Al Azhar University located in Cairo, Egypt, as the fount of Sunni religious knowledge. Al Azhar, considered the preeminent religious school in Sunni Islam, has been in existence since 969, when it was founded by the Fatimid Caliph Almiz. When necessary, scholars in residence will issue *Fatwas* as exigencies dictate. However, OBL correctly points out that the autocratic leader of Egypt, President Hosni Mubarak, maintains close control even of the scholars of Al Azhar. See also note 11 above regarding Egypt's control of the *Ulema* (Islamic scholars).

24. There are ten violations, or "voiders," that strip Islam from a believer. For more information please see the Forward.

25. The reference is to the Saudi royal family's tribal tradition of receiving their subjects at their *Majlis* (councils) to hear grievances and receive petitions. See generally, "Politics of Saudi Arabia," *Wikipedia, the Free Encyclopedia*, at www.en.wikipedia.org/wiki/Politics_of_Saudi_Arabia.

26. The reference to "falsehood" cannot be overly emphasized. Islam is grounded on the concept of rejecting idolatry, false prophets, and falsehood. Muslims consider Muhammad (PBUH) to be the last in the lineage of the Old Testament prophets and falsehood practiced by ostensible Islamic clerics is akin to apostasy.

27. Islam forbids the charging of *Riba* (usury, which includes interest on lent money): *Holy Quran*, 2 (Al-Baqarah [The Cow]):275.

28. The Saudi kingdom is roiling with dissention because of its autocratic government and the extravagant lifestyles of the Saudi royal family and its approximately 4,000 profligate princes. Add to this the popularity of OBL within the kingdom, and the mix becomes volatile. See OBL's 1995 Letter to King Fahd, *infra*, for a listing of his grievances against the Saudi regime. See generally, Faiza Saleh Ambah, "Moves Toward Reform Wane in Saudi Arabia," *Christian Science Monitor*, October 4, 2004, at www.csmonitor.com/2004/1004/p06s01-wome.html; "Human Rights in Saudi Arabia: A Deafening Silence," *Human Rights Watch Backgrounder*, December 2001; Joseph A. Kechichian, "Testing the Saudi 'Will to Power:' Challenges Confront Prince Abdallah," *Middle East Policy Council*, Vol. X, Winter 2003, at www.mepc.org/public_asp/journal_vol10/0312_kechichian.asp.

29. The reader must understand that OBL's words as expressed in this speech must not be taken lightly. The United States' invasion of Iraq has given his message deep traction in the Islamic world, especially among the young people to whom the instant speech was primarily addressed. It is from the young that OBL recruits his *Mujahideen*. The Iraq War has not furthered the United States' declared "war against terrorism." Rather, as predicted by President Hosni Mubarak before the outbreak of hostilities, the Iraq War has probably created "a hundred Osama bin Ladens." If anything, President Mubarak's estimate fell far short of the actual figure, which continues to grow each day that United States military forces occupy Iraq and kill Iraqis. Since the Iraq invasion, worldwide terrorist incidents have exponentially increased: from 175 in 2003 to 634 in 2004. The Bush administration's answer has been to discontinue the State Department's annual report of terrorist incidents. See Jonathan S. Landay, "U.S. Eliminates Annual Terrorism Report," *The Seattle Times*, April 16, 2005. See also, Anonymous, *Imperial Hubris: Why the West Is Losing the War on Terror*, pp. 212-214 (Brassey's, Inc. 1st. Ed. 2004).

CHAPTER 14

1. OBL videotape which first aired on *Al-Jazeera Television* on September 11, 2003.

2. OBL refers to the United States invasion of Afghanistan on October 7, 2001, and of Iraq on March 20, 2003 He claims that the invasions, especially that of Iraq, had been planned six months before the 9/11 attacks on the World Trade Center in New York and the Pentagon in Washington, DC. As early as February 1, 2001, the Bush administration convened a meeting

300 Osama Bin Laden: America's Enemy In His Own Words

of the National Security Council exploring strategies aimed at effecting regime change in Iraq. Military options were discussed. On September 13, 2001, at a subsequent NSC meeting, actually a war planning session after the infamous 9/11 attacks, Deputy Secretary of Defense Paul Wolfowitz raised the subject of attacking Iraq as "doable." See Ron Suskind, *The Price of Loyalty*, pp. 84-87, 186-188 (Simon & Schuster 2004). After returning to the White House on September 12, 2001, President Bush confronted his counterterrorism czar, Richard A. Clarke, and in no uncertain terms, pressed Mr. Clark to find a connection between the 9/11 attacks and Iraq, to the latter's dismay. Earlier that day, Mr. Wolfowitz again raised the possibility of bombing Iraq in retaliation for the 9/11 attacks. Apparently, Iraq hosted more targets of opportunity than did Afghanistan, the locale from which al-Qaeda operated. See Richard A. Clarke, *Against All Enemies*, pp. 30-33 (Free Press 2004). Later that day, President George W. Bush confronted Mr. Clark and indicated that the former wanted a rationale by which to attack Iraq in response to the 9/11 attacks. On December 28, 2001, General Tommy Franks, then commanding the war in Afghanistan, secretly briefed President Bush, National Security Advisor Condolezza Rice, Secretary of State Colin Powell, Secretary of Defense Donald Rumsfeld, and C.I.A. Chief George Tenet about secret plans for the invasion of Iraq. Bob Woodward, *Plan of Attack*, pp. 52-66 (Simon & Scheuster 2004).

3. For a more thorough discussion of the *Wahhabi* belief in *Jihad*, and of offensive and defensive *Jihad*, see the Forward.

4. Jarir ibn Atiyah ibn l-Khatafa, b. 650, one of the greatest poets of the Umayyad period, known for his sharp barbs aimed at rivals. "Jarir," *Encyclopaedia Britannica Online* at www.britannica.com/eb/article/?tocId=9043384.

5. OBL lists some of the names of the 9/11 hijackers. A complete list of their names follows: From Boston: American Flight 11 - Muhammad Atta, Abdul Aziz Omari, Satam al Suqami, Wail al Shehri, and Waleed al Shehri; United Flight 175: Marwan al Shehhi, Fayez Banihammad, Mohand al Shehri, Ahmed al Ghamdi, and Hamza al Ghamdi; From Washington Dulles: American Flight 77 – Khalid al Mihdhar, Majed Moqed, Hani Hanjour, Nawaf al Hazmi, and Salem al Hazmi (brothers); Newark, New Jersey: United Flight 93: Saeed al Ghamdi, Ahmed al Nami, Ahmad al Haznawi, and Ziad Jarrah. *The 9/11 Commission Report,* pp. 1-4 (Authorized Edition 2004).

6. A *Hadith* is an authenticated "tradition" of the Prophet Muhammad, (PBUH), that exemplifies his words and deeds. See the Forward for a discussion of *Hadith* scholarship.

7. OBL apparently paraphrases the Prophet Muhammad (PBUH). "Do not seek a coward for advice for he makes things look harder for you; and do not ask a stingy man for advice for he will fail you... And let it be know to you that cowardice, stinginess, and greediness are traits that have mistrust (in God) in common." Sheikh Mirza Hussein (b. 1838), *Mustadrak Al-Wasail*, from the book of guidelines of companionship, www.imamreza.net/eng/imamreza.php?id=1012.

8. As previously stated herein, defensive *Jihad* is invoked when the lands of Islam are attacked by non-believers (non-Muslims). In response, Muslims are supposed to rise up and defend the lands against the attackers. Under appropriate circumstances, killing is justified in the cause of defensive *Jihad*. OBL is saying to those who do not accept the necessity of killing during defensive *Jihad* to refrain from dissuading those who are convinced that killing is appropriate. Again, for a discussion of defensive *Jihad* see Anonymous, *Imperial Hubris: Why the West Is Losing the War on Terror*, pp. 6-8, 17 (Brassey's, Inc. 2004). Of course, OBL has said that he is engaged in a defensive *Jihad* against the military encroachments of the United States and Western military forces in Saudi Arabia and in the Arabian (Persian) Gulf states generally, and of course, in Afghanistan and Iraq. He also includes the occupation of Palestinian lands by Israel and attacks on Muslims anywhere in the world as sufficient to invoke defensive *Jihad*. The Editor is unable to locate the quoted material.

9. The verse is widely known and was authored by the Tunisian poet Abou al Kacem

Echebbi (1909-1934), see Webspawner at www.webspawner.com/users/binkhaldun6.

10. *Hadith al Qudsi* 3/3, Chapter 22, *IslamAcademy.com*, www.islamacademy.com/modules/wfsection/article.php?articleid=6&page=2. *Hadith al Qudsi* are sayings of the Prophet (PBUH) related through divine inspiration. Only the *Holy Quran* contains verbatim words of God. The *Hadith* are not verbatim, unlike the *Holy Quran*. See generally, "Fatwa Bank," *IslamOnLine.net,* January 9, 2003; www.islamonline.net/Fatwa/english/FatwaDisplay.asp?hFatwaID=20516. Recall that *Hadiths* are authenticated traditions (words and deeds) of the Prophet Muhammad (PBUH). See the Forward for more information.

11. By "agent governments," OBL refers to the governments of the countries from which the 9/11 hijackers hailed. He brands these governments as "agents" of the West because of their acceptance of Western values or the presence of Western military forces on their soil, as well as their questionable Islamic credentials. Twelve of the thirteen hijackers used as "muscle" to overcome the passengers were from Saudi Arabia: Satam al Suqami, Wail al Shehri, Waleed al Shehri, Abdul Aziz al Omari, Ahmed al Ghamdi, Hamza al Ghamdi, Mohand al Shehri, Majed Moqed, Salem al Hazmi, Saeed al Ghamdi, Ahmad al Haznawi, and Ahmed al Nami. Fayez Banihammad came from the UAE. Of the pilots: Mohamed Atta was Egyptian, Ziad Jarrah was born in Lebanon, Marwan al Shehi was born in the UAE, Nawaf al Hazmi was a Saudi (his brother was Salem al Hazmi), Khalid al Mihdhar was a Saudi, and Hani Hanjour was born in Saudi Arabia. See generally *The 9/11 Commission Report, supra*, p. 231 and Appendix.

12. *Hadith*, "A believer is not bitten from the same hole twice." Reported by Al-Bukhari, Muslim, Ahmad, Abu dawood, and ibn Majah (*Hadith* scholars). See "Certain Qualities of Believers," *Al-Jazeerah.info*, www.aljazeerah.info/Islam/Islamic%20subjects/2004%20subjects/June/Certain%20Qualities%20of%20Believers,%20Adil%20Salahi.htm; also, Abdullah Jibrit Oyekan, "Accommodating *Kufr* [non-believers]," *Salaam*, www.salaam.co.uk/knowledge/kufr.php. Sahih Muslim, *Hadith*, Book 042, No. 7137: see www.usc.edu/dept/MSA/.

13. Consistent with the *Wahhabi* creed, OBL advocates the creation of an Islamic nation that knows no national boundaries and that adopts the *Sharia*, i.e., Islamic law, as the law of the *Ummah* (Islamic nation). Presently, Sudan has adopted the *Sharia* as its rule of law, and in many Islamic countries, e.g., in Egypt, *Sharia* is the rule of law applied to family matters like marriage, divorce, and estate distribution.

14. *Ulema* refers to Islamic scholars, including clerics. OBL obviously rejects those of the *Ulema* who reject his views. More information can be found in the Forward.

15. OBL refers to Muhammad's (PBUH) daughter, Fatima. *Hadith* of Bukhari, vol. 8, Book 81, No. 779.

16. Islam is based on Five Pillars. More information can be found in the Forward regarding these pillars..

17. Without exception, OBL views the Middle East regimes as corrupt and ruled by apostates. He states that government- sponsored Imams pay lip-service to Islam; and religious rituals are permitted so long as they pose no threat to the government.

18. Abu-Jahl was Amr bin-Hisham, an early enemy of the Prophet Muhammad (PBUH), who led the Meccan army against the Prophet (PBUH) and his followers at the Battle of Badr in 624. He was killed in the battle. Abu Jahl literally means "Father of Folly," a mock name given to him by the Muslims. His real name was Amr ibn Hisham. See "Abu Jahl," *Comparative Index to Islam*, www.answering-islam.org.uk/Index/J/abu_jahl.html; also, "The Avowed Enemy – The Devout Mujahid," originally published in the 20th issue of *Nida/ul Islam Magazine*, September-October 1997, at www.islam.org.au/articles/20/ikrimah.htm.OBL refers specifically to a well-known *Hadith*: Sahih Bukhari, *Hadith*, Vol. 4, Book 53, No. 369, at www.usc.edu/dept/MSA/.

19. OBL again refers to the corrupt regimes of the Middle East, especially those of the Arabian (Persian) Gulf States, i.e., the "desert Arabs," who failed to join the *Mujahideen* (Islamic warriors) and instead spent dozens of years "preparing" to join.

20. *Holy Quran*, 9 (At-Taubah [The Repentance]):46.
21. *Holy Quran*, 8 (Al-Anfal [The Spoils of War]):24.
22. *Holy Quran*, 9 (At-Taubah [The Repentance]):24.

CHAPTER 15

1. Broadcast by *Al-Jazeera Television* on October 12, 2003.
2. *Holy Quran*, 66 (At-Tahrim [The Prohibition]:9.
3. Al-Bukhari, Vol. 3, *Hadith* 660. "He who is killed while protecting his property is a martyr, and he who is killed while defending his family, or his blood, or his religion is a martyr." Narrated by Sa'id Ibn Sayet, *Hadith* 4754, Abu Dawud. See Mamarinta Omar Mababaya and Dr. Norlain D. Mababaya, "Islam: The Complete Way of Life (Some Proofs from the Qur'an and the Authentic Hadith)," at www.wefound.org/texts/Islam_files/IslamComplete.htm, at p. 9 of 58 pages.

4. Saad bin Ibaadah, a leader of the Medina-based Khazraj tribe, who was a competitor of Abu Bakr for appointment as Caliph after the death of Muhammad (PBUH) in 632. Abu Bakr was appointed. Saad never recognized Abu Bakr's appointment for the duration of the latter's life, nor did he pray or perform the *Haj* (pilgrimage) to Mecca during the leadership of Abu Bakr.

Muhammad bin Abdullah bin Hasan al-Muthanna bin Hasan bin Ali was promoted by his father as the *Mahdi** during the second Abbasid caliphate in ca. 770 and was a Shi'ite opponent of Mansur, the second Abbasid caliph.

* The concept of the "Mahdi" (the guided one) differs between Sunni and Shi'ite Islam. In the Sunni tradition, the Mahdi will appear during the last days of the world and will precede the second coming of Jesus. Each will work together to bring justice on Earth. Jesus will slay the false Messiah, known as the *Dajjal*. Jesus will then marry, have a family, and die on Earth.

The Shi'ites believe that the Mahdi is the twelfth (last) Imam (in the context of religious leader) who is alive but in hiding after his birth in 868. He went into occultation at age five. At the end of times, he will return to Earth, destroy the false Messiah and usher in an era of peace.

See "Mahdi," *Wikipedia, the Free Encyclopedia*, at www.en.wikipedia.org/wiki/Mahdi; and "The Messiah and the Mahdi: One and the Same Person," *Alislam*, at www.alislam.org/library/mandm.html.

Khalid ibn al Walid, the most famous of the Muslim generals, headed Caliph Abu Bakr's armies and enforced Abu Bakr's rule throughout the then Islamic Empire. Al Muthanna ibn Harithah, chief of Banu Shayban, a clan of Banu Bakr, had distinguished himself in the battle of Dhu Qar against the Persians. He was responsible for reconciling the clans of Banu Bakr when Khalid entered their territories. Al Muthanna, his brother Al-Muanna, and their men were allowed to join the Islamic army, which then defeated the Persians in 633 in present-day Kuwait.

Yusuf al-Din aka Salah al-Din (1138 - 1193) ("Saladin" in the West) was the Kurd (note OBL's appeal to the Kurdish minority in Iraq) who led the Muslim armies in the reconquest of Jerusalem from the Crusaders in the year 1187. The Crusaders of the First Crusade had seized that holy venue in the year 1099. See Dr. Mansoor Alam, "Islamic History: Part 1 – The Death of the Prophet (PBUH)," www.tolueislam.com/Bazm/Mansoor/MA_history_1.htm; "['Aalim Network QR] Muhammad Dhu-Nafs Azakiya," August 31, 1997, question answered by Syed Muhammad Rizvi, www.al-islam.org/organizations/aalimnetwork/msg00430.html;"Al Futuhat: The Muslims' Historical Campaigns," *Muslim American Society*, September 5, 2003, www.masnet.org/history. asp?id=423; Karen Armstrong, *Holy War,* pp. 235, 257-260 (Second Anchor Books Edition December 2001).

5. Again, for a thorough discussion of the meaning and nature of *Jihad*, see the Forward. Suffice it to say herein that to OBL *Jihad* signifies far more than an internal "struggle." He is speaking of defensive *Jihad*, or holy war, against those infidels who have attacked Islam.

6. After the Prophet Muhammad's (PBUH) death in 632, the Islamic empire expanded both

West and East. To the East, Al Hajjaj ibn Yusuf al Thaqafi (714) had been appointed governor of the Eastern provinces in 694. His generals conquered Kabul in 700 A.D; Balkh in 705; Bukhara, Samarkand, and Khawarizm (modern Khiva) between 710 and 712 ; Farghanah in 713 ; Kashgar (Chinese Turkestan) in 715 ; Al-Shas (Tashkand) in 751 ; and entered Sind (India) in 711. He advanced to Nirun (modern Hyderabad) and reached as far as Multan. "Al-Futuhat:The Muslims' Historical Campaigns," *Muslim American Society*, September 5, 2003, www.masnet.org/history. asp?id=423

7. In OBL's *Wahhabi* view of Islam, *Jihad* is seen as the sixth pillar of the religion and an obligation of all Muslims. Again, see the Forward for a thorough discussion of the *Wahhabi* view of *Jihad* as Islam's sixth pillar.

8. By Nation, OBL refers to the *"Ummah,"* Arabic for the people, more specifically, the nation of Islam, i.e., the "nation" of true believers (Muslims) without regard to national boundaries. See the Forward for a discussion of the *Ummah*.

9. OBL rails at those Iraqis who have chosen to participate in the local legislative councils organized by the Coalition Provisional Authority, the administrative authority led by Paul Bremmer III and imposed by the occupying U.S. and coalition military forces. See generally, Major Scott Caldwell, "Councils Give Citizens a Voice in Neighborhood Government," *Defend America News*, U.S. Department of Defense News About [sic] the War on Terrorism, April 27, 2004, at www.defendamerica.mil/articles/apr2004/a042704b.html.

The term "astray" has special significance in Islam in that it refers to the Al-Fatihah, the first chapter (*Sura*) of the *Holy Quran*, comprising only seven verses. These verses are recited together as the single, most recited prayer in Islam. It would be repeated before, during, and after regular prayers, before meals, before travel, during stressful times, during thankful times, and most probably is on the lips of every Muslim at death.

Holy Quran, 1 (Al-Fatihah [The Opening]):1 – 6.

10. The Baath (Arabic for "insurrection" or "renaissance") Party was formerly known as the Baath Arab Socialist Party. It is a secular, Arab nationalist party. Its early proponents were Zaki al-Arsuzi, Salah al-Din al-Bitar, and Michel Aflaq. The party was officially founded in Damascus, Syria, on April 7, 1947. The Iraqi branch was formed in 1954. In 1963, the Baath Party came to power in Syria and in Iraq. The Syrian and Iraqi parties differed in ideology and became separate entities. The Baath Party's rule in Iraq came to an end with the toppling of the regime of Saddam Hussein (arrested on December 14, 2003, by United States military forces in May 2003.) The Baath Party remains in power in Syria, led by the strongman Bashir Assad. See "Baath Party," *The Syrian Encyclopedia*, at www.damascus-online.com/se/hist/baath_party.htm.

The Kurds of Iraq have several secularized political parties: the Kurdistan Democratic Party, the Patriotic Union of Kurdistan, the Kurdistan Women Union, the Kurdistan Toilers Party, the Kurdistan Socialist Democrat Party, the Democratic National Union of Kurdistan, the Kurdistan Liberation Party, to name a few. See T.F. Mills, et. Al., "Iraqi Kurdistan: Political Parties," September 27, 1997, at www.flag.de/FOTW/flags/krd%7Diq.html; and "Kurdistan," November 12, 2004, at www.politicalresources.net/kurdistan.htm.

11. Hamid Karzai was declared the President of Afghanistan on October 26, 2004 [after a national election]. He is widely viewed as having been assured of his office by strong support from the United States after its overthrow of the Taliban regime in 2001. For example, the U.S. government provided him with helicopters with which to canvass Afghanistan. He was the only presidential candidate with such means of transportation. President Karzai remains mostly in Kabul protected by American special forces troops and employees of the Vinnel Corporation, a security company headquartered in the United States and long suspected as a Central Intelligence Agency front. The Taliban have regrouped in Afghanistan and continue to mount an insurgency against the Karzai government. Notwithstanding Mr. Karzai's election, Afghanistan remains riven by dissention and violent confrontations between the government and its many warlords

and between the warlords themselves, and between the government and a revitalized Taliban. See "Official: Karzai Wins Afghanistan's Presidential Election," *Aljazeera.com*, October 26, 2004, at www.aljazeera.com.

Mahmoud Abbas was temporarily appointed as Prime Minister of the Palestinian Authority in March, 2003, after Palestine Liberation Organization Chairman Yasser Arafat was placed under house arrest in his compound at Ramallah, West Bank of the Occupied Territories by Israeli Defense Forces. Mr. Abbas resigned the following October after a power struggle with Mr. Arafat. On November 11, 2004, Mr. Abbas was elected as Chairman of the Palestinian Liberation Organization after Mr. Arafat's death. In January, 2005, Mr. Abbas was elected President of the Palestinian Authority. See "Mahmoud Abbas," *Wikipedia, the Free Encyclopedia*, www. en.wikipedia.org/wiki/Mahmoud_Abbas; "Profile: Mahmoud Abbas," *BBC News*, January 10, 2005, at www.news.bbc.co.uk/2/hi/middle_east/1933453.stm.

12. The "road map" refers to a plan to achieve Israeli-Palestinian peace propounded by the "quartet" (the United States, the European Union, Russia, and the United Nations), first outlined in a speech by President George W. Bush on June 24, 2002. The *Intifada* refers to the *Al-Aqsa, or Second, Intifada* that began on September 8, 2000, when the then Israeli opposition leader Ariel Sharon and 1000 of his bodyguards provocatively visited the Noble Sanctuary (*Al-Haram Ash-Sharif* in Arabic) (aka the Temple Mount, *Har HaBayt* in Hebrew) in the Old City of Jerusalem. More about the *Intifada* can be viewed in the Forward. See generally, "Road Map for Peace," *Wikipedia, the Free Encyclopedia*, www.en.wikipedia.org/wiki/Road_map_for-peace and /wiki/Al-Asqa_Intifada.

13. Besides the Islamic youth, OBL outlines roles for all Muslims in defensive *Jihad*. He relies on one of the most well-known *Hadiths** in Islam. Sahih Muslim, *Hadith*, Book 001, No. 0081: See: www.usc.edu/dept/MSA/.

14. The term "*Mujahideen*" refers to Islamic warriors.

15. Sahih Bukhari, *Hadith*, Vol 1, Book 2, No. 35, See "Interesting Quotes from the Hadith on Jihad," Christian Apologetics & Research Ministry, www.carm.org/islam/Hadith_Jihad.htm, See also www.usc.edu/dept/MSA/.

16. The Rabia, Mudar and Kurdish are among the dominant tribes/clans located in Iraq. In the Iraqi culture, the people tend to bond with particular groups: family, tribe, clan, village, etc. Tribal-clan loyalties are important because "[s]haming is the primary instrument with which Iraqi Arab society enforces conformity." Kurdish tribal practices are not unlike those of the Iraqi Arab tribes; however, the Kurds are not Arabs. Ethnically, they are more closely related to the Iranians. They inhabit portions of Iraq, Iran, Syria, Armenia, and Turkey. "Kurds," *Columbia Encyclopedia, Sixth Edition, 2001*, www.bartleby.com/65/Kurds.html; "Societal Framework," *Globalsecurity. org*, www.globalsecurity.org/military/world/iraq/society.htm.

17. OBL obviously refers to the September 11, 2001, attacks on the World Trade Center. The human and economic costs of the 9/11 attacks were enormous by any standard. 2,792 people were killed outright. In September, 2003, the world-wide cost of 9/11 was estimated to have been one trillion dollars. Of that sum, $500,000,000,000 was borne by the United States alone. Business Staff, "Sept. 11 Economic Toll: $1 Trillion," *The Oakland Press, Online Edition*, September 7, 2003.

18. In fiscal 2003, the United States' annual budget deficit was actually $374.8 Billion. *Financial Statements of the United States Government for the Years Ended September 30, 2003, and September 20, 2002*. See also Sue Kirchhoff, "Federal Deficit Hits Record $374.2 Billion," *USA Today*, October 20, 2003.

19. These are Iraqi provinces over which the Iraqi government and the United States and coalition forces exercised little or no control in October 2003. For example, the city of Fallouja is located in Anbar province and was only wrested from the control of the Iraqi insurgency in mid-November, 2004, at a cost to the United States Marines, who led the attack on Fallouja, of

71 killed and 623 wounded. See Patrick J. McDonnell and John Hendren, "Fallouja Fight Among Deadliest in Years for US; Last Month's Battle Left 71 American Troops Dead and 623 Injured," *Los Angeles Times*, December 2, 2004.

20. OBL refers to the First Crusade, called by Pope Urban II on November 25, 1095. Karen Armstrong, *Holy War*, p. 3 (Anchor Books 2001).

21. OBL refers to the Battle of the Trench (Ditch) in the year 627 in which the city of Medina, occupied by the Prophet Muhammad (PBUH) and his followers, was besieged by some 10,000 troops from the city of Mecca. The besiegers were led by Abu Sufyan, who had become the Prophet's arch-enemy. A trench dug around Medina by the Prophet's forces prevented Abu Sufyan's army from gaining entry into Mecca, and after repeated failed attempts, Abu Sufyan and his army returned to Mecca. www.angelfire.com/ny/dawahpage/hist3.html; "Muhammad," *Wikipedia, the Free Encyclopedia,* www.en.wikipedia.org/wiki/Muhammad.

22. Al-Tawba (Taubah) is Sura (Chapter) 9 (The Repentence) also (The Ultimatum); and Al-Anfal (The Spoils of War) is Sura 8 of the *Holy Quran*.

23. In all of these venues, Muslims are under attack. For a more complete discussion of Chechnya, Kashmir, and the Philippines, please see the Forward.

CHAPTER 16

1. Videotape broadcast on *Al-Jazeera Television* on October 18, 2003.

2. In the West, Israel is perceived as the only true democracy in the Middle East. In the Middle East, Israel is not perceived as a democracy because of the relegation of the Israeli Arabs to second-class citizenship in Israel proper and Israel's brutal occupation of the Occupied Territories. On the treatment of Israeli Arabs in Israel, see generally: "Israeli Arabs, Land and Arab Refugees," U.S. Library of Congress, December 9, 2004, at www.countrystudies.us/israel/23. htm; Barbara Piett, "Israeli Arabs Struggle to Fit in," *BBC News*, January 26, 2003, at www.news. bbc.co.uk/2/hi/middle_east/2691357.stm; and Peter Berkowitz, "Israel's House Divided," *The Weekly Standard*, April 12-19, 2004, issue, at www.weeklystandard.com/Content/Public/Articles/ 000/000/003/950mqrrk.asp.

3. OBL views all of Israel, including the Occupied Territories, as occupied Palestine.

4. The Caliphate refers to the leader of the Islamic nation, or *Ummah*. For more information about the Caliphate please see the Forward.

5. As of July 15, 2005, 1,760 United States soldiers have been killed in Iraq, and over 13,498 have been wounded. Of the killed, 1,623 of them died after May 1, 2003, the day President George W. Bush, while dressed in a U.S. Navy flight suit, declared "mission accomplished" and an end to major hostilities in Iraq while standing on the deck of a U.S. Navy aircraft carrier steaming off the coast of San Diego, California. "Casualties," *Wall Street Journal*, July 15, 2005.

6. The first full day of the Iraq War was March 20, 2003. As late as March 17, 2003, the Bush administration was concerned that the United Nations would enact a counter-resolution to clarify its opposition to the use of force in Iraq. The only U.N. action prefatory to the War was Resolution 1441, which did not authorize the use of force. As an alternative to the U.N., the Bush administration cobbled together a coalition, which it called the "coalition of the willing," consisting of thirty countries: Afghanistan, Albania, Australia, Azerbaijan, Colombia, Czech Republic, Denmark, El Salvador, Eritrea, Estonia, Georgia, Hungary, Iceland, Italy, Japan, Latvia, Lithuania, Macedonia, Netherlands, Nicaragua, Philippines, Poland, Romania, Slovakia, South Korea, Spain, Turkey, United Kingdom and Uzbekistan. Of this "coalition," only Australia, Denmark, Poland, and the United Kingdom actually provided military forces for the War. After hostilities ceased, some other countries sent military forces to assist in reconstruction, but for the most part the coalition has significantly eroded since March of 2003. For example, Spain, the Dominican Republic, and Honduras have withdrawn their forces, and Poland intends to do so in the near future. Costa Rica has asked to be removed from the list. The coalition did not achieve

the desired goal of legitimizing the Iraq War in the eyes of most of the world. At this writing, the Bush administration continues to try to engage the U.N. in the rebuilding of Iraq while his coalition continues to disintegrate.

See generally, Bob Woodward, *Plan of Attack*, pp. 364-365, 401 (Simon & Schuster 2004); Prof. Stephen Zunes, "President Bush Fails to Make His Case," *AlterNet*, October 8, 2002, at www.alternet.org/waroniraq/14255/; Prof. Stephen Zunes, "UN Resolution Does Not Authorize US to Use Force Against Iraq," *Common Dreams News Center*, November 14, 2002, at www.commondreams.org/views02/1114-03.htm; and Steve Schifferes, "US Names 'Coalition of the Willing,'" *BBC News*, March 18, 2003, at www.news.bbc.co.uk/2/hi/americas/2862343.stm; "Members of the 'Coalition of the Willing,'" *Fahrenheit [9/11 by Michael Moore]*, October 7, 2004, at www.newsaic.com/f911chap6-7.html; and "Italy Plans Withdrawal, Further Eroding U.S.-Led Coalition," Associated Press, *MSNBC.com*, March 15, 2005, at www.msnbc.com.

7. The reference is to Abd al-Malik, the fifth Umayyd Caliph. He was born in 646 and died in 705. He reigned as Caliph between 685 and 705. His early reign was characterized by Byzantine intrusions into his provinces and an uprising in 682, who occupied Mecca and declared himself Caliph. In 692, Mecca was re-conquered and Al-Zubayr killed. See "Abd al-Malik B. Marwan (646-705), The Fifth Umayyad Caliph, Reigned 685-705," at www.princeton.edu/~batke/itl/denise/abdmalik.htm; and "Abd al-Malik," *Wikipedia, the Free Encyclopedia*, October 10, 2004, last modified, at www.en.wikipedia.org/wiki/Abd-al_ibn_Marwan.

8. Kuwait was and remains a staging venue for the insertion of United States military forces into the Iraq theater of operations. See "Kuwait Is US Key Partner in Combating Terrorism: Rumsfeld," *China View*, December 9, 2004, at www.news.xinhuanet.com/english/2004-12/09/content_2311126.htm; and Brian Ballou, "Disgruntled Soldiers Put Rumsfeld on Defensive," *Boston Herald*, December 9, 2004, at www.news.bostonherald.com/international/view.bg?articleid=57939.

9. See endnotes 5 and 6, *infra*. The Bush administration's primary stated rationale for the Iraq War was Iraq's possession of weapons of mass destruction. No such weapons were found after the conclusion of the War. Controversy continues to swirl around the question whether the administration "wagged the dog" in declaring war on Iraq. See generally, Byron York, "The Truth About Bush's 'Lies,'" *National Review Online*, June 16, 2003, www.nationalreview.com/york/york060303.asp; and Bill Nichols, "U.N.: Iraq Had No WMD After 1994," *USA* Today, March 2, 2003, at www.usatoday.com/news/world/iraq/2004-03-02-un-wmd_x.htm. See also the Forward, where Deputy Secretary of Defense Paul Wolfowitz is quoted as saying that the WMD rationale was merely a convenient consensus-builder.

10. OBL obviously refers to the attacks of September 11, 2001, on the World Trade Center in New York City and on the Pentagon in Washington, D.C.

11. For OBL's most immediate post-9/11 published statement, see his October 7, 2001, statement, *infra*. Prior to his October 7th statement, he gave an interview to a South Asian publication in which he denied any involvement in 9/11. See OBL's interview with *Ummat Newspaper*, Karachi, Pakistan, September 28, 2001, reprinted in English at www.robert-fisk.com/usama_interview_ummat.htm.

12. OBL refers to his stated intention to remove all United States and Western military forces (which he views as the new Crusaders) from the sites of the Holy Places, i.e., the cities of Mecca and Medina in Saudi Arabia, as well as from the Arabian Gulf States themselves.

CHAPTER 17

1. OBL statement broadcast on *Al-Jazeera Television* on January 4, 2004.

2. More information about *Jihad* and Mustafa Kemel Ataturk can be found in the Forward.

3. The *Ummah* means the Islamic nation without regard to national boundaries.

4. This refers to the overwhelming Christianity of the U.S. and its coalition partners.

5. More information regarding the Caliphate can be seen in the Forwad.

6. More information regarding the Bush administration's rationale for launching the Iraq War and more specifically Mr. Wolfowitz's comments about the rationale used for the war can be seen in the Forward.

7. This mosque is located in Jerusalem on the Noble Sanctuary (*Al-Haram Ash-Sharif*), also known as the Temple Mount in the West. More information regarding Al-Quds and The Noble Sanctuary can be viewed in the Forward and in endnote 12 of OBL's Statement of October 12, 2003.

8. More information regarding *Mujahideen* and the Road Map for Peace," can be found in the Forward.

9. OBL refers to the Arabian (Persian) Gulf States such as Saudi Arabia, Kuwait, United Arab Emirates, Qatar, etc.

10. More information regarding the original Crusades can be found in the Forward.

11. Muhammad (PBUH) sent messengers to the *Ghasasinah*, an Arab tribe under the Roman Empire near the Syrian border. The Prophet (PBUH) asked the people to convert to Islam, but they refused and killed the messengers. They were then attacked and defeated by the Muslims. The battle occurred at a place named *Mou'tata* in the eighth month of the *Hijra*, which means migration and refers to Muhammad's (PBUH) immigration from the city of Mecca to the city of Medina in the year 622. In the year 638, the Muslim calendar was adopted, designating the year of the *Hijra* as the first year of the new Muslim calendar. Jamil Abdul-Razzak, "History of Islam, Idris Mosque at www.idrismosque.com/history.html; "Hijra (Islam)," *Wikipedia, the Free Encyclopedia*, at www.en.wikipedia.org/wiki/Hijra_(Islam).

12. OBL refers to the Jewish occupation of Jerusalem and of the occupation of Iraq by United States and coalition forces as a result of the continuing Iraq War.

13. OBL consistently refers to the Saudi Arabian cities of Mecca and Medina as the Two Holy Places. More information regarding these two cities can be found in the Forward.

14. Here, OBL is criticizing the official *Ulema*. More information regarding the *Ulema* can be found in the Forward.

15. OBL refers to the 1990 invasion of Kuwait by Iraq and the response by the neighboring countries, including Saudi Arabia, which invited the United States and Western coalition forces into their venues in order to liberate Kuwait in what became known as the 1991 Persian Gulf War.

16. See the "Joint Defense and Economic Cooperation Treaty Between the States of the Arab League," June 17, 1950, February 2, 1951, and February 16, 1952, at www. jewishvirtuallibrary.org/jsource/Peace/arabdef.html. See also, Abdullatif Al-Mannawi, Ashraq "Drama as Arab League Summit," *Asharq Alawsat, Arab News, [cited at] Al-Jazeerah News*, March 2, 2003, at *aljazeerah.info*. The article documents the March 2, 2003, Arab League meeting at which the leaders from the twenty-two nations comprising the Arab League strongly opposed the anticipated attack on Iraq by the United States and its limited "coalition of the willing" after having failed to achieve the United Nation's Security Council's consensus in support of military action against Iraq.

17. In unleashing the Iraq War, the United States gained tacit permission from Saudi Arabia, Jordan, Kuwait, Qatar, and Bahrain to use bases located in their countries from which to conduct military activities in support of the War. Bob Woodward, *Plan of Attack*, at pp. 112, 136, 230, 264, and 330 (Simon & Schuster 2004). General Tommy Franks actually commanded the War from the Prince Sultan Air Base in Saudi Arabia. *Id.* at p. 378.

18. OBL means the general prohibition of a Muslim killing a Muslim, or alternatively, a Muslim country making war on another Muslim country.

Holy Quran, 4 (Al-Nisa [The Women]:29.

19. Saddam Hussein was arrested by United States Army personnel on December 14, 2003. "Saddam Hussein Arrested in Iraq," *BBC News*, December 14, 2003.

20. Iraq invaded Iran on September 22, 1980. The war lasted until August 20, 1988. The Shah of Iran was overthrown in 1979 and replaced by a theocracy led by the Supreme Leader Ayatollah Khomeini. For an extensive treatment of the United States' support for Saddam Hussein during the Iran-Iraq War, see "Shaking Hands with Saddam Hussein: The U.S. Tilt toward Iraq, 1980-1984," *National Security Archive Electronic Briefing Book No. 82*, Joyce Battle, Editor, February 25, 2003, George Washington University, at www.gwu.edu/~nsarchiv/NSAEBB/NSAEBB82/; and "Iran-Iraq War," *Wikipedia, the Free Encyclopedia*, at www.en.wikipedia.org/wiki/Iran-Iraq_War.

21. OBL refers to the Gulf Cooperation Council ("GCC"), consisting of the Arabian (Persian) Gulf States of Bahrain, Kuwait, Oman, Qatar, Saudi Arabia, and the UAE (United Arab Emirates). The Council was formed on May 25, 1981, for the ostensible purpose of "coordination," a euphemism for security. Political disagreements have hindered efforts at collective security and interchangeability of equipment and shared commands. The then pending Iran-Iraq War was the catalyst for the formation of the GCC. Though joint forces have been organized, there roles remain vague, especially regarding whether they may intervene in domestic emergencies. See "Gulf Cooperation Council [GCC]," *GlobalSecurity.org*, at www.globalsecurity.org/military/world/gulf/gcc.htm.

22. Kharijite (Arabic: *Khawarji*, meaning those who seceded) Islam refers to one of the earliest Shi'ite (*Shiia*) sects that left the followers of Ali, cousin and son-in-law of the Prophet Muhammad (PBUH). The Kharijites rebelled against Ali because of the willingness of the followers of Ali to arbitrate the then pending dispute with Mu'awiya, governor of Damascus, as to who would be the new Caliph after the Caliph Uthman was killed in 656. The Kharijites believed that the choice was a matter of divine judgment. A struggle for succession ensued between Ali and Mu'awiya. Ali defeated the Kharijite rebellion, but their movement survived and one of their number assassinated Ali, who had risen to become Caliph, in 661. Ironically, and tragically, the Kharijites pioneered the killing of Muslims whom they considered to be heretics. The sect was concentrated in Southern Iraq in the late 7th and early 8th Centuries.

See www.globalsecurity.org/military/intro/islam.htm and /islam-kharijite.htm and /islam-salafi.htm.

23. On May 12, 2003, "Al Qaeda suicide car bombs struck three expatriate compounds in Riyadh," Saudi Arabia. Anonymous, *Imperial Hubris: Why the West Is Losing the War on Terror*, p. 97 (Brassey's, Inc. 2004).

24. *Al-Hall Wal Aked*, literally, "Those who loose and tie" – a reference to righteous people who can remove and appoint rulers in the Islamic tradition. See Muhidden Ivn Arabi, *Alfutouhat Qurtobi*, pp. 908, 2119, 2568, 2578, and 3102. And in *Tafseer Al Qurtobi* at p. 219.

25. *Sunnah* refers to the example (i.e., words and deeds) of the Prophet Muhammad (PBUH), as recorded in the *Hadiths*, compilations of the traditions of the Prophet (PBUH).

26. See endnote 21 of OBL's statement of February 11, 2003, infra, for a discussion of the Muslim conquest of the Eastern Romans.

CHAPTER 18

1. Originally broadcast by *Al-Jazeera Television* on April 15, 2004.

2. Of course, "September 11th" refers to the al-Qaeda attacks on the World Trade Center in New York City and on the Pentagon in Washington, D.C., on September 11, 2001. "March 11th" refers to the coordinated bombings of four commuter trains at the height of the morning rush hour in Madrid, Spain, on Thursday, March 11, 2004. Members of a Moroccan Islamic Combat Group have been arrested for the bombings. No link between al-Qaeda, OBL and the Moroccan group has been established. 191 people were killed and 1,800 were wounded. The bombing occurred on the penultimate day of campaigning before the Sunday national elections. Prime Minister Jose Maria Anzar's decision to send Spanish troops to Iraq to assist the United States in the Iraq War

was highly unpopular with the Spanish public. In the aftermath of the bombings, his government was soundly defeated at the polls the following Sunday. The bombings were perceived as the catalyst for his removal, and for the subsequent recall of Spain's troops in Iraq by his successor, Socialist Jose Luis Rodriguez Zapatero. Observers consider the ouster of the Anzar government and the withdrawal of the Spanish troops from Iraq to be a political triumph for al-Qaeda. See "March 11, 2004, Madrid Attacks, *Wikipedia, the Free Encyclopedia*, March 11, 2004, www. en.wikipedia.org/wiki/11_March_2004_Madrid_attacks; see also, James A. Phillips, "Spain's Retreat After the Madrid Bombings Rewards Terrorism, *The Heritage Foundation*, March 16, 2004, Web Memo No. 448 at www.heritage.org/Research/Europe/wm448.cfm.

 3. Ahmad Yassin was the founder and spiritual leader of Hamas, acronym for *Harak Al-Muqawamah Al-Islamiyyah* (Arabic for "Islamic Resistance Movement"). On March 22, 2004, in the occupied Gaza Strip, the 66-year-old wheelchair-bound paraplegic was assassinated by a missile launched from an Israeli attack helicopter as he was leaving a mosque after dawn prayers. Seven Palestinian bystanders also died in the attack. Israel called the assassination another step in its policy of "extrajudicial execution" of its perceived enemies. Sheikh Yassin, as he was referred to because of his role as an Islamic cleric, and Muhammad Taha founded Hamas in late 1987. Hamas seeks to end the Israeli occupation of the Gaza Strip and the West Bank as well as the state of Israel itself. It regards all Palestinian lands as an Islamic homeland. Its military wing is known as the *Izz al-Din al –Qassam* Brigade. It also supports a variety of social service activities in the Occupied Territories such as orphanages, hospitals, and mosques. Canada and the United States have designated Hamas as a terrorist organization. See "Terrorist Group Profiles: Hamas," Naval Postgraduate School, Dudley Knox Library, at www.library.nps.navy.mil/home/tgp/hamas. htm; "Hamas," *Wikipedia, the Free Encyclopedia*, at www.en.wikipedia.org/wiki/Hamas; "World Continues to Protest Sheikh Yassin's Assassination, *Al-Jazeera Information Center*, March 28, 2004, at www.aljazeerah.info/; and "Amnesty International Strongly Condemns the Assassination of Sheikh Yassin," March 22, 2004, at www.amnesty.nl/persberichten/NK-PB0428.shtml.

 4. As of November 13, 2004, Haliburton (a company formerly headed by Vice President Dick Cheney), through its subsidiary Brown and Root, had been awarded contracts worth more than $1.7 billion by the Pentagon for services in support of the Iraq War. The company also anticipates further earnings on the magnitude of hundreds of millions of dollars under a no-bid contract awarded by the U.S. Army Corps of Engineers. Michael Dobbs, "Halliburton's Iraq Contracts Exceed $1.7 Billion," *Washington Post*, August 28, 2003.

 5. OBL is referring to the March 11th bombings in Madrid.

 6. The Soviets first invaded Afghanistan in the winter of 1979. The Russians first invaded oil-rich Chechnya in 1994, withdrew in 1996, and then invaded again in 1999. They remain there fighting a vicious war against Islamic rebels seeking independence. See "Chechnya Goes to Polls in Wake of Airline Terror Claim," *Sunday Herald*, August 29, 2004, at www.sundayherald. com/44391.

 7. The United States invaded Afghanistan on October 7, 2001. It invaded Iraq on March 20, 2003.

 8. OBL refers to the stationing of United States troops in Saudia Arabia prefatory to, during, and after the 1991 Persian Gulf War.

 9. Operation Restore Hope was the name of the United States military incursion into Somalia in 1993. On October 3, 1993, militia loyal to Somali warlord Farah Aideed shot down two U.S. Blackhawk helicopters over downtown Mogadishu, killing 18 U.S. Rangers. The U.S. withdrew its forces from Somalia shortly after the incident. See Richard A. Clarke, *Against All Enemies*, pp. 84-89 (Free Press 2004); and "Somalia," *Military.com*, at www.military.com/. See the Forward.

 10. Every key European nation, including France and Germany, who opposed the Iraq War, rejected OBL's offer of a peace treaty. Jill Lawless (*Associated Press*), "al-Qaida Treaty Rejected,"

San Francisco Examiner, April 16, 2004, www.sfexaminer.com.

CHAPTER 19

1. Excerpts broadcast on Al-Jazeera Television on October 29, 2004, two days before American voters cast their votes in the 2004 United States Presidential election. An almost unfathomable complete translation was offered by the United States government and reprinted in the *Washington Post* on November 1, 2004. This Editor now offers the reader an understandable English translation. This is the famous statement that OBL directed to America during the final week of the 2000 Presidential election. Senator John Kerry, President George W. Bush's opponent, has said that he believes that the statement influenced the outcome of the election in the President's favor. See "Exclusive: Kerry Says UBL Tape Cost Him Election," *Fox News Channel*, November 21, 2004, at www.foxnews.com/story/0,2933,139060,00.html.

2. See the Forward for a discussion of the selection of the English translation of the Holy Quran for use in this book as well as a discussion about the *Wahhabi* creed of Sunni Islam, the dominant creed on the Arabian Peninsula.

3. President George W. Bush's Speech to a Joint Session and Congress and to the American People, September 20, 2001: "They hate our freedoms... of religion... of speech... to vote and assemble and disagree..." www.whitehouse.gov/news/releases/2001/09/print/20010920-8.html.

4. The nineteen young Arab Muslim men who carried out the attacks on 9/11/2001.

5. In the tradition of Islam, any reference to a deceased person will evoke a prayer for God's mercy on them.

6. By Nation, Mr. Bin Laden refers to the *Ummah*, the world's Muslims without regard to national borders.

7. More information regarding the Lebanese Civil War can be found in the Forward.

8. More information regarding the post 1991 Gulf War sanctions against Iraq can be found in the Forward.

9. The C.I.A. was instrumental in the empowerment of the Baathist Party in Iraq in 1963, overthrowing the anti-American and anti-corporatist Abdul Karim Kassem, who led the military coup in 1958 that overthrew the Iraqi monarchy. Saddam Hussein became President of Iraq in 1979. See Richard Sanders, "Regime Change: How the C.I.A. put Saddam's Party in Power," October 24, 2002, at www.hartford-hwp.com/archives/51/217.html. See also, Gerald Butt, "Saddam Hussein Profile," *BBC News,* January 4, 2001, at www.news.bbc.co.uk/1/hi/world/middle_east/1100529.stm.

10. *Time Magazine*, interview with OBL, January 11, 1999, vol. 153, no. 1. Rahimullah Yusufzai, a journalist who worked for Pakistan's *The News* conducted the interview. No interview by anyone named Scott representing *Time Magazine* occurred in 1996. The *Time* interview may be seen at www.robert-fisk.com/usama_interview_timemagazine.htm.

11. Mr. Arnett interviews OBL in March, 1997. It may be read at the Robert Fisk website cited in the previous endnote.

12. No such meeting occurred. In 1998, OBL met with John Miller of ABC News on May 28, 1998. Likewise, it may be accessed at the Robert Fisk website cited in endnote 10.

13. This is an obvious reference to the bombing of the United States embassies in Dar es Salaam, Tanzania, and Nairobi, Kenya on August 7, 1998. More information regarding the bombing can be found in the Forward.

14. On December 29, 1992, a hotel at which U.S. troops en route to Somalia were staying. The soldiers had already left. Two Austrian tourists were killed. U.S. intelligence believes that this was Al Qaeda's first terrorist attack. See the Forward.

More information regarding the attack on the U.S.S. *Cole* can be found in the Forward.

15. Abdul Bari Atwan is the editor of *Al-Quds al Arabi* Arabic-language newspaper published in London, England. He interviewed OBL in 1996. Unfortunately, an English-language

version of the interview is not presently available.

16. Robert Fisk interviewed OBL on December 6, 1996. The reader may access the interview at Mr. Fisk's website, cited in endnote 10, *infra*.

17. The Uniting and Strengthening America by Providing Appropriate Tools Required to Intercept and Obstruct Terrorism, aka the "U.S.A. Patriot Act," enacted on October 26, 2001, Public Law 107-56. OBL's criticism of the Patriot Act strikes a responsive chord in America: see Eric Lichtblau, "Coalition Forms to Oppose Parts of Antiterrorism Law [Patriot Act]," *New York Times*, March 25, 2005.

18. Before becoming President of the United States, George W. Bush was governor of Texas. His brother, Jeb Bush, is the governor of Florida.

19. OBL refers to the U.S. presidential election of 2000, which was characterized by allegations of voter fraud in the state of Florida. The United States Supreme Court interceded and stopped the counting of ballots. George W. Bush was declared to be the winner by some 168 votes. The state's electoral votes carried him past the 270 needed to win the presidential election. See *Bush v. Gore*, 531U.S. 98 (December 12, 2000).

20. *Mujahedin* refers to an Islamic warrior. OBL refers to the Soviet invasion in Afghanistan, which began in the Winter of 1979 and ended after the signing of the Geneva Accords on April 14, 1988.

21. The estimated cost to Al Qaeda in mounting the 9/11 attack.

22. More information regarding the human and economic costs of 9/11 can be seen in the Forward.

23. Johnathan Weisman and Thomas E. Ricks, "Increase in War Funding Sought, *Washington Post*, October 26, 2004, page A01. The Bush administration is seeking an emergency allocation of $70 billion. Thus far, the Afghanistan and Iraq Wars have cost a total of $225 billion since the invasion of Iraq.

24. Muhammad Atta has been identified as the leader of the 9/11 attacks. This is the first instance of a rank having been assigned to him by Al Qaeda or OBL. A complete list of their names follows: From Boston: American Flight 11 - Muhammad Atta, Abdul Aziz Omari, Satam al Suqami, Wail al Shehri, and Waleed al Shehri; United Flight 175: Marwan al Shehhi, Fayez Banihammad, Mohand al Shehri, Ahmed al-Ghamdi, and Hamza al-Ghamdi; From Washington Dulles: American Flight 77 – Khalid al Mihdar, Majed Moqed, Hani Hanjour, Nawaf al Hazmi, and Salem al Hazmi (brothers); Newark, New Jersey: United Flight 93: Saeed al Ghamdi, Ahmed al Nami, Ahmad al Haznawi, and Ziad Jarrah. *The 9/11 Commission Report*, pp. 1-4 (Authorized Edition 2004).

25. At the moment of the 9/11 attacks, President Bush was visiting an elementary school reading a children's book entitled *My Pet Goat* to a class of children. He apparently continued to read to them after being informed of the strike against the first tower and continued to read to them until after the strike against the second tower. This sequence of events has been memorialized in real time in the Michael Moore documentary, *Fahrenheit 911* (2004). Expanding on OBL's observation, President Bush's careening course around the country in Air Force One after leaving Texas the morning of the attacks and his reluctance to return immediately to Washington gave much pause in many circles when weighing his leadership qualities. See the sequence of the immediate post-9/11 events memorialized in James Bamford, *A Pretext for War*, pp. 62-92 (Doubleday 2004); and Richard A. Clarke, *Against All Enemies*, Chapter 1 (Free Press 2004).

26. See Chapters 7 and 8 of the *9/11 Commission Report*, *supra*. Chapter 8 is aptly entitled "The System Was Blinking Red."

27. OBL is referring to the civilian casualties in the Iraq War. Although the United States government does not officially count civilian casualties in the Iraq War, recent estimates indicate that as many as 100,000 Iraqis have died since the U.S. invasion. *News@Nature.com*, October 29,

2004, "100,000 Civilians May Have Died in Iraq Conflict.") As of July 15, 2005, 1,760 American soldiers have been killed in Iraq since President Bush declared an end to hostilities on May 1, 2003, and more than 13,000 have been wounded. "Casualties," *Wall Street Journal*, July 15, 2005.

28. Sahih Bukhari, *Hadith*, Vol. 5, Book 59, No. 597: at www.usc.edu/dept/MSA/.

29. Israel frequently bombs or rockets densely populated Palestinian neighborhoods in the Occupied Territories of the West Bank and the Gaza Strip in operations aimed at the extrajudicial assassination of perceived enemies. Innocent bystanders are often killed. For an example, see "Five Palestinian Bystanders Killed, 12 Injured in an Israeli Occupation Assassination Attempt on an Activist in Gaza," *Aljazeerah.info*, August 18, 2004, at www.aljazeerah.info.

30. The Editor is unable to find the source of the quotations or the poem.

CHAPTER 20

1. This audio taped statement was originally broadcast on various internet websites on December 16, 2004.

2. By the "land of the Two Holy Mosques," OBL refers to the mosques at Mecca and Medina in Saudi Arabia. More about these cities and the *Haj* can be found in the Forward.

3. The original text refers to the "rulers of Riyadh." Riyadh is the capital of Saudi Arabia and the seat of the government of the Saudi monarchy led by the Saud royal family. Riyadh's governor is Salman, brother of King Fahd. Anthony Shadid & Steve Coll, "At a Crosroads, Saudi King Tests the Winds of Reform," *Washington Post*, August 18, 2005.

4. "*Mujahideen*," *Wordreference.com*, at www.wordreference.com/definition/mujahadeen. Please note that various accepted spellings characterize this Arabic-English transliteration, e.g., *mujahadeen, mujahidin*, etc.

5. *Holy Quran* 7 (Al-Araf [The Heights or The Wall with Elevations]):163.
Holy Quran, 4 (An-Nisa [The Women]):154.

6. *Holy Quran*, 89 (Fajr [The Break of Day]):11-14.

7. *Holy Quran*, 5 (Al Maida [The Table Spread (with Food)]):78-79.

8. Al-Hakim al Naysaburi, a *Hadith* scholar who created fifty classifications of *Hadith* and is known for his work, *Ma'rifah 'Ulum al Hadith*. See translation by *JihadUnspun.com* at www.jihadunspun.com.

9. Abu Daoud, *Hadith*, Book 37 No. 4325.

10. *Holy Quran*, 24 (An-Nur [The Light]):63.

11. *Holy Quran*, 11 (Hud [Prophet]):114.

12. Islam distinguishes between major and minor sins. More information regarding these sins can be found in the Forward.

13. *Kufr* - Infidelity, non believing in, and showing ungratefuleness to God and not believing in Him and in Islam (apostasy). See "Kufr," Islamic Glossary at www.usc.edu/dept/MSA/reference/glossary/term.KUFR.html.

14. There are ten violations, or "voiders," that strip Islam from a Muslim. More about the "ten voiders" can be seen in the Forward.

15. In April, 1994, in London, England, OBL formed the Committee for Advice and Reform (a.k.a. Advice and Reform Committee) in Saudi Arabia to prosecute reform in that country. More about the committee and OBL getting his citizenship stripped by Saudi Arabia can be seen in the Forward.

16. "There is no god but God," the fundamental monotheistic pillar of Islam.

17. *Holy Quran*, 11 (Hud [The Prophet]):112.

18. *Holy Quran*, 11 (Hud [The Prophet]):117.

19. Sahih Muslim, *Hadith*, Book 001, No. 0062: at www.usc.edu/dept/MSA/. See also, "The Hadiths, No. 21," FortyHadith.com, at www.fortyhadith.iiu.edu.my/hadith21.htm.

20. *Holy Quran*, 8 (Al-Anfal [The Spoils of War]):63.

21. *Holy Quran*, 7 (Al-Araf [The Heights or the Wall with Elevations]):96.

22. More information regarding the *Caliphate* can be viewed in the Forward.

23. More information regarding the *Rashidoon* can be viewed in the Forward.

24. More information regarding Ibn Taymiya and Wahhabism can be viewed in the Forward.

25. As previously stated in the Forward, *Wahhabis* seek to recreate the Muslim *Ummah* (Islamic nation) and to build a global Islamic community in the likeness of the first three generations of Muslims, the Companions (*Sahabah*) of the Prophet (PBUH), their immediate followers (*Tabiun*), and the followers of the *Tabiun*.

26. OBL refers to autocratic regimes that conduct elections in form but not in substance. In Yemen and Jordan, the royal families are omnipotent. In Egypt, President Mubarak is an autocrat presently seeking an unprecedented fifth term as president and grooming his son to ascend to power. See endnote 37 of the Epilogue.

27. OBL refers to the ouster of Sharif Hussein, the *Emir* of Mecca, from Saudi Arabia by Abdul Aziz ibn Saud, the founder of the Saudi monarchy, and his British benefactors.

28. He refers to the close ties between the United States and Saudi Arabia.

29. Saudi King Fahd had been debilitated since suffering a stroke in late 1995. Crown Prince and First Deputy Prime Minister Abdullah bin Abd al Aziz acted as the *de facto* regent until August 1, 2005, when the King died and Crown Prince Abdullah became King. See "The Man at the Center: Saudi Prince Abdullah," *The Estimate*, Vol. XV, No. 2, January 25, 2002, at www.theestimate.com/public/012502c.html.

30. Saudi Defense Minister Prince Sultan bin Abdul Aziz; and Saudi Interior Minister Prince Naif Bil Abdul Aziz. The Saudi Royal Diwan is the primary executive office of the King, and his principal advisors have offices in the Royal Diwan. See "The Royal Diwan," www.countrystudies. us/saudi-arabia/48.htm, of the United States State Department, citing to the Library of Congress. See endnote 32, *infra*, for an example of the removal of a Crown Prince – Prince Hassan of the Royal Kingdom of Jordan.

31. Born Ibn Saud, King Saud (1902 - 1969) ruled Saudi Arabia from 1953 to 1964. Ostensibly, he was removed because he had brought serious financial crisis to the Kingdom in 1958. His brothers appointed his brother, Faisal, to succeed him. Ultimately, Saud was exiled from Saudi Arabia in November, 1964, and later died in Athens, Greece in 1969. Unfortunately, it was King Saud who etched into the minds of Americans the stereotype of the profligate "Arab Sheikh" when he and his entourage of Cadillacs, red carpets, servants, and "wives" arrived in the United States for a high-profile visit in 1957. See "King Saud," *Encyclopedia of the Orient*, at www.i-cias.com/e.o/saud.htm.

32. In late 1998, Jordan's King Hussein spent six months in the United States at the Mayo Clinic undergoing treatment for cancer. Shortly before his death on February 7, 1999, he replaced his brother, Prince Hassan, with his eldest son, Prince Abdullah, as the Crown Prince. On King Hussein's death, Prince Abdullah, then 31, became King. Prince Hassan was age 51 and had been Crown Prince for the past thirty-four years. King Abdullah's Mother was English, and his appointment grated many in the Middle East who wondered how a man of half-Arab blood with limited Arabic-language skills could lead the Hashemite family, descendents of the Prophet Muhammad (PBUH). Eighteen-year-old Prince Hamza, the full-blood son of King Hussein and his fourth wife, the popular Queen Noor, was designated to be Crown Prince. However, on November 27, 2004, King Abdullah removed Prince Hamza as Crown Prince. No successor has been announced as of this writing. See Martin Asser, "World: Middle East Analysis: Jordan's Succession Saga," *BBC News*, February 6, 1999, at www.news.bbc.co.uk/1/hi/world/middle_east/272678.stm; "King Hussein Ponders Change in Succession to Jordan's Throne," *CNN.com*, January 22, 1999, at www.cnn.com/WORLD/meast/9901/22/jordan.king/; "Hussein's Illness Raises Succession Concerns," *Al-Ahram Weekly Online*, Issue No. 388, 30 July – 5 August 1998, at www.weekly.ahram.org.eg/1998/388/re3.htm; and "Jordan Crown Prince Relieved of Title,"

Aljazeera.net, November 28, 2004, at www.english.aljazeera.net/NR/exeres/14554311-E5A6-48AF-B5B4-45E8CAFBA9E1.htm.

33. Al-Azhar University, located in Cairo, Egypt, is considered to be the preeminent religious instructional school in Su.nni Islam. It was founded in 969 by the Fatimid Caliph Almiz. Presently, the Egyptian government keeps a close eye on the religious doctrines being espoused by Al Azhar's scholars to ensure that they stay within bounds of the government's view of Islam. More information regarding the Americanization of schools and the Wahhabi creed of Islam can be viewed in the Forward.

The *quid pro quo* between the Sauds and the *Wahhabis* was that the former would govern and the latter would provide the regime with religious legitimacy and care for the pastoral needs of the people. Neither would interfere with the other. Thus, from a practical standpoint, it is unlikely that the Saudi government has much incentive or ability to restrain or redirect the puritanical teachings of Wahhabism. For an interesting discussion of this Saudi conundrum, see Fareed Zakaria, "The Saudi Trap," *Newsweek Magazine*, June 28, 2004, at www.fareedzakaria.com/articles/newsweek/062804.html.

34. For example of Saudi Arabia's attempts to mollify the United States and temper its religious curricula, see "Saudi Arabia Suspends 900 Imams," *BBC News*, March 17, 2004, at www.news.bbc.co.uk/1/hi/world/middle_east/3520822.stm.

35. *Holy Quran*, 10 (Yunus [Jonah]):15.

36. The secular Jordanian monarchy and government is not a favorite of OBL's. The founding of modern Jordan relates back to the British government's post-World War I installation of the Hashimite Abdullah ibn Hussein in the previous Ottoman Turkish territory known as Transjordan. The British government granted Jordan independence in 1923, subject to Britain's post-World War I mandate from the League of Nations. Abdullah's son, Talal, was mentally ill and deposed. He was succeeded by his son, Hussein, born in 1935. Of course in the 1967 Israel-Arab War, Jordan lost the West Bank of Palestine to Israel. In 1970, as a ramification of the 1967 defeat, open warfare in Jordan broke out between King Hussein's government and Yasser Arafat's Palestinian Liberation Organization, which was trying to organize a government opposing the monarchy. Hussein's army defeated the Palestinians in 1970 in a campaign referred to by the Palestinians as "Black September" because of the massive casualties among their civilians. Many of the Palestinians fled to Lebanon. By 1979, Arafat and Hussein had reconciled, the impetus being Egypt's then pending peace with Israel. Then in 1994, Israel and Jordan signed a peace agreement. King Hussein died in 1999, succeeded by Abdullah. Many Palestinians view Abdullah as just another despot, portraying Jordan as synonymous with collusion with Israel and betrayal of the Palestinians. See generally, "Jordan," *Infoplease.com*, at www.infoplease.com/ipa/A0107670.html; and Iqbal Jassat, "Jordan's Abdullah Continues Betrayal of Palestine," at www.mediareviewnet.com/Jordan.htm.

Regarding Morocco, King Muhammad VI succeeded his unpopular and repressive father, King Hassan II, in 1999. But Morocco remains ruled by a secularized monarchy. Initially, Muhammad VI loosened the monarchy's grip on the country when he first assumed power, allowing moderate Islamist parties to operate legally and releasing political prisoners that had filled his father's notorious prisons. However, with the occurrence of terrorist attacks in Casablanca in 2002, the government enacted new anti-terrorism laws and stepped up its campaign against perceived extremists. Some rights groups claim the new laws erode human rights. In February 2004, Muhammad VI also enacted a new family law, called the Mudawana, like its predecessor, but which grants more rights to women. It has been opposed by religious conservatives. See Abdesalam Maghraoui, "Political Authority in Crisis: Muhammad VI's Morocco," *Middle East Report, Morocco in Transition, Report 218*, Spring 2001, at www.merip.org/mer/mer218/218_maghraoui.html; and Pascale Harter, "Divorce Divides Morocco and West Sahara," *BBC News*, August 4, 2004, at www.news.bbc.co.uk/1/hi/world/africa/3532612.stm.

37. Please see the Forward for more information regarding the use of Saudi military bases by U.S. forces.

38. In July of 2004, Saudi Foreign Minister Saud al-Faisal actually proposed to United States Secretary of State Colin Powell to send Muslim troops into Iraq to restore order. In October 2004, the Iraqi interim government rejected the offer, expressing concerns about occupying troops from a neighboring country. See Elise Labott, "Saudi Plans Muslim Troops in Iraq," *CNN.com*, July 28, 2004, at www.cnn.com/2004/WORLD/meast/07/28/powell.saudi/; and "Iraq Rejects Saudi Troops," *Rediff.com*, October 19, 2004, at www.rediff.com/news/2004/oct/19saudi.htm.

39. See the Forward for more information regarding General Franks's using a Saudi air force base to conduct the Iraq War.

40. On January 17, 2003, the BBC reported on a Saudi plan to topple Saddam Hussein by encouraging Iraqi generals to overthrow him, on the promise of a United Nations resolution of amnesty for the perpetrators. See "Saudi Plan to Toppel Saddam," *BBC News World Edition*, January 17, 2003, at www.news.bbc.co.uk/2/hi/middle_east/2667051.stm.

41. See the Forward for a list of the ten violations leading to apostasy.

42. Please see the Forward for more information regarding King Saud's financial aid from the British.

43. OBL refers to the recent book by Bob Woodword, *Plan of Attack*, in which he chronicles the Bush administration's planning of the Iraq War. He specifically documents a meeting convened on January 11, 2003, before the outbreak of hostilities on March 19, 2003, during which Vice President Cheney briefed Prince Bandar on the "plan of attack." The meeting was also attended by Secretary of Defense Donald Rumsfeld and Chairman of the Joint Chiefs of Staff Richard B. Myers. Bob Woodward, *Plan of Attack*, pp. 263-266 (Simon & Schuster 2004).

44. OBL refers to the Arab League Summit convened in Beirut, Lebanon, March 27-28, 2002. At the Summit, the Saudi Arabian government introduced what became known as the "Abdullah Initiative," a Middle East peace proposal floated by Crown Prince Abdullah of Saudi Arabia. He offered to normalize relations with Israel on condition of a withdrawal to the latter's 1967 borders and an acceptance of an independent Palestinian state with Jerusalem as its capital. See "Arab League Peace Initiative, 2002," at www.al-bab.com/arab/docs/league/peace02.htm; and "League of Arab States: Arab Summit Beirut, 27-8 March 2002, *One World-Nations Online*, at www.nationsonline.org/oneworld/arab_peace_plan.htm.

45. In April, 2004, the Saudi government agreed to establish an investment fund for the reconstruction of Iraq. See "Saudi Arabia Agrees to Set Up Fund to Aid Iraqi Regeneration," *Iraq Procurement*, April 10, 2004, at www.iraqdevelopmentprogram.org/.

46. See the Forward for a discussion of OBL's frayed relationship with the government of Saudi Arabia.

47. *Holy Quran*, 12 (Yusuf [Prophet Joseph]):76.

48. *Holy Quran*, 2 (Al-Baqarah [The Cow]):275.

49. Saudi Arabia has been intensely criticized by Islamists because it has allowed the presence of banking institutions that earn interest on deposits. Commonplace on the streets of Saudi Arabia are banks like the British-Saudi Bank, the American-Saudi Bank, etc. These banks are authorized by Section B, Article 1, of the Saudi law, enacted by the King's Edict No. M/5. *Sharia* (Islamic law) courts were forbidden to intervene by the Specialization Law, Articles 20 and 21. Also, Saudi Arabia sits on the boards of the International Monetary Fund and the Arab Monetary Fund. See "Saudi Arabia Is Not an Islamic State – Saudi Arabia Deals in Riba," *Islamic-State.Org*, at www.islamic-state.org/saudi/riba.shtml.

50. King Hussein of Jordan was opposed to the American invasion of Kuwait and attempted to achieve a peaceful withdraw of Iraqi forces from Kuwait. Palestinians comprise over 50% of Jordan's population and generally were supportive of Saddam Hussein, who in turn had supported the *Intifada* uprising against Israel's occupation of Palestinian lands. See endnote 36, *infra*, for a

discussion of the negative perceptions of King Hussein because of his contacts and peace treaty with Israel. See also, Eqbal Ahmad, "King Hussein's Dual Legacy," *Dawn-Opinion*, February 14, 1999, at www.geocities.com/CollegePark/Library/9803/eqbal_ahmad/eqbal_king_hussein. html; and "Assessment for Palestinians in Jordan," *Data*, University of Maryland, citing U.S. Department of State Human Rights Reports for 1993 and 1994, at www.cidcm.umd.edu/inscr/mar/assessment.asp?groupId=66302.

51. Saudi Arabia's Crown Prince Abdullah visited Jordan in 1998 after an eight-year hiatus brought about by the Jordanian King's perceived support for Saddam Hussein during the Gulf War in 1991. Crown Prince Abdullah then attended the King's funeral in 1999. (King Hussein died on February 7, 1999.) See "1998 King Hussein Agenda" at www.kinghussein.gov.jo/archive6.html; and Caroline Faraj, "Queen Mourns Beloved Husband," *Jordan Times*, February 8, 1999, at www.ismaili.net/timeline/1999/19990208b.html.

52. Gamal Abdel Nasser, leader of Egypt, 1954 - 1970; Anwar Sadat, President of Egypt, 1970 - 1981; and Colonel Muammar al-Qaddafi, who seized power in Libya via a bloodless military coup in 1969 and assumed dictatorial power in 1970. For a discussion of Saudi Arabia's checked history with these venues and Arab nationalism generally, see "Saudi Arabia: Arab Nationalism," *Country Study*, 2004, U.S. Department of State, U.S. Library of Congress, at www.countrystudies.us/saudi-arabia/60.htm. OBL refers to the Arab League Summit convened in Beirut, Lebanon, March 27-28, 2002. At the Summit, the Saudi Arabian government introduced what became known as the "Abdullah Initiative," a Middle East peace proposal floated by Crown Prince Abdullah of Saudi Arabia. He offered to normalize relations with Israel on condition of a withdrawal to the latter's 1967 borders and an acceptance of an independent Palestinian state with Jerusalem as its capital. See "Arab League Peace Initiative, 2002," at www.al-bab.com/arab/docs/league/peace02.htm; and "League of Arab States: Arab Summit Beirut, 27-8 March 2002, *One World-Nations Online*, at www.nationsonline.org/oneworld/arab_peace_plan.htm.

53. *Holy Quran*, 6 (Al-An'am [The Cattle]):162-163.

54. *Holy Quran*, 2 (Al-Baqarah [The Cow]):9.

55. *Holy Quran*, 4 (An-Nisa [The Women]:61.

56. In response to demonstrations for reform that occurred in Saudi Arabia's capital, Riyadh, in mid-December 2004, the Saudi government sentenced fifteen demonstrators, including one woman, to public floggings and prison terms ranging from two to six months and between 100 and 250 lashes. The public floggings are a message cautioning against further demonstrations. Note that this incident occurred in the milieu of President George W. Bush's war in Iraq and overall campaign to bring democracy to the autocratic regimes in the Middle East. Hassan M. Fattah, "Saudi Court Orders Lashings for 15 Demonstrators," *New York Times*, January 13, 2005; Reinout van Wagtendonk, "Bush's Vision of Middle East Democracy," *Radio Netherlands*, November 7, 2003, at www.www2.rnw.nl/rnw/en/currentaffairs/region/northamerica/us031107. html.

57. Al Qadi Ayad (1118 – 1166), an Imam in *Tafsir* (the science by which the *Holy Quran*'s teachings, interpretations, and rulings are understood and derived) and *Hadith*, a *Faqih in usul* (a Jurist), a scholar in the Arabic language was from Ceuta, under Spain, then an enclave of Morocco. In his magnum opus *Ash Shifa*, he describes a biographical account of the life of Prophet Muhammad's (PBUH) character by his acuteness, eloquence, his nobility, his intellect, forbearance, decency, excellent conduct, his compassion and his justice amongst other qualities. We read about the immense value placed on him by His Lord and his nobility in this world and the Hereafter." AbuBakr Karolia, "The Best of Creation – The Walking Qur'an," *Nuradeen.com*, October 27, 2003, at www.nuradeen.com/Contributions/TheBestOfCreation.htm

58. *Holy Quran*, 33 (Al-Ahzab [The Confederates]):36.

59. OBL refers to the multi-ethnic, mostly non-Pashtun, opposition forces which opposed the Taliban's imposition of power over Afghanistan. Controlling perhaps 5% of Afghanistan in

the northern Panjshir valley, the Northern Alliance became the surrogates for American ground forces when the United States "invaded" Afghanistan on October 7, 2001, to ferret out al-Qaeda and dispatch the Taliban, whose leader, Mullah Muhammad Omar, had refused to hand OBL over to the United States. Fiona Symon, "Afghanistan's Northern Alliance, *BBC News*, September 19, 2001, at www.news.bbc.co.uk/1/hi/world/south_asia/1552994.stm; and "Who Are the Northern Alliance?", *BBC News*, November 13, 2001, at www.news.bbc.co.uk/1/hi/world/south_asia/1652187.stm.

60. OBL refers to Kharijite (*Khawarji*, meaning those who seceded) Islam, one of the earliest Shi'ite sects. Originally, the were followers of Imam Ali ibn Abdi Talib (b. ca. 570), the fourth Caliph. His followers believed him to be the only true successor to the Prophet Muhammad (PBUH) because of his direct blood lineage as the Prophet's cousin and son-in-law. However, the Kharijites rebelled against Ali because of his willingness to arbitrate the then pending dispute with Mu'awiya, governor of Damascus, as to who should be the new Caliph after the Caliph Uthman was killed in 656. The Kharijites believed that the choice was a matter of divine judgment. Ali defeated their rebellion, but their movement survived. In 661, one of their members assassinated Ali, who had become the fourth Caliph. From a political movement supporting Ali, Shi'ism [literally, the party of Ali] evolved into a religious formulation that today represents approximately 10-15% of all Muslims. See also endnote 22 of OBL's speech of January 4, 2004, *infra.*; and "Shites," *Infoplease*, at *www.infoplease.com/ce6/society/A0844916.html.*

61. Several assassination attempts against OBL are rumored to have occurred during his stay in Sudan between 1991 and 1996. For a discussion, see "Bin Laden's Life in Sudan – Into the Development of Osama's Viewpoints," *Jihad Unspun*, November 21, 2001, at www.jihadunspun.com/BinLadensNetwork/background/blyis.html.

62. OBL refers to an incident that occurred in 1924, when the violence-prone *Wahhabi* followers of the Al-Saud family (now backed by the British, who had ceased their support of Sharif Hussain), led by the future founder of Saudi Arabia, Abdul Aziz ibn Saud, massacred the inhabitants of Taif in Southern Saudi Arabia, killing approximately 1000 people and terrorizing the remainder of the Arabian Peninsula. In December, 1925, Saudi forces occupied Medina, and in January, 1926, Abdul Aziz ibn Saud declared himself to be the king of the Hijaz (i.e., Arabia). See Naseem ul-Haq, "Al-Saud: The West's Custodians of the Haramain [holy cities of Mecca and Medinah]," *MuslimMedia.com*, at www.muslimedia.com/archives/special-edition/hajj/hajj2.htm. In conquering the Arabian Peninsula with the assistance of their British patrons between 1918 and 1926, the Sauds "repeatedly massacred rival tribes, executing hundreds of people, including women and children. Members of the Al-Saud family personally beheaded many of them." Often the Al-Sauds executed their enemies after their capture, and by the time they seized control of the whole peninsula, they had publicly executed 40,000 people and had carried out approximately 350,000 amputations (of the arms of poor caught stealing bread). Craig Unger, *House of Bush, House of Saud*, pp. 85-86 (Scribner 2004).

63. Imam an-Nawawi, d. 1277, born as Yahya ibn Sharaf al-Nawawi, who became a versatile Islamic scholar, leaving behind numerous works, including Forty Hadith and Al-Muqasis (Manual of Islam). See "Imam an-Nawawi," *Bysiness.co.uk*, at www.bysiness.co.uk/Ulemah/bionawawi.htm; also, "An-Nawawi's Forty Hadeeth," at www.Hadith.8m.com/Hadith1.html. See also, *FortyHadith.com*. OBL refers to the *Al-Muqasis*, Tenet 1.4: "Everything that is necessarily known by Muslims to be of religion." See Nuh Ha Mim Keller, translator, "Chapter One - Fundamentals of Faith and Sacred Law," *Al-Muqasis – Al-Nawawi's Manual of Islam*, excerpt, at www.bysiness.co.uk/excerpts/exceptmuqasid1.htm.

64. Sahih Bukhari, *Hadith*, Vol. 3, Book 39, No. 531: *Hadith*, Book 019, No. 4366:, at www.usc.edu/dept/MSA/. See also, "Appendix I, Jihad and Expulsion of Non-Muslims from Islamic Countries," at www.bharatvani.org/books/jihad/app1.htm.

65. See previous endnote.

66. *Holy Quran* 7 (Al-Araf [The Heights or The Wall with Elevations]):163.
Holy Quran, 4 (An-Nisa [The Women]):154. Sahih al-Bukhari, *Hadith* No. 3403."

67. OBL is quoting a *Hadith* written by Sahih Bukhari in several different forms: Book 53, Vol. 4, No. 410; Book 53, Vol. 4, No. 411 and Book 73, Vol. 8, No. 196; Book 73, Vol. 8, No. 197. Book 86, Vol. 9, No. 96. Note that this Editor believes that the following sentence, "The worst traitor is a general Amir," is OBL's own description of his view of Saudi Arabia's rulers in the context of the quoted *Hadith*. See www.usc.edu/dept/MSA.

68. *Holy Quran*, 22 (Al-Hajj [The Pilgrimage]):25.

69. *Holy Quran*, 27 (An-Naml [The Ants]):34.

70. OBL refers to arms accords negotiated between the UK and Saudi Arabia, beginning in 1986 with *Al Yamamah* (the "dove") I, the purchase of aircraft and related military equipment for the sum of 5 billion British pounds. In 1988, *Yamamah II* was negotiated. It was valued at approximately 16 billion British pounds. In perspective, however, between 1990 and 2000, Saudi purchased approximately 40 billion dollars (U.S.) in arms from the U.S. and 10 billion dollars in arms from France. See generally, Chrissie Hirst, "The Arabian Connection: The UK Arms Trade to Saudi Arabia," *Campaign Against Arms Trade*, at www.caat.org.uk/information/publications/countries/saudi-arabia.php; and "Saudi Arabia, Arms Sales Tables, Total Licenses/Agreements 1990-2000," Federation of American Scientists at www.fas.org/asmp/profiles/saudi_arabia.htm.

71. The Saudi royal family's profligate ways are well-known throughout the world. The cost of Kind Fahd's palaces has been conservatively estimated to reach two billion dollars. Fareed Zakaria, "The Saudi Trap," *Newsweek Magazine*, June 28, 2004, at www.fareedzakaria.com/articles/newsweek/062804.html.

72. *Holy Quran*, 18 (Al Kahf [The Cave]):79.

73. Khalid al Mihdhar and Nawaf al Hazmi were the two 9/11 hijackers who visited San Diego in the year 2000. They were from Mecca. They were both aboard the plane that struck the Pentagon.

74. OBL refers to the 1979 seizure of the Grand Mosque of Mecca (*Masjid Al-Haram*), which houses the Kaba, by Islamic militants led by Juhaiman al-Oteibi. Saudi Arabian military forces attacked the occupied mosque, dozens were killed on both sides, and Al-Oteibi and others surrendered. He and 62 of the captured rebels were subsequently executed at various locations throughout Saudi Arabia. See article by Fareed Zakaria, cited at endnote 71, *infra*.

75. OBL refers to Yusuf al-Hajjaj, governor of Iraq and Hind [India] and Sind [Persian/Iranian frontier, Indus Valley' from 694 to 714, under the caliphs Abd al-Malik (692 - 705) and his son and successor Walid I (705 - 715). In 711, he appointed his nephew, then seventeen-year-old Muhammed al-Qasim to lead an army of conquest into Sind and Hind, not to spread Islam but rather to eradicate piracy and protect commerce. Hajjaj instructed Al-Qasim to "give quarter (*Aman*) to any of the inhabitants of Sind who ask for it, but not to the residents of Debal," which was the first city conquered by Al-Qasim. Al-Qasim subsequently defeated Dahir, king of Sind, at the battle of Ar-Rur in 712 Al-Qasim sent Dahir's head and those of the other "chiefs of Hind" to Al-Hajjaj. Dahir's defeat completed the Muslim conquest of Al-Hind. See Andre Wink, *Al-Hind: The Making of the Indo-Islamic World*, Vol, 1, pp. 202-204 (Oxford University Press (Delhi) 1990). This Editor believes OBL is referring to Al-Hajjaj's enlightened command of Al-Qasim, listening to his general, instructing him logically and successfully, and ensuring that Quranic practices were implemented wherever the army touched.

76. OBL's figure may be inflated. For more information regarding the Gulf War sanctions, please view the Forward.

77. Sahih Bukhari, *Hadith*, Book 40, Vol. 3, No. 552: Book 40, Vol. 3, No. 553: Also, Book 54, Vol. 4, No. 535: See also, Sahih Muslim, *Hadith*, Book 26, No. 5570: Book 26, No. 5573: Book 32, No. 6345: Book 32, No. 6346: Book 32, No. 6348: see http://www.usc.edu/dept/MSA/

78. "If all the inhabitants of the heavens and the earth join hands to kill a Muslim, God will

cast all of them to Hell on their faces." Quoted from Shaykn Abdullaah As-Subayyil, "Prohibition of Shedding Protected Blood," *Islamic Forum*, October 4, 2004, at www.forums.gawaher.com/lofiversion/index.php/t91.html.

79. *Holy Quran*, 4 (An-Nisa [The Women]):93.

80. Sahih Bukhari, *Hadith*, Book 83, Vol. 9, No. 4: see www.usc.edu/dept/MSA/.

81. The killing of a Muslim is forbidden in hundreds of recorded traditions (*Hadith*) of the Prophet (PBUH). For example, Sunan Abu-Dawud, *Hadith*, Book 39, No. 4487: " * * * I heard the Apostle of God (PBUH) say: It is not lawful to kill a man who is a Muslim except for one o the three reasons: *Kufr* (disbelief) after accepting Islam, fornication after marriage, or wrongfully killing someone, for which he may be killed." see www.usc.edu./dept/MSA/ also, "PA Mufti Calls Upon Muslims Not to Join U.S. Coalition Against Terrorism," *Middle East Research Institute*, No. 278, October 1, 2001, at www.memri.org/bin/articles.cgi?Page=subjects&Area=middleeast&ID=SP27801.

82. Imam Al-Nisai, *Hadith*, (ca. 278 A.H./900 A.D.), at http:www.quran-hadith-index.com/.

83. *Holy Quran*, 9 (At-Taubah [The Repentance]):114.

84. *Holy Quran*, 60 (Al-Mumtahanah [The Woman to Be Examined]):4.

85. OBL refers to the beheading of American hostage Paul Johnson by al-Qaeda militants in Saudi Arabia in June 2004. Mr. Johnson was a contract employee who maintained Apache attack helicopters for the Saudi government and armed forces and had lived in Saudi Arabia for over a decade. See "Al Qaeda Militants Kill American Hostage," *CNN.com*, June 18, 2004, at www.cnn.com/2004/WORLD/meast/06/18/saudi.kidnap/.

86. The covenant is an important Islamic principle. Muslims may enter into covenants with their enemies when the former are weak and certain conditions are present. Generally, any covenant should not exceed ten years, during which time the Muslims are to strengthen themselves for the resumption of *Jihad*. Once of sufficient strength, the covenant is to be voided and the enemy informed of the voidance. If the enemy unilaterally attacks Muslims anywhere, the covenant is canceled. See Abu Haitham al-Hijazee, "Understanding Covenants in Islam," *Jihad Unspun*, January 22, 2005, at www.jihadunspun.com.

87. *Holy Quran*, 4 (Al-Nisa [The Women]):112.

88. Until 2003, Saudi Arabia had contributed 15.4 million dollars (U.S.) to Yasser Arafat's Palestinian Authority every two months. After Chairman Arafat's death, much of the money remains unaccounted for. Paul Martin, "Will $1 Billion Be Buried With Arafat?," *The Washington Times*, November 8, 2004.

89. OBL refers to the March 1996 Conference of Peacemakers convened at Sharm El-Sheikh, Egypt. The Saudi Foreign Minister Prince Saud al-Faisal attended the conference and expressed a "collective commitment to peace" and condemned violent acts directed at "innocent civilians" in Tel Aviv, Israel, and the Occupied Territories of Palestine. He urged a resumption of the peace process based on the principles expressed at the Madrid Conference (convened between October 30 and November 1, 1991.) The Sharm El-Sheikh Conference was attended by approximately one-half of the Arab League members and issued a communiqué that condemned "all acts of terror- including terrorism against Israel and Israelis." See "1996 Speech, Prince Saud's Speech at Peacemaker Conference, Sharm al-Shaikh," *Royal Embassy of Saudi Arabia*, Washington, D.C., a www.saudiembassy.net/1996News/Statements/SpeechDetail.asp?cIndex=459; Nevine Khalil, "Marathon Diplomacy Carries the Day, *Al Ahram Weekly On-Line*, No. 446, September 9-15, 1999; and Hillary Mann, "Policy Watch: Arab Anti-Terror Efforts: Assessing An Arab League Initiative," *The Washington Institute for Near East Policy*, No. 294, January 13, 1998, at www.washingtoninstitute.org/templateC05.php?CID=1173.

90. See endnote 37, *infra*.

91. See endnote 38, *infra*.

92. See endnote 44, *infra*.

93. Sahih Muslim, *Hadith*, Book 001, No. 0196: at www.usc.edu/edu/dept/MSA/.

94. OBL refers to Ahmad ibn Muhammad Hanbal (780 - 855), the Muslim jurist and theologian who founded the Hanbali school (*Fiqh*) of Sunni Islam. See the Forward for more information regarding Hanbal and the *Fiqh*.

95. *Holy Quran*, 7 (Al-Araf [The Heights or The Wall with Elevations]): 113.

96. OBL paraphrases the *Holy Quran*'s "turning back" verse, 3 (Al-Imran [The Family or Imran]):114.

97. Sahih Bukhari, *Hadith*, Vol. 4, Book 52, No. 192. See www.usc.edu/dept/MSA/.

98. OBL refers to Al Qaeda operatives or sympathizers who have been killed. Gunman attacked the United States consulate in Jeddah, Saudi Arabia, on December 6, 2004. Several people were killed. "Arms Cache Found in Car in Jeddah," *Washington Times*, December 23, 2004, at www.washingtontimes.com/.

99. See above endnote 64, documenting a *Hadith* in which the Prophet Muhammad (PBUH) instructed his followers to expel the Jews and Christians from the Arabian Peninsula.

100. *Holy Quran*, 57 (Al-Hadid [Iron]):22.
Sahih Al-Timidhi (831 - 901) was an Islamic scholar who studied under Imam Bukhari, Imam Muslim, and Imam Abu Dawd. For more information about Timidhi, please see the Forward.

101. *Holy Quran*, 52 (At-Tur [The Mount]):48.
Holy Quran, 3 (Al Imran [The Family of Imran]):73.

102. OBL refers to the Battle of the Trench (Ditch) in the year 627 in which the city of Medina, occupied by the Prophet Muhammad (PBUH) and his followers, was besieged by some 10,000 troops from the city of Mecca. The besiegers were led by Abu Sufyan, who had become the Prophet's arch-enemy. A trench dug around Medina by the Prophet's forces prevented Abu Sufyan's army from gaining entry into Mecca; and after repeated failed attempts, Abu Sufyan and his army returned to Mecca. See www.angelfire.com/ny/dawahpage/hist3.html; "Muhammad," *Wikipedia, the Free Encyclopedia*, www.en.wikipedia.org/wiki/Muhammad.

103. *Holy Quran*, 33 (Al-Ahzab [The Confederates]):21.

104. The Prophet Muhammad (PBUH) said, "Great rewards are given for great trials, and when God loves a people, He tests them. Whoever accepts the trial cheerfully earns His good pleasure, and whoever resents it earns His displeasure." Cited at *Ihyae Uloum Addean*, Abou-Hamed Al-Ghazali, pp.1436, 1382, 1423; and *Nuzhat Almajales ws Muntakhab Annfaes*, by Assafouri, p. 68 The Prophet Muhammad (PBUH) said "Geat Rewards are given for great trials and when God loves a people, He tests them. Whoever accepts the trial cheerfully earns His good pleasure, and whoever resents it earns His displeasure."

105. A poem by OBL, seemingly based on *Holy Quran*, 2 (Al-Baqarah [The Cow]):155-157.

106. *Holy Quran*, 4 (An-Nisa [The Women]):104.

107. *Hadith*: "It has been reported by Ahmed and Tabarani that the Prophet (PBUH) said: 'There will always remain a group in my Ummah [Islamic nation] who shall remain steadfast upon the truth. Who shall always remain dominant over their enemies, those who oppose them will never be able to harm them except the occasional inconvenience that they will suffer. And they will remain dominant in this way until the Decree of God (i.e., Day of Judgment).' The Sahaba asked 'Ya Rasul Allah (PBUH) where will they be?' The Prophet (PBUH) said: 'in Bayt al-Maqdis and its surrounding areas.'" See www.mpacuk.org/content/view/250/34/. Another reference may be found at *Fadhael Alqudss*, by Ibnul-Jawzi, p. 6.

108. *Holy Quran*, 20 (Ta-Ha [T.H.]):72.

109. The Shah of Iran was overthrown on April 1, 1979.

110. OBL probably is referring to Romanian dictator Nicolae Ceausescu, who was overthrown in 1989 and executed along with his wife, Elena, by a mob in Bucharest.

111. See endnote 31, *infra*.

EPILOGUE

1. For a viewpoint directly from the Middle East, see Muqtedar Khan, "Clear and Present Danger," *Al-Ahram Weekly*, Issue No. 643, June 19-25, 2003, at www.globalpolicy.org/empire/ analysis/2003/0619danger.htm. Finally, the best source of polling in the Middle East is the Pew Research Center. See "A Year After Iraq War," *Pew Research Center*, March 16, 2004, at www. people-press.org/reports/display.php3?ReportID=206.

2. After the Prophet Muhammad (PBUH) died in 632, the Muslims appointed successors, known as Caliphs, to lead Islam. Later, the Shi'ite Muslims broke from mainstream, or Sunni, Islam because they insisted that the Caliph be related to the Prophet (PBUH) by blood. The Caliphate was dissolved in 1924 by Turkish President Mustafa Kemel Ataturk, whose republican government succeeded the Ottoman Empire whose Sultan had been acting as the Caliph. Over the centuries the Caliphate was controlled by various dynasties, e.g., the Abbasids and the later Ottomans. See the Forward.

3. Sahih Muslim, Hadith, Book 001, No. 0081: See www.usc.edu/dept/MSA/.

4. Ghabram Soref, President of American University, Kuwait, "An Arab Liberal Looks at the Postwar Middle East," *The Washington Institute for Near East Study, Soref Symposium*, 2003, www.washingtoninstitute.org/templateC07.php?CID=142.

5. "Mubarak Warns of 100 Bin Ladens," *CNN.Com*, March 31, 2003, at www.cnn. com/2003/WORLD/meast/03/31/iraq.egypt.mubarak.reut/.

6. Michael Mainville, "U.S. Bases Overseas Show New Strategy," *Pittsburg Post-Gazette*, July 26, 2004, at www.globalsecurity.org/org/news/2004/040726-us-bases.htm; Paul Starobin, et. al., "The Next Oil Frontier," *BusinessWeekOnline*, May 27, 2002, at www.businessweek.com/ magazine/content/02_21/b3784008.htm.

7. On December 28, 2001, General Tommy Franks, then commanding the war in Afghanistan, secretly briefed President Bush, National Security Advisor Condolezza Rice, Secretary of State Colin Powell, Secretary of Defense Donald Rumsfeld, and C.I.A. Chief George Tenet about secret plans for the Invasion of Iraq. Bob Woodward, *Plan of Attack*, pp. 52-66 (Simon & Scheuster 2004).

8. "Backgrounder: The President's Quotes on Islam – In the President's Words: Respecting Islam," www.whitehouse.gov/infocus/ramadan/islam.html; "Reactions by Mainline Christians, A Muslim Group, Etc. to Verbal Attacks on Muslims," *Religious Tolerance*, May 9, 2003, at www. religioustolerance.org/reac_ter18c.htm.

9. See "Muslims Angered by Baptist Criticism," *CNN.com*, June 13, 2002, at www. archives.cnn.com/2002/ALLPOLITICS/06/13/cf.crossfire/; Prof. Juan Cole, "Mohammed Was a Terrorist?," *History News Network*, October 7, 2002, at www.hnn.us/articles/1018.html; "Pat Robertson Attacks Islam," Transcript of *Hannity & Colmes*, September 18, 2002, at *Muslim Access*, www.muslimaccess.com/articles/islamophobes/pat_robertson.asp; "Cover Story: Anti-Islam," Religion and Ethics, *PBS*, December 20, 2002, at www.pbs.org/wnet/religionandethics/ week616/cover.html; "General Says 'War on Terror' a Religious Struggle, Muslims Worship Idol," *Muslim American Society*, October 16, 2003, at www.masnet.org/news.asp?id=563; General: Sorry About Islam Remarks," *CBSNews.com*, October 18, 2003, at www.cbsnews. com/stories/2003/10/21/attack/main579249.shtml; Mustafa Abdel Halim, "U.S. Muslim Groups Consider Boycotting Bush Iftar," *IslamOnline.net*, October 27, 2003, at www.islamonline.net/ English/News/2003-10/27/article09.shtml.

10. See "Bush Administration Documents on Interrogation," *Washington Post*, June 23, 2004; Dan Eggen and R. Jeffrey Smith, "F.B.I. Agents Allege Abuse of Detainees at Guantanamo Bay," *Washington Post*, December 21, 2004; R. Jeffrey Smith and Dan Eggen, "New Papers Suggest Detainee Abuse Was Widespread," *Washington Post*, December 22, 2004; Carol D. Leonnig, "Further Gitmo Detainee Abuse Alleged," *Washington Post*, December 25, 2004; "New

U.S. Memo Backs Off Torture Arguments," *Associated Press-The New York Times*, December 31, 2004; Dan Van Natta, Jr., "Growing Evidence U.S. Sending Prisoners to Torture Capital Despite Bad Record on Human Rights, Uzbekistan is Ally," *The New York Times*, May 1, 2005; "Periscope: Gitmo – SouthCom Showdown," *Newsweek Magazine*, May 9, 2005 ("interrogators, in an attempt to rattle suspects, flushed a Quran down a toilet") (article later retracted but seventeen Muslims died during the protests); Eric Schmitt, "No Criminal Charges for Officer at Abu Ghraib Interrogations," *The New York Times*, May 12, 2005; David Johnson, "Terror Suspects Sent to Egypt by the Dozens, Panel Reports," *The New York Times*, May 12, 2005; Musadeq Sadeq, "Anti-U.S. Violence Erupts in Afghanistan," *Washington Post*, May 12, 2005; and Carlotta Gall, "Muslim' Anti-American Protests Spread From Afghanistan," *The New York Times*, May 14, 2005.

11. As will be discussed below, most Muslims live in democracies and Islam teaches tolerance, not intolerance. Regarding womens' rights, a word is in order. First, Islam was the first of the great religions to grant women protection and property rights. Womens' rights vary across the Middle East and South Asia. In fundamentalist Saudi Arabia they may not vote or even drive. In conservative Iran, they do not wear the burka, are equal to men in the workplace, are members of parliament, vote, and drive. In Pakistan a woman has previously ruled as Prime Minister. Moreover, many women in Muslim countries are quite comfortable with their status according to the *Sharia* (Islamic law). For example, in Iraq today female political leaders are advocating the adoption of the *Sharia's* protections for women as an element of the finalized constitution. Every major religion, including Islam, can improve the status of women. For example, there were no women candidates considered for appointment as Pope after the recent death of John Paul II. Orthodox and Conservative Judiasm's exclusively-male rabbis rail at Reform's female rabbis. The U.S. is best advised to let the Muslims themselves determine the status of women in the various cultures that comprise the Islamic world. Even a superficial reading of the three Arab Human Development Reports issued by the United Nations between 2002 and 2005 suggests that many Muslim venues can ill-afford to continue to waste the skills, knowledge, and abilities of fifty percent of their populations.

Regarding the *Sharia* in Iraq, see Jill Carroll, "Iraqi Women Eye Islamic Law," *Christian Science Monitor*, February 25, 2005.

12. David E. Kaplan, "Investigative Report: Hearts, Minds, and Dollars: in an Unseen Front in the War on Terrorism, America Is Spending Millions... To Challenge the Very Face of Islam," *U.S. News and World Report*, p. 22, April 25, 2005.

13. *9/11 Commission Report*, pp. 47-70, 374-383 (Authorized 1st. Ed. 2004). See also Bill Tammeus, "Giving Islam Short Shrift," *Kansas City Star*, August 7, 2004, at www.campus-watch.org/article/id/1237.

14. "Fast-Growing Islam Winning Converts in Western World," *CNN Interactive*, April 14, 1997, at www.cnn.com/WORLD/9704/14/egypt.islam/; Hossein Askari, "US Middle East Policy: A New Start?," *In The National Interest*, February 2005 at www.inthenationalinterest.com/Articles/February%202005/February2005askariPFV.html.

15. *Holy Quran*, 2 (Al-Baqarah [The Cow]):62.

16. Karen Armstrong, *Holy War*, pp. 178-179 (Anchor Books 2001).

17. See "Jews," *MSN Encarta*, at www.encarta.msn.com/encnet/refpages/search.aspx?q=jews; Lewis Lipkin, "French Anti-Semitism: From the Middle Ages to the Dreyfus Affair," June 1, 2002, Think Tank-Israel, at www.think-Israel.org/frenchAS.html; and Sarine Roffe, "The Jews of Aleppo," *JewishGen:SeafardSIG*, at www.jewishgen.org/SefardSIG/AleppoJews.htm.

18. See "The Arab Israeli Conflict: History Palestine, Jordan, etc., at *Arab2.com*, www.arab2.com/biography/Arab-Israeli-Conflict-mid.htm. This is an excellent web site with links to the original maps and documents.

19. "Palestinian Detainees Go on a Hunger Strike, Calls for Freedom Mount on Palestinian Detainees' International Day," *Palestinian Media Center, Aljazeerah Info*, April 16, 2005, at www.aljazeerah.info/News%20archives/2005%20News%20Archives/April%202005%20News/ 16%20n/Palestinian%20Detainees%20Go%20on%20a%20Hunger%20Strike,%20Calls%20for% 20Freedom%20Mount%20on%20Palestinian%20Detainees'%20International%20Day.htm.

20. For information about Israel's incursion into Lebanon and Mr. Sharon's responsibility for the massacres, see the treatment and links found at "Israeli Politics: Information Regarding Sabra and Shatila," *Palestine Monitor*, at www.palestinemonitor.org/israelipoli/sabra_shatilla_ links.htm ; Richard H. Curtiss, "Leah Rabin's Frankness Gets Mixed Media Reviews," *Washington Report on Middle East Affairs*, February/March 1996, at www.washington-report. org/backissues/0296/9602048.html. For a discussion of President Bush's comments about Mr. Sharon, see Glenn Kessler, "Bush Sticks to Broad Strokes," *Washington Post*, June 3, 2003, at www.washingtonpost.com/ac2/wp-dyn?pagename=article&contentId=A5423-2003Jun2&notFound=true.

21. Phil Brennan, "Israel's Population Bomb in Reverse," *NewsMax.com*, October 19, 2002, at www.newsmax.com/archives/articles/2002/10/18/181802.shtml.

22. Daniel Mandel, "Flight into Egypt," *Australia/Israel & Jewish Affairs Council*, June 2000, www.aijac.org.au/review/2000/256/flight.html.

23. Tom Raum, "Bush Shifts War Rationale From Iraqi Arms, *KansasCity.com*, the Kansas City Star, September 8, 2003, at www.kansascity.com/mld/kansascity/news/breaking_ news/6722744.htm; and Mark Sandalow, "News Analysis: Record Shows Bush Shifting on Iraq War – President's Rationale for the Invasion Continues to Evolve," *San Francisco Chronicle*, September 29, 2004, www.sfgate.com/cgi-bin/article.cgi?file=/c/a/2004/09/29/MNGE590O711. DTL.

24. Jim Shea, "A Whole New Meaning to Texas Hold 'Em," *The Salt Lake Tribune*, April 30, 2005, at www.sltrib.com/portlet/article/html/fragments/print_article.jsp?article=2699615.

25. "Bush-Abdullah Meeting Focused on Oil Prices," *Arab News - Middle East North Africa Financial Network*, April 27, 2005, at www.menafn.com/qn_news_story_s.asp?StoryId=89584.

26. "Egypt Frees Muslim Brotherhood Men," *Aljazeera.net*, April 10, 2005, at www.english. aljazeera.net/NR/exeres/0B8D1B0E-E2AA-42FD-83AC-4E79EA9E0C92.htm.

27. Tyler Marshall, "U.S. Chooses Stability Over Quick Reform," *LA Times*, June 25, 2005.

28. *"Islamists Dominate Saudi Municipal Elections,"* Associated Press, The Jerusalem Post, April 23, 2005, at www.jpost.com/servlet/Satellite?pagename=JPost/JPArticle/ShowFull&cid=111 4222833202&p=1078397702269.

29. Don Van Natta, Jr., "Growing Evidence U.S. Sending Prisoners to Torture Capital Despite Bad Record on Human Rights, Uzbekistan is Ally," *New York Times*, May 1, 2005, at www.sfgate.com/cgi-bin/article.cgi?file=/c/a/2005/05/01/MNGE5CI9MO1.DTL.

30. Matthew Lyn, "Europe Buries the Hatchet with Qaddafi to Tap Oil," *Bloomberg.net*, October 18, 2004, at www.quote.bloomberg.com/apps/news?pid=10000039&refer=columnist_ lynn&sid=aVjRu6M654nU.

31. Scott Wilson and Daniel Williams, "A New Power Rises Across Mideast," *Washington Post*, April 17, 2005.

32. Warren Hoge and David E. Sanger, "Iran to Resume Nuclear Plans, Official States at U.N. Conference," *The New York Times*, May 4, 2005; "Work Related to Enrichment to Resume Within Days, Iran Says," *Los Angeles Times Wire Services*, May 10, 2005.

33. Fareed Zakaria, *The Future of Freedom*, p. 120 (W.W. Norton & Co., 1st. Ed., 2003).

34. See "Armed Conflict Events Data, Algerian Civil War, 1992-Present," at http://www. onwar.com/aced/data/alpha/algeria1992.htm.

35. Kaplan, *U.S. News & World Report, supra*, p. 29.

36. Farid Zakaria, *supra*, at p. 129. Most Muslims live in the democratic countries of India

and Indonesia.

37. Megan K. Stack, "Mubarak Keeps Egypt Guessing in Interview: The Long Time President's Seven-Hour Tete-a-Tete with a Reporter on TV Is a Journey to the Past, and His Critics Find in It Little Hope for Change," *Los Angeles Times*, May 1, 2005, at www.latimes.com.

38. See Muhammad Bailony, "Islam and Democracy: Between Tradition and Ideology," *Senior Honors Thesis*, Department of Political Science, University of California, San Diego, March 28, 2005.

39. See "Current List of Foreign Terrorist Organizations and Other Terrorist Organizations," *Center for Defense Information*, April 5, 2005, at www.cdi.org/friendlyversion/printversion. cfm?documentID=384 ; Patrick Goodenough, "Chinese Muslim Terror Suspects Cleared; Fearful of Going Home," *CBSNEWS.COM*, October 29, 2004, at www.cnsnews.com/ViewPrint. asp?Page=/ForeignBureaus/archive/200410/FOR20041029b.html; and "China: Uighur Muslim Separatists – Updated Special Report," *Virtual Information Center,* March 20, 2003, www.vic-info.org/RegionsTop.nsf/0/c8a851e5a7f3d35f0a256cef000b7ce9?OpenDocument. Regarding China's foreign currency reserves, see "The China Currency Exchange Rate Problem: Facts and Policy Options," The U.S.-China Economic and Security Review Commission, May 9, 2005, at www.uscc.gov/researchpapers/2005/05_05_09currency_exchange_rate.htm.

40. See "Chechnya Goes to Polls in Wake of Airline Terror Claim," *Sunday Herald*, August 29, 2004, at www.sundayherald.com/print/44391.

41. See "Q & A: Kashmir Dispute," *BBC News*, November 25, 2002, at www.news.bbc. co.uk/1/hi/world/353352.stm. See also, "India: Gujarat Massacre Cases Sabotaged," *Human Rights Watch News*, July 1, 2003, at www.hrw.org/press/2003/06/india070103.htm.

42. Harish Dugh, "Economy: Europe, US Set to Fall to Cheap Indian Labour," *The Financial Express*, May 15, 2005, at www.financialexpress.com/print_latest.php?content_id=87904; Amol Sharma, "India Winning Higher-Status Jobs from US," *Christian Science Monitor*, June 18, 2003, at www.csmonitor.com/2003/0618/p01s03-wosc.html.

43. Max V. de Leon and Jefferson Antiporda, "Terrorist Links a Daunting Challenge for RP – Zoellick." *The Manila Times*, May 6, 2005, at www.manilatimes.net/national/2005/may/06/yehey/top_stories/20050506top6.html.

44. Muhammad Sahmi, "Iran's Nuclear Program. Part II: Are Nuclear Reactors Necessary?," *Payvand's Iran News*, October 3,2003, at www.payvand.com/news/03/oct/1022.html.

45. Deb Riechmann, "Bush Urges Saudis to Boost Oil Production, *Associated Press*, *Chicago Sun-Times*, April 25, 2005, at www.suntimes.com/output/terror/cst-nws-bin04.html; "Bush Pushes; Will Oil Costs Budge?," *CBSNews.com*, April 25, 2005, at www.cbsnews.com/stories/2005/04/25/politics/main690561.shtml.

46. Robert L. Hirsch, Roger Bezdek, and Robert Wending, SAIC Corporation, "Peaking of World Oil Production: Impacts; Mitigation; & Risk Management," February 2005, at www.energybulletin.net/4638.html.

47. Mark Christopher, "China Ravenous – and Dangerous," *Houston Chronicle*, May 7, 2005, at www.cfr.org/pub8085/mark_christopher/appetite_for_oil_china_ravenous_and_dangerous.php.

48. "Saudi-funded charities have been implicated in backing jihadist movements in some 20 countries." Kaplan, *U.S. News & World Report, supra*, p. 29.

49. Jan Mouawad and Simon Romero, "Unmentioned Energy Fix: A 55 M.P.H. Speed Limit," *New York Times*, May 1, 2005.

50. "Saudi Aramco," Ministry of Petroleum & Mineral Resources, Kingdom of Saudi Arabia, at www.mopm.gov.sa/html/en/saudico_e.html.

51. Robert L. Hirsch, et. al., Id.; Maryann Mott, "Alaska-Refuge Drilling Approved by U.S. House," *National Geographic News*, April 21, 2005, at www.news.nationalgeographic.com/news/2005/04/0421_050421_alaskadrilling.html.

52. In order, the three holiest places in Islam are Mecca, home of the *Masjid* (Mosque) *al Haram* that houses the *Kaba*; Medina, the city to which the Prophet Muhammad migrated from Mecca in 622, and which houses his tomb at the Mosque of the Prophet (*Masjid al Nabawi*); and the *Masjid Al-Aqsa* on the *al-Haram ash-Sharif* (The Noble Sanctuary aka Temple Mount in the West) in Jerusalem (*Al-Quds*). www.islamonline.net/iol-english/dowalia/news-26-11/topnews9. asp.

53. For a provocative discussion of United States militarism and U.S. military bases in the Middle East, see Chalmers Johnson, *The Sorrows of Empire: Militarism, Secrecy, and the End of the Republic*, at pp. 226-253 (Metropolitan Books, 1st Ed. 2004).

54. Bob Woodward, *Plan of Attack*, at p. 378 (Simon & Schuster 2004).

55. Phyllis Bennis, "The Iraqi Constitution," *Foreign Policy in Focus*, March 17, 2004, at www.fpif.org/cgaa/talkingpoints/0403iraq-const_body.html.

56. Greg Palast, "Adventure Capitalism," *Information Clearing House*, October 26, 2004, at www.informationclearinghouse.info/article7146.htm.

57. Bruce Fein, "Flawed Interim Constitution," *The Washington Times*, March 23, 2004, at www.washtimes.com/commentary/20040322-082831-2551r.htm.

58. "Al-Mahdi Army/Active Religious Seminary/Al-Sadr's Group," *GlobalSecurity.Org*, April 27, 2005, at www.globalsecurity.org/military/world/para/al-sadr.htm.

59. Deb Riechmann, "Bin Laden Draws Rare Mention from Bush," *Chicago Sun-Times*, March 4, 2005, www.suntimes.com/output/terror/cst-nws-bin04.html.

60. Anonymous (Michael Scheuer), *Imperial Hubris: How the West Is Losing the War on Terrorism*, pp. 212-214 (Brassey's, Inc. 2004); "War on Iraq Could Drain US Anti-Terror Campaign: Report," *English People*, reporting an article in the *Washington Post* of September 1, 2002, at www.english.people.com.cn/200209/02/eng20020902_102459.shtml.

61. "100,000 Civilians May Have Died in Iraq Conflict," at www.nature.com/news/2004/041025/full/041025-20.html, October 29, 2004.

62. "Rumsfeld memorandum to General 'Dick' Meyers, Paul Wolfowitz, Gen. 'Pete' Pace, and 'Doug' Feith, subject: Global War on Terrorism," October 16, 2003, at Dave Moniz and Tom Squitieri, "Defense Memo: A Grim Outlook," *Information Clearing House*, October 22, 2003 (*USA Today*), at www.informationclearinghouse.info/article5047.htm.

63. "Iraq Death Toll Tops 270 in 9 Days," *MSNBC News*, May 6, 2005, at www.msnbc. msn.com/; James Tarabay, "No Sign of Government Strategy for Defeating Insurgents," Turkish Weekly, The New Anatolian, May 6, 2005, at www.turkishweekly.net/comments.php?id=997.

64. Milan Rai, "News & Analysis: Turning Point Fallujah: How US Atrocities Sparked the Iraqi Resistance," *ElectronicIraq.Net*, May 4, 2005, at www.electroniciraq.net/news/1947.shtml.

65. Milan Rai, Id.

66. "Fallujah," *Wikipedia, the Free Encyclopedia*, at www.en.wikipedia.org/wiki/Fallujah; Milan Rai, Id.

67. "US Probes Zarqawi Hospital Visit," *News.Com.Au*, May 6, 2005, at www.news.com. au/story/0,10117,15196352-23109,00.html.

68. Jim Landers, "Iraq's Unsecured Ammo Dumps Providing Explosives for Insurgency," *The Dallas Morning News*, December 22, 2004, at www.duluthsuperior.com; John Diamond, "Small Weapons Prove the Real Threat in Iraq," *USA Today*, September 29, 2003, at www. usatoday.com/news/world/iraq/2003-09-29-cover-small-arms_x.htm.

69. Thom Shanker, "Pentagon Says Iraq Effort Limits Ability to Fight Other Conflicts," *New York Times*, May 3,2005.

70. Bob Dart, "Draft May Be Needed in a Year, Military Analysts Warn," *Cox News Service*, March 3, 2005, at www.truthout.org/docs_2005/033105C.shtml.

71. Anthony H. Cordesman, "Outside View: Restructuring U.S. Military," *Washington Times* (*UPI*), April 15, 2005, at www.washingtontimes.com/upi-breaking/20050414-094312-4386r.htm;

Roland Watson, "Young Turn Their Backs on Life in US Military," *Times Online*, May 14, 2005, at www.timesonline.co.uk/article/0,,11069-1611339,00.html.

72. See "President Bush Reaffirms Resolve to War on Terror, Iraq, and Afghanistan," *White House Press Release*, March 19, 2004, at www.whitehouse.gov/news/releases/2004/03/20040319-3.html; Douglas Jehl, "Iraq May Be Prime Place for Training of Militants, C.I.A. Report Concludes," *New York Times*, June 22, 2005.

73. See generally, Seymour Hersh, *The Price of Power: Kissinger in the Nixon White House* (Summit Books 1st. Ed. 1983).

74. In 1998, OBL was interviewed by *Al-Jazeera Television*. He was asked whether he would submit to a trial by the Taliban regime (and the application of Sharia [Islamic law]) in Afghanistan, which he considered to be a pure Islamic regime. OBL responded that he would submit to the jurisdiction of any Sharia (Islamic law) court not influenced by infidels and if the court were one in which the prosecutor and the accused could stand together. But he would not participate in such a court if the United States were the prosecutor. In that case, he would have to become a prosecutor himself and charge the U.S. with many crimes against Muslims. See the interview at www.robert-fisk.com/usama_interview_aljazeera.htm.

This Page Left Intentionally Blank For Notes

Selected Bibliography

"100,000 Iraqi Civilians May Have Died in Iraq Conflict,"*News@Nature.com*, October 29, 2004.

9/11 Commission Report, pp. 47-70, 374-383 (Authorized 1st. Ed. 2004).

"A Biography of Osama Bin Laden," *PBS: Frontline*, at www.pbs.org/wgbh/pages/frontline/shows/binladen/who/bio.html.

"A History of the Israeli-Palestinian Conflict: 1991-2001," *Promises* (Justine Shapiro, B.Z. Goldberg, and Carlos Bolado), PBS, at www.pbs.org/pov/pov2001/promises/timeline.html.

"A Year After Iraq War," *Pew Research Center*, March 16, 2004, at www.people-press.org/reports/display.php3?ReportID=206.

Abdel-Halim, Mustafa , "Top Brass Under Fire for Calling Allah 'Idol,'" *IslamOnline.com*, October 17, 2003, at www.islamonline.net/English/News/2003-10/17/article06.shtml.

"Abdullah Azzam: The Godfather of Jihad," *Perspectives on World History and Current Events: Middle East Peace Project*, at www.pwhce.org/middleeast.html.

Aboulafia, Richard, "The End of the Saudi Aircraft Market?," Industry Insights: *Aerospace America*, November, 2003, at www.aiaa.org/aerospace/Article.cfm?issuetocid=424&ArchiveIssueID=44.

Advanced Legal Studies Institute, "Islamic Classical Legal Texts," at www.nyazee.com/islaw/alsi%20Islamic%20Law%20Series.html.

Al-Jazeera Television 1997 Interview with Osama Bin Laden, at www.robert-fisk.com/usama_interview_aljazeera.htm.

Alam, Mansoor, Dr., "Islamic History: Part 1 - The Death of the Prophet (PBUH)," www.tolueislam.com/Bazm/

Mansoor/MA_history_1.htm.

"Al-Futuhat:The Muslims' Historical Campaigns," *Muslim American Society*, September 5, 2003, www.masnet. org/history.asp?id=423

Al-Hijazee, Abu Haitham, "Understanding Covenants in Islam," *Jihad Unspun*, January 22, 2005, at www. jihadunspun.com.

Al-Hilali, Muhammad Taqu-ud-Din, Dr., and Dr. Muhammad Muhsin Khan, *Interpretation of the Meanings of the Noble Qur'an in the English Language*, Islamic University, Al Midihah Al Munawwarah, Saudi Arabia, published by Darussalam Publishing, Seventeenth Revised Edition, April, 1997.

Ali, Abdullah Yusuf, Translator, *The Holy Quran* (1st. Ed. 1934, Khalil Al-Rawaf Copyright 1946).

"Al-Zawahari Calls Muslims to Resist Under a United Leadership," *ArabicNews.com*, October 2, 2004, at www. arabicnews.com/ansub/Daily/Day/041002/2004100203.html.

Anonymous (Michael Scheuer), *Imperial Hubris: How the West Is Losing the War on Terrorism*, (Brassey's, Inc. 2004).

Anthony, John Duke, "Saudi Arabian-Yemeni Relations: Implications for U.S. Policy," *ArabiaLink.com*, June 28, 2000, at www.arabialink.com/Archive/GWDigests/GWD2000/GWD_2000_06_19.htm#GWP1.

"Appendix B: Background Information on Terrorist Groups, Patterns of Global Terrorism - 2000," Released by the Office of the Coordinator for Counterterrorism, U.S. State Department, April 30, 2001, at www.state.gov/s/ ct/rls/pgtrpt/2000/2450.htm.

"Arab League Peace Initiative, 2002," at www.al-bab.com/arab/docs/league/peace02.htm.

"Arabic Timeline," at www.princeton.edu/~batke/itl/scroll/600tx.html.

"Armed Conflict Events Data, Algerian Civil War, 1992-Present," at http:www.onwar.com/aced/data/alpha/ algeria1992.htm.

Armstrong, Karen, *Holy War: The Crusades and Their Impact on Today's World* (Second Anchor Books Edition, December 2001).

Askari, Hossein Askari, "US Middle East Policy: A New Start?," *In the National Interest*, February 2005 at www.inthenationalinterest.com/Articles/February%202005/February2005askariPFV.html.

"Ataturk," *Voyager.com*, at www.turkiyeninrehberi.com/eng/turkiye/ataturk/hayati.asp.

Azzam, Sheikh Abdullah, "Chapter 1: Defense of Muslim Lands: *The First Obligation After Iman [Belief]*," Islamistwatch.org, at www.islamistwatch.org/texts/azzam/defense/chap1.html.

"Baath Party," *The Syrian Encyclopedia*, at www.damascus-online.com/se/hist/baath_party.htm.

"Backgrounder: The President's Quotes on Islam - In the President's Words: Respecting Islam," www. whitehouse.gov/infocus/ramadan/islam.html.

Bailony, Mohammed, "Islam and Democracy: Between Tradition and Ideology," Senior Honors Thesis, Department of Political Science, University of California, San Diego, March 28, 2005.

Ballou, Brian, "Disgruntled Soldiers Put Rumsfeld on Defensive," Boston Herald, December 9, 2004, at www. news.bostonherald.com/international/view.bg?articleid=57939.

Bamford, James, *A Pretext for War* (Doubleday 2004).

Bard, Mitchell, "The Al-Aksa Intifada," Jewish Virtual Library, 2004, at www.jewishvirtuallibrary.org/source/

Peace/intifada2.html

Bard, Mitchell, "The Jews of Tunisia," citing the April 17 and 23, 2002, issues of the *Washington Post*, Jewish Virtual Library, at www.jewishvirtuallibrary.org/jsource/anti-semitism/tunisjews.html

Battle of Yarmuk," *Wikipedia, the Free Encyclopedia* at www.en.wikipedia.org/wiki/Battle_of_Yarmuk.

Bennis, Phyllis, "The Iraqi Constitution," *Foreign Policy in Focus*, March 17, 2004, at www.fpif.org/cgaa/talkingpoints/0403iraq-const_body.html.

Berkowitz, Peter, "Israel's House Divided," *The Weekly Standard*, April 12-19, 2004, issue, at www.weeklystandard.com/Content/Public/Articles/000/000/003/950mqrrk.asp

"Bin Laden's Life in Sudan - Into the Development of Osama's Viewpoints," *Jihad Unspun*, November 21, 2001, at www.jihadunspun.com/BinLadensNetwork/background/blyis.html.

Brennan, Phil, "Israel's Population Bomb in Reverse," *NewsMax.com*, October 19, 2002, at www.newsmax.com/archives/articles/2002/10/18/181802.shtml.

Brown, Archie, Prof., "Reform, Coup, Collapse: The End of the Soviet State," *BBC News*, December 10, 2001, at www.bbc.co.uk/history/war/coldwar/soviet_end_01.shtml.

"Bush-Abdullah Meeting Focused on Oil Prices," *Arab News - Middle East North Africa Financial Network*, April 27, 2005, at www.menafn.com/qn_news_story_s.asp?StoryId=89584.

"Bush Administration Documents on Interrogation," *Washington Post*, June 23, 2004.

"Bush Administration's Legal Debate Over Torture, Interrogation Policies, Treatment of Enemy Combatants and Detainees, and the Applicability of Prisoner of War Status," *FindLaw.Com,* at www.news.lp.findlaw.com/hdocs/docs/torture/powtorturememos.html.

"Bush Clarifies View on War against Terrorism," *MSNBC.com*, August 31, 2004.

"Bush Pushes; Will Oil Costs Budge?," *CBSNEWS.com*, April 25, 2005, at www.cbsnews.com/stories/2005/04/25/politics/main690561.shtml.

Bush v. Gore, 531U.S. 98 (December 12, 2000).

Business Staff, "Sept. 11 Economic Toll: $1 Trillion," *The Oakland Press, Online Edition*, September 7, 2003.

Butt, Gerald, "Saddam Hussein Profile," *BBC News*, January 4, 2001, at www.news.bbc.co.uk/1/hi/world/middle_east/1100529.stm.

"Caliph," *Wikipedia, the Free Encyclopedia*, www.en.wikipedia.org/wiki/Caliph.

Carroll, Jill, "Iraqi Women Eye Islamic Law," *Christian Science Monitor*, February 25, 2005.

"Casualties - US vs. NVA/VC," recommended by *The History Channel*, at www.rjsmith.com/kia_tbl.html.

"Chapter 2: The Islamic Concept of Tawheed (Monotheism)," Tawhed al-Ibaadah, www.ahya.org/tjonline/eng/02/2tawheed.html.

"Charity Blames Invaders for Iraq 'Health Disaster,'" *Guardian Unlimited*, November 30, 2004, at www.guardian.co.uk/Iraq/Story/0,2763,1363083,00.html.

Chen, David W., "New Study Puts Sept. 11 Payout at $38 Billion," *New York Times*, November 8, 2004.

"China: Uighur Muslim Separatists - Updated Special Report," *Virtual Information Center*, March 20, 2003, www.vic-info.org.

Christopher, Mark, "China Ravenous - and Dangerous," *Houston Chronicle*, May 7, 2005, at www.cfr.org/pub8085/mark_christopher/appetite_for_oil_china_ravenous_and_dangerous.php.

Chughtai, Shaheen, "Profile: Kingdom of Saudi Arabia," *Aljazeera.net*, October 14, 2003, at www.english.aljazeera.net.

Clark, Richard, *Against All Enemies* (Free Press 2004).

Cole, Juan, Prof., "Muhammad Was a Terrorist?," *Center for History and News Media*, October 7, 2002, at www.hnn.us/articles/1018.html.

Coll, Steve, *Ghost Wars* (The Penguin Press 2004).

"Commanding Heights, Saudi Arabia, Overview," *PBS*, at www.pbs.org/wgbh/commandingheights/lo/countries/sa/sa_overview.html.

Comment, "Why Greater Israel Vision Has Perished," *The Observer/Guardian Unlimited*, January 11, 2004, at www.observer.guardian.co.uk/comment/story/0,6903,1120533,00.html.

"Contemporary Chronology of Iraq," at www.firethistime.org/contempchrono.htm.

Conversion of Gregorian dates to Hijra dates, or vice versa, see www.rabiah.com/convert/.

Cordesman, Anthony H., "Outside View: Restructuring U.S. Military," *Washington Times (UPI)*, April 15, 2005, at www.washingtontimes.com/upi-breaking/20050414-094312-4386r.htm.

Country Reports on Human Rights Practices - Saudi Arabia, 2002, March 31, 2003, U.S. Department of State.

"Cover Story: Anti-Islam, Religion and Ethics," *PBS*, December 20, 2002, at www.pbs.org/wnet/religionandethics/week616/cover.html.

Current List of Foreign Terrorist Organizations and Other Terrorist Organizations," Center for Defense Information, April 5, 2005, at www.cdi.org.

Dart, Bob, "Draft May Be Needed in a Year, Military Analysts Warn," *Cox News Service*, March 3/, 2//5, at www.truthout.org/docs_2005/033105C.shtml.

Davis, Douglas, "Mossad Warned CIA of Attacks - Reports," *The Internet Jerusalem Post*, September 17, 2001, at www.prisonplanet.com/mossad_warned_cia_of_attacks.html.

De Rooij, Paul, "Palestinian Misery in Perspective," *Arabic Media Internet Network*, June 1, 2004, at www.amin.org/eng/paul_de_rooij/2004/jun01.html.

Deans, Bob, "America's Popularity Plunges Worldwide," *Seattle Post-Intelligencer*, December 5, 2002 at www.seattlepi.nwsource.com/national/98525_poll05.shtml.

Dobbs, Michael, "Halliburton's Iraq Contracts Exceed $1.7 Billion," *Washington Post*, August 28, 2003.

"Dr. Ayman al-Zawahiri," Perspectives on World History and Current Events: *Middle East Project*, at www.pwhce.org/zawahiri.html.

"East Timor," *Wikipedia, the Free Encyclopedia*, at www.en.wikipedia.org/wiki/East_Timor.

Eggen, Dan and R. Jeffrey Smith, "FBI Agents Allege Abuse of Detainees at Guantanamo Bay," *Washington Post*, December 21, 2004.

"Egypt Frees Muslim Brotherhood Men," *Aljazeera.net*, April 10, 2005, at www.english.aljazeera.net/NR/exeres/0B8D1B0E-E2AA-42FD-83AC-4E79EA9E0C92.htm.

"Exclusive: Kerry Says UBL Tape Cost Him Election," *Fox News Channel*, November 21, 2004, at www.foxnews.com/printer_friendly_story/0,3566,139060,00.html.

"Fallujah," *Wikipedia, the Free Encyclopedia*, at www.en.wikipedia.org/wiki/Fallujah.

"Fast-Growing Islam Winning Converts in Western World," *CNN Interactive*, April 14, 1997, at www.cnn.com/WORLD/9704/14/egypt.islam/.

Fattah, Hassan M., "Saudi Court Orders Lashings for 15 Demonstrators," *New York Times*, January 13, 2005.

"Fatwa Bank, Details of Fatwa, What Are the Major Sins?," October 21, 2003, *IslamOnline.net*, at www.islamonline.net/fatwa/english/FatwaDisplay.asp?hFatwaID=106447.

Fein, Bruce, "Flawed Interim Constitution," *The Washington Times*, March 23, 2004, at www.washingtontimes.com.

"Fighting Islam's Fierce Moro Warriors - America's First War with Suicidal Islamic Warriors," *Military History Magazine*, April 2002, at www.freerepublic.com/focus/news/654540/posts.

Financial Statements of the United States Government for the Years Ended September 30, 2003, and September 20, 2002.

Fisk, Robert, Web Site, interviews with Osama Bin Laden, at www.robert-fisk.com/.

Fournier, Ron, "Bush Mocks Bin Laden As Evil Man," *Associated Press*, December 14, 2001, at www.multimedia.belointeractive.com/attack/response/1214bushvideo.html.

"France: Facts and Figures, Military," *World Sites Atlas*, adopted from *CIA World Fact Book 1998*, at www.sitesatlas.com/Europe/France/frastats.htm.

Full Text of Human Rights Record of US in 2004," *People's Daily Online*, March 3, 2005, at www.english.people.com.cn/200503/03/print20050303_175406.html.

Gall, Carlotta, "Muslim' Anti-American Protests Spread From Afghanistan," *New York Times*, May 14, 2005.

Gardner, Beth, "A Cleric Who Stuck to His Guns," *Associated Press - MSNBC*, May 27, 2004, at www.msnbc.msn.com/id/5078153.

Gates, John M., The U.S. Army and Irregular Warfare, "Chapter Three: The Pacification of the Philippines," November 2002, at www.wooster.edu/history/jgates/book-ch3.html.

Gellman, Barton and Thomas E. Ricks, "U.S. Concludes Bin Laden Escaped at Tora Bora Fight," *Washington Post*, April 17, 2002.

"General Says 'War on Terror' a Religious Struggle, Muslims Worship Idol," *Muslim American Society*, October 16, 2003, at www.masnet.org/news.asp?id=563.

"General: Sorry About Islam Remarks," *CBSNews.com*, October 18, 2003, at www.cbsnews.com/stories/2003/10/21/attack/main579249.shtml.

"Geneva Peace Initiative Set to Take Off," www.aljazeerah.info/, December 1, 2003.

"Genghis Khan," *Wikipedia, the Free Encyclopedia*, www.en.wikipedia.org/wiki/Genghis_Khan.

Ghabram Soref, President of American University, Kuwait, "An Arab Liberal Looks at the Postwar Middle East," *The Washington Institute for Near East Study*, Soref Symposium, 2003, www.washingtoninstitute.org/templateC07.php?CID=142.

Grossman, Andrew, "Finding the Law: Islamic Law (Sharia)," *LLRX.com*, August 1, 2002, updated August 11, 2002, at www.llrx.com/features/islamiclaw.htm.

"Gulf Cooperation Council - GCC," Arab German Consulting, at www.arab.de/arabinfo.gcc.htm.

"Gulf States Face Unemployment Problems," *Migration News*, February, 1995, at www.migration.ucdavis.edu/mn/.

Guzman, Gregory, "Christian Europe and Mongol Asia," *Essays in Medieval Studies 2*, at www.illinoismedieval.org/ems/VOL2/2ch13.html.

Gwynne, Rosalind, Department of Religious Affairs, University of Tennessee, "Draft: Al-Qaida and Al- Qur'an: The 'Tafsir' of Usamah bin Ladin," September 18, 2001, at www.web.utk.edu/~warda/bin_ladenand_quran.htm.

Haddad, G.F., "Imam Ahmad," edited and published by Syed Adad Ali, at www.geocities.com/alkuraan_alhuda/imams/Imam_humbul.htm.

Haddad, G.F., "Abu Hanifa" and "Greatest of Abu Hanifa," *Living Islam*, 2001, at www.livingislam.org/ahanifa_e.html.

Hadith Collection – "Bukhari," Spiritual Health Learning Community Center; www.spiritual-health.org/Sufi/Community/Bukhari/81.htm.

"Hamas," *Wikipedia, the Free Encyclopedia*, at www.en.wikipedia.org/wiki/Hamas.

Heges, Stephen J., "Military to Leave Saudi Arabia," *Chicago Tribune*, April 30, 2003, www.globalsecurity.org/org/news/2003/030430-psab01.htm.

"Hegira," *The Columbia Encyclopedia, 6th Ed., 2001*, at www.bartleby.com/65/he/Hegira.html.

Henshaw, John Mitchel, "Israel's Grand Design: Leaders Crave Area from Egypt to Iraq," *Media Monitor*, reprinting an article that first appeared in *The American Mercury Magazine* in the spring of 1968, at www.mediamonitors.net/johnhenshaw1.html.

Henzel, Christopher, "The Origins of Al-Qaeda Ideology," National Defense University, National War College, pp. 5-6, April 20, 2004.

Hersh, Seymour, "King's Ransom," *The New Yorker*, October 22, 2002.

Hersh, Seymour, *The Price of Power: Kissinger in the Nixon White House* (Summit Books 1st. Ed. 1983).

Hirsch, Robert L., Roger Bezdek, and Robert Wending, SAIC Corporation, "Peaking of World Oil Production: Impacts; Mitigation; & Risk Management," February 2005, at www.energybulletin.net/4638.html.

Hirst, Chrissie, "The Arabian Connection: The UK Arms Trade to Saudi Arabia," *Campaign Against Arms Trade*, at www.caat.org.uk/information/publications/countries/saudi-arabia.php.

"Historic Kyoto Treaty Inked Without the World's Biggest Polluter the US," *Agence France Presse*, February 16, 2005, at www.commondreams.org/headlines05/0216-12.htm.

Hooker, Richard, "Islam: The Abbasid Dynasty," www.wsu.edu/~dee/ISLAM/ABASSID.HTM.

Hourani, George F., translator, "Averroes," *Islamic Philosophy Online Project*, at www.muslimphilosophy.com/ir/fasl.htm.

"How Much Did the Gulf War Cost the US? Appendix P," Conduct of the Persian Gulf War, The Final Report to the U.S. Congress by the U.S. Department of Defense, April, 1992, at www.people.psych.cornell.edu/~fhoran/gulf/GW_cost/GW_payments.html.

"Hubal, the Moon God of the Kaba," Islam: Truth or Myth, at www.bible.ca/islam/islam-moon-god-hubal.htm.

"Human Rights in Saudi Arabia: A Deafening Silence," *Human Rights Watch Backgrounder*, December 2001.

"Ibn Rushd (Averroes), 1126-1198 CE," *Islamic Philosophy Online Project*, at www.muslimphilosophy.com/ir/art/ir100.htm.

"Ilm of Hadiths," at www.geocities.com/~abdulwahid/hadith/ilm_hadith.html.

"Imam Abu Hanifa," *Islamonline.com*, July 15, 2004, at www.islamonline.com/cgi-bin/news_service/profile_story.asp?service_id=855

Al-Tirmidhi [Imam Al-Tirmidhi], full name Abu Isa Muhammad ibn Isa ibn Musa ibn al-Dahhak al-Sulami al-Tirmidhi (824-892), *Wikipedia, The Free Encyclopedia*, at www.en.wikipedia.org/wiki/Al-Tirmidhi.

"India: Gujarat Massacre Cases Sabotaged," *Human Rights Watch News*, July 1, 2003, at www.hrw.org/press/2003/06/india070103.htm.

"Interesting Quotes from the Hadith on Jihad," Christian Apologetics & Research Ministry, www.carm.org/islam/hadith_jihad.htm, quoting from the online source of the Hadith, which is found at www.usc.edu/dept/MSA/fundamentals/hadithsunnah/bukhari/.

"International Criminal Court," *Human Rights Watch*, www.hrw.org/campaigns/icc.

"International Day of Action," *The Guardian*, October 17, 2001, at www.cpa.org.au/garchve4/1067day.html.

"Interview of Usama Bin Ladin by John Miller - May 1998," *ABC News*, at www.robert-fisk.com/usama_interview_john_millerabc.htm.

"Intifada Timeline," *Al-AhramWeeklyOnline*, Issue No. 710, 30 September to 6 October, at www.weekly.ahram.org.eg/print/2004/710/fo5.htm.

"Iran-Iraq War," *Wikipedia, The Free Encyclopedia*, at www.en.wikipedia.org/wiki/Iran-Iran_War.

"Iraq Death Toll Tops 270 in 9 Days," *MSNBC News*, May 6, 2005, at www.msnbc.msn.com/

"Iraq Rejects Saudi Troops," *Rediff.com*, October 19, 2004, at www.rediff.com/news/2004/oct/19saudi.htm.

"Iraq Surveys Show 'Humanitarian Emergency,'" *UNICEF Information Newsline*, August 12, 1999, www.unicef.org/newsline/99pr29.htm.

"Iraq WMD Report Enters Political Fray," *CNN.com*, October 4, 2004, at www.edition.cnn.com/2004/ALLPOLITICS/10/07/wmd.iraq/.

"Islam," *Global Security.com* at www.globalsecurity.org/military/intro/islam.htm and /islam-kharijite.htm and /islam-salafi.htm.

"Islamic Calendar," *Islam.com*, at www.islam.com/IslamCalen.htm.

"Islamic Classical Legal Texts," at *Advanced Legal Studies Institute*, www.nyazee.com/islaw/alsi%20Islamic%20Law%20Series.html.

"Islamists Dominate Saudi Municipal Elections," *Associated Press, Washington Times*, April 24, 2005, at www.ap.washingtontimes.com/dynamic/stories/S/SAUDI_ELECTIONS?SITE=DCTMS&SECTION=HOME.

"Israel, Military Cooperation with the United States," at www.country-data.com/cgi-bin/query/r-6860.html.

"Israeli Arabs, Land and Arab Refugees," Country Studies, U.S. Library of Congress, December 9, 2004, at www.countrystudies.us/israel/23.htm.

"Israeli Politics: Information Regarding Sabra and Shatila," *Palestine Monitor*, at www.palestinemonitor.org/israelipoli/sabra_shatilla_links.htm.

"Italy Plans Withdrawal, Further Eroding U.S.-Led Coalition," *Associated Press, MSNBC.com*, March 15, 2005, at www.msnbc.msn.com/id/7193188/.

Jaffa, Eric, "The Mistreatment of Iraqi Prisoners: More Than Six People Involved," *MoveLeftMedia*, at www.moveleft.com/moveleft_essay_2004_05_09_if_bush_were_truly_sorry_about_the_prisoners_in_iraq.asp.

"Jews," *MSN Encarta*, at www.encarta.msn.com/encyclopedia_761567959/Jews.html.

Johnson, Chalmers, *The Sorrows of Empire: Militarism, Secrecy, and the End of the Republic*, (Metropolitan Books, 1st Ed. 2004).

Johnson, David, "Terror Suspects Sent to Egypt by the Dozens, Panel Reports," *New York Times*, May 12, 2005

"Jordan Crown Prince Relieved of Title," *Aljazeera.net*, November 28, 2004, at www.english.aljazeera.net/NR/exeres/14554311-E5A6-48AF-B5B4-45E8CAFBA9E1.htm.

"Kaaba," *Wikipedia, the Free Encyclopedia*, at www.en.wikipedia.org/wiki/Kaaba.

Kaplan, David E., "Investigative Report: Hearts, Minds, and Dollars: in an Unseen Front in the War on Terrorism, America Is Spending Millions . . . To Challenge the Very Face of Islam," *U.S. News & World Report*, p. 22, April 25, 2005.

Kechichian, Joseph A., "Testing the Saudi 'Will to Power:' Challenges Confront Prince Abdallah," *Middle East Policy Council*, Vol. X, Winter 2003, at www.mepc.org/public_asp/journal_vol10/0312_kechichian.asp.

Kennicott, Philip, "An About-Face on America," *The Washington Post*, August 24, 2004, p. C1.

Kessler, Glenn, "Bush Sticks to Broad Strokes," *The Washington Post*, June 3, 2003, at www.washingtonpost.com/ac2/wp-dyn?pagename=article&contentId=A5423-2003Jun2&notFound=true.

Khan, Muqtedar, "Clear and Present Danger," *Al-Ahram Weekly*, Issue No. 643, June 19-25, 2003, at www.globalpolicy.org/empire/analysis/2003/0619danger.htm.

"Khobar Towers Bombing," *Wikipedia, The Free Encyclopedia*, www.en.wikipedia.org/wiki/Khobar_Towers_bombing

"King Hussein Ponders Change in Succession to Jordan's Throne," *CNN.com*, January 22, 1999, at www.cnn.com/WORLD/meast/9901/22/jordan.king/.

"King Saud," *Encyclopedia of the Orient*, at www.i-cias.com/e.o/saud.htm

Kirchoff, Sue, "Federal Deficit Hits Record $374.2 Billion," *USA Today*, October 20, 2003.

"Kitaab At-Tawheed (The Book of Tawheed [Oneness of God])," found at www.islamicweb.com/beliefs/creed/abdulwahab/.

"Kurdistan," November 12, 2004, at www.politicalresources.net/kurdistan.htm.

"Kurds," *Columbia Encyclopedia, Sixth Edition, 2001*, www.bartleby.com/65/ku/Kurds.html.

"Kuwait Is US Key Partner in Combating Terrorism: Rumsfeld," *China View*, December 9, 2004, at www.news.xinhuanet.com/english/2004-12/09/content_2311126.htm.

"Kuwait Will Not 'Americanize' Textbooks," *Jihad Watch*, January 2, 2004, at www.jihadwatch.org/archives/000542.php.

Labott, Elise, "Saudi Plans Muslim Troops in Iraq," *CNN.com*, July 28, 2004, at www.cnn.com/2004/WORLD/meast/07/28/powell.saudi/.

Ladah, Michael S. and Suleiman I. Ajlouni, "Mr. Bush, What About Israel's Defiance of UN Resolutions: An Open Letter to George W. Bush," *Media Monitors*, September 29, 2002, at www.mediamonitors.net/michaelsladah&suleimaniajlouni1.html.

Lamb, Karin, "Worries Arise About Fate of Arafat Financial Empire," *Seattle Times*, December 11, 2004.

"Land of Israel," *Wikipedia: The Free Encyclopedia*, www.en.wikipedia.org/wiki/Eretz_Yisrael.

Landers, Jim, "Iraq's Unsecured Ammo Dumps Providing Explosives for Insurgency," *Dallas Morning News*, December 22, 2004.

Laville, Sandra, "Saudi Names the Cleric Filmed with Bin Laden," *News.Telegraph*, December 15, 2001, at www.telegraph.co.uk/news/main.jhtml?xml=/news/2001/12/15/wvid15.xml.

Lawless, Jill, "Al-Qaida Treaty Rejected," *San Francisco Examiner (Associated Press),* April 16, 2004.

"Leading Saudi Dissident 'Freed,'" *BBC News*, March 25, 2003, at www.news.bbc.co.uk/1/hi/world/middle_east/2885647.stm

"League of Arab States: Arab Summit Beirut, 27-8 March 2002," *One World-Nations Online*, at www.nationsonline.org/oneworld/arab_peace_plan.htm.

Leonnig, Carol D., "Further Gitmo Detainee Abuse Alleged," *Washington Post*, December 25, 2004.

Lichtblau, Eric Lichtblau, "Coalition Forms to Oppose Parts of Antiterrorism Law, *New York Times*, March 23, 2005.

Lipkin, Lewis, "French Anti-Semitism: From the Middle Ages to the Dreyfus Affair," June 1, 2002, *Think Tank-Israel*, at www.think-Israel.org/frenchAS.html.

"List of Islamic Terms in Arabic," *Wikipedia, the Free Encyclopedia*, at www.answers.com/topic/list-of-islamic-terms-in-arabic.

Lothar, "The Axis of Evil: US, Pakistan, Israel, & Saudi Arabia,"January 29, 2005, at www.matrix.bangkokpost.co.th/forums/print.php?Message_ID=7919.

Luwaran.com at www.luwaran.com.

Macintyre, Ben, *The Man Who Would Be King: The First American in Afghanistan*, p. 46 (Farrar, Stauss and Groux, 1st Ed. 2004).

"Mahmoud Abbas," *Wikipedia: the Free Encyclopedia*, www.en.wikipedia.org/wiki/Mahmoud_Abbas.

Mainville, Michael, "U.S. Bases Overseas Show New Strategy," *Pittsburg Post Gazette*, July 26, 2004, at www.globalsecurity.org/org/news/2004/040726-us-bases.htm.

"Major Sins," www.themodernreligion.com/misc/hh/major_sins.htm.

Malik Muwatta, Hadith, at www.usc.edu/dept/MSA/fundamentals/hadithsunnah.

"Malnutrition Rising Among Iraqi Children," Associated Press, The Register-Guard, Eugene, Oregon, USA, November 23, 2004, at www.registerguard.com/news/2004/11/23/a2.int.hunger.1123.html.

Mann, James, *Rise of the Vulcans - The History of Bush's War Cabinet* (Viking- The Penguin Group - 2004).

Manville, Michael, "U.S. Bases Overseas Show New Strategy," *Pittsburg Post-Gazette*, July 26, 2004, at www.globalsecurity.org/org/news/2004/040726-us-bases.htm.

"March 11, 2004, Madrid Attacks," *Wikipedia, the Free Encyclopedia*, March 11, 2004, www.en.wikipedia.org/wiki/March_11_2004_Madird_attacks.

Marquardt, Eric, "Losing the Hearts and Minds," *Power and Interest News Report*, June 22, 2003, at www.pinr.com/report.php?ac=view_report&report_id=60&language_id=1.

Martin, Patrick, "US Accelerates Preparations for Invasion of Iraq," *World Socialist Web Site*, January 4, 2003, at www.wsws.org/articles/2003/jan2003/iraq-j04.shtml.

McDonnell, Patrick J.and John Hendren, "Fallouja Fight Among Deadliest in Years for US; Last Month's Battle Left 71 American Troops Dead and 623 Injured," *Los Angeles Times*, December 2, 2004.

McKillop, Andrew , "Per Capita Oil Demand and World Oil Demand Growth," September 20, 2004, at www.vheadline.com/readnews.asp?id=22842.

McLuhan, Marshall, *Understanding the Media: the Extensions of Man* (McGraw Hill 1964).

"Medina," *Wikipedia, the Free Encyclopedia*, at www.en.wikipedia.org/wiki/Medina.

"Mid East Maps: Map of UN Partition Plan for Palestine - 1947," at www.mideastweb.org/unpartition.htm.

"Middle East and North Africa: Information and Interior Ministers Must Tackle Clampdown on Freedom of Expression," Amnesty International, January 17, 2003, at www.web.amnesty.org/library/Index/ENGMDE01001 2003?open&of=ENG-300.

"Middle East: Attitudes Toward the United States," Congressional Research Service, CRS Report for Congress, the Library of Congress, December 31, 2001, at www.fpc.state.gov/documents/organization/7858.pdf.

"Military Forces in the Middle East," *Houston Chronicle*, March 18, 2003, www.globalsecurity.org/org/news/2003/030318-military02.htm.

Mills, T.F., et. al., "Iraqi Kurdistan: Political Parties," September 27, 1997, at www.flag.de/FOTW/flags/krd%7Diq.html.

Momayezi, Nasser, "Islamic Revivalism and the Quest for Political Power," *The Journal of Conflict Studies*, University of New Brunswick, Vol. XVII, No. 2, Fall 1997, at www.lib.unb.ca/Texts/JCS/bin/get.cgi?directory=FALL97/articles/&filename=MOMAYEZI.html.

"Moro Islamic Liberation Front," Federation of American Scientists: Intelligence Resource Program, at www.fas.org/irp/world/para/milf.htm.

"Moro National Liberation Front (MNLF)- Terrorist Group Profile," *MIPT-Terrorism Knowledge Base*, at www.tkb.org/Group.jsp?groupID=202.

Morris, Edmund, *Theodore Rex* (Random House 2001).

"Most of U.S. Forces Withdrawn From Saudi Arabia," *USA Today*, August 28, 2003, www.usatoday.com/news/washington/2003-08-28-ustroops-saudiarabia_x.htm.

Mott, Maryann, "Alaska-Refuge Drilling Approved by U.S. House," *National Geographic News*, April 21, 2005, at www.news.nationalgeographic.com/news/2005/04/0421_050421_alaskadrilling.html.

Mouawad, Jan and Simon Romero, "Unmentioned Energy Fix: A 55 M.P.H. Speed Limit," *New York Times*, May 1, 2005.

"Mubarak Warns of 100 Bin Ladens," *CNN.com*, March 31, 2003, at www.cnn.com/2003/WORLD/meast/03/31/

iraq.egypt.mubarak.reut/.

"Muhammad," *Wikipedia, the Free Encyclopedia*, www.en.wikipedia.org/wiki/Muhammad.

"Muslims Angered by Baptist Criticism," *CNN.com*, June 13, 2002, at www.archives.cnn.com/2002/ ALLPOLITICS/06/13/cf.crossfire/.

Natta, Dan, Jr., "Growing Evidence U.S. Sending Prisoners to Torture Capital Despite Bad Record on Human Rights, Uzbekistan is Ally," *New York Times*, May 1, 2005.

"New U.S. Memo Backs Off Torture Arguments," *Associated Press - New York Times*, December 31, 2004.

Nichols, Bill, "U.N.: Iraq Had No WMD After 1994," *USA Today*, March 2, 2003, at www.usatoday.com/news/ world/iraq/2004-03-02-un-wmd_x.htm.

Osama Bin Laden interview with *Ummat Newspaper*, Karachi, Pakistan, September 28, 2001, reprinted in English at www.robert-fisk.com/usama_interview_ummat.htm.

Osama Bin Laden: A Chronology of His Political Life, *PBS: Frontline*, at www.pbs.org/wgbh/pages/frontline/shows/binladen/etc/cron.html.

Ottaway, David B., "U.S. Eyes Money Trails of Saudi-Backed Charities," *Washington Post*, August 19, 2004, at www.washingtonpost.com/wp-dyn/articles/A13266-2004Aug18.html.

Oyekan, Abdullah Jibri, "Accommodating Kufr [apostates, non-believers]," *Salaam*, www.salaam.co.uk/ knowledge/kufr.php.

"Palestinian Detainees Go On a Hunger Strike, Calls For Freedom Mount On Palestinian Detainees' International Day," Palestinian Media Center, *Aljazeerah Info*, April 16, 2005, at www.aljazeerah.info/News%20archives/ 2005%20News%20Archives/April%202005%20News/16%20n/Palestinian%20Detainees%20Go%20on%20a% 20Hunger%20Strike,%20Calls%20for%20Freedom%20Mount%20on%20Palestinian%20Detainees'%20Intern ational%20Day.htm.

"Pat Robertson Attacks Islam, Transcript of Hannity & Colmes, September 18, 2002," at *Muslim Access*, www. muslimaccess.com/articles/islamophobes/pat_robertson.asp.

"Periscope: Gitmo - SouthCom Showdown," *Newsweek Magazine*, May 9, 2005.

Phillips, James A. Phillips, "Spain's Retreat After the Madrid Bombings Rewards Terrorism" *The Heritage Foundation*, March 16, 2004, Web Memo No. 448 at www.heritage.org/Research/Europe/wm448.cfm.

Piett, Barbara, "Israeli Arabs Struggle to Fit in," *BBC News*, January 26, 2003, at www.news.bbc.co.uk/2/hi/ middle_east/2691357.stm.

"Poet Flattered by Bin Laden's Attention," *FoxNews.com*, January 6, 2002, at www.foxnews.com/ story/0,2933,42314,00.html.

"Politics of Saudi Arabia," *Wikipedia: The Free Encyclopedia*, at www.en.wikipedia.org/wiki/Politics_of_Saudi_ Arabia.

Pollack, Kenneth M., *Arabs at War: Military Effectiveness, 1948-1991* (University of Nebraska Press 2002).

Praust, Jordan, Prof., "The Common Plan to Violate the Geneva Conventions," *Jurist: Legal Intelligence, University of Pittsburg School of Law*, May 25, 2004, at www.jurist.law.pitt.edu/forum/paust2.php.

"President Bush Reaffirms Resolve to War on Terror, Iraq, and Afghanistan, White House Press Release, March 19, 2004, at www.whitehouse.gov/news/releases/2004/03/20040319-3.html.

"President George W. Bush's Speech to a Joint Session and Congress and to the American People, September 20,

2001: "They hate our freedoms . . . of religion . . . of speech . . . to vote and assemble and disagree . . .." www. whitehouse.gov/news/releases/2001/09/print/20010920-8.html.

"Prince Faisal bin Turki's Speech in U.K on Saudi Energy Industry," Royal Embassy of Saudi Arabia, Washington, D.C., December 2, 2000, at www.saudiembassy.net/2000News/Statements/SpeechDetail. asp?cIndex=347.

"Prince Naif Ibn Abdul Aziz Reiterates the Keeness of the Council of Arab Interior Ministers to Enhance Security and Stability in the Arab World," *Ain-Al-Yaqeen*, January 24, 2003, at www.ain-al-yaqeen.com/ issues/20030124/feat5en.htm.

"Q & A: Kashmir Dispute," *BBC News*, November 25, 2002, at www.news.bbc.co.uk/1/hi/world/353352.stm.

"Qatar, Saudi Arabia Sign Border Agreement," *People's Daily*, March 22, 2001, at www.english.people.com. cn/english/200103/22/eng20010322_65657.html.

"Quraish," *Wikipedia, the Free Encyclopedia*, at www.en.wikipedia.org/wiki/Quraish.

Rahman, Fazlur, "Hadith, General Information," www.mb-soft.com/believe/txw/hadith.htm also see www. geocities.com/~abdulwahid/hadith/ilm_hadith.html.

Rai, Milan, "News & Analysis: Turning Point Fallujah: How US Atrocities Sparked the Iraqi Resistance," *ElectronicIraq.Net*, May 4, 2005, at www.electroniciraq.net/news/1947.shtml.

Randall, Kate, "Iraqi Child Deaths Have Doubled Under UN-Imposed Sanctions," *World Socialist Web Site*, August 14, 1999, www.wsws.org/articles/1999/aug1999/iraq-a14.shtml.

Raum, Tom, "Bush Shifts War Rationale From Iraqi Arms," *KansasCity.com, the Kansas City Star*, September 8, 2003, at www.kansascity.com/mld/kansascity/news/breaking_news/6722744.htm.

"Reactions by Mainline Christians, A Muslim Group, Etc. to Verbal Attacks on Muslims," *Religious Tolerance*, May 9, 2003, at www.religioustolerance.org/reac_ter18c.htm.

Rees, Matt, "Mohammed al-Durra," *Time Magazine Pacific*, No. 51, December 25, 2000, at www.time.com/ time/pacific/magazine/20001225/poy_mohammed.html.

Reichmann, Deb, "Bin Laden Draws Rare Mention from Bush," *Chicago Sun-Times*, March 4, 2005, www. suntimes.com/output/terror/cst-nws-bin04.html.

Reichmann, Deb, "Bush Urges Saudis to Boost Oil Production, *Associated Press, LA Times*, April 25, 2005, at www.latimes.com/news/nationworld/politics/wire/sns-ap-bush-saudi-arabia,1,3680754.story?coll=sns-ap-politics-headlines.

"Report on International Religious Freedom: United Arab Emirates," Jewish Virtual Library, www. jewishvirtuallibrary.org/jsource/anti-semitism/relunitedarabemirates00.html.

"Rights Groups Dismayed by Afghan Strongman's Post," *Reuters*, March 3, 2005, at www.afghanchat.com/ article3103.html.

"Road Map for Peace," *Wikipedia, the Free Encyclopedia*, www.en.wikipedia.org/wiki/Road_map_for_peace.

Roberts, Paul Craig, "A Country Destroyed," April 20, 2004, www.lewrockwell.com/roberts/roberts38.html.

Roffe, Sarine Roffe, "The Jews of Aleppo," *JewishGen:SeafardSIG*, at www.jewishgen.org/SefardSIG/ AleppoJews.htm.

Rubin, Michael, "Sanctions on Iraq: A Valid Anti-American Grievance?," *Middle East Review of International Affairs* (MERIA), vol. 5, no. 4, December 2001, www.meria.idc.ac.il/journal/2001/issue4/jv5n4a6.htm.

Rumsfeld memorandum to General "Dick "Meyers, Paul Wolfowitz, Gen."Pete" Pace, and "Doug" Feith, subject: Global War on Terrorism," October 16, 2003, at Dave Moniz and Tom Squitieri, "Defense Memo: A Grim Outlook," *Information Clearing House,* October 22, 2003 (USA Today), at www. informationclearinghouse.info/article5047.htm.

"SA Mufti Calls Upon Muslims Not to Join U.S. Coalition Against Terrorism," *Middle East Research Institute,* No. 278, October 1, 2001, at www.memri.org/bin/opener.cgi?Page=archives&ID=SP27801.

"Saddam Hussein Arrested in Iraq," *BBC News,* December 14, 2003.

Sadeq, Musadeq, "Anti-U.S. Violence Erupts in Afghanistan," *Washington Post,* May 12, 2005.

Sahih al-Tirmidhi, "Hashi Al-Eritre," *Islamic Forum,* December 20, 2004, citing to www.gawaher.com/index.php?act=Search&CODE=show&searchid=3aa27ac52f546cb8c7a79ca149e25c99&sea rch_in=posts&result_type=posts&highlite=sahih+al+tirmidhi

Sahih Bukhari, Hadith, at www.usc.edu/dept/MSA/fundamentals/hadithsunnah/bukhari/052.sbt.html.

Sahih Muslim, Hadith, at www.usc.edu/dept/MSA/fundamentals/hadithsunnah/muslim/001.smt.html.

Sahmi, Mohammad, "Iran's Nuclear Program. Part II: Are Nuclear Reactors Necessary?," *Payvand's Iran News,* October 3,2003, at www.payvand.com/news/03/oct/1022.html.

Sandalow, Mark, "News Analysis: Record Shows Bush Shifting on Iraq War - President's Rationale for the Invasion Continues to Evolve," *San Francisco Chronicle,* September 29, 2004, at www.sfgate.com/cgi-bin/ article.cgi?file=/c/a/2004/09/29/MNGE590O711.DTL.

Sanders, Richard, "Regime Change: How the CIA put Saddam's Party in Power," October 24, 2002, at www. hartford-hwp.com/archives/51/217.html.

"Saudi Arabia offers initiative to promote economic development and political participation across all Arab countries," Saudi Embassy, January 21, 2003, at www.saudiembassy.net/2003News/Press/PressDetail.asp?cYea r=2003&cIndex=68.

"Saudi Arabia Is Not an Islamic State - Saudi Arabia Deals in Riba," *Islamic-State.Org,* at www.islamic-state. org/saudi/riba.shtml.

"Saudi Arabia Plagued by Dissent, Economic Instability," *Jewish Institute for National Security Affairs,* September 1, 1996, at www.jinsa.org/articles/articles.html/function/view/categoryid/111/documentid/297/ history/3,2359,947,653,111,297.

"Saudi Arabia Suspends 900 Imams," *BBC News,* March 17, 2004, at www.news.bbc.co.uk/1/hi/world/middle_ east/3520822.stm.

"Saudi Arabia, Arms Sales Tables, Total Licenses/Agreements 1990-2000," *Federation of American Scientists* at www.fas.org/asmp/profiles/saudi_arabia.htm.

"Saudi Arabia, Country Analysis Briefs," Energy Information Agency, United States Department of Energy, at www.eia.doe.gov/cabs/saudi.html.

"Saudi Arabia," *Wikipedia, the Free Encyclopedia,* at www.en.wikipedia.org/wiki/Saudi_Arabia.

"Saudi Arabia," *Encarta.com* at www.encarta.msn.com/encnet/refpages/search.aspx?q=saudi+arabia.

"Saudi Arabia: Arab Nationalism," Country Study, 2004, U.S. Department of State, U.S. Library of Congress, at www.countrystudies.us/saudi-arabia/60.htm.

"Saudi Arabia: History and Culture," *U.K. Travel Guide,* at www.uk.holidaysguide.yahoo.com/p-travelguide-7577-saudi_arabia_travel_guide-i.

"SAUDI ARABIA: Saudi Clerics Forbid Muslims to Watch US Arabic Channel [Al Hurra]," *The Straits Times*, March 8, 2004, reproduced in *Asia Media: The Asia Pacific Media Network*, UCLA Asia Institute, at www.asiamedia.ucla.edu/article.asp?parentid=8702.

"Saudi Aramco," Ministry of Petroleum & Mineral Resources, Kingdom of Saudi Arabia, at www.mopm.gov.sa/html/en/saudico_e.html.

"Saudi Cash Joins Forces with Nuclear Pakistan," *Financial Times*, August 4, 2004, at www.inn.globalfreepress.com/modules/news/article.php?storyid=645.

"Saudi Plan to Topple Saddam," *BBC News World Edition*, January 17, 2003, at www.news.bbc.co.uk/2/hi/middle_east/2667051.stm.

"Saudi Scholar Forbids Taking Part in Attacking Iraq," *ArabicNews.com*, Marach 7, 2003, at www.arabicnews.com/ansub/Daily/Day/030307/2003030714.html.

"Saudi Sentences Reformist to 5 Years," *DefenseSupplier.com*, reprinting UPI press release dated September 14, 2004, at www.defensesupplier.com.

"Saudis Confront Extremist Ideologies: Anti-Terror Forum Is Latest Sign of Changing Attitudes," *Washington Post*, February 6, 2005.

"Saudis Divided Over Foreign Troops Presence in Riyadh," February 19, 2001, Saudi Arabia: An NCO Reports [sic], August 15, 2001, at www.d-n-i.net/fcs/comments/c424.htm.

"Saudi-U.S. Relations: A Future of Steady Growth," *The Washington Times*, A Special I International Report, September 22, 2000, at www.internationalspecialreports.com/middleeast/00/saudiarabia/2.html; and www.infopedia.ruv.net/19/1967.html.

"Saudi-US Relations Information Service Newsletter Special Supplement: Terrorists Strike Multiple Targets in Riyadh," May 13, 2003, at www.saudi-us-relations.org/newsletter/saudi-relations-supplement-5-13.html

Schifferes, Steve, "US Names 'Coalition of the Willing,'" *BBC News*, March 18, 2003, at www.news.bbc.co.uk/2/hi/americas/2862343.stm.

Schmidt, Susan, "Spreading Saudi Fundamentalism in U.S.: Network of Wahhabi Mosques, Schools, Web Sites Probed by FBI," *Washington Post*, October 2, 2003.

Schmidtt, Eric, "No Criminal Charges for Officer at Abu Ghraib Interrogations," *The New York Times*, May 12, 2005.

Schwartz, Stephen, *The Two Faces of Islam* (Doubleday November 2002).

"Serbs Sorry for Srebrenica Deaths," *BBC News World Edition*, November 10, 2004, at www.news.bbc.co.uk/2/hi/europe/3999985.stm.

Shanker, Thom , "Pentagon Says Iraq Effort Limits Ability to Fight Other Conflicts," *New York Times*, May 3, 2005.

Sharma, Amol, "India Winning Higher-Status Jobs from US," Christian Science Monitor, June 18, 2003, at www.csmonitor.com/2003/0618/p01s03-wosc.html.

Shea, Jim, "A Whole New Meaning to Texas Hold 'Em," *The Salt Lake Tribune*, April 30, 2005, at www.sltrib.com/portlet/article/html/fragments/print_article.jsp?article=2699615.

"Sheikh Omar Abdul Rahman," at www.islam.co.za/saiin/abdulrahman.html.

"Shites," *Infoplease*, at www.infoplease.com/ce6/society/A0844916.html.

Slevin, Peter and Mike Allen, "Bush: Sharon a Man of Peace," *Washington Post*, April 19, 2002.

Smith, R. Jeffrey and Dan Eggen, "New Papers Suggest Detainee Abuse Was Widespread," *Washington Post*, December 22, 2004.

"Societal Framework," *Globalsecurity.org*, at www.globalsecurity.org/military/world/iraq/society.htm.

"Somalia," *Military.com*, at www.military.com/Resources/HistorySubmittedFileView?file=history_somalia.htm.

"Somalia: Human Rights Developments," *Human Rights Watch*, 2004, at www.hrw.org/reports/1994/WR94/Africa-08.htm.

Soref, Ghabram, President of American University, Kuwait, "An Arab Liberal Looks at the Postwar Middle East," *The Washington Institute for Near East Study, Soref Symposium, 2003*, www.washingtoninstitute.org/templateC07.php?CID=142.

Spolar, Christine, "14 'Enduring Bases' Set in Iraq," *Chicago Tribune*, March 23, 2004, www.globalsecurity.org/org/news/2004/040323-enduring-bases.htm.

Stack, Megan K., "Mubarak Keeps Egypt Guessing in Interview: The Long Time President's Seven-Hour Tete-a-Tete with a Reporter on TV Is a Journey to the Past, and His Critics Find In It Little Hope for Change," *Los Angeles Times*, May 1, 2005, at www.latimes.com.

Starobin, Paul, et. al., "The Next Oil Frontier," *Business Week Online*, May 27, 2002, at www.businessweek.com/magazine/content/02_21/b3784008.htm.

"Struggle for Peace: Special Section," *CNN.Com*, www.cnn.com/WORLD/struggle_for_peace/.

"Sudanese Celebrate Peace Treaty," *ABC News*, January 9, 2005, at www.abcnews.go.com/International/wireStory?id=398719.

"Sudanese JEM Rebel Leader Opts for Darfur Criminal Court," *Sudan Tribune*, May 3, 2004, at www.sudantribune.com/article.php3?id_article=9390.

Sun Tzu, *The Art of War*, translated by Samual B. Griffith (Oxford University Press 1963).

Sunan Abu-Dawud, Hadith, at www.usc.edu/dept/MSA/fundamentals/hadithsunnah/abudawud/039.sat.html.

Suskind, Ron, *The Price of Loyalty* (Simon & Schuster 2004).

Symon, Fiona, "Afghanistan's Northern Alliance, *BBC News*, September 19, 2001, at www.news.bbc.co.uk/1/hi/world/south_asia/1552994.stm.

Tammeus, Bill, "Giving Islam Short Shrift," *Kansas City Star*, August 7, 2004, at www.kansascity.com/mld/kansascitystar/living/religion/9337928.htm.

Tandler, Stewart, "Abu Hamza Accused of Inciting Hate and Murder," *Timesonline*, October 20, 2004, at www.timesonline.co.uk/printFriendly/0,,1-2-1319188-2,00.html.

Tarabay, James, "No Sign of Government Strategy for Defeating Insurgents," *Turkish Weekly, The New Anatolian*, May 6, 2005, at www.turkishweekly.net/comments.php?id=997.

Teitelbaum, Joshua, "Holier than Thou, Saudi Arabia's Islamic Opposition," *The Washington Institute for Near East Policy*, Executive Summary, 2000, at www.washingtoninstitute.org/templateC04.php?CID=53.

"Ten Things Which Nullify Ones [sic] Islam," at www.idrismosque.com/vio.html.

"Terrorist Group Profiles: Hamas," Naval Postgraduate School, Dudley Knox Library, at www.library.nps.navy.mil/home/tgp/hamas.htm.

"The Arab Israeli Conflict: History Palestine, Jordan, etc.," at *Arab2.com*, www.arab2.com/biography/Arab-Israeli-Conflict.htm.

"The Arab League Peace Plan,'" *Jewish Virtual Library*, March 27, 2002, at www.jewishvirtuallibrary.org/jsource/Peace/arabplan.html.

"The Arab Peace Initiative," *Middle East Web*, March 28, 2002, at www.mideastweb.org/saudipeace.htm.

"The Assad Era," *Country Studies*, at www.country-studies.com/syria/the-assad-era.html.

"The Avowed Enemy - The Devout Mujahid," originally published in the 20th issue of *Nida-ul Islam Magazine*, September-October 1997, at http:www.islam.org.au/articles/20/ikrimah.htm.

"The Battle of Jamal (Camel)," *Islamic Occasions Network*, at www.ezsoftech.com/islamic/jamal.asp.

"The Battle of Uhud," Muslim American Society, Minnesota Chapter, at www.masmn.org/documents/Books/Safiur_Rahman_Mubarakpuri/Raheeq_Al_Maktoom/408.htm.

"The Best Generations," Islam and New Zealand Muslim Community, May 14, year unknown, at www.nzmuslim.net/article101.html.

"The China Currency Exchange Rate Problem: Facts and Policy Options," *The U.S.-China Economic and Security Review Commission*, May 9, 2005, at www.uscc.gov/researchpapers/2005/05_05_09currency_exchange_rate.htm

"The Franklin 'Prophecy:' Modern Anti-Semitic Myth Making," at www.adl.org/special_reports/franklin_prophecy/franklin_intro.asp.

"The Man at the Center: Saudi Prince Abdullah," *The Estimate*, Vol. XV, No. 2, January 25, 2002, at www.theestimate.com/public/012502c.html.

"The Ottoman Empire: A Chronological Outline," at www.turizm.net/turkey/history/ottoman.html.

"The Power of Saudi Arabia's Islamic Leaders," *Middle East Quarterly*, September 1999, quoting in turn Abir, "Saudi Arabia: Government, Society, and the Gulf Crisis," p. 178. See www.meforum.org/article/482.

"The Royal Diwan," www.countrystudies.us/saudi-arabia/48.htm, of the United States State Department, citing to the Library of Congress.

Thornton, Ted, "Muhammad and Early Islamic Period 570-632 C.E.," at www.nmhschool.org/tthornton/mehistorydatabase/muhammad_and_early_islamic_perio.htm.

Thornton, Ted, Civil War in Lebanon, History of the Middle East Database, www.nmhschool.org/tthornton/mehistorydatabase/civil_war_in_lebanon.htm.

"Thoughts on the Ten Commandments," www.etori.tripod.com/commandments.html.

"Timeline on Terror Prisoners' Treatment," *Newsday.com*, January 6, 2005, at www.newsday.com/news/nationworld/world/wire/sns-ap-prisoner-abuse-timeline,0,7785463.story.

"Tirmidhi (209-279 H)," Sunnah.org, at www.sunnah.org/historyScholars/imam_tirmidhi.htm.

"Toting the Casualties of War: Beth Osborne Daponte Talks About Her Estimates of Iraq's Gulf War Dead Got Her in Deep Trouble with the White House," *Business Week Online*, February 6, 2003, at www.businessweek.com/bwdaily/dnflash/feb2003/nf2003026_0167_db052.htm.

"Transcript of Osama Bin Laden Interview by Peter Arnett," *CNN*, March 1997, at www.robert-fisk.com/usama_interview_cnn.htm.

"Twenty-Six Saudi Scholars Address Message to the Iraqi People," *Site Institute (The Search for International Terrorist Entities)*, Site Publications, November 7, 2004, at www.siteinstitute.org/bin/articles.cgi?ID=publicatio ns10504&Category=publications&Subcategory=0.

"Two U.S. Allies Review Islamic Curricula at Schools, Mosques," *World Tribune.com*, May 21, 2003, at www.216.26.163.62/2003/me_egypt_05_21.html.

"U.S. Bomb Damages Mosque," *CNN.com*, November 16, 2001, at www.archives.cnn.com/2001/WORLD/ asiapcf/central/11/16/ret.mosque/.

"U.S. Bombing Watch: Archive of U.S. Bombings, Invasions, and Occupations of Iraq (Methodology History of U.S. Bombing Watch)," *Colorado Campaign for Middle East Peace*, December 31, 2004, at www.ccmep. org/usbombingwatch/2003.htm.

"U.S. Forces Order of Battle - 26 December 2004," *Global Security.Org*, at www.globalsecurity.org/military/ops/iraq_orbat_041226.htm.

"U.S. Military Budget for FY 2003," International Institute for Strategic Studies, U.S. Department of Defense, at the Center for Arms Control and Non-Proliferation, at www.armscontrolcenter.org/archives/000568.php.

"U.S. Probes Zarqawi Hospital Visit," *News.Com.Au*, May 6, 2005, at www.news.com.au/ story/0,10117,15196352-23109,00.html.

"U.S. Pulls Out of Saudi Arabia," *BBC News*, April 29, 2003, www.news.bbc.co.uk/2/hi/middle_east/2984547. stm.

"U.S.: Restore Rights Undercut by Post 9-11 Policies: Congress Should Act on Legislation to Protect Basic Rights in the United States," *Human Rights Watch*, June 16, 2004, at www.hrw.org/english/docs/2004/06/16/ usdom8773_txt.htm.

Ul-Haq, Naseem, "Al-Saud: The West's Custodians of the Haramain [holy cities of Mecca and Medinah]," *MuslimMedia.com*, at www.muslimedia.com/archives/special-edition/hajj/hajj2.htm.

Unger, Craig, *House of Bush, House of Saud* (Scribner 2004).

"UNHRC Releases 2001 Global Refugee Statistics," *EuropaWorld*, June 21, 2001, at www.europaworld.org/ week87/unhcr21602.htm.

United States Army, *Interim Field Manual 03-7.22, Counterinsurgency Operations* (2004).

"United States Efforts to Undermine the International Criminal Court: Legal Analysis of Impunity Agreements," *Human Rights Watch*, www.hrw.org/campaigns/icc/docs/art98analysis.htm.

University of Southern California data base of the Hadith collections of the works of Sahih Bukhari, Sahih Muslim, Abu-Dawud, and Malik Muwatta in English at www.usc.edu/dept/MSA/reference/searchhadith.html.

"USS Cole," *Wikipedia, the Free Encyclopedia*, at www.en.wikipedia.org/wiki/USS_Cole_bombing.

Van Natta, Dan, Jr., "Growing Evidence U.S. Sending Prisoners to Torture Capital Despite Bad Record on Human Rights, Uzbekistan is Ally," *New York Times*, May 1, 2005.

Van Wagtendonk, Reinout, "Bush's Vision of Middle East Democracy," *Radio Netherlands*, November 7, 2003, at www.www2.rnw.nl/rnw/en/currentaffairs/region/northamerica/us031107.html.

"Violations of Islam," www.idrismosque.com/vio.html.

"Wahhabism," *GlobalSecurity.Com*, see www.globalsecurity.org/military/intro/islam.htm and /islam-kharijite. htm and /islam-salafi.htm.

Walley, Cherilyn A., "A Century of Turmoil: America's Relationship with the Philippines," *Special Warfare*, September 2004, at www.findarticles.com/p/articles/mi_m0HZY/is_1_17/ai_n8573960.

"War on Iraq Could Drain US Anti-Terror Campaign: Report," *English People*, reporting an article in the *Washington Post* of September 1, 2002, at www.english.people.com.cn/200209/02/eng20020902_102459.shtml.

Watson, Roland, "Young Turn Their Backs on Life in US Military," *Times Online*, May 14, 2005, at www.timesonline.co.uk/article/0,,11069-1611339,00.html.

Weisman, Jonathan and Thomas E. Ricks, "Increase in War Funding Sought," *Washington Post*, October 26, 2004.

Whalen, Christopher, "In Somalia, the Saudi Connection," *Washington Post*, October 17, 1993.

"What Are the Trade-Offs?," Feminist Budget, Feminist Majority Foundation, February 1996, at www.feminist.org/other/budget/budget5.html.

"What is the Palestinian Authority and How Did It Originate?," *Palestine Facts*, Israel 1991 to Present PA Origins, at www.palestinefacts.org/pf_1991to_now_pa_origin.php.

Wheatcroft, Andrew, *Infidels* (Random House 2003, 2004).

"When Suspicion Is Mistaken as Proof - the Sorry Tale of Khalid al-Fawwaz," *Salaam.com*, March 6, 2003, reprinted from the February 20, 2003, edition of the Financial Times, at www.salaam.co.uk/themeofthemonth/january03_index.php?l=29%82%22=0.

"Who Are the Northern Alliance?", *BBC News*, November 13, 2001, at www.news.bbc.co.uk/1/hi/world/south_asia/1652187.stm.

"Who Were His Friends," *IslamOnline.net*, August 8, 2003, at www.islamonline.net/English/introducingislam/Prophet/Companions/article01.shtml.

Wilson, Scott and Daniel Williams, "A New Power Rises Across Mideast," *Washington Post*, April 17, 2005.

Wink, Andre, *Al-Hind: The Making of the Indo-Islamic World, Vol. 1*, (Oxford University Press [Delhi] 1990).

"Wolfowitz Comments Revive Doubts Over Iraq's WMD," *USA Today*, May 30, 2003, at www.usatoday.com/news/world/iraq/2003-05-30-wolfowitz-iraq_x.htm.

Woodward, Bob, *Plan of Attack* (Simon & Schuster 2004).

"Karzai: 'Don't Spray Poppies'", *CBSNews.com*, January 31, 2005, www.cbsnews.com/stories/2004/11/18/world/main656576.shtml.

"Work Related to Enrichment to Resume Within Days, Iran Says," *Los Angeles Times Wire Services*, May 10, 2005.

"The Life and Death of Shaikh Yasin," *Al-Jazeera Net*, March 24, 2004, at www.english.aljazeera.net/NR/exeres/7995E32C-9686-40DA-97AD-2E0D5EABF6D1.htm.

"World Military Expenditures and Arms Transfers (WMEAT) 1996," U.S. Arms Control and Disarmament Agency, at www.fas.org/man/docs/wmeat96/.

"World War I," at www.countrystudies.us/syria/8.htm.

Wright, Robin, and Thomas E. Ricks, "Bremer Criticizes Troop Levels: Ex-Overseer of Iraq Says U.S. Effort Was Hampered Early On," *Washington Post*, October 4, 2004.

"Yemen Admits 'Terrorist Act' Behind Tanker Blast," *IslamOnline.net*, October 17, 2002, at www.islamonline.net/English/News/2002-10/17/article12.shtml.

Yoo, John C. and James C. Ho, Yoo NYU Combatants.Doc, August 1, 2003.

Yoo, John C. Robert J. Delahunty, "The Geneva Convention Isn't the Last Word," *San Francisco Chronicle*, at www.sfgate.com/cgi-bin/article.cgi?f=/c/a/2005/02/02/EDGAOB45OE1.DTL.

York, Byron, "The Truth About Bush's 'Lies,'" *National Review Online*, June 16, 2003, www.nationalreview.com/york/york060303.asp.

Zakaria, Fareed , "The Saudi Trap," *Newsweek Magazine*, June 28, 2004, at www.fareedzakaria.com/articles/newsweek/062804.html.

Zakaria, Fareed, *The Future of Freedom* (W.W. Norton & Co., 1st. Ed., 2003).

Zunes, Stephen, Prof., "President Bush Fails to Make His Case," *AlterNet*, October 8, 2002, at www.alternet.org/waroniraq/14255/.

Zunes, Stephen, Prof., "UN Resolution Does Not Authorize US to Use Force Against Iraq," *Common Dreams News Center*, November 14, 2002, at www.commondreams.org/views02/1114-03.htm.

This Page Left Intentionally Blank For Notes

Index